DATE DUE

APR 1 7 1994		
APR 2 2 1994		

LABOR RELATIONS IN THE FEDERAL GOVERNMENT SERVICE

LABOR RELATIONS IN THE FEDERAL GOVERNMENT SERVICE

By Murray B. Nesbitt

Queens College
City University of New York

The Bureau of National Affairs, Inc. Washington, D.C.

Library of Congress Cataloging in Publication Data

Nesbitt, Murray B.
    Labor relations in the Federal Government service.

    Includes index.
    1. Collective bargaining—Government employees—
United States—History. 2. Trade-unions—
Government employees—United States—History.
I. Title.
HD8008.N38   331.89'041'353   75–44255
ISBN O–87179–225–7

Printed in the United States of America
International Standard Book Number: 0–87179–225–7

To the memory of Sterling Denhard Spero
and my father, Daniel Nesbitt

FOREWORD

Years, indeed decades, before trade union organization and action by public employees had become everyday headlines in the press, Sterling Spero recognized that public sector labor relations was a subject to which scholarly attention must be paid. But Dr. Spero was a lonely pioneer, more like Leif Ericson than Columbus, in that it took years for explorers to begin following in his footsteps. Nonetheless, he continued to work in this field and inspired his students to join his explorations. Dr. Murray Nesbitt, a research fellow in the New York University Institute of Labor Relations, was one of this select group.

Work on this book was begun by Professor Spero under a modest grant from the New York University Institute of Labor Relations. But after a brief effort on the early sections Dr. Spero was obliged to discontinue all work on this study because of other pressing obligations. He therefore turned the entire project over to Dr. Murray Nesbitt, who proceeded with the work to its conclusion as its sole author. In this book, Nesbitt provides a comprehensive and very much up-to-date review and analysis of labor relations within the Federal Government. That the book is topical is obvious to the most casual reader of metropolitan dailies. It is, perhaps, even more topical than many may recognize; for the long era of rapid growth in the size of public sector employment appears to have ended, with cutbacks and retrenchment the current rule and the prospect of only slow expansion resuming even when happier economic circumstances return. Labor relations were not easy during the expansion period, but they are likely to be significantly more difficult in the more constrained environment in which we are likely to be living for some time. This book provides the necessary historical perspective, for it deals with earlier, not entirely dissimilar, periods. Equally important, it tells us where we are now with respect to federal labor relations, at a level of understanding not matched elsewhere in print.

The credit for this book, of course, belongs entirely to Dr. Nesbitt, its author. Without pretending to claim any share of this credit, I am bound to say that the Graduate School of Public Administration of New York University is proud to have been the institutional home of Professor Spero during much of his career and Dr. Nesbitt as a graduate student and to have fostered research on public sector labor relations long before it was a popular subject for research. Our institutional contributions have been modest ones, but we are happy to bask in the reflected light from Sterling Spero's pioneering efforts and Murray Nesbitt's significant contributions to the understanding of some critical public issues.

DICK NETZER
Dean, Graduate School of
Public Administration
New York University

PREFACE

The very existence and direction of this work is owed to Sterling D. Spero, pioneer author in the field of public employee unionism and Professor Emeritus in the Graduate School of Public Administration of New York University. It was through his personal drive and interest that the author began this study that was to be almost a decade in preparation. Throughout this period, the author was deeply indebted for his constant support, advice, consultation, and direction. Moreover, Dr. Spero made important contributions to the book itself in the coverage of the early historical development of federal labor relations in Chapters I through IV, XVIII, and XIX. His fertile mind was a continuous source of inspiration and encouragement. The book would not have been written without him.

A greatly appreciated grant by the Institute of Labor Relations of New York University under the direction of Thomas G. S. Christensen and Bruno Stein was especially helpful during the early stages of the study. The late Dean Ray Harvey of the Graduate School of Public Administration helped initiate the study and always cheered the work on. Indeed, this undertaking could not have been carried on without the cooperation of literally scores of persons: government officials, union leaders at the national and local levels, elected representatives, rank and file federal workers, and many knowledgeable private individuals. Not only are their names too numerous to attempt to list but many of the contributors preferred to remain anonymous.

Acknowledgements which no mere lines of preface can repay must be made to: Morris Biller of the New York Metro Area Postal Union, Jean Coutourier of the National Civil Service League, Jacob Finkelman of the Public Service Staff Relations Board of Canada, Wilfred V. Gill of the Federal Labor Relations Council, Anthony F. Ingrassia and L. David Korb of the Office of Labor-Management Relations in the U.S. Civil Service Commission, Maxwell Lehman of the New York State Charter Revision Commission, John A. McCart of the Government Employes' Council, Thomas Milazzo of the U.S. Civil Service Commission's New York Region, the late Otto Pragan of the AFL-CIO, the

Hon. Spottswood W. Robinson III, Judge of the U.S. Circuit Court of Appeals, Newell B. Terry of the U.S. Department of the Interior, and Louis S. Wallerstein of the Federal Employee Management Relations Division in the U.S. Department of Labor. A sincere word of deep appreciation is also due my wife and family for their cheerfulness in support and forcefulness in encouragement.

Queens College   MURRAY B. NESBITT
Flushing, New York

TABLE OF CONTENTS

PART I

THE TRADE UNION SCENE

CHAPTER I

THE NATIONAL GOVERNMENT AND PUBLIC UNIONISM

Executive Order 10988, issued by President Kennedy in January 1962, brought labor relations in the federal civil service a step closer to the standards long required in private industry. While this order obliged government authorities to deal with their employees through unions of their choosing and opened the way for collective bargaining, it still left final decision over bargainable issues and procedures in the hands of the employing authorities or the central personnel agency. Thus the hand of the sovereign obtruded into the bargaining process in ways that negated the principle of equality of the parties upon which collective bargaining is based.

This was not surprising since the concept of the subordination of the public employee to the government as a sovereign employer had long been accepted doctrine in the American public service. There the formula that "the state determines its relations with its servants" had been interpreted to require a personnel system based on unilateral employer action.

When the Kennedy order was issued, the great majority of federal civil servants, apart from the postal employees and blue-collar workers in the industrial-type services, were unorganized. Except for the officers of the regular craft unions, few leaders of employee organizations and fewer government administrators were experienced in the ways of labor-management negotiation. The limits placed upon collective bargaining in the executive order were in part a recognition of this fact and in part a manifestation of the reluctance of employing officials to accept limitations on the unilateral authority they had so long exercised.

The historical expression of sovereignty is found in the doctrine of the divine right of kings, which asserted that "divinely appointed" kings could do no wrong. The doctrine offered a rationalization for the acts of a central crown government in preserving its royal prerogatives over the rival centers of power in developing national states. Introduced into nineteenth-century American political thought to justify rival claims to ultimate power by both state and federal authorities, the doctrine found little expression in public employment—that is, until government officials acting in the name of the state in its capacity as employer sensed a threat in the rise of civil service unionism to the exercise of their managerial powers.

The unilateral system of personnel administration under which the federal civil service developed was not solely the product of sovereign authority. Administrative powers are derived from many policy decisions regarding the organization and management of public services. The policy decision in the Kennedy order to substitute consultation and negotiation with employee representatives for managerial unilateralism was a sovereign decision to alter federal personnel administration. It was, nevertheless, only a part of the total fabric.

Sovereignty is but a weighty word used to identify the powers of the state to make and execute public policies through its established governmental organs. The concept presumes an ultimate legal authority inhering in the state which transcends the powers of individuals and groups in its domain. The practical exertions of such legal authority, however, are far from absolute in modern democratic societies. Today, ultimate governmental actions stem from several sources of power. This is particularly true in the United States with its federal system, its written constitutions limiting the powers of government, a bicameral Congress whose members are chosen on different bases, and a separation of legislative and executive powers, the exercise of which is subject to judicial review. Furthermore, the whole governmental complex operates within the context of a highly pluralistic society, freely organized in nongovernmental political, economic, religious, and social groups. Public policy is the resultant of the competing pressures of these groups upon the organs of government.

Government employees functioning as citizens, as voters, and as a distinct economic group in a changing American society have been able to challenge the claims of employer unilateralism and gradually establish an area of countervailing rights for themselves. In legal theory these rights, expressed in legislation, executive orders, and agency regulations, are concessions by the sovereign employer and may be overridden by him.

A distinction must be made, however, between the final authority of the sovereign employer in law and the reality of his capacity to exercise such power. The ability to exert authority is increasingly qualified by new institutions which acquire social roots, economic power, and political relationships that give them a life of their own. There are many things which governments may do legally but which they cannot enforce practically. It is highly unlikely after new bargaining rights are granted to public employees or are achieved by them that they could be substantially curtailed once solidly established. This would probably be true in spite of legal reservations insuring ultimate overriding sovereign authority.

Thus, the most thoroughgoing and successful collective bargaining procedure in the federal service, that of the Tennessee Valley Authority (TVA), operates under the proviso:

"The parties recognize that TVA is an agency of and is accountable to the government of the United States of America. Therefore TVA must operate within the limits of its legally delegated authority and responsibility." [1]

Such reminders of ultimate sovereign authority are not characteristic of the American service alone. The key provision of the British Whitley Council system which states that agreements "shall become operative" when officially reported was immediately made subject to a "clarifying interpretation" [2] declaring, "the government has not surrendered and cannot surrender its liberty of action in the exercise of its authority and the discharge of its responsibility in the public interest." [3]

These reservations of sovereign authority have been compared to "management rights" in private employment. The analogy, however, is incomplete. Reservations in private industry seek to exclude from the bargaining table certain issues involving the employer's power to run his business. The Kennedy order on Employee-Management Cooperation, it is true, required that a specific management-rights clause be included in all collective agreements made under it. But the reservations of sovereign authority go beyond such a declaration. They constitute a unique overriding power without counterpart in private employment, a power which ostensibly may even be exercised on an ex post facto basis.

A. FEDERAL POLICIES FROM RESTRAINT TO TOLERATION

The unilateralism of the governmental employer has never gone entirely unchallenged in this country. When union activity

---

[1] Tennessee Valley Authority, *General Agreement*, with Tennessee Valley Trades and Labor Council, August 6, 1940, revised to date, Art. II, Sec. 1.

[2] J. H. Macrae-Gibson, *The Whitley System in the Civil Service*, 1922, p. 12.

[3] Leonard D. White, *Whitley Councils in the British Civil Service*, 1933, p. 12.

first appeared in the federal service in the 1830s during the presidency of Andrew Jackson, the government claimed no special status clothing it with rights and privileges beyond those of other employers. The "laborers, workmen and mechanics" in the navy yards and other public works belonged to the same unions as private or municipal employees. The government resisted their demands where it was able and yielded where pressure or labor market conditions made it expedient or necessary to do so. But it did not challenge employee rights to unionize, demonstrate, use political pressure, or strike.

It was not until the postal workers, who were distinctively government employees rather than laborers or mechanics who might work for anyone, began to organize in the late 1880s and 1890s that government began to oppose employee activity on principle and to claim a special status as employer. The laborers and mechanics were backed by the political power of the large outside organizations which represented them. The postal workers, on the other hand, were completely beholden to patronage-appointed postmasters and supervisors who hired them and fired them with few statutory or administrative restrictions, and determined their pay, assignments, and working conditions as though they were their chiefs' private hirelings. The rising organizations represented a challenge to the system. Employing officials denounced them for interfering with constituted authority and feared them as threats to their political bases.

At first resistance was left to the local postal authorities. But by the mid-1890s the local movements had gained sufficient national cohesion and outside support from the organized labor movement and other political quarters to arouse the opposition of the administration in Washington. An order by President Cleveland's postmaster general, William L. Wilson, in 1895 marked the first of a series of executive actions seeking to stamp out organized employee activity.

The Cleveland-Wilson order forbade any employee, upon pain of removal, to visit Washington "whether on leave with or without pay for the purposes of influencing legislation before Congress." The postal organizations were attempting no industrial action such as the demonstrations and strikes of the Jackson era. Their methods were lobbying, election activity, and other political pressures conducted first in clandestine and then in open affiliation with the general labor movement.

President Theodore Roosevelt viewed such conduct as interference with the authority of the Executive to manage the business of the government and a violation of the principle of the political neutrality of the civil service to which, as a pioneer civil service reformer, he ardently adhered.

The result was the first of the famous "gag" orders forbidding employees "either directly or indirectly, individually or through associations, to solicit an increase in pay or to . . . attempt to influence in their own behalf any other legislation whatsoever . . . save through the heads of the department in or under which they serve." [4]

Though aimed specifically at the postal organizations, the order was couched in terms which covered the whole federal service. But when protests were made privately to the President by representatives of the politically influential national printing trades unions in the Government Printing Office, the representatives were assured that the order would not apply to their members.[5]

In 1909 President William H. Taft extended the Roosevelt restrictions to forbid any official or subordinate employee to "respond to any request" from Congress or its members "except through or as authorized by the head of his department." [6] This order was a by-product of the economy and efficiency movement. The further suppression of employee organization activity was not the President's central concern. His interest, rather, was in laying the groundwork for implementing the economy-efficiency philosophy with the introduction of an executive budget and an orderly, hierarchically organized administration with clear lines of authority climaxing in the hands of the chief executive.

Civic and academic circles supported the order as a contribution to essential administrative reform. The National Civil Service Reform Association viewed it as under-pinning for an anonymous and politically neutral civil service.[7] Professor Henry Jones Ford, of Princeton, one of the country's leading political scientists, hailed the order as an essential step toward a responsible executive budget. It would, he said, prevent "the Administration's estimates from being crossed up by estimates privately submitted to Congress." [8]

Independent efforts by employee organizations for improved working conditions involving higher costs interfered with the process of executive budget making and "crossed up" Administra-

---

[4] Executive Order, January 25, 1902. In 1906 the order was reissued to include independent government establishments in addition to the executive departments.

[5] Interviews with union representatives, one of whom later became an official of the Government Printing Office.

[6] E.O. 1142, November 28, 1909.

[7] *Report of the National Civil Service Reform Association,* 1912.

[8] Henry Jones Ford, *The Cost of Our National Government,* 1910, pp. 115-116.

tion estimates. The conception of orderly administration upon which the economy-efficiency movement was based assumed that only the Executive and his alter-ego deputies, who "could trace their authority to the people" and were legally responsible for controlling the orderly operations of the government services, could properly speak for the people to the Congress.[9] Apparently it was taken for granted that orderly democratic administration required an authoritarian administrative process.

To the postal workers and their increasingly militant organizations the Taft order was another hard twist to the bind already tying down their freedom to operate. Instead of serving as a prelude to a new era of governmental order and efficiency, the Taft "gag" ushered in a period marked by extremely low morale within the civil service. Its results were unrest, defiance of orders, work stoppages, and threats of formal strikes.

The government's answer was an uncompromising anti-union campaign resorting to the use of informers and spying by postal inspectors even to the extent, as Senator Robert M. LaFollette of Wisconsin charged, of violating the privacy of the mails.[10] Organizations not favored by the Department were outlawed and leaders and active members severely disciplined or discharged.[11]

The net result was an intensified anti-gag campaign culminating in the passage on August 24, 1912, of the Lloyd-LaFollette Act. The legislation, passed as a rider to a post office appropriation act, was largely a product of leadership by the American Federation of Labor (AFL). Key provisions were drawn up under the guidance of President Samuel Gompers.

The Lloyd-LaFollette Act marked a major turning point in the history of civil service unionism. For half a century, until the Kennedy order of 1962, it remained the most important piece of legislation affecting the rights of federal employees. Its central purpose, to nullify the gag orders, was accomplished by the provision:

> "The right of persons employed in the civil service of the United States either individually or collectively to petition Congress or any member thereof or to furnish information to either House of Congress, or to any committee or member thereof, shall not be denied or interfered with." [12]

---

[9] Sterling D. Spero, *The Labor Movement in a Government Industry* (New York: George H. Doran Co., 1924), pp. 21-22. Reprinted New York: Arno Press and New York Times, 1971.

[10] *Congressional Record*, 62nd Cong., 2nd Sess., 1912, p. 10729. See also Sterling D. Spero, *op. cit.*, pp. 167-168.

[11] Spero, *op. cit.*, pp. 139-180.

[12] 37 Stat. 555, August 1912.

Other portions of the act attempted to put an end to the anti-union activities of the postal authorities by requiring procedures intended to stop removals for organization activity. These provided that removals might be made only for "such cause as will promote the efficiency of the service and for reasons given in writing" with an opportunity to reply to the charges. And it was specifically provided that membership in postal labor organizations "not affiliated with any outside organization imposing an obligation or duty" to strike against the United States did not constitute cause for removal or demotion. The clause on affiliation, the work of President Gompers, has been interpreted as recognizing the right to affiliate with the AFL since, as a federation of autonomous unions, it had no power to impose an obligation upon its affiliates to strike.

The act had little immediate effect on the attitude of management officials. Although gradually modifying some of their more blatant anti-union tactics, most officials continued to be uncooperative, if not actually hostile to organized employee activity.[13] Restrictions on the power of removal notwithstanding, dismissals for union activity continued. The law stated that no examination of witnesses, trial, or hearing was required except in the discretion of the officer making the removal. Employing authorities had little difficulty in firing active unionists by stating causes for removal other than organization activity. The courts refused to examine the reasons given by administrators, thus allowing their actions to stand.[14]

Rebuffed by the managing authorities, employee organizations, freed from the gag order, turned to Congress for redress and improvement. Close relations were built up between unions and congressional committees. Some employees, taking advantage of the door opened by the law, made individual approaches to their congressman, a practice in the long run of advantage neither to the service nor the employee body as a whole.

Pressures for official recognition of unions by administrative authorities began in the mid-1930s with the introduction of President Franklin D. Roosevelt's New Deal programs to end the ravages of the Depression and bring the country's social legislation abreast of the times. The New Deal brought about a tremendous rise in federal employment.

---

[13] Spero, *op. cit.*, pp. 186-228.
[14] Levine v. Farley and Howes, 107 F 2d 186 (1939) ; see Sterling D. Spero, *Government as Employer* (New York. Remsen Press, 1948) , pp. 40-43. Reprinted, Carbondale, Ill.: Southern Illinois University Press, 1972.

The newcomers were young, enthusiastic partisans of the burgeoning labor movement. Many with union backgrounds became impatient with the tactics of federal employee organizations and were eager to project the methods of private labor relations into the setting of their new employment. This quickly produced a marked change in the temper of the service and created a cleavage between the newcomers and the employees of the older established agencies. The National Industrial Recovery Act and later the Wagner Act giving government support to the organization of labor resulted in an unprecedented rise in trade union membership in both the new Congress of Industrial Organizations (CIO) and old AFL unions.

Federal workers could hardly have remained unaffected. Through new or expanded locals of the old federations and a new CIO affiliate they launched campaigns for improved conditions and expanded rights using militant tactics patterned after those of the outside labor movement—tactics such as picketing, mass demonstrations, and rough talk. The shortcomings of the Lloyd-LaFollette Act were emphasized, and voices were raised demanding collective bargaining with the government. Some congressmen became alarmed, and there were calls for legislation to suppress this militancy and make civil service collective bargaining illegal.

At this point President Roosevelt, unable to accept an invitation to attend the Twentieth Jubilee Convention of the National Federation of Federal Employees (NFFE), seized the opportunity to state his attitude toward federal employee-management relations in a letter to NFFE President Luther C. Steward.[15] The President's immediate purpose was to forestall threatened congressional action which might hamstring the Administration's control over personnel policy and hamper fruitful developments in employment relations going forward in some agencies.

According to Otto S. Beyer, presidential labor advisor, who played a leading role in its drafting, the letter was intended to strengthen the leadership of the established organizations by approving their objectives and methods and decrying the militant tactics of the challenging newcomers.

The President wrote:

"Reading your letter of July 14, 1937, I was especially interested in the timeliness of your remark that the manner in which the activities of your organization have been carried on during the past

---

[15] Letter dated August 16, 1937.

two decades 'has been in complete consonance with the best traditions of public employee relationship.' Organizations of government employees have a logical place in government affairs.

"The desire of government employees for . . . objectives of a proper employee relations policy, is basically no different from that of employees in private industry. Organization on their part to present their views on such matters is both natural and logical. . . ." [16]

The letter then went on to say that "militant tactics have no place in the functions of any organization of government employees," and to condemn strikes of public employees as "unthinkable and intolerable." It closed with a paragraph underscoring the limits of collective bargaining between government and its employees.

The letter, despite its support for employee organization, did nothing to move employing authorities towards more understanding and positive employee-management relations policies. Unconventional militant tactics did subside after the letter was written. However, they are accepted today as a matter of course. The comments on the strike were a ritualistic repetition of standard condemnations of a weapon to which no responsible federal employee union of that day had any intention of resorting. On the other hand, the paragraph dealing with collective bargaining quickly became the most influential official pronouncement on federal labor relations between the Lloyd-LaFollette Act and the Kennedy order. Although the letter succeeded in its immediate purpose of stopping antibargaining legislation, its practical result was to impose an effective barrier against the extension of collective bargaining. This part of the letter was quoted in personnel handbooks as a statement of presidential policy declaring that collective bargaining in the federal service was "impossible."

The much quoted paragraph read:

"All government employees should realize that the process of collective bargaining, as usually understood, cannot be transplanted into the public service. It has its distinct and insurmountable limitations when applied to public personnel management. The very nature and purposes of government make it impossible to bind the employer in mutual discussions with employee organizations. The employer is the whole people, who speak by means of laws enacted by their representatives in Congress. Accordingly, administrative officers and employees alike are governed and guided, and in many cases restricted by laws which establish policies, procedures and rules in personnel matters." [17]

---

[16] *Ibid.*
[17] *Ibid.*

The key phrases "as usually understood" and "to represent fully and bind the government" were ignored, and stress was laid upon the limitations which legally distinguished collective bargaining in the public service from that in the private sphere. Thus a statement intended to forestall legislation seeking to arrest efforts toward more cooperative employment relationships became a barrier to the extension of such efforts.

The year 1937, which saw the publication of the Roosevelt letter, also saw the publication of the *Report of the President's Committee on Administrative Management.* The committee's study group on personnel administration, headed by Floyd W. Reeves and Paul T. David, inquired into the state of employer-employee relations. It reported that not only were administrative officials generally "reluctant to recognize and confer with representatives of employee groups," but also that such groups "frequently appear to encounter passive if not active opposition." [18]

President Franklin D. Roosevelt, notwithstanding his vigorous support of trade unionism in private industry and his recognition in the letter to Steward of the "natural and logical" role of employee organization in government, not only took no action to alter the situation to which Reeves and David called attention but also ignored the following proposal in their report:

> "The majority of employees in any professional, group or craft or other appropriate unit should have the right to determine the organization person or persons to represent the group, craft or unit in joint conference with administrative officials or representatives of such officials." [19]

Had this proposal been implemented, a program along the lines of that set forth in the Kennedy order might have had a quarter-century headstart. What actually happened, however, was that with the exception of the few agencies where sophisticated cooperative labor relations were developing, the great majority of the employees continued to turn to Congress for improvement, and employing officials continued to point to the letter to Steward to justify their refusal to enter into negotiated arrangements with their employees.

B. MOUNTING PRESSURES FOR CHANGE

With legislation thus made the principal vehicle for determining working conditions, employee organizations became adept at lobbying and developed an extraordinarily expert knowledge of

---

[18] Floyd W. Reeves and Paul T. David, *Personnel Administration in the Federal Service,* 1937, p. 2.
[19] *Ibid.,* p. 54.

the complex mysteries of the legislative process. The employing agencies, for their part, developed similar expertise. Thus the congressional committee became the arena in which contests over employment relations took place. Sometimes, as under the personnel classification laws, a mechanical system placed heavy restrictions on the administrator's discretion. At other times the detailed application of broad general legislation was left to the sole judgment of the employing official.

As personnel problems grew in complexity, both employers and employees became increasingly critical of this system, the former for its inflexibility, the latter for its unilateralism. The constructive potential of collective bargaining demonstrated in TVA, the Department of the Interior, and the Government Printing Office stimulated demands for its introduction into the other branches of the service, and the rapid spread of bargaining in municipal employment lent further impetus to these demands.

Pressure for change came from outside the service as well as within. Shortly after the war, in 1946, the National Civil Service League (NCSL), the progenitor and watchdog of the merit system, issued a report on *Employee Organization in the Public Service*. It endorsed collective bargaining and exclusive recognition of the bargaining agent, saying:

> "The head of a public agency must at all times be free to accept petitions or requests for conferences from any source, but he should reserve any 'agreements' for conferences with the group representing the majority." [20]

The word "agreement" was enclosed in quotation marks because, the report explained, "normally a 'contract' with an employee organization in the public service represents an advisory group judgment which an administrator is willing to accept, not a technical instrument regarded as binding the government in the future to a contract resulting from group pressure." [21] Yet the League recognized the fact that legislation could make contracts legally binding, saying: "An unequivocal grant of power to an administrative agency over a matter covered in an agreement is necessary, if its government to which it is subordinate is to be bound by the agreement." [22]

All of this was far in advance of general federal practice. Yet it was descriptive of practices rapidly developing in municipal employee relations. During the decade and a half following the

---

[20] National Civil Service League, *Employee Organization in the Public Service*, 1946, p. 16.

[21] *Ibid.*, p. 19.

[22] *Ibid.*, p. 18.

League's 1946 report, scores of agreements were consummated between municipalities and employee organizations in all parts of the country. New York, Philadelphia, and Cincinnati formally adopted city-wide systems of collective bargaining. Several states passed laws requiring the practice in their municipalities.

In 1960 another committee of the National Civil Service League issued a statement largely repetitive of the position taken in its 1946 report. It espoused collective negotiation under exclusive recognition, informal and morally binding agreements, limited dues checkoff, and advisory arbitration.[23] Although this statement actually added little to the earlier proposals, it came when the times were riper and thus had a greater impact on public policy. The influential columnist of the *Washington Daily News*, John Cramer, commenting under the heading "Report Plugs Collective Bargaining," said the League statement "puts that conservative organization several million light-years ahead of the federal government."[24]

At the same time, the League staff in a statement of its own accompanying the policy declaration found "the federal government lagging behind other jurisdictions, in spite of the growing awareness of the need for better employee-management cooperation." There is, said the staff, "neither a uniform system nor consistent executive interest in its possibilities."[25]

During the 15 years between the two NCSL reports the two Hoover Commissions addressed themselves to the subject. The task force on civil service of the 1949 Commission found that the government had lagged behind American industry in improving employer-employee relations and that, while federal employees were given "some degree of protection against abuse, discrimination, and unjust treatment," they were "not provided a positive opportunity to participate in the formulation of policies and practices which affect their welfare."[26] The task force went on to recommend that "the President should require the heads of departments and agencies to provide for employee participation in the formulation and improvement of Federal personnel policies and practices."[27] The Commission's only practical suggestion, falling far short the Reeves-David proposals in 1937 for exclu-

23 *Good Government,* Spring 1965, pp. 22-26.
24 *Washington Daily News,* December 2, 1960.
25 Murray B. Nesbitt, *Employee Organizations in the Public Service* (Staff Report; New York: National Civil Service League, 1960) , pp. 16-17.
26 U.S. Commission on Organization of the Executive Branch of the Government, *Report,* 1949, pp. 125-126.
27 *Ibid.*

sive recognition, was the establishment of joint councils composed of employee representatives and supervisory officials.

The second Hoover Commission, finding no progress during the intervening six years, declared in 1955 that "the Federal government has lagged behind other organizations in recognizing the value of providing formal means for employee-management consultation." [28]

In addition, the American Bar Association (ABA) began to show a cautious interest in public employment relations. A Committee on Labor Relations of Government Employees was established under the chairmanship of Professor H. Eliot Kaplan of New York University, the country's leading authority on civil service law and for many years the leader of the civil service reform movement. After studying the problem for three years the committee issued its first report in 1952. It made no concrete proposals but contented itself with the hope that "a sound program could be developed here if there were a reasonable and common sense approach . . . on the part of both public officialdom and employee representatives, with mutual respect for each others prerogatives and privileges." [29]

But when the same committee offered its next report three years later, its tone was different. The earlier bland generalities and pious hopes gave way to sharp criticism of the government's evasiveness on meeting the issue. The report declared:

> "A government which imposes on other employers certain obligations in dealing with their employees may not in good faith refuse to deal with its own public servants on a reasonably similar favorable basis, modified, of course, to meet the exigencies of the public service. It should set the example for industry by being perhaps more considerate than the law requires in private enterprise." [30]

Subsequent reports by the ABA continued to note the federal lag in comparison not only with private enterprise but also with the rapid spread of collective bargaining in local government.

Sentiment crystallized by the 1946 report of the National Civil Service League and the first Hoover Commission's comments prompted the Federal Personnel Council, an official body made up of agency personnel directors, to issue a memorandum on "Effective Relationships with Organized Employee Groups in the

---

[28] U.S. Commission on Organization of the Executive Branch of the Government, *Report of the Task Force on Personnel and Civil Service,* 1955, p. 110.

[29] American Bar Association, Section of Labor Relations Law, Committee on Labor Relations of Government Employees, *Proceedings,* 1952, p. 143. Permission to reprint this article from the Labor Law Report was obtained from the American Bar Association and its Section of Labor Relations Law, 1969.

[30] *Ibid., Proceedings,* 1955, p. 5.

Federal Service." [31] The statement was admittedly negative in emphasis, and it was not until after it had been distributed to the employing authorities that the unions were consulted—a striking indication of the existing state of federal labor relations. Just over a year later, in August 1952, a new "suggested guide," apologetically labelled "a proposal by Federal Directors of Personnel," was sent to department and agency heads. According to the Council, the suggestions, revised after consultation with the unions, were put in "positive rather than negative form."

The revised document added nothing to the generalities of the Roosevelt letter to Luther C. Steward. After repeating the standard declaration that employees had the right to join or refrain from joining lawful organizations which did not assert the right to strike, it went on to suggest that employee organizations be encouraged "and insofar as practicable be requested to discuss questions of personnel policy" with agency officials and that "policies and procedures governing personnel policies should be published and made available to all employees. . . ." [32]

The effect of these feeble proposals was nil. Six years after their publication, Rocco Siciliano, Special Assistant for Personnel Management to President Eisenhower, issued a letter to agency heads calling upon them to evaluate their labor relations practices. He also asked the Civil Service Commission to include a review of agency practices in its regular inspections and to report to him periodically its findings regarding their effectiveness and conformity to the directives in the *Federal Personnel Manual.*

On the basis of the reports sent to him Siciliano concluded, "Although there has been some definite improvement, much remains to be done. Employee relations are not uniformly good throughout all federal establishments." [33]

Meanwhile the efforts toward the modernization of employment relations were moving ahead on other fronts. Frustrated by executive inaction, employee organizations turned to Congress for legislation to implement the guarantees of the Lloyd-LaFollette Act. The first bill to require union recognition was introduced in 1949, the year of the first Hoover Commission report. Between that date and the publication of the Kennedy order, literally dozens of proposals for legislation requiring union recognition and

---

[31] Issued in 1951.

[32] U.S. Civil Service Commission, Federal Personnel Council, *Suggested Guide for Effective Relationships With Organized Employee Groups in Federal Civil Service,* August 1952.

[33] Rocco C. Siciliano, "Employee—Management Relations in the Federal Government," *Good Government,* January 1960, p. 4.

collective bargaining were deposited in the congressional hopper. Most of these introductions were mere formalities to please union leaders resident in the member's district. One, however, received serious attention and was actually on the verge of enactment when the Kennedy executive initiative for union recognition and bargaining forestalled it. Beginning in 1952 hearings were held on this measure, the Rhodes-Johnston Bill, in several Congresses. The bill had strong union support. It was favorably reported out in both Houses several times but never reached the floor for a vote.

The final bill, presented in 1961, recognized "the right . . . of a union of government employees to present grievances on behalf of their members without restraint . . . or reprisal," and provided that any administrative officer violating such right was subject to suspension, removal, or other penalties deemed proper by the head of his agency.[34] It required conferences upon union request not only on specific personnel matters but upon "matters of policy affecting working conditions, work procedures, automation, safety, in-service training, labor-management cooperation, methods of adjusting grievances, transfers, appeals, granting of leave, promotions, demotions, rates of pay and reduction in force." [35]

The requirement, it should be noted, was for conference, not collective bargaining. This procedure, known as joint consultation, had been in effect in much of British private industry since the Whitley Report following the First World War and had been required by law in British nationalized industry since the mid-1940s. A clear distinction was made there between collective bargaining, which results in binding contracts, and consultation, which is an advisory process leaving final decision to management. The Rhodes-Johnston Bill made no mention of this all-important characteristic of "conference" or consultation, although it did deal with the two processes in separate sections.

The bill conferred "authority and obligation" upon management and unions "to bargain collectively with each other on terms and conditions of employment." It provided for several steps in the resolution of bargaining impasses. The first called for mediation by the Federal Mediation and Conciliation Service (FMCS). If no resolution was achieved, either party could refer the impasse to a proposed new agency, the Government Labor-Management Relations Panel, consisting of a chairman and four

---

[34] U.S. House of Representatives, *H.R. 12*, 87th Cong., 1st Sess., 1961, Sec. 201 (a) .

[35] *Ibid.*, Sec. 201 (b) (1) .

to eight members appointed by the President. If the impasse could not be brought to an end by this panel, it could order formal hearings and issue a final and binding award. The bill also contained provisions for final and binding arbitration of grievances by special boards of three—one member chosen by the union, one by the employing agency, and a third by these two members or by the Secretary of Labor if no agreement could be reached regarding the selection of the third member.[36] Such concepts, in varied form, were to appear in numerous bills in the 1960s and were clearly reflected in both the Kennedy and Nixon orders.

Government spokesmen strongly opposed the Rhodes-Johnston bill, declaring that it would upset the whole sytem of personnel administration; hold up management decisions through what might prove to be endless conference; and shift authority from responsible agency heads, the Civil Service Commission, and the Comptroller General to the new Government Labor-Management Relations Panel or outside arbitrators. Numbers of administrators agreed with Chairman Philip Young of the U.S. Civil Service Commission that existing rules and regulations were adequate for handling employment relations.[37] Others held that such changes as might be necessary should be made by executive action.

Administrators feared that the proposed legislation might open a Pandora's box of complications extending far beyond the well-intentioned specific objectives of the legislation.[38] One serious concern, not widely expressed, recognized that laws once on the books are subject to amendment and extension as well as to judicial interpretation. The way would thus be open to expanded congressional intrusion into executive processes and to growing judicial interference in personnel administration, long the bane of state and local governments.

These fears and doubts notwithstanding, the continuing failure to take steps toward effecting the proposals of official and civic bodies for the modernization of federal labor relations brought increasing support for union recognition legislation. One of the

---

[36] *Ibid.*, Secs. 403, 501.

[37] U.S. Senate, Committee on Post Office and Civil Service, *Hearings,* 84th Cong., 2nd Sess., 1956, p. 125. At these hearings the Civil Service Commission issued a statement entitled "A Short History of the Civil Service Commission's Position on Employee-Management Relations Bills." See pp. 256, ff.

[38] For excellent analyses of the proposed union recognition legislation see Wilson R. Hart, *Collective Bargaining in the Federal Civil Service* (New York: Harper & Brothers, 1961) , pp. 17-37, and Willem B. Vosloo, *Collective Bargaining in the United States Federal Service* (Chicago: Public Personnel Association, 1966) , pp. 45-56.

vigorous supporters of such legislation was Senator John F. Kennedy. He not only gave favorable testimony at earlier committee hearings [39] but just before his election to the Presidency reiterated his support for the Johnston bill. In an effort to garner as many votes as possible in a tight race, Kennedy wrote to a prominent postal official that he "always believed that the right of federal employees to deal collectively with the federal departments and agencies . . . should be protected." Noting his "great interest and regret that the Congress adjourned without acting upon Senator Johnston's bill," he concluded: "I should think that a Democratic 87th Congress with Democratic leadership from the White House could deal effectively with the proposal." [40]

Once in office, President Kennedy quickly acquired a perspective toward the complexities of administration which he could not get from a Senate seat. Although the bill he endorsed was already pending in the new Congress, he proceeded to undercut it by appointing a Task Force on Employment-Management Cooperation to review and make recommendations on federal employment relations. His executive order quickly followed. "This action," said Wilson R. Hart, a keen observer of federal labor policy, "pulled the rug from under the government unions just as they were about to pluck the golden apple. It not only deprived them of the prize," he continued, "but made them like it." [41]

Judging by the comments of union officials, there seemed to be little regret over the substitution of executive action for legislation. John A. McCart, operations director of the Government Employes' Council (GEC), now servicing over one million members of AFL-CIO affiliated unions of federal employees in all branches of the service, called the executive order "the most momentous development in the history of [government] labor relations since the enactment of the Lloyd-LaFollettee Act in 1912." [42]

President B. A. Gritta of the Metal Trades Department, AFL-CIO, called the order "a real milestone in establishing the rights

---

[39] U.S. Senate, *Hearings,* 1956, *op. cit.,* p. 36.

[40] Letter from John F. Kennedy to John W. Ames, Publicity Director, Illinois Federation of Postal Clerks, October 31, 1960. Cited in Harry A. Donoian, *The Government Employes' Council: Its Organization and Operations* (Washington: Government Employes' Council, 1968), p. 49.

[41] Wilson R. Hart, "The U.S. Civil Service Learns to Live with Executive Order 10988: An Interim Appraisal," *Industrial and Labor Relations Review,* January 1964, p. 205.

[42] U.S. Department of Labor, Office of Employee-Management Relations, *Proceedings of the Institute on Employee-Management Cooperation,* March 8, 1963, p. 33.

of government workers to organize, obtain exclusive recognition of their unions, to engage in genuine collective bargaining and to negotiate signed agreements." [43]

The late President E. C. Hallbeck of the United Federation of Post Office Clerks, one of the leading supporters of the recognition bills, noted that the order for the "first time set forth a government policy with positive approval of union activity in the federal service." [44]

One dissenting voice was that of Vaux Owen, president of the independent NFFE. The order, he protested, imposed an adversary relationship upon federal employment based on "outside union thinking" with a progressive development of practices associated with collective bargaining in industry. This, he asserted, might lead to strikes against the government. [45]

Nathan Wolkomir, president of a large local of the NFFE, expressing opposition in even stronger terms, told the union's national executive council that the Task Force report "will create in employee-management relations . . . a tower of Babel . . . a class distinction between one group of civil servants and others . . . a divide and conquer contest between employee groups creating animosities, hatreds and opportunists. . . ." [46]

Yet two years later, when it became apparent that failure to take advantage of the Kennedy order was undermining the Federation, Wolkomir broke with Owen and defeated him for the national presidency on a platform pledging to "milk the order to dryness." [47] Thus the last major holdout against the order was brought into line. By this time the federal establishment was well into a labor relations experience that culminated in the first Nixon order and the momentous national events of 1970.

---

[43] Metal Trades Department, AFL-CIO, *Proceedings,* Fifty-first Convention, November 11, 1963, pp. 3, 14.

[44] Quoted in *Management Relations With Organized Public Employees* (K. O. Warner, ed.) (Chicago; Public Personnel Assn., 1963), p. 228.

[45] *Ibid.,* pp. 232-233.

[46] *The Federal Employee,* December, 1964, pp. 8-9.

[47] *Ibid.*

CHAPTER II

THE BLUE-COLLAR UNIONS

In the early 1830s, during the Presidency of Andrew Jackson, artisans and laborers employed by the Federal Government in its public works joined with private and municipal employees in a movement to reduce their hours of labor to 10 a day. The federal workers were organized not as government employees but as "laborers, workmen, and mechanics" in unions that included private, municipal, and federal employees. These unions made no distinction between public and private employers. Their tactics included demonstrations, during which "employment ceased" and "business was at a standstill," long strikes, and political pressure.

A. EARLY STRUGGLES FOR COMPARABILITY

The Federal Government, more insulated from direct pressure than private employers or local government, was the last employer in the principal industrial centers to grant the shorter day. It did so usually after long resistance and only where the local authorities and private employers had already yielded. In Washington, D.C., where private employers successfully opposed the 10-hour day, a strike at the navy yard failed. In Philadelphia, on the other hand, where the municipal and private employers acceded, an executive order by President Jackson compelled the naval authorities to yield. This order came after a protracted strike at the navy yard climaxed by a mass meeting of "citizens, mechanics and workingmen," which sent a committee to Washington to obtain the President's intervention.

The Philadelphia experience brought the holdout Baltimore federal authorities into line after the workers threatened a strike, declaring that they "positively refused to be governed by the old system." Other federal works in Maryland shortly complied. The Maryland success was followed before long in New York City, where the Federal Government was again the last employer to yield.

Just as the political weight of the 10-hour victory in Baltimore brought the other federal works in Maryland into line, so the success of the movement in Philadelphia and New York City brought the shorter day into effect in the rest of New York State and Pennsylvania.

The long day continued to prevail, however, at federal works in other centers. To bring these places into line the convention of the National Trades Union, the first national labor federation in the United States, initiated a drive for congressional action. Convention delegates attacked the policy of federal officials holding back waiting for other employers to take the lead. Such officials, declared an irate delegate, "abused the trust imposed upon them" and placed themselves "in the attitude of selfish employers when they should have been first to set the example. . . ." [1]

The legislative effort failed because Congress, in line with the beliefs of the time, deemed it best "to leave such matters to the parties themselves for regulation." [2] Legislating on hours of labor was regarded as an unwarranted interference with freedom of contract. One representative declared, "Why we might just as well prescribe by law what sort of clothes a man should wear, or what time he should eat his dinner! A man who is free should be left to make his own contracts!" [3]

But the policy of leaving it to the parties failed outside of the leading industrial centers. In five of the eight states where federal plants were located 12- to 15-hour days remained the rule.[4] The labor unions, having failed locally and in Congress, decided to concentrate their political efforts on the executive. The Panic of 1837 interrupted these plans; but when normal conditions returned, pressure on President Martin Van Buren was renewed. The result was an executive order signed on March 31, 1840, establishing the 10-hour day on all federal public works.

The Van Buren order not only wiped out inequalities in federal labor standards; it by-passed the policy of following prevailing community standards and substituted national uniformity by executive regulation in place of the crude collective bargaining which had been taking place between the unions and local fed-

---

[1] J. R. Commons & E. A. Gilmore, *Documentary History of American Industrial Society*, Vol. VI, pp. 232-233.
[2] *Congressional Debates*, 24th Cong., 2nd Sess., 1836, p. 2892.
[3] *Ibid.*, p. 2890.
[4] The long day remained in effect in Massachusetts, Rhode Island, Virginia, New Hampshire, North Carolina, and the District of Columbia.

eral officials. The order also raised federal standards above those of other employers, thereby, for the first time, making the government a model employer setting standards for others to follow.

Only two years after the Van Buren order, the shipbuilding crafts began to agitate for an eight-hour day. The ships' carpenters and caulkers led the way and shortly won an eight-hour day on old work at the Charlestown Navy Yard. In 1854 eight hours became the standard day for the whole caulker craft. By the outbreak of the Civil War the more important private yards were operating on an eight-hour schedule and were attracting some of the most skilled workmen away from the navy yards. To prevent this drain, Congress in 1861 passed the first law requiring that hours and wages in navy yards conform to those prevailing in the locality.[5] Determination was left to the yard commandant. A similar act passed the following year made the local commandant's determinations subject to the review of the Secretary of the Navy.[6]

The prevailing-rate acts of 1861 and 1862 were the first legislative declarations of governmental labor policy. They broke no new ground, but they did give congressional sanction to a policy which, though recognized as desirable, was often resisted by installation authorities. Furthermore, although the policy laid down by the law specifically applied to navy yards, it was an expression of the intent of Congress and thus eventually became a guide for other federal industrial services.

This was demonstrated at the Government Printing Office, which became a federal agency in January 1861 after purchase from its private owners. The Washington printers union, the Columbia Typographical Society, demanded an eight-hour day in all the shops in town, the new Government Printing Office included. The union, however, in consideration of the many complications attending the transfer of the plant to government ownership, decided to withhold its demand until a more opportune time. This came two years later when the printers and bookbinders were seeking the elimination of irregularities in their pay scale to bring them up to the level of the rest of the city. When the Superintendent of Printing refused their demands, the two unions threatened to strike. When the time for the walkout came, however, the printers refused to go out, leaving the bookbinders to carry the burden alone.

The strike lasted seven weeks and aroused bitter feelings. A company of marines was placed on guard at the Printing Office

---

[5] 12 Stat. 330, December 21, 1861.
[6] 12 Stat. 587, July 16, 1862.

while the strikers picketed the railroad station and the roads leading into Washington to prevent the importation of strike-breakers. A compromise settlement was finally arrived at under which the superintendent agreed to pay the prevailing wage and promised to join with the union in asking Congress to legislate an eight-hour day. He held that he was without power to reduce hours without legislative consent.

It was not until after the Civil War, according to George E. Seibold, the historian of the Columbia Typographical Society, that " the seed sown in the early days of the Society for an eight-hour day began to take root in 1865, the movement having spread to other trades." As during the 10-hour-day agitation, "mass meetings, torchlight processions, and other means were employed to arouse public interest." [7]

In 1866 the printers demanded an eight-hour day from October to May, leaving the 10-hour schedule in force the rest of the year. The private printing shops resisted this demand and issued a lengthy protest against granting it in the government plant. Before long, however, the private plants conceded while the government still held out. A strike followed and the superintendent came to terms, stating in a letter to the union:

> ". . . evidence of the acquiescence by the employing printers of the city in the adoption by the Society of the eight-hour rule is before me . . . I feel authorized thereby and therefore will pay four dollars per diem for eight hours' labor hereafter in accordance with the scale adopted by the Society." [8]

The eight-hour movement, beginning as noted in 1865, concentrated on government service, thus testing the efficacy of the model-employer concept. The movement's first successes occurred in the area of municipal employment a year before the victory in the Governnment Printing Office. Boston adopted the first eight-hour ordinance covering all city workers in September 1865. Baltimore, Detroit, Chicago, New York, and smaller cities soon followed.

The federal employees, instead of attempting to bring federal operations in various cities into line one by one, decided to concentrate on Congress, believing this to be a quicker and easier method of achieving success for all federal industrial workers. The process proved more difficult and frustrating than expected. Although a law was finally passed in 1868 providing that eight hours constituted a day's work for all "laborers, workmen and mechan-

---

[7] George E. Seibold, *Historical Sketch of Columbia Typographical Union Number 101*, 1915, p. 25.

[8] *Ibid.*, Letter dated October 22, 1866.

ics" in federal employ,[9] it took four years to achieve satisfactory implementation. The act failed to provide specifically, as President Van Buren's 10-hour order had done, that the shorter day was not to be accompanied by a reduction in daily pay.

Immediately after the passage of the act, the Secretary of War, John M. Schofield, reduced pay by 20 percent, the equivalent of the hours reduction. Similar action by Gideon Welles, Secretary of the Navy, followed.

When the Grant Administration came to office in 1869, Adolph E. Borie, the new Secretary of the Navy, attacked the eight-hour law as "embarrassing and injurious to the interests of the Navy," and urged its repeal. "The demagogues in Congress," he wrote, "enacted the law regardless of the public interest and dare not repeal it whatever may be their conviction." Borie followed this attack by reissuing his predecessor's 20-percent wage cut. In this he was buttressed by an opinion of the Attorney General. He did this despite a House resolution declaring that the act was not to be so construed. The immediate result of Borie's order was a strike in the Philadelphia Navy Yard followed by the organization of "eight-hour leagues" and "workingmen's associations," including both government and private employees, in all parts of the country.

In May 1869 President Grant issued a proclamation directing that no reduction in daily wages paid by the government to "laborers, workmen, and mechanics" should be made "on account of such reduction of hours of labor." [10]

Despite the demonstrations of labor organizations and demands for the removal of offending officials, interpretations of the law in violation of the President's proclamation continued for another three years. In May 1872 the President issued a second proclamation specifically directing "all officers of the executive departments of the government . . . to make no reduction in wages . . . on account of reduction of hours of labor." [11] Five days later Congress finally settled the issue by a joint resolution restoring to all employees sums withheld because of the reduction of hours between the date of the passage of the law and the President's proclamation. During the consideration of the joint resolution attempts to repeal the original eight-hour law failed.

There are several significant aspects to government labor relations in both the 1830s and the 1860s. The labor movement

---

[9] 15 Stat. 77, June 1868.
[10] Proclamation by the President, May 29, 1869.
[11] Proclamation by the President, May 13, 1872.

treated the government-employer the same as it treated other employers, using every available kind of pressure, including the strike. Government made no claim to special rights as an employer and asked no special consideration from its employees. The doctrine of the sovereign employer, which later became a dominant factor in public employment relations, was not asserted. Collective bargaining between the parties, though less sophisticated and elaborate than the process today, nevertheless was a fact. The various trade unions set their scales and presented them to their employers, who accepted or rejected them or reached compromise agreements. In both public and private employment, exchanges of letters or oral acceptances took the place of the formal contract upon which the parties now set such store.

The Panic of 1873 and the long depression that followed brought labor union activity in the navy yards and arsenals to a standstill. Recovery did not begin until a program for modernizing the military establishments got under way after the Spanish-American War.

By this time the character of the unions seeking to organize the works had changed from the loose and rather amorphous groupings of earlier years to tightly organized craft unions affiliated with the AFL. At the same time, the works commanders had also become more conscious of themselves as military professionals and more jealous of their authority than their predecessors had been. During the labor movements of the 1830s and 1860s the authorities resisted the employees' demands but did not question their right to make them. By the turn of the century, on the other hand, the new generation of commanders were insisting that they could deal only with individuals and refused to meet with union representatives.

The issue came to a head at the Rock Island Arsenal shortly after the end of the Spanish-American War. The machinists, making up the largest craft and strongest union in the plant, issued a formal complaint alleging that they were obliged to work "under military regulations," that men were dismissed for the most trivial and arbitrary reasons, that constant discrimination was practiced against union members, and that their wages were the lowest in any federal establishment. When after repeated requests the commanding officer continued to refuse to meet with a union committee, the international office authorized a strike.[12]

---

[12] Sterling D. Spero, *Government as Employer* (New York: Remsen Press, 1948), p. 94. Reprinted Carbondale, Ill.: Southern Illinois University Press, 1972.

The War Department then entered the controversy and agreements were reached between the Secretary of War and the International Association of Machinists (IAM). The agreements provided that the men's grievances would be corrected and that no reprisals would be taken against the strikers. Arsenal commanders were ordered to receive representative grievance committees and to refer to the department all matters which they could not settle at the plant level.

On the basis of these promises the men returned to work only to have the commander ignore the agreement, demonstrating again the difficulty of obtaining local compliance with central policy. Only a third of the strikers were reemployed, and among these all who refused to leave the union were soon fired.

The strike did, however, bring a lasting gain in the establishment of grievance committees. The Navy soon followed the policy of the arsenals by establishing its own grievance committees. Such steps ended the insistence of military officers that they could deal only with individuals and marked the beginning of more realistic labor policies.

The new dispensation led gradually to a growth of trade unionism. By 1904 the machinists had become sufficiently strong to require the establishment of a division in their international union, known as District 44, to handle the affairs of government employees. Prior to the formation of the district, sentiment had been growing for the federation of all the mechanical employees. The establishment of District 44 emphasized organization along craft rather than intercraft or industrial lines. Although it strengthened the largest craft and seemed to harden the decision of the craft unions to organize in established form, it did not end support for organization along more inclusive lines. Two years after the creation of District 44, William L. Cain, its secretary-treasurer, a leading advocate of a broader union, headed a new organization, the National League of Government Employees (NLGE). Declaring that the League was intended to supplement rather than displace the craft unions, Cain attempted to retain his office in District 44.

The NLGE spread rapidly, attracting members from all the crafts, which found themselves at a disadvantage because of their higher dues. Begun in the navy yards, it soon extended into the army arsenals and continued to grow for the next five years despite the fact that the AFL, on the insistence of the crafts, declared it a dual organization and cautioned union members to shun it.

B. THE FIGHT OVER TAYLORISM

About 1911 opposition to the introduction of the Taylor system of scientific management became the dominant concern in the federal industrial services. The campaign was fought on two fronts, industrially with stoppages and strikes and politically with efforts for so-called anti-stopwatch legislation. Although the League joined this fight, it could not match the influence that the craft unions, with their ties to the organized labor movement, were able to bring to bear.

There were work stoppages in many plants when supervisors tried to make time studies or put other aspects of the Taylor system into effect. When an attempt was made to apply the system in the foundry at the Watertown Arsenal, the molders union, after indicating its opposition to the commanding officer with no effect, obtained authority from the international union to strike. The strike was called when several men were discharged for refusing to submit to time tests. The molders were out for a week. They returned when the War Department promised that all grievances would be thoroughly investigated, that the discharged employees would be reemployed, and that no reprisals would be taken against the strikers.

The strike hardened the attitudes of both the unions and the Ordnance Department of the Army. It led the unions to a decision to seek the solution of their problem through legislation rather than resistance at the plants. It also led the Ordnance Department to redouble its efforts to install the Taylor system regardless of employee resistance.

The concern of the unions extended beyond the issue in government shops. These, the unions feared, were being used as laboratories for testing the Taylor system and as demonstration centers to publicize it to private industry.[13]

Three days after the Watertown strike the House of Representatives established a special committee to study and report on the applicability of the Taylor system to government work. The committee's report contained what was probably the first official reference to the possibility of collective bargaining regarding federal working conditions. Various features of the Taylor system should be introduced, the report declared, "only with scrupulous care that the workman shall have full opportunity for increasing his earn-

---

[13] International Association of Machinists, Official Circular No. 12, April 26, 1911.

ings without risk of strain, for collective bargaining if he should so desire and for easy and direct appeal to management. . . ." [14]

The Army Ordnance Department, ignoring these qualifications and reasoning that "the selection of any system of shop management must be to a great extent a matter of administration," [15] went on with its plans in the face of overwhelming employee opposition.[16] When provisos in the Army and Navy appropriation acts denying funds for the use of "a stop watch or time measuring device" for job time study passed the House and were pending in the Senate, the Chief of Ordnance, General William L. Crozier, resorted to various ruses to defeat the measures. He ordered the suspension of premium payments with no increase in base pay. Since base pay under the Taylor plan was lower than standard straight rates, the employees were actually suffering a pay reduction below prevailing rates. General Crozier declared that he did this so that the employees would "understand what they were threatened with." When asked whether his action was intended to lead the workers to oppose the pending bills, he admitted that he acted "for the purpose of allowing them to protest if they wanted to." [17]

Such bureaucratic evasion of the intent of Congress was further demonstrated when the Army Appropriation Act, effective July 1, 1915, was signed on March 4, 1915. The very next day or, in the general's words, "as soon as the issue was determined by the passage of the bill," premium payments and time studies were resumed. The pleasure of the employees at again receiving higher compensation was hailed by the Department as a vindication of its stand. Still determined to carry out his policies, the general quickly found ways by which he "saved" the workers "from the disadvantages of the legislation." [18] Taking advantage of the technicality that anti-Taylor provisions were contained only in the Army Appropriation Act, he continued Taylor practices in those arsenals whose funds came from other acts not containing the prohibitions. He also found ways of evading the law elsewhere. Although his efforts were admittedly designed to evade the expressed will of Congress, the Controller of the Treasury and the Judge Advocate General had little choice but to uphold them as conforming to the letter of the law.

14 U.S. House of Representatives, *Report No. 403,* 62nd Cong., 2nd Sess., March 9, 1912, p. 7.

15 *Ibid.*

16 U.S. Senate, *Document No. 800,* 63rd Cong., 3rd Sess., 1915, pp. 13-16.

17 U.S. House of Representatives, Committee on Labor, *Hearings,* 64th Cong., 1st Sess., 1916, pp. 174-175.

18 *Congressional Record,* 63rd Cong., 3rd Sess., 1915, p. 31.

Discontent in the shops rose, and the IAM had great difficulty in preventing a strike, which it wanted to avoid in order not to interfere with delicate negotiation: it was engaged in with the War Department. Eventually the loopholes in the anti-Taylor legislation were closed. After negotiations with the unions following refusal of the employees to cooperate in further experimentation, the Department dropped its efforts.

The result was that for many years federal shops were stopped from managerial experimentation with measured standards of production and the adoption of many modern management methods. This might well have been avoided if the Ordnance Department of the Army had cooperated with its employees through "collective bargaining . . . and direct appeal to management" as the House Committee investigating the Taylor system had recommended.

C. WARTIME SPURS TO COOPERATION

The campaign against the Taylor system was carried on by the various craft unions cooperating informally but without any central organization. Many employees, however, were dissatisfied. In April 1915 an attempt was made at the Norfolk Navy Yard to form a federation of the crafts within the AFL, to be called the United States Federation of Government Navy Yard and Arsenal Employees. Although the attempt failed, it led the Metal Trades Department of the AFL to permit all local unions in the yards and arsenals, whether or not they were in a strict sense metal trade unions, to form metal trades councils. The need for this step was demonstrated by the speed with which metal trades councils were established.

Strengthened organization enhanced the influence of the unions with Congress. It did not, however, move them significantly closer to a more formalized and effective role in the Ordnance Department of the Army. Although, according to President Alifas of District 44, officials made no attempt to prevent employees from belonging to unions,

> "they apparently still resent the interference of organized labor in what they consider their affairs. While they are ready at all times to receive, listen and at times act upon the suggestions and wishes of representatives of organized labor, an effort is continuously made to impress upon us that they are not making arrangements with us." [19]

The Chief of Ordnance, General Crozier, declared: "We do not deal with representatives of the union except as they repre-

---

[19] *The Federal Machinist,* September-October, 1921, p. 4.

sent our own employees. We deal with committees representing the employees and those committees may also be committees or officers of labor unions." [20] While he had himself, he said, often talked with union officials who were not arsenal employees, he did not allow arsenal commanders to do this.[21]

The Navy, according to President Alifas, evinced a more cooperative attitude at the departmental level, but the policy did not readily seep down to local commanders. This again demonstrated the difficulty of achieving cooperation from local officials in the implementation of departmental or administration labor policies.

During the First World War the necessity of keeping government plants manned and operating efficiently brought about a decided liberalization of labor relations practices. Commanders were explicitly forbidden to discriminate against union members and were ordered to deal fully, frankly, and cooperatively with union representatives. These policies continued for a short time after the war's end, but when demobilization was completed and the regular officers replaced the reserve officers, the services reverted to their older attitudes.

The reversion occurred without departmental objection in the Army. In the Navy, however, when Assistant Secretary Franklin D. Roosevelt received complaints that officers were refusing to meet committees of union men, he ordered a stop to such practices and directed "that shop committees, union or otherwise, are always to be received and listened to." [22] Carrying this policy to the national level, Roosevelt arranged to have a union representative named by the president of the AFL placed on the Central Wage Board of Review. This body passed upon the recommendations of local wage boards regarding prevailing rates.

World War II caused a further liberalization of labor policy. The War Department under a program of decentralization ordered local commanders to establish grievance procedures and recognize the right of employees "to join or refrain from joining unions." [23]

Early in 1941, two years before the War Department took these steps, the Secretary of the Navy called a conference of union representatives of all yards and stations and invited them to "air their gripes." So many gripes were aired that the Department reconsidered its plan to assemble a similar conference every four months and never called another meeting.

---

[20] House *Hearing* cited, note 17.
[21] *Ibid.*
[22] Letter of August 5, 1919.
[23] War Department, Administrative Memo. W-6, January 1943.

During the following year the Secretary addressed a letter to all commanding officers requesting them to deal with their employees through their chosen representatives according to "accepted industrial relations procedures." Although the letter ended with an exhortation "to join in this crusade for greater harmony in the navy family," it proved exceedingly difficult to obtain full compliance in the field. "The attainment of harmony," wrote one high officer, "required more than exhortation; it required reorientation of an inherited way of thought." The Department, however, appeared to derive sufficient satisfaction from the results of its efforts to report that labor-management policy discussion was widespread, "and in many places cordial and rewarding."

The ultimate result of these efforts for better labor relations was the incorporation of the following paragraph in the Navy's *Personnel Policies for Employees Handbook:*

> "Although a navy yard, as a government agency, cannot enter into collective bargaining agreements with any group of employees, it is the desire of the management in formulating policies and procedures to consider the wishes and viewpoints of the workers. It is the policy of yard management, therefore, to meet with any employee or group of employees for discussion of mutual problems. To that end employees are encouraged to elect, from shops or offices, representatives to meet with management for their common advantage." [24]

This remained the official statement of the Navy's labor relations policy until President Kennedy's executive order on Employee-Management Cooperation.

D. DEVELOPING CHANGES

Since the Kennedy order unionism among the blue-collar workers, especially in the military installations, has undergone substantial changes. District 44 of the IAM, which since 1904 has served as the clearing house, legislative arm, and in many respects the leader of the skilled crafts, was abolished. In its place the international union established the IAM Government Employees Department and announced the tripling of the staff assigned full time to organizing and servicing federal employees. The president of the old District 44 became the coordinator of the new department, with assistant coordinators assigned respectively to the eastern and western halves of the country. Special full-time international representatives were assigned to organizing activities and to the handling of grievances. In announcing the reorganization, IAM President Roy Siemiller said:

---

[24] Sterling D. Spero, *op. cit.*, p. 104.

"We feel that with our new Government Employees Department we are now in a position to build the strongest union in the federal service. . . . The results should be a quickening improvement in working conditions, prompter handling of grievances and a stronger voice for federal blue collar workers in Washington." [25]

Even before the establishment of the new department the IAM had broken established AFL-CIO jurisdictional boundaries. The Kennedy order made it possible for any organization which could meet its requirements to seek exclusive recognition. Taking full advantage of the opening, the IAM set out to organize whole installations, including not only blue-collar workers belonging in other union jurisdictions but white-collar workers as well. This was largely a defensive measure. IAM was meeting increasing competition from other organizations which were also seeking broad exclusive contracts. Some came from groups of crafts federated in metal trades councils without machinist members. Most of it, however, came from industrial unions which ignored craft lines. One of the IAM's principal competitors was the American Federation of Government Employees (AFGE), a sister AFL-CIO affiliate. Though barred by its charter from organizing workers belonging within the jurisdiction of other affiliates, the AFGE has ignored these strictures and at one time admitted that 45 percent of its members were blue collar workers.[26] Further discussion of this situation will be found in Chapter IV dealing with the general unions of federal employees.

The independent National Federation of Federal Employees and a new and vigorous organization, the National Association of Government Employees (NAGE), have also been organizing blue-collar workers. These unions have the advantage of being completely free of AFL-CIO jurisdictional barriers.

The rise of NAGE has been astonishing. The organization began as a veterans' association at the Watertown Arsenal in Massachusetts, where it established an enviable record of successful handling of veterans' grievances and defense of veterans' rights under the Veterans Preference Act of 1944.

At the first election for an exclusive bargaining agent at the Watertown Arsenal, NAGE won by a substantial majority over the IAM local. Some of the winning issues were "no union bosses," "a young and growing organization," "conflict of interest in IAM between government union and industry union members," and "industrial versus craft unionism."

---

[25] "A New Day for Federal Workers", *The Machinist*, November 10, 1966.
[26] *Federal Times*, October 26, 1966.

NAGE repeated its pattern of success in other military installations in New England. It soon spread across the country to arsenals, naval stations, air force depots, and Federal Aviation Agency and Space Agency centers, winning craftsmen, technicians, and white-collar workers. Before long, unlike the earlier movements seeking to bridge craft union lines at the navy yards and arsenals, it successfully challenged the crafts and the old established general unions, the NFFE and the AFGE as well. This competition between NAGE and the two older general unions is injecting a new dimension into government blue-collar unionism.

The Kennedy order gave unions an official status for which they had long been pressing. For military management, this required a radical change of attitude. In practice, the kind of relationship implied in the statement quoted from the Navy's personnel handbook meant little. The unions were present. There were few consultations with their representatives. When such sessions did occur, management seldom asked union representatives for advice or suggestions. It usually used the sessions to acquaint the representatives with decisions already made. The Kennedy order changed this situation. It made union recognition by management obligatory and opened the way for unions to play a part in the determination of working conditions which they had sought in vain for decades.

CHAPTER III

THE POSTAL UNIONS

It was in the Postal Service that the decisive contest over unionization in the federal service took place. Though the weapons were different from those used by both sides in private industry, the contest was equally sharp.

Prior to its reorganization, the Postal Service was organized .as a government department whose head, the Postmaster General, was a member of the President's Cabinet. Of all Cabinet departments it was the least concerned with the politics of public policy and most involved in the politics of partisan patronage. Nearly every Postmaster General was an active participant in the management of party organization. Many served as chairmen of the national committee of the President's political party and managed presidential election campaigns.

Until the Pendleton Civil Service Commission Act in 1883 laid the basis for the merit system, the post office in each locality was treated as an adjunct of the local organization of the party nationally in office. Employees were appointed by the local postmaster and paid out of sums credited to each post office. Appointments and duty assignments were made in collaboration with the local political organization.

The passage of the Civil Service Commission Act weakened the hold of congressmen and local politicians on the service. As it relaxed dependence of the employees on their political sponsors, it also led sponsors to lose interest in their former proteges. The employees, thrown on their own resources, began to seek protection through self-organization.

A. THE POSTAL EMPLOYEES ORGANIZE

In those days the service was composed of three large categories of employees: city letter carriers, post office clerks, and railway postal clerks. The city carriers, the most homogeneous group, were all engaged in the same kind of work. Their chances of promotion to supervisory grades were comparatively small. Aside from assignment to lighter routes, there were few favors that the individual carrier could receive. The only improvements he could expect were those that came to the group as a whole. This absence of the prospect of personal preferment saved the letter carriers from much of the factionalism that has bedeviled the organizing efforts of other postal workers, and it has made them one of the most thoroughly organized occupations in the entire labor movement.

Carrier organization did not start from scratch after the passage of the Pendleton Act. Local associations had existed in a number of cities since the establishment of the city delivery service in 1863. Though organized as benefit societies and social clubs, these groups soon became interested in working conditions. They quickly assumed the political coloration of the local machine and obtained results by trading favors with the party leaders.

Problems incapable of local solution were handled by delegations to Washington nominally elected by the local carriers but actually chosen by the local society. The delegations quickly found it necessary to unite their Washington efforts through a temporary legislative committee to serve during the legislative session. The committee soon assumed permanent status and designated a permanent secretary. The first incumbent was John F. Victory, the founder of *The Postal Record,* a magazine which ultimately became the official organ of the National Association of Letter Carriers (NALC) when it was formed in 1890.

The Carriers' principal objective was an eight-hour day. An eight-hour law, won by the blue-collar workers, had been on the books since 1868. The Post Office Department, however, refused to apply it to the postal service on the ground that "postal employees were neither laborers, workmen, nor mechanics," categories of employees specifically mentioned in the act.

The campaign for an eight-hour day was part of a general nationwide movement led by the central labor organization of the time, the Noble Order of the Knights of Labor. Begun in the late 1860s, the movement was interrupted by the depression of 1873-1879, but revived with the return of prosperity and reached its climax about the time the postal employees began their serious organizing efforts in the mid-1880s. When their attempt to extend the eight-hour act of 1868 failed, the letter carriers in a number of large cities turned to the Knights of Labor for help and formed local assemblies of the labor order operating as ruling factions within the established local associations.

This affiliation gave a tremendous spur to the carriers' efforts. In 1888, two years after the formation of the first local Knights' assembly in New York, Congress overrode vigorous opposition from the postal authorities and passed a letter carriers' eight-hour law. Organization leaders were fired for minor infractions of the rules. Active employees were harassed by deliberately imposed inconveniences such as assignments to undesirable routes far from their homes or the imposition of extra duties. In New York, 150 men were suspended as "detriments to the service" but were later reinstated on Washington's orders after intercession by the national office of the Knights of Labor.

Departmental opposition did not stop after the passage of the eight-hour law. For three months the authorities openly ignored it. They then adopted a policy of deliberate evasion even more flagrant than that attempted by the War and Navy Departments after the passage of the Act of 1868. The new law provided that "eight hours shall constitute a day's work for letter carriers. . . . [I]f any carrier is employed a greater number of hours a day than eight he shall be paid extra for the same in proportion to the salary now fixed by law." [1] The Department interpreted eight hours a day to mean 56 hours a week, so that a carrier who worked nine hours a day for six days and was off on Sunday owed the Department two hours at the end of the week. After five years of litigation the U.S. Supreme Court upheld an order of the Court of Claims invalidating the Department's interpretations and requiring the government to adjust thousands of claims for overtime totaling almost $3,500,000. [2]

Meanwhile, the post office clerks were engaged in a parallel struggle for organization against much greater odds. The term "postal clerk" is a misnomer. The force includes both men and women engaged in a great variety of occupations. Only a small minority are engaged in work which can properly be called clerical. The central function of the force is the distribution of mail in post offices, which involves a variety of tasks ranging from manual labor—most of which is now done by the special classification of workers called mail handlers—to postal tasks requiring specialized knowledge and skill, particularly in a period of increasing automation.

While the nature of the carrier service encouraged solidarity, that of the clerical force led to factionalism, split ranks, and competing organizations. The clerk could look forward to more desirable assignments and to promotions to supervisory ranks which

1 25 Stat. 157 (1888).
2 Post v. U.S., 148 U.S. 124 (1893).

depended to a great extent on political favor. This competition for personal advancement was a source of dissension and individual politicking. It enabled the administration to play favorites, to encourage factionalism, pitting one group against another with the purpose of breaking up the clerks' organizations or controlling them if they could not be disrupted.

Attempts to organize the postal clerks began as early as 1879 with the formation of ad hoc committees and conferences in several cities. The movement gradually spread. In 1884, the year after the passage of the Civil Service Commission Act, a meeting of local representatives was held in Washington which urged the passage of a salary classification law. Congress showed no interest.

This defeat led to sharp differences among the clerks, with one faction insisting on pressing salary reform as the first order of business and the other opting for taking immediate advantage of the eight-hour movement and climbing on the bandwagon with the support of the Knights of Labor.

Stimulated by the passage of the carriers' eight-hour law, the clerks, early in 1889, united their local associations in a National Association of Post Office Clerks. Its immediate objectives were an eight-hour day together with the abolition of uncompensated overtime. The passage of a wholly inadequate salary classification act the next year further stimulated differences over priorities, encouraging the postal authorities to play the hour and salary advocates against each other. These efforts at disruption were accompanied by the dismissal of the officers of the New York Association, the largest and most active branch, and the disciplining of other active members. To forestall further official reprisals those who replaced the dismissed officers tried to appease the Department by inviting the admission of supervisors to membership. The national officers of the newly formed National Association supported the step. This sparked a secession from the National Association and the formation of a new organization, the United Association of Post Office Clerks.

The atmosphere of the service was such that several of the seceding locals were reluctant openly to take sides and remained outside both national groups. In New York, the majority faction secretly organized an assembly of the Knights of Labor which remained intact after the branch formed the United Association.

The favor-currying policies had supporters among the carriers as well as the clerks. The results were scandal and corruption that damaged both the clerks' and carriers' movements. Among the letter carriers, exposure and correction came from within the association. Protests by the clerks to President Theodore Roosevelt led to an official investigation and action by the White House.[3]

Dangerous as these scandals were, they proved to be an episodic and nonrecurring threat as the tone of the service rose with the strengthening of the merit system. The major challenge to organization unity and stability continued to be the division over methods and tactics.

When the National Association of Letter Carriers was founded in 1890, two years after the Knights of Labor had achieved the passage of the carriers' eight-hour law, a strong movement developed to bring the NALC into the labor order. A schism lasting several years ensued, during which the Knights' assemblies and the carriers' association attempted to function separately. The break was finally healed by a compromise and an apparent patronage deal which left the Knights' assemblies intact, made the Knights' national head president of the NALC, and placed the chief of the New York assembly on the NALC's executive board. By this time, the mid-1890s, the Knights of Labor were rapidly losing strength. Within a few years they disappeared as a significant force, thus bringing the split in the carriers' association to final solution. By the end of the 1890s the NALC had become a strong and well-knit organization.

The postal clerks' situation, however, was different. The Department bestowed its favors on the leaders of the National Association. The United Association, virtually barred from contact with the authorities and lacking the strength to influence legislation, was ready, after less than three years, to make concessions. The result was the formation of the United National Association of Post Office Clerks, which became known as the UNAPOC. Under the merger agreement supervisors above the grade of foremen were barred from membership, but all officials except postmasters who were members of the old National were permitted to continue their membership.

The formation of the UNAPOC merely shifted the controversy over departmental control of organization policy from one between two rival associations back to one between two factions in the same organization. Several of the local groups which had refused to take sides during the split demonstrated their lack of confidence in the new group by continuing to remain independ-

---

[3] Sterling D. Spero, *The Labor Movement in a Government Industry* (New York: Macmillan and Co., 1927), Chapters V, VI. Reprinted New York: Arno Press, 1971.

ent. In Chicago, where the independent association had affiliated with the Knights to protect it from departmental domination, opposition to the UNAPOC was particularly strong.

With the Knights rapidly losing ground, the AFL, seeking to fill the void and capitalize on the sentiment for labor affiliation, invited the postal workers to join its ranks. Two years later, in 1900, the Chicago clerks responded and received a local charter as the Chicago Post Office Clerks Union.

Affiliation with the AFL quickly became a major issue in the established postal organizations. It was brought to the floor of both the UNAPOC and Letter Carriers' national conventions and after bitter contests was rejected upon the recommendation of their respective leaderships. These contests left serious wounds. The Letter Carriers managed to maintain their unity, but the clerks suffered serious defections. Dissident members in a number of cities broke with their national association and formed AFL local unions. A few years later, in 1906, these unions united in the National Federation of Post Office Clerks with a national charter from the AFL.

B. REPRESSION AND CONFLICT IN THE POST OFFICE

Meanwhile, in an attempt to halt the push for policies the government was not ready to accept, President Theodore Roosevelt in 1902 issued his first gag order forbidding employees of the executive departments to seek to influence legislation in their behalf "individually or through associations—save through the heads of the departments." The gag extended an order of President Cleveland's Postmaster General William L. Wilson forbidding postal employees on pain of dismissal "to visit Washington, whether on leave, with or without pay, for the purpose of influencing legislation." An order by President Taft in 1909 went so far as to prohibit answering congressional requests for information.

The Roosevelt and Taft gag orders remained in effect for over a decade. The morale of the service was never lower than during those years. Taking their cue from the White House, postal division heads and bureau chiefs proceeded to outlaw organizations whose policies they opposed. Their orders were enforced by harsh penalties. Spying was resorted to freely, even to the extent of violating the privacy of the mails.

Grievances remained uncorrected, while both working conditions and the quality of service deteriorated. Yet, with the exception of unionized clerks, the established organizations not only took no action to oppose the gag but, in their efforts to maintain good relations with the Department, accepted it as a recognized rule of federal employment. This policy did not go unchallenged, however. As working conditions deteriorated, militant factions arose in the ranks of the Letter Carriers' and the Railway Mail Associations, while the UNAPOC suffered defections to the AFL-affiliated National Federation.

The fourth large group, National Rural Letter Carriers' Association, believed for a time that they could circumvent the gag because their official paper, the *RFD News*, was owned by a man who was neither an employee of the service nor a member of the association. The Department, however, indicating that the words "directly or indirectly" in the gag order meant what they said, soon brought the association to terms. But owing to the political connections of the rural carriers and their influence along their routes, the Department never succeeded in reducing their union to the same degree of subservience as the UNAPOC, the NALC, and the Railway Mail Association (RMA).

The unrest caused by the gag was most severe in the railway mail service which was responsible for the transportation of mail and its distribution on trains and in railway terminals. Its skilled distributors were regarded as the aristocrats of the service. Yet, standards of safety and sanitation had been permitted to decline to a scandalous state. A number of bad wrecks occurred in which many clerks were injured or killed when the wooden mail cars were smashed between heavy metal equipment. When clerks attempted to call this condition to public attention, the Department issued an order, the "wreck gag," forbidding employees to make any public comment on accidents or to say anything which might disturb the Department's "respectful relations with railroads." [4]

In the midst of this crisis Postmaster General Hitchcock issued orders to "take up the slack" in the railway mail service. Work was speeded up, routes combined, layoff periods reduced, crews cut, and the filling of vacancies forbidden—all on the eve of the Christmas rush. Virtual strikes occurred on some mid-Western runs, the most significant on the Tracy-Pierre run in North Dakota when clerks refused to take on extra work. Formal strikes were threatened elsewhere. Morale and efficiency plummeted. Mail remained unworked for days, with thousands of sacks transferred to sidetracked cars to await distribution by clerks called to work during their layoff periods.

---

[4] *Ibid.*, pp. 130-133.

Fearful of upsetting its departmental "stand-in," the leadership of the RMA failed to meet the crisis. Its inaction brought a smoldering, two-pronged rebellion to a head. One group of militants organized an opposition in the divisional and local units of the association in order to oust the national leadership. Another, seeking faster action, broke away from the RMA and established an independent Brotherhood of Railway Postal Clerks. The results were immediate. The "slack orders" were revoked and full departmental support was given for legislation to improve the safety and sanitation of mail cars.

The Brotherhood, however, did not stop there, but joined with the National Federation of Post Office Clerks in a major effort to repeal the Roosevelt and Taft gag rules as the employees' "fundamental grievance." A raucous though ably edited paper, *The Harpoon,* which later became the official organ of the Brotherhood, spearheaded the fight. It put on a vigorous campaign to raise funds and secure the reinstatement of the suspended Tracy-Pierre "strikers." When a Senate Committee shelved a provision requiring steel mail cars, *The Harpoon* urged the clerks to "refuse to ride" on cars they considered unsafe.

The new Brotherhood affiliated with the AFL and together with the union of post office clerks enlisted the powerful aid of President Samuel Gompers in the anti-gag fight. On August 24, 1912, a memorable date in civil service history, Congress passed the Lloyd-LaFollette Act, which outlawed the presidential gag orders. It guaranteed the right to lobby and nullified the Department's anti-union regulations recognizing the right of postal employees to organize and affiliate with outside organizations. It imposed an obligation not to strike against the government. The Act's wording, which had been approved by President Gompers prior to passage, allowed federal employees to join the AFL.[5]

Sooner than expected the guarantees of the Lloyd-LaFollette Act demonstrated their value, for President Wilson's Postmaster General, Albert S. Burleson, quickly proved a bold and implacable opponent of employee organization. In his effort to make not only the Post Office balance its budget but return a surplus to the Treasury, he attacked postal labor legislation enacted in the wake of the anti-gag fight. Legislation provided for eight hours of actual service to be worked within 10 hours and one rest day in seven. Burleson attempted to reduce salaries wherever he could find a loophole in the law to allow it. He opposed the employees' efforts to win pay increases to meet rising wartime prices, declar-

---

[5] *Union Postal Clerk,* August 1912, p. 1.

ing that they were "receiving three times as much as those fighting in the trenches." He attacked affiliation with the AFL and demanded the immediate repeal of the Lloyd-LaFollette Act.

When Burleson attempted to put part of his economy program into effect by administrative action, the employees' organizations, taking advantage of their new legal guarantees, went to Congress and obtained quick revocation of his acts. It had become apparent that attempts to cooperate with Burleson's administration were futile. The militant factions in the RMA and the NALC, which had become active during the anti-gag campaign, grew in strength. The National Federation of Post Office Clerks gained members at the expense of the UNAPOC.

Burleson attempted to counter these tendencies by removing the national officers of all the postal organizations except the UNAPOC from their postal jobs. Far from cowing the organizations, the move actually strengthened them by forcing them to employ their officers on a full-time basis, thus removing the constant threat of disciplinary action that the Department had held over them.

In a bold move to strengthen the militant factions in the old associations the National Federation of Post Office Clerks, whose constitution had always contained a provision supporting the principle of one big postal union, obtained a new charter from the AFL expanding its jurisdiction to the whole postal service. It was renamed the National Federation of Postal Employees. When carriers and railway mail clerks began to join it in large numbers, the two craft associations forestalled disruption by agreeing to affiliate with the AFL if the new union would surrender its charter and return to its old clerks' jurisdiction. A few years later the acts of affiliation taken by the NALC's and the RMA's conventions were affirmed by referenda.

The ferment also affected the Rural Letter Carriers' Association. A small body of carriers on routes radiating from urban centers withdrew and received an AFL charter as the National Federation of Rural Letter Carriers.

When Postmaster General Burleson left office on March 4, 1921, the *Union Postal Clerk,* the official organ of the National Federation, ran his picture over the legend:

"A Citizen of Austin—Mr. Burleson of Austin, Texas Who Almost Succeeded in Finishing What Ben Franklin Started—Our Postal Service. If His Involuntary Retirement Brings Him the Joy It Brings Us He Is A Happy Mortal."

The new Postmaster General, Will H. Hays, announced that Burleson's policies would be "completely reversed." It was his intention, he said, to "humanize the postal industry" and make the employees "partners in the enterprise." In his first report Postmaster General Hays declared: "I have met and am meeting and want to continue to meet the heads of all postal organizations just as often as it is convenient for them to see me. This, I understand, is a change in practice."

It was indeed, but there were, nevertheless, many features of Hays' personnel policy which made the unions suspicious and uneasy. The center of that policy was a system of local consultative committees headed by a National Service Relations Council. This council was composed of two representatives of each of the postal organizations; the AFL affiliates; and rival independent supervisors and postmasters' associations, the latter made up of political appointees. Under this set-up the employee groups which pursued a "stand-in" policy together with those representing the managerial bureaucracy and political appointees who owed their jobs to the Administration had a majority vote in the council. Furthermore, the Postmaster General openly expressed his disapproval of labor affiliation in an address to the UNAPOC convention in which he said, "We shall treat all alike, but shall cooperate so closely together that there will be no need of affiliations."

The regular unions believed the service relations system was a company union device intended to undermine them, and this gradually brought about the council's downgrading and eventual abandonment. The unions preferred to deal directly with Congress on basic employment conditions and to this end built one of the most successful lobbies at the Capitol.

In 1924 the postal organizations demonstrated their power when they obtained the passage of a salary bill increasing scales above levels desired by the Administration. President Coolidge vetoed the bill but Congress adjourned before the veto message was received. When the House met again after the President's overwhelming victory at the polls, all of his enhanced prestige and political clout could save the veto by only a single vote.

The great test of postal unionism came with the Depression of the 1930s. The volume of mail fell by more than one third. Pressure for wage cuts and layoffs finally resulted in the first wage reductions in the history of the federal service in the form of a month's furlough. This form of cut, amounting to $8\frac{1}{3}$ percent, was favored by the unions over a straight reduction since it maintained statutory salary rates. When the Roosevelt Administration came into office, a straight 15-percent salary cut was enacted.

This led to attacks on the union leadership by organized insurgents who insisted that the union officers "supinely surrendered to the economizers." Hardest hit were the substitutes, the lowest rung in the service ladder. These were civil service employees appointed after competitive examinations and were not to be confused with temporaries or provisionals taken on during holiday rush periods. The "subs," in short, were apprentices awaiting regular assignment. Although obliged to be on call for a full tour of duty, they did not receive annual salaries but were paid hourly rates and were called to work only when regulars were away or when the mails were too heavy for them to handle.

The steep decline in postal business caused by the Depression together with the economy wage cuts hit the substitutes hard. In many large city offices substitutes on duty for a whole week earned as little as six dollars. Impatient with the big unions for what they called neglect of their plight, the substitutes in several large cities formed the National Association of Substitute Postal Employees (NASPOE). Its membership included dissidents from the Federation, UNAPOC, and NALC. Lacking the legislative contacts and experience of the established unions, which incidentally were not neglecting the substitute problem, the new group turned to militant tactics.

A march on Washington demanding a "job for every substitute" was followed by a highly publicized report by Postmaster General Farley pointing to a postal surplus of nearly $5 million. But instead of using this money to improve the plight of his exploited employees, Farley set out to increase the surplus by more economies. On top of the 15 percent salary cut he sought to institute payless vacations for regular postal employees, a four-day payless furlough, and the curtailment of the employment of substitutes.

The effect was not unlike that of Hitchcock's "slack orders." The efficiency of the mail service declined. Sacks awaiting distribution and delivery piled up while idle trucks stood outside the post offices. Deliveries and collections in the residential sections were sharply curtailed.

Another march on Washington followed. The established unions entered the campaign and applied their traditional methods of publicity and political pressure so effectively that Postmaster General Farley was obliged to backtrack and rescind his orders.

The most significant long-range result of the "rebellion of the substitutes" and the formation of NASPOE was the thrust it gave to a new drive for one big union of postal workers. This had always been a stated objective of the National Federation of Post Office Clerks, but after the abandonment of its experiment with industrial unionism during the Burleson period the goal became rather academic.

Building on this sentiment, NASPOE, which organized all substitutes regardless of craft, called upon all substitutes and sympathizers in the regular unions to join in a one-big-union movement cutting across craft lines. These lines together with the UNAPOC-Federation split blocked efforts to prevent cuts and improve working conditions and service standards. The result was the establishment of the Committee for One Organization, which soon became known as the Committee for One. Communist influence was clearly present in the movement, which was supported by a Communist paper, the *Red Write-Up*. Openly distributed in front of all the large post offices, the paper not only supported the Committee for One but also urged a vote for the Communist ticket on Election Day.

The Committee was thus revealed as a group interested in splitting the established organizations and forming a Communist-controlled postal union. The next step followed shortly with the transformation of the Committee into the Postal Workers of America. Few clerks and carriers joined. Most members came from the postal laborers (later called mail handlers), the motor vehicle employees, and substitutes. Apparently no attempt was made to reach the railway mail clerks.

Economic recovery gradually changed the picture. Conditions among the substitutes improved to the point where their problems ceased to be a major issue and NASPOE was disbanded. Members of the Postal Workers of America also began to abandon their organization and join the regular unions. This, however, not only was a result of the passing of the postal crisis but also reflected a change in Communist Party tactics from independent "red unionism" to infiltration into and collaboration with established unions. Although a nucleus of sincere industrial unionists, chiefly among the mail handlers, motor vehicle employees, and fringe groups, remained, the movement became insufficiently representative to survive.

C. THE ONE-BIG-UNION CONCEPT

The demise of this movement by no means signaled the end of sentiment for industrial unionism. Strong support for it existed in every postal craft except possibly the rural carriers. The need for cooperation among the unions had always been recognized. A Joint Council of Affiliated Postal Organizations, representing the unions affiliated with the organized labor movement, has existed since the 1920s.

As federal labor relations matured under the Kennedy order the advisability of increased united strength in negotiating with management intensified. With the advent of the U.S. Postal Service, it became a virtual necessity. Indeed, it was almost to be expected that establishment of the new semi-independent agency would greatly stimulate postal mergers. Over the years, however, unity has been a long time coming and is not yet assured.

Earlier, a significant merger was effected between the UNAPOC and the Clerks' Federation, ending 60 years of fruitless, wasteful rivalry. The old Railway Mail Association, later renamed the Postal Transport Association, whose ranks were decimated by the drastic curtailment of railway mail service, joined the new clerks' union now known as the United Federation of Postal Clerks (UFPC). A merger of the small affiliated rural letter carriers organization with the National Association of Letter Carriers had already taken place.

Two important national groups that cut across craft classification still functioned independently. One was the National Alliance of Postal and Federal Employees, an organization of black postal workers of all classifications, and the National Postal Union (NPU), which broke away from the postal federation in 1958 over the issue of the under-representation of large city locals.

The NPU's powerful Manhattan-Bronx Postal Union (MBPU), for example, won exclusive recognition under the Kennedy order in the Bronx and New York post offices. It had a larger membership among the clerks than the Federation had in New York City, with some members among the carriers and substantial strength in the smaller postal crafts such as the special delivery messengers, mail handlers, motor vehicle workers, and maintenance employees.

The NPU was firmly committed to the goal of industrial unionism and tried hard to heal its split with the clerks. A merger agreement was carefully worked out between officers of the two organizations but was rejected by the UFPC at a special convention called in early 1966. The plan failed to achieve the required two-thirds majority by only 22 votes.[6] However, negotiations were continued, and a revised merger agreement was submitted to the

---

[6] United Federation of Postal Clerks, AFL-CIO, *Proceedings*, Special Convention, Cleveland, Ohio, April 1966, pp. 71-75.

regular national convention in August. Despite the support of its late president, Roy Hallbeck, and the officers of the United Federation, the convention, reflecting the greater voting weight of the smaller locals, rejected merger again, this time by a far wider margin.

Nevertheless, merger negotiations continued. Hallbeck expressed the leadership's views in both organizations when he declared:

> "We have paid a frightful price for disunity. It has had its effect in the Congress; it's had its effect in administrative circles. Our dealings with the Department have been something less than completely satisfactory . . . the Department has always had the advantage of being able to play both ends against the middle to the great disadvantage of those we represent." [7]

When merger negotiations were renewed in 1968, the cry of "one big postal employees union" was supported by claims of such management tactics.

In 1966, the issues had been narrowed substantially. Some fear was expressed over the financial condition of the NPU health benefits program. Major Federation opposition, however, was to NPU's adherence to the one-man, one-vote principle which, combined with the increased delegate representation of large locals at national conventions, would have furthered the imbalance between city and rural power and tended to "swallow up" the smaller locals.[8] Under the UFPC constitution, however, one third of the rural vote could always defeat the merger.

The NPU declared that it would continue its efforts to unite all postal workers in a single union, despite its two rebuffs from the Clerks' Federation. Strengthened by increasing membership and healthy finances, it voted for another merger attempt at its 1968 convention. Nevertheless, the resolution insisted that the merger committee adhere to prior NPU policies on industrial unionism, referendum election of officers, voice and vote roll calls at national conventions, and national convention representation.[9]

This round of merger negotiations lasted almost a year. In May 1969 both unions announced that proceedings had reached an impasse. Amid mutual complaints of intransigence, a deadlock again occurred over the two issues essential to the NPU position—a roll-call convention vote and proportionate representation on the merged national executive board. The NPU then considered its

---

[7] *Ibid.*, p. 1.

[8] United Federation of Postal Clerks, AFL-CIO, *Biennial Report to National Convention,* August 8, 1966, p. 6.

[9] *Government Employee Relations Report,* No. 259 (1968) , pp. A-11, E-1.

only alternative to be greater organizational activity in all postal areas.[10] Nevertheless, the door was kept open for further merger negotiations by the UFPC's new president, Francis F. Filbey, while the NPU affirmed its availability for merger talks with all unions.[11]

A number of smaller unions affiliated with the AFL-CIO still remained independent of the larger unions, although their merger with the clerks or carriers seemed logical. The National Association of Special Delivery Messengers could have been combined with the carriers. The National Association of Post Office Mail Handlers could logically have been absorbed by the Clerks' Federation or the NPU. Quite a stir ensued, therefore, when a special convention of the Mail Handlers voted to join the half-million strong Laborers' International Union of North America (LIUNA), AFL-CIO, in April 1968. The LIU, a "mixed" union represented about 30,000 government workers, primarily at the state, county, and city levels. It was planned that a special Mail Handlers Division would be set up within the LIUNA, and that the power, finances, and resources of the larger union would strengthen this group's influence with Congress, bargaining power, and organizational efforts.[12]

The merger was plagued by internal dissension, court suits, financial difficulties, and alleged dilatory tactics in implementing the agreement. Michigan mail handlers tried to enjoin the special convention. One group of national officers sought to enjoin the president and other officers from undermining and frustrating the merger. There was a question of the constitutionality of the special convention. Just before his death, President McAvoy of the Mail Handlers went to court to void the merger.[13]

The NPU, unlike the UFPC, was unhampered by the niceties of the AFL-CIO no-raiding agreement and embarked on a lively organizational campaign that could only benefit from the internal troubles of the Mail Handlers. In this they met with some success. The NPU displaced the Mail Handlers in Dayton, Ohio, and got informal recognition in Detroit.[14] In New York City the president of the large Mail Handlers Local 1 joined the Manhattan-Bronx Postal Union and urged all officers and members to do likewise. The president of the Bronx local followed suit.[15] The

10 *The Union Mail,* June 1969, pp. 3, 4.
11 *Government Employee Relations Report,* No. 300 (1969), pp. A-4, A-5.
12 *Ibid.,* No. 241 (1968), pp. A-6, A-7.
13 *Ibid.,* No. 264 (1968), pp. A-3, A-4; No. 273 (1968), pp. A-15, A-16.
14 *Ibid.,* No. 256 (1968), p. A-6; No. 260 (1968), p. A-1.
15 Manhattan-Bronx Postal Union, NPU, *The Union Mail,* March 1969, pp. 1, 3, 8.

MBPU claimed that almost 600 mail handlers came over to their organization.[16] Nevertheless, it was reported that the Mail Handlers were doing well in the organizing competition. Despite NPU inroads, they won 10 of 11 consecutive representation elections after the merger and displaced the NPU in the large Philadelphia Post Office.[17]

D. THE MERGER MOVEMENT

Such diverse maneuverings by all the unions concerned were dwarfed, however, by the merger efforts that followed passage of the Postal Reorganization Act. The whole issue was now placed in an entirely new perspective. Impending negotiations with the new quasicorporate Postal Service strongly militated toward greater unity in collective bargaining. This concern was enhanced substantially by a hard management approach to the first round of negotiations under the Act at both the national and local levels. Indeed, the first working contract was not arrived at until the 90-day bargaining period, the 45-day fact-finding stage, and the further 45 days' bargaining mandated by the Act were fully expended. The final step would have been the binding arbitration undesired by both sides. The negotiations had been carried on with the vehement and condemnatory comments that had unfortunately come to characterize postal collective bargaining. Against this dilatory background, major organizational mergers were consummated and the first steps initiated toward attaining "one big postal union."

For years many postal union leaders and observers of the field had believed that eventually the service would be represented by two major unions based essentially upon community of interest. Employees working inside, such as clerks, mail handlers, and maintenance staffs, would naturally form one union, according to this view; letter carriers, special delivery messengers, motor vehicle operators, and all employees working outside the post office would merge into another. To a degree this pattern was adhered to, for the inside workers acted first. But thus far the major outside unions, those representing the carriers, have maintained their independence.

The United Federation of Postal Clerks led the way. By December 1970, after several months of negotiations, a merger agreement was signed by the UFPC, the National Association of Post Office and General Services Maintenance Employees, and the

[16] *Government Employee Relations Report,* No. 287 (1969), p. A-4.
[17] *Ibid.,* No. 271 (1968), p. A-6; No. 252 (1968), p. A-6.

National Federation of Post Office Motor Vehicle Operators. Essentially, craft divisions were maintained, and the inside-outside differences presented no difficulty. The Special Delivery Messengers, another outside group, signed the merger agreement only a month later. All four unions were affiliates of the AFL-CIO. The UFPC contributed some 175,000 members, and the three other groups brought the total to more than 200,000.[18]

The major plum was the NPU and its large membership. An industrial union of primarily inside workers, it crossed craft lines. Its greatest strength lay in the urban centers. The groundwork had already been laid for merger; disagreements were now clearcut. Merger committees met and national officers of the AFL-CIO sought to resolve the major differences that were blocking full agreement.[19] Finally in March 1971 it was announced that a merger agreement acceptable to the NPU and particularly its 27,000 member Manhattan-Bronx Postal Union had been reached and signed.[20] After a favorable referendum vote on the merger and a new constitution, the American Postal Workers Union (APWU) would become a reality.

Aside from the usual questions of personalities, leadership, finances, and organizational structure that plague all merger efforts, several important issues, old and new, had to be surmounted for the NPU to join. The obstacles that frustrated prior attempts at merger were overcome by provisions for all national officers to be elected by referendum ballot votes mailed directly to the home of each member. The new conglomerate union would follow the industrial concept of a single postal union, but national craft departments or councils would preserve craft identities. The NPU's fear of rural convention dominance was allayed by the provision of proportionate representation at national conventions with one vote for each 25 members right down the line. Extensive local autonomy within the structure of a strong national organization was written into the constitution.[21]

With these issues resolved, ratification of the new merger and constitution became possible. Returns from all five unions showed 152,601 (96 percent) *for* and only 6,456 *against* the consolidation. This was not surprising. The need was there and the constitution was a truly democratic and modern document. The strength of a single union of approximately 320,000 members could

---

18 New York Letter Carriers, Branch 36, NALC, *Outlook,* January-February 1971, p. 3.
19 Manhattan-Bronx Postal Union, NPU, *News Flash,* February 17, 1971.
20 *New York Times,* March 4, 1971.
21 Manhattan-Bronx Postal Union, NPU, *The Union Mail,* April 1971, pp. 1, 2.

not be gainsaid. The point was not lost on George Meany, who observed, "The merger included the entry into an AFL-CIO union of the largest unaffiliated organization of postal workers." [22]

Four postal unions still remained outside the APWU. The invitation to join the merger had been extended to all.[23] The largest, the National Association of Letter Carriers (some 212,000 strong), had taken a watch-and-wait attitude while its merger committee worked with the Clerk's Federation. After the first major consolidation took place, the NALC and UFPC merger Committees "reported progress and a display of agreement on the part of all members." [24] Later, however, Carrier President James Rademacher chose to tread softly before fully committing himself.

For years sentiment for industrial unionism was prevalent among the rank and file in the larger offices. The New York branch of the Carriers in the late 1950s endorsed not only postal industrial unionism but one big union for all federal employees. Thousands of employees in many agencies demonstrated their support by joining the New York Carriers, which they regarded as the vehicle for the achievement of that objective. The national officers, however, put an end to the effort and forced the branch to return the noncarrier members to their established jurisdictions. More recently, during the difficulties following the 1970 strike the N.Y. Carriers Branch 36 and the MBPU conducted local area merger talks, none of which came to fruition.[25]

This concern for merger was not, however, a local sentiment alone. The national leadership of the NALC was always open to the possibilities of consolidation.When the Affiliations Committee reported to the NALC national convention in 1970, it stated:

> "The objective of this committee as mandated by past conventions has been to seek ways and means of closer relations with other labor unions and to work toward the merger of all postal unions. ... Our National Officers have always been willing to work with any other Union for the benefit of the postal worker. Through the years the NALC has been actively interested in the formation of ONE UNION of postal employees . . . ." [26]

Four plans were considered—complete merger of all postal unions, a federation of postal unions, the old alternatives of "outside" crafts merging with the Carriers and "inside" crafts with

---

22 David L. Perlman, "The Surge of Public Employe Unionism," *The American Federationist,* AFL-CIO, June 1971, p. 2.

23 The *New York Times,* March 4, 1971.

24 *The Postal Record,* January 1971, p. 7.

25 New York Letter Carriers, Branch 36, NALC, *Outlook,* April 1970, p. 1; Manhattan-Bronx Postal Union, NPU, *News Flash,* April 15, 1970, May 26, 1970.

26 National Association of Letter Carriers, 47th Biennial Convention, *Proceedings,* August 16-22, 1970, p. 32.

the Clerks, or complete independence for the NALC.[27] The clear intention was to continue merger efforts among all postal groups. Realistically the Committee concluded: "One big union or federation will come about only when all postal unions and their officers put aside their differences and jealousies and work together to achieve their common goal."[28]

After the momentous postal mergers, NALC President Rademacher was reported to be considering the additional alternatives of leaving the AFL-CIO entirely or possibly affiliating with the Teamsters.[29] This was part and parcel of his cautious attitude. He believed that the APWU would have to be fully ratified by its own rank and file and prove that it would be mutually beneficial to both the APWU and the NALC before the Carriers would even entertain steps to join.[30] Rademacher was concerned over the extensive assets the NALC would bring to any merger. Their value demanded that great care be exercised in their disposition. He declared: "NALC has millions of dollars of assets in real estate and insurance which we are not about to turn over to a merged group of unions without something substantial in return."[31] In question were the headquarters building worth over $4 million and other property assets, planned and existing. One of these, Nalcrest, the union's retirement home community in Lake Wales, Fla., represented an investment of some $4.5 million. Also involved were substantial assets in mutual benefit association—specifically, the Carriers Life Insurance Department—and a well-financed health benefit program.[32] Rademacher expressed his general sentiment in these words: "[A]s the oldest and most respected of all unions representing government workers, we do not intend to turn our assets, our membership and our prestige over to any group or groups until we are confident that in so doing, we would be acting in total support of the welfare of our membership."[33]

The independent National Rural Letter Carriers Association appeared resolved to continue its separatist position. Although postal reform has removed politics from future selections for these positions, the 30,000-odd rural carriers are mainly political

---

27 *Ibid.*, pp. 33-34.

28 *Ibid.*, p. 34.

29 Dennis Mullin "NALC Seen Taking Long Look at Postal Union Merger Merits," *Federal Times*, March 31, 1971.

30 James H. Rademacher, President, NALC, *The Postal Record*, April 1971, pp. 4-5.

31 *Ibid.*

32 Gerald Cullinan, Assistant to the President, NALC, *Interview*, August 17, 1971.

33 James H. Rademacher, *op. cit.*, p. 5.

appointees. They have always exhibited unique qualities of conservatism, independence, and loyalty towards their organization. The NALC made several attempts during the 1940s and 1950s to recruit them but to no avail, although a small minority of rural carriers joined the NALC. The Rural Carriers had national exclusive recognition and joined the Council of American Postal Employees (CAPE), which was established to present a united position during the first negotiations with the Postal Service. Cooperation ended there, however, and their craft "community of interest" has served to prevent any move towards merger.[34]

The National Alliance of Postal and Federal Employees comprises some 40,000 government workers, mostly blacks. With membership predominantly from the Postal Service, it nevertheless crosses craft lines. Its prime interest has been in developing a militant, forceful program for defending black interests against encroachment. Not only has it refrained from joining the merger movement, but it has unhesitatingly accused the seven national exclusive unions and the Postal Service of harassing black employees and subtly removing them from their jobs by relocating postal installations away from the core areas of the urban centers.[35] Under the recognition procedures of the Postal Reorganization Act, it is unlikely that the Alliance can achieve exclusive recognition, except possibly in jurisdictions with an overwhelmingly black postal population. Moreover, it is highly questionable whether it could effectively be heard as the voice of black rights if submerged in a much larger organization. Its prime function as civil rights watchdog could thus be seriously compromised in such a merger.

Considering these difficulties, the prospects for a single industrial union of postal workers are not assured. The Alliance and Rural Letter Carriers may not join, while the Mailhandlers and Letter Carriers may. If the price of the NALC's joining is a realignment into two unions of "inside" and "outside" workers with provisions for united bargaining, there will still be difficulties with the APWU and its industrial union concept. Should all postal unions ultimately combine, however, an organizational giant of some 700,000 workers will come into being. This would be one of the most prestigious elements of the American labor movement.

---

[34] Gerald Culliman, *op. cit.*

[35] "Seven Unions Accused of Working Against Black Postal Employes," *The New York Times*, August 11, 1971; "Negroes Accuse Postal Service," *The New York Times*, August 12, 1971.

There is another real possibility by which membership could be expanded to more than one million members. In the Federal Government it has been common practice for industrial, proprietary-type enterprises to deal with "mixed" unions. It is quite natural for workers, particularly in the traditional crafts, to organize accordingly regardless of whether they work for public or private employers. For years, the TVA, Interior Department, Alaska Railroad, Department of Defense, and others have dealt with such unions whether individually or in Trades Councils.[36] Under changed postal conditions, it would be neither illogical nor unusual for "mixed" unions of postal and other communications workers to develop as the Postal Service becomes more and more like a private-sector business. Postal workers would merely be revising old organizational patterns as their employer changed emphasis and direction.

Thus it was not surprising that in 1972 moves began to ally the large affiliated postal unions with their communications counterparts in the AFL-CIO in a single organization. Efforts by the APWU and the powerful Communications Workers of America (CWA) to effect a merger may have been the strongest impetus for NALC President Rademacher to reconsider joining. The CWA resolved in convention to work for a merger and began discussions with the APWU. President Filbey of the Postal Workers committed himself to present the issue to his convention in April 1972. Rademacher made public a letter received from Joseph A. Bierne, President of the CWA, suggesting the adoption of a similar resolution at the July 1972 NALC Convention. Bierne hoped the NALC would act affirmatively on the merger. The convention, as a preliminary to action, empowered a merger committee "to meet with those who are proposing an international union of all workers in the communication field." [37] Rademacher himself was reported to recognize the inevitability of a comprehensive alliance of communications and postal trade unions.[38] Despite opposition cries of "merger now," the recommendation was adopted that the committee "talk merger with the CWA during the next two years and report back to the convention in 1974." Merger efforts thus continued apace.[39]

---

[36] See Chapters II, XV, XVI, XIX.
[37] National Association of Letter Carriers, Bulletin #19, July 3, 1972.
[38] See Joseph Young, *Washington Evening Star,* July 6, 1972, p. A-2.
[39] National Association of Letter Carriers, 48th Biennial Convention, Bulletin #22, July 15, 1972.

Chapter IV

UNIONS IN THE CLERICAL, TECHNICAL, AND PROFESSIONAL SERVICES

More than million and a quarter federal employees outside the postal and industrial services work in every agency of government. One in five, a tenth of the whole federal service, works in metropolitan Washington. The rest are stationed over the length and breadth of the land and in far corners of the world. The overwhelming majority, 44 percent of the total federal employment, are in the classified service, their compensation fixed under the Classification Act and the Pay Acts of 1962 and thereafter. Another segment, accounting for about 7 percent, are in special services constituting the white-collar branches of the TVA, the United States Public Health Service, the Coast Guard, exempt categories in the Veterans Administration, and other federal hospitals and institutions, along with various branches of the Department of Justice, including the FBI. These special services together with those under the Classification Act represent almost every civil occupation from charwoman to zoologist, from astronomer to stone cutter.

Aside from the fact that they are all civil servants, these workers in scores of different agencies have little cohesion or feeling of common interest with employees outside of their own branches. The customs inspector in New York or Seattle has little in common with the mine inspector in Montana or Pennsylvania, or the teacher in an Indian School in New Mexico with the physicist in the Bureau of Standards.

It is hardly surprising that these employees have been the last to seek organization and the most difficult to organize. Such benefit societies and social organizations as did spring up among them from time to time did not follow the pattern of the postal societies and develop into labor unions. Although professional aloofness, white-collar snobbery, and the disparateness of the services account for this in large part, these have not been the only factors. Another major factor has been the role of the employees in the Washington departments. Although representing only one fifth of the classified personnel, the Washington employees down to World War I largely set the tone and attitude of the field.

A. THE FIRST WHITE-COLLAR EFFORTS

Nearly all the employees in Washington, even after the passage of the Civil Service Act in 1883, continued to owe their jobs and allegiances to congressmen and politicians back home. Under the law, Washington jobs were apportioned among the several states in proportion to population. Although the apportionment system is now virtually dead, many employees still maintain close relations with their congressmen. In earlier times, before the great expansion of the service beginning with the New Deal and the Second World War, a larger proportion of the service worked in the capital. Here in this most politically sensitive spot everyone from Cabinet secretaries to "government girls" took their cues from the powers in the White House or in Congress. Franklin K. Lane, President Wilson's Secretary of the Interior, called Washington "a place where everyone is afraid of everyone and the protective sense is abnormally developed." Although these attitudes became modified in the field, the tone of the capital could still be felt and hardly provided a climate conducive to the growth of employee organization.

The first serious attempt to form a nonpolitical organization to defend and promote the interests of the employees outside the post office and the crafts was made in 1896 when a group of customs employees in New Orleans suggested "the propriety of organizing a National Association of Civil Service Employees on lines similar to those of the National Carriers Association." [1]

The purpose of the association was to break the hold of local politicians on the employees whose pay and working conditions, as in the Post Office before the clerks and carriers classification acts, were virtually fixed by the local office heads acting in conjunction with leaders of the political machines. Local associations were formed in response to the New Orleans call in more than a dozen cities from New York to New Orleans to San Francisco. In 1896 delegates met in Washington and resolved:

"The employees of the Classified Civil Service are declared to be, in law and in fact, employees of the Government, and they do not, by reason of their employment, owe any duty to any political party, nor to any political leader. They are in no sense the private em-

---

[1] Correspondence with L. P. Ault, the organization's prime mover.

ployees of any officer of the Government whose official duties constitute him the superior officer of others, and they have not surrendered in the least degree their status as American citizens, with every right to act unitedly in their own interests." [2]

The association declared its central purpose to be "to inaugurate and conduct a campaign of Civil Service education which will have the effect of strengthening the growing sentiment for Civil Service Reform." Resolutions condemned the continuance of appointment and removal for political reasons. Legislation was sponsored requiring that cause for removal be stated in writing as required much later in the Lloyd-LaFollette Act.

A committee was sent to see President Proctor of the Civil Service Commission to offer the association's cooperation in the promotion of civil service reform. It was rebuffed. As the official custodian of civil service reform, the commissioner wanted no assistance or cooperation from civil service employees. "Mr. Proctor received us coldly," said association president L. P. Ault. "He gave us no encouragement whatsoever." [3]

The rebuff put the National Civil Service Association out of business as a labor organization and auxiliary of the civil service reform movement. The association, however, made one major contribution to good administration and better employment relations by launching the movement for civil service retirement. An association bill providing for a contributory retirement system was introduced in Congress in 1897 and reintroduced at each following session until the organization went out of existence. While the association's chief weakness was its inability to make headway among the politically oriented employees in the Washington offices, retirement was one issue which caught their interest. When the association disbanded in 1900, the United States Civil Service Retirement Association took its place. The retirement movement was greatly strengthened by the support of the National Association of Letter Carriers. However, bitter conflicts between factions supporting contributory retirement on the one hand and straight pension plans on the other held up legislation for nearly 20 years while the rival groups fought each other in the courts. By that time, the National Federation of Federal Employees had been organized, and it played a leading role in the passage of the Retirement Act of 1920.

Meanwhile, efforts to organize the Washington service came to naught. In 1911 the *Civil Service Advocate,* the organ of one of the retirement associations, suggested that the retirement issue be

---

2 National Civil Service Association, *Proceedings,* 1896, p. 10.
3 Correspondence with President L. P. Ault of the Association.

dropped and energy concentrated on securing higher salaries. In a poll taken by the *Washington Times,* 70 percent of the 12,600 employees casting ballots supported a salary increase regardless of retirement legislation. Yet no movement for higher pay developed. The gag rule obviously made a salary campaign difficult, but it also became an excuse for inaction. Despite the vigorous activity among postal groups for removal of the gag, the Washington employees remained aloof and allowed the postal workers to carry the battle for them.

It appeared that nothing could arouse the departmental employees. In 1912 Congress passed a measure limiting the tenure of civil service employees to seven years. While the measure was pending, a mass meeting of protest was called, not by the departmental workers, but by the National Federation of Post Office Clerks. Though well advertised and pushed, only 96 employees came to the meeting to defend their jobs against the spoilmen's threat.

President Oscar F. Nelson of the Postal Clerks angrily addressed the gathering, saying:

"If I were a member of Congress and knew that only ninety-six out of thousands who were affected attended, I would vote for the limited tenure bill because if they were not more interested in their welfare, than such attendance indicated, I would take it for granted that they favored the proposition to legislate them out of a job." [4]

Congress evidently assumed the correctness of Nelson's views and passed the bill. The AFL and the postal union strongly urged President Taft's veto, which, as a supporter of the merit system, he readily gave.

A number of attempts were made around this time to issue papers or magazines devoted to the interests of the Washington employees. The most notable were the *Departmental Journal* and the *Government Clerk.* The ventures failed to rouse the Washington corps not only to any efforts at united action but apparently even to interest in their common concerns. This contrasts with the central role which journals played in the organization of postal workers and local government employees. The *Postal Record,* a privately owned magazine, played a leading role in the formation of the National Association of Letter Carriers. Its editor, John F. Victory, became the association's first national secretary, the NALC assuming ownership of the magazine. The *R.M.S. Bugle* predated the establishment of the Railway Mail Associa-

---

[4] National Federation of Federal Employees, *Summary of Proceedings of the First and Second Conventions,* 1919, pp. 73-74.

tion and did much to arouse sentiment among the railway postal clerks for the establishment of their organization. *The Harpoon,* under the editorship of Urban A. Walter, was instrumental in the exposure of the disgraceful working conditions in the Railway Mail Service and in the fight against the departmental and presidential gag orders. Its efforts led to the formation of the Brotherhood of Railway Postal Clerks and to the ultimate victory of the militant wing in the RMA. The *R.F.D. News* led to the formation of the National Rural Letter Carriers Association. Though it continued to be individually owned, it became the association's "official organ," and its editor-owner, Wisdom D. Brown, became the organization's leader. The purpose of this arrangement was to assure greater freedom in exposing the rural carriers' position in the face of administration pressures on their association, which was heavily weighted with employees who owed their appointments to political patronage.

In local government a privately owned weekly, *The Chief,* long served as a voice for New York's municipal employees. Its owner-editor organized and led the Civil Service Forum, which remained the dominant employee organization for many years. In the same way, a New Jersey journal, *The Civil Service,* led the principal employee organization in that state. In New York State, *The Civil Service Leader,* an independently owned weekly, became the organ of the powerful state Civil Service Employees Association.

Even today outside journalism plays a leading role in keeping federal employees abreast of governmental developments and in supporting their efforts for their occupational protection and advancement. Columnists for the major daily newspapers in Washington have become leading makers of civil service opinion. The *Federal Times,* an independent Washington paper, plays a role in federal service affairs equal to that which the independent civil service weeklies have long played among public employees in New York City.

B. INTERNECINE STRIFE: DISSENSION OVER CLASSIFICATION AND THE AFL

Despite the long and persistent lethargy of the employees in the classified service, their activities were stimulated anew by the anti-gag fight, the passage of the Lloyd-LaFollette Act, and the success of the postal unions in combatting the hostility of Postmaster General Burleson's administration. Again, as a decade and a half earlier, the customs service was first to move. Local associations of customs inspectors were formed at several major ports at the call of the employees in New York and late in 1912 united in the National Association of Customs Inspectors. Though at first attempting to function as a general labor organization, the association because of its limited membership decided to ignore economic concerns and rather to work with the Treasury to improve the administration of the service and to defend employees against what it regarded as unjust charges. In defending aggrieved employees the association followed the practice of taking cases only if convinced of their innocence.

Two local unions affiliated directly with the AFL in 1913 and 1914. The first, a union of general jurisdiction, was formed in San Francisco; the second, a small local in the Treasury Department, finally broke the ice in the Washington service. No additional progress was made, however, until a congressman from Kansas, William P. Borland, introduced a bill to increase hours of labor from seven to eight a day without increased compensation. Borland, proud of his record as a "friend of labor," was shocked to find that the Washington employees, instead of greeting his measure with their usual complaisance, protested vigorously. Borland assumed that he was merely correcting the favored status of federal employees by bringing the working conditions in line with those of other workers.

The AFL, however, took the position that the diminution of working standards, regardless of their superiority to those generally prevailing, was a threat to the interests of the labor movement. Under the leadership of a group in the office of the Quartermaster General of the Army, which quickly obtained an AFL charter, a mass meeting was called to fight the Borland amendment. The hall was packed and hundreds were turned away for lack of room. AFL President Gompers and Secretary Morrison addressed the crowd.

The Borland rider was overwhelmingly defeated in the House, largely as a result of AFL pressure. The effect on the employees both in Washington and in the field was astonishing. Inquiries came to President Gompers from city after city. The AFL put organizers in the field. By the end of the summer of 1917 delegates of 64 local federal employee unions with 10,000 members gathered in Washington and under Gompers' leadership launched the National Federation of Federal Employees.

The jurisdiction of the new union was exceedingly broad. It covered all civil employees of the Federal Government and of the District of Columbia except postal employees and "those exclusively eligible to membership in any other existing national or international organization affiliated to the American Federation of Labor." The latter exclusion was eventually to cause a great deal of trouble.

The constitution contained a strong no-strike clause. The union president, Luther C. Steward, laid great stress on the significance of affiliation with the AFL, saying:

> "Federal employees, as wage earners, have interests in common with all wage earners and the AFL is the big central American organization of all wage earners—We need support of our fellow workers to win our cause but we owe them our support in return. The National Federation of Federal Employees is a trade union and the obligations of trade unions are mutual."

The new union's first test was a second attempt by an angry Congressman Borland to overcome his earlier defeat with another try at lengthening the hours of labor. Though his measure this time passed both Houses, the NFFE with the AFL's strong support induced President Wilson to veto it. Following this victory the NFFE and its labor allies carried the fight into Borland's district in Missouri and in a primary campaign in which the vetoed bill was a clear-cut issue defeated the Congressman by a large majority. Two national officers of the NFFE campaigned openly.

One of the major problems before the federal service in the years immediately following World War I was the inadequacy of the pay scales, exacerbated by the gross inequities which crept into them as a result of the haphazard expansion of the service. Basic pay for the clerical grades was set by an act of 1854 and for the subclerical grades by an act of 1866. New agencies created in the meantime were staffed with employees whose pay was fixed by new law and regulations that took little account of established standards. The doubling of the service during World War I added to the confusion. New employees were recruited at new levels while older employees, often in the same offices, continued under scales more than a half century old. It was not unusual to find supervisors making less than their subordinates. The morale of the service reached so low a point at the war's end that it was difficult to keep the service adequately manned and to carry on the operations of many agencies.[5]

At the NFFE's initiative a congressional Joint Commission on Reclassification, which became known as the Keating Commission after its chairman, Representative Clarence Keating, was set up.

---

[5] See two articles by Mary Connyngton in *Monthly Labor Review,* June 1920 and December 1920.

Its report, a landmark in public personnel administration, found that the government had no standard for fixing pay, no plan for relating salaries to the character of work performed, no system of promotion or advancement, and no adequate provision for such important matters as working space, illumination, ventilation, rest rooms, and medical and surgical emergency relief.[6] The report recommended the classification of the service in the District of Columbia into grades and classes with compensation fixed on the basis of comparable pay for comparable work. The ultimate result was the Classification Act of 1923.

It took over four years from the publication of the report to the passage of the Act. They were years of intense political activity on the part of the NFFE to overcome resistance in congressional and party quarters where the manipulability of the old system was preferred to the regularity and order provided by the Joint Commission's proposals. Vocal opposition came from the Bureau of Efficiency, the governmental agency for research in administrative management. The Bureau insisted that position classification was its function and opposed the creation of the Reclassification Commission. It was especially critical of the leading role the NFFE played not only in the creation of the Joint Commission but also in the conduct of its work. The union helped to recruit and organize the Commission's staff and along with other employee organizations in Washington was officially represented on its working committees. Instead of hailing this first attempt in the federal service at government-employee cooperation, the Bureau condemned it as a dangerous innovation that turned a prime management function, which "belonged in the hands of responsible officials," over to "subordinate employees who could not trace their authority to the people."[7]

Encouraged by the success of its cooperation with the union, the Reclassification Commission suggested that the relationship be made permanent by the creation of a Civil Service Advisory Commission. This was to consist of 12 members, six to be designated by the President to represent the administrative staffs and two each from the manual, clerical, and professional services to represent the employees. The advisory group was to provide for the selection of personnel committees in each department and bureau "to assist in improving the morale and efficiency of the serv-

---

[6] U.S. House of Representatives, *Report of the Congressional Joint Commission on Reclassification of Salaries, House Document 686,* 66th Cong., 2nd Sess., 1920, p. 54.

[7] Interview with Herbert D. Brown, Chief of the Bureau of Efficiency, and other Bureau officials, 1922.

ice, and in making suggestions and recommendations as to personal service regulations, methods, and organization of work, working conditions, health and safety." [8]

This first proposal for employee-management cooperation in the federal service was attacked by the Bureau of Efficiency as an attempt to make "employee interference in personnel matters permanent." The NFFE, sensing a threat to its campaign for reclassification, allowed the proposal to fade away. This concession, however, did little to ease the way for reclassification. The struggle became enmeshed in high politics. Senator Reed Smoot of Utah, chairman of the Appropriations Committee, and his allies in both Houses set out to block reclassification.

The campaign for the bills incorporating the Keating Commission's proposals was led by a group called the Joint Committee on Reclassification, an ad hoc body not to be confused with the Keating Congressional Joint Commission, which had ceased to exist after it completed its report. The new joint committee was composed of trade unions both in and outside of Washington and was supported by civic organizations and reform groups.

The joint committee's bill was blocked by a rival measure drawn by the Bureau of Efficiency and sponsored by Senator Smoot and his counterpart in the House, Representative Wood. The ensuing deadlock continued through session after session until the White House intervened in March 1923 and forced the passage of a compromise measure, the Classification Act of 1923. One wholesome result of the compromise was a slight reduction in the number of grades and classes into which the service was divided. Its key provision, which placed the implementation of the law in the hands of an *ex officio* body, the Personnel Classification Board, rather than in the Civil Service Commission alone, was a clear victory for the Smoot-Bureau of Efficiency forces. This *ex officio* agency was composed of representatives of the Civil Service Commission, the Bureau of Efficiency, and the Bureau of the Budget. The NFFE objected strongly on the grounds that there was no authority to which the board was responsible, that the Bureau of Efficiency was hostile to the kind of classification the law required, and that the Bureau of the Budget was more interested in keeping expenses down than in fixing equitable wages.

That NFFE's fears were justified was quickly demonstrated. The Smoot faction, operating through the Bureau of Efficiency, dominated the Board, using its position to reward and punish

---

[8] Report of the Joint Commission, *op. cit.*, pp. 131-132.

federal employees and agencies according to the exigencies of patronage and Smoot faction policies. Representative Frederick R. Lehlbach, Chairman of the House Civil Service Committee and a fellow Republican, charged on the House floor that the Personnel Classification Board had deliberately violated every provision of the law except the clause creating it.[9] Over the protest of the Civil Service Commission member, the Board refused to carry out specific requirements of the Act and, according to the House Civil Service Committee, "made no classification at all and attempted to impose a plan which the Congress had rejected." [10]

The classification which finally emerged gave practically no salary increases. Such raises as were given were small amounts required to bring the old scale, including the flat cost-of-living bonus granted after the war, up to the new scale set in the law. According to the union, about 90 percent of the employees were classified on the basis of salary plus bonus, that is, their current rate of pay. The remaining 10 percent were rewarded for playing the game with the Smoot-Bureau of Efficiency alliance or punished for refusing to play. In one office, cards calling for identical duties were classified in three different grades. Three bureaus in the Department of Labor—Women's, Children's, and Labor Statistics—which had beaten the Smoot group in a tug of war over appropriations were punished by classification as minor bureaus. Statisticians and economists in one of these bureaus were classified as clerks, while those with the same qualifications and responsibilities in the Department of Agriculture were classified as professionals at twice the salary.

Inequities in the law's administration and refusal of the Personnel Classification Board to extend provisions of the Act to the field services, where inequities were even greater than in Washington, soon backfired on the NFFE. Discontent was especially great in large and cohesive services like customs and immigration, which began to move on their own for salary increases. A benefit society among the immigration people which had never before behaved like a labor union urged separate salary legislation. The customs employees formed a new Customs Service Association to embrace all customs personnel, including the already well-organized inspectors. Bills were introduced for salary increases. President Luther C. Steward of the NFFE reluctantly opposed these bills, arguing that separate efforts by various employee groups threatened to undermine the Federation's efforts to obtain an or-

---

[9] Speech by Hon. Frederick R. Lehlbach in the House of Representatives, February 12, 1924, p. 8 (published as a pamphlet by the Government Printing Office) .
[10] U.S. House of Representatives, *Report No. 315*, 68th Cong., 1st Sess., 1924.

derly, systematic handling of the total salary problem. Although many customs workers understood Steward's position and remained loyal to the NFFE, as the new customs association had originally urged, a large group in New York and some other eastern ports withdrew from the NFFE in protest.

Other disappointed groups also began to drop out of the union. The decline in membership was not checked or reversed until the passage in 1928 of the Welch Act, which increased pay and directed the Personnel Classification Board to survey the field service for reclassification.

In 1931 a chastened and reformed Board issued its final report, which contained an apparently innocent proposal that was to tear the federal employees' union movement apart. The offending proposal called for the extension of the classification principle throughout the federal service, including the skilled crafts. Suspicion bred by the breadth of the NFFE's jurisdiction was already eroding relations between it and the craft unions. The NFFE charter, drawn by Samuel Gompers himself, covered persons eligible for membership in established AFL unions if they already belonged to the union of primary jurisdiction. A number of federal workers in the crafts and trades had joined the NFFE, especially at installations where they constituted only a few craftsmen among many white-collar and general workers. Some of these members were not in good standing in their craft unions when they joined the Federal Employees. Others failed to maintain their craft dues after joining, a situation on which the NFFE found it difficult to check.

The craft union's officials, especially in the metal and building trades, charged the NFFE with "rustling" and "raiding" their members. Similar charges had been made by AFL unions against one another since the birth of the AFL and were frequently accompanied by bitter controversy, sometimes leading to temporary withdrawal from the Federation.

The craft leaders, however, refused to treat the NFFE's trespasses as just another jurisdictional dispute. Unlike the usual AFL controversy, more than two unions were involved. Nearly all the metal trades and several other unions were aligned against the NFFE. They were apparently as much concerned with the threat of industrial unionism to craft jurisdiction as they were with the defection of a comparatively small number of members. The issue became exaggerated in the minds of the craft leaders into a struggle for the perpetuation of craft unionism against an incompatible type of organization.

John P. Frey, of the AFL Metal Trades Department, charged that the NFFE by its support of the Final Report of the Classification Board revealed its intent to extend its jurisdiction over all craftsmen. He called on the AFL at its convention in Vancouver to reverse its repeated stands in favor of classification and oppose the NFFE's measure.

The suggestion that the skilled crafts be included in the classification system had first been made in the Keating Report in 1920. Then the NFFE, at the insistence of the crafts, withdrew its support for the proposal, making clear that it had no intention of forcing craftsmen into classification schemes if they preferred not to be included. NFFE now repeated this offer regarding the recommendation in the Final Report. The postal unions and NFFE implored the leaders of the craft unions not to press their hostile resolution. The controversy over the handful of craftsmen who had joined the Federation could, they said, easily be solved as similar controversies had been in the past. But the craft leaders, obsessed with suspicion of the Federation's industrial union ambitions, pushed their resolution through the convention.[11]

The leadership of the Federal Employees, denied AFL support for its major legislation program, believed that it had no choice but to recommend withdrawal from the AFL. At this point AFL President William Green, who had succeeded Gompers, made belated conciliatory overtures. These came too late, however. The leardership of the NFFE had committed itself. In very light balloting in which but half the membership participated, the Federal Employees, by a vote of 16,335 to 11,406, voted to leave the AFL.[12]

If the AFL convention, dominated by the craft leaders, blundered in denying an affiliate the support to which it believed it was entitled, the NFFE likewise blundered, especially after conciliatory gestures were finally made, in choosing to sever its ties with the labor movement. The NFFE, after all, owed its inception to the AFL and had always, with the possible exception of the National Federation of Post Office Clerks, laid greater emphasis on its labor solidarity than any other union of federal workers. Many opponents of disaffiliation regarded the move as a desertion of principle. The majority of the Washington membership voted against withdrawal, as did sizable blocs in other large cities.

---

11 American Federation of Labor, *Proceedings*, 1931, p. 125.
12 For reports on the two sides of the controversy see John P. Frey, *The Story May Now be Told*, 1933; and National Federation of Federal Employees, *History of the Break in Affiliation with the American Federation of Labor*, 1933.

President Luther C. Steward, cognizant of the significance of this pro-AFL sentiment within the Federation and conscious of his own and his union's background, made frequent statements such as, "We feel that the proper place for an organization of federal employees is affiliation with the general labor movement and withdraw with great reluctance." [13] The AFL, however, instead of using such declarations together with the pro-AFL sentiment, proceeded to make the breach permanent by chartering a new union, the American Federation of Government Employees.

AFGE's arrival on the scene was soon followed by the election of President Franklin D. Roosevelt and the launching of the New Deal. Thousands of militant, labor-conscious youths entered the federal service to man the New Deal agencies. A cleavage deeper than that between the two unions quickly developed inside the ranks of the AFGE. The New Dealers supported militant trade union tactics such as the expanding labor movement was practicing in private employment. These included demonstrations, picketing, and loud public demands. The membership in the old-line departments opted for quiet legislative efforts such as those the NFFE had practiced for years before its break with the labor federation.

The militants quickly turned their pressures into a challenge to the AFGE leadership. The gauntlet was thrown down when General Hugh S. Johnson, administrator of the National Recovery Administration (NRA), fired John L. Donovan, president of the NRA local lodge, following a disorderly demonstration by a delegation led by him in the administrator's office. Abusive attacks on Johnson followed. A joint committee of AFGE and NFFE picketed the administrator's office carrying placards accusing him of anti-unionism even as he was trying to persuade private employers to deal with unions of their employees.

Although the AFGE leadership supported the local lodge, both the local lodge and national AFGE officers disavowed responsibility for the tactics used when Johnson submitted the dispute to arbitration. This disavowal was implemented at the AFGE convention in New York the following autumn by amendments to the national constitution forbidding picketing and strikes and limiting delegations to government offices to not more than five persons.

This action intensified the fight for control of the union. Between the close of the New York convention and the opening of

---

[13] Correspondence, April 25, 1932.

the next, nearly a dozen local lodges had been suspended for violating the anti-picketing clause and other national regulations. When the next convention met the national leadership took further measures to strengthen its position by requiring each new local lodge to serve a probationary period as a temporary affiliate in order to give the national office time to "observe the conduct, character, and qualifications of the applicants," [14] and thus protect itself against infiltration by its opponents.

When the economic recession of 1937 was reaching its low point, an economy drive was launched in Congress. The militants, fearing pay cuts and furloughs similar to those imposed in the early Roosevelt years, demanded that the AFGE depart from its traditional legislative methods and adopt more vigorous and less restrained tactics. When the national leadership refused, declaring that such methods would do more harm than good, seven Washington lodges defied the national office, formed a Committee Against False Economy, and called a mass meeting. The national leadership suspended the rebellious locals, which thereupon attacked the AFGE and the AFL as "undemocractic and ineffective" and requested the Committee for Industrial Organization, the forerunner of the Congress of Industrial Organizations (CIO), to admit them to membership and launch an all-out drive for a mass organization of federal employees. The Committee acceded and a new union, the United Federal Workers of America (UFWA), was formed.

The new movement fell far short of its announced objective. Although the UFWA constitution repeated all the restrictions on striking, picketing, and mass tactics contained in the charters of the older unions, the circumstances of its birth caused the great body of federal workers to shun it. Furthermore, it soon became obvious to Jacob Baker, the provisional president designated by the CIO, and to numbers of members who joined seeking a more militant union, that Communists were gaining a dominant place in the organization. Baker's resignation, when a convention assembled at the end of the union's provisional status, helped to make this state of affairs clear to many prospective members.

However, the UFWA, without practicing the noisy tactics of the AFGE dissidents who brought it into being, was responsible for significant innovations in federal union practice. Instead of confining its operations to legislative activity, it emphasized the handling of grievances and complaints to a far greater extent than did the other unions. It presented evidence both orally and

[14] *The Government Standard,* December 23, 1936.

in writing to the Bureau of the Budget and was the first federal employee union to obtain statements of personnel policy in white collar agencies. It referred to these efforts as "shop activities" and "collective bargaining," thus stressing its role as a "real union" rather than just another "employee lobby."

During World War II and as long as the entente with the Soviet Union lasted, the UFWA assumed the role of a superpatriotic organization. But when the war ended and the union found itself faced with the prospect of little growth in its comparatively small membership, it merged with the CIO's union of local government employees, the State, County, and Municipal Workers of America, whose leadership was even further to the left than that of the federal workers' union. In the merged organization, the United Public Workers of America (UPWA), the federal membership was in a decided minority.

The first UPWA convention, held in the spring of 1946, adopted a resolution calling for an end to American efforts to isolate the Soviet Union and demanding the withdrawal of British and American troops from "friendly countries," including Greece, China, the Philippines, and India. It refused, however, to adopt a resolution calling for the withdrawal of Soviet troops from Poland, Bulgaria, and other east European nations.[15]

The compounding of this blunder by the adoption of a provision on strike policy brought about a drop in federal employee membership to a mere 5,000[16] from 38,000 at the time the merger took place. The strike provision extended the policy of the local government union to the merged union. It provided that a local union contemplating a strike must first receive the permission of the national president. Congress reacted quickly with its first outright antistrike legislation depriving an employee of his salary for membership in a union "asserting the right to strike against the United States" and requiring an affidavit from every employee declaring that he was not a member of such an organization.[17] The president of the UPWA attemped to counteract the disastrous effect of the strike policy and the resulting antistrike legislation by issuing a long explanation holding that the strike proviso did not apply to federal employees.

Anticommunist members who still believed that the union could serve a useful purpose formed a Build the Union Committee with centers in a dozen cities "to adhere firmly and loyally to

---

[15] Sterling D. Spero, *Government as Employer*, pp. 198, 199.
[16] This was exclusive of 15,000 Panamanian employees in the Canal Zone organized in 1946.
[17] Public Law 419, 79th Cong., July 3, 1946.

national CIO policy" and restore public confidence "by divorcing our union from divisive ideological policies and practices." [18] The decline and loss of confidence had gone so far, however, that the rescue effort made no headway. Expulsion from the CIO in the early 1950s along with other allegedly Communist-dominated unions brought the rapid disintegration and final disappearance of the UPWA, leaving the field once more to the NFFE and the AFGE.

C. UNION REACTIONS TO THE KENNEDY ORDER

Whether it was their rivalry, aggravated by the period of triple unionism, or merely apathy on the part of the employees to whom they appealed, the NFFE and the AFGE showed no significant growth until the issuance of the Kennedy executive order.

The two unions gave the executive order strikingly different receptions. To John Griner, president of the AFGE, it offered "an unparalleled opportunity for management and non-management employees to demonstrate their ability to cooperate in the public interest and in the interest of those who have chosen the federal service as a career." [19]

To Vaux Owen, president of the NFFE, the order threatened the best interests of the employees by pitting "management" against "rank and file" in an adversary relationship based on "outside union thinking" posing a threat of the "progressive development of practices associated with collective bargaining in industry." [20] Holding the order an unconstitutional exercise of executive authority, Owen led the NFFE to institute an unsuccessful court action to prevent its implementation.[21]

Meanwhile the AFGE, taking full advantage of the order, won scores of exclusive recognition agreements. Its membership grew at a rate exceeding that of any union in the country, while the NFFE suffered a membership decline of some 30 percent, falling from a high of 60,000 to 42,500 in September 1964.

These apparent results of Owen's policy sparked a revolt against his leadership led by Nathan T. Wolkomir, NFFE's national vice president. Seeking to forestall the opposition, Owen advised limited compliance with the order at the local level. However, a few scattered locals representing some 3,000 members

---

[18] Build the Union Committee, *Statement of Policy*, October 26, 1947.
[19] Quoted in *Management Relations With Organized Public Employees* (K. O. Warner, ed.) (Chicago: Public Personnel Association, 1963), p. 222.
[20] *Ibid.*, pp. 232-233.
[21] National Federation of Federal Employees, *et al.* v. Paul H. Nitze, Secretary of the Navy, *et al.*, Civil Action No. 1380-64, D.D.C., September 29, 1965.

had already sought and won exclusive recognition. The ice was broken by Wolkomir's own local, representing 2,100 employees at the Air Force base at Rantoul, Ill. At the national convention in September 1964 Wolkomir defeated Owen for the presidency by a vote of 326 to 317. The vote was close, but this has usually been true of votes overthrowing a sitting union administration.[22]

Moving to reverse his predecessor's policy, Wolkomir declared that the NFFE had "finally and officially found Executive Order 10988." [23] A vigorous organizational drive followed, Wolkomir noting that unlike the AFGE, whose charter forbade it to organize wage board workers, the independent NFFE was free of the jurisdictional restrictions which the AFL-CIO placed upon its affiliates. "Our strength," he declared, "is not in maintaining a 'semiprofessional' union but a union in its true connotation—a union for all federal employees." [24]

It was easier, however, to announce the NFFE's new look than to give it substance. The vote for the new policy had been close. A large part of the membership had favored the old order, and the union was still bound by many old commitments. The convention which elected the new regime had at the same time voted approval of the lawsuit to invalidate the executive order and approved the outgoing president's report denouncing exclusive recognition as alien to the traditions of the service. Thus, Wolkomir could announce, "We intend to use the Executive Order and milk it to dryness," [25] and at the same time attack one of the order's central concepts, exclusive recognition, as having created a "melody of chaos" by developing union power structures and causing management to lose ground.[26] But as the new regime became entrenched and more confident, concessions to past attitudes diminished. Exclusive recognition was sought and won for installation-wide units of blue-collar and white-collar workers.

The AFGE, despite its charter bar against the admission of wage-board workers, admitted that it had been organizing such workers since its establishment in 1932 even though NFFE's break with the AFL resulted from similar but less flagrant juris-

---

[22] Note the close votes ousting the leadership of Carey in the International Union of Electrical Workers, MacDonald in the United Steel Workers, Zander in the State, County and Municipal Employees. Reuther's victory in the UAW in 1945 was by the narrowest of margins.

[23] Remarks before the Washington Chapter of the Public Personnel Association, October 27, 1964.

[24] National Federation of Federal Employees, *Convention Proceedings,* 1964.

[25] Remarks before Washington Chapter, Public Personnel Association, October 27, 1964.

[26] Remarks before the Federal Conference on Employee-Management Relations, November 1964.

dictional violations. Today a large percentage of AFGE members are in the wage-board category. President Griner insisted that by appointing him to serve on a committee to review wage-board policies, the AFL-CIO gave tacit approval to his organizing activities.[27]

The advantages to which the NFFE had looked were thus partially balanced by the AFGE's organizing efforts. This sharpened competition between the two organizations. Their relations were characterized by claims, counterclaims, and recriminations similar to those which had gone on for decades between the independent and AFL postal clerks' organizations before they merged.

The issue of affiliation with the AFL-CIO has been the central issue between the NFFE and AFGE, as it was for more than half a century between the two postal clerks' unions. Each group customarily hails its election victories as presaging the quick demise of its rival. The AFGE's election victories over its unaffiliated rivals sounded the "death knell for independents, be they company unions or mere dues collection agencies."[28] "Not a week passes," Wolkomir retorted, "but the NFFE welcomes into its ranks numbers of disillusioned former members and whole locals of the AFGE."[29]

The fact is that the Kennedy order stimulated the growth of both unions. The NFFE recovered its earlier losses and the AFGE, ignoring the jurisdictional limitations of the AFL-CIO, became the largest union of federal workers.

The AFGE, however, was not the only union to ignore jurisdictional boundaries. Nor was the NFFE its only competitor. The National Association of Government Employees began as an independent challenger of the crafts in the industrial establishments of the military services, as many other organizations had done before.[30] It branched out and competed with AFGE and NFFE among classes of employees which they had regarded as their preserve. The new organization's resourceful and energetic leadership grasped the opportunities offered by the Kennedy order to seek local exclusive recognition for white-collar clerical and technical employees wherever it could win their adherence. It won representation for Veterans Administration hospital employees, Federal Aviation Agency traffic controllers, Space Agency technical personnel, and blue- and white-collar employees in all parts of the country.

27 *Federal Times,* October 26, 1966.
28 *The Government Standard,* October 7, 1966.
29 *The Federal Times,* October 26, 1966.
30 Cf. Chapter II.

The AFGE defeated NAGE in a contest involving a white-collar group at Portsmouth, N.H. NAGE, in turn, defeated AFGE in two Veterans Administration hospitals, one in Brockton, Mass., and one in Coatesville, Pa. In January 1967 NAGE won exclusive recognition for 3,200 workers at the Army Depot at Pueblo, Colo., where AFGE already had a number of small units. The AFGE subsequently accused the NAGE of dishonest organizing methods, claiming that it had distributed illegal prepaid membership cards as it had done earlier at the Naval Air Station at South Weymouth, Mass. The AFGE requested a second card check in both cases, but the NAGE refused. The employing agency accepted the results of the vote for NAGE.

Craft unions also have paid little heed to jurisdictional boundaries. The International Association of Machinists as well as craft federations such as the Metal Trades Councils have won exclusive recognition for whole installations, including white-collar employees, in the same way that the AFGE has won similar installation-wide recognition of bargaining units, including skilled craftsmen.

In one important instance the IAM brought charges against the AFGE under the anti-raiding provisions of Article XXI of the AFL-CIO constitution. A local of the IAM had won exclusive recognition at the aircraft service base of the Federal Aviation Agency's Aeronautical Center in Oklahoma City in 1963 and signed a collective agreement with the base the next year. In 1965, the employing agency withdrew recognition after the IAM was unable to show support of a majority of the employees. When the AFGE quickly moved to take the IAM's place, the latter filed a raiding complaint under the AFL-CIO constitution. It claimed that the AFGE had induced its members to defect; had ignored the craft's established collective bargaining relationship, causing it to lose its exclusive recognition; and by its hurry to take the IAM's place had prevented the latter from repairing its relations with its former members. The umpire in the dispute, David L. Cole, citing precedents established in decertification cases in private industry, declared that "the same principle is applicable to government employment relationships" and ruled that the action of the AFGE was in violation of the AFL-CIO constitution.[31]

Though significant for decertification cases, this ruling had little effect on the scramble for recognition in disregard of tradi-

---

[31] Ruling of Umpire David L. Cole, May 5, 1966, Text in *Government Employee Relations Report*, No. 148 (1966), p. F-1.

tional jurisdictional bounds. In addition, the AFGE raised several questions which umpire Cole left unanswered, the most pertinent of which concerned how the anti-raiding restrictions of the AFL-CIO squared with the Kennedy order's guarantee of freedom to join any organization.[32]

The AFL jurisdictional restrictions afford certain advantages to independents. AFGE President Griner admitted in his report to the union's 1966 convention that despite several hearings to clear up jurisdictional issues, there were a number "of undecided problems in this area that must be adjudicated in the future." [33] Some unions consider it a violation of AFL-CIO rules for one union to accept membership cards from members in another affiliated union. Griner called refusal to accept such cards a violation of the Standards of Conduct promulgated under the order, holding that it could lead to the withdrawal of exclusive recognition. "We must examine this and other problems shortly," he said, because "independent unions have no restrictions concerning raiding which gives them a decided advantage over AFL-CIO affiliates." [34]

That the order opened the door to recognition for any organization which could qualify was in keeping with existing conditions of federal employment. However, the resulting proliferation of employee organizations seeking to block out protected preserves was hardly contemplated by the framers. It was their belief that the order would lead to the establishment of strong and stable organizations able to exercise a balancing influence in negotiations with employing agencies. While the order strengthened the big national unions, it at the same time created problems arising out of intense competition for recognition among unions big and small with aims and programs which often actually clash. The result was not only to dilute the political strength of the unions and weaken their countervailing power in dealing with employing agencies but also to divide their unity of action in their legislative relations.

D. THE PROFESSIONAL ASSOCIATIONS

Many small organizations of technical specialists and professionals, some serving in a single agency, also sought the prestige and stability which comes from exclusive recognition. Some of these organizations had never before functioned as labor unions.

---

[32] *Ibid.*
[33] American Federation of Government Employees, *President's Report to the Convention,* September 1966.
[34] *Ibid.*

Examples are the Federal Plant Quarantine Inspectors National Association, the Federal Tobacco Inspectors Mutual Association, the National Association of Federal Veterinarians, the National Association of Government Inspectors, the National Labor Relations Board Professional Association representing the lawyers in that agency, and the Patent Office Professional Association representing the lawyers and other professionals in its agency.

Most federal professional groups continue to oppose collective bargaining as "unprofessional." They eschew the use of the order and continue to seek their objectives by the traditional pre-10988 methods of employee organizations—that is, publicity, lobbying, and consultation with agency administrators. Some of these organizations function solely as professional societies in both public and private agencies and take no position on the propriety of professionals joining labor unions. Other groups, of which the National Society of Professional Engineers is an example, strongly oppose unionization. Founded in 1934 at a time when the expanding labor movement was attempting to organize engineers, scientists, and technicians, this group's declared purpose was "the promotion of the professional, social, and economic interests of the Professional Engineer . . . beyond the scope of the technical societies." [35] In a 1966 pamphlet addressed to government engineers the Society declared:

> "Collective bargaining by professional engineers is in conflict with the basic principles of a professional individual. The individual responsibility and independent judgment required of a professional engineer are incompatible with the regimentation fundamentally inherent in unionism." [36]

The division among professional workers over the issue of union membership is by no means confined to the federal service, but it is a more significant issue there because of the existence of large unions which have enrolled professionals from their beginning.[37] Professional employees strongly committed to organized labor—for example, those in the Department of Labor—have opted for the affiliated AFGE. Others still seeking the support of a strong general union but with reservations about formal ties with organized labor have joined the NFFE, which has always made a special pitch to professionals. In its earliest years the NFFE had a smoothly functioning Scientific and Technical Sec-

---

[35] National Society of Professional Engineers, *Professionalism or Unionism—Which Choice for the Engineer in Government?,* 1966.

[36] *Ibid.*

[37] See statement of Arbitrator Nathan Clayton, on ability of professional associations to function as employee representatives under E.O. 10988. *Government Standard,* August 30, 1963.

tion, which it later abandoned. It is at present making strong efforts to attract professional and managerial employees, especially personnel officers, who are regarded as arms of management and are therefore excluded from common bargaining units with rank and file workers. There was nothing in the Kennedy order, the NFFE has pointed out, to prevent the organization of separate personnel officer or supervisory units.[38]

Strongly opposing these efforts, Vincent E. Jay, for nearly a quarter century an active member of NFFE, gave up his membership and took the lead in founding the Federal Professional Association (FPA). Later explaining his move in a letter to NFFE President Wolkomir, he said:

"A long-time (24 years) member, former officer and employee of the NFFE, I know its activities and its members as few individuals do. The fact that it is now a labor union (which it pretends not to be) should be clear to everyone.

"The fact that it cannot fairly represent both wage board and other non-professional *and* managerial employees ought to be equally clear. The vast difference between the needs and desires of non-professional employees on the one hand, and the professional and managerial personnel on the other hand, precludes fair and proper representation of all.

"So let's make a deal. Non-professionals occasionally apply for membership in FPA and we, of course, refuse them. We will be glad to refer these people to you, if you will refer professionals and managers to FPA." [39]

The FPA was founded in 1962 after two years of inquiry and discussion by a group of federal professionals in Washington. It was organized on an individual membership basis. Through publicity and legislative activity it sought to obtain such economic benefits for professional employees as implementation of salary comparability with prevailing professional pay as already provided in principle by the Salary Reform Act of 1962, improved travel privileges and allowances, and different treatment for professionals from that accorded other employees. To obtain the latter objective it advocated, after a referendum of its membership, the establishment of a distinct professional category, presumably a category like that in the British Civil Service, rather than the professional classification in the pre-1949 Classification Act. The FPA has also sought to remove the Bureau of the Budget's restric-

---

[38] Under President Nixon's E.O. 11491, Secs. 7 (e) , 10 (b) (1) , and 24, supervisors may organize but their associations may no longer be recognized as "employee organizations." Instead, consultations are to be afforded them outside the established labor relations system.

[39] Federal Professional Association, *Press Release,* Letter to Nathan T. Wolkomir, August 2, 1966.

tions on the number of higher grade positions. It has championed legislation providing for increases in legislative and judicial salaries tied to increases in the civil service. It is also interested in post-entry for professional employees and has expressed the possibility of establishing a federal staff college.[40]

The FPA's very broad definition of "professional" extends to categories of government specialists and technicians, including personnel and budget officers as well as managerial employees; the latter are rather broadly defined in order to make little distinction between supervisors and executive managerial officers. The FPA engaged Robert Ramspeck, who had served as chairman of both the House Civil Service Committee and the United States Civil Service Commission, as consultant and legislative representative. Yet, despite Ramspeck's great prestige and the dedication of its leadership, it has grown with frustrating slowness. By 1967, for example, its membership had barely reached a thousand of an estimated 250,000 of the service eligibles.

Perhaps the principal factor in the failure of eligible members to join FPA in large numbers is the existence of many professional societies to which federal employees may belong. These include national professional groups like social work and nursing societies, bar and medical associations, and technical, engineering, and scientific societies, most of whose members are not in the federal service. In addition, there are many more bureaus or departmental groups, some local and some national. Several, as indicated above, sought and won exclusive bargaining rights under the Kennedy order. Others have preferred to operate in their accustomed ways outside the order.

During 1966 the FPA and the Organization of Professional Employees of the Department of Agriculture (OPEDA) initiated a series of meetings of representatives of some two dozen associations of varying size, ranging from a few hundred to OPEDA's 7,000, to devise ways of inter-organization cooperation.[41] Toward the end of 1966 six of these groups formed the National Federation of Federal Professional Organizations (NFFPO). They were

---

[40] Federal Professional Association, *A Federal Staff College, Report of a Panel Discussion,* August 1966.

[41] *The Federal Times,* June 29, 1966, and December 7, 1966. Among participants were the Patent Office Society, the National Society of Professional Engineers, the Association of Senior Engineers, the Association of Naval Weapons Engineers and Scientists, the Air Traffic Control Association, the National Association of Federal-State Employees, the Functional Section of Professional Engineers in Government, the District of Columbia Society of Professional Engineers and the D.C. Chapter of the Special Libraries Association. Also present was the National Association of Federal Veterinarians which had won exclusive recognition under the order.

OPEDA, the Federal Veterinarians, the Patent Office Professional Association, the Air Traffic Controllers, the Society of Professional Engineers, and the Association of Senior Engineers, Naval Ship Systems Command.[42]

FPA, despite its early initiative in the movement, not only stayed out of the NFFPO but opposed it. Its primary reasons were inadequacy of financing and the dissimilarity of the affiliates in size and professional purity. An FPA statement said, concerning size, that "a 100-member affiliate can negate the vote of a 1000-member affiliate." On the subject of professional purity the statement pointed out that "OPEDA includes . . . such categories as 'professional secretaries' and 'professional clerks' whose problems and desires are not really those of true professionals and executives and the NSPE's [National Society of Professional Engineers] Federal membership is dwarfed by its membership in industry."[43] The FPA, holding itself out as an alternative to the NFFPO, expressed the hope that the movement would "solidify the affiliates' interest in joint action and impel them to reconsider FPA's standing offer of affiliation under FPA."[44]

At the beginning of 1967 Mr. Ramspeck threw a bombshell into the FPA by threatening to resign unless it showed signs of more rapid growth. If "members do not bring in large numbers of additional members," he said, the organization might just as well "cease to exist."[45] In consequence, a membership drive was begun. A merger was effected with the National Society of Federal Engineers, Scientists, and Allied Professions, and an affiliation agreement on a federation basis was made with the National Association of Naval Technical Supervisors. Ramspeck was sufficiently satisfied with the progress to stay on as consultant.

The question still remains in the minds of many federal professionals, however, whether a general association attempting to include and cater to all professionals can meet economic needs as effectively as the big unions and serve professionals' needs as well as the specialized organizations. In the days before the Kennedy order the problem was simple. But since then many groups that never before functioned as labor unions have sought to use the order despite doubts in some impartial quarters regarding their capacity adequately to represent their members as labor unions. Even some large and well established professional organizations, such as the National Association of Internal Revenue Employees

42 *The Federal Times,* December 7, 1966.
43 The Federal Professional Association, *Newsletter,* November 1966.
44 *Ibid.*
45 *Government Employee Relations Report,* No. 173 (1967) , p. A-10.

(NAIRE)[46] and the American Nurses Association, ran into trouble because, as professional bodies, they had always had supervisory and management officials in their membership.

It will be remembered that the Kennedy order specifically stated that no unit established for exclusive recognition may include "both professional employees and non-professional employees unless a majority of such professional employees vote for inclusion in such unit." [47] The order also excluded managerial officials and their subordinates from the same bargaining unit. These clauses caused serious problems for both the big general unions and the professional associations like NAIRE and the American Nurses Association in their efforts to secure exclusive recognition.

Thus, the big unions which seek inclusive membership outside the Postal Service are faced with a dual problem of the skilled craft workers on the one hand and the professional, management, and supervisory employees on the other. In a sense this situation represents another example of the struggle between inclusive, industrial-type unionism and specialized organizations such as craft and technical-professional groups.

---

[46] Since August 1973, the National Treasury Employees Union.

[47] E.O. 10988, Sec. 6. This provision was fully retained in E.O. 11491, Sec. 10 (b) (4) , and in the Postal Reorganization Act, 84 Stat. 719; 39 U.S.C. Sec. 1202, August 12, 1970.

PART II

THE EVOLUTION OF THE FEDERAL LABOR POLICY

CHAPTER V

THE LAW AND FEDERAL
COLLECTIVE BARGAINING

A. THE CONSTITUTIONAL FRAMEWORK—THE
SOVEREIGNTY DOCTRINE
AND THE DELEGATION
OF POWERS

The fulcrum for the policies that set public service labor relations apart from its private counterpart is reliance upon the sovereignty doctrine. This emphasis, adopted and maintained by public management, has served to define and limit union status, action, and the extent of collective bargaining.

As with all legal doctrines, however, interpretation and application still remain subject to modification and change by courts, legislatures, and executive practice. This flexibility of the legal system serves to meet the needs of a changing society and to conform the law to consensus in the body politic. Under our constitutional system and the stare decisis of the judicial process, many fundamental concepts, from states' rights to civil liberties, have undergone extensive revision with the shifting pressures of broad social and economic movements. So also, how the courts interpret the sovereignty doctrine in labor matters in the immediate future will have practical ramifications for the daily conduct of government employee relations. Its interpretation has been questioned and its practical application has been even more extensively modified. The end result has been a steady lessening of the once unquestioned refusal to countenance any deviation from the uniqueness of the traditional practice of public service staff relations.

Simply stated, the sovereign employer reserves the power to determine the terms and conditions of employment of its civil servants. The sovereignty of the United States, at law, lies in all the people and is represented by their elected legislators and executives. It is often overlooked, however, that within our constitutional system, the manner and extent of exerting the sovereign prerogatives of the people are always subject to diverse interpretations. The law is clear that the people, through the legislature, cannot totally abdicate legislative authority to the executive, independent agencies, or third parties. Literal application of this principle would preclude any system of collective bargaining. Our law, however, is replete with well-developed principles of the delegation of power. These include delegations from the legislature to the executive or to independent regulatory agencies by congressional action and delegations by the executive to its agencies by executive order. It therefore follows that judicial interpretation of the doctrine of delegation of sovereign powers could just as easily embrace a system of collective negotiation. It could be seen as action by the chief executive in the exercise of his own constitutional executive powers or as an accepted execution of delegated congressional powers.[1]

A fundamental issue before legislatures and courts today is whether to adhere to the strict sovereign concepts which legally obstruct labor programs or adopt collective representation systems within the frame of reference of judicially accepted principles of constitutional delegation of power. The latter choice is a natural concommitant of the executive personnel function. This does not necessarily imply a total abandonment of the governmental process to government fixed by collective bargaining agreements. It merely indicates a greater area of permissive interaction between executives and labor representatives in the fixing of working conditions through a mutual sharing of authority. Under this interpretation there is no abdication of sovereign prerogative.

Tests set down by the Supreme Court for the delegation of power permit an executive program entailing extensive bargaining. Congressional budgetary control does not preclude presidential discretion in the execution of a budget. With growing union strength and awareness on the part of public employees of their own problems, those avenues that permit greater flexibility and accommodation are to be preferred to a compulsive adherence to sovereign principles. Principles of sovereign immunity preclude the state's being forced into any contractual relation against its will. No aspect of the doctrine's development at Anglo-Saxon common law, however, would bar the executive's voluntary par-

---

[1] For an excellent contemporary treatment of congressional delegation of power to the executive branch and its limiting safeguards, see Louis Fisher, "Delegating Power to the President," *Journal of Public Law,* Emory University Law School, Vol. 19, No. 2, 1970, pp. 251-282.

ticipation in a collective bargaining system by presidential order or by legislative enactment.

The power of the American executive has been formidably expanded by a steady stream of congressional delegations consistently upheld by the courts. Delegation is rooted in the "non-absolutism" of our system of separation of powers. Within the constitutional framework there are innumerable instances of the "commingling of powers." The principle of the separation of powers was never intended to be inviolate or sacrosanct. As expressed by James Madison in *The Federalist Papers*,[2] the system of checks and balances which was to serve as a hold on arbitrary government was to work through the medium of a sharing of powers. The natural result of the willingness of the branches to share their powers was the inordinate growth of executive power through the delegation of legislative authority. Indeed, the so-called fourth branch of government—the independent agencies—evolved from the eagerness of Congress to delegate functions.

It has long been accepted that the most numerous and important of the President's powers are those that he receives from Congress. In executing the sovereign legislative prerogatives, he has steadily been given more and more discretion. This is true despite the limitations, criteria, and guidelines included to control their execution. The relaxation of restraints upon delegation, whether given to executives or administrative agencies, was essential and inescapable for modern, complex government to operate. Legislative acts cannot anticipate each possible facet of daily administration. They are essentially statements of basic policy whose enforcement rests primarily upon executive ability and interpretation. For this, the President is given extensive legislative and judicial powers subject to review.

The courts have consistently legitimitized this expansion of delegated executive discretion. The Supreme Court on only two occasions has declared delegations to public authorities unconstitutional, and both were emergency measures of the Great Depression. In *Panama Refining Co. v. Ryan,* the "Hot Oil" Case, the Supreme Court struck down the National Industrial Recovery Act's provision authorizing the President to prohibit interstate shipment of oil produced or withdrawn from the market contrary to state regulations. In doing this, the court relied on the statute's fatal lack of policy and standards against which presidential policy could be weighed, leaving "the matter to the President without standard or rule to be dealt with as he pleased."[3] In the

---

[2] Hamilton, Madison, Jay, *The Federalist Papers,* Nos. 47, 48.
[3] Panama Refining Co. v. Ryan, 239 U.S. 388, 55 S.Ct. 241 (1935).

famed Schecter Case, presidential authority to approve codes of fair competition was considered to be so unfettered, loose, and vague as to constitute "a roving commission." Said Mr. Justice Cardozo: "This is delegation running riot. No such plenitude of power is susceptible of transfer." [4]

As Kenneth Culp Davis has emphasized, the delegation in both cases was not to an administrative agency which followed established procedures and was traditionally oriented towards due process protections for the affected parties. Thus, in the absence of executive disorganization on the scale prevailing in the 1930s, Davis believes, the "Hot Oil" Case would be decided differently today. Moreover, the lesson of the Schecter Case has been well learned. Congress has scrupulously avoided excessive, vague delegations of power since that decision. In short, according to Davis, "[i]n absence of palpable abuse or true congressional abdication, the non-delegation doctrine to which the Supreme Court has in the past often paid lip service is without practical force." [5]

A perennial objection to expanding executive discretion is the doctrine *"Delegata potestas non potest delegari"*— a power already granted may not again be delegated. Rooted in the system of separation of powers, it would in theory require that Congress, whose powers are delegated to it by all the sovereign people, not delegate these powers to the executive or to private parties. The latter category could easily be read to include labor unions entering into collective bargaining agreements. The doctrine has never been specifically overruled as a matter of law, but its effectiveness as a barrier to greater executive discretion in exercising the powers of sublegislation has been negligible. It is true that the elder Mr. Justice Harlan declared in *Field* v. *Clark* in 1892:

> "That Congress cannot delegate legislative power to the President is a principle universally recognized as vital to the integrity and maintenance of the system of government ordained by the Constitution . . . Legislative power was exercised when Congress [in the Tariff Act of 1890] declared that the suspension should take effect upon a named contingency. What the President was required to do was simply in execution of an Act of Congress." [6]

The Court, nevertheless, upheld a delegation of power to the President to suspend provisions of the Tariff Act regarding the free importation of particular articles if he ascertained that foreign

---

[4] Schecter Poultry Corp. v. U.S., 295 U.S. 495, 55 S.Ct. 837 (1935).
[5] Kenneth Culp Davis, *Administrative Law and Government* (St. Paul: West Publishing Co., 1960), p. 55.
[6] Field v. Clark, 143 U.S. 649, 692, 693, 12 S.Ct. 495, 504 (1892).

states had imposed such duties that he deemed to be reciprocally unequal and unreasonable.[7]

This presidential power to act under legislative grant was established very early in *The Brig Aurora* v. *U.S.*, wherein the Court sustained a power granted to the President to revive the Non-Intercourse Act of 1809 when, in his judgment, certain conditions were deemed to exist.[8] The presidential tariff power has been steadily increased. In 1928 the executive power to raise or lower tariff rates by 50 percent in order to equalize costs of production here and abroad was upheld under the Tariff Act of 1922.[9] Presidential discretionary powers in tariff settling have expanded to this day.

The comprehensive scope and diversity of the great areas of executive discretion that have been upheld by the courts conceivably could include a collective bargaining system without violating concepts of sovereignty. The maxim that sovereign congressional powers cannot be delegated has been effectively circumvented in the courts through two major lines of interpretation—first, that the control of Congress is nominally retained in the fixing of standards to guide the executive; and second, that the criteria and wording of the delegated powers are so broad, vague, and all-encompassing as to invite greater and greater executive discretion. In the administration of foreign affairs the executive has great freedom to exert the discretionary powers in areas delegated to him as beyond the ability, knowledge, and effectiveness of the Congress. These inherent sovereign powers in foreign relations were interpreted as descending directly from the Crown and were clearly upheld as beyond the detailed scrutiny and control of Congress in the landmark case *United States* v. *Curtiss-Wright Export Corporation*.[10] In the domestic sector, although the Supreme Court has insisted upon the retention of more congressional control, delegated executive power has continued to grow and diversify.

Professor Corwin clearly described the characteristic instances of congressional delegation. Essentially, they are those laws which go into operation upon the occurrence of some event to be determined by some other authority, executive or administrative; or those laws which delegate a considerable measure of choice regarding the very content and application of the statute.[11] While

---

[7] *Ibid.*
[8] The Brig Aurora v. U.S., 7 Cranch 382 (1813) .
[9] Hampton and Co. v. U.S., 276 U.S. 396, 48 S.Ct. 348 (1928) .
[10] U.S. v. Curtiss-Wright Export Corp., 299 U.S. 304, 57 S.Ct. 216 (1936) .
[11] Edward S. Corwin, *The President: Office and Powers* (New York: New York University Press, 1948) , p. 150.

maintaining, in principle, the prohibition against delegation, the Supreme Court has upheld expanded executive discretion time and time again upon standards which are really quite broad. It has permitted a wide spectrum of authority as being in "the public interest" or for "public convenience and/or necessity." This was also the case in defining "unfair labor practices" and "unfair trade practices" and in fixing "just and reasonable rates." Similar general guidelines have supported programs ranging from the regulating of houses of ill-repute near army camps to revising precipitately the corporate structure of public utility holding companies.[12] The areas of delegated legislative powers are too diversified to catalog here.[13] Suffice it to say that the concept is an integral part of our constitutional fabric, one which is regularly applied in normal periods and more frequently relied upon in times of economic stress or war.

It is also well established that the President may subdelegate powers to department and agency heads. The virtual impossibility of complete personal supervision led to early court recognition of this need.[14] The power to subdelegate, so actively applied in the executive personnel function, was recognized by Congress in 1950 when it authorized the President, within certain limitations, to delegate to department or agency heads any of his functions.[15] In short, the delegation and subdelegation procedure has been an essential support of vital national programs. It was particularly needed to implement depression, war, labor relations, and economic controls legislation. Executive discretion is inherent in, for example, the national programs to meet natural disasters and to conduct the war on poverty.

In the personnel field, however, these concepts have been effectively allied with the sovereignty doctrine to resist collective bargaining systems. Corollary maxims were successfully defended in many courts which declared that it was an inherent function of the legislature, acting for the people, to determine the working conditions obtaining in the public service and that neither the

---

12 McKinley v. U.S., 249 U.S. 397, 39 S.Ct. 324 (1919); American Power and Light Co. v. SEC, 329 U.S. 90, 67 S.Ct. 133 (1946).
13 Buttfield v. Stranahan, 192 U.S. 270, 24 S.Ct. 349 (1904), standards for tea imports; U.S. v. Grimaud, 220 U.S. 506, 31 S.Ct. 480 (1911), regulating forest preserves; Yakus v. U.S., 321 U.S. 414, 64 S.Ct. 660 (1944), war emergency price controls; U.S. v. Curtiss-Wright, 299 U.S. 304, 55 S.Ct. 216 (1936), prohibition of armaments sales to belligerent countries; Opp Cotton Mills v. Administrator, 312 U.S. 126, 61 S.Ct. 524 (1941), fixing minimum wages. These citations merely scratch the surface as to cases permitting executive leeway in administering legislative policies.
14 Wilcox v. Jackson, 38 U.S. (13 Peters) 498 (1839); Williams v. U.S., 42 U.S. (1 Howard) 290 (1843); Ludecke v. Watkins, 335 U.S. 160, 68 S.Ct. 1429 (1948).
15 64 Stat. 419 (1950); 65 Stat. 712 (1951), 3 USCA Secs. 301-303.

legislature nor the executive could abdicate their powers by delegating their functions to a third, private party such as a labor union or an arbitrator.

Characteristic of court attitudes on this point was the 1947 Missouri decision of *Springfield* v. *Clouse,* where a declaratory judgment was sought under a new state constitution. The court disagreed in the strongest terms with the union's argument that cities had the legal right to enter into collective agreements, emphasizing that:

> "The principle of separation of powers is stated in the Constitution. . . . This establishes a government of laws instead of a government of men; a government in which laws authorized to be made by the legislative branch are equally binding on all citizens including public officers and employees. . . . The members of the legislative branch represent the people and speak with the voice of all people, including those who are public officers and employees. . . . Laws must be made by deliberation of the lawmakers and not by bargaining with anyone outside the law-making body. . . .
>
> "Under our form of government, public office or employment never has been and cannot become a matter of bargaining and contract. This is true because the whole matter of qualifications, tenure, compensation and working conditions for any public service, involves the exercise of legislative powers. Except to the extent that all the people have themselves settled any of these matters by writing them into the Constitution, they must determine by their chosen representative who constitutes the legislative body. It is a familiar concept of constitutional law that the legislature cannot delegate its legislative powers and any attempted delegation thereof is void. If such powers cannot be delegated, they surely cannot be bargained or contracted away; and certainly not by any administrative or executive officers who cannot have any legislative powers." [16]

Although protecting the administrator's discretion, the court still insisted that the standards governing his discretion must remain a matter of legislative prerogative. Collective contracts were deemed to be infringements upon the statutory powers of the municipal civil service commission.[17]

Such declarations epitomize the conservative judicial approach to public labor relations that still obtains in the majority of jurisdictions. From the plethora of cases already enumerated recognizing advanced executive discretion in a great variety of vital activities, it becomes clear that the issue of public employee labor relations has been singled out for special application of the sovereignty and nondelegation concepts. These concepts have been retained and continue to serve public management as arguments

---

[16] City of Springfield v. Clouse, 356 Mo. 1230, 1239; 206 S.W.2d 539, 544, 545 (1947).

[17] *Ibid.* at 1251, 206 S.W.2d at 544-546.

upon which to fall back for reserve support. Nevertheless, it is equally clear that executive action and statutory expansion of executive personnel power have permitted outstanding exceptions to such judicial prohibitions at all levels of government. From President Martin Van Buren's administration to the passage of the Postal Reorganization Act of 1970, the simple expedient of preserving executive authority and/or reserving final executive or legislative approval has permitted mutual agreement upon public service working conditions by both formal and informal means.[18] Under such provisions, sovereign immunity was left undisturbed. Indeed, the remarkable expansion of collective bargaining programs at the state and local levels clearly indicate that a reexamination of these concepts is already well advanced. Essentially, they are being reformed and crystallized in a new crucible of practical, often emergency, operational pressures and work stoppages and rapidly changing executive, judicial, and employee attitudes.

B. EXPANDING EXECUTIVE DISCRETION AND COLLECTIVE BARGAINING

It is pertinent to note the background against which executive discretion has been exercised in federal staff relations. As has been pointed out, the Jackson and Van Buren Administrations relied upon discretion as an inherent part of the executive function, a view entirely supported by congressional intent. In the growing labor unions of the 1830s and 1860s no distinctions were made in membership between public and private employees. Government executives did not conceive of themselves as a separate, unique breed of employers. Significantly, government labor relations were deeply involved in the contemporary political battles raging at the local level. The relative success of early organized labor's demands upon government in the arsenals and navy yards depended primarily on labor's comparative success against the private employers of a particular municipal or regional area.

Sovereignty was not involved. Executive responsibility for government labor policy was the order of the day. Harsh suppression by many executive officers during the Jacksonian era was merely another reflection of the laissez-faire attitude towards incipient unionism which permeated the entire industrial structure of the nation. Congress left government labor relations to the executive. It rarely interfered and the federal executive enjoyed complete

---

[18] U.S. House of Representatives, *H.R. 17070*, 91st Cong., 2nd Sess., 1970, Sec. 116; 84 Stat. 722, Sec. 208, August 12, 1970.

independence and unusually great management discretion in personnel relations. An informal, rather crude process of collective bargaining accordingly evolved. The fixing of hours and wages, the core of true collective bargaining, was never really considered except in terms of executive discretion. As the late Professor Leonard D. White pointed out:

> "As far as Congress was concerned, its policy was to leave the hiring and firing of craftsmen and laborers to the unregulated discretion of executive officers. So far as the latter were concerned they were like any other employers and could hire and fire as circumstances dictated." [19]

No legislation governing public labor relations was seriously considered, just as Congress throughout the nineteenth century would not regulate hours and wages in private industry. To the House Committee on Public Buildings in 1838 the demand for an hour's reduction evoked the avowal that the time and price of labor were matters unsuited to legislative action.[20] In short, as Professor White declared:

> "The management of the public offices was recognized by Congress to be an executive function. The executive offices imposed no restrictions on their own authority to hire, to assign to duty, to favor or disfavor, and to remove at will." [21]

If executives acted to improve federal working conditions in the 1830s, they did so primarily because of the political pressures of local labor parties and not because of strong unionism. The workingmen's parties of the 1830s appeared in New York, Philadelphia, and Boston and won many local victories in a variety of cities from upstate New York and New England to Zanesville, Ohio. They influenced much of Jacksonian politics and policies in the cities although they were of less importance nationally. Worker-oriented political organizations such as the New York Locofocos were forces with which President Van Buren had seriously to contend.[22]

Thus it was by executive order that Van Buren in 1840 established federal policy on the hours and wages of government workers. Local unions and the National Trades' Union for years had been petitioning Congress and local installation executives to adopt the 10-hour day. Concerned with votes on the eve of a pres-

---

[19] Leonard D. White, *The Jacksonians* (New York: The Macmillan Company, 1954), p. 406.

[20] U.S. House of Representatives, *Report No. 886,* 25th Cong., 2nd Sess., May 11, 1838.

[21] Leonard D. White, *op. cit.,* p. 410.

[22] Joseph G. Rayback, *A History of American Labor* (New York: The MacMillan Co., 1959), pp. 70-72, 84-87.

idential election, Van Buren ordered the uniform adoption of the 10-hour day at all federal works. His order read:

> "The President of the United States, finding that different rules prevail at different places as well in respect to hours of labor by persons employed in the public works under the immediate authority of himself and the Departments as also in relation to the different classes of workmen, and believing that much inconvenience and dissatisfaction would be removed by adopting a uniform course, hereby directs that all such persons, whether laborers or mechanics be required to work only to the number of hours prescribed by the ten-hour system." [23]

By supplementing the order with a prohibition against reducing wages in accordance with the reduced working day, the President in substance legislated a considerable increase in pay.[24] He did much, therefore, to launch the "government as model employer" concept.

It is important to note at this point how the issue of pay is a focal point for the conflict between executive discretion and legislative control. The sovereign employer concept places pay determination squarely in the legislature. It is this argument which has successfully obstructed the adoption of effective collective negotiation systems. Nevertheless, this view is relatively new; for long the federal executive was given extensive discretion in pay matters within the prescribed limitations of total budgetary allotments and general maximum pay statutes. Union attitudes today vary little from their traditional position that employees must participate in the pay-fixing process.[25]

While federal administrators had the power to fix wages, a crude form of negotiation was practiced without congressional interference. Federal Government processes during the nation's developmental years naturally lent themselves to great executive discretion. Morton Godine points out that from 1795 to 1853 Congress generally left the fixing of wages for clerks and other employees to the department heads. Given a "lump sum" appropriation, each department fixed the number and pay of its employees. This created many discrepancies and was further complicated by legislation allowing executives to hire only in accordance with "statutory rolls," which again endeavored to fix

---

[23] *Niles Weekly Register,* December 26, 1840, p. 59.

[24] *Ibid.*

[25] B. A. Gritta, as President of the Metal Trades Department, AFL-CIO, for example, in an interview of July 23, 1964, stated that the first two years under the Kennedy order produced only restrictive bargaining; that there was no real collective bargaining since the basic subject areas were covered by law. Congress still fixed wages. The postal unions gave wage bargaining high priority in the legislative maneuvering prior to adoption of an independent postal service in 1970. It is to be expected that other federal unions will feel entitled to similar benefits.

the number and pay of employees.[26] Even after the statutes of 1853 and 1854 sought to provide equal pay for equal work for clerical employees and State Department workers, department heads were still given the responsibility to classify their working forces. As Paul Van Riper puts it, throughout this period and even on through the years following the Pendleton Act, "Position-classification and salary administration presented . . . a peculiar combination of administrative discretion and congressional whim." [27]

It is clear, therefore, that early congressional efforts to control or regulate the government establishment were not motivated by a desire to reassert inherent legislative hegemony over the service as a manifestation of sovereignty. It was an issue of civil service reform—not labor relations. The statutes introducing classification-compensation schedules and other major aspects of the merit system were not intended primarily to deter growing restlessness of employees or their organizations. They were natural expressions of public revulsion to the excesses of the spoils system during administrations from President Grant through Cleveland.

In point of fact, employee organizations preferred congressional uniform standards and merit principles to the unpredictable independence of federal executive officers in the various installations. Substantial, disparate inequities had resulted from the latter. To federal employees, statutory reform was preferable to the spoils politics that influenced federal executives at local levels in the management of their offices.[28] Yet it is important to note that even during the formative period from 1853 on and beyond 1883, administrative discretion was not impaired substantially. It was still the department executive who had the primary function of introducing classification systems both before and after the Pendleton Act. Van Riper remarks that as late as the 1880s, "Salaries and duties basically reflected political and social rather than administrative theories." [29]

Even more indicative of the great reliance of Congress upon administrative discretion in the personnel function is the wage-board system of determining prevailing rates for federal blue-collar workers. Again, the essential ingredient is final administrative determination. The entire procedure represents an unusually

---

[26] Morton R. Godine, *The Labor Problem in the Public Service* (Cambridge: Harvard University Press, 1951) , pp. 219-220.

[27] Paul Van Riper *History of the U.S. Civil Service* (Evanston: Row, Peterson and Co., 1958) , pp. 54, 151-152.

[28] Morton R. Godine, *op. cit.*, p. 220.

[29] Paul Van Riper, *op. cit.*, p. 152.

clear case of legislative delegation delimited by only the simplest, broadest standards to guide its administrative execution. Established in the early years of the Civil War, the prevailing-rate concept was forced by labor market pressures. By 1861 the attractions of private employment had to be equalled in order to stabilize the labor market and avoid obstructing the war effort in the navy yards. Now more than a century old, the prevailing-rate concept has vast application and is continually being reexamined. In his memorandum calling for the coordination of wage board activities, President Johnson noted that by November 1965 this pay-fixing program affected more than 617,000 federal employees in the trade, craft, and manual labor occupations involving payroll expenditures of over $4 billion annually.[30]

There was nothing in the early statutes specifically delineating the procedures to be adopted for fixing prevailing-wage rates. The first law of 1861 merely declared:

> "That the hours of labor in the Navy yards of the United States shall be the same as in private shipyards at or nearest the port where such yard is established, and the wages to be paid to all employees in such yards shall be, as near as may be, the average price paid to all employees of the same grade in private shipyards or work shops in or nearest to the same vicinity, to be determined by the Commandant of the Navy yard." [31]

But the law in this form was considered too constricting and was quickly changed to permit even greater executive leeway and discretion. It provided:

> "That the hours of labor and the rates of wages of the employees in the Navy yards shall conform as nearly as is consistent with the public interest with those of private establishments in the immediate vicinity of the respective yards to be determined by the Commandants of the Navy yards, subject to the approval of the Secretary of the Navy." [32]

This basic policy remains essentially unchanged. Only the methods for fixing pay have been modified. Ultimate executive authority has been retained.

The rate-fixing procedures first adopted might well have been different had the processes of collective bargaining been as well developed in the 1860s as they are today. There were no restrictions in the statute itself to prevent Navy officials from resorting to bargaining. The time was not propitious, however, primarily because of the weakness of employee organizations. The process adopted was essentially a procedure which retained, above all, ad-

---

[30] *Message for Chairman Macy,* November 16, 1965.
[31] 12 Stat. 330, December 21, 1861.
[32] 12 Stat. 587, July 16, 1862.

ministrative initiative, control, and final approval. The many wage boards were composed primarily of management officials and representatives who conducted the various local and regional pay surveys as data collectors and reporters.[33] Employee or employee union participation was substantially excluded. The prevailing-rate wage-survey system was and is the general practice in the Defense Department, National Aeronautics and Space Administration (NASA), Bureau of Engraving and Printing, Bureau of the Mint, the Coast and Geodetic Survey of the Commerce Department, the TVA, and the Department of Interior's Bonneville Power Administration (BPA) and its Bureaus of Indian Affairs, Mines, and Reclamation, among many other agencies.[34]

Nevertheless, the very existence of great administrative discretion in the wage board system and the relative strength of blue-collar unions have militated towards greater union participation in the wage-setting process through the wage-board machinery itself. To some union officers the survey technique presents a major possible avenue to bring "true" negotiating into government employment, for here the unions are able to "dicker" over that most essential of issues—wages. To many other leaders this end can be achieved only through new legislation providing full wage bargaining rights.[35]

The power to participate in the fixing of wages is derived from the survey system itself. All parties conversant with classification-compensation practice are well aware of the determining influence on final wage data that the choice of areas, jobs, and companies to be solicited will have. The choice of methods to be used in gathering and presenting the wage data is equally important.[36] It is a relatively simple matter to influence wage data by selecting high, low, or average-paying firms in the survey sample, to cite only one possible gambit. Unions, of course, made every effort to participate in all such functions. The concern, therefore, of federal management officials over "excessive" union participation in the wage survey process was readily understanda-

---

[33] See Chapter XIX for a discussion of recent revisions in the federal prevailing rate procedures.

[34] U.S. Department of Labor, Bureau of Labor Statistics, *Collective Bargaining Agreements in the Federal Service, Late Summer 1964*, BLS Bulletin No. 1451, August 1965, pp. 28-31. This survey of about 209 agreements noted that stipulations regarding wage surveys appeared in 55 contracts covering the following agencies: Commerce, Air Force, Army, Navy, HEW, Interior, Treasury, CAB, FAA, ICC, VA and the Tariff Commission. See Chapter XIX for wage coverage in detail.

[35] Interview with William H. Ryan, as President, District 44, IAM and Leo C. Sammon, Business Representative, District 44, IAM, July 28, 1964.

[36] Chas. W. Brennan, *Wage Administration* (Homewood, Ill.: Richard W. Irwin, Inc., 1963), pp. 203-220.

ble. Nevertheless, many of the contracts written under E.O. 10988 reflected management acceptance of prevailing-rate determination as a form of collective bargaining. Some agreements provided for union notice and participation, with union members as data collectors and observers on survey committees. Others established union rights to request surveys and to recommend inclusion or exclusion of jobs or firms from the survey sample. There are avenues of appeal.[37] That some unions were, for a time, content with the system was indicated by provisions accepting current wage-fixing procedures as satisfactory.[38]

Perhaps the clearest recognition of mutuality in wage determination under the prevailing-rate principle was developed in the Interior Department. There the executive policy of affirmatively promoting participation developed an oft-used contractual provision which is self-explanatory. Thus the 1964 agreement between the Bureau of Indian Affairs and the Maritime Trades Council provided:

> "When rates of pay or working conditions affecting employees . . . *are to be determined through the process of collective bargaining,* both parties shall be guided by the principle of conforming to prevailing rates and practices in the locality of the Vessel's area of operations for similar job classifications and work activities. Prior to such negotiations the Area Director and the Council shall set up a joint fact-finding committee for the purpose of establishing any relevant facts pertaining to rates of pay, job comparability, and working conditions. Consideration shall be given by the negotiating committees in their negotiations to any facts so established and to such other evidence as may be submitted by either party." [39]

Variations of this joint factfinding technique for wage board workers are generally used in such Interior agencies as the Bonneville Power Administration, Bureau of Mines, Bureau of Reclamation, and others.[40]

---

[37] U.S. Department of Labor, Bureau of Labor Statistics, *op. cit.,* p. 29.

[38] U.S. Coast Guard, *Basic Agreement,* between Coast Guard Aircraft Repair & Supply Base, Elizabeth City, N.C., and IAM Lodge 2203, March 3, 1964, Article XIV.

[39] U.S. Department of the Interior, *Basic Agreement,* between Bureau of Indian Affairs, Juneau Area, and "Council," July 25, 1963, Secs. 9.02, 9.03 (emphasis added).

[40] U.S. Department of Interior, *Basic Agreement,* between Bonneville Power Administration and Columbia Power Trades Council, June 30, 1963, Sec. 8.

———, Memorandum of Agreement, between Bonneville Power Administration and AFGE Lodge No. 928, July 2, 1965. Secs. 6.01, 6.02, 6.03.

———, *Basic Agreement,* between Bureau of Mines, Morgantown Research Center and AFGE, Lodge No. 1995, January 17, 1962, Art. IV, Secs. 3, 4, 5.

———, *Basic Agreement,* between Bureau of Reclamation, CRSP Power Operations Office and IBEW, Local 2159, January 8, 1965, Article V.

See Chapters XVI, XIX.

Executive discretion within the confines of broad legislative direction can thus develop collective systems which set pay levels just as other negotiable items are determined. There is no violation of the sovereignty doctrine. In this regard there are certain definite similarities in the present federal labor policy. The original 1862 statute required the approval of the Secretary of the Navy of all pay rates set by local commandants. The wording of the statute has not only remained essentially the same but reservations in the Kennedy and Nixon orders repeated this basic management prerogative.[41] Thus approval by the head of the agency is still mandatory before any agreements can be effectuated. By simply requiring executive approval of all agreements which at law could be questioned as illegally concluded with unaccountable third parties, any charge of violation of the sovereignty principle was effectively blocked. The executive can thus act with greater freedom to implement legislatively delegated programs or effect policies under his own executive powers.

Executive discretion in the control and administration of governmental personnel is a fundamental axiom of our tripartite system. It is an extensive power whether derived from the President's basic constitutional power as the Chief Executive or from congressional delegations.[42]

Ever since the introduction of civil service reform, the President's administrative discretion has been affirmed and expanded. The Pendleton Act itself, in 1883, despite its provisions to provide independence and impartiality in the new Civil Service Commission (CSC), left it largely to the discretion of the President to determine the extent of coverage of federal personnel under the system. The CSC was clearly ordered to act as an aid to the President in effectuating the Act.[43] Thus the entire philosophy of civil service reform retains the principle that the President exerts a particular personnel authority. John Millett observed that the power to determine which federal employees shall or shall not have their status controlled by civil service rules carries with it the great responsibility to oversee generally the satisfactory performance of the entire system of personnel management.[44] From the inception of the Act, two basic threads of development have been evident. First, by executive action from President Arthur on, we see the gradual extension of the Act's coverage from

---

[41] E.O. 10988, Sec. 7; E.O. 11491, Sec. 15.

[42] U.S. *Constitution,* Article II, Secs. 1, 3.

[43] 22 Stat. 403, January 16, 1883.

[44] John D. Millett, *Government and Public Administration* (New York: McGraw-Hill Co., 1959) , p. 337.

13,900 positions in 1884 to about 86 percent of the entire executive branch on the occasion of the Act's 75th anniversary.[45] Second, and most essential to executive action in the field of labor relations, is the President's assumption of the mantle of forceful leadership in the area of modern personnel management, the better to transform the federal service into an effective instrument of modern administration.

The executive order has been the major instrument of positive personnel policy. In addition to reaching new heights in expanding civil service coverage under the Ramspeck Act of 1940,[46] President Roosevelt used the executive order to establish divisions of personnel supervision and management in the departments, thus expanding the functions of departmental personnel officers. He revitalized the Council of Personnel Administration, which, in later form, was to become a potent factor in improving administration, and he supported agency in-service training programs.[47] These orders implemented progressive personnel practices. President Truman speeded the conversion from war to peace by replacing the temporary war regulations with a reaffirmation of the CSC as the central personnel agency. By these acts, he provided leadership for all the federal service and delineated the functions of all agencies in the personnel field.[48] In an historic action, Truman ordered the establishment in 1948 of a Fair Employment Board to seek the end of discrimination in the executive branch based on race, color, religion, or national origin.[49] It was also by executive order that this policy was carried forward in 1955, 1961, and 1965.[50]

Thus it can be seen that executive action need not await legislative initiation to embark on major personnel programs. Congress establishes the general policy governing basic areas such as civil service coverage, classification, veterans' preference, political neutrality, and basic pay schedules. This precludes neither extensive executive discretion within the statutory boundaries nor executive initiative in administration. It is both logical and reasona-

---

[45] Charles Cooke, *Biography of an Ideal* (Washington: U.S. Civil Service Commission, 1959) , p. 57.

[46] E.O. 8743, April 23, 1941; 54 Stat. 1211, November 26, 1940. 5 U.S.C. 681-684.

[47] E.O. 7916, June 24, 1938.

[48] E.O. 9691, February 4, 1946.

[49] E.O. 9980, October 21, 1948.

[50] By E.O. 10590, on January 18, 1955, President Eisenhower replaced this Board with the President's Committee on Government Employment Policy. This was again superseded when President Kennedy issued E.O. 10925 in 1961 establishing a more independent President's Committee on Equal Employment Opportunity. On September 24, 1965, President Johnson by E.O. 11246 transferred its functions entirely to the CSC in the interests of streamlining and strengthening the civil rights effort.

ble to conclude that the same conditions should obtain in the realm of labor relations. Of course, special legislation permitted extensive collective bargaining in the TVA, BPA, Government Printing Office, Alaska Railway, Inland Waterways Corporation, St. Lawrence Seaway, and now the Postal Service. Its acceptance in these areas was assured because of reservations of approval by the executive providing that such agreements did not violate the concepts of sovereignty. It should follow, therefore, that prior localized executive efforts at collective negotiations and expansion of collective bargaining under the federal government-wide cooperation program do no violation to the sovereignty concept so long as the necessary legal reservations are observed.

C. THE EMPLOYEE-MANAGEMENT COOPERATION PROGRAM BEFORE THE COURTS

The Chief Executive's power to initiate and administer a labor relations program has been consistently upheld by the courts. The sovereignty issue has not been raised and has not, therefore, acted as an obstructive force in the program's development. In the settlement of private labor disputes, the Supreme Court has refused to recognize any nebulous "inherent" power in the President to act beyond constitutional or congressionally granted powers. The famed "steel seizure" case was careful to recognize an executive power to take over the steel mills only if authorized by some statute or the Constitution but not otherwise.[51]

In 1965, in a decision of vital importance to the constitutionality of the Kennedy order, Judge Spottswood W. Robinson, then of the U.S. District Court for the District of Columbia, recognized the essential difference when he declared:

"The plaintiff's [National Federation of Federal Employees] position, simply and solely, is that the Order is legislation and that the President cannot pass laws, and the only authority relied upon is Youngstown Sheet and Tube Company v. Sawyer. But a President's policy pronouncement to the executive agencies of the Federal Government can in no way be assimilated to an order seizing private property. Youngstown is clearly inapposite here." [52]

Thus the Supreme Court has shown a willingness to uphold great executive discretion if implemented within the executive prerogative. Moreover, the Court has exhibited a reluctance to

---

[51] Youngstown Sheet & Tube Co., et al. v. Sawyer, 343 U.S. 579, 72 S.Ct. 863 (1952).

[52] National Federation of Federal Employees, et al. v. Paul H. Nitze, Secretary of the Navy, et al., Civil Action No. 1380-64 (D.D.C., September 29, 1965). Unpublished opinion, p. 12.

interfere with or obstruct presidential programs lest it commit an unwarranted invasion by the judiciary into areas that are constitutionally within the executive purview.

The lower courts have consistently followed this reasoning in cases where the initiation and administration of the new federal labor program has been questioned. The prerogative of the President to embark on a public employee relations program without congressional authorization has been consistently upheld as a part of his executive personnel function.

An early case brought in the federal courts to test the effectiveness of President Kennedy's Executive Order 10987 involved this issue. This order granted government employees the right to appeal within an agency against administrative decisions to take adverse action against them.[53] It was issued simultaneously on January 17, 1962, with E.O. 10988, which also provided that all employees in the competitive civil service were to have the same rights as veterans to appeal to the CSC in adverse-actions proceedings.[54] The case involved an employee of NASA who was discharged for falsifying overtime reports and thus obtaining overtime compensation fraudulently.[55] After exhausting her remedies under the NASA appeals system, the appellant appealed to the CSC under E.O. 10988. The CSC upheld NASA, leaving the appellant's dismissal undisturbed. The appeal was based on the ground that no formal review had been made of the entire official appellate record and the transcript of the evidence in passing judgment. It was claimed that procedural due process was not afforded. Important to the issue of executive discretion was the underlying question of the court's willingness to police the administrative actions of agencies moving under executive direction and following the basic standards set by the Civil Service Commission.

Circuit Court Judge McGowan refused to intrude the court into an area of internal procedural regulation of personnel. He adhered to the traditional tests for judicial self-restraint in administrative matters, stating:

". . . But as long as the agency action is neither arbitrary nor capricious, this would seem to be a matter for the agency's judgment. As has been noted above, this is an area where judicial interference is misconceived, pregnant as it is with possibilities of disturbing the

---

[53] E.O. 10987, *Agency System for Appeals from Adverse Actions*, January 17, 1962, Sec. 1.

[54] E.O. 10988, *Employee-Management Cooperation in the Federal Service*, January 17, 1962, Sec. 14.

[55] Agatha Mendelson v. John W. Macy, Jr., et al., 356 F.2d 796, No. 19310 (C.A. D.C. 1966). See also Joseph Young, "The Federal Spotlight," *Washington Star*, August 20, 1965.

orderly and uniform personnel administration envisaged by Congress." [56]
The administrative procedures and the actions of both NASA and the CSC were entirely upheld as not unreasonable or arbitrary. There was substantial compliance with internal regulations. Above all, the court declined to "substitute its judgment for that of an administrative agency." [57] This basic tenet of administrative law effectively supports executive power.

A major test [58] of executive discretion in federal labor relations developed when the Manhattan-Bronx Postal Union, affiliated with the independent National Postal Union, contested a decision of Postmaster General Gronouski. He had determined to withhold the union's certification as the exclusive representative of the New York Post Office because of the department's "60 percent" rule in representation elections. Although E.O. 10988 required only a majority for certification as the exclusive representative, ample provision was left to empower the CSC, agency heads, and the Temporary Committee on Implementation of the Federal Employee-Management Relations Program to fix policy, rules, and regulations governing the recognition of organizations as exclusive representatives.[59] The Temporary Committee had recommended that, where a union won less than an absolute majority, the election not be considered valid if less than 60 percent of the eligible employees cast ballots. The CSC endorsed this policy and transmitted the recommendation to all affected agencies, and in May 1962 the Post Office Department issued a Postal Bulletin explaining the rule as it was to apply to the first elections under E.O. 10988.[60] Under these procedures the MBPU was designated as the exclusive representative of mail handlers by virtue of an election in June 1962.

Another election was held in May and June of 1964. The MBPU received 2,493 votes, or 66.6 percent, while Local 1 of the National Association of Post Office Mail Handlers, Watchmen, Messengers, and Group Leaders, an AFL-CIO affiliated craft organization, received 1,156, or 30.9 percent. However, of 6,535 eligible voters, only 3,729, or 57.06 percent, had actually voted. Therefore, the 60-percent rule was not satisfied. The union was accordingly informed it would not be recognized as the exclusive agent for mail handlers at the New York Post Office of this

[56] *Ibid.*, at 800.
[57] *Ibid.*
[58] Manhattan-Bronx Postal Union, *et al.* v. Gronouski, 350 F.2d 451, No. 18,882 (C.A. D.C. 1965).
[59] E.O. 10988, Secs. 6, 10, 12, 13.
[60] Manhattan-Bronx Postal Union, *et al.* v. Gronouski, *supra,* at 453.

group. Instead, both it and its competitor were offered formal recognition.

Its protest rebuffed by a federal district court, the MBPU appealed, arguing that the Post Office had arbitrarily narrowed the President's order by requiring 60-percent participation when Section 6 (a) of the order stated that a mere majority would suffice for exclusive recognition. The union also claimed that the court had jurisdiction through its equity powers to grant relief and require the Postmaster General to recognize it as the exclusive bargaining agent.

The opinion of the court of appeals, by Judge McGowan, affirmed the district court's dismissal, addressing itself to the issues of executive discretion, the separation of powers, and the sovereignty question. Judge McGowan, within the framework of the sovereignty doctrine, upheld the executive's prerogative to conduct a government labor relations program. He affirmed upon two fundamental grounds, namely:

> "Appellants' suit, in effect, is one against the United States which cannot be maintained without its consent. Moreover, the right they seek to assert in this instance is not, in our view, *appropriate for judicial vindication.*" [61]

He laid out his reasoning point by point. First, he cited the Supreme Court's holding that simply naming an individual as defendant does not make a suit any less a suit against the United States. The main question remained, that is, whether the relief nominally sought against an officer was really relief sought against the sovereign. A suit against the sovereign has been clearly defined as one where "the judgment sought would require the payment of public funds or entail the transfer of public lands, or . . . would interfere with the public administration by either restraining the Government from acting or requiring it to act." [62] This was such a case, the judge reasoned, since the aim of the appeal was to oblige the Postmaster General to recognize the union.

However, Judge McGowan emphasized that it is equally well accepted that there can be circumstances in which specific relief against an officer is not relief against the United States. In this regard, he noted that the Supreme Court has recognized exceptions to the general rule of sovereign immunity; that actions will lie if (1) officers act beyond their statutory powers and (2), even though they act within the scope of their authority, the powers themselves or the manner in which they are exercised are consti-

---

[61] Manhattan-Bronx Postal Union *et al.* v. Gronouski, *supra,* at 454 (emphasis added).

[62] *Ibid.*; see also Dugan v. Rank, 372 U.S. 609, 83 S.Ct. 999 (1963).

tutionally void.[63] In short, when an officer acts beyond his authority, he is not doing the business of the sovereign as he is empowered to do it, or he is doing it in a way the sovereign has forbidden. In such a case, specific relief would lie against the officer. However, such was not the situation regarding the Post Office Department's action under E.O. 10988, in the judge's view.

What the court of appeals affirmed in this decision was the sovereign prerogative of the President to institute a labor program and to allow his officers extensive discretion to administer it. The court firmly supported departmental discretion as an adjunct to presidential action. It declared, in regard to the 60-percent rule:

". . . The Postmaster General's responsibility for the administration of Government employment policies and regulations within the Department is unquestioned. By the terms of the order, he, like the heads of other agencies was, in his administration of the Post Office Department, directed to carry out the policies therein expressed. He was instructed to adopt appropriate regulations and procedures to achieve that purpose. Presumably the President foresaw that such regulations and procedures should not be uniform throughout the Government, for he left their formulation and adoption to the heads of the various agencies. It would thus appear that the President intended to allow his subordinates some considerable flexibility in the implementation of his objective." [64]

As to the issue of judicial intervention in what it deemed to be an executive program, the court used perhaps even stronger language. Almost Jeffersonian in his treatment of the program as essentially a "political question," Judge McGowan called for judicial restraint. To the claim that the District Court should have exerted its general equity powers, he responded:

". . . Those powers have on occasion in the past been successfully invoked to secure relief against various representatives of the federal establishment. But it has been commonly recognized that, in order to avoid the rock of sovereign immunity, on the one hand, and to maintain a reasonably acute sensitivity to the fundamental implications of the separation of powers, on the other, the occasion must be a compelling one." [65]

What better statement of presidential prerogative and discretion in labor matters than the court's observation that:

"Executive Order 10988 represents in essence a formulation of broad policy by the President for the guidance of federal employing agencies. It has no specific foundation in Congressional action, nor was it required to effectuate any statute. It could have been with-

---

63 Dugan v. Rank, *supra*, at 621-622; Larson v. Domestic and Foreign Commerce Corp., 337 U.S. 682, 689-690, 69 S.Ct. 1457 (1949) ; Malone v. Bowdoin, 369 U.S. 643, 82 S.Ct. 980 (1962) .

64 Manhattan-Bronx Postal Union, *et al.* v. Gronouski, *supra,* at 454-455.

65 *Ibid.,* at 456.

drawn at any time for any or no reason. It represented simply one President's effort to move in the direction of what he had been advised by his experts would be an improvement in the efficiency of federal employment. As we have indicated he imposed no hard and fast directives on the many different kinds of federal employees; and he left large areas for the exercise of discretion at levels below the summit, although he went to some pains to provide continuing advisory services from those people and agencies within his administration equipped with special knowledge or experience in personnel matters.

"The President did not undertake to create any role for the judiciary in the implementation of this policy. The question of his power to do so aside, he was, at least in this matter of determining representational rights, emulating the example of Congress, which has shown a marked disinclination to intrude equity courts into this process." [66]

The real point at issue here was not whether the 60-percent rule was just and warranted. The rule itself was widely opposed by public employee unions and by important elements in federal management. Secretary of Labor Wirtz, addressing the Metal Trades Council in 1963, voiced the view that such a voting rule was wrong and that, as a consensus on this procedure developed among the agencies, he would do his utmost to resolve this and other major problems.[67]

Another important question left unanswered by this decision concerned the relatively unlimited executive discretion in the federal system's administration. The MBPU, NAIRE, NFFE, and other federal unions felt keenly their inability to appeal agency interpretations under E.O. 10988. From the unions' point of view there were no real reins on management's interpretation and administration of the ground rules for carrying out the Employee-Management Cooperation (EMC) program. Since the essence of the program was mutuality and cooperation, they desired more than simply negotiating agreements. They wanted to participate in implementing the program. This concern was their prime motivation for resorting to judicial review of administrative action. Obviously, revisions and improvements in management procedures and policies were needed to satisfy such complaints. Yet Secretary Wirtz believed federal executives had come a longer way under E.O. 10988 than in any other period of management in this country. He declared:

"I think it is one of the great accomplishments of the last two years that it has been possible to establish so quickly so effectively,

---

[66] *Ibid.*

[67] W. Willard Wirtz, *Address*, to the 51st Convention of the Metal Trades Department, AFL-CIO, New York, November 11, 1963, pp. 97-98.

a pattern for unionization, representation and bargaining in the Federal Government, the pattern that, of course, had been set before, that we are making very great strides forward in this particular area." [68]

Of great importance was the manner in which the court of appeals, by refusing to place judicial reins upon executive discretion, assured and protected the power to institute a government-wide labor relations program. The federal program which, from its inception, steadily took on many aspects of traditional collective bargaining, was thus upheld without excessive reliance upon the obstructive concepts of the sovereignty doctrine.

Finally, one cannot ignore the implications of the Supreme Court's denial of certiorari when this dispute was again appealed in 1966.[69] It is true such action does not carry with it any official expression of opinion of the Court on the merits of a case. Moreover, the reasons both substantive and procedural for denying certiorari are legion. Nevertheless, any action by our highest court is of tremendous importance, especially in this vital area where it has rarely expressed its views. Moreover, this is the only major litigation under the new federal program actually to reach the Supreme Court.

The McGowan decision actually constituted strong *stare decisis* when the National Association of Internal Revenue Employees contested an interpretation of the Kennedy order by the Internal Revenue Service. The district court, in January 1965, had dismissed NAIRE's challenge to the IRS's decision to exclude criminal investigators from coverage under Section 16 of the order. That section specifically permitted the exclusion of those elements performing intelligence investigation or security functions if the head of the agency determined that their inclusion would be inconsistent with national security requirements. When the dismissal was appealed to the Court of Appeals for the District of Columbia, the MBPU opinion was the major basis for affirmation. The court held that if the Secretary of the Treasury had erred in his interpretation, relief would have to be sought elsewhere and not in the District Court.[70]

An attack by the NFFE upon the new program was far more fundamental. It went to the core of the issue by questioning E.O. 10988's constitutionality. The main thrust of its legal attack was

---

68 *Ibid.*, pp. 96-97.
69 Manhattan-Bronx Postal Union, *et al.* v. O'Brien, 382 U.S. 978, 86 S.Ct. 548 (1966).
70 National Association of Internal Revenue Employees v. Dillon, 356 F.2d 811 (C.A. D.C. 1966).

that the order was unauthorized by either the Constitution or any congressional statute and represented action beyond the constitutional authority of the President. This litigation reflected the vigorous opposition of the NFFE to the program when first introduced. NFFE's attitude eventually progressed from the outright rejection by former President Vaux Owen of the basic philosophy underlying the order to the more positive position of his successor, Nathan T. Wolkomir. Vaux Owen believed the executive order promoted conflict, not cooperation, and was a means by which outside labor unions would acquire power over federal employees. Mistrusting the program as the product of Secretary of Labor Goldberg's experiences in the private labor field, he was dead set against the exclusive recognition provisions of Section 6 and collective bargaining generally.

The NFFE, independent and professionally oriented, had been experiencing serious difficulty because of the conflict-of-interest provisions of the program. It was further plagued by increased competition from the AFGE, IAM, and other organizations. Many of its members holding supervisory positions had voluntarily relinquished their membership in NFFE or were made to do so in many instances in order to retain their positions. On September 14, 1962, the NFFE National Convention adopted a resolution which, in part, called upon the President to eliminate the order's exclusive recognition provisions and, failing that, congressional negation of Section 6. It also resolved to exert every possible effort to remove the conflict-of-interest impediments.[71]

In June 1964 NFFE instituted suit [72] to declare the order unconstitutional after the U.S. Naval Marine Engineering Laboratory at Annapolis, Md., rejecting the NFFE's request for formal recognition under Section 5 of the order, followed Arbitrator Thomas Holland's decision that the IAM be recognized as the exclusive representative of machine shop employees. The suit charged that E.O. 10988 was unconstitutional because it permitted the Secretary of the Navy to abdicate the authority given him by Congress by following the arbitrator's decision. The NFFE's complaint pointedly noted that in just under two years its membership nationally had decreased by 6,108, to 41,493, and that of the Annapolis local from 291 to 161.[73] The Secretary of

---

[71] Vaux Owen, in *Management Relations With Organized Public Employees* (K. O. Warner, ed.) (Chicago: Public Personnel Assn., 1963), pp. 231-232, 234.

[72] NFFE, *et al.* v. Nitze, Secretary of the Navy, *et al.*, Civil Action No. 1380-64 (D.D.C., 1965), unpublished opinion. Reported in *Government Employee Relations Report*, No. 109, October 11, 1965.

[73] *Government Employee Relations Report*, No. 40, (1964), pp. F-1, F-5.

the Navy, it was charged, in following the arbitrator's decision had violated the federal statutes which defined his duties and required that any substantial transfer or reassignment of his duties be reported to Congress.

The district court, in an opinion by Judge Spottswood W. Robinson, III, noted that "the action seeks . . . a declaration that the Order itself is invalid and an injunction that would broadly restrain any and all implementation of it." [74] The court found that the NFFE had no standing to sue. The language of the decision, although qualifying and descriptive, decidedly recognized the collective bargaining process in the federal program as a valid executive measure. The court asserted:

"As both the Task Force and the President recognized, collective bargaining in the Federal Service is much less potent than its counterpart in private employment. The Order remains faithful to the executive responsibilities of Federal officials and the limitations inevitably flowing therefrom. . . . Moreover, the Order, as its history shows, commits the formulation and execution of the bargaining process, as other matters, to the administrative discretion and arrangement of the individual agencies. If there can be any basis for legitimate criticism of the bargaining in the Laboratory machine shop it cannot be directed against the Order itself." [75]

Taking an approach similar to that of Judge McGowan's later opinion, Judge Robinson held that E.O. 10988 was an executive policy directive and that there was no intent that the judiciary participate in its effectuation. Recognizing that the issue of the NFFE's standing presents "a fundamental and sensitive question of separation of powers between the executive and judicial branches of government," he reminded the parties that interference by the courts would produce "nothing but mischief." [76]

In support of the constitutionality of the entire EMC program, the court declared:

"The Order attacked in this litigation was the fruitage of a beneficent purpose to improve employee-management relations in federal operations through a general policy as to union recognition in the executive branch. Its objectives embraced the employees' betterment as well as increased efficiency in the Federal work force. The fact that the President did not create judicially enforceable rights does not make these benefits any less real. It means only that in case of dispute each branch of the Government is to remain in its proper sphere, and that appeal is to be made to the agency head or the Chief Executive, and not the courts." [77]

---

[74] NFFE, et al. v. Nitze, et al., unpublished opinion, p. 8.
[75] Ibid., pp. 10-12.
[76] Ibid., p. 14.
[77] Ibid., pp. 14-15.

With the election of Nathan Wolkomir in 1964 came a new approach by the NFFE to the opportunities afforded by the order.[78] The union's executive council voted to refrain from further litigation over the order's constitutionality, deciding instead to direct its efforts toward resolution of the conflict-of-interest issue through internal executive channels.[79]

It is apparent that the judicial reefs of the sovereignty doctrine no longer prevent the adoption of federal collective bargaining systems. The constitutionality of such programs remains inviolate since they are conducted within the existing and accepted framework of constitutional powers for the carrying out of presidential policy and congressional legislation. The sovereign principle was resurrected when convenient in the past to oppose collective action. It is now apparently being purposefully deemphasized in order to implement a program of greater collective action. As NALC President Jerome J. Keating commented to the AFL-CIO Constitutional Convention in December 1965:

> "We find less and less individuals who occupy executive positions in government who feel that they are sovereigns. The old idea that every man who works for the government is a sovereign has disappeared to a great extent." [80]

The use of executive authority to promote labor relations programs has not reduced by one jot the efforts of federal unions to solidify their gains through congressional action. As the EMC program developed and many dissatisfactions evolved over policies and procedures, even greater union legislative efforts were mounted. "Collective bargaining by law" was the catchword. Legislative efforts were hastened by increased pessimism over executive initiative to reform the program. This was particularly acute during the period prior to President Nixon's issuance of E. O. 11491 in October 1969. There was also great dissatisfaction with the course of collective bargaining in the Post Office Department and other agencies. The Postal Reorganization Act[81] fulfilled the postal unions' desire for a labor-management relations program established by statute. Federal unions generally seek to have Congress bring labor relations under an independent board or panel. Should this happen for the entire federal establishment, the sovereignty doctrine will have been effectively removed as a factor in labor relations.

---

[78] Nathan T. Wolkomir, "President Wolkomir Describes NFFE's Revitalized 'New Look,'" *The Federal Employee,* December 1964, Vol. XLIX, No. 12, p. 8.

[79] *Government Employee Relations Report,* No. 111 (1965), p. A-1.

[80] *Government Employee Relations Report,* No. 119 (1965), p. A-7.

[81] 84 Stat. 719; 39 U.S.C. Sec. 101, August 12, 1970.

CHAPTER VI

NATIONAL POLICY SINCE 1962

A. THE EXECUTIVE LANDMARKS

That collective negotiation was not new to the federal service was fully borne out by the findings and recommendations of the Kennedy Task Force. Some of the agencies it examined had collective bargaining procedures closely approximating those of private industry. Indeed, in some cases the procedures were superior in efficiency and human relations factors. One such agency, Interior's Bonneville Power Administration, has often been singled out on this score. It cannot be argued that the BPA is a government corporation or independent regulatory commission. The BPA is a large administrative unit within a regular executive department.

With minor exceptions, all the Task Force proposals for the future were already contemporary policy in one federal agency or another.[1] Indeed, some units with advanced procedures had stood up well under the test of time. This simple fact of life in federal labor-management relations influenced the wording and spirit of the report to the President. Among the major emphases of the report was the clear intent to further labor-management relations by executive action—by presidential order which established public policy without legislation. To some degree, the executive channel removes legalistic obstructions to advanced labor relations by the simple expedient of deemphasizing their importance. Possible constitutional limitations or the alternative use of legislation for setting up a labor relations program were hardly mentioned in the report.

This does not imply that the intention of the Task Force was to denigrate the methods guaranteed by the Lloyd-LaFollette Act but simply that the new program was to be an executive policy administratively carried out. If unions believed they could

[1] President's Task Force on Employee-Management Relations in the Federal Service, *Report*, November 30, 1961, p. iii.

109

accomplish more by legislative lobbying, that path was still open to them. The Task Force merely emphasized that basic goals could be achieved by the executive branch without legislation; collective negotiation could be a matter of everyday administration. The only recommendation submitted that would have required congressional action was the voluntary checkoff of organization dues.

The executive approach continues to be the essential federal policy. Despite innumerable congressional bills submitted to revise diverse aspects of the federal program, Presidents Johnson, Nixon, and Ford chose to follow in Kennedy's footsteps in labor matters. Mr. Nixon's postal policy was the only exception. On September 8, 1967, Mr. Johnson appointed a President's Review Committee on Federal Employee-Management Relations patterned upon the 1961 Kennedy Task Force.[2] Chaired by Secretary of Labor W. Willard Wirtz, it again included John W. Macy of the Civil Service Commission and Robert F. McNamara of the Defense Department.[3] Mr. Johnson's desire was to continue the direction labor relations had taken under the Kennedy order—to determine what the program had accomplished, where it was deficient, and what adjustments were needed to ensure "its continued vitality in the public interest."[4]

When President Nixon took office, a similar Study Committee[5] continued to review and assess federal labor history under E.O.

---

[2] Chaired by Secretary of Labor Arthur J. Goldberg, the Kennedy Task Force included John W. Macy, Jr., Chairman of the Civil Service Commission; David E. Bell, Director, Bureau of the Budget; Robert F. McNamara, Secretary of Defense; J. Edward Day, Postmaster General; and Theodore C. Sorensen, Special Counsel to the President. The alternates were James J. Reynolds, Assistant Secretary of Labor; Richard J. Murphy, Assistant Postmaster General; William D. Carey, Executive Assistant Director, Bureau of the Budget; Carlisle P. Runge, Assistant Secretary of Defense; Wilfred V. Gill, Assistant to the Chairman, Civil Service Commission; Lee C. White, Special Counsel to the President. Daniel P. Moynihan, Special Assistant to the Secretary of Labor, served as Staff Director and Ida Klaus, Counsel to the New York City Department of Labor, served as Consultant.

[3] Also appointed to the Johnson Review Committee were Lawrence F. O'Brien, Postmaster General; Charles L. Schultz, Director of the Budget; and Joseph A. Califano, Jr., Special Assistant to the President. Louis S. Wallerstein, of the Office of Federal Employee-Management Relations in the Labor Department, served as Staff Director. By the time its report was unofficially published, Charles J. Zwick represented the Budget Bureau, W. Marvin Watson was Postmaster General, and Clark M. Clifford was Secretary of Defense.

[4] U.S. Office of the President, *Memorandum on Employee Organizations and Agency Management*, September 8, 1967.

[5] The 1969 Nixon Study Committee included Robert E. Hampton, Chairman of the Civil Service Commission; Melvin R. Laird, Secretary of Defense; George P. Shultz, Secretary of Labor; Winton M. Blount, Postmaster General; and Robert P. Mayo, Director of the Bureau of the Budget. Wilfred V. Gill's particular role in developing federal labor policy was again brought home. He served on all three study groups as the alternate member for the Civil Service Commissioner. As Executive Director of the Federal Labor Relations Council, he helped issue its report supporting E.O. 11616 in 1971.

10988. Its motivations were essentially those of the Johnson Review Committee. From the resulting recommendations and action taken by Mr. Nixon, it was clear that the work conducted under Secretary Wirtz was heavily relied upon.

The report and recommendations issued by the Nixon group in August 1969 were similar in many respects to the Johnson committee report, which had no official standing. There were, however, departures from the latter's recommendations that reflected the management-oriented thinking of the Nixon Administration. These were incorporated, on October 29, 1969, in President Nixon's Executive Order 11491,[6] which superseded E.O. 10988 when it came into force on January 1, 1970.

Despite underlying similarities in policy recommendations, the findings of the Johnson and Nixon committees were undeniably different in tone and attitude. The Nixon Study Committee's expressions of proposed policy, for example, in the areas of union security, management rights, representation elections, checkoff, and the superiority of laws and regulations, consistently evidenced a more conservative viewpoint than did policy statements of the Johnson Review Committee. The Study Committee explicitly laid out union liabilities and urged that unions be more forcefully regulated. The Nixon order achieved several long overdue reforms, but the overall approach of the Nixon program rankled many union leaders because it failed to make the substantive changes they deemed necessary.

There had been little doubt in 1961 that the Federal Government wanted to set a public policy making collective employee relations an ordinary part of its executive function for personnel management. The differences between collective dealing in the private and public spheres were recognized and it was made clear that the entire program was to be subject to existing acts of Congress. It was believed, nevertheless, that when federal law, administrative discretion, the merit system, and the public good were considered, sufficient areas of common interest could be found to warrant instituting a program of collective dealing that would bring mutuality to the formulation of public personnel policy. The approach under President Johnson was the same.

B. THE POLICY OF DECENTRALIZATION

While the Kennedy Task Force called for the establishment of a government-wide labor policy, it emphasized ultimate agency

---

[6] *Executive Order 11491: Labor-Management Relations in the Federal Service,* October 29, 1969.

independence and responsibility for implementation of the program:

> "In proposing a government-wide policy on employee-management relations we are not proposing the establishment of uniform government-wide practices. The great variations among the many agencies of the government require that each be enabled to devise its own particular practices, in cooperation with its own employees. Our object is to lay down the general policies which should guide such efforts." [7]

In line with this policy, the Kennedy order was directed specifically to agency heads. While the Labor Department and the CSC were responsible only for servicing the program, the individual agency was responsible for finally fulfilling it.

This division of responsibility must be viewed in the light of the broad spectrum of policies that had developed in the labor relations of the many federal agencies. The more independence afforded agency administration under the order, the greater was the opportunity to perpetuate existing agency practices in vital areas.

Forty years have passed since the NLRB undertook the gargantuan task of interpreting policies on, among others, appropriate bargaining units, exclusive recognition rights, representation elections, conflicts-of-interest, and unfair labor practices. Now that policies on many of these issues have been set for federal employees, comparable responsibility and administrative and judicial discretion have been granted to agency heads regardless of the specificity of the executive orders.

Substantial arguments can be made for this approach. Macy applauded the general support of federal agencies for the adoption of a government-wide policy to provide guidelines for devising programs tailored to particular agency needs. However, he noted that many agencies had presented differing views and proposals as to what that policy should be. He also emphasized that the problems of each agency vary. Issues of appropriate recognition were complicated by diverse employee group affiliations. The same problems that plagued the NLRB in fixing standards for determining appropriate bargaining units appeared in government as well.[8] Macy concluded that:

> "Variations in patterns of employee affiliation, in the array of employee groups, and in the size and situations of Federal agencies

---

[7] Task Force, *op. cit.*, p. iv.

[8] John W. Macy, Jr., " 'New Era' in Employee-Management Relations," *Civil Service Journal,* January-March 1962, p. 3.

dictated against an attempt to fashion a standard system and detailed procedures to be followed on a Government-wide basis." [9]

Warren B. Irons, executive director of the CSC during the Kennedy Administration, saw the delegation of responsibility to the agencies as the prerequisite of a fundamental decision. The choice had to be made between changing the basic structure and concept of the whole federal program in one stroke and fostering progressive change within its existing framework. What was sought, he believed, was evolutionary change without undue delay or difficulty within the system. The major advantage of delegating responsibility to the agencies was that it allowed each agency to suit the program to its specific needs. The broad language of the Kennedy order, in fact, encouraged local managers to experiment in implementing the program, free of the restrictions that a detailed, centrally controlled policy would impose. Built-in flexibility, he contended, promoted an effective program.[10] Although this freedom permitted varying rates of compliance with the program, Irons, after two and one-half years of the program, stated that agency management generally had done an "exceptional job in placing a sensitive and complex new program into effect."

1. Implementation

Implementation of the program entailed two basic phases for the agency—setting policies and procedures and implementing them. As to the first phase, Section 10 of E.O. 10988 was explicit in providing that no later than July 1, 1962, the head of each agency was to issue appropriate policies and regulations for the implementation of the order. These were expected, among other things, to include a clear statement of employee rights and to set the policies and procedures for recognizing employee organizations, determining appropriate bargaining units, and consulting with unions, other organizations, and individual employees. As far as practicable and appropriate, the formulation of these policies was to be carried on in consultation with employee representatives.[11] There was no rush to comply with the July 1 deadline.

The Committee on the Law of Government Employee Relations of the American Bar Association pointed to the federal program's lack of centralized procedural decision making in the very first year E.O. 10988 was in effect. The Committee noted, however, that during this initial phase there was relatively little

---

[9] *Ibid.*

[10] Warren B. Irons, "Employee Management Cooperation: The Federal Program in Perspective," *Public Personnel Review,* July 1964, p. 148.

[11] E.O. 10988, Sec. 10.

open controversy between agencies and union organizations. This was attributed to a number of factors. First, the great mass of complicated directive material generated by the order might have created a substantial obstacle to understanding and assimilation. Second, much of the order's exact language was reproduced in agency regulations, particularly on those matters which were specifically set forth and from which variation was neither feasible nor practicable. In many instances, the order was clear and insistent upon issues which were and still are controversial. For example, new regulations merely repeated the language of the order in provisions pertaining to management prerogatives, statutory limitations, and employees' rights to join or to refrain from joining an organization. Provisions dealing with unit restrictions, conflicts of interest, the individual employee's right to consult directly with his supervisor, the use of government time and facilities, and the collection of dues generally also were repeated verbatim in the individual agency's policies and regulations.[12]

Despite conscious attempts to reduce friction, disputes were precipitated by the agency action of fixing substantive provisions while ostensibly establishing agency procedures. Thus, the ABA committee pointed out that some agencies included built-in preferences for large appropriate units in their procedures for unit determination. This action was contrary to union views that a particular military installation might comprise several separate appropriate units, a view which reflected policies followed in private industry.[13]

In setting program procedures, certain agencies incorporated substantive policies pertaining to the crucial issue of the proper subject areas for bargaining. The order and the Code of Fair Labor Practices stipulated that an agency must negotiate with an exclusively recognized organization. They also stipulated that the areas for negotiation should include all personnel policies and practices and matters affecting working conditions that were of concern to organization members, subject to law and within agency discretion. The ABA committee noted that while some agencies accepted this fairly broad policy, others spelled out the areas of possible negotiation in precise detail directly in the new regulations. In the area of conflict of interest, agency regulations

---

[12] American Bar Association, Section of Labor Relations Law, Committee on Law of Government Employee Relations, *Report*, "The Federal Government's Employee Management Cooperation Program," Chicago, 1963, pp. 126-133. Permission to reprint this article from the *Labor Law Report* was obtained from the ABA and its Section of Labor Relations Law, 1969.

[13] *Ibid.*, pp. 131-132.

also set down varying substantive provisions of great import to the organizations concerned.[14]

Since all collective negotiations were conducted subject to agency regulations, it was a simple matter for agency heads to preclude discussion of certain items. They could either exempt the items in advance from the area of negotiation or later unilaterally revise the regulations, which, of course, negated existing contracts. There is little doubt that the controversy surrounding negotiable subjects contributed to agencies' hesitancy to comply with the Kennedy order, despite agency protestations that they accepted the system as a long overdue step forward.

Of all federal agencies, according to Wilson Hart, only the Labor and Agricultural Departments acted before the July 1 deadline. Furthermore, as Chairman Macy himself conceded, by the end of 1962 some agencies still had not complied with the order's requirement that regulations be issued to implement the program.[15]

Commenting upon the responsibility of agency management to contribute to the fostering of stability among employee unions, the ABA committee declared:

"Here we must express reservations. The program is based upon a policy of decentralization which puts each agency in a posture of employer and law-giver at one and the same time . . . .

"Most agencies are too devoted to their own regulations . . . . They must learn that regulations are not holy writ. They can be changed or modified . . . and they can also be discussed and negotiated. Emphasis upon regulatory supremacy can stifle collective bargaining, and can force unions to continue the political approach to their problems which the program was, in part, meant to eliminate.

"The program also suffers from lack of a guiding philosophy. The policy is clear, but its implementation may be affected by the personal views of hundreds of agency officials scattered from coast to coast. There is little evidence that the agencies are able to enforce top-level policy effectively enough to prevent wide variations in the program as a whole." [16]

In the second phase, where the emphasis shifted to the operational processes of negotiation and consultation, agencies could have chosen to foster the purposes of the program or to delay, minimize, or water down the executive policy. Many agencies took the former path while others endeavoured to maintain previous attitudes of toleration within the new framework of the

---

[14] *Ibid.*, pp. 132-133.
[15] Wilson R. Hart, "The U.S. Civil Service Learns to Live with E.O. 10988," *Industrial and Labor Relations Review*, January 1964, p. 203.
[16] American Bar Association, *op. cit.*, pp. 142-143.

order. It was in this phase that the loudest complaints of union leaders were voiced. They either accused agencies of falling short of program objectives or presented criticisms challenging the entire structure of the new program. Generally their criticisms were motivated by disappointment with the rate of progress of federal labor relations, as compared with private-sector labor relations practice.

The late Otto Pragan, of the AFL-CIO Education Department, reflected the views of union leaders after two full years of living with the Kennedy order. Addressing the Government Employes' Council, he commented that the new program, especially its collective bargaining aspects, had the potential for bringing real equality to the bargaining table. Yet even though 80 percent of the postal workers, 20 percent of the blue-collar workers, and 5 percent of the classified employees had negotiated or were negotiating collective agreements, Pragan asserted that many of the principal grievances of union representatives were still unsatisfied. At the close of 1963 Pragan pointed out:

> "that government management is now less inclined to carry out the high spirited statements they made at the time the Order was issued. They are also less inclined to make bilateral collective bargaining the very base of labor management relations in the Federal service. The scope of collective bargaining varies from agency to agency—it swings from hostile opposition, often meaningless reiteration and rewriting of existing regulations and provisions in personnel manuals to sometimes meaningful and genuine bargaining. Too often management takes a legalistic approach which does not bring about a real change in personnel policies and practices but degrades the collective bargaining agreement to an appendix of the personnel manual. The greatest disappointment with this concept of collective bargaining, as we see it in many government departments, is that management does not accept in good faith the intent and purpose of the Executive Order, which even within its limited scope provides for bilateral and meaningful collective bargaining in the federal service." [17]

2. The Initial Experience

The decentralized control that made possible the varied spectrum of agency compliance manifested itself in the bargaining phase. More than two years after the order such early contracts as that of the Army Pictorial Center with the NFFE, Local 1106; the Office of the Supervisor of Shipbuilding, Camden, N. J., with

---

[17] Otto Pragan, "Union Experiences under the Executive Order," *Remarks*, before Government Employes' Council at AFL-CIO Convention, New York, November 19, 1963; also in GEC *Bulletin*, No. 2, January 16, 1964.

the American Federation of Technical Engineers, Local 198; and Philadelphia Army Engineers District with the National Marine Engineers Beneficial Association relied practically entirely, by reference and incorporation, on the FPM.[18] It should be noted, however, that in following years meaningful contracts were written by these unions, the postal unions, the Metal Trades Department, the IAM, the National Maritime Union, the AFGE, and many others.

In the early bargaining phase, however, there was considerable disparity among the agencies in willingness to arrive at actual negotiated agreements. The Bureau of Labor Statistics' review of 209 contracts arrived at by mid-1964 revealed great variations in the time required to reach agreement. Although it generally took from four to nine months to write a contract after the granting of exclusive recognition, in some cases it took as little as three months and in others as many as 19 months.[19] Managerial reluctance to comply with the Kennedy order was underscored by the fact that, as of 1965, more than one half of all agencies with exclusively recognized unions had failed to come to any agreement whatsoever.[20] Moreover, outside the Post Office Department the number of exclusives was a relatively small fraction of the potential number throughout the federal establishment. As of November 1968 only 28 percent of the white-collar employees and 67 percent of the blue-collar workers were in exclusive units and less than half the federal workforce operated under negotiated agreements.[21] While this picture had improved by 1970, 42 percent of all federal eligibles still had not achieved exclusive recognition, and 54 percent of the qualifying workforce was not covered by a negotiated agreement.[22] By November 1974 the picture had improved substantially, with 1,142,419 employees in exclusive units and 984,553 under contracts, not counting the Postal Serv-

---

[18] U.S. Department of the Army, *Agreement,* between Army Pictorial Center, Long Island City, U.S. Army, New York, and National Federation of Federal Employees, Local 1106, July 11, 1963; U.S. Department of the Navy, *Agreement,* between Office of Supervisor of Shipbuilding, Camden, N.J., and American Federation of Technical Engineers, Local 198, AFL-CIO, June 9, 1964; U.S. Department of the Army, *Agreement,* between Army Engineers District, Philadelphia, Pa., and National Marine Engineers Beneficial Association, AFL-CIO, January 1, 1964.

[19] U.S. Department of Labor, Bureau of Labor Statistics, *Collective Bargaining Agreements, Late Summer, 1964,* Bulletin No. 1451, August 1965, p. 7.

[20] U.S. Civil Service Commission, Employee-Management Relations Section, *Listing of Exclusive Recognitions and Negotiated Agreements in Federal Agencies Under E.O. 10988, July 1965.*

[21] Wilfred V. Gill, Director, Office of Labor-Management Relations, U.S. Civil Service Commission, *Statement,* before U.S. House of Representatives, Subcommittee on Postal Operations, April 25, 1969, p. 12.

[22] U.S. Civil Service Commission, Office of Labor-Management Relations, *Union Recognition in the Federal Government, November 1970,* June 1971, p. 15.

ice.[23] Among other things, the increase indicated a significant improvement in management cooperation with program goals.

Union representatives often expressed the view that the new policy was designed to foster the process of collective bargaining. However, most believed it was falling short of that end. Certain unions with long experience in collective bargaining were able from the outset to negotiate sound and meaningful contracts. The majority, however, were concerned primarily with acquiring and solidifying their initial recognition as bargaining agents. Accordingly, they settled at first for agreements that were far from satisfactory to them, with the intent of bettering their position in each succeeding round of negotiations. In government, this means seeking to duplicate, as far as possible, the labor relations practices in private industry—"real" collective bargaining, arbitration, impasse resolution machinery, and for some organizations the right to strike.

3. Efforts at Reform

The deficiencies of decentralization were fully recognized by the 1967 Johnson Review Committee. When its draft report was finally published early in 1969 on an unofficial basis, its first recommendation called for increased central authority in overall program decision making.[24] The Committee reviewed the motivations of the Task Force in vesting authority in agency heads under the guidance and with the assistance of the Labor Department and the CSC. It concluded that the desired ends had been achieved in part, but not without adverse effects. In its view, union complaints of inequality in dealings with management, especially when agencies acted unilaterally or failed to act, combined with the appearance of bias in "one-sided processes" in E.O. 10988, "strengthened labor demands for program supervision by a central authority and for impartial, third-party handling of disputed matters." [25] The Committee, therefore, recommended the formation of a supervisory body to be known as the Federal Labor Relations Panel. This was to have consisted of the chairman of the CSC, the Secretary of Labor, and the chairman of the NLRB.[26]

---

[23] _____ _Union Recognition in the Federal Government, November 1974,_ February, 1975. See FPM Bulletin No. 711-32, March 1975, p. 1.

[24] President's Review Committee on Employee-Management Relations in the Federal Service, _Draft Report,_ April 1968, in U.S. Department of Labor, _56th Annual Report, 1969,_ Attachment B, p. 4.

[25] _Ibid.,_ p. 5.

[26] _Ibid.,_ pp. 4, 6.

A supervisory body with somewhat different membership was established by President Nixon's Executive Order 11491. The FLRC was to be chaired by the CSC chairman and included the Secretary of Labor. The NLRB chairman, however, was replaced by an "official of the Executive Office of the President and such other executive officials as the President may designate."[27] By E.O. 11616 of August 1971 the membership of the FLRC was changed so that the director of the Office of Management and Budget was fixed as the third member of the Council.[28] The director of the OMB at that time was George P. Shultz; as Secretary of Labor he had served on the Study Committee, and he was thus well qualified for FLRC membership.

The Nixon Study Committee report urged that the FLRC "oversee" the entire federal labor relations program.[29] This was not intended to deprive the Council of a role in the determination and clarification of policy and procedure, especially in the areas of appropriate unit, representation procedures, unfair labor practices, and internal union affairs. In certain of these areas provisions were made for direct action by the Assistant Secretary of Labor for Labor-Management Relations.[30] However, the principal medium for overseeing the entire program was to be the Council's appellate function in instances where the parties cannot resolve their differences in the normal course of events. In the course of settling disputes the FLRC was to build up a body of administrative precedents controlling policy and procedure that could be used to decide future disputes. The essential functions and relationships of both the Council and the Assistant Secretary were maintained in President Fords' E.O. 11838.[31] The Council, it was hoped, would influence individual agencies to adhere more closely to national labor policy. To handle impasse resolution, a separate unit, the Federal Service Impasses Panel, was established within the Council by E.O. 11491.

It was never intended that the Civil Service Commission or the Labor Department be deprived of their continuing functions of servicing and administering the labor-management relations program. Both the Review Committee led by Secretary Wirtz and the Nixon group held that, despite its authority, the Council

---

27 E. O. 11491, Sec. 4 (a) .

28 E. O. 11616, *Labor-Management Relations in the Federal Service*, August 26, 1971, Sec. 3.

29 President's Study Committee, *Report and Recommendations on Labor-Management Relations in the Federal Service*, August 1969, pp. 2, 6-8.

30 *Ibid.*, pp. 18, 25-30.

31 *Ibid.*, pp. 6-8, 25-26, 37, 48-51; E.O. 11491 as amended by E.O. 11838, February 6, 1975, Sec. 4.

should use "calculated restraint" in its duties in order that the agencies and labor organizations be left "free to work out their differences to the maximum extent possible without damaging the overall program." [32] Thus a considerable degree of decentralization was to be retained. The primary decisions controlling daily labor relations were still left to the executives in the departments and agencies. So established policies could be perpetuated, and the Civil Service Commission could maintain its place in the program's evolution.

C. THE PROBLEM OF SEMANTICS

Operational disagreements between unions and management often stem directly from differing concepts as to the basic intent and spirit of the federal program. Both contend that the program supports their respective views. Federal management insists that the Task Force and Kennedy order officially recognized the inherent uniqueness of government employment, a factor which has prevented the complete imposition of all private labor relations practices on federal agencies. The more militant unions either contend that private-sector labor practices are what the order originally contemplated or seek, in the course of effectuating the program, to have general labor relations concepts adopted. They accomplish their ends by pressing continuously for individual agency interpretations and acceptance of practices that parallel those in the private sphere as much as possible.

Task Force member John W. Macy emphasized time and again that the Kennedy executive order was not intended to duplicate private labor practices but rather was meant to cater to the particular needs of the federal service. He pointed out that controlling statutes, the public interest, and concern for the preservation of the merit system were features distinguishing public from private employee relations. The federal labor relations program, premised on these controlling features, combined certain procedures of private labor relations with the practices already accepted in the government service.[33] The Task Force was insistent on the need to distinguish between public- and private-sector labor relations:

> "Despite the obvious similarities in many respects between conditions of private and public employment, the Task Force feels that the equally obvious dissimilarities are such that it would be neither

---

[32] Review Committee, *op. cit.*, pp. 6-7, and Study Committee, *op. cit.*, p. 8. Here, as in many other segments of the Study Committee's report, there was extensive reliance upon the exact language of the Johnson Review Committee's draft report.
[33] John W. Macy, Jr., "Employee Management Cooperation in the Federal Service," *Personnel Administration*, Vol. 26, No. 1, January 1963, pp. 11, 13, 14.

desirable, nor possible, to fashion a federal system of employee-management relations directly upon the system which has grown up in the private economy." [34]

Collective bargaining proved the major obstacle to agreement in the dispute over the differences between public- and private-sector labor relations. The Civil Service Commission took a straightforward stand. In its training materials, compiled in order to guide the agencies, it supported in detail the proposition that E.O. 10988 did not introduce collective bargaining, in the full sense of the term, into the federal service.[35] It rested its case on the doctrine of sovereignty and the primacy of the public interest.

Management reluctance to use the language of labor relations rankled the unions. It was not a surface difference but one that symbolized the profoundly held concepts of federal cooperation as the Commission saw them. Otto Pragan had pointed out that if federal executives wished to consider themselves model employers, they had to follow the practices of model employers in our industrial society, who, within the law, achieve labor-management consensus through collective bargaining. In Pragan's view, government management had a long way to go before achieving such leadership. Long before the Johnson Review Committee, he cautioned that any new examination should result in an order which "should not be afraid to substitute the meaningful terms 'union' and 'collective bargaining' for the timid terms 'employee organization' and 'employee-managment cooperation.' " [36]

Times have decidedly changed. Wilfred V. Gill, director of the Office of Labor-Management Relations in the CSC, reflected the mood. Involved with the EMC program from its start, he anticipated no radical departure from the Kennedy order's basic philosophy of cooperation:

> "This is more than a high-sounding word in the title of the present program. It means that I don't believe we will move into the 'class-struggle' approach which characterized labor-management in industry during the formative 30s and seems to be working today in some of the states and cities. My personal belief is that cooperation is the only realistic objective in public employee unionism. We are 'locked' in together, management and employees, in common responsibility of service to the public—management cannot lock out

---

[34] Task Force, op. cit., p. 7.

[35] U.S. Civil Service Commission, *Employee-Management Cooperation in the Federal Service,* Basic Training Materials, August 1962, pp. 1.02-1.04.

[36] Otto Pragan, "Is Prvate Sector Industrial Relations the Objective in the Federal Service?" Industrial Relations Research Assn., Annual Spring Meeting, Milwaukee, Wisconsin, May 6, 1966 pp. 47-48.

the employees; the employees cannot strike, so we have to live together and cooperate in the best way possible." [37]

The 1961 Task Force had called for an "affirmative willingness" in management's attitude toward "collective dealing," using the latter term with all the limits implied in the governmental context.[38] In 1967, Task Force member Gill, who later served as Executive Director of the Federal Labor Relations Council, described what he believed to be the limits of a program of "affirmative willingness" in management:

"To encourage forthright collective bargaining and other dealings with recognized unions in the full range permitted by E.O. 10988, on the one hand our limits should be guarding against concession at the expense of the public interest merely to achieve labor-management peace and, at the other end of the spectrum, rigidity or mismanagement that so infringes employee or union rights as to bring about public demonstrations or work stoppages." [39]

The Johnson Review Committee acknowledged existing union discontent over management's unwillingness to accept fully the lexicon of private labor relations. There was some movement toward acceptance in the proposal that the term "employee organization" be replaced by the term "labor organization," as used in our general labor laws. The Review Committee proposed that "labor organization" be defined as:

"any lawful organization of any kind, or any employee representation group which exists for the purpose, in whole or in part, of dealing with federal agencies concerning grievances, personnel policies and practices, or other matters affecting the working conditions of their employees. . . ." [40]

Further change was evidenced in the Review Committee's willingness to discuss the issues in terms of "bargaining," "collective bargaining," and "collective bargaining agreements." It is true that almost all of its draft report employed traditional governmental terms. Nevertheless, the fact that "collective bargaining" was referred to on a number of occasions was a gain for labor.

The Nixon Study Committee, however, was scrupulously careful not to use the term "collective bargaining" in reference to federal negotiations. The term was used in reference to bargaining in the private sector only.[41] In other instances it was deleted

---

[37] Wilfred V. Gill, "Employee-Management Cooperation in Interior," *Interior Department,* Personnel Conference, Albuquerque, New Mexico, October 18, 1967, p. 93.

[38] Task Force, *op. cit.,* p. 11.

[39] Wilfred V. Gill, *op. cit.,* pp. 93-94.

[40] Review Committee, *op. cit.,* pp. 50-51.

[41] Study Committee, *op. cit.,* pp. 20, 39.

entirely from language that was otherwise carried over from the Review Committee draft report.[42] Nevertheless, the Study Committee recognized the need to emphasize the word "labor" in future developments. Thus E.O. 11491 substantially adopted the Review Committee's proposed definition of "labor organization," established a Federal Labor Relations Council, and changed the title of the EMC program to "Labor-Management Relations in the Federal Service." [43]

The experience of the postal work stoppages and strike in 1969 and 1970 virtually obliterated such delicate nuances in President Nixon's language and thinking, particularly about the Post Office Department. In his message on postal reform he declared:

> "I propose that the new United States Postal Service be empowered to engage in collective bargaining with recognized employee organizations over wages, hours and working conditions generally with negotiating impasses being finally resolved, if necessary, by binding arbitration." [44]

The Nixon Administration reform bill made complete, consistent, and broad use of the terms "collective bargaining," "labor organization," and "labor disputes" in a manner reminiscent of the Wagner and Taft-Hartley Acts. Although the bill had application only to POD, the lesson was not lost to the nonpostal unions.

D. A LABOR RELATIONS PROGRAM ON THE INDUSTRIAL MODEL?

The trend toward the use of labor relations terms and concepts might well have been expected from the makeup of the 1961 Task Force and the language of its report. Its acceptance of certain views established a spirit of change that spurred unions to action. By the Task Force's own admission certain private-sector labor relations procedures might apply within the Federal Government.[45]

This admission was an opening wedge for labor. It was quite possible that another situation similar to that created by the Luther Steward letter [46] might have developed. The policy stated in that letter became scripture for those agencies seeking to avoid

---

[42] Ibid., pp. 2, 45.
[43] E. O. 11491, Preamble, Secs. 2 (e), 4, 6. Under the Kennedy order the program became widely known as the Employee-Management Cooperation (EMC) program.
[44] U.S. House of Representatives, Message from the President, 91st Cong., 2nd Sess., April 16, 1970, p. 3.
[45] Task Force, op. cit., p. 7.
[46] See p. 10.

collective bargaining, in spite of the fact that its author, President Roosevelt, had praised the collective bargaining practices of the TVA. The Task Force recognized the disparities between public and private labor-management relations, and therefore Task Force statements conceivably could have been used in the same way that the Steward letter was to provide grounds for some agencies to resist the extension of private practices in the federal service. But since the Task Force also agreed that certain private labor practices should be adopted, in many agencies unions were able to promote fuller collective bargaining.

The labor orientation of the Task Force was part and parcel of the total philosophy of the Kennedy Administration. A prominent characteristic of the new leadership was a positive and, above all, activist policy in all labor relations matters, pressed by Arthur J. Goldberg, the President's accomplished and much publicized Secretary of Labor. The failure to revise federal employment practices by legislation had caused Mr. Kennedy some disappointment as a Senator. It was thus believed that after his election he would view possible changes in the federal service more favorably. In point of fact, the greatest evidence of Mr. Kennedy's pro-labor sentiment was his appointment of Goldberg as Secretary of Labor.

Goldberg had a well-earned reputation as an astute negotiator. Well versed in the in-fighting of collective bargaining, he had the ability to influence and compromise in order to achieve negotiated settlements, traits he developed as counsel for the United Steelworkers after World War II in fierce negotiations with big steel. He was one of that union's major strategists and became a close associate of many CIO leaders. One of the architects of the AFL-CIO merger (and its major historian [47]), he became the new organization's special counsel. Prior to the passage of the Landrum-Griffin Act, in the face of adverse publicity resulting from Teamster Union scandals uncovered by the McClellan Committee, it was Goldberg who drew up the AFL-CIO's self-regulating Code of Ethics. Goldberg's position and reputation in the labor movement clearly presaged the independent role he would play in government.

Six months after taking office, President Kennedy appointed Goldberg chairman of the Task Force on Employee-Management Cooperation in the Federal Service. In labor matters, Goldberg towered over the other Task Force members and their alternates. According to Wilson Hart, he chaired the group with extraordi-

---

[47] Arthur J. Goldberg, *AFL-CIO, Labor United* (New York: McGraw-Hill, 1956).

nary adroitness and recruited its key staff members.[48] He was among the first to give any form of recognition to an employee group under the new system.

The Task Force, staffed with liberal activists, favored the legitimate interests of organized labor. Among the many factors that prevented the private labor relations system from being fully incorporated in the federal service, two stand out. First, the Task Force policy recognizing basic dissimilarities between private and public employment was officially sanctioned by the Kennedy order. Second, the primary responsibility for enacting the provisions of the Kennedy order was given to the Civil Service Commission, the personnel arm of the Presidency. The Labor Department was responsible for matters such as administering the advisory arbitration of grievances and deciding appropriate bargaining unit questions, while the CSC and the Labor Department were mutually responsible for, among other activities, developing the Standards of Conduct and the Code of Fair Labor Practices. There was no intimation that the CSC was to set aside its chief function of personnel administration. Major policy changes were inhibited by executive policy and the very structure of the federal personnel administration maintained to implement the EMC program.

Among the major issues that the CSC encountered during the developmental stage of the EMC program were the problems of conflict of interest, the need for central authority, the 60-percent rule in representation elections, the scope of negotiation, appropriate bargaining unit issues, and government neutrality toward employees' union activities. The CSC's final decisions on these questions in almost every instance hinged upon the degree to which it was willing to adopt private labor practice.

During this stage it was only natural for federal labor unions to cite accepted industrial practices and to urge their adoption. This search for precedent was recognized in an article by David S. Barr written after two years of the program. Noting that people naturally rely upon their previous experiences to cope with new situations, he stated that:

"[A]s soon as the various branches of government, the unions, and the employees were confronted with this new wrinkle in the face of the federal service they began to cast about for a meaningful historical context or mold into which the new program could be comfortably poured. The sense of urgency surrounding the quest was due, in large part, to the fact that the Order itself was broadly phrased

48 Wilson R. Hart, "The U.S. Civil Service Learns to Live With E.O. 10988," *Industrial and Labor Relations Review,* January 1964, p. 206.

and its 'legislative history'—a rather terse, 27 page report—devoid of sufficient explication.

"The most natural inclination, at least on the part of labor organizations, was to turn to the National Labor Relations Act. Here was a readily available body of law that had successfully withstood the test of time since its beginnings in 1935. It governed labor-management relations in much the same way, it appeared, as the Order was to govern such relations in the public sector. The Act was, after all, something that lawyers, union leaders, administrators and arbitrators had become familiar with. The feelings of most federal agencies (with such obvious exceptions as the National Labor Relations Board and Department of Labor) were precisely to the contrary. They were almost totally unfamiliar with the act or the decisions of the NLRB and therefore strongly suspected the motives of those who would impose upon them a set of principles which had been formulated without their participation. Moreover, the agencies had been entrusted with the responsibility of promulgating regulations to implement the Executive Order and the intrusion of 'established' doctrine would necessarily lessen their scope of power and freedom to handle their own affairs." [49]

Decentralized program implementation and substantial executive discretion at the agency level were fundamental program policies. There is little doubt that the absence of any general adoption of settled NLRB principles fostered these policies. Barr pointed out that the order's history did not "clearly suggest a reliance upon or rejection of the NLRA as a helpful guide." [50] Still, much of the language and many provisions of the order were taken almost directly, and presumably intentionally, from the NLRA. Such being the case, Barr believed that "the nearly 30 years of successful experience under the act would undoubtedly prove useful. While not binding, as such, decisions of the NLRB should be deemed highly relevant to the proper interpretation of the Executive Order." [51]

In confrontations with federal labor organizations, the Civil Service Commission insisted that it had looked to private experience in developing policy proposals. Defending the CSC against a claim of failure to recognize sufficiently the importance of general labor experience, Macy made it clear that the CSC was not unwilling to learn from the private sector. Stating the definitive Commission policy, he declared that "staff work on the development of policy proposals both in the Commission and in the

[49] David S. Barr, "Executive Order 10988: An Experiment in Employee-Management Cooperation in the Federal Service," *Georgetown Law Journal*, Vol. 52, Winter 1964, pp. 422-423. Quoted by permission.
[50] *Ibid.*, p. 426.
[51] *Ibid.*, p. 428.

agencies regularly includes, where appropriate, study of pertinent private sector provisions and experience." [52] He went on to say that the National Labor Relations Act "neither governed nor controlled" federal labor relations policy, which was significantly different from private labor law in a number of aspects.[53]

E. THE ROLE OF THE CIVIL SERVICE COMMISSION

Over the years, particularly during the Kennedy and Johnson Administrations, the Commission chairman assumed more and more of the role of spokesman for the President in labor matters. This increasingly close relationship necessarily enhanced the degree of executive discretion exercised by the chairman. It also provided many opportunities for the chairman to make his views known to the President during the formulation of policy.

The evolution of this President-CSC chairman relationship has been clearly traced by Chester G. Hall from Hoover onward. Hall noted that the formal general staff procedures of the Eisenhower Administration were replaced by informal procedures under Kennedy. Presidential tasks were now to be fulfilled by using people, not organizations. Thus, Kennedy, recognizing a great need for an adviser on personnel management, relied, like Eisenhower, upon the Commission chairman, and for the post chose John Macy. While the CSC chairman's duties were expanded, his position was less official than it had been under Eisenhower. Macy, according to Hall:

> "received no publicized charter for his White House duties, but with Presidential access and support plus specific Presidential tasks to carry out, he became in fact the untitled adviser to Kennedy on all civilian personnel matters. This designation and use of the Chairman by Kennedy was both the most complete and the least publicized example among all the approaches of Presidents assuming control of the Civil Service Commission in order to make it a personnel arm." [54]

Throughout the 1960s the CSC maintained a consistent set of personnel policy goals vis à vis federal unionism: The Commission sought "to discern what the true role or function of unionism

[52] John W. Macy, Jr., "The Federal Employee-Management Cooperation Program," *Industrial and Labor Relations Review,* Vol. 19, July 1966, p. 557.

[53] For a most interesting and hard-hitting dialogue upon the thesis that there existed a Civil Service Commission "approach" as opposed to a more private-practice-oriented, Labor Department "approach" to administering the federal program see: Wilson R. Hart, "The Impasse in Labor Relations in the Federal Civil Service," *Industrial and Labor Relations Review,* Vol. 19, January 1966, pp. 175-189, and John W. Macy, Jr., *Ibid.,* pp. 549-561, for a spirited defense.

[54] Chester G. Hall, Jr., "The U.S. Civil Service Commission: Arm of the President?" *Public Personnel Review,* Vol. 28, April 1967, p. 118.

should be in government and how the existing institutions and arrangements for personnel administration should react or adjust to union influence." [55] Policy objectives, aimed at encouraging unionism in the Federal Government, were stated in terms that characterized unions primarily as aids to management. Unions were to spur management to act on employee problems and were to cooperate with management in promoting job safety and communicating employee attitudes. Union support was to be enlisted in improving federal personnel management in areas such as equal opportunity, the employment of youth and the handicapped, and improved service. Of course, unions were expected to continue to seek justice for employees and to defend the rights of individuals and groups. The full scope of "agency-union consultation and negotiation" as authorized by law was to be supported, but concessions were not to be made at public expense merely to achieve labor-management peace. Moreover, "rigidity or mismanagement which would so infringe employee or union rights as to bring about demonstrations, work stoppages or other militant objections" was to be avoided.[56]

Despite the efforts of the Commission, many rank-and-file union members believed that its labor relations functions should be curtailed, or even, perhaps, entirely eliminated. Thus Thomas R. Donohue, executive assistant to AFL-CIO President George Meany and formerly an Assistant Secretary of Labor under President Johnson, expressed typical union views in an address before the Collective Bargaining Forum in New York City in 1969. Contesting the fundamental and official position that federal service is based upon the civil service concept, he emphasized that the civil service concept is "ancillary to federal employment, it is that part of the federal employment concept which is designed to insure fairness and equity in hiring and tenure, in promotion and assignment." [57] Donohue believed it was wrong that a concept designed to ensure fairness should preclude other systems of securing equity, particularly when such systems were desired by a majority of the workers. Thus, if union security measures such as the union shop were deemed "inappropriate" to the civil service

---

55 Wilfred V. Gill *Remarks,* at National Conference of the Society for Personnel Administration, Washington, June 6, 1968, p. 1.

56 *Ibid.,* pp. 2, 3.

57 Thomas R. Donohue, Address before the Collective Bargaining Forum, Institute of Collective Bargaining and Group Relations, New York, May 12, 1969, entitled "The Future of Collective Bargaining in the Federal Government," in *Collective Bargaining Today* (Washington: The Bureau of National Affairs, Inc., 1970), p. 167.

concept, then, conceivably, union grievances about promotions would be equally inappropriate.[58]

Donahue seriously questioned the efforts of the Commission to expand its labor relations role by appointing field staff to advise agencies on labor matters. He drew a precise distinction between the functions of a central personnel agency and a governmental industrial relations adviser, warning that in government as in private industry no employer could afford "to fuzz" the distinctions between personnel management and labor relations. Since the Labor Department possessed industrial relations expertise, he proposed that it be recognized and used.[59]

Public employee unions at all levels of government consistently have sought independence within the agencies administering their labor relations. Reflecting union desires for independence, Donohue deplored efforts to make the Civil Service Commission "the central focus of a new labor relations structure on the theory that it is capable of doing the work that should be done by an impartial agency." Casting the CSC as an arbitrator of labor disputes would, he believed, "confuse its role as the representative of the personnel interests of the agencies." [60] That no major policy revision would be forthcoming he inferred from President Nixon's "unfortunate" act of selecting the chairman of the CSC to head the committee charged with revising federal labor practices.[61]

Within the limitations of law and executive directives, the CSC has shown flexibility and a willingness to innovate in numerous areas. However, so long as it functions principally as a central personnel agency, it will be subject to union criticism that it has not gone far enough. Many unions assume that the Commission, in the last analysis, must identify with management—and "its philosophical frame of reference invariably reflects an illiberal approach, although it is clothed in progressive terminology." [62] If new legislation establishes guiding principles and a regulatory board similar to the NLRB, the problems of incorporating private practice will be lessened. Certain unions still hope there will be such legislation. But so long as this is not the case and the EMC program is guided by the Commission, the CSC must be expected to continue to operate as it has—as an enlightened and amenable yet traditional central agency for personnel administration.

---

58 *Ibid.*
59 *Ibid.*, p. 167.
60 *Ibid.*, pp. 167-168.
61 *Ibid.*, p. 169.
62 Sidney A. Goodman, President, National Postal Union, *Letter*, to Louis Wallerstein, Staff Director, Review Committee on Federal Employee-Management Relations, October 17, 1967, p. 5.

F. THE WORK OF THE PRESIDENT'S
REVIEW COMMITTEE

The debate over central administration was a major cause for the delay in the issuance of, and the eventual failure to adopt, the recommendations of the Johnson Review Committee. These recommendations were finally published in early 1969 as an appendix to the Department of Labor's 56th annual report. It was thus made public after the uncertainties and disruptions of the national political campaign but before the Johnson Administration left office. As a draft report, however, it had "no official status," as Secretary Wirtz was careful to point out.[63]

This hard fact culminated a period of expectation, particularly on the part of the federal unions, that was replete with frustration and dissatisfaction. The Review Committee held hearings in October 1967, and it was generally known that the report had been completed by April 1968. Yet no official action seemed forthcoming. Rumors were freely circulating in Washington that the report was languishing "on the President's desk." In the face of mounting apprehensions that no executive order would issue, all those associated with the Review Committee, whether in the Labor Department, Civil Service Commission, or the agencies, were uncommunicative. Before long, however, it became known that the delay was due primarily to dissatisfaction with the recommendations on the part of some agencies, particularly the Department of Defense.

This fact was officially confirmed upon issuance of the draft report when Secretary Wirtz disclosed that a "series of developments (including changes in membership of the Committee) precluded either final agreement on the Draft Report or any transmittal to the President." [64] Former Assistant Secretary of Labor Donohue later corroborated its nontransmittal to the White House and generally described the objections of the Defense Department that blocked such transmittal.[65] He emphasized that the recommendations had incorporated compromises in an effort to achieve unanimity among the five members of the Committee. After the draft had received tentative approval by all in April 1968, the report was sent to each committee member for signature of the letter of transmittal to the President. Four of the agency heads signed the draft report. However, Secretary of Defense Clark Clifford refrained from granting it final approval. It appeared

---

[63] Review Committee, op. cit., p. i.
[64] Ibid., p. 4.
[65] Thomas R. Donohue, op. cit., pp. 168, 169.

that he had insurmountable objections to the authority proposed for the recommended Federal Labor Relations Panel. [66]

Clifford took issue with the proposal granting the Panel authority to make final and binding decisions resolving negotiation impasses. As Donohue pointed out, the Secretary was convinced this authority was in conflict with his power and responsibility for the administration of his agency—a position, Donohue noted, that was not shared by the rest of the Committee.[67] On the issue of impasse resolution, it was unacceptable to Defense that the decisions of other federal executives should be binding on the Defense Department. Donohue declared that the other Committee members were simply unwilling at that juncture "to negotiate down from that point." [68]

Although the draft report was never transmitted to the President, Secretary Wirtz felt compelled to make it available to the public in spite of its unofficial status. His reason for doing so, he explained, was that "it reflects the serious and responsible contributions of a wide variety of informed people to a subject of national interest." [69] Publication served to inform all concerned with the federal labor scene of the contemporary trend of official thinking, and this was a necessary spur to continued progress. Moreover, the work of the Review Committee was eventually used to good advantage by the Nixon Study Committee.

As a result of the delay, the AFL-CIO and individual unions expanded their lobbying efforts for legislation to improve collective bargaining in the federal establishment. At the AFL-CIO 1969 convention in Miami, the AFL-CIO Executive Council adopted a statement calling for the appointment of a committee to formulate legislation. The committee, composed of the presidents of the foremost federal service unions, worked out an acceptable draft bill and presented it in June 1969 at the hearings before the House Subcommittee on Postal Operations. The proposed legislation received full union publicity. Nevertheless, the unions had little hope of success in view of the conservative tenor of the Congress.

A consensus prevailed among labor leaders and government executives alike that Mr. Nixon would issue a new executive order. Several announcements of impending action were made extending the time for tentative issuance. It was widely expected

---

66 *Ibid.*
67 *Ibid.*, p. 169.
68 Thomas R. Donohue, *Panel Discussion*, The Collective Bargaining Forum, New York, May 12, 1969.
69 Review Committee, *op. cit.*, p. i.

that any executive action would be limited by the same ground rules. Considerations similar to those that had governed the Kennedy and the Johnson study groups still controlled. These limited possible changes to innovations that could be effected within the executive branch without the necessity of enabling legislation or new expenditures.

Executive Order 11491, when finally issued, provided greater uniformity by establishing a central authority in the Federal Labor Relations Council. Although the FLRC was not the independent agency that the unions sought in proposed legislation, it was a step toward such an agency even though it was composed entirely of executive officers.[70] It differed from the agency envisioned in the Johnson Committee report in that it did not extensively process bargaining impasses. A separate Federal Service Impasses Panel was created to resolve negotiation deadlocks. This function contributed to the Defense Department's reluctance to approve the draft report. President Nixon, however, incorporated the essentials of the Study Committee's report in his order, including its recommendations on impasse resolution. The Impasses Panel was given the power to "settle the impasse by appropriate action." [71] Only the Panel could decide whether the parties could use arbitration or third-party factfinding with recommendations.

In addition, E.O. 11491 further defined the activities of the Civil Service Commission. CSC was to continue to offer agencies guidance in labor-management relations and help develop training programs. Agency operations were to be reviewed for conformance to the order and the merit system. On the basis of these reviews, the CSC was to report periodically to the FLRC with its recommendations for improvements. Together with the Labor Department, it was to continue to collect and disseminate vital statistics and information.[72] Now, however, the Commission was given the responsibility of providing administrative support and services to the Council and to the Impasses Panel.[73]

In fulfilling its guidance and service functions, the Commission continues to fulfill its essential purpose as a personnel-administration-oriented agency. However, the ultimate responsibility for administering the program and fixing overall policy now resides in the Federal Labor Relations Council, not in the Commission or the Labor Department. If the Council's functions are clearly

---

[70] See Chapter XXI.
[71] E.O. 11491, Sec. 17.
[72] E.O. 11491, Sec. 25 (a) (b) .
[73] Ibid., Secs. 4, 5, as amended by E.O. 11616, Sec. 3.

delineated and understood and its authority is not diffused, it can maintain the independence necessary to deal effectively with the unique problems of the labor relations program.

As required by the order, the FLRC twice conducted extensive general reviews of the labor relations program. Its recommendations for improvements were fully carried out by new executive orders. After a review of some 18 months, including three days of hearings in April 1974, the Council's report became the basis of President Ford's Executive Order 11838 amending the Nixon orders. The Ford order primarily provided for consolidation of bargaining units and increased the scope of negotiations, and it confirmed and solidified the structure of the FLRC. President Ford, in a statement accompanying the order, stressed the importance of good labor relations in his Administration, noting that seldom had there been "greater need of cooperation in making Government more effective and cohesive." [74]

---

[74] President Ford, Statement on Issuance of E.O. 11838, February 6, 1975; see also U.S. Civil Service Commission, *Consultant*, 1 FLMC 75-4, February 28, 1975; E.O. 11491, Sec. 4 (b).

CHAPTER VII

THE EXECUTIVE ORDERS—THE GROUND RULES FOR ORGANIZATION AND NEGOTIATION

In simplest terms, the new industrial relations program embodied in E.O. 10988 sought to provide federal employees with a greater opportunity to participate in the administration of their jobs. Employee organizations were recognized as essential contributors to the effective conduct of public business. Orderly and constructive labor relations were sought as aids to efficient government administration and the employees' well-being.[1] Within the context of these stated policies, the Kennedy order endeavored to define the rights and duties of employees, unions, and management. In so doing, it set down provisions which stemmed fundamentally from private labor relations experience. Most of the new policies were to the liking of the major unions.

The degree to which private labor practices or existing governmental policies were used depended upon certain basic approaches to labor relations in the Federal Government. These approaches were definitively expressed in the Task Force report and Kennedy order and served to regulate the extent to which public and private policies were incorporated. For example, the troublesome problem of scope of negotiations was governed by ample provisions preserving the superiority of statutes, agency regulations, and Civil Service Commission directives. The limitations on executive discretion, insistence upon final departmental approval of agreements, and extensive enumeration of inviolate

---

[1] E.O. 10988, Preamble. President Nixon's E.O. 11491 deleted the statement that employee participation contributed to the effective conduct of public business. In its stead, the Preamble declared: "The public interest requires high standards of employee performance and the continual development and implementation of modern and progressive work practices to facilitate improved employee performance and efficiency." Although the change indicated a somewhat greater management orientation, the remaining preamble clauses were generally similar to those of the Kennedy order.

management prerogatives served to prevent any wholesale super-imposition of private labor practices.[2] These provisions were entirely in keeping with the sovereignty doctrine. A more detailed treatment of the limitations on collective bargaining is found in Chapter XX.

Prime considerations in the program were the promotion of the public interest and the preservation of the merit system. As many labor practices consonant with these objectives were to be introduced as possible. It was early apparent that NLRB policies and private labor practices would be the initial points of reference. However, the possibility of their adoption was measured in terms of their acceptability under the controlling philosophies of federal personnel administration. Union complaints in myriad administrative disputes were directly attributable to essential differences in basic policy interpretation.

A. EMPLOYEE RIGHTS AND UNION SECURITY

Among the greatest advances made under the Employee-Management Cooperation program were the rights and privileges granted to individual employees and to their unions. These were lauded or decried by unions in direct proportion to their similarity to rights in private practice. Reflecting Task Force recommendations, the order explicitly declared that federal employees:

> "shall have, and shall be protected in the exercise of the right, freely and without fear of penalty or reprisal, to form, join and assist any employee organization or to refrain from any such activity. Except as hereinafter expressly provided, the freedom of such employees to assist any employee organization shall be recognized as extending to participation in the management of the organization and acting for the organization in the capacities of an organization representative including presentation of its views to officials of the executive branch, the Congress or other appropriate authority." [3]

Furthermore, it stated:

> "The head of each executive department and agency shall take such actions consistent with law, as may be required in order to assure that employees in the agency are apprised of the rights described . . . and that no interference, restraint, coercion or discrimination is practiced within such agency to encourage or discourage membership in any employee organization." [4]

Much of this language was taken directly from the Wagner Act. The right of self-organization and the right to form, join, or assist

---

[2] E.O. 10988, Secs. 1 (b), 6 (b), 7 (1), 7 (2).

[3] E.O. 10988, Sec. 1 (a); President's Task Force on Employee-Management Relations in the Federal Service, *Report*, November 30, 1961, Sec. A, pp. iv, ii, E.O. 11491 retained the original wording with only slight variation.

[4] *Ibid.*

labor organizations were couched in the same terms as its old Section 7. The Kennedy order essentially restated that Act's prohibitions upon employer interference with these rights, support of company unionism, or discrimination for or against a particular labor organization.[5]

It would be misleading to imply that the Kennedy order was the first attempt to invoke standards for government which theretofore had been applied solely to private industry. Protection of individual and union rights had been growing steadily at both the local and the national levels of government. Even some of the more orthodox national agencies, in accordance with prevailing CSC policy, already had assured the right to organize and join unions. The Air Force statement of policy, for example, was typical in this regard. It advised that:

> "Civilian employees of the Air Force, like employees of other organizations, have the statutory right to organize and to express their views collectively. This right is inherent in our democratic system. Air Force employees are free to join or not to join unions. . . . Employee groups are free to pursue activities consistent with their purposes and within the limits of governing directives. Prompt consideration will be given to group proposals and petitions." [6]

While established federal policies such as those of the CSC and the Air Force were based on toleration and agency choice, new policies under the Kennedy order were based on a clear statement of required government-wide rights, with affirmative provisions to protect those rights. The new rights were greatly welcomed. Nevertheless, unions took a dim view of those aspects that they felt reflected the philosophy of the Taft-Hartley Act. Reaching beyond the domain of collective employee rights, the Taft-Hartley Act granted privileges to the individual worker apart from his status as a union member. Organized labor viewed the Taft-Hartley or Labor-Management Relations Act of 1947 as an attempt to establish an independent channel of communication between individual employees and management. Unions viewed this as a direct attempt to undermine their strength and potential for growth.

Militant federal employee unions, therefore, saw the order's protection of the right "not to join" a union as paralleling the right-to-work laws sanctioned by the Taft-Hartley Act.[7] They

---

[5] 49 Stat. 452, 29 U.S.C., Secs. 157, 158 (1935).

[6] U.S. Department of the Air Force, *Manual*, 40-1, AFE2-4, Sec. 3, March 24, 1954.

[7] 49 Stat. 452, 29 U.S.C. Secs. 175, 178 (1) (2) (3), 164 as amended by Public Law 101, 80th Cong., 1st Sess. (1947).

took the same view of the Task Force's recommended union security prohibition.

In addition to his right not to join a union the individual employee, regardless of union membership, was permitted to bring matters of personal concern to the attention of his superiors and pick his own representative in a grievance or appellate action.[8] In short, while the order sought to establish a favorable climate for union membership, it managed to keep the road clear for nonunion employees to achieve the same benefits. According to John Macy among the core considerations of the program was the government's "special obligation to recognize the rights of non-organized employees, as well as those affiliated with employee organizations."[9] Employee-rights provisions clearly incorporated precedents already set in our national labor laws. They just happened to be the precedents that the public employee unions would have preferred be left out of federal policy.

In a relatively short period of time, the question of union security took on far greater importance for organized public labor than individual employee rights. After only six years of the federal program, the concept of union security came under close scrutiny.[10] At the local level, some very strong agreements incorporated provisions for "modified" and regular union shops or other types of union security. Such was not the case at the federal level, but the controversy succeeded in creating quite a stir.

The issue of union security can present a direct confrontation between merit and trade-union principles in government. Whereas the merit system removes political strings from the appointive process, a closed or union shop or similar security provisions adds the requirement of union membership. Innovations in the hiring or retention process aimed at achieving union security must, therefore, reflect changing views on the meaning of "merit" within the trade-union context.

The basic controversy has been assessed in these terms:

"Where the selection of personnel is made on a compositive basis under some form of merit system, the closed shop in the strict sense of the term is impossible, for the closed shop implies the supplying of personnel by the union or its selection from the union ranks either through hiring halls or otherwise. A more frequent demand of government employee unions has been the union shop. . . . Whether or not this device would fit into a competitive merit sys-

[8] E.O. 10988, Secs. 1 (a) , 3 (c) (1) , 8 (a) (b) .

[9] John W. Macy, Jr., "New Era in Employee-Management Relations," *Civil Service Journal,* January 1962, p. 2.

[10] See Chapter XI for a discussion of union security in relation to the federal checkoff experience.

tem depends on the specific requirements of the legislation under which the system is set up." [11]

The typical union approach was well expressed by Arnold Zander, former president of the American Federation of State, County and Municipal Employees (AFSCME), in a 1960 communication to the National Civil Service League. Zander said:

"Once a union has been granted bargaining rights for all employees in a bargaining unit by the democratic principle of majority representation, it follows that the will of the majority of the employees should become effective for the minority as well. All of the employees should be required to join the employees' union and to pay dues to support the organization by equivalent tax or dues. It has been our experience, as well as that of most other unions, that the union shop tends to promote responsible unionism by providing union security. The union shop promotes harmony in collective bargaining.

"There is a fundamental difference between labor unions and organizations of a political, cultural or religious nature. In a modern society there is moral justification for compulsory membership in labor organizations if the purposes of such organizations are clearly designed to serve the needs of all the workers, and these needs can be achieved only by collective action and decision. Nonmembers as well as members, benefit from the efforts of the union. It is only fair that workers who benefit from the efforts of the union be required to share the costs." [12]

At the local level, this characteristic trade union practice has gained limited acceptance in public employment. A study conducted in 1960, for example, recorded that 10 out of 120 jurisdictions had accepted the union shop.[13] Nevertheless, the drive for union security has continued. Indeed, some remarkable contracts have been written.

In April 1961, for example, the City of Philadelphia entered into a union-shop agreement with the AFSCME. It was constituted as a "modified union shop" in order to circumvent certain statutory requirements. This "forced unionism," as its opponents termed it, required that a new employee join the union within six months of entering the service. A two-week period was, therefore, provided, during which a newly hired employee could leave the union if he so desired. The contract was hailed by Zander as a bellwether for similar agreements in other major American cities.[14]

---

[11] Sterling D. Spero, *Government as Employer* (New York: Remsen Press, 1948), p. 378. Reprinted Carbondale, Ill., Southern Illinois University Press, 1972.

[12] Arnold Zander, *Letter*, to National Civil Service League, June 20, 1960, p. 6.

[13] Murray B. Nesbitt, "The Civil Service Merit System and Collective Bargaining" (unpublished Ph.D. dissertation, Graduate School of Public Administration; New York University, 1962), pp. 220-222.

[14] *Ibid.*, pp. 177-185.

Seven years later AFSCME President Jerry Wurf noted a 60-percent membership increase over a four-year period. For his union, then fast approaching the 400,000-member mark, Wurf emphasized the need to promote union security advances, particularly the agency shop, at all local levels. He pointed out that 275 AFSCME contracts contained union security measures. The AFSCME had potential jurisdiction over nine million local government workers. Union security, its leadership believed, was among the elements that conceivably could make AFSCME the largest union in the country.[15]

In New York City, where AFSCME made great gains, the city administration followed a policy of promoting the interests of exclusively recognized unions to promote stability and manageable negotiations. Mayor Lindsay acted administratively and restricted the privilege of checkoff of union dues to unions achieving exclusive representative status. New York's highest state court upheld the Mayor's action.[16] AFSCME, the United Federation of Teachers, and other organizations in the city actively pressed for greater union security, whether in the form of a union shop, agency shop, or maintenance-of-membership provisions.

The union security movement in the cities was, perhaps, even more pronounced in Canada, where M. Z. Prives early discovered 29 cases of the union shop and two of the closed shop in questionnaires returned by 16 unions.[17] In the United States the trend has been restricted primarily to local public employee unions; however, its implications were not lost on the federal employee unions, which pressed for union security whenever reform of the federal system came before the Congress or the executive branch.

In earlier years, the Government Printing Office had flirted with the closed shop, and the Inland Waterways Corporation had made use of the union shop. At the time of the Task Force study, however, no major federal agency had conceded any such union security measures. Even agencies that enjoyed relatively advanced labor relations programs avoided recognition of the closed or the union shop. Some agencies permitted exclusive recognition for purposes of negotiation, but the path was always kept officially clear for hearing the views of minority unions and individual em-

---

15 *Government Employee Relations Report*, No. 247 (1968), p. AA-1. It now claims over 700,000 members.

16 In Re Herbert S. Bauch, President, Local 832, International Brotherhood of Teamsters v. City of New York, 21 N.Y. 2d 599; 289 N.Y. Supp. 2d 951 (1968).

17 M. Z. Prives, *Unionism and the Merit System in Municipal Relations in Canada* (Montreal: Canadian Federation of Mayors and Municipalities, 1958), p. 55. See also Murray B. Nesbitt, *op. cit.*, pp. 205-273.

ployees. Above all, no employee was required to join a union during the recruitment and appointment process.

Not even the labor relations practices of the Tennessee Valley Authority, which closely paralleled those in the private sector, extended to compulsory union membership. The TVA Trades and Labor Council mounted determined efforts to achieve union security through collective bargaining. It succeeded only in having the 1951 General Agreement include the statement that union membership is "advantageous to employees and to management, and employees are accordingly encouraged to become and remain members of the appropriate unions." [18] However, the effect of this provision should not be underestimated. From its inception the TVA encouraged union membership as a matter of administrative policy, if not as a contract requirement. TVA policy far exceeded the view of the Task Force on union security by considering union membership as a favorable factor in determining merit and efficiency in appointments and promotions. TVA's contract with its white-collar workers also encouraged union membership, not only for the reasons already stated but also to promote improved labor relations, employee efficiency, and greater understanding of and striving toward TVA policy objectives.[19]

Thus the policy recommended by the Task Force in 1961 was already government-wide in application and represented the traditional federal approach toward union security. This approach had been described in a National Civil Service League policy statement:

> "Both the closed and union shop of private industry are inappropriate in the public service. There is an obligation on the public official and the employee association alike not to interfere with the individual employee's free right to decide for or against joining an employee association." [20]

Of all its recommendations, the Task Force was most adamant upon this point. Echoing the NCSL, it asserted that "[t]he union shop and the closed shop are inappropriate to the Federal Service." [21] Such provisions, it declared, were contrary to the civil service concept upon which federal employment is based.[22]

---

[18] Harry L. Case, *Democracy in Administration: A Study of Personnel Policy in TVA*, Tennessee Valley Authority, May 1954, pp. 31, 32. See also TVA, *General Agreement*, with TVA Trades and Labor Council, negotiated August 6, 1940, revised July 1, 1951, and February 3, 1964, Art. III, Sec. 2.

[19] TVA, *Articles of Agreement*, between TVA and Salary Policy Employee Panel, Negotiated December 5, 1950, Revised February 4, 1955, and Reaffirmed May 7, 1964, *Supplementary Agreement* 5, Sec. B. For further discussion, see Chapter XV.

[20] National Civil Service League, *Statement of Policy—Employee Organizations in Government*, November 1960, Sec. VI (a).

[21] Task Force Report, Sec. K, p. v.

[22] *Ibid.*, p. 25.

By late 1967 there had been no change whatever in management's attitude, and the agencies remained silent upon the issue before the Johnson Review Committee. Over the intervening years, however, federal unions had begun to speak more frequently and more openly for union security, expressing their own desires and reflecting the increasing demands of local government organizations. The union position was officially stated by George Meany in testimony before the Review Committee. Commenting upon union willingness, in both public and private labor relations, to represent all workers in a unit, he decried the lack of support from nonmembers enjoying the benefits of union representation and urged that the union shop or agency shop be permitted:

> "We do not believe there is any legal or constitutional prohibition against the negotiation of labor-management union security agreements which bring all workers in an appropriate unit into the membership of the appropriately recognized labor organization. The dues checkoff is already in effect for union members where formal or exclusive recognition exists. It is entirely appropriate for negotiated agreements to specify that those workers in the covered unit shall become dues paying union members or shall support the union with regularly checked off payments equal to the regular union dues." [23]

The insistent demands of the many union representatives testifying insured that the question of union security would at least have to be considered and studied by the Johnson Review Committee. Yet there was never any reason to expect radical departures by the Federal Government from the original Task Force position. Nevertheless, the remote possibility that the President might, by executive order, authorize some form of union or agency shop triggered a well-publicized and forceful reaction from the right-to-work advocates. Since the Committee report had not yet been issued, its possible position on union security became a subject of great speculation and confusion.

The reticence of CSC Chairman Macy was obvious when he listed some of the questions that were under consideration by the Committee. At a press interview, he remarked that "union security as it relates to something more than dues checkoff" was being considered.[24] Joseph Young's *Washington Star* column indicated that private-sector union security policies would not be found in any new federal policy. Young predicted that the Review Committee "would reject any requirement that employees in exclusive

[23] George Meany, President, AFL-CIO, *Statement*, before President's Review Committee, October 23, 1967, p. 13.
[24] *Government Employee Relations Report*, No. 241 (1968), p. A-8.

recognition units be required to join unions or pay union dues in order to hold their jobs." [25]

Young's prediction was correct, and even today the government's position on compulsory union membership is essentially unchanged. The significance of the push for greater union security was the cumulative effect of this and other disputes on the possibility for change and progress. Management and labor were almost unanimously agreed that vital revisions in policy and procedure were needed in many areas. The time for change was at hand, and the necessary hearings and deliberations had been properly conducted. It would have been lamentable indeed if pressure groups concerned with one issue among so many had been able to stifle advances in all areas.

The union-security dispute came to a head in mid-1968 during the period of preparation for the national political conventions. Whether this coincidence was a factor or not, the Review Committee's report remained unissued throughout the period of the national campaigns. National labor policy was a relatively minor issue in the 1968 election. In addition labor's power to influence legislation had waned somewhat over the years, and there was a substantial public reaction against public employee unionism as a result of state and local disputes affecting the citizen's everyday life. The natural reluctance to make major political decisions in a crucial election year combined with the desire to tread softly in an area of such great public concern may well have contributed to the failure to revise the federal program.

As it turned out, neither the Johnson nor the Nixon study group intended to expand union security beyond the existing checkoff provisions. The differences in the general tenor of both Committees' reports, however, were visible in their respective comments. The Johnson Review Committee acknowledged labor testimony in favor of greater union security and generally admitted the value of such measures for producing stable labor relations. It stated, "The utilization of such measures enables labor organizations to devote their efforts to the establishment of constructive labor-management relationships." [26] Nevertheless, the Committee recommended only a strengthening and improvement of the checkoff "at this time." Having proved itself as a stabilizing influence, the checkoff was credited with bringing status and

[25] Joseph Young, "The Federal Spotlight," *Washington Star*, April 19, 1968.
[26] President's Review Committee on Employee-Management Relations in the Federal Service, *Draft Report*, April 1968, in U.S. Department of Labor, *56th Annual Report*, 1969, Attachment B, p. 48.

maturity to the unions.[27] To foster greater stability, the Committee therefore recommended that revocation of dues withholding be permitted only once a year instead of twice a year, as was then the practice.[28]

No such references or recommendations appeared in the report of the Nixon Study Committee. Not only was the overall security issue not considered, but the one recommendation on union security simply called for the continuance of the voluntary dues withholding program—that is, maintenance of the status quo.[29] On the other hand, in its discussion of negotiations the report used strong and affirmative language to insure the right not to join a union. It declared:

> "The present Order has provided that employees shall have the right, freely and without fear of penalty or reprisal, to join and assist any employee organization or to refrain from any such activity. We recommend that this right remain unimpaired.
>
> "To avoid any misunderstanding on this subject we recommend that the new Order provide that any provision in a negotiated agreement relating to payment of money to an organization must be based on voluntary written authorizations by the individual employee." [30]

President Nixon's order fully adopted this proposal. It required that the basic provisions of all contracts expressly include a statement that "nothing in the agreement shall require an employee to become or to remain a member of a labor organization, or to pay money to the organization except pursuant to a voluntary written authorization by a member for the payment of dues through payroll deductions." [31] This language in Section 12 (c) of E.O. 11491 effectively prohibited the negotiation of any stronger union security provisions. Specifically, it foreclosed any possibility of union shop, agency shop, or maintenance-of-membership provisions. The policy was fully retained by President Ford's E.O. 11838 of February 1975.

As the decade of the 1960s waned, it appeared that federal service union security would remain a dead issue well into the future. Such was not to be the case. In less than six months the postal strike precipitated a remarkable change in presidential thinking on the security question. As will be discussed in Chapter XVII, one of the most cherished goals of the Nixon Administration was

---

[27] *Ibid.*
[28] *Ibid.*, p. 49. See also Chapter XI.
[29] President's Study Committee, *Report and Recommendations on Labor-Management Relations in the Federal Service,* August 1969, pp. 55, 56.
[30] *Ibid.*, pp. 4, 42.
[31] E.O. 11491, Sec. 12 (c) .

the establishment of an independent, corporate postal service. It became apparent under the pressure of the stoppages and the political opportunity for reform they created that the Administration was willing to make concessions on union security if this would speed the approval of the new postal-service concept. And the unions, it appeared, were willing to accept an independent Postal Service in order to attain their bargaining goals.[32]

As a result of the postal negotiations the right-to-work dispute was publicly aired again. Under the threat of continued mail stoppages the Administration and the seven craft unions with national exclusive recognition arrived at a memorandum of agreement on the combined issues of postal reorganization and salary increases in mid-April 1970.[33] In line with the new governmental policy towards postal workers, labor relations now fell within a statutory framework requiring collective bargaining over all aspects of wages, hours, "and in general, all matters . . . subject to collective bargaining in the private sector." [34] Thus the National Labor Relations Act (NLRA) was to apply wherever consistent with the new postal law. As to the "right to work," therefore, Section 14 (b) of the Taft-Hartley Act would govern. This section permitted postal unions to bargain over union security and secure union shop agreements in those states that had no right-to-work statutes. The applicability of the NLRA provision was incorporated into Administration and union-supported legislation in both the House and the Senate.[35] When asked whether a government employee should have to join a union to keep his job, Meany testified that under the NLRA the government as employer would have to act as would private employers who signed union shop agreements.[36] The Administration's position on Section 14 (b), however, was rejected in the House, where strong right-to-work opposition was marshalled to stall its passage.

---

[32] See Chapter XVII. See also U.S. House of Representatives, Committee on Post Office and Civil Service, *Hearings on H.R. 17070,* testimony of George Meany, 91st Cong., 2nd Sess., April 23, 1970, p. 90; James Rademacher, president, National Association of Letter Carriers, *The Postal Record,* September 1970, p. 18, and testimony in U.S. Senate, Committee on Post Office and Civil Service, *Hearings,* 91st Cong., 1st Sess., November 25, 1969, pp. 800-810.

[33] U.S. Senate, Committee on Post Office and Civil Service, *Hearings on S. 3613, Postal Modernization,* 91st Cong., 2nd Sess., April 23, 1970, pp. 1083-1085.

[34] *Ibid.,* p. 1083.

[35] U.S. Senate, *S. 3842,* 91st Cong., 2nd Sess., May 1970, Sec. 1309; U.S. House of Representatives, *H.R. 17966,* 91st Cong., 2nd Sess., June 8, 1970, Sec. 222. Similarly permissive provisions were in *H.R. 4* and *H.R. 11750,* 91st Cong., 1st Sess., 1969 prior to the March 1970 strike.

[36] U.S. House of Representatives, Committee on Post Office and Civil Service, *Hearings on H.R. 17070, Postal Reform,* 91st Cong., 2nd Sess., April 23, 1970, p. 95.

The House bill, H.R. 17070, was changed to give an employee the right to refrain from joining a union. The Senate however, by a small margin, retained the Section 14 (b) approach in its bill, leaving union security as one of the differences to be resolved by the conference committee dealing with H.R. 17070. For fear, among other things, that the House conferees might retreat from the House bill's right-to-work position, the House of Representatives, under the leadership of Rep. David Henderson of North Carolina, passed a resolution on June 18 directing them to adhere completely to the House's stand on H.R. 17070. It was clear that strong opposition in the House would defeat the conference bill if it included a union security provision, thus further delaying postal reform. The final bill contained an explicit right-to-work provision,[37] in which form it was quickly passed and signed by the President.

Although disappointed over their defeat on the right-to-work issue, the postal unions were not prepared to forego other advances toward full collective bargaining because of it. On balance, it was a minor loss to crafts such as the letter carriers, which enjoyed high rates of union membership.

George Meany pledged that the AFL-CIO would soon renew the fight for "genuine collective bargaining for all aspects of employment for all civilian workers of the federal government."[38] Yet the fate of union security legislation restricted to the Postal Service left little doubt as to the outcome of any attempt to enact such legislation for the remainder of the federal service. The policy as set forth in E.O. 11491 was to be the rule for some time to come.

B. THE PROGRAM AND THE MERIT SYSTEM

The EMC program adopted two fundamental positions on the merit system. First, it accepted employee organizations as useful and compatible partners in a personnel system based on merit. It then established protections against modification of the merit system that strengthened federal unions might eventually propose. Essentially, it recognized that conflicts between merit and union principles could easily occur in such areas as recruitment, promotion, reductions in force, union security, and increased union participation in the management function.

[37] 84 Stat. 737; 39 U.S.C. Sec. 1209 (c) (1970). "Each employee of the Postal Service shall have the right, freely and without fear of penalty or reprisal, to form, join or assist a labor organization or to refrain from any such activity, and each employee shall be protected in the exercise of this right."

[38] U.S. House of Representatives, Committee on Post Office and Civil Service, *Hearings,* 91st Cong., 2nd Sess., April 23, 1970, p. 85.

For years a prime element in the uneasiness surrounding the growth of public unionism had been the threat that it allegedly represented to the merit system. Merit principles supposedly eliminate from the public service the personal and arbitrary influences of politics and favoritism. They provide equality of opportunity for all qualified citizens. The only standard for selection in hiring and promotion is merit, proved in fair competition. Unions, on the other hand, traditionally seek to influence or control the hiring process and to advance the interests of union members in promotion, demotion, assignments, and other tenure areas. Labor organizations also strive for union security whenever possible. There is little doubt that these two systems of personnel principles can seriously clash in the public service if reasonable accommodations are not made.

M. Z. Prives, in a study made for the Canadian Federation of Mayors and Municipalities in 1958, pointed out that during the initial stages of the fight for a merit system organized labor is the merit system's natural ally, since labor also suffers because of political patronage. Because a union must seek to gain a foothold before it can present more substantial demands, it will support the merit system not only on principle but also because the groundwork for recognition and fruitful negotiations is more easily laid under a merit system. Prives concluded, however, that:

> "Once well entrenched . . . the union becomes interested, in turn, in the protection of its membership from outside competition, as well as betterment of their conditions. Two related aims will emerge: The impositions on municipal hiring (closed shop or a degree of union security) and the desire to gain participation in management functions. At this point a clash with the management side may occur." [39]

As public service unionism continues to grow, we are witnessing a redefinition of the basic terms "merit," "seniority," and "security." New evaluations are being made as the influences of each conceptual system interact over the years. One can reasonably conclude that these influences were clearly recognized by the Task Force. The basic compatibility of collective action through labor organizations and a merit civil service was confirmed in this observation:

> "The Task Force wishes . . . to note its conviction that there need be no conflict between the system of employee-management relations proposed in this report and the Civil Service merit system, which is and should remain the essential basis of the personnel policy of the Federal Government.

---

[39] M. Z. Prives, *op. cit.;* see also Murray B. Nesbitt, *op. cit.*

"The principle of entrance into the career service on the basis of open competition, selection on merit and fitness, and advancement on the same basis, together with the full range of principles and practices that make up the Civil Service system govern the essential character of each individual's employment. Collective dealing cannot vary these principles. It must operate within their framework." [40]

This view was incorporated in the Task Force's recommendation on the scope of consultations and negotiations. Its general effect was restrictive. To be negotiable, issues of working conditions and personnel policies had to be "within the limits of applicable federal laws and regulations, and consistent with *merit system principles*." [41] The Task Force report noted that the major employee organizations were well aware of these limitations. Nevertheless, in confirmation of Prives' thesis, they expressed a willingness to negotiate under the restrictive requirements of law and merit. The report declared that it was still quite possible to negotiate in such areas as working conditions, promotion standards, grievance procedures, safety, transfers, demotions, reductions in force, etc., and to do so in a manner consistent with merit system principles. [42]

There was no provision in the Kennedy order that referred directly to the merit system. However, there were repeated requirements that all aspects of the program be "consistent" and "consonant," not "incompatible" with law; "subject to law and policy requirements"; "governed by policies set forth in the Federal Personnel Manual"; and, finally, "conform to standards issued by the Civil Service Commission." These requirements constituted protections for the merit principles inherent in civil service statutes. [43]

The new labor relations program did not contemplate a radical departure from the classical merit approach to federal personnel policy. There was no sudden acceptance of union criteria in those areas that were considered negotiable matters, even within the limits of the new system. Nevertheless, in the thousands of contracts negotiated since January 1962 some of the standards and practices of private-sector unionism have assuredly been introduced. Private-sector influences are to be found particularly in clauses dealing with grievance procedures, disciplinary actions, working conditions, leaves, pay surveys, checkoffs, safety committees, promotions and assignments, and position classifications.

The Kennedy order did, however, preserve those aspects of the merit system that were directly in conflict with traditional labor

---

[40] Task Force Report, p. 8.
[41] *Ibid.*, Sec. E, p. v (emphasis added).
[42] *Ibid.*, p. 18.
[43] E. O. 10988, Preamble, Secs. 1 (a), (b), 3 (c), 6 (b), 7 (l), 8 (a), 11, 13 (b), 14.

union objectives and operating methods. The basic hiring and promotion process was governed by statute. And the right to strike was effectively precluded by denying recognition and the benefits of the program to any organization that asserted such right.[44] This policy merely confirmed existing federal statutes forbidding strikes by government employees.

The Nixon Administration adopted a pragmatic approach. It reaffirmed its support of the merit system and proposed changes only where these were deemed necessary to eliminate existing deficiencies. No massive overhaul was contemplated. Where prior labor experience was beneficial, it was to be applied. Thus, the members of the Nixon Study Committee unanimously believed their recommendations would "strengthen the usefulness of labor-management relations as a constructive force in matters affecting the well-being of employees, in full compatibility with the civil service merit system which remains the cornerstone of governmental personnel policy." [45] Management's hand was strengthened in a number of respects, and statutory limitations were further emphasized. Yet the Committee declared that desired changes could be effected without disrupting the continuing program, and that in formulating its proposals it had been "mindful of the desirability of preserving the features of Executive Order 10988 which have worked well." [46] This policy was still in force in 1975 after two extensive reviews of the program by the Federal Labor Relations Council.

---

44 Task Force Report, Sec. B., pp. iv, 13; E.O. 10988, Sec. 2.
45 Study Committee, *op. cit.*, p. 5.
46 *Ibid.*, pp. 4, 5.

Chapter VIII

RECOGNITION—THE KEY TO FEDERAL POLICY

Federal union leaders quickly agreed that the provisions for recognition and negotiation were among the greatest advances afforded by E.O. 10988. Recognition conferred on unions an official status previously denied in the federal service. The hope was early and often expressed that the Kennedy order's recognition provisions could, in time, bring to the remainder of the federal service the sophisticated kind of collective bargaining practiced in the TVA and other proprietary-type agencies. The establishment of a government-wide policy at least offered some promise of achieving this end.

The applause, nevertheless, was accompanied by criticism. Unions feared that local management control over the qualifications for acceptance as an "employee organization," the appropriate-unit issue, and the scope of negotiations would obstruct successful collective bargaining. Most union leaders remained deeply concerned over recognition, claiming that the order did not go far enough.

In many ways the recognition provisions sought to preserve existing practices. Arguments had been proffered by management to the effect that, although the law did not require private employers to deal with organizations not representing a majority of the workers, the unique characteristics of government service generally and the federal service in particular demanded that communication and consultation also be maintained with nonmajority groups. This view underlay the special protections afforded veterans, religious, and social organizations.

The special relationships already existing between various agencies and veterans organizations were recognized and preserved. These organizations had developed services designed to protect the privileges and benefits Congress had granted veterans, and it was felt that their activities would not conflict with the new recognition procedures.[1] This view was also taken of the wide variety of social and religious organizations that had dealt with management on a limited basis in the areas of their particular concern. In August 1971, E.O. 11616 added professional organizations to those enjoying such privileges.[2] It was thought that management should continue its consultation with these groups even if there were exclusive recognition. Under accepted practice a majority representative normally would be present at any consultations on issues involving the entire unit. But since the Kennedy and Nixon orders did not allow management consultation with nonmajority groups on "matters of general employee-management policy," no provision was made for the exclusive representative to be present.[3]

Both the Kennedy and Nixon orders also provided that the individual employee, whether a union member or not, could always bring personal matters directly to his appropriate superior. Regardless of the form of recognition in his unit, the employee could also pick his own representative in grievances or appeals.[4] There was little new in this provision. Protection of the employee's private route to his superior had always been a part of the CSC's policy, and Section 9 (a) of the Taft-Hartley Act had long provided that any employee or group of employees could present grievances and have them adjusted without the intervention of the exclusive bargaining representative.[5] In 1971, E.O. 11491 was amended to limit radically collective bargaining over traditional grievance procedures, taking them out of the scope of negotiations and returning them to control by law and regulation. The individual's right, regardless of the form of recognition, to use the statutory grievance procedures and pick his own defense representative was thus affirmed.[6]

Union proponents in and out of government are inclined to believe that extensive provisions for independent employee or group action have a weakening effect on the status and strength of an incumbent majority union. Their views reflect a fear that

---

[1] President's Task Force on Employee–Management Relations in the Federal Service, *Report*, November 30, 1961, pp. iv, 16; E.O. 10988, Sec. 3 (c). This was retained intact by E.O. 11491, Sec. 7 (d) (2).

[2] E.O. 11491, Sec. 7 (d) (3) as amended reads: "Recognition of a labor organization does not preclude an agency from consulting or dealing with a religious, social, fraternal, professional or other lawful association, not qualified as a labor organization with respect to matters or policies which involve individual members of the association or are of particular applicability to it or its members."

[3] E. O. 10988, Sec. 3 (c) ; E.O. 11491, Sec. 7 (d) (3).

[4] *Ibid.*

[5] 49 Stat. 453, 29 U.S.C. Sec. 159 (a) (1947).

[6] E.O. 11616, Sec. 5 amending Sec. 7 (d).

such provisions lead employees to believe that unions are unnecessary and that they can achieve on their own all that unions can gain for them. A powerful counter argument contends that the simple existence of such independent alternatives constitutes a necessary spur which forces the majority union to represent employees better and produce results. It is either that or face the alternative of a dwindling membership.

A. TRANSITION UNDER E.O. 10988

The Kennedy order established three basic forms of recognition: informal, formal and exclusive.[7] The form of recognition applying in a particular case was made dependent upon the proportion of employee organization members present or voting for a union in the unit in question.

Informal recognition was described by the Task Force as simply an extension of the right of any government employee to be heard. It gave an organization the right to present its views on matters of interest to its members. This right merely reflected established agency policies of soliciting and considering employee and employee-group views in the formation of future personnel policy, and was, as before, essentially permissive in character. Management was not obligated to hear all organizations with informal recognition—nor, probably, could it because of the amount of time this would consume and the mechanics it would involve. Informal recognition could exist concurrently with formal or exclusive recognition.[8] Although in essence a continuation of existing personnel policy, informal recognition represented a potential threat to the authority of another union having formal or exclusive recognition in the same unit.

Formal recognition was to be afforded all organizations representing 10 percent of the employees in a unit where no exclusive recognition had been granted. Therefore, several formal recognitions could exist concurrently and, perhaps, not conflict with several informal-recognition relationships. Formal recognition could not, however, co-exist with exclusive recognition. The prime advantage of formal recognition was that it granted the right to broad consultation. By this grant, management was required to consult on the formulation and execution of all personnel policies of interest to the membership of the organization. While the organization did not have the right to act on behalf of the entire unit, it was afforded the opportunity to raise issues with manage-

---

[7] E.O. 10988, Secs. 3, 4, 5, 6.

[8] Task Force, *op. cit.*, pp. iv, 12, 13; E.O. 10988, Sec. 4 (a) (b) .

ment and to present its views in writing for management's required, and hopefully careful, consideration.[9]

The great value of consultation was much evidenced by this provision. Many union leaders considered the requirement that management discuss issues both locally and nationally one of the major contributions of the Kennedy order. They believed that a relatively intangible factor in the success of the program was management's simple realization that it was now compelled at least to sit down and talk before it could change any rules or regulations.

The provision for national formal recognition was used as an extremely effective instrument for consultation and indirectly helped to solve many problems that developed in local units with exclusive recognition. National formal recognition became as highly prized by unions such as the AFGE, for example, as exclusive recognition in local installations. As recommended by the Task Force, the order provided that an agency head could grant national formal recognition to organizations which, in his opinion, had a sufficient number of locals or total membership within the agency to warrant such a grant. This resulted in effective consultation in numerous instances. The AFGE sought and achieved national formal recognition in almost all agencies. It was considered a valuable tool for ironing out local differences informally at the national level. Local executives, for example, might vary widely concerning the permissive scope of negotiations under Section 6 (b), or might indulge in alleged unfair labor practices. Both conditions could easily be remedied by a quick directive from the national agency head. National formal recognition thus provided another valuable channel through which union views were made known. It was also thought that when local executives were not present, national officers were likely to be more amenable to adjustments since an opportunity was presented to save face for all concerned. In short, under this provision, appeals directly to the agency head or his representative could result in broad solutions through consultation on pressing national and local matters. Although emphasis was placed on exclusive recognition by observers of the program, the palpable advantages of consultation at the national level were fully appreciated. Later they were clearly manifested in the reforms of E.O. 11491.

Under Section 6 of the Kennedy order, an employee organization that met all requirements for formal recognition and had been chosen by a majority of the employees in an appropriate

---

[9] Task Force, *op. cit.*, pp. iv, 12-14; E.O. 10988, Sec. 5 (a) (b).

union was to be recognized as the unit's exclusive representative. The provision was adapted from what has become our national labor relations code. With the exception of the strong management prerogatives and the lack of centralized agency control, the basic concepts of recognition, the test for appropriate bargaining units, and the required exclusions therefrom were directly traceable to similar policies in our private national labor law and NLRB decisions.

Wilson R. Hart reflected the views of most observers in judging that of all those things permitted by the Kennedy order that had been frowned on in the past, the most significant innovation was the exclusive-bargaining-agent principle. Although long embodied in our national labor policy, and founded in the concept of majority rule in republican government, it was strongly resisted by practically all federal agencies.[10] The Task Force itself noted that exclusive recognition had been adopted in only a small number of federal agencies.[11] The TVA, the Interior Department, the Alaska Railroad, and the Government Printing Office were the leading examples.

Government acceptance of the practice, however, had grown considerably over the years. As far back as 1937, in the Report of the President's Committee on Administrative Management, Reeves and David proposed:

"The majority of the employees in any professional, or craft, or other appropriate unit should have the right to determine the organization, person, or persons to represent the group, craft or unit in joint conference with administrative officials or the representative of such officials." [12]

According to Gordon Clapp, formerly of the TVA,

"The whole practical point of majority representation is that it helps achieve orderly relations between groups of workers and the small few who administer the agency. Majority representation and exclusive recognition of the majority is a device for fixing responsibility and encouraging leadership and the acceptance of obligations." [13]

Nevertheless, in his classic work Clapp later admitted that the TVA was unique in its adoption of majority rule. He pointed to Luther C. Steward's letter to him declaring that majority rule

---

[10] Wilson R. Hart, "Government Labor's New Frontier Through Presidential Directive," 48 *Virginia Law Review* 901 (1962).

[11] Task Force, *op. cit.*, p. 14.

[12] U.S. President's Committee on Administrative Management, *Report of the Committee*, Part II; Reeves and David, *Personnel Administration in the Federal Service*, Washington, 1937, p. 112.

[13] *Good Government*, July-August 1941, p. 39.

was "certainly not a live issue in the federal service." [14] That statement, however, was made in the early 1940s. Attitudes have changed considerably since then.

For example, in 1941 the National Civil Service League declared that "a contract for exclusive recognition of any one organization is incompatible with the nature of public administration." [15] Clapp predicted, however, that government officials and employees would reexamine their position on this issue in the light of the passage and general application of the National Labor Relations Act.[16] Thus, in 1946 the NCSL, on addressing itself to the issue of whether a majority organization in an appropriate unit should be given exclusive recognition, recommended:

> "In short, the head of a public agency must at all times be free to accept petitions or requests for conferences from any source, but he should reserve any agreements for conferences with the group representing the majority." [17]

In 1960 an NCSL policy statement, considered in depth by the Task Force, recorded the substantial changes that had occurred in the League's approach to acceptance of the principle of exclusive recognition. As to whether the principle was desirable, it stated:

> "A public agency must accept petitions or requests for conference from any source. However, multiplicity of unions in a unit can create internal rivalries and be wasteful of the time of an administrator.
>
> "In case of numerically large units with a homogeneous type of work exclusive recognition of the majority will often be mutually satisfactory. Where there is a substantial diversity in the character of the work of the employees of a unit, it would seem undesirable to promote exclusive recognition." [18]

In spite of reservations, the NCSL accepted the fundamental principle of exclusive recognition, and saw fit to support and recommend collective negotiation and written agreements.

By the mid-1950s there was considerable evidence that governmental jurisdictions were becoming more favorably inclined towards exclusive recognition. The New York City Department of Labor, after surveying 55 jurisdictions at all levels, disclosed that

---

[14] Gordon R. Clapp, *Employee Relations in the Public Service* (Chicago: Civil Service Assembly, 1942), pp. 93, 94.

[15] *Good Government*, May-June, 1941, p. 23.

[16] Clapp, *op. cit.*, p. 94.

[17] National Civil Service League, *Employee Organizations in the Public Service,* New York, 1946, pp. 15, 16.

[18] National Civil Service League, *Employee Organizations in Government,* New York, 1960, p. 3; see also Murray B. Nesbitt, National Civil Service League, *Staff Report,* New York, 1960, pp. 10, 11.

87.5 percent of the jurisdictions extended some form of recognition. The most frequent practice—in 61.9 percent of the cases—was to recognize the union as the exclusive agent for all employees in a unit. Members-only recognition on an exclusive basis was extended by 26.2 percent, while plural recognition was afforded by 11.3 percent. Admittedly, the majority of these agencies were of the type engaged in "public works" activities or were primarily composed of blue-collar workers, but the findings of the NYC Department of Labor nevertheless evidenced a distinct trend.[19]

The unique character of civil service notwithstanding, the Task Force in accepting exclusive recognition incorporated a fundamental aspect of private labor relations in the Federal Government. It adhered to the prevalent trend in also adopting the inseparable concepts of the written contract and collective negotiations. Necessarily, the program also accepted the problems inherent in these concepts. Outstanding among these were determining appropriate units, conducting elections, and preventing unfair labor practices. The Task Force eliminated the knotty and perennial problem of affiliation when it declared:

> "As a general proposition, recognition should, under the conditions specified below, be granted to any trade union, association, council, federation, brotherhood or society having as a primary purpose the improvement of working conditions among federal employees; and any craft trade or industrial union whose membership may include both federal employees and employees in private organizations." [20]

In summary, the new attitude was clearly evident in the statement that:

> "Wherever exclusive recognition is now practiced in the federal government it has proved successful, and the federal officials concerned have unanimously recommended its adoption elsewhere in the government.

> "The Task Force accepts the view that in appropriate circumstances exclusive recognition is wholly profitable and in such circumstances will permit the development of stable and meaningful employee management relations based upon bilateral agreements. Such agreements may, of course, be reached between management and a single employee organization or, alternately, a council of organizations. It is to be expected that there will be circumstances in which employees, although organized, may not wish exclusive recognition. However, the general federal practice

---

[19] New York City, Department of Labor, *Extent of Recognition and the Bargaining Unit in Public Employment,* Monograph No. L.R. 3; New York, May 1955, pp. 7, 8.

[20] Task Force, *op. cit.,* p. 13.

should be to provide for exclusive recognition in an appropriate unit wherever a majority of employees desire it." [21]

Adherence to private-sector practice was remarkable on the question of recognition. Criteria for appropriate units spelled out in the Kennedy order rested primarily upon an intent to insure a clear and identifiable community of interest among the employees. No unit was to be established solely on the basis of the extent of employee organization in the proposed unit. These guidelines and the exclusion of managerial, personnel, professional, and supervisory employees are traceable to similar provisions in the Taft-Hartley amendments and NLRB decisions. The provision in Section 3 (b) relieving an agency of the duty to determine recognition questions for at least 12 months from the date of any prior determination of exclusive recognition had its counterpart in Section 9 (c) (3) of the amended National Labor Relations Act. The rationale for the provision granting, with exclusive recognition, the right to be represented at all discussions between management and other employees or employee representatives concerning grievances, personnel policies, or matters affecting general working conditions was found in Section 9 (a) of the NLRA.

E.O. 10988 specified that an organization exclusively recognized must speak, act, and negotiate for all employees in the unit, without discrimination and regardless of their membership or nonmembership in the majority union. No other organization could be formally recognized, although organizations of fewer members could continue informal relationships. The exclusively recognized union was the only voice that could speak for all and with whom management could negotiate and reach bilateral agreements.[22]

To round out the rights of unions under exclusive recognition, management was given definite responsibilities. Not only were executives compelled to negotiate with unions but also they were specifically required to meet at reasonable times in order to do so. In the first two years of the program, the requirement to meet at reasonable times was stated in rather broad terms. As the bargaining process developed, unions were able to secure contract provisions that set fixed meeting dates for negotiations. This was considered necessary since it was believed that strong local agency control over meeting times had on occasion permitted some resort to dilatory tactics. Management also had to confer on questions of

---

[21] *Ibid.,* p. 15.
[22] *Ibid.,* pp. iv, 12, 14-16; E.O. 10988, Sec. 6 (a) (b) .

the scope and the execution of a written document incorporating any agreement reached by the parties.[23] In the area of management rights, there were several elements not derived from private-sector practice, specifically, the extensive reservations maintaining managerial discretion, agency approval, and statutory superiority throughout the negotiating process. These were set forth at length in Sections 6 (b) and 7 (1) (2).

The grant of exclusive recognition also incorporated the Task Force's guidelines for controlling the scope of consultation and negotiation. These provisions eventually became a knotty source of continuing conflict. Section 6 and Section 7 limitations on the scope of negotiations and the power given local management to fix the items of negotiation prior to bargaining sessions were particularly frustrating. Unions often alleged that with these weapons managers could eliminate from the areas of discussion issues that unions considered both essential and well within the executive's discretion as outlined in the order. The severe implications of the running dispute over scope of negotiations are more closely examined in Chapter XX.

The Kennedy order officially established the policy of requiring a written agreement. Written agreements had long been recommended by the National Civil Service League and had become standard operating procedure in most jurisdictions with advanced labor relations. On the pressing issue of the resolution of bargaining impasses, the order implemented the Task Force's view that arbitration should not be used as a means of settlement. Although it recommended that resolution methods should be devised on an agency-by-agency basis, no particular techniques were suggested beyond the authorization for advisory arbitration of grievances. New contracts written in the first seven years after the promulgation of the order sought to resolve impasses through factfinding panels, conciliation and mediation, and referral to higher echelons, but no agency agreed to advisory arbitration. This problem is more fully dealt with in Chapter XIV.[24]

B. CONSOLIDATION UNDER E.O. 11491

In setting up the three types of agency recognition, E.O. 10988 provided for a process through which labor organizations could gradually acquire the strength and expertise necessary for their

---

[23] E.O. 10988 Sec. 6 (a) (b).

[24] See also Chapter XVI, which discusses, among other things, the Bonneville Power Administration's use of advisory arbitration to resolve impasses on wage disputes. Its mediation-advisory arbitration provisions were written into pre-E.O. 10988 contracts.

new role as true bargaining agents. Some unions could build their representative character by taking advantage, step by step, of the lesser forms of recognition.[25] The question arose as to whether the recognition policy was essentially a transitional measure and had sufficiently fulfilled its purpose. This issue was exhaustively examined by the Johnson Review Committee.

Although in mid-1969 unions pressured Congress to enact a broadened labor law for the entire Federal Government, they had little expectation of success. Encouraged by pronouncements by CSC and other officials, however, they did anticipate action by President Nixon. Improvements thus were to be effected by executive action, and the consensus was that the impending revisions would be based essentially upon the findings and recommendations of the Johnson Review Committee.

The Johnson committee proposed revisions affecting all three forms of recognition. The new recommendations to a large extent mirrored the views of both management and labor. For example, the position of the AFL-CIO, as presented in the testimony of George Meany, was clearly discernible in many of the final recommendations.[26] This position, especially in regard to informal recognition, had received the unanimous support of the affiliated unions testifying and, in addition, was widely concurred in by many agency representatives.

Foreshadowing a recommendation by the Nixon Study Committee, the Johnson Review Committee called for the abolition of informal recognition in an effort to strengthen exclusive representation as the major form of relationship. Some unions still found informal recognition to be a useful device, but they were decidedly in the minority. The Committee recognized the transitional character of this form of recognition and agreed with the "substantial number of both union and agency officials" who believed that it had "outlived its usefulness as a positive force in promoting sound labor relations." The Committee formally recognized union complaints that such recognition was inappropriate where another union was exclusively recognized and that it detracted from the "dignity and prestige" of the exclusive union. Management testimony also confirmed the negative aspects of informal recognition. It encouraged fragmentation, created overlapping re-

---

[25] Sterling D. Spero, "Collective Bargaining in American Public Service," *Professional Public Service,* Professional Institute of the Public Service, Vol. 41, No. 11, November 1962, p. 9. Also in AFL-CIO, Department of International Affairs, *Free Trade Union News,* August 1962.

[26] George Meany, President, AFL-CIO, *Statement,* before President's Review Committee, October 23, 1967.

lationships, and caused undue administrative burdens; moreover, unions with such recognition lacked "the strength to contribute substantially to stable labor relations."[27]

The practice of formal recognition as it had developed under the Kennedy order was also slated for radical surgery. The Johnson group believed that formal recognition should be retained at the local level with certain modifications in substance and requirements, but that recognition at the national level should be entirely replaced by a new system designated "national consultation." The Nixon Study Committee recommended that local formal recognition be eliminated entirely.

Although the Review Committee declared that most of its witnesses favored continuation of local formal recognition, there were some glaring divergencies of opinion on this point within the ranks of both labor and management. Although the AFL-CIO position fully rejected informal recognition, it nevertheless concurred that formal recognition "at least permits a union to represent its members and, therefore, often affords such organization a better opportunity to obtain exclusive recognition." [28] Meany was far more concerned with national consultation, and therefore the AFL-CIO position did not overly emphasize the formal recognition issue.[29] AFGE president John Griner, however, vigorously defended formal recognition as a valuable means of effecting fuller communication and dialog that could serve as an open forum to bring employee problems to management's attention. Noting that over half of AFGE's active lodges enjoyed exclusive status, Griner asserted that the remainder, which had formal recognition, were pressing for exclusive recognition and would achieve it in the near future. He believed, therefore, that formal recognition should be strengthened, not eliminated.[30] On the other hand, William Ryan of the Machinists grouped local formal and informal recognition together and called for their total abolition. Citing arguments echoed by management witnesses, he concluded that only with exclusive recognition could the federal

[27] President's Review Committee on Employee-Management Relations in the Federal Service, *Draft Report,* April 1968, in U.S. Department of Labor, *56th Annual Report, 1969,* Attachment B, pp. 20-23. See also, President's Study Committee, *Report and Recommendations on Labor-Management Relations in the Federal Service,* August 1969, pp. 8, 11-12.

[28] George Meany, *op. cit.,* p. 7.

[29] *Ibid.,* pp. 6-8.

[30] John F. Griner, President, American Federation of Government Employees, AFL-CIO, *Statement,* before President's Review Committee, October 23, 1967, pp. 4-7.

service "eventually reach the plateau of genuine collective bargaining."[31]

Management positions also varied on the question of local formal recognition. Nevertheless, it is both meaningful and indicative of executive thinking that the agencies with the greatest experience in labor relations and the largest numbers of employees enjoying some form of recognition called for the elimination of all forms of local recognition other than exclusive recognition. Thus, the Post Office representative, while conceding that minority recognition may have been appropriate during the transitional period, called for its elimination where exclusive recognition was appropriate; to do otherwise would impair stable labor relations and unduly burden management.[32] The Army was equally adamant in opposing minority recognition, declaring:

> "Five years ago, formal recognition provided a powerful aid to union organizing efforts since it provided the union with such rights as dues checkoff and consultation on new or revised personnel policies and practices. We feel that the infant of five years ago has matured rapidly and is now a healthy, robust youngster who no longer needs this step stool to get to the bargaining table." [33]

The Navy's view was most concise on this point. It recommended:

> "That the Executive Order provide for exclusive recognition only. We believe that informal recognition could be dropped immediately and that formal recognition could be phased out over a reasonable period such as two years. These eliminations would remove conflicts resulting from overlapping recognitions, and provide for strong and clear-cut representation by unions." [34]

This position was supported by such agencies as the Treasury Department and General Services Administration. However, its major advocate was the Interior Department, whose many years of experience enabled it to declare with authority that an organization with exclusive representation rights is really "the sole point of communication and negotiation on matters affecting all employees in the unit.[35]

---

[31] William H. Ryan, National Coordinator, Government Employees Department, International Association of Machinists, AFL-CIO, *Statement*, before President's Review Committee, October 23, 1967, p. 3.

[32] Anthony F. Ingrassia, Director, Labor Relations Division, U.S. Post Office Department, *Statement*, before President's Review Committee, October 26, 1967, p. 4.

[33] U.S. Department of the Army, *Statement*, before President's Review Committee, October 1967, pp. 7-8.

[34] Randolph S. Driver, Deputy Under Secretary of the Navy for Manpower, *Statement*, before President's Review Committee, October 1967, p. 5.

[35] Newell B. Terry, Director of Personnel, U.S. Department of the Interior, *Statement*, before President's Review Committee, October 27, 1967, p. 6.

The Review Committee, however, recommended retention of local formal recognition in the belief that it served a useful purpose in the development of positive employee-management relations. Revisions were, nevertheless, recommended to ensure a more accurate estimate of the intensity of employee desires and to grant consultation rights only to those organizations representing a meaningful portion of the workers.[36] Furthermore, and essentially in deference to the many expressions in favor of exclusive recognition alone, the areas of consultation for formal recognition were to be clearly limited. All matters involving new personnel policies and practices that affected the working conditions of all the employees were to be discussed solely with the exclusively recognized labor organization.[37]

The Nixon Study Committee departed radically from the position of the Johnson group by refusing to retain local formal recognition. It was viewed as causing the same confusions and difficulties as informal recognition. Although it had served a useful purpose in the past, the Study Committee asserted that recently it had "produced problems which hinder the development of stable and orderly labor relations." It was difficult to maintain "an appropriate difference in the rights and obligations" of formal recognition as compared with those of exclusive recognition.[38]

This position constituted a major step forward. By discontinuing the two lesser forms, the Study Committee firmly established, without qualification, the supremacy of local exclusive recognition. In this it followed established private practice and the pronounced trend in local government. In calling for the end of formal recognition, it declared:

> "The prevailing form of recognition today is exclusive. Over 50 per cent of the Federal workforce is now covered by exclusive—far greater than the coverage in private employment. Clearly, employees and labor organizations no longer need the special assistance in organizing provided by formal recognition, and its continuance is not warranted in view of the problems involved in administering multiple forms of recognition." [39]

As the Committee recommended, E.O. 11491 proscribed the issuance of new formal recognitions and provided for the phasing out of those already in existence.[40] Subsequently this order was amended by E.O. 11616 to eliminate all formal and informal recognitions as of August 26, 1971.[41]

---

[36] Review Committee, *op. cit.*, p. 24.
[37] *Ibid.*, pp. 24, 25.
[38] Study Committee, *op. cit.*, p. 13.
[39] *Ibid.*, pp. 13-14.
[40] E.O. 11491, Sec. 8.
[41] E.O. 11616, Sec. 6.

The concept of national formal recognition was not abandoned, however. Management and labor representatives alike had urged that a means of communication at the national level—in addition to exclusive recognition—be retained. Responding to this urging, the Johnson Review Committee had recommended that national consultation rights be extended to organizations meeting specified criteria. Its proposed Federal Labor Relations Panel was to be charged with the establishment of government-wide standards for a national consultation system. National consultation rights were not to be granted in any instance where a labor organization already enjoyed national exclusive recognition.[42] Moreover, the Review Committee emphasized that national consultation should not include the right to negotiate an agreement. This was intended to strengthen further the concept of exclusive recognition.

The Committee sought to delineate clearly the difference between national consultation and national exclusive recognition rights. It recommended that national consultation should include the right to notification of any proposed agency changes in personnel policies that might affect the employees represented by the organization in question and the right to comment on such proposals, submit alternatives, and receive an agency reply if duly requested. National consultation also was to guarantee a union the opportunity to take affirmative action by suggesting personnel policy changes. Further, it was to afford the right to confer and to submit written views to the agency with the knowledge that suggestions would receive careful consideration. Opportunity to appeal agency actions withholding national consultation rights was to be provided.[43].

The Committee's detailed enumeration of the proposed national consultation rights actually fortified the status of exclusive recognition. Its effect was to limit the employee coverage and the scope of consultation in a manner that precluded inroads into the negotiation process, which was reserved to organizations enjoying exclusive recognition.

The Nixon Study Committee concurred in these recommendations, making only minor changes,[44] and the concept of national consultation rights subsequently was embodied in E.O. 11491. The task of establishing qualifications was assigned to the new Federal Labor Relations Council. Such rights may not be granted

---

[42] Review Committee, op. cit., pp. 26, 27.
[43] Ibid., p. 28.
[44] Study Committee, op. cit., pp. 14-17.

if another union possesses national exclusive recognition for the unit. Granting national consultation rights does not preclude an agency from dealing on the national level with other unions on matters affecting their membership. These rights must be terminated by the agency if the labor organization ceases to qualify under the established criteria. Unions seeking eligibility for national consultation rights may refer their cases to the Assistant Secretary of Labor for Labor-Management Relations for decision.[45] Further appeal is possible to the Council itself.[46]

1. The 60-Percent Rule

The Johnson Review Committee reinforced its support of exclusive recognition by recommending changes to remove some of the obstructions and misunderstandings that had created confusion. Slated to go were the 10-percent membership requirement and the 60-percent representative vote rule. Both policies had caused many administrative difficulties in the determination of majority status. Executive Order 10988's requirement that at least 10 percent of the employees in a unit had to be union members before exclusive recognition could be granted had not been particularly beneficial. The unnecessary administrative problems this requirement had created warranted its elimination. The Review Committee recommended that "exclusive representation rights should be granted to the labor organization designated by a majority of the employees in an appropriate unit in a manner similar to that used in the private sector." [47]

A major step toward adopting the traditional process for selecting an exclusive majority representative was the Committee's move to recommend rejection of the 60-percent vote rule. This rule had not been set forth in E.O. 10988 but had been established administratively in accordance with recommendations of the President's Temporary Committee on Implementation. The furor it created among federal unions did not abate during the life of the Kennedy order.

The rule provided that no representation election could be considered valid unless at least 60 percent of the employees available and eligible to vote in a unit actually participated in the election. Union leaders viewed the rule as violating the basic tenets of the democratic process and denigrating the rights of the majority. The rule had been strongly criticized by the American

45 E.O. 11491, Sec. 9 (a) , (b) , (c) .
46 *Ibid.*, Sec. 4 (c) (1) .
47 Review Committee, *op. cit.*, p. 29.

Bar Association and other impartial observers of federal labor relations. Its enforcement had caused unions to resort to diverse means to entice as many employees as possible to vote. Union practices such as offering door prizes or holding raffles invariably created questions of undue influence and precipitated challenges to elections.[48] According to George Meany, the 60-percent rule gave "unjustified weight to stay-at-home non-voters." [49] Thus, the Review Committee helped terminate a long-smoldering dissatisfaction when it recommended abandonment of the rule in favor of the principle that a representative should be selected only on the basis of a majority of those voting.[50]

These long-overdue reforms of representation rules were incorporated into federal labor relations practice under the Nixon order. Section 10 (a) effectively abolished both the 10-percent membership requirement and the 60-percent representation vote rule.[51] The Study Committee went a step further than the Review Committee, however, rejecting authorization cards, checkoff authorizations, and other methods of determining a majority representative in favor of election by secret ballot.[52] Under the provisions of E.O. 11491, secret-ballot elections were to take place under the supervision of the Assistant Labor Secretary. Elections must now be held to determine whether a union is to be recognized, whether it is to lose its recognition, or whether it is to be replaced by another organization. These requirements were affirmed in E.O. 11838 of February 1975, which also reflected the Federal Labor Relations Council's refusal to return to the 60-percent rule. In any event, the Assistant Secretary already possessed the authority to invalidate an election if the number of ballots cast failed to represent the true wishes of the unit.[53]

---

[48] A typical situation arose in December 1967 during an election involving the Manhattan-Bronx Postal Union, affiliated then with the independent National Postal Union, and the National Association of Post Office Mail Handlers. Much was at stake. The certification as exclusive representative would have covered about 7,800 mailhandlers in the New York Post Office and 11,000 handlers in the New York Region. The MBPU offered an opportunity to win a savings bond to all who came to vote. After a resounding election win, complaints were levelled at the MBPU by the Mail Handlers' union, and it was not until February 1968 that the Post Office denied the protest and sustained the election results. MBPU officials conceded that their only motivation in encouraging greater participation was to satisfy the 60-percent rule. Interview with Morris Biller, President, Manhattan-Bronx Postal Union, Jan. 8, 1969. See *The Union Mail*, Vol. 11, No. 1, February 1968, p. 1.

[49] George Meany, *op. cit.*, p. 14.

[50] Review Committee, *op. cit.*, p. 29.

[51] E.O. 11491, Sec. 10 (a) (d) .

[52] Study Committee, *op. cit.*; Review Committee, *op. cit.*, pp. 51, 52.

[53] E.O. 11491, Sec. 10 (d) ; Federal Labor Relations Council, *Amendments to E.O. 11491 With Report and Recommendations*, Washington, 1975, pp. 18-20.

2. Appropriate-Unit Problems

The confusion over national exclusive recognition created by President Kennedy's Temporary Committee on Implementation was finally resolved by the Johnson and Nixon study groups. A policy statement of the Temporary Committee had discouraged the establishment of units for national exclusive recognition. Both study groups encouraged them, however, by declaring that at the present level of development:

> "determinations as to the appropriateness of such units should be based upon the same criteria used in determining the appropriateness of any other unit requested for the purpose of exclusive recognition." [54]

In keeping with this approach, national exclusive recognition was clearly sanctioned by Section 9 (a) of the Nixon order.

The recognition process enables government to fix the character of appropriate bargaining units and to set the procedures for certification. This attribute was not lost upon both the Johnson and Nixon groups. In advancing exclusive recognition they also established new standards and criteria for appropriate units. Some of these broadened the previously limited grounds for unit determination. Others established new policy in areas of continuing controversy. Finally, new procedures were instituted to administer the recognition process.

In recommending changes, both committees emphasized improving agency performance and strengthening policies that had been sought by management throughout the EMC program. Thus, the Kennedy criterion for fixing appropriate units—an identifiable "community of interest" among employees—had been strongly criticized as inadequate. In both the public and the private sector this issue had always presented difficult problems. To ensure more effective labor relations both the Johnson and Nixon committees therefore recommended that the factors of "effective dealings" and "efficiency of agency operations" should also be considered as relevant criteria. The Nixon order established these factors as additional bases for unit determination. [55]

The Nixon Study Committee emulated private practice on the issue of guard units. The Committee noted that private-sector collective bargaining units of other employees are not deemed appriate if they also include plant guards. Nor are labor unions permitted to represent guards if they admit employees other than

---

[54] Review Committee, *op. cit.*, p. 30; Study Committee, *op. cit.*, p. 21.

[55] Review Committee, *op. cit.*, pp. 43-44; Study Committee, *op. cit.*, pp. 19-20; E.O. 11491, Sec. 10 (a). For an extensive discussion of appropriate-unit provisions, see Chapters IX and XXI.

guards to membership or are affiliated with parent organizations that permit nonguard membership. The Committee concluded that federal labor relations had advanced to the point at which the same standards should apply. It therefore recommended that private-sector requirements should be made mandatory in the federal service. Executive Order 11491 accordingly decreed that both of the criteria noted above should govern in the future establishment of appropriate units. However, in 1975, E.O. 11838 abandoned the policy of separate guard representation. The Federal Labor Relations Council found that private-sector conflicts of interest among guards did not materialize under the federal strike ban. Prior special treatment of guards had only encouraged instability, unit fragmentation, and union rivalries. President Ford's order accordingly rejected separate guard units and provided for guards representation along with all other employees.[56]

The Kennedy order had taken a strong stand against possibilities of conflict of interest.[57] This created great confusion and discontent, particularly for organizations that included among their membership both supervisors and subordinates who might have been employed by the same agency and have sought representation in the same appropriate unit. Many labor unions for years had included employees in both categories. Serious disagreements over appropriate units for such employees arose in many agencies and created much dissatisfaction. Considerable testimony before the Johnson Review Committee was devoted to the issue of supervisors and, as a result, recommendations were submitted that sought to crystallize federal policy. The Review Committee called for a clearer and fuller alignment of supervisors with management, and the Nixon Study Committee enlarged upon this view.[58]

In pursuance of the Kennedy policy of clearly defining management's role, the Nixon group essentially concurred with the Review Committee in stating:

"We view supervisors as a part of management, responsible for participating in and contributing to the formulation of agency policies and procedures and contributing to the negotiation of agreements with employees. Supervisors should be responsible for representing management in the administration of agency policy and labor-management agreements including negotiated grievance systems, and for expression of management viewpoints in daily communication with employees. In short, they should be and are part of agency management and should be fully integrated into that management." [59]

---

[56] Study Committee, *op. cit.*, p. 20; E.O. 11491, Sec. 10 (b) (3) (c) ; E.O. 11838, Secs. 2, 10, 11; Federal Labor Relations Council, *op. cit.*, pp. 7-8.
[57] E.O. 10988, Sec. 6 (a) . For further discussion, see Chapter IX.
[58] Review Committee, *op. cit.*, pp. 30–33.
[59] Study Committee, *op. cit.*, p. 22.

To implement this policy the Study Committee proposed that the definition of "supervisor" applied in private industry be adopted in the federal service. Since supervisors are part of management, it recommended that no recognition be granted any unit that included supervisors or managerial executives. Thus, no recognition would be afforded for mixed units or for units that consisted only of supervisors. The Committee stipulated further that no supervisor should be allowed to participate in the management or representation of labor organizations also representing nonsupervisory employees. Supervisors were to be excluded from current formal or exclusively recognized units and from contract coverage not later than one year from the date of the anticipated Nixon order. Renewal of recognition would be permitted only for those managerial or supervisory units that "historically or traditionally represented the management officials or supervisors in private industry" and also held exclusive recognition at the time of the new order. Executive Order 11491 adopted these policies in the exact language of the Study Committee's report. All supervisors that failed to meet the stipulated exceptions were to be excluded from recognition units and contract coverage by December 31, 1970.[60]

Although omitted from the recognition process, supervisory organizations were still deemed entitled to an essentially permissive form of consultation. The Nixon Study Committee believed that such organizations should be allowed the chance to consult with higher management executives, and it urged the agencies to establish means whereby "supervisors and associations of supervisors are afforded the opportunity to participate in a meaningful way in the management process and have their problems fairly considered." [61] In line with the general policy, even consultation was predicated upon a supervisory association's being independent of any labor union or federation and having no relationship with groups holding recognition for nonsupervisory employees.

Recognizing the nebulous status of supervisory associations, both the Johnson and Nixon committees recommended that a review of agency arrangements for dealing with supervisors and their organizations be conducted. This concern culminated in the Federal Labor Relations Council's 1975 recommendations, which were embodied in E.O. 11838. No changes had been proposed after the Council's first general review in 1971. But by 1975, according to the FLRC, "intramanagement communications and consultation with supervisors and associations of supervisors [had] reached the stage where they would be dealt with more appropriately outside

---

[60] *Ibid.*, pp. 21-24; E.O. 11491, Secs. 10 (b) (1), 24 (a) (d).
[61] Study Committee, *op. cit.*, pp. 23-24.

the Executive order." Thus, the policy of further separating supervisors from the general labor relations program was strengthened.
The Council believed agency responsibility to consult with supervisors and their associations would continue effectively under the
Federal Personnel Manual system, as would supervisory checkoff
privileges. E.O. 11838 retained the fundamental policy of excluding genuine supervisory positions from bargaining units. However,
the definition of "supervisor" was narrowed so as not to include
persons who merely did minimal performance evaluation of other
workers and possessed no real supervisory authority. "Work
leaders" and employees having only sporadic supervisory duties
had already been classified nonsupervisory in interpretations by
the Assistant Secretary. True supervisors were thus more clearly
defined and their full integration into management was solidified
by maintaining the policy that prevented unions from representing supervisors in agency grievance and appeal machinery.[62]

C. IMPLICATIONS FOR ADMINISTRATION

The Nixon Administration fully carried out the recommendations of both the Johnson and Nixon study committees in the
area of recognition. Independent unions believed the emphasis
upon exclusive recognition amounted to favoritism towards large,
entrenched national organizations. Despite this belief, it is undeniable that the greater acceptance of exclusive recognition is a
major characteristic of the general movement toward the formalization of government labor relations. The trend is evident at
state and local levels as well. In Canada, federal and provincial
systems have been enacted to provide majority representation.
States such as Oregon, Wisconsin, New York, Connecticut, and
Massachusetts, among others, have sought to institutionalize the
public collective bargaining process, as have many municipalities.
Because of diverse factors such as the size, mission, and administrative structure of governments and the character and organization of local labor unions, the needs of different jurisdictions necessarily vary. No single system of labor relations administration
could be expected to service all governments with equal efficacy.
Certain characteristics can be applied generally, however; one
such characteristic is exclusive recognition of the majority representative. Executive Order 11491 brought to the federal establishment the recognition concept of the private sector that had already achieved wide acceptance in local government.

[62] *Ibid.*, p. 24; E.O. 11838, Secs. 1, 6, 16; Federal Labor Relations Council, *op. cit.*,
pp. 14-16; *Federal Personnel Manual*, Chap. 251; FPM Supplement 990-1, Civil
Service Regulations, Part 550. See also *Government Employee Relations Report*,
No. 592 (1975), pp. A-10, A-11.

Part III

CONTRACTS AND POLICIES

Chapter IX

BASIC FEDERAL POLICY AND THE PREAMBLE CONTRACT

A. THE PRECEDENTS OF CONTRACT EXPERIENCE

Several considerations influence collective agreements between any government and its employees' unions. For example, laws and regulations can serve to solidify the unilateral power of the employer and to fortify the procedures evolved to exert its authority. In this regard, the exclusion of certain contract areas from bilateral negotiation because of overriding statutes and executive practices has already been noted. It was quite possible for a conservative agency, confirmed in its reluctance to cooperate with unions, to scrape by with minimal adherence to the Kennedy order. Furthermore, the agency could easily jeopardize good-faith bargaining simply by issuing new regulations that obstructed agreements both before and after negotiations.[1]

Over the years, experience in negotiation and contract-writing had been acquired by certain federal agencies where collective bargaining long had been practiced. The numerous contracts they had concluded necessarily influenced unions and management faced with the prospect of a formally recognized policy of cooperation. Under such circumstances, the natural inclination of the parties was to imitate and adopt agreements that ostensibly had served them well over the years. The TVA, Department of Interior, Alaska Railroad, and Government Printing Office did in fact rely upon past contracts. This reliance was especially noticeable in the agreements of the Interior Department, which had mapped out a system of formal collective bargaining at the departmental level that called for two types of negotiated agreements. First, there were the Basic Labor Agreements concerned primarily with matters of broad principle, policy, and procedure. These gov-

---

[1] American Bar Association, Section of Labor Relations Law, Committee on Law of Government Employee Relations, *Report*, Chicago, 1965, pp. 330-331. See also Chapter XX.

171

erned the fundamental issues under negotiation and set forth basic terms of agreement in core areas. They were augmented by Supplementary Labor Agreements, meant to implement, with specificity, the general policies already established. Supplementary agreements dealt with such matters as conditions, pay, and detailed work rules and standards.[2]

Perhaps the most outstanding adaptation of this format under the Kennedy order was worked in the Post Office Department's national basic agreements with the six, later seven, major craft postal unions.[3] These agreements were viewed as bellwether contracts not only because of the large number of workers they covered but also because of the detail, strength, and completeness of their provisions. In the 1968 agreement there were seven national supplemental agreements for particular crafts dealing with, among other items, heavy-duty compensation, hourly rates, and seniority.

Under the new program many unions, such as the AFGE, NAGE, and NFFE, made good use of established techniques. This was the result of two basic factors: their desire to fashion contracts which would be effective and flexible, and their desire to retain formulas that had withstood the test of time.

However, excessive reliance upon contract patterns established prior to the Kennedy order contained serious pitfalls and disadvantages. Many factors militated against the total imposition of one agency's contract policies upon those of another agency. The most basic of these was the fact that agencies have different functions that require contract agreements suited to specific needs. In addition, employees may be organized on different bases—craft, industrial, installation, regional, and so on. Their unions may differ in leadership, organization, and philosophical approach to collective bargaining.

There were fundamental differences in the early contracts negotiated under the Kennedy order. Accords first entered into by sophisticated unions such as the Metal Trades Department, National Maritime Union, or the International Association of Machinists were generally conceded to be "genuine collective bargaining agreements." They were, in the main, forceful,

    [2] U.S. Department of the Interior, Bureau of Reclamation, *General Agreement,* between Columbia Basin Project and the Columbia Basin Trades Council, October 1959; *Supplementary Agreement,* No. 1, July 1960.
    ———, *General Agreement,* between Region 1 and IBEW, Local 283, March 1960; *Supplementary Agreement,* June 1960.
    ———, *General Labor Agreement,* Parker Davis Project and the Colorado River Power Trades Council, December 1951, Revised September 1960; *Supplementary Agreement,* December 1960.
    [3] U.S. Post Office Department, *Agreements,* March 20, 1963; June 18, 1964; September 24, 1966; and March 8, 1968.

comprehensive contracts that dealt specifically with as many areas as the unions could bring to the bargaining table within the limitations of law and regulation. They were basic agreements on real bargaining issues, at least to the degree possible under E.O. 10988. On the other hand, especially in the very early negotiations, certain basic agreements were little more than agreements to agree, or "preamble agreements." [4] Very often supplementary agreements did little to rectify the situation. They merely added specific provisions to the basic contract in the exact language of the executive order. Another perpetuating technique was to repeat in the contract's terms the existing regulations of the agency's personnel manual.[5] Some agreements even went so far as to include references to the precise citation in the personnel manual after each contract clause. These practices, however, steadily decreased with the acquisition of greater bargaining sophistication by both sides.

B. THE PREAMBLE AGREEMENTS

It is important to note the extent and character of preamble-type "agreements to agree." They reflected the weakness of unions newly established in bargaining units and/or the implacability of local executives seeking to implement the Kennedy order conservatively. The contracts reflected the level of mutuality that existed between unions and management and the attitude of management toward promotion or discouragement of unionism in its agency.

In their first dealings with management, unions will accept

---

4 U.S. Department of Health, Education, and Welfare, Social Security Administration, *Agreement,* between Philadelphia Payment Center and AFGE, Lodge 2006, January 9, 1964.

U.S. Department of Defense, *Agreement,* between Kincheloe Air Force Base and NFFE, Local 32, September 10, 1963.

U.S. Railroad Retirement Board, *Agreement,* with AFGE Lodges Council, September 23, 1963.

U.S. Department of Labor, *Agreement,* with AFGE Lodge 12, January 1963.

U.S. Department of Health, Education, and Welfare, Social Security Administration, *Agreement,* between Headquarters and Payment Center, Baltimore, and AFGE Lodge 1923, October 3, 1963.

5 U.S. Department of the Army, *Agreement,* between Tobyhanna Army Depot and AFGE Lodge 1647, May 31, 1963.

U.S. Department of Health, Education, and Welfare, Social Security Administration, *Agreement,* between the Philadelphia (Northeast) District Office and AFGE Lodge 2327, February 28, 1964.

U.S. Department of the Navy, *Agreement,* between Supervisor of Shipbuilding, Camden, N.J., and American Federation of Technical Engineers, Local 198, June 9, 1964.

U.S. Department of the Army, *Agreement,* between Army Pictorial Center, Long Island City, and NFFE Local 1106, July 11, 1963.

U.S. Department of the Army, *Agreement,* between Army Engineer District, Philadelphia, and National Marine Engineers Beneficial Association, January 3, 1964.

only a little in the hope of greater gains later on. At this point the union desires mainly to "get a foot in the door." Because the unions' initial goal was to secure status and recognition, first contracts were very often weak and merely declaratory. This was especially true in bargaining units comprising the previously unorganized, white-collar, classification-act workers.

Before union negotiators had acquired the membership support and know-how they needed to force more substance into contracts, they were quite content merely to get a contract. As Cohany and Neary, surveyors for the Bureau of Labor Statistics, commented:

> "Approximately 30 per cent of the nonpostal agreements were in essence recognition agreements, in that, for the most part they provided little else than a restatement of various sections of the Executive Order, general pledges of cooperation, and a statement on duration. Such arrangements were relatively more frequent in bargaining units for classified than for wage-board employees. Covering agencies and unions unaccustomed to negotiating activities they thus essentially represent a desire to embody exclusive recognition rights into a written agreement." [6]

Some of the extremes to which these preamble contracts went were remarkable. The January 1964 contract between the Army Engineers District in Philadelphia and the Marine Engineers' Beneficial Association essentially constituted a statement of management rights and of union acquiescence to management direction. A statement of policy first spelled out broad areas in which executive prerogatives were retained. Then, in the substance of the agreement, 15 of 19 specific provisions either referred directly to a civilian personnel regulation that was to govern the item or provided for union agreement with some other executive action that was to control the particular issue. Items that were not so limited included such earthshaking issues as passes for association representatives, time for meals, condition of quarters, and provision that the engineer on watch was not required to do work away from the engine room. Such issues as grievances, wages, hours, disciplinary proceedings, overtime, holidays, promotion, and the like were expressly based upon then-prevailing regulations and Army-Air Force wage-board procedures.[7] In essence, the "agreement" constituted a simple rewriting of the agency regulations in the language and format of a labor contract.

---

[6] Harry P. Cohany and H. James Neary, "Collective Bargaining Agreements in the Federal Service," *Monthly Labor Review*, Vol. 88, No. 8, August 1965, p. 945.

[7] U.S. Department of the Army, *Agreement*, between Army Engineer District, Corps of Engineers, Philadelphia, and National Marine Engineers' Beneficial Association, AFL-CIO, January 3, 1964.

What was, therefore, the basic purpose of these preamble-type contracts? For the unions, they represented achievement of recognition and a written agreement—a weak contract, perhaps, but a start. For the agencies, they established rules and limits to govern the negotiating process. The accords did not actively or affirmatively promote the unionization process. Concessions were held to a minimum, and items deemed negotiable were put down for eventual determination by supplemental agreements. While the substance of preamble contracts was weak, their provisions and form were important and bear closer examination; for they were a written embodiment of the traditional and conservative agency approach toward collective bargaining.

Practically all such agreements contained an opening statement of policy or preamble of specific character. In general, this was a laudable assertion of intent setting forth the purposes to be accomplished by the parties under the contract. While overflowing with declarations of worthy objectives, such contracts, tended to avoid hard-core issues. The essentially general language of the "preamble" contract was evident in the early agreement of the Kincheloe Air Force Base and the NFFE, which began as follows:

> "The Air Force recognizes: the right of employees to organize and express their views collectively; that participation of employees in the formulation and implementation of personnel policies affecting them contributes to effective conduct of Air Force Business; that the efficient administration of the Air Force and the well-being of its employees require that orderly and constructive relationships be maintained between the Union and management officials; and that effective employee-management cooperation in the public service requires a clear statement of the respective rights and obligations of the Union and Employer." [8]

The contract went on to recite basic employee rights and to describe a very limited area for collective negotiation. Mostly it was given over to statements of management rights and reservations, with few details on substantive changes.

Among the basic policy issues generally set forth in the preamble contract was a powerful statement of management rights. Many private-sector unions question the need for such clauses, and the alert union in industry will endeavor to prevent their insertion entirely. Under the provisions of E.O. 10988 and the directives of the CSC and the agencies implementing these contracts, inclusion of a detailed management-rights clause was man-

---

[8] U.S. Department of the Air Force, *Memorandum of Agreement*, between Kincheloe Air Force Base, Michigan, and NFFE, Local 32, September 10, 1962, Sec. 2. The phrasing of this fairly typical clause derived primarily from the statement of purposes in the Kennedy order itself.

datory. Because of the major questions of management prerogatives and legislative limitations upon executive discretion
(examined in detail in Chapter XX), the agencies followed a
fixed policy of including stock clauses to assure the preservation
of management prerogatives. At the state and local levels, unions
often have succeeded in placing curbs on management rights in
such areas as union security, classification, promotion, seniority,
and merit rating. Because of the extensive application of federal
laws, however, a high degree of uniformity has been maintained
in order to insure retention of management rights in these areas
—a sore point to federal unions, as was made abundantly clear to
the Johnson Review Commitee.

Contract uniformity was easily accomplished throughout the
government by requiring adoption of the exact language of the
Kennedy order's basic policy. Specific clauses were clearly spelled
out by the CSC and relayed through departmental directives to
local negotiators. These clauses reappeared unchanged in virtually all contracts. For example, the management-rights provisions in Section 7 of E.O. 10988 appeared in the Employee-Management Cooperation chapter of the *Federal Personnel Manual*.[9] For
the Veterans Administration, this same provision was found with
only slight variation in the *VA Personnel Manual* [10] and the VA
guide [11] intended to aid field station officers in becoming familiar
with the format of the basic agreement. The guide made mandatory the inclusion of this fundamental clause and its specific language. Furthermore, it cautioned that care should be exercised in
the negotiation of any basic or supplemental agreement provisions which might have the effect of negating the management
clause.[12] The clause subsequently appeared without variation in,
for example, the early contract between the VA Hospital in Tuscaloosa, Ala., and Lodge 131 of the AFGE. The basic clause read
as follows:

> *"Mutual Rights and Obligations*
> "A. In the administration of matters covered by this agreement
> and amendments and supplements, officials and employees are gov-
> erned by the provisions of any existing or future laws or regula-
> tions, including policies set forth in the Federal Personnel Manual,
> the VA Policy Manual MP-5 and published department policies
> which may be applicable, and the Agreement and supplements and

---

[9] U.S. Civil Service Commission, *Federal Personnel Manual*, Chap. 711, Subchap.
7-4 (a), 2 (a), 2 (b). (1963).

[10] U.S. Veterans Administration, *Personnel Policy Manual*, MP-5, Chapter 20,
Pars. 10 (a), 10 (b), 19 (b).

[11] U.S. Veterans Administration, Office of Assistant Administrator for Personnel,
Employee Management Cooperation—The Basic Agreement, June 1963, p. 2.

[12] *Ibid.*

amendments thereto shall at all times be applied subject to such laws, regulations and policies.

"B. Nothing in this agreement . . . shall restrict the VA in exercising its right in accordance with applicable laws and regulations to:

"1. Direct employees of the VA.

"2. Employ, promote, transfer, assign and retain employees in positions within the VA, and to suspend, demote, remove or take other disciplinary action against employees.

"3. Relieve employees from duties because of lack of work or other legitimate reasons.

"4. Maintain the efficiency of the government operations entrusted to the VA.

"5. Determine the methods, means and personnel by which such operations are to be conducted.

"6. Take whatever actions may be necessary to carry out the mission of the VA in situations of emergency." [13]

The Nixon order carried forward the same philosophy and language. Section 12 of E.O. 11491 virtually duplicated Section 7 of the Kennedy order and often appeared in its entirety in federal agreements. Section 12 (a), however, did vary the language sufficiently to preserve existing accords against changes in agency regulations unless such changes were required by law or the regulations or agreements of higher authority. Although contracts thus remained unquestionably subject to law and regulation, there was some protection against capricious agency changes at the local level for the duration of existing agreements.[14]

Having first laid out the broad areas of restriction, the agreements very often included a definition of those matters held appropriate for negotiation. Uniformity and consistency were achieved on negotiable items, since negotiable-issues clauses were also attuned directly to CSC interpretations as set forth in the *Federal Personnel Manual*.[15] Most agencies considered that the

---

[13] U.S. Veterans Administration, *Basic and Supplemental Agreements*, between VA Hospital, Tuscaloosa, Ala., and Lodge 131, AFGE, November 27, 1963, Sec. IV, A, B.

[14] E.O. 11491, Sec. 12. The section was repeated closely, for example, in the following: U.S. Department of the Navy, *Agreement*, between Pearl Harbor Naval Shipyard and Honolulu Metal Trades Council, April 15, 1970, Art. II, Secs. 1, 3; U.S. Department of Commerce, *Multi-Unit Agreement*, between Weather Bureau and Eleven AFGE Locals, August 24, 1970, Art. II; U.S. Department of Commerce, *Agreement*, between National Ocean Survey and National Maritime Union, October 1, 1970, Art. II; U.S. Department of Health, Education and Welfare, *Master Collective Bargaining Agreement*, between Social Security Administration, Bureau of District Office Operations, Boston Region, and AFGE, New England Council of Social Security Locals, February 24, 1971, Art. V, Secs. 1-3; U.S. Department of the Navy, *Negotiated Agreement*, between Navy Exchange, Roosevelt Roads, Puerto Rico, and National Maritime Union, January 21, 1971, Art. II.

[15] U.S. Civil Service Commission, *op. cit.*, Subchap. 7-3 (a) (b) (1963).

following clause, with some variation in phrasing, should be required in contracts: [16]

> "It is agreed that matters appropriate for consultation and negotiation between the employer and the union are policies, programs and procedures related to working conditions including but not limited to such matters as safety, training, labor-management cooperation, employee services, methods of adjusting grievances, appeals, granting of leave, promotion plans, demotion practices, pay practices, reduction in force practices, and hours of work. All matters which are governed by law or regulation wherein the employer has no discretion including but not limited to wages, salaries, overtime rates and similar pay matters, holidays, leave accrual, life and health insurance coverage, retirement, annuities, and injury and unemployment compensation will not be subject to negotiation between the parties hereto." [17]

To a large degree this was more than a mere definition of negotiable areas. The consistency with which this almost universal clause was followed in the actual terms and provisions of the contracts was remarkable. The contracts reiterated the allowed areas in the very titles of the clausal provisions.

Each of the enumerated issues was covered in most contracts. It was, therefore, with the enlargement of these permitted areas that unions were most concerned. The *Federal Personnel Manual* was clear that these negotiable "matters will vary according to the extent to which personnel management authorities are delegated within an agency and the needs and interests of employees." [18] This was in line with the CSC's policy of decentralized negotiations, and engendered the hope in unions that at the local level they might succeed in expanding bargaining issues.

Contracts written under the Nixon order continued the practice of using stock clauses and in some instances expanded it. For example, many negotiators wrote accords similar to the one written for the Naval Weapons Center at China Lake, Calif., effective through 1972. That contract incorporated by reference and repetition the entire section on unfair labor practices and standards of conduct for unions called for in the Kennedy order and spelled out in Section 19 of the Nixon order.[19]

---

[16] U.S. Veterans Administration, Office of the Assistant Administrator for Personnel, *Employee Management Cooperation—The Basic Agreement*, June 1963, p. 3.

[17] U.S. Department of the Air Force, *Memorandum of Agreement*, between Hickam Air Force Base, Hawaii, and AFGE, Lodge 882, November 2, 1964, Art. VI, Sec. 1.

[18] U.S. Civil Service Commission, *op. cit.*, Subchap. 7-3 (a) (1963).

[19] U.S. Department of the Navy, *Agreement*, between Naval Weapons Center, China Lake, Calif., and Indian Wells Valley Metal Trades Council, April 17, 1970, Art. I, Sec. 3; Art. IV, Sec. 6.

C. RECOGNITION AND RELATED CLAUSES

The collective bargaining process under the EMC program also evolved the use of certain typical clauses which were far more than mere reiterations of Kennedy order policy and management interests. These were basic clauses rooted in private-sector labor relations. Since a prime union concern in the inauguration of the new federal program was the achievement of status and recognition—indeed, since the concept of exclusive recognition was the program's keystone—all contracts, of both the preamble and the truly substantive type, set forth the names and jurisdiction of the parties precisely and recognized their special position.

This is not a routine matter. The naming of a labor organization as the recognized contracting party in an agreement very probably constitutes the culmination of serious inter-union and union-agency disputes over the basic collective bargaining relationship. Fundamental power struggles are almost always involved. Recognition is, of course, essential. However, the clauses also recite the prerequisites for a claim for recognition by another union. Decertification of a union is assured if a stated set of conditions come into being. The final agreement, then, may well represent the end result of forceful, competitive, and heated organizational campaigns.

The appropriate-unit question is treated relatively early in the average federal agreement. This issue is vital to unions since it delineates the area of their operating jurisdiction and the number of employees they are to represent. The contract therefore may again reflect the disputes, generally with the agency, as to what the appropriate bargaining unit should be. Under E.O. 10988 this issue conceivably could have been resolved unilaterally by agency executives, or by mutual agreement, or by executive conformance with an arbitrator's advisory award as provided for under Section 11 of the order. The eventual appropriate unit may also represent the end result of inter-union rivalries and power plays. As in private industry, competing unions will press for determinations that will make appropriate those units in which they have the greatest organized strength and, therefore, the best chance of victory in the ensuing election. This is so despite the government's avowed policy that appropriate-unit issues are to be determined without regard to the extent of organization, a policy taken bodily from the labor law of the private sector. Thus, the final unit is likely to have been formed as a result of union rivalry, fixed agency policy, and/or powerful union pressures.

As already noted, unit-determination procedures, originally under the jurisdiction of agency heads, were formalized under E.O. 11491 and placed within the jurisdiction of the Assistant Secretary of Labor for Labor-Management Relations. The Assistant Secretary thus conducts representation elections and certifies unions with exclusive recognition. President Ford's E.O. 11838 insured that he would continue to do this only through secret ballot elections. Appeals from his decisions are made to the Federal Labor Relations Council, which retains the final authority to decide. It was believed that a central authority of interagency character could build up a relatively independent body of policy on the question of appropriate units.[20]

Union claims to membership in the appropriate governmental units and executive order policy are the bases upon which recognition clauses are formulated. Under the EMC program, exclusive recognition has been granted departmentwide nationally in only a few instances, primarily in the Post Office. The most common unit is a mixed unit of wage-board and nonprofessional classification-act employees at a particular installation. Other common types of units were made up of wage-board employees alone, craft employees, guards, graded and/or ungraded employees, and supervisory or professional employees.[21]

It is essential that a union, having achieved recognition, continue to enjoy the support of a majority of the employees in the unit. The continued validity of an agreement can depend upon the union's success or failure in demonstrating continued majority support. The BLS reported that approximately two thirds of federal agreements by August 1964 called for the cancellation of the contract at any time by mutual agreement or when it was determined that the union no longer qualified for exclusive recognition. Other contracts provided that after the first year a showing that at least 30 percent of the employees desired a new unit determination would be ground for a new election. This reflected able and cautious bargaining on the part of management and had

    [20] E.O. 11491, Secs. 4, 6; Federal Labor Relations Council, *Amendments to E.O. 11491 With Report and Recommendations*, Washington 1975, pp. 18-20.

    [21] See U.S. Department of Labor, Bureau of Labor Statistics, *Collective Bargaining Agreements in the Federal Service, Late 1971*, Bulletin No. 1789, April 1973, pp. 2, 6, 7. This study found the mixed unit to be most prevalent, particularly in large defense-agency bargaining units. The August 1965 BLS study found that, outside the Post Office, wage-board units surpassed mixed units, with Classification Act units far behind. This merely reflected the varying levels of union organization in 1964. See BLS Bulletin No. 1451, August 1965, pp. 6-7.

the inevitable effect of directing unions into more positive action and affirmative service in order to maintain leadership positions.

Perhaps the best type of recognition clause developed defined the exact types of employees in the unit and set forth the union's functions in both the bargaining and grievance procedures. For example, the following clause, from an early Blue Grass Army Depot agreement, appeared in a great number of IAM contracts:

"The Employer recognizes that the Union . . . is the exclusive bargaining agent under the provisions of Executive Order 10988 for all employees in the unit, composed of (graded), (ungraded), direct hire civilian employees in job ratings and position classifications appearing on the eligible to vote list furnished by the Employer, and in any other occupations hereafter added which are not excluded by Executive Order 10988, Section 6 (a) and, the Union hereby recognizes the responsibilities of representing the interests of all such employees with respect to grievances, personnel policies, practices and procedures or other matters affecting general working conditions at the Blue Grass Army Depot, Richmond." [22]

Although the 1964 BLS survey of 209 contracts stated that all agreements examined contained recognition clauses defining the unit, it was still possible to write an accord without recognizing the union in specific terms. Thus, the 1964 Philadelphia Payment Center agreement failed to declare that the employer recognized the union as the exclusive representative of all employees in the unit. A statement to that effect is basic in a union accord. The contract dealt with recognition only through fringe references to "units for which exclusive recognition is accorded" and the union's agreement that "the employees of the unit it represents should loyally and effectively perform loyal and efficient services." There was recognition of the activities of union officials and stewards, but at no point was there an outright recognition of the union as the exclusive bargaining agent. [23]

Another important aspect of the recognition provisions concerns the role of the union in grievance procedures. Section 8 of the Kennedy order provided that only exclusively recognized unions could write agreements covering grievance machinery. Such unions sought contracts setting forth their responsibilities not only as the bargaining agent but as the employees' grievance representative. The union was required to represent all

---

22 U.S. Department of the Army, *Basic Agreement*, between Blue Grass Army Depot, Richmond, Ky., and Fort Estill Lodge 859, IAM, March 10, 1964, Art. I, Sec. 1.

23 U.S. Department of Health, Education and Welfare, *Basic Agreement*, between Social Security Administration, Philadelphia Payment Center, and AFGE, Lodge 2006, Art. XI, Sec. 2, Arts. IV, VI, Secs. 1 and 2.

employees in the unit, regardless of union membership. Specific references to the union's general responsibility in grievance procedures served to enhance its position and promote the employee's urge to rely upon union aid in time of need. Before the major changes in grievance procedure in 1971 and 1975, this was of primary concern to unions operating under contracts which for many years allowed two sets of grievance machinery, one provided by the agreement and the other existing by virtue of prior agency practice. Since the employee could choose which procedure to follow and whether or not he desired union grievance representation, a clause in the contract providing for union responsibility was most advantageous. In the absence of such a clause, the individual employee would be more likely to act independently. Therefore, agencies amenable to greater union participation signified their willingness by agreeing to clauses that particularly specified union responsibility to represent the interests of all employees "with respect to grievances, personnel policies, practices and procedures or other matters affecting their general working conditions."[24]

Extensive consideration of grievance contracts is provided in Chapter XIII. Suffice it here to say that the Nixon order formalized prior practices permitting the continuance of contracts with dual grievance systems, that is, with both the "agency" procedure and the "negotiated" machinery. However, it officially provided that if the parties so desired the negotiated procedure could be made the sole grievance machinery available to resolve individual employee grievances and contract disputes. This reform was short-lived, however, since amendments to E.O. 11491 restored to individual employees their right to handle their own grievances.

An important innovation under E.O. 11491 was the introduction of binding arbitration as one of the final steps in the grievance procedure; the Kennedy order had permitted only advisory arbitration. Many new contracts incorporated binding arbitration during 1970 as a result.[25]

The 1971 amendments to E.O. 11491 radically revised the permitted scope of negotiated grievance procedures. A procedure for the consideration of grievances over the interpretation or application of contract language was made mandatory, and such grievances could be taken to arbitration by either the agency or the

24 U.S. Department of the Navy, *Basic Agreement*, between U.S. Naval Ordnance Plant, York, Pa., and IAM, Tyson Lodge 175, February 13, 1963, Art. 1.
25 U.S. Department of the Navy, Naval Weapons Center, China Lake, Calif., *Agreement*, April 17, 1970, Art. XXXII, Sec. 1 (a) ; U.S. Department of the Navy, Pearl Harbor Shipyard, *Agreement*, April 15, 1970, Art. XVII, Sec. 1.

exclusive representative. (However, the right of individual employees to present such grievances and have them adjusted without the intervention of the union was recognized.) Grievances on all other matters, including matters for which statutory appeals procedures existed, were not to be subject to negotiated procedure but were to be handled "under any procedure available for the purpose."[26]

As described in Chapter VIII, the Nixon order took a firm stand on supervisors and guards. In time supervisors were to be eliminated entirely from exclusive units. This clarification of policy was offered as preventing conflicts of interest. Until revised by the 1975 Ford order, new units of guards were to be separate exlusive units. Guards' unions could not include other government workers or be affiliated with organizations that did.[27] Exclusionary clauses, therefore, restated most of the order's policy and were considered more or less mandatory by management. While varying the wording slightly, the 1971 agreement at the Navy Exchange at Roosevelt Roads, Puerto Rico, was typical. It described the unit and then excluded "managers, supervisors, guards, professional employees, personnel employees in the Navy Exchange Civilian Personnel Office other than clerical employees and all military personnel." [28]

In accordance with Kennedy and Nixon policy, professionals were also generally excluded unless a majority of them voted to be included in a combined appropriate unit made up substantially of nonprofessionals. Very often, the contracts listed by title the supervisory employees to be excluded or merely stated that the contracts covered all nonsupervisory personnel. They would repeat the entire definition of "supervisor" found in Section 2 (c) of the order. Under the Kennedy order the fundamental policy of the Civil Service Commission and the agencies remained infrangible on conflict of interest. Their position was hotly contested by public service unions whose membership comprised substantial numbers of supervisors and subordinates alike.

The CSC's position was firmly upheld by E.O.11491, which emulated the private sector in defining the nature and functions of supervisors. The Federal Labor Relations Council, commenting

[26] E.O. 11616, Sec. 13; Federal Labor Relations Council, *Labor Management Relations in the Federal Service, Amendments to E.O. 11491 With Report and Recommendations*, Washington, August 1971, pp. 3-7.

[27] E.O. 11491, Secs. 2 (c), 10 (b), 24 (a); E.O. 11838, Secs. 2, 10, 11.

[28] U.S. Department of the Navy, *Negotiated Agreement*, between Navy Exchange, U.S. Naval Station, Roosevelt Roads, Puerto Rico and the Industrial, Technical, and Professional Government Employees Division of the National Maritime Union, February 10, 1971, Art. I, Sec. 2.

on the amendments incorporated by E.O.11616, admitted to careful study and consideration of the supervisor issue. In no way, however, did it react to the suggestion that the Administration "relax restrictions against the inclusion of supervisors holding union office." Indeed, the Council's 1975 proposal integrated supervisors even more effectively into the management structure.[29]

D. TERM OF CONTRACT AND RENEGOTIATION

The 1965 BLS study of collective bargaining agreements in the federal service reported that more than 90 percent of the agreements examined specified a term of one year, subject to provisions calling for automatic renewal for an equal period. The majority of the remaining 10 percent were two-year contracts. In almost all instances a notice of termination was required. The study also noted that in about 80 percent of these agreements there was ample provision for renegotiation by mutual consent of any of the contract's provisions or new supplemental agreements.[30] Renegotiation provisions are an important part of the contract, since they keep the collective bargaining agreement up to date and responsive to a changing economy.

A typical renegotiation clause is to be found in the 1971 NMU contract at the Naval Station in Puerto Rico, which provided:

> "This agreement . . . shall remain in effect for two years from the date of its approval by the Navy Resale System Office. At the written request of either party, the parties shall meet to commence negotiations on a new agreement on the sixtieth (60th) day prior to the expiration date of this agreement. . . . In the absence of a written request from either party for renegotiation by the 60th day prior to its terminal date, this Agreement shall automatically be renewed for two (2) additional years and will thereafter continue to do so on a reoccurring basis provided that it is brought into conformance, as required, with current published agency, including Navy Resale System Office, policy and regulations." [31]

Concerning renegotiation during the contract term, the agreement stated:

> "[The agreement] may be opened for amendment by mutual consent of the parties at any time. Any requests for amendment

---

[29] Federal Labor Relations Council, *Amendments to E.O. 11491 With Accompanying Report and Recommendation,* August 26, 1971, p. 14; _____, *Amendments to E.O. 11491 With Accompanying Report and Recommendations,* Washington, 1975, pp. 11-17.

[30] U.S. Department of Labor, Bureau of Labor Statistics, *Collective Bargaining Agreements in the Federal Service, Late Summer 1964,* Bulletin No. 1451, August 1965, pp. 11, 12. The second BLS study of 1973 did not examine this aspect in detail. It did note that 15 percent of the 671 agreements studied provided that existing accords should continue in effect until replaced by a new contract. See BLS Bulletin No. 1789, April 1973, pp. 70-71.

[31] U.S. Department of the Navy, Navy Exchange, U.S. Naval Station, Roosevelt Roads, Puerto Rico, *Negotiated Agreement,* February 10, 1971, Art. XXV, Sec. 1.

shall be in writing and must be accompanied by a summary of the amendment proposed. Representatives of the Employer and the Union shall meet within fifteen (15) calendar days after receipt of such request to reopen the agreement for amendment and negotiations shall be limited to those proposals covered in the summary. Agreement shall be evidenced by written amendment duly executed by both parties." [32]

The importance of this clause cannot be doubted, for negotiation is a continuing process, particularly during the formative years of a collective bargaining relationship. Federal negotiators adopted similar clauses very early in the Kennedy program and increased their use over the next decade.

It is to be noted that these renegotiation clauses require mutual consent for reopening of the contract. Management—or the union, for that matter—remains free to insist that the original accord be observed for its full term. The only outright obligation imposed on the parties is that if negotiations actually are consummated, any changes must take the form of a written agreement.

Management rights were again protected at the final stages of the average contract by making the agreement subject to any future changes in law or agency regulations. This policy has been maintained during the entire federal labor relations program. The following clause, with variations, has appeared in a majority of contracts:

"Modification or amendment of this agreement resulting from changes in applicable laws, regulations or policies issued by higher authority after the date of this agreement, the implementation of which is mandatory and not discretionary with the Employer, will be made by written notification to the Council indicating the modification and basis therefore . . . ." [33]

Some accords at least have provided for consultation over conforming the contract to changes in policy. The following appeared in the Pearl Harbor Naval Shipyard agreements from 1964 through May 1972:

"Amendments to this agreement may be required because of changes in applicable laws and regulations of appropriate authorities made after the effective date of this agreement. In this event, the parties will meet as soon as possible for the purpose of negotiating new language which will bring this agreement into conformity with such changes." [34]

[32] *Ibid.*, Art. XXV, Sec. 2 (a) . The BLS study of April 1973 found such renegotiation clauses in 88 percent of 671 accords in effect in 1971. See BLS Bulletin No. 1789, April 1973, pp.11-12.

[33] U.S. National Aeronautics and Space Administration, *Agreement*, between Goddard Space Flight Center and Washington Area Metal Trades Council, October 1964, Art. XXV, Sec. 5.

[34] U.S. Department of the Navy, *Agreement*, between Pearl Harbor Naval Shipyard and Honolulu, Hawaii, Metal Trades Council, May 1970, Art. XXVI, Sec. 2. Also appearing in *Agreement* between the parties for April 3, 1964, Art. XXIX, Sec. 5.

CHAPTER X

THE SUBSTANTIVE PROVISIONS

When the Kennedy order opened the way for collective bargaining in the federal service, many observers wondered what there was to bargain about. Did not the order's reservations regarding management rights and sovereign prerogatives deny the equality of the parties upon which collective bargaining is posited? Were not the things that really mattered—wages, hours, working conditions, and fringes—covered by law or regulations based on legislation? Finally, even if a field for joint negotiation might be staked out, could government managers and personnel men overcome their habits of unilateral action and accommodate themselves to the bargaining process?

The American Bar Association, whose Committee on Law of Government Employee Relations published annual reports on the early operations of the order, raised such questions when the EMC program was first instituted. A year later, however, the ABA committee found that most government officials had "been meeting the challenge" and that "meaningful agreements were being negotiated." [1] The Committee concluded that "both agencies and unions have had a great deal to negotiate about and that a wide range of subjects were both negotiable and negotiated," [2] including the following:

"shift assignments; schedules of tours of duty; call-back pay; union participation in apprentice programs; job posting; within-grade increases; a requirement that supervisors submit written statements giving reasons for refusing to promote a qualified candidate; distribution of the agreement; merit staffing; dues check-off; union's right to be present at any grievance, disciplinary or appeal hearing and to make its views known; a non-employee union official's right

---

[1] American Bar Association, Section of Labor Relations Law, Committee on Law of Government Employee Relations, *Report*, Chicago, August 1964, p. 361. Permission to reprint this article from the Labor Law Report was obtained from the ABA and its Section of Labor Relations Law, 1969.
[2] *Ibid.*

186

to visit the installation during working hours; joint fact-finding committees; and impasse procedure." [3]

This kind of negotiation was the avowed goal of organized government labor. As IAM official Theodore Vanderzyde declared to federal personnel officers in 1963, the unions would not be satisfied with contracts that simply parroted the order. He stated that with truly cooperative management, his union was able to write agreements that "illustrate what may be accomplished in the way of industrial peace and harmony"—to write accords that "parallel those in the private sector." Among the more substantive provisions of IAM agreements he included uniform grievance procedures, promotion systems, policies on distribution of overtime, and rules governing leave. There were also clearly defined hours of work and basic workweek, participation in wage surveys, holiday work policies, safety measures, and other important negotiable issues.[4]

Chairman John W. Macy, Jr., of the Civil Service Commission found that progress under the EMC program compared favorably with the development of collective bargaining in the first years after passage of the National Labor Relations Act. Macy believed that

> "considering the nature of the program, and thinking back upon the experience of the private sector of the economy in the early days of the Wagner Act, the acceptance of the program by federal officials has been impressive. No doubt some federal managers did not personally like the obligations placed upon them by the program. There have been, and probably will continue to be, scattered instances of resistance; but regardless of personal feelings, federal managers overwhelmingly demonstrated their sense of responsibility and their understanding of the program." [5]

A. HOURS OF LABOR—WORKDAY AND WORKWEEK

Hours of labor have been a major issue in federal labor relations since the 10-hour movement of the 1830s. In government, the hours question has been closely tied to the issue of wages. There was once a popular AFL slogan which ran:

> "Whether you work by the week or the day
> Decreasing the hours increases the pay."

Various statutes fix the federal workweek at eight hours a day and 40 hours a week. While the workweek can only be changed

---

[3] *Ibid.*

[4] *Government Employee Relations Report,* No. 12 (1963), pp. A-1, A-2.

[5] John W. Macy, Jr., "The Federal Employee-Management Cooperation Program," *Industrial and Labor Relations Review,* Vol. XIX, July 1966, p. 549.

through legislation, its administration opens a broad field for negotiation.[6] This situation is no different from that in the private sector, where collective agreements regulate the implementation of basic workday and week.

By negotiating contracts within the general outline of the statutes, agencies and unions varied the nature of the workday and workweek to a remarkable degree and to the increased satisfaction of the employees. There also are numerous issues so related to hours of work as to seem almost inseparable from them. Some of these, such as overtime, shift periods, meal periods, rest periods, leaves, and holidays, were accepted as proper subjects for collective negotiation. The extent of federal bargaining on these vital issues diminished some of the differences between public- and private-sector contracts. While few government agencies have accords that fully compare with those in industry, there is an undeniable trend toward the inclusion of hours provisions almost as comprehensive and meaningful as those in the private sector.

Agencies and unions with labor relations experience exhibited new energy in contract-writing under the impetus of the Kennedy order. Provisions on such subjects as hours of work, overtime, holidays, and the various types of leave took up a considerable portion of the contracts, especially in the blue-collar agreements.

IAM's 1962 contract with the Louisville Naval Ordnance Plant was typical of many comprehensive agreements. Spelling out the details of shifts and other working hours within the framework of statutory prescriptions, the agreement provided:

"When one shift is employed, the starting time shall not be earlier than 7:00 A.M., except where it is necessary to depart from this time to meet the needs of the operation. The lunch period under this rule will not be paid for unless worked. When a second or third shift is scheduled, 3 days notice will be given to the affected employee. When 2 shifts are employed the starting time of the first shift shall not be earlier than 7:00 A.M., and the second shift shall start immediately following the close of the first shift. The lunch period under this rule will not be paid for unless worked. When three shifts are employed the starting time of the first shift shall not be earlier than 7:00 A.M., and the starting time of each of the other two shall be regulated accordingly.[7]

---

[6] In 1963 the AFL-CIO adopted a resolution offered by the Government Employes' Council to reduce the federal workweek to 35 hours without a reduction in pay. It was believed that the Government would thus set an example for private industry for improving general working conditions. AFL-CIO, Fifth Constitutional Convention, *Policy Resolutions*, Government Employes' Programs, Pay (c), adopted November 1963, New York; published Washington, February 1964, p. 172.

[7] U.S. Department of the Navy, *Basic Agreement*, between U.S. Naval Ordnance Plant, Louisville, Ky., and IAM, Lodge No. 830, 1962, Art. VI, Sec. I.

Additional contract provisions barred the employer from varying the basic workweek for any employee unless his job related directly to the protection of property, security, health, and other vital matters. Even here the employer agreed to prior consultation with the union to determine the jobs to be placed in this special category. The contract also provided that should the employer interrupt or suspend operations when fewer than four hours had been worked, the employee was to be paid for four hours. If operations continued for more than four hours but less than eight, the employee was to be paid for eight hours. There was to be no charge against annual or sick leave. Provision was also made for clean-up time at the end of each shift for the purpose of returning tools and cleaning machinery.[8]

The Charleston Naval Shipyard's 1966 contract with the Metal Trades Council allowed for clean-up time before lunch and after the work shift to enable employees who had been in contact with toxic materials considered health hazards to take the necessary precautions. Inequities in the allotment of such clean-up time were declared to be appropriate items for discussion between the union steward and supervision. Reasonable time was also allowed for stowing tools and equipment, removing fire hazards, and securing work areas after each shift. The determination of this time allowance was declared a subject for mutual discussion.[9]

In 1968 the third major agreement negotiated at the Charleston Naval Shipyard was hailed as exemplifying the best type of union contract attainable under the Kennedy order.[10] It was the culmination of collective bargaining that over the decade had substantially expanded the scope of negotiation. Union rights and duties were spelled out with clarity and precision. The Metal Trades Council cited 47 new and beneficial changes in an agreement that was already considered among the most advanced in substantive content.

Hours and shifts were more than merely defined. The provisions governing their administration were expanded and called for greater union notice, consultation, and participation than had previously been required. Traditional union values were clearly discernible in the new procedures. For example, new understandings controlled assignments to service-type functions that had to

---

[8] *Ibid.*, Secs. 2, 3, 4.
[9] U.S. Department of the Navy, *Agreement*, between Charleston Naval Shipyard and Charleston Metal Trades Council, AFL-CIO, 1966, Art. VII, Secs. 8-11.
[10] U.S. Department of the Navy, *Agreement*, between Charleston Naval Shipyard and Charleston Metal Trades Council, AFL-CIO, 1968.

be performed over periods exceeding the five-day week or the clearly fixed eight-hour work shifts. The employer agreed to keep to the minimum the number of employees assigned to a workweek other than Monday to Friday. Such employees were to be assigned on a rotating basis in order of increasing seniority. It was also agreed that the Shipyard would notify the union in advance of any proposed changes in the basic workweek, and consult with it if desired. It was stipulated that only if there were "compelling considerations which dictate a need for the change" would the basic workweek be varied.[11]

Consideration for the employee's well-being was a prime concern of the agreement. Employees whose workweek was to be changed were to be notified before midnight of the Wednesday prior to the workweek during which the change was scheduled. In addition, changes generally had to last at least three weeks,[12] thus permitting the employee some degree of preparation and organization. Changes in assignments to service-type functions could be for periods of less than three weeks; but, at least, it was agreed that the nonwork days of employees placed on a rearranged workweek would be consecutive whenever practicable.[13] Notice and consideration were thus implicit in the contract terms.

Assignments to night shifts came in for special consideration. So long as selections resulted in a balanced work force, the swing and graveyard shifts were put on a voluntary basis. In the event that the supply of volunteers exceeded the demand, seniority was to be the basis for selection. If there were insufficient volunteers, assignments were to be made on a rotating basis starting with the reasonably qualified employee with least seniority.[14]

The detail of this 1968 accord was remarkable in its concern for the human needs of the employees. Volunteers for night-shift work were not to have their shift disturbed except upon their request or if the workload required some adjustment. If the latter case, the Shipyard agreed "to minimize to the maximum the impact of such adjustments on employees."[15] The normal night shift tour was set for the usual 90 days, and every reasonable effort was to be made to avoid changing an employee's regular shift hours from one night shift to the other when he completed a normal night-shift tour. Volunteers could indicate in advance

---

[11] *Ibid.*, Art. VIII, Secs. 3, 4.
[12] *Ibid.*, Art. VIII, Sec. 5.
[13] *Ibid.*
[14] *Ibid.*, Art. VIII, Sec. 11.
[15] *Ibid.*

whether they preferred to limit their tour to 90 days or stay on the night shift for an indefinite period. Under no circumstances could volunteers who chose the indefinite assignment be replaced on the night shift without their consent. Considerations were also provided for involuntarily assigned personnel. Finally, on the request of the chief steward, exceptions to the shift procedures were to be granted employees for physical disabilities or for prior military or educational commitments, to cite some possibilities.[16]

It was clearly stipulated that each employee had to be at the job site ready for work at his scheduled time. However, if the employer required him to perform any work before or after his regular shift hours, or if he was directed merely to report at a designated place at a specified time prior to the scheduled start of his shift, all such time was to be considered compensable at the appropriate rate of pay.[17] Sunday was to be compensated at premium rates if included in the basic workweek. Finally, the accord specified that employees were not required to accept any instructions, job assignments, or turnovers in connection with their work prior to the scheduled starting time.[18]

The 1968 Charleston Naval Shipyard accord was a prime indicator of the continuing trend toward more substantive agreements. It serves as an example of the detail, sophistication, and substance that could be achieved in contract writing under the Kennedy order.

Agreements under the Nixon order continued the trend toward detailed hours clauses. The 1970 NMU accord with the National Ocean Survey, for example, went beyond a definition of the basic workweek to a detailed catalogue of hours clauses covering day workers; rest periods; security and anchor watches; hours of labor in port; sea watches; meal hours; hours for quartermasters, yeomen and pharamacists' mates; deck, engine, and steward department hours rules.[19]

Comprehensive overtime administration was often provided for in contracts. For example, in addition to setting the rate of time and one-half after eight hours worked in a day, the Louisville Ordnance Plant contract specified procedures intended to bring equity into overtime distribution and at the same time recognize

---

16 *Ibid.*

17 *Ibid.*, Art. VIII, Sec. 12.

18 *Ibid.*, Art. VIII, Secs. 13, 14.

19 U.S. Department of Commerce, Environmental Science Services Administration, *Agreement*, between National Ocean Survey and NMU, 1970. See also U.S. Department of the Navy, *Agreements*, between Military Sealift Command and NMU, 1971.

the needs and responsibilities of the workers. If employees were called in for overtime, they were to be paid for at least two hours at the overtime rate. Employees were permitted to refuse overtime work unless they had received at least a day's notice. However, in times of national emergency employees were expected to make every effort to work a reasonable amount of time when necessary. Ungraded workers were not to be laid off during regular working hours in order to equalize time when operations made overtime necessary. There were also specific provisions to protect graded employees. The contract further required that overtime be distributed as equally as possible among the different classes of employees insofar as the nature of the work permitted. Records were required for overtime worked and were subject to union inspection.[20]

Other contracts contained provisions setting forth the order in which overtime was to be assigned and gave employees the opportunity to refuse overtime. Some agreements provided overtime pay for work outside of the regular schedule, including Saturdays and Sundays. In 25 percent of the agreements examined in the Bureau of Labor Statistics' 1965 survey, management retained the right to vary the hours of work but only after notice to or consultation with the union.[21] The incidence increased to over 50 percent of the accords reported on in 1973.[22]

Year after year the scope of contracts broadened, and the handling of various items became more and more sophisticated and specific. An accord concluded between the AFGE and the Social Security Administration in 1966 set forth a clear schedule of priorities for overtime distribution based upon the performance of the employees competing for it. When volunteers exceeded the number needed, journeymen at the top of their grade whose performance met or exceeded production standards were to have first preference. Following in order were lower grade workers whose production was at or above par; employees who had done the work before and journeymen of lower standards; other personnel in the operating function; and those outside the operating func-

---

[20] U.S. Department of the Navy, Louisville Naval Ordnance Plant, *Basic Agreement*, 1962, Art. VI, Sec. 5.

[21] U.S. Department of Labor, Bureau of Labor Statistics, *Collective Bargaining Agreements in the Federal Service, Late Summer 1964*, BLS Bulletin No. 1451, August 1965, pp. 13-15.

[22] ———, *Collective Bargaining Agreements in the Federal Service, Late 1971*, BLS Bulletin No. 1789, April 1973, pp. 16-18. This study reported that 88 percent of the agreements analyzed had overtime equalization clauses; that half of these (253 contracts) allowed the right to refuse overtime. Ninety-six out of 671 accords called for premium pay for weekend work.

tion. Specific provisions governed which trainees could or could not receive overtime. It was also provided that no employee could qualify for overtime whose current work was unsatisfactory, as demonstrated by his performance records.[23]

Sophisticated overtime-distribution provisions were also to be found in the 1968 Charleston Naval Shipyard accord. Employees within an occupational job rating constituted the group within which nondiscriminatory distribution was to be made. To insure fairness, the contract required that:

> "The status of equity will be audited by the cognizant Chief Steward or his designated representative and the Shop or Office Head five times, at the end of six months, twelve months, sixteen months, twenty months and twenty-three months after the effective date of this agreement. The object of this review is to either establish an acceptable explanation for any alleged inequity in overtime assignments, or to agree on remedies to resolve imbalances." [24]

Unresolved issues were to be processed either under the procedures for interpretation of the contract or through the grievance machinery, both of which culminated in advisory arbitration.[25]

Provision was made for the full utilization of employees during overtime assignments, and at least two hours' pay was guaranteed in the case of a call-in. If an employee reported late, he was not to be denied the remainder of an overtime assignment so long as another worker had not replaced him and the need for his work still remained.[26]

The 1971-72 NMU contract with the National Ocean Survey reflected the complexity of specialized shipboard work. Detailed provisions covered authorization, computation, checking, and payment of overtime and penalty pay time at sea. Drills, inspections, and examinations required by law or emergency were not deemed overtime. Security and anchor watches, supper relief, line handling during exceptional tides, the cleaning of water tanks, rest periods, and midnight lunches all were treated in terms of overtime. Equally detailed terms governed working hours and overtime for vessels in port.[27]

---

[23] U.S. Department of Health, Education and Welfare, Social Security Administration, *Supplemental Agreement No. 3*, between SSA Headquarters Bureaus, Baltimore, Md., and AFGE, SSA Lodge No. 1923, 1966, Art. IV, Secs. 1-5.

[24] U.S. Department of the Navy, Charleston Naval Shipyard, *Agreement*, 1968, Art. IX, Sec. 3.

[25] *Ibid.*

[26] *Ibid.*, Art. IX, Secs. 8-11.

[27] U.S. Department of Commerce, Environmental Science Services Administration, *Agreement*, between National Ocean Survey and NMU, 1971, Appendix I, Art. III, Secs. 1-22.

B. ADMINISTRATIVE AND SICK LEAVE

Among the essential fringe benefits closely related to working time are leaves and holidays. Many agreements have taken note of existing policies by formalizing them in the contracts. The treatment of administrative leave—time paid for but not worked because of unexpected circumstances—in the 1962 Machinists' contract previously cited is an example of this. Such leave was to be granted to workers scheduled but unable to report because of extremely adverse weather conditions. Those who did report were to be considered in a work status and their services utilized.[28] Similar rules were prescribed for machine breakdowns, interruptions caused by fire, power failure, or other unforeseen emergencies, and acts of God. The 1970 accord at the Naval Weapons Center, China Lake, Calif., allowed for administrative excusals from duty without charge to annual or sick leave when employees were prevented from working by interruptions or suspension of operations during their regular shift hours.[29] Such provisions are found in many contracts. Recently, stricter controls have been placed on the granting of administrative leave. Depending on whether notice of the disruption can be given or not, some installations provide for either the assignment of other work or, to a limited degree, the involuntary use of annual leave.[30]

While sick leave is governed by statute, the administration of sick leave is in many cases governed by contract. The 1962 IAM contract, for example, called for approval of sick leave if the incapacitated worker gave notice as soon as possible to his immediate supervisors or someone delegated to receive notice.[31] Going a step further, the 1964 Charleston contract with the Metal Trades Council described the means of notification necessary and the purposes for which sick leave would be granted in advance.[32] The particulars of these provisions were even more extensively described in the 1966 and 1968 Charleston agreements, which provided that:

> "An employee unable to report to work due to sickness or injury shall notify his shop or office by telephone, or by a fellow employee within three hours after the beginning of his shift on the first day

---

[28] U.S. Department of the Navy, Louisville Naval Ordnance Plant, *Basic Agreement,* 1962, Art. VI, Sec. 6.

[29] U.S. Department of the Navy, China Lake Naval Weapons Center, *Agreement,* 1970, Art. XVI, Sec. 4.

[30] U.S. Department of the Navy, Pearl Harbor Naval Shipyard, *Agreement,* 1970, Art. X, Secs. 1, 2.

[31] U.S. Department of the Navy, Louisville Ordnance Plant, *Basic Agreement,* 1962, Art. VIII.

[32] U.S. Department of the Navy, *Agreement,* between Charleston Naval Shipyard and Charleston Metal Trades Council, 1964, Art. IX, Secs. 2, 3.

of absence and on each Monday thereafter until he returns to duty. When it is not practicable to make a telephone call, notification may be made by letter, post-card or telegram. Such notification is necessary for the employer to place the employee in a paid sick leave, paid annual leave, or leave without pay status, as appropriate, and shall not in itself be justification for approval or disapproval of sick leave.

"Sick leave, if accrued shall be granted for medical, dental or optical examination or treatment or for securing diagnostic examinations or x-ray. Sick leave for these purposes shall be requested in advance, and the amount requested shall be limited to that amount which is reasonable for the specified request." [33]

Contracts frequently require a medical certificate for leave approval, thus reflecting management's legitimate interest in eradicating abuse and the employees' concern for protecting their leave privileges. Since the EMC program's inception many agreements have contained statements in which the union, recognizing the importance of sick leave and the obligation of the employee to use it only for valid reasons, has agreed to support management in its efforts to stop sick-leave abuses.[34] In addition, unions have made efforts to protect workers against any intimidation that would inhibit their legitimate use of sick leave. An AFGE agreement, for example, specified that:

"The employer shall not publicly post individual or group sick leave records. Nor will sick leave statistics be displayed publicly for the purpose of any competition which would have the effect of discouraging the proper use of sick leave." [35]

One of the most comprehensive regulations on sick-leave abuses stated:

"Except as hereinafter provided, employees shall not be required to furnish a medical certificate to substantiate requests for sick leave unless such leave exceeds three work days continuous duration. It is agreed and understood that the Employer has the right to require that an employee furnish a medical certificate for each absence that he claims is due to illness on the following basis: (a) There is substantial evidence that the employee has abused sick leave privileges over the previous twelve months period; (b) The Employer has counselled the employee in respect to the use of his sick leave, a record of such counselling is on file, and the sick leave record of the employee subsequent to the counselling does not indicate improvement; (c) And the employee has been furnished writ-

---

[33] U.S. Department of the Navy, *Agreement*, between Charleston Naval Shipyard and Charleston Metal Trades Council, 1966, Art. XII, Secs. 2, 3.
[34] U.S. Department of the Navy, *Agreement*, between Puget Sound Naval Shipyard and the Bremerton Metal Trades Council, 1963, Art. XI, Sec. 1.
[35] U.S. Department of the Air Force, *Memorandum of Agreement*, between San Antonio Air Materiel Area, Kelly Air Force Base, Texas, and AFGE, Local 1617, 1970, Art. XIII, Sec. 10.

ten notice that he must furnish a medical certificate for each absence which he claims was due to illness. Such written notices will not be filed in the employee's official personnel file. It is further agreed that the Employer will review the sick leave record of each employee required to furnish a medical certificate for each absence which he claims was due to illness at least annually, and upon request of the employee semi-annually, and where such review reveals no substantial evidence that the employee has abused sick leave privileges during the review period, the employee will be notified in writing that a medical certificate will no longer be required for each absence which is claimed as due to illness for periods of three days or less." [36]

At the Charleston shipyard, the provisions governing advance sick leave were specifically laid out in the 1966 and 1968 agreements; in the first contract in 1964, reference had been made only to the applicable regulations, including the Navy Civilian Personnel Instructions. In the 1968 agreement a clause was inserted to make it clear that the contract was to "supersede any prior or existing practice, policy or instruction that conflicts with the provisions herein in all matters within the discretion and authority of the Employer."[37] Although the parties were still subject to the general limitations on bargaining, there was a growing reliance upon negotiations and specific contract terms, particularly in regard to medical certification, illness occurring at work, doctors' examinations, and the return to employment.

The sick leave clauses were highly indicative of the extent to which old and new policies could be formalized and reduced to detailed, substantive contractual terms. During the EMC program federal contracts have begun to exhibit the same features that characterized private industry accords. Increasingly they sound the same, look the same, and even weigh the same as their counterparts in the private sector.[38]

C. ANNUAL LEAVE AND HOLIDAYS

Annual leave and holiday provisions in the federal service are controlled by statute and, therefore, remain basically nonnegotiable. These areas have been the subjects of extensive bargaining in private industry. Federal union leaders naturally desire more leeway in negotiating vacation and holiday time. Although aware that only Congress can make basic changes, some unions have been able to negotiate more equitable procedures for the administration of leave policies. Although in their early stages of devel-

---

[36] U.S. Department of the Navy, Charleston Naval Shipyard, *Agreement,* 1968, Art. XII, Sec. 4.

[37] *Ibid.,* Art. V, Sec. 3.

[38] See U.S. Department of Labor, BLS Bulletin No. 1789, *op. cit.,* pp. 32-34.

opment many contracts provided simply that annual leave and holidays would be granted in accordance with the appropriate regulations, increasingly they set forth detailed administrative procedures.[39]

The scheduling of vacations is a difficult managerial problem as well as a matter frequently of deep concern to workers. Negotiators therefore developed clauses which protected agency needs by requiring that requests for annual leave be submitted reasonably far in advance and by making leaves subject to overriding installation workload and manpower requirements. Some agencies also grant annual leave time for religious holidays subject to the same conditions.

Since the number of holidays is governed by statute, many contracts did no more than list the legal holidays authorized by the Federal Government. Others, such as the detailed AFGE accord at Kelly Air Force Base, set forth the rules for holiday observance in considerable detail. Dates for the several holidays were given, and the days to be observed in lieu of holidays falling on non-work days were specified—Friday in the case of Saturday holidays and Monday in the case of Sunday holidays, for employees scheduled for the normal Monday-through-Friday workweek. Rules for the payment of premium rates to employees working on holidays, whether within or without the basic workweek, also were set forth.[40]

The practices detailed in the AFGE agreement may well have been only a restatement of established agency policy. Nevertheless, their clear affirmation in the contract at least served to demonstrate to employees that their representatives were actively involved in the administration of leave practices.

D. LEAVE FOR UNION ACTIVITIES

Agreements increasingly sanctioned leaves of absence for union activity, a type of leave now officially recognized. In the BLS contract survey of 1973, 57 percent of the sample made some provision for such leave.[41] Many contracts permit the union to designate certain members as eligible for leave either to accept union office or to attend a union convention or meeting. Whenever pos-

---

[39] *Ibid.*, pp. 30-32. The 1973 BLS study reported that about 75 percent of the accords examined provided for vacation scheduling; about 30 percent considered annual leave forfeiture; and almost two thirds dealt with sick leave.

[40] U.S. Department of the Air Force, *Memorandum of Agreement,* between San Antonio Air Materiel Base, Kelly Air Force Base, Texas, and AFGE, Local 1617, 1971, Art. XII, Secs. 1, 2, 3.

[41] U.S Department of Labor *op. cit.,* pp 60-61.

sible, the union must give the agency prior written notice.[42] A 1966 Machinists contract, for example, contained the following provision:

> "One employee will be granted annual leave or leave without pay as necessary to accept temporary union positions or to attend conventions or meetings of the union not to exceed 30 days, provided the union submits the request to the employer at least 30 days in advance of the date the absence is to commence. Consideration will be given to requests submitted less than 30 days in advance." [43]

Although in most contracts, as in the above example, the maximum leave period was relatively short, some agreements envisioned rather lengthy periods of leave. For example, the 1966 Defense Printing Service in Washington agreed with the Lithographers that leave without pay would be granted for "up to one year, provided such employee can be spared from his job without serious detriment to plant operations." [44] The AFGE Field Labor Lodges agreement with the Labor Department went further, declaring that:

> "Employees who are selected to serve in the capacity of AFGE union representative or officer which requires absence from the job will be granted annual and/or without pay leave for the necessary periods up to two years. For elective offices, such leave may be extended for the term of the office of the officer." [45]

One of the more liberal union leave provisions was written into the 1965 AFGE basic agreement with the Bonneville Power Administration. It reflected the BPA's long history of successful labor relations. This provision permitted employees to take leave for up to a year to accept positions with the union, provided they had at least a year of service. It also specified the terms of rehiring for employees who elected to remain with the union beyond the one-year period:

> "If at the end of that period [one year] they wish to remain with the union, they will resign their Federal employment with the understanding that when they wish to return to the Administration they will be reemployed subject to the following conditions: (a) The individual must have acquired career or career conditional status." [46]

---

[42] U.S. Department of the Navy, *Basic Agreement,* between Naval Ordnance Plant, Louisville, Ky., and IAM, Lodge No. 830, 1964, Art. XI.

[43] U.S. Department of the Navy, *Agreement,* between Naval Marine Engineering Laboratory, Annapolis, Md., and IAM, Lodge No. 174, 1966, Art. XIII, Secs. 1, 2.

[44] U.S. Department of Defense, *Agreement,* between Defense Printing Service— Navy Publications and Printing Service Office, Washington, and Lithographers Int'l Union, AFL-CIO, Lodge No. 98-L, 1966, Art. XV, Sec. 2.

[45] U.S. Department of Labor, *Agreement,* between U.S. Department of Labor and National Council of Field Labor Lodges, AFGE, 1966, Art. 24, Sec. i. Renewed in *Agreement,* January 28, 1970.

[46] U.S. Department of the Interior, *Basic Agreement,* between Bonneville Power Administration and AFGE, Lodge No. 928, 1965, Sec. 14.01.

Among other conditions, an individual had to give 30 days' notice of his desire for reemployment. If all conditions were satisfied, he was to be offered the first vacancy to occur in his branch of the trade at the grade he left or at a lower grade. While he could refuse to accept a lower grade position, he was required to accept a position equal in grade to the one he left or forfeit all reemployment rights. After returning, an employee was barred from further union leave for a term equal to the period of his absence or two years, whichever was less.[47]

Administrative leave provisions sometimes have been coupled with arrangements permitting union representatives to perform day-to-day union activities on working time. The Labor Department's 1970 accord with AFGE Local 12 recognized that "reasonable time spent by union officials in the conduct of union-management business under Executive Order 11491 contributes to the development of orderly and constructive employee management relations." [48] Time off during working hours was therefore allowed for such activities as grievance handling, consultation with management, and participation in the work of joint union-management committees, including related preparation and travel.[49] The accord further provided for administrative leave for union representatives to attend training sessions relating to matters within the scope of E.O. 11491.[50]

E. OTHER LEAVE

Among other types of leave covered in federal labor contracts are personal leave without pay and leave or time off from work to fulfill civic duties or responsibilities. On the issue of personal leave without pay, one IAM agreement, after affirming the right of employees to apply for such leave for valid reasons, stated that such leave normally should not exceed one year and was subject to the approval of the commanding officer. A provision important to the individual worker declared that the employer would provide work at the end of the leave period within the rating held by the employee at the time of his departure. Moreover, the employer recognized the bumping and retreating rights of the worker in a situation in which his status might have been affected by reduction-in-force actions during his absence.[51] Generally, law

---

[47] Ibid.
[48] U.S. Department of Labor, General Agreement, between Washington Metropolitan Area and AFGE, Local 12, 1970, Art. IV, Sec. C (1).
[49] Ibid.
[50] Ibid., Art. IV, Sec. D.
[51] U.S. Department of the Navy, Louisville Naval Ordnance Plant, Basic Agreement, 1964, Art. X.

and regulations govern the accrual of rights pertaining to retirement and coverage under life insurance and health benefit programs during personal leave.

In some contracts, primarily in defense installations, comprehensive provisions were set forth allowing an employee to fulfill his civic responsibilities without prejudice to his employment status. Thus, a Navy agreement allowed paid time off for jury duty and qualification for such duty. Administrative time also was granted not only for voting in elections and referenda but for registration when this could be accomplished only during working hours. Clauses pertaining to charity drives declared that the union and the employer would cooperate in worthwhile campaigns but that employees would be subjected neither to pressure to contribute nor to reprisals for refusing to participate. An employee required to testify as a witness in official or private court proceedings was to be granted leave, pay, and expenses, depending on the type of litigation involved and the nature of his appearance.[52] Clauses covering such eventualities appeared in 30 to 36 percent of the contracts in the 1973 BLS study.[53]

F. CONDITIONS OF WORK

Contracts increasingly have detailed the terms governing a variety of working conditions, such as lunch periods, cleanup time, rest periods, and time for stowing tools and equipment. The Bureau of Labor Statistics 1965 study found rest periods of 10 to 15 minutes in 4 percent of contracts, clothing allowances in 5 percent, and cleanup time in 18 percent.[54] The corresponding frequencies in the 1973 BLS study were 38 percent, 40 percent, and 38 percent, respectively.[55]

Safety measures, an essential ingredient of good working conditions, have received increasing attention also, particularly in the blue-collar agreements. Typical of safety clauses found in contracts is the following provision from a Navy agreement:

"No employee shall be required to work on or about moving or operating machines or in areas where conditions exist that are unsafe or detrimental to health without proper precautions, protective

---

[52] U.S. Department of the Navy, Naval Weapons Center, China Lake, Calif., *Agreement*, 1970, Art. XVII, Secs. 1-7.

[53] Voting arrangements, 36 percent; jury-duty provisions, 35 percent; charity-drive clauses, 30 percent.

[54] U.S. Department of Labor, BLS Bulletin No. 1451, *op. cit.*, p. 17.

[55] *Ibid.*, BLS Bulletin No. 1789, pp. 19-21.

equipment, and safety devices determined to be necessary by the Shipyard Safety Division." [56]

According to the Navy agreement, no workman is to be permitted to work alone or beyond the call or observation of other employees if the work is deemed hazardous. If the employee believes the work is dangerous to his health, the supervisor is required to inspect the job before assigning duties. If doubt remains, the supervisor must refer the problem to the Shipyard Safety Division for further guidance. [57] The 1965 Langley Research Center agreement formally granted the employee the right to refuse alleged unsafe work until a final decision was made by the appropriate safety officer.[58] A common safety feature of the more advanced contracts is assumption by the employer of the responsibility for furnishing necessary protective clothing and equipment. The Langley contract made first-aid training available to employees, required first-aid kits in each shop, and made provision for increased medical treatment in the more serious cases. It also provided that on the day of injury there was to be no loss in pay or charge to annual or sick leave. It even went so far as to declare that the lack of air conditioning was detrimental to efficiency and that the employer would make every reasonable effort to make work areas comfortable and would discuss with the unions the actions necessary to achieve this end.[59]

By mid-1964, according to the Bureau of Labor Statistics, approximately a third of federal contracts contained safety provisions, ranging from simple policy statements of union-management cooperation to detailed safety committee provisions.[60] The frequency of safety clauses increased rapidly thereafter. By late 1971 overall policy statements were found in 18 percent of contracts, up from 5 percent.[61]

Perhaps the most important development in occupational safety has been the establishment of joint safety committees, which were provided for in 58 percent of the contracts in the 1971 BLS sample.[62] These committees serve primarily as watchdogs, meeting periodically to discuss safety problems with employer and union representatives and to make recommendations

[56] U.S. Department of the Navy, Charleston Naval Shipyard, *Agreement*, 1968, Art. XX, Sec. 5.
[57] *Ibid.*
[58] NASA, Langley Research Center, *Agreement*, 1965, Art. XIII, Sec. 2.
[59] *Ibid.*, Art. XIII, Secs. 4-7.
[60] U.S. Department of Labor, BLS Bulletin No. 1451, *op. cit.*, p. 20.
[61] *Ibid.*, BLS Bulletin No. 1789, pp. 23-25.
[62] *Ibid.*, pp. 25, 26.

to the employer for their resolution. The 1968 Charleston Naval Shipyard contract, for example, provided for a safety planning committee consisting of the Shipyard commander, his designated representatives, and a Metal Trades Council safety committee composed of five members, including the Council safety representative. The planning committee was to meet monthly. A corrective procedure was established for settling safety disputes through a system of appeals. Council representatives were counseled to be alert in the course of their daily work for unsafe practices, equipment, and conditions, including environmental conditions, that represented industrial health hazards. The first step in the dispute-settlement procedure was discussion by the shop steward and the immediate supervisor. Resolution was next to be attempted by the chief shop steward and the shop head. The third step called for referral to the safety division head and the Council safety representative, who were to meet with the shop head and the steward to review the matter. Disputes still unsettled were to be brought before the safety planning committee for final determination. Council representatives were to receive full pay for time spent at safety meetings.[63]

Working conditions clauses range from the general to the very detailed, according to the needs of the particular bargaining unit. General provisions require the employer to bear the full expense of special tools, clothing, and equipment. An example of an exceptionally detailed approach is provided by the 1968 Charleston Naval Shipyard agreement, which covered the following matters: provision of food on remote assignments, assignment of reserved parking spaces to handicapped employees, furnishing of transportation for the treatment of occupational illnesses, participation by the union in cafeteria administration, and provision of adequate protective clothing and special safety equipment.[64] One contract went so far as to assure that the employer would request a draft deferment for any apprentice in the unit who maintained satisfactory grades and shop performance.[65] Another listed the factors for determining the "effective" temperature, that is, the temperature calculated from the thermometer, relative humidity, rate of air movement, and heat radiation from the sun. When the effective temperature reached 85 degrees, workers with known heart conditions would cease manual labor; when it reached 88 degrees, all

---

[63] U.S. Department of the Navy, Charleston Naval Shipyard, *Agreement*, 1968, Art. XXI, Secs. 1-3.
[64] *Ibid.*, Art. XXXI, Secs, 2-8, 13, 14.
[65] NASA, Langley Research Center, *Agreement*, 1965, Art. XVI, Sec. 8.

would discontinue heavy manual labor and take frequent breaks, usually 10 minutes per hour. Workers incapacitated by work-related injuries or illnesses were to receive only light duty where possible. The employer agreed to appraise and improve health services on the base.[66]

G. UNION PRESENCE

The provisions of the Kennedy order granting recognition and negotiating rights to unions also enhanced their status in their dealings with management. The special position granted unions with exclusive recognition was formalized in contract clauses which helped insure the maintenance of that position. Among such clauses were provisions authorizing leave for union activities, giving unions special status in the new wage-fixing procedures,[67] and, especially, enabling union representatives to perform the day-to-day activities necessary to their representation functions and to solidify the union's exclusive status. Since union security measures common in private industry were not permitted under the EMC program, government-employee unions worked within the order's limitations to strengthen their position with both management and employees. They accomplished this primarily through contractual guarantees of representation and visitation rights and the establishment of procedures to carry on union business and publicize the union's function.

Both the Kennedy and Nixon orders strictly differentiated between official and unofficial union business. Agreements generally paraphrased Section 9 of the Kennedy order restricting certain activities on government time. By 1971, almost 60 percent of the BLS contract sample followed the 1963 NFFE accord, which stated:

> "In the interests of efficient conduct of Government business and economical use of government time, and in order to draw a reasonable distinction between official and non-official activities, those activities concerned with internal union business, membership meetings, solicitation of membership, dues, campaigning for union offices, conduct of elections for union offices and distribution of literature will be conducted outside of regular working hours." [68]

The government has taken a positive attitude toward official relations between management and labor. Strong blue-collar unions

---

[66] U.S. Department of the Air Force, San Antonio Air Materiel Area, Kelly Air Force Base, *Memorandum of Agreement*, 1971, Art. XXVII, Secs. 6-8.

[67] See Chapter XIX.

[68] U.S. Department of the Army, *Agreement*, between Army Pictorial Center, Long Island City, N.Y., and NFFE, Local 1106, 1963, Par. 5.

took the first steps in organizing formal union/management relations, and were followed by white-collar unions and unions newly involved in organizing the blue-collar trades. Many contracts fixed specific times at periodic intervals for both sides to discuss negotiable items. In the more advanced accords, for example, the 1968 Charleston Naval Shipyard agreement, it was provided that upon the request of either party meetings would be called promptly to resolve such issues as might arise. This contract further provided for a great many privileges calculated to strengthen the union's position. Records were to be kept of all meetings; union officers and stewards were to receive copies of management instructions, notices, and pertinent memoranda and were to be apprised of all current, pending, and predicted changes in shipyard workloads. Space on bulletin boards was alloted for exclusive union use in publicizing the purpose, date, time, and place of its recreational and social activities, union elections, appointments, and meetings. Other materials could be posted by mutual agreement between the employer and the union, but management reserved the right to review submitted postings. This gave management some protection against misuse of bulletin boards, while leaving the union in a more favorable position than it had enjoyed under many earlier agreements.[69]

Of utmost importance are the clauses governing union rights of representation and visitation. In almost 100 percent of the contracts in the 1973 BLS study there were provisions governing the work of stewards and union representatives. One half of these accords afforded visitation rights to nonemployee union officers.[70] In essence, union-rights provisions fix the number of representatives and define their duties and privileges. The Pearl Harbor Naval Shipyard accord, effective through 1972, formally stated the need to recognize Metal Trades Council representatives in appropriate levels and areas for the proper administration of the agreement. The administration and interpretation of the accord, as well as day-to-day union-management relations, were conducted through the president of the Metal Trades Council and the head of the Employee Relations Division. Meetings were to be held once a month or more frequently between the Shipyard commander or his representatives and a five-member Council committee to discuss appropriate matters. Stewards and chief stewards were to be

---

[69] U.S. Department of the Navy, Charleston Naval Shipyard, *Agreement*, 1968, Art. III, Secs. 1, 2, 4-9. See also U.S. Department of Labor, *op. cit.*, p. 53, in which it was stated that 78 percent of the accords studied allowed for some union-affairs publicity.

[70] U.S. Department of Labor, *op. cit.*, pp. 54-58.

appointed at a ratio of one to every 100 employees on each shift in every shop or department. Five additional stewards could be appointed if the MTC deemed it necessary. The Council could designate representatives to handle matters above the shop group or division level. Up-to-date lists of all the aforesaid stewards, officers, and representatives were to be supplied and maintained by the Council.[71]

Management's approach has often shown a positive and accommodating attitude in facilitating union activities. At Pearl Harbor all stewards and committeemen were allowed reasonable time off without loss of pay to carry out their responsibilities. Reasonable time off during regular hours was afforded for the preparation of agendas for the meetings with the employer. Representatives were permitted to leave their work areas and enter other areas, and supervisors were required to give priority to their requests to move about. Special considerations governed the work assignments of shop stewards, and, in recognition of the need to keep each union representative in the same unit with the men he represented, the transfer of stewards from one shop, workshift, or workweek to another was barred unless compelled by work commitments.[72]

As in most defense installation contracts, management at the Pearl Harbor Naval Shipyard agreed to provide space for union meetings and for filing materials.[73] It also granted reserved parking privileges to the Council on the basis of one place for each affiliated local union.[74] General union visitation rights were assured by a clause that required the yard to make all necessary arrangements for authorized representatives of affiliated unions to visit the shipyard at reasonable times to conduct appropriate business.[75] The 1968 Charleston agreement even enumerated procedures to insure the appointment of acting stewards for sea-trial runs and temporary duty stations.[76] The contract flatly encouraged management officials to cooperate in all authorized union activities.[77]

These provisions taken together place the union in a preferred position that increases the likelihood of its retention as unit rep-

[71] U.S. Department of the Navy, Pearl Harbor Naval Shipyard, *Agreement,* 1970, Art. III, Secs. 1-5.

[72] *Ibid.,* Art. III, Secs. 6-10.

[73] *Ibid.,* Art. III, Sec. 11.

[74] *Ibid.,* Art. XXIII, Sec. 8.

[75] *Ibid.,* Art. III, Sec. 12.

[76] U.S. Department of the Navy, Charleston Naval Shipyard, *Agreement,* 1968, Art. IV, Sec. 12.

[77] *Ibid.,* Art. VI, Sec. 11.

resentative. They serve as a substitute for the stabilizing influence which the union shop or other forms of union security forbidden in the federal service afford in private labor relations. Every contract clause which enhances the image of the union as the sole employee representative contributes to this end. One of the most effective provisions is the clause that allows the union to be present at discussions between the employer and individual employees, who may not be union members. This union privilege is claimed whenever the subject matter deals with grievances and personnel policies and practices affecting the general working conditions for which the union must bargain and assume a major responsibility.[78] Thus the union member is assured of representation while the nonmember is made to realize that his problem can be dealt with only within the context of the collective agreement.

In the 1970 Pearl Harbor agreement the position of the union was buttressed by the shipyard's agreement to inform all newly hired employees, as part of their job orientation, of the role of the exclusively recognized union. Orientation for new employees was also to include introduction to the chief steward during the first two weeks on the job, and the latter was permitted to give the new man a private briefing on the contractual relationship at the installation.[79]

Steps such as these—even something as simple as permitting union officials to wear identifying decals on their helmets [80]—are of great psychological importance to the unions. The effectiveness of such measures, taken at the early stages of employment, depends to a great extent upon the attitude of the employer. Many employers tend to maintain an attitude of strict neutrality, as they would toward competing organizations or toward unionism versus nonunionism. This principle of neutrality, imbedded in Civil Service Commission guidelines, was intended to apply essentially to situations preceding the recognition of an exclusive bargaining agent. Its projection into situations where an exclusive agent has been recognized runs counter to the concept of recognition, a fact which some employing officials do not appear to understand. It nevertheless remains true that the manner in which orientation programs are conducted reflects the particular employer's attitude towards the recognized union.

---

[78] U.S. Department of the Navy, Pearl Harbor Naval Shipyard, *Agreement*, 1970, Art. II, Sec. 4 (c) .

[79] *Ibid.*, Art. XXIII, Sec. 1; Art. III, Sec. 6.

[80] *Ibid.*, Art. III, Sec. 6.

The use of official time for union activities was the subject of considerable controversy under E.O. 11491. As already noted, both the Kennedy and the Nixon order prohibited the use of government time for purely internal union affairs such as organizational drives, dues collection, meetings, and so forth. Section 9 of the Kennedy order, however, permitted the use of official time for consultations and meetings with recognized organizations "whenever practicable." For years, therefore, accords made extensive provision for· such activities. It was left to the individual agency to insist, if it so desired, that negotiations be conducted during the nonduty hours of the union representatives.[81] As a result, contracts varied considerably until the Nixon order dispelled any doubts on the issue by flatly prohibiting employees, as union representatives, from using "official time when negotiating an agreement with agency management."[82]

Unions viewed this provision as a serious backward step. The Government Employes' Council reflected labor's attitude when it testified before the Federal Labor Relations Council prior to the issuance of E.O. 11616. It advocated the granting of administrative leave for union participants officially involved in unit determination, hearings, unfair labor practice hearings, and bargaining deadlocks. The Nixon order policy was termed "punitive, repressive," and an "unnecessary impediment to attaining satisfactory labor relations." [83]

But the Federal Labor Relations Council concluded that the results of this provision were both good and bad. Among its unfavorable effects were the difficulty of scheduling sessions and "delays in completing negotiations because of a union's inability to provide representation." Its benefits were found in better advance preparations for negotiations and greater efficiency in using meeting time.[84] On balance, the Council believed that a return to the use of some official time for negotiations would be most salutary. A modification of the Nixon policy to permit a limited, reasonable use of the official time of the parties would "enlarge the scope of negotiations and promote responsible collective bargaining." However, such use was to be expressly limited "to maintain a rea-

---

[81] E.O. 10988, Sec. 9.
[82] E.O. 11491, Sec. 20.
[83] Government Employes' Council, AFL-CIO, *Statement to the Federal Labor Relations Council on E.O. 11491,* October 7, 1970, pp. 4, 5.
[84] Federal Labor Relations Council, *Labor-Management Relations in the Federal Service, Amendments to E.O. 11491 With Report and Recommendations,* Washington, August 1971, p. 11.

sonable policy with respect to union self-support and an incentive to economical and businesslike bargaining practices." [85]

The entire issue was viewed as a proper subject for negotiation. The Council, however, recommended that limitations on the use of official time should be in alternative forms, either a maximum of 40 hours or a maximum of one half the total time spent on bargaining during duty hours. Such limitations applied to duty hours used by union representatives not only for negotiations but also for preliminary preparations, mediation, and impasse resolution if necessary. It was clear that overtime, premium pay, or travel expenses were not authorized. It was specified that the number of union representatives ordinarily should not exceed the number of management negotiators.[86] Almost all of these recommendations were incorporated in Section 20 of E.O. 11616.

Executive Order 11616 served to lessen friction and practical difficulty in an area already fraught with disagreement. It allowed unions to preserve and advance the privileges achieved since 1962 that enhanced their effectiveness as exclusive bargaining agents. The amendments apparently succeeded, for when the Council reviewed the issue again in 1975 it concluded that no radical changes in policy were warranted. Strong evidence indicated less conflict over official-time disputes and substantially less use of the maximum time permitted for negotiations under E.O. 11616. Both sides seemed contented with the Assistant Secretary's elimination of financial losses previously incurred by employees when they served as hearing witnesses or election observers. The FLRC concluded that "the existing policies on official time have, on balance, stimulated the businesslike conduct of labor relations while minimizing financial hardships on individual employees and should be retained without modification." [87]

---

[85] *Ibid.*
[86] *Ibid.*
[87] Federal Labor Relations Council, *Labor-Management Relations in the Federal Service, Amendments to E.O. 11491 With Report and Recommendations,* Washington, February 1975, pp. 73-77.

CHAPTER XI

THE CHECKOFF AGREEMENTS

The withholding of union dues is closely related to the union security issue. With the union shop forbidden by both E.O. 10988 and E.O. 11491, it was not surprising that federal employee unions brought pressure to bear to have the checkoff of union dues broadly adopted in government agencies. The practice already was common in state and local government contracts as well as in private industry.

State and local jurisdictions with dues checkoff provisions followed the lead of the Taft-Hartley Act governing private industry by insisting that dues withholding be voluntary. A written authorization typically is required of each individual employee, who retains the right to revoke the withholding authority, generally after a specified period of time. This limitation, however, has failed to inhibit the widespread use of dues withholding in the public service. In the early 1960s Arnold Zander, president of the American Federation of State, County and Municipal Employees, noted that over 80 percent of AFSCME's membership was on checkoff—an early indication of the mounting cooperation of governments in the growth of public unionism.[1] The Kennedy Task Force confirmed this development, commenting, in addition, that checkoff was included in 71 percent of the major accords in private industry. The Task Force recognized checkoff as an important means of insuring the stability of union membership and of freeing union leaders for more pressing duties.[2] This sentiment was expressed in substantially the same form in the reports of the Johnson and Nixon study groups.[3]

---

[1] Arnold Zander, *Letter*, to National Civil Service League, June 20, 1960, p. 6.

[2] President's Task Force on Employee-Management Relations in the Federal Service, *Report*, November 30, 1961, p. 21.

[3] President's Review Committee on Employee-Management Relations in the Federal Service, *Draft Report*, April 1968, in U.S. Department of Labor, *56th Annual Report, 1969, Attachment B*, pp. 48-49; President's Study Committee, *Report and Recommendations on Labor-Management Relations in the Federal Service*, August 1969, pp. 55-56.

Such official endorsements notwithstanding, the Federal Government lagged far behind other sectors in accepting the checkoff.[4] The Kennedy Task Force noted that this was one of the most frequent issues raised by unions at its hearings. It believed that the lag was due to prevalent interpretations of federal statutes that prohibited payroll deductions unless specifically authorized by law. Of the federal agencies, only the Tennessee Valley Authority and the Bonneville Power Administration permitted dues withholding. They could do so because their statutory authority was broad enough to allow personnel activities beyond the usual proscriptions, a freedom not then afforded the remainder of the federal establishment.[5] Because of these restrictions, the Task Force recommended that voluntary dues withholding be permitted, with costs borne by the recipient organization, if authorized by Congress.[6]

The Kennedy order did not contain a checkoff provision. This was in line with the intent of the Task Force to fashion a program which could be implemented completely by presidential action. It is important to note that the restricting statutory factor was cited by those who helped formulate the program as one of the major obstructions to founding an independent central authority or "board" for its administration. They believed that existing Civil Service Commission and Labor Department facilities were more than ample to fulfill the proposed tasks, and that a new agency with its large appropriations for personnel and machinery would require full congressional action. Essentially the same reasoning was reflected in the 1967 and 1969 reviews of the EMC program.

Before Congress acted on the checkoff issue, Comptroller General Joseph Campbell ruled in January 1963 that authority already existed permitting the CSC to authorize agencies to make dues payroll deductions just as deductions were made for the payment of income taxes.[7] President Kennedy then requested the Commission to:

> "initiate the necessary action to develop regulations, standards and
> procedures to permit departments and agencies to operate a system

---

[4] A questionnaire survey conducted in early 1961 disclosed how the incidence of checkoff increased at each lower level of government. Only two of 21 federal agencies answering provided the service. However, 12 of 25 state governments and 37 of 51 cities responding permitted dues withholding. See Murray B. Nesbitt, "The Civil Service Merit System and Collective Bargaining" (unpublished Ph.D. dissertation, Graduate School of Public Administration, New York University, 1962), p. 232.

[5] Task Force Report op. cit.

[6] Ibid., Sec. H, pp. v, 21.

[7] See Government Employee Relations Report, No. 4 (1963), pp. A-6, F-1-F-4; and Public Law 87-304, Secs. 5, 6 (September 26, 1961).

of voluntary withholding of employee organization dues for members who elect to pay dues in this fashion. In developing these instructions the withholding of dues should be viewed as a service that the departments and agencies may provide to employee organizations that have been granted formal or exclusive recognition." [8]

CSC Chairman Macy proceeded to appoint a group which drafted a proposed procedure for a voluntary system of union dues withholding. The draft procedure was studied by a prominent union committee appointed by AFL-CIO president Meany.[9] There was considerable disagreement over the costs of setting up and maintaining the program, the inclusion of temporary employees, and the discretion to be given to individual agencies in implementing the plan.[10]

Setting a deadline of January 1, 1964, for implementing the procedure, the CSC issued its final regulations on voluntary dues checkoff. It was anticipated that initially about 500,000 employees would fall under the new checkoff provisions. The rules permitted the agencies considerable flexibility in granting checkoff to unions with formal or exclusive recognition at the local or national levels.[11] According to Macy,

> "Dues withholding must be entirely voluntary on the part of employees, be based on individual authorization, and permit employees to revoke the authorization at six-month intervals. The cost of dues withholding is paid by the employee organization and not by the Government. A standard fee in the amount of two cents for each deduction has been established to cover the cost of this service." [12]

Action was immediately taken on the plan. The Department of the Interior and the Department of Defense were the first agencies to adopt regulations permitting the checkoff for qualified organizations,[13] but it was the Post Office Department in December 1963 that was the first major agency to conclude a "Memorandum of Understanding" providing the checkoff service. The memoran-

---

[8] Office of the President, *Memorandum*, May 21, 1963.

[9] The Committee was chaired by Andrew J. Beimiller, Director, Department of Legislation, AFL-CIO and included John F. Griner, American Federation of Government Employees; B. A. Gritta and Clayton W. Bilderback, Metal Trades Department; E. C. Hallbeck, United Federation of Postal Clerks; Jerome J. Keating, National Association of Letter Carriers; and William H. Ryan, International Association of Machinists.

[10] *Government Employee Relations Report*, No. 3 (1963) pp. A-10, A-11.

[11] U.S. Civil Service Commission, *Federal Employees Pay Regulations*, Part 25, Subpart F, and FPM Letter No. 550-5, October 10, 1963.

[12] John W. Macy, Jr., *Letter to the President*, January 17, 1964.

[13] U.S. Department of the Interior, *Memorandum on Voluntary Allotments for the Payment of Dues to Employee Organizations*, November 13, 1963; U.S. Department of Defense, *Directive 1426.4—Voluntary Allotments for Payment of Dues to Employee Organizations*, November 27, 1963.

dum covered the 13 employee organizations then granted exclusive or formal recognition at the national level.[14]

The movement quickly gathered momentum. Between January and late summer of 1964, 37 agreements incorporated dues checkoff procedures. Some of these were concluded even before the CSC regulations were issued with the understanding that they would go into effect when officially permissible.

As finally promulgated by the CSC, dues checkoff regulations were not fully satisfactory to the unions, which believed that an employee's authorization should be effective for at least a year, as was the case in the private sector. The CSC standards provided that employees could withdraw their voluntary authorizations twice yearly, six months apart.

Checkoff was not to be considered a matter of right, and thus fell within the definition of a negotiable issue. This was due to the CSC's directive that dues withholding had to "be viewed as a service that the departments and agencies may provide to employee organizations." [15] Checkoff therefore remained a matter of choice for each agency. Moreover, CSC rules dictated that before an employee could authorize dues allotments, there had to be a mutual arrangement in writing, within the framework of CSC instructions, between the agency and the employee organization to insure the smooth functioning of the dues-allotment program.[16] Since extensive requirements had been laid down for implementation of the checkoff, the issue became an essential bargaining point.

As a result of the discretion given agencies, checkoff provisions have taken many forms. In some contracts, dues withholding is conducted in accordance with Commission regulations, while in others it is governed by extensive administrative procedures. In essence, however, the detailed contracts paraphrased the *Federal Personnel Manual* and agency directives issued in accordance with CSC policy. In the 1966 Defense Printing Service contract with the Lithographers and Photoengravers it was agreed that voluntary allotment procedures would follow agency directives and instructions, which made the unions primarily responsible for the administrative and cost burdens. Thus, the union had to explain the voluntary nature of the program to employees, pay for and distribute the allotment forms prescribed by the Comp-

---

[14] U.S. Post Office Department, *Regional Letter,* Subject: Dues Withholding, RL Na 63-194, December 13, 1963.

[15] U.S. Civil Service Commission, *Federal Personnel Manual,* Part 550.

[16] *Ibid.*

troller General, deliver them to the agency, and pay two cents for each deduction.[17] The administrative details of the checkoff procedure proliferated in the IAM, NAGE, and Metal Trades Council contracts, which accounted for a large proportion of defense installation agreements.[18] In many instances the checkoff became the subject of supplementary agreements spelling out specific union and management responsibilities.[19]

The remarkable growth of checkoff provisions has been described by a CSC report prepared to meet union and management information needs, It disclosed that as of January 1968 there were 1,762 union dues-withholding contracts; 811,336 federal employees had voluntarily authorized the checkoff of union dues. Projecting the annual amount of monies to be withheld for the calendar year 1968 by simple multiplication, the total reached an imposing $23,268,000, and for a number of reasons the eventual amount deducted would be greater still. Union cost for the deductions totaled only about $300,000.[20]

Among the interesting points noted by the CSC dues checkoff survey was the great disparity in organization strength that existed between the AFL-CIO affiliated and independent unions. Whereas the AFL-CIO affiliates collected over $18,108,000 under 1,268 contracts, the independents received only $5,159,000 under 494 contracts.[21] Thus, although the EMC program was designed to permit all organizations to make their way, up till 1974 the established unions successfully had maintained their leadership position throughout the government service.[22]

When the issue of dues withholding came before the President's Review Committee in 1967, it was again related to the union security question. George Meany, speaking for the AFL-CIO and strongly supported by the individual affiliated unions, stated that union security agreements should be permitted. He

17 U.S. Department of Defense, *Agreement and Letter of Understanding*, between Printing Service-Navy Publications and Printing Service Office, Washington, and Lithographers and Photoengravers International Union, Local 98-L, AFL-CIO, 1966, Art. XII.

18 U.S. Department of the Navy, *Agreement*, Between Pearl Harbor Naval Shipyard and Honolulu, Hawaii Metal Trades Council, 1964, Art. VII, Secs. 1-9. Renegotiated to date.

19 U.S. Department of the Interior, *Supplementary Agreement No. 3*, between Bonneville Power Administration and AFGE, Lodge 928, 1964. Renegotiated to date.

20 U.S. Civil Service Commission, Office of Labor-Management Relations, *Voluntary Union Dues Allotments in the Federal Government 1968* (Washington, 1969), pp. iii, 8.

21 *Ibid.*, p. 49.

22 U.S. Civil Service Commission, Office of Labor-Management Relations, *Union Recognition in the Federal Government, Statistical Report*, Nov. 1974 (Washington, March 1975), p. 23.

saw no constitutional or legal bar to their negotiation. He called essentially for acceptance of the union shop or the agency shop, thus bringing to the federal level the demands increasingly faced by state and local governments. Meany declared:

"The dues checkoff is already in effect for union members where formal or exclusive recognition exists. It is entirely appropriate for negotiated agreements to specify that those workers in the covered unit shall become dues paying union members or shall support the union with regularly checked-off payments equal to the regular union dues." [23]

Meany's only specific recommendation to improve the checkoff practice was that the revocation period be changed from six months to one year. This was a clear indication of federal-union satisfaction with the system—no surprise, considering the effectiveness of the collections. According to Meany, experience showed "little or no dissatisfaction"; so it was "clearly unnecessary to have a revocation period twice a year." [24]

Although the Review Committee was not prepared to incorporate either the union shop or the agency shop into the federal program, it was quite willing to accept the one-year revocation period. Like the AFL-CIO it considered the checkoff as part of the union security issue, but it declined to comment on the broad recommendations submitted for more far-reaching union security provisions. Nevertheless, it recognized the "value of union security measures in producing stable labor-management relations" and saw their use as enabling labor organizations to devote their efforts to the establishment of constructive relationships. [25]

In the last analysis, the only union security technique that the Committee would countenance for the program was dues withholding. The checkoff was credited with bringing stability, status, and maturity to federal labor organizations, and was the only form of union security to be "strengthened and improved at this time." [26]

The Review Committee proposed that CSC regulations be amended to permit exclusive unions to negotiate accords with only an annual revocation for dues checkoff. Revocation also would occur if the Union's recognition was terminated or if the employee left the unit or was expelled or suspended from the labor organization. Organizations with formal recognition or na-

---

[23] George Meany, *Statement*, before President's Review Committee, October 23, 1967, p. 13.
[24] *Ibid.*, p. 15.
[25] Review Committee, *op. cit.*, p. 48
[26] *Ibid*, p. 49.

tional consultation rights were still to be held to the six-month revocation rule.[27]

The Nixon Study Committee was not as impressed by the
AFL-CIO recommendations as its predecessor. Opting for the status quo, it urged that employees continue to be allowed to revoke
their authorizations at six-month intervals. The other conditions
for revocation suggested by the Johnson Committee were incorporated in the Study Committee Report[28] and implemented by
E.O. 11491. In addition, the Nixon order authorized voluntary
dues allotments for management and supervisory officials if permitted by agency agreements with their respective professional
associations.[29]

When the program came under review by the Federal Labor
Relations Council in 1970, several recommendations were made
to revise the dues-withholding policy. With informal and formal
recognition eliminated from the national program, some suggested that dues checkoff be permitted regardless of recognition.
Others believed that unions with secured national consultation
rights should be permitted checkoff.[30] The Council, however, continued to limit dues withholding privileges to exclusively recognized organizations.

One major innovation recommended by the Council was
achieved by Section 21 of E.O. 11616. The recovery of costs for
processing voluntary allotments was changed from a directive into
a proper subject for collective bargaining. E.O. 11491 had mandated that all accords for checkoff contain a provision obliging
the agency to recover the costs of making deductions. The Council believed that such a uniform policy was no longer desirable:
the checkoff service charge had become "a meaningful economic
item suitable for bargaining between the parties in the same way
as other matters governing the labor-management relationship."
An agency could agree to make no service charge at all or accept
a charge below actual costs if other benefits achieved in the contract warranted such action.[31] On the other hand, an agency
might insist upon a higher rate for the deductions. In the absence
of strict controlling regulations on this point, an agency could
calculate its costs as it saw fit, raising them well above the two-
cent deduction if it desired.

---

[27] *Ibid.*

[28] Study Committee, *op. cit.*, pp. 55-56.

[29] E.O. 11491, Sec. 21 (a) , (b) .

[30] Federal Labor Relations Council, *Report and Recommendations on Labor-Management Relations in the Federal Service,* June 1971, p. 15.

[31] *Ibid.*, pp. 12-13.

While the benefits of the checkoff system have been amply demonstrated by the federal experience,[32] other forms of union security remain untested at the federal level. There is little expectation that the government will radically change its conservative approach to the union security issue. Accordingly, the union shop and the agency shop remain very much in the future.

In the Council's 1975 review the union concept of checkoff again confronted the federal view. Labor sought a uniform, overall policy that would continue dues withholding during contract renegotiations. Unions felt their bargaining threatened by the constant possibility of management stopping checkoff privileges pending arrival at a new agreement. In line with E.O. 11616 policy, the Council chose to keep dues withholding "subject to the dynamics of negotiations." Rejecting the idea of uniform agency prescriptions during this critical period, the FLRC concluded that the experience and expertise gained by the parties over the years would insure responsible bargaining over checkoff substance and procedures.[33] The federal policy of complete checkoff negotiation was accordingly unaltered by the Ford order. It remains a powerful factor in the collective bargaining process.

---

[32] By late 1971, 68 percent of the accords examined by the BLS authorized the checkoff. See *Collective Bargaining Agreements in the Federal Service, Late 1971*, BLS Bulletin No. 1789, April 1973, pp. 54, 58-60.

[33] Federal Labor Relations Council, *Report and Recommendations on Labor-Management Relations in the Federal Service*, February 1975, pp. 68-69. See also *Government Employee Relations Report*, No. 592 (1975) p. A-16.

CHAPTER XII

UNION PARTICIPATION IN PERSONNEL MANAGEMENT

In the Federal Government the traditional approach to personnel management held that a scientific and relatively impersonal system of administration, if efficiently carried out, contained within itself the solution to the difficulties of the civil servant. It also held that since many of the benefits fought for so vigorously in private industry were provided by law in government service, public employees would follow personnel directives with greater harmony and acquiescence. It was quite the opposite psychological impulse, however, which lay behind the organization of public employee unions and the negotiation of collective bargaining agreements for federal workers.

The underlying need of employees to participate collectively in deciding personnel policy has long been recognized. According to O. Glenn Stahl:

"A union is something belonging to the employee. What it seeks and what it does is a part of him. It provides a feeling of identification with the securing of certain personnel objectives that is not present when the solution to personnel policies—even when they are highly acceptable—is handed to the workers by management. Employees want to do some things for themselves, no matter how enlightened an organization's personnel administration is." [1]

The EMC program nurtured this employee desire, which led, ultimately, to greater union involvement in personnel administration.

From the traditional executive's point of view the conduct of personnel matters was a managerial prerogative. In the discussion of management rights in Chapter IX it was pointed out that the management-rights clause, required in federal contracts by CSC regulations, retained management control over direction, promo-

---

[1] O. Glenn Stahl, *Public Personnel Administration*, (5th Ed.; New York: Harper & Row, 1962), p. 225.

tion, transfer, demotion, and other personnel matters relating to federal employees. Such control was declared necessary to maintain efficiency and to carry out the mission of the agency. Required "subject" clauses relegated the agreement to a subordinate position in relation to existing and future agency rules and regulations.[2] The federal contracts negotiated most recently have to some extent sidestepped "subject" clauses by calling for consultation over new departmental rules whenever suggested rule changes might involve the terms of the negotiated agreement. Agreements now tend to emulate the former Post Office Department agreement, which provided that wherever conflicts occurred between the contract and the agency personnel manual, the contract was to govern.

Items pertaining to working conditions, time, and pay are among the most important of union bargaining objectives in the federal service. But in addition to these, under the EMC program there has been increased union participation in such personnel areas as promotions and assignments, reductions in force, rehiring, job descriptions and ratings, interstation transfers, apprentice programs, and training. Only those clauses most representative of the general trend toward union involvement are examined below.

A. PROMOTIONS AND ASSIGNMENTS

Within the guidelines set down by CSC regulations, the more advanced contracts contain a variety of arrangements on the policies and procedures governing promotions and assignments. Sixty-five percent of the contracts reported by the BLS in 1973 had clauses governing the promotion process.[3] Some of these clauses were very specific as to the precise procedures both for promotion and for union participation in the promotion process.

Recent contracts have incorporated detailed assurances of union representation. For example, the AFGE contracts with the Air Force, the Labor Department, and the Bonneville Power Administration contained strong provisions governing promotion, merit staffing, and reassignment. The AFGE agreement through 1973 at the San Antonio Air Materiel Area declared:

"In order to reduce employee dissatisfactions in the promotion system and to build employee confidence in its operation, it is essential that the Union be involved in promotion actions to the ex-

---

[2] E.O. 11491, Section 12(a), as previously noted, did protect agreements during their current term from agency regulation changes that were not required by law or higher authority.

[3] U.S. Department of Labor, Bureau of Labor Statistics, *Collective Bargaining Agreements in the Federal Service, Late 1971*, BLS Bulletin No. 1789, April 1973, pp. 36-40.

tent that it may reassure all employees that they have received fair and impartial consideration. Not only will the Union's presence allow employees to place more assurance in the promotion plan, but it should limit the number of formal, protracted, inquiries required by the filing of formal grievance and equal employment complaints. With the foregoing in mind, the parties agree that when designated by employees, Union representatives will be permitted to post audit the records used as a basis for screening and ranking the employee." [4]

The Labor Department accord with AFGE Local 12 in the Washington Area was a renewal of one of the first agreements in the federal program. Extremely detailed, it contained a 14-page merit-staffing provision—the longest in the contract—introduced by a special preamble emphasizing the dual responsibilities of the parties for administering the merit-staffing program.[5] In addition to referring to the CSC's Federal Merit Promotion Policy, found in Chapter 335 of the *Federal Personnel Manual,* which formed the basis of the Labor Department's merit system, the accord incorporated extensive provisions for implementing the program. Union participation was assured by the requirement that the union be supplied with copies of all advertised vacancies, certifications, and selection lists. Local 12 was to be advised of the qualifications for positions. It was to cooperate with management in finding alternatives to the Federal Service Entrance Examination for unit employees seeking beginning professional positions. Local 12 representatives could be present at performance evaluations of employees by their supervisors. The union was to be consulted on the naming of impartial persons to the lists from which merit-staffing panels were to be drawn.

In addition, the AFGE agreement made provision for union review of merit-staffing actions. The union had the right to request an examination of the record if it believed that a violation of the merit-staffing article had taken place. Review of a merit-staffing action could be initiated by either the union or the department in question and was to be conducted at employee-management meetings below the departmental level. The authority to decide cases was clearly delineated. Departmental meetings on specific merit actions were to be resorted to only when necessary to emphasize broad problems which either party was presenting.

Union concern over the reassignment of employees within a unit was expressed in a different form in the AFGE-Bonneville

[4] U.S. Department of the Air Force, *Memorandum of Agreement,* between San Antonio Air Materiel Area, Kelly Air Force Base, Texas, and AFGE, Local 1617, 1970, Art. XVI Sec. 5.

[5] U.S. Department of Labor, *Agreements,* between Labor Department, Washington Area, and AFGE Lodge 12, 1970, Art. XI Secs. A, D, E, F.

Power Administration agreement. Conceding the union's interest in reassignments, the BPA agreed that before appointing an employee to a primary vacancy, it would inform the union of the circumstances surrounding the appointment and would give it 10 days to present its position.[6]

In the areas of promotion, work assignments, and reductions in force, unions are striving to obtain the same goals and policies that are found in private labor relations. The more advanced federal contracts are invariably concerned with the traditional doctrines of promotion from within and seniority. They specify procedures for permanent promotions after temporary appointments and for the fullest union cooperation and participation in the entire promotion process.

High on the list of union priorities is a policy of promotion from within. The promotion clause in the 1968 Charleston Naval Shipyard agreement was representative of the more advanced federal contracts. The clause declared:

> "When filling positions up to and including first level supervisory positions under Plan A of the Navy Merit Promotion Program, the Employer will normally select employees from existing appropriate registers. However, the Employer may elect to use other methods, such as repromotion, reinstatement or transfer, as authorized by applicable regulations. In this connection, the Employer agrees to use to the maximum extent, the skills and talents of employees within the Shipyard in order to achieve the resulting benefits of higher morale and reduced turnover, and where all factors among candidates under consideration are substantially equal, will select employees for such positions from among qualified candidates employed within the Shipyard." [7]

Some agencies have stated their promotion policy in terms of geographical limits. For example, one Federal Aviation Agency agreement declared that the Aircraft Services Base was to be the normal area from which employees who were members of the unit would be considered for promotion. Specific limitations on promotion were also set for other personnel of the agency. Thus, outside employees of the FAA who were not a part of the Aircraft Services Base could not compete for promotion to positions in the unit. Competition was permitted only when the area of consideration had to be enlarged either because there were fewer than five outstanding and well-qualified candidates within the contractual area or because of other circumstances beyond the

6 U.S. Department of the Interior, *Memorandum of Agreement,* between the Bonneville Power Administration and AFGE, Lodge 928, 1965, Sec. 1-1303.

7 U.S. Department of the Navy, *Agreement,* between Charleston Naval Shipyard and Charleston Metal Trades Council, AFL-CIO, 1968, Art. XIV, Sec. 1.

control of the employer.[8] In regard to qualifications, the 1967 second-round agreement at NASA's Goddard Space Flight Center stipulated that:

"The first area of consideration [for promotions] is the Goddard Space Flight Center. In those cases where outside applicants are clearly better qualified they may be selected. In the event of such selection, at the time the decision is made, the Council will be notified and given the opportunity to review the selection record." [9]

Federal promotion provisions do not invest the seniority principle with the importance that it enjoys in private labor relations. The relationship between seniority and merit in promotion remains one of the major areas of dispute in public employee unionism. While in private labor relations seniority is viewed by some as outweighing all other factors, it is still relegated to a secondary position in government service. In the federal service a typical seniority provision might be that where the qualifications of the best two or more candidates are equal, the employee with the greatest departmental service is to be selected.[10]

Some contracts are quite specific on the issue of seniority. The Laborers' Union contract with the Philadelphia Naval Supply Depot, for example, defined seniority as "total continuous service . . . without regard to periods of absence, whether in a leave with pay or leave without pay status." [11] It further stated that if an employee was involuntarily separated without cause and then rehired within one year, he was not to lose seniority.[12] Other provisions governed the application of seniority factors. Thus, the contract detailed how:

"Within any particular job classification, seniority shall be the deciding factor in determining job assignments, leave preference, and retention in employment, other than those terminations from employment which are based on disciplinary offenses or unsatisfactory performance. If all other factors are equal, senior employees shall be given preference in promotion to a higher classification." [13]

Pay aspects and effective dates of temporary promotions have also been the subjects of negotiation. A large majority of blue-col-

---

[8] Federal Aviation Agency, *Basic Agreement,* between the Aircraft Services Base, Oklahoma City, Okla., and IAM, Lodge 960, AFL-CIO, 1964, Art. XI, Sec. 2.

[9] National Aeronautics and Space Administration, *Negotiated Agreement Under E.O. 10988,* between Goddard Space Flight Center and Washington Area Metal Trades Council, AFL-CIO, 1967, Art. XVI, Sec. 5.

[10] See U.S. Department of Labor, *Agreement,* with AFGE, National Council of Field Labor Lodges, 1966, Art. XIX, Sec.b (1) , (c) .

[11] U.S. Department of the Navy, *Negotiated Agreement,* between U.S. Naval Supply Depot, Philadelphia, Pa. and Laborers' International Union of North America, AFL-CIO, Local 1041, 1965, Art. XXI, Sec. (1) .

[12] *Ibid.*

[13] *Ibid.,* Sec. 2.

lar and "mixed" unit agreements provide, as did the Goddard Space Flight Center accord, that any nonsupervisory employee who is temporarily assigned to a higher level position for a period in excess of 30 calendar days is to be temporarily promoted and to receive the rate of pay for the position to which he was assigned.[14] The 1968 Charleston agreement went a step further, stipulating that certain temporary promotions would be made whenever it could be reasonably determined, at the time of an appointment, that the assignment would exceed 30 calendar days.[15]

In their attempt to extend promotion provisions unions have sought more publicity on the notification and release of promotion action results and the protection of employees' promotion rights, and as much union participation as possible in the selection and appeals processes. The desire for publicity is served by provisions that require the employer to advertise, through posting on official bulletin boards, promotion opportunities for all positions in the unit, supervisory or otherwise. The announcement period for such vacancies is often seven or 10 calendar days prior to the closing date for filing applications. Some contracts provide for the acceptance of applications even after the closing date, provided it can be shown that there are extenuating circumstances.

Contract provisions cover such items as the type and number of positions under the promotion plan and the provisions governing the consideration of employees for promotion. Although standards for the qualification, evaluation, and selection of employees are controlled essentially by CSC regulations, unions have influenced them in many ways. For example, the Goddard Space Flight Center agreement provided counseling for promotion applicants whose experience and training precluded them from consideration. Records including the following data had to be kept on all promotions: selection standards used, areas of consideration, and names of employees selected for promotion. All unsuccessful candidates had to be notified as soon as possible, usually within two weeks after the selections had been made. Finally, employees actually selected were to be released as soon as possible from their present positions, normally two weeks from the date of their selection.[16]

---

[14] National Aeronautics and Space Administration, Goddard Space Flight Center, *Agreement*, 1967, Art. XVI, Sec. 14.

[15] U.S. Department of the Navy, Charleston Naval Shipyard, *Agreement*, 1968, Art. XIV, Sec. 4.

[16] NASA, Goddard Space Flight Center, *Agreement*, 1967, Art. XVI, Secs. 1, 2, 3, 6, 7, 9-13.

The Office of Economic Opportunity's 1971 headquarters agreement with the AFGE set merit-staffing procedures which adhered to the Federal Merit Promotion Policy. One selection process was provided for nonsupervisory positions and another for supervisory positions or grade levels above GS-12. The headquarters personnel officer rated all candidates for nonsupervisory jobs while a promotion panel rated supervisory candidates. Promotion panels were composed of three employees in positions equal to or higher than the job to be filled. They were to be as well qualified as possible for the job under consideration. Where possible, not more than one panel member was to be from the same office. One representative from management participated as a nonvoting advisor to the panel. A union representative could be present, but only as a nonvoting observer, if a unit member was being considered.[17]

The union presence was specifically fostered by the provision that:

"In addition to its non-voting seat on all Promotion Panels, the Union will provide evaluative feedback to management on the whole Merit Promotion Plan. The Employer agrees to consult with the Union on rating systems, the weighing of rating criteria, the system for constituting, and convening Promotion Panels, and the location of candidates career ladder occupations or any other changes in the promotion system." [18]

Other AFGE accords varied the dual selection process to fit the professional needs of the agency.[19]

A provision in the Labor Department's field employees' 1966 agreement evidenced a growing union influence in the last stages of decision making in the promotion process. In cases of abuse, the union could overturn promotion actions at the agency level by appeal to a higher authority:

"Delegated authority to approve personnel actions subject to the merit staffing plan will be withdrawn, at the discretion of the Secretary [of Labor], where there are found to be repeated or flagrant violations of the merit staffing plan and/or this Agreement." [20]

The concern of employees and unions over federal promotion and rehiring policies before and during the Kennedy program was not lost on the Civil Service Commission. For 10 years it had

17 Office of Economic Opportunity, *Agreement,* with AFGE, Local 2677, Washington, 1971, Art. 19, Secs. 3 (c) , 4, 5, 6.

18 *Ibid.,* Sec. 8.

19 U.S. Department of Labor, Washington Area, *Agreement,* 1970, Art. XI, Sec. F (2) .

20 U.S. Department of Labor, Field Offices, *Agreement,* 1966, Art. XIX, Sec. B (12) . The provision was renegotiated unchanged.

been engaged in a thorough study of federal merit promotion practices. As in other internal studies, such as those of the new wage-fixing procedures, it solicited the views of agencies and unions in formulating its final proposals. The CSC's recommendations, submitted in early 1968, reflected a number of union positions exemplified by promotion clauses of the more advanced accords under the Kennedy order. Few unions would have disagreed with Chairman Macy's comments that the new federal policy would "greatly improve the process of identifying and selecting the best candidates for advancement opportunities" and would "assure that merit principles are complied with, eliminate weaknesses that were the cause of employee dissatisfaction . . . and help strengthen employee confidence in the fairness of merit promotion procedures in their agencies." [21]

Union officials could be expected to oppose excessive reliance on merit alone and assuredly would find fault with other aspects of the plan. However, the general provisions of the program assuring that employees were fully informed about promotion policies and procedures and promotional opportunities jibed perfectly with contract promotion clauses. While unions welcomed opportunities to become involved in the development or revision of agency promotion policies, their beliefs in the essentially negotiable nature of promotion issues and their concern for seniority presaged unavoidable disagreements.

Under current practice, each agency head is responsible for developing and publishing promotion guidelines and merit-promotion plans applicable within his agency. Agency merit-promotion programs continue to be operated under the principles and procedures established by the CSC's Federal Merit Promotion Policy.[22]

Instituted in September 1968, the Federal Merit Promotion Plan required that employees be permitted to indicate their interest in particular positions, types of positions, or positions in certain locations. If demoted other than for cause, they were to be given special consideration for repromotion. No agency requirements were to be higher than the Commission's qualification standards. Ranking procedures were to employ appropriate job-related criteria for identifying the best qualified candidates, and supervisory appraisals of performance were to be considered as one part of the ranking process. Length of service or experience was to be used as one of the ranking factors only when it

---

21 *Government Employee Relations Report*, No. 237 (1968), p. A-2.

22 U.S. Civil Service Commission, *Federal Personnel Manual*, Chap. 335, Subchap. 2-3, March 9, 1971.

could be clearly and positively related to the quality of performance or when there was a tie among candidates. Supervisory positions were to have special promotion plans, and employees selected for first-level supervisory jobs were required to have special training.

Promotions were not to be based on personal relationships or favoritism. An employee could be selected from a list of eligibles from a regular civil service examination to fill a higher position in his own agency only if he would rank among the best qualified under competitive promotion procedures. In filling a position by transfer or by reinstating a former employee, an agency had to assure that the person selected would rank with the best qualified agency employees if the position had known promotional potential or was at a higher grade than the last position held by the candidate.

Formal employee complaints about promotions were to be made under the grievance machinery. Written tests were ruled out for promotion unless they were required by the CSC, met the strict guidelines developed by the CSC, or were given prior approval by the Commission.[23]

The new policy had a mixed reception among union leaders. Their views were well represented by John A. McCart, operations director of the AFL-CIO's Government Employees' Council. Reflecting the basic union premise that promotion policies constitute an appropriate matter for negotiation, he stated that the new policy would inhibit full collective bargaining. The CSC's regulations, he believed, should protect the promotion provisions of existing contracts and allow for even wider bargaining whenever exclusive recognition was granted to new employee groups. In the interests of innovation and experimentation, the promotion program should be aimed at stimulating "imaginative negotiations rather than circumscribing the subject."[24]

Although McCart found some of the recommendations desirable, his ideas for improving the Commission's proposals illustrated the underlying union interests traditionally applied to promotion situations. In defense of the concept of "promotion from within," he called for provisions giving employees in a unit unrestricted opportunity to compete, subject only to the rights of demoted or separated workers. Applicants outside of the unit

---

[23] Public Personnel Association, *Personnel News,* Vol. 34, No. 8, May 1968, pp. 21, 23.

[24] John A. McCart, *Letter,* to John W. Steele, Chief, Program Systems and Instructions Division, Bureau of Policies and Standards, Civil Service Commission, April 15, 1968, p. 1.

should be considered only when no qualified inside employee had applied. To do otherwise would restrict "the aspirations of employees entitled to compete on the basic principle of promotion from within."

As to the FMPP's insistence upon supervisory appraisals as one of the ranking factors, he reported that union experience with such appraisals had been generally poor. Their use permitted supervisors to influence the selection process, thus inviting favoritism and detracting from true impartiality.

On the basic issue of seniority, McCart crystallized union thinking when he stated:

> "The draft extends very grudging recognition to this element in determining the promotion qualifications of workers. Permitting its use only when directly associated with an individual's work related performance or in resolving equal qualifications will inhibit agencies from using the factor. Because there are so many other elements available to evaluate qualifications, seniority is rarely used to 'break ties,' even where present agency policy recognizes it. In effect, the Commission's strained description of the performance-seniority relationship will actually discourage agencies from attempting to use it. We feel stongly that an employee's performance and promotion potential are enhanced by length of experience. The validity of our position is supported in other phases of Federal personnel policy—lateral advancement in the pay systems and reduction in force. Certainly, recognition by Congress of this factor as a measure of an individual's work value should impel the Commission to extend it to the promotion process. It is difficult for us to comprehend the Commission's traditional refusal to discern the practical application of the seniority principle to another fundamental aspect of personnel operations –the opportunity for advancement." [25]

The FMPP thus precipitated another confrontation between merit and seniority principles. While it is logical that the Civil Service Commission should feel compelled to preserve and foster merit principles, it is equally logical for unions to strive for a concept that has served them well in private industry.

Under the present federal program, contracts may provide that annual performance evaluations made by supervisors are to be used in rating candidates for promotion. Seniority is only one of several evaluation criteria. These criteria were spelled out as follows for rating examiners, merit staffing panels, and selecting officers in the 1970-1971 Labor Department accord:

> "Evaluation of candidates will be based on a review of each individual's total background to determine the extent to which he meets the following criteria:

---

[25] *Ibid.*, pp. 2, 3.

(1) The best combination of education and experience required for the specific job to be filled.

(2) Personal traits—such as ability to work with others, to exert leadership, or to supervise—to the extent they are required by the specific job to be filled.

(3) Past and present job performance as related to the requirements of the job to be filled.

(4) Length of service in the grade below that of the job to be filled, or in a higher grade, to the extent that such service is related to the current requirements of the specific job to be filled." [26]

B. DEMOTIONS, REPROMOTIONS, AND REDUCTIONS IN FORCE

Federal unions have shown as much concern over downgrading, demotion, layoff, and reassignment of workers as they have over promotion policy. Occasional demotions or firings are justifiably based upon disciplinary proceedings, but large movements cannot be attributed to employee fault and are due, rather, to administrative changes in organization or policy or the cutting of funds for particular programs. The size of the federal service fluctuates. It expands with each crisis on the international and national scene and shrinks in size when the emergency has ended. War, depression, and national social disturbances have all contributed to these expansions and contractions. For the federal employee and his union this fact presents a real and pressing problem. Their concern was early expressed in the contracts under the Kennedy order, particularly those of blue-collar and mixed bargaining units, and is now increasingly manifest in the white-collar agreements. By 1971, for example, 57 percent of the accords in the BLS study called for union participation in RIF circumstances. In 1964 only 15 percent had so provided. [27]

What are the unions most concerned with under such conditions? Of most consequence to unions in a reduction in force are the questions of who will be dismissed and the order of layoff. Among the many factors considered in deciding these questions are employment tenure, veterans' preference, efficiency, and seniority. Are the employees to be simply demoted, possibly setting off a chain reaction of "bumpings," or are they to be laid off outright?

---

[26] U.S. Department of Labor, Washington area, *Agreement,* 1970, Art. XI, Secs. F (2) (e) , G (2) (c) . See also U.S. Civil Service Commission, *Federal Personnel Manual,* Chap. 335, Subchap. 3-6, March 9, 1971.

[27] U.S. Department of Labor, Bureau Labor of Statistics, BLS Bulletin No. 1789, pp. 40-43.

Unions also seek a voice in the policies applicable to rehiring, repromotion, and reassignment once the emergency causing the reduction in force has ended. Contracts since 1963 have emphasized unions' need for advance notice and their desire to participate in the administration of changes. Unions want to know, in advance, what an agency intends to do in order to minimize the adverse effects of cutting staff and to participate, as much as possible, in the decisions controlling reductions and rehiring. Thus, in spite of the fact that CSC regulations set basic policy, unions have sought in their agreements to share responsibility for the essentially managerial function of reductions and demotions just as they endeavored to influence the promotion process.

When demotions or dismissals are the result of employee wrongdoing, their administration is governed by provisions for disciplinary action. While these provisions may or may not mention demotion specifically, it is covered in the phrase "other disciplinary action." When downgrading is specified, it generally has followed the form established in the Philadelphia Naval Supply Depot agreement with the Laborers' Union, which permits a union representative or observer to be present "at all formal hearings held in connection with the suspension, demotion or removal of an employee of the Unit under the disciplinary action procedure." [28]

As in private industry, federal employee unions are concerned with easing the transitional affects of demotions and dismissals, and are eager to influence the rehiring process. This is clearly evidenced in the reduction-in-force provisions. The 1963 AFGE agreement at the Redstone Arsenal indicated some of the major union concerns in demotion other than for disciplinary reasons. In that agreement the provision covering routine organizational personnel changes declared that:

> "The Employer agrees that cases of demotions that result from gradual changes in duties will be made according to the seniority principles contained in the Reduction in Force Regulations except where it can be shown how or why a specific individual must be demoted. It is also agreed that arbitrary downgrade of positions to meet fiscal limitations is prohibited." [29]

Federal employee unions share the same fears as all organized labor in the face of advancing technology. At times the union-

---

[28] U.S. Department of the Navy, Philadelphia Naval Supply Depot, *Negotiated Agreement*, 1965, Art. XVII, Sec. 1.

[29] U.S. Department of the Army, *Agreement*, between U.S. Army Missile Support Command, Redstone Arsenal, Ala., and AFGE Lodge 1858, 1963, Art. XIX, Sec. 2.

management conflict over technological change in the Federal Government has been bitter. Nevertheless, acceptance of the inevitable was expressed in the Metal Trades Council's agreement at the Puget Sound Shipyard. There the union sought to influence the reduction-in-force situations by stipulating that:

> "It is agreed that the Employer, to the extent consistent with the Shipyard's manpower requirements, will make a reasonable effort to reassign employees whose positions are eliminated due to automation or adoption of labor saving devices. It is agreed that the Employer will make a reasonable effort to train employees where necessary for reassignment, whose positions are eliminated because of automation or the adoption of labor saving devices, provided cost of such training is not excessive and if the employee has the necessary aptitude as determined by the Employer." [30]

The clause might well have been taken out of a private industrial labor contract.

The 1968 Charleston Navy Yard agreement incorporated more extensive RIF provisions. It called for reassignments and demotions as alternatives to layoffs and for the maintenance of reemployment priority lists.[31] The agreement also set forth what classes of employees were to receive priority and how they were to receive it and gave workers the alternative of demotion to layoff.[32]

Union policy is to invoke all measures possible to keep people working. The Puget Sound compact called for the shipyard to make a reasonable effort to avoid or minimize a reduction in force by adjusting the staff through promotion, reassignment, or transfer of employees to available vacancies for which they were qualified.[33] Such provisions were not restricted to blue-collar agreements. Similar ones were included in the 1966 accord between the Boston District of the Internal Revenue Service and the independent National Association of Government Employees, covering over 1,000 professional employees. Like many blue-collar contracts, this NAGE accord included a provision insuring that the bumping and retreat rights of the employees involved in a layoff were to be governed by the applicable statutes and CSC

---

[30] U.S. Department of the Navy, *Agreement,* between Puget Sound Naval Shipyard and Bremerton Metal Trades Council, AFL-CIO, 1965, Art. XVII, Sec. 3.

[31] U.S. Department of the Navy, Charleston Naval Shipyard, *Agreement,* 1968, Art. XVII, Secs. 2, 3. See also U.S. Department of the Navy, Pearl Harbor Naval Shipyard, *Agreement,* 1970, Art. XI; U.S. Department of the Navy, Naval Weapons Center, China Lake, Calif., *Agreement,* 1970, Art. XXVI.

[32] U.S. Department of the Navy, Charleston Naval Shipyard, *Agreement,* 1968, Art. XVII, Sec. 4.

[33] U.S. Department of the Navy, Puget Sound Naval Shipyard, *Agreement,* 1965, Art. XVII, Sec. 1.

regulations.[34] NAGE's substantial experience with the New England blue-collar workers was thus applied in the white-collar and professional areas.

Of equal importance to the unions are the repromotion and the rehiring processes. Some repromotion clauses go beyond RIF situations and are general in their application. For this reason, they are sometimes included in the promotion provisions. Thus, in contracts such as that covering the Washington, D.C., Naval Station, previous demotions were considered as part of the selection procedure in promotion.[35]

The China Lake Naval Weapons Center accord, effective through 1972, typified the more advanced agreements. In line with the Federal Merit Promotion Policy, employees who had been permanently in first-level supervisory positions but who were demoted as the result of reduction in force were to be automatically certified in the group of "highly qualified" applicants and given special consideration in filling first-level supervisory vacancies. Permanent nonsupervisory workers demoted through RIF actions were to "be given preferential consideration by selecting officials for repromotion to such positions as vacancies arise." These rights were granted for two years to employees meeting the qualification standards.[36] The accord even provided:

> "In case of demotions in lieu of separation by reduction in force action, the Employer agrees to give such employees who apply for promotions under the Federal Promotion Plan equal consideration for promotion along with other eligible candidates to ensure that the best qualified persons are selected to fill existing vacancies." [37]

The typical rehiring clause required that reemployment priority lists be maintained and that employees be rehired under CSC regulations governing appointments from such lists. The 1967 agreement at the NASA Goddard Space Flight Center provided for two reemployment priority lists, one for permanent appointments required by the *Federal Personnel Manual* and one for temporary appointments established by contract, which protected for a period of two years the employee's rights to placement on

---

[34] U.S. Treasury Department, *Agreement,* between the Internal Revenue Service, Boston District, and NAGE, Local R 1-30, 1966, Art. XVI, Secs. 1-4.

[35] U.S. Department of the Navy, *Basic Negotiated Agreement,* between U.S. Naval Station, Washington, D.C., and Washington Area Metal Trades Council, AFL-CIO, 1964, Art. XVI, Sec. 9.

[36] U.S. Department of the Navy, Naval Weapons Center, China Lake, Calif., *Agreement,* 1970, Art. XXVII, Secs. 1, 2.

[37] *Ibid.,* Art. XXVII, Sec. 3.

the list for permanent appointments. Rehiring was done on a seniority basis.[38]

As noted, unions sought involvement in the personnel function primarily through advance notice of and participation in personnel actions. A clause widely used by the AFGE was succinct yet comprehensive in its statement of the union's function in reduction-in-force situations. Its 1970 accord with Federal Prison Industries, Inc., for example, provided:

> "The Employer shall notify the Union of all pending reduction in force actions when the Employer is reasonably sure that such actions are inevitable. The reduction in force is to be accomplished in accordance with the statutory requirements and the Civil Service Commission rules and regulations. The Union shall be notified in writing of the number of employees and the competitive levels affected initially, the date action is to be taken, and the reason for the reduction in force. The Employer will consult with the Union concerning efforts to minimize the adverse affects on employees." [39]

The merit promotion policy of the Civil Service Commission necessarily involved demotion and repromotion. The union attitude toward the FMPP, typified by the Government Employes' Council, was that "the entire program should be available for negotiation in exclusive units," at all levels—local, intermediate, and national—whenever necessary.[40]

Concerned primarily with the protection of existing employee rights, the GEC called for reliance on seniority and promotion from within. It was content that the CSC plan required the promotion of the holder of a reclassified job. However, it felt constrained to recommend:

> "For those demoted without personal cause, entitlement to repromotions to the same or intervening positions is a matter of right. This right should take precedence over normal competitive process. Failure to select a demoted employee must be justified in writing, and made available to the demoted individual." [41]

Thus, traditional merit concepts and union seniority principles again confronted one another. While the FMPP remains oriented towards the competitive process rather than seniority, unions will not cease their efforts to influence policy or demotions and repromotions. Although compromise has been achieved to some degree

---

[38] National Aeronautics and Space Administration, Goddard Space Flight Center, *Negotiated Agreement*, 1967, Art. XVIII, Sec. 3.

[39] U.S. Department of Justice, *Master Agreement*, between Bureau of Prisons, Federal Prison Industries, Inc., and AFGE Council of Prison Locals, 1970, Art. 25, Sec. a.

[40] John A. McCart, *Letter*, to John W. Steele, April 15, 1968, p. 5.

[41] *Ibid.*, p. 4.

in local government, comprehensive absorption of the seniority principle at the expense of merit is not in line with continuing federal labor policy.

C. POSITION CLASSIFICATION

In the management of personnel, position classification is a basic necessity serving many purposes. Outstanding among these in government is the maintenance of a unitary system which sets each job in its proper horizontal and vertical setting and serves as a basis for equitable pay scales. Purists in administration who recognize classification as a personnel function are disturbed, particularly at the local levels, over the deep encroachments of budgetary officers into this area.

Union attitudes, at least in regard to certain sectors of local government, emphasize the conviction that much of traditional classification theory is obsolete and that classification itself should be deemed a proper subject for collective bargaining. In New York City, for example, classification questions have been bargained over since 1963. Union leaders there have publicly called for abandonment of the classification system. Actually, in New York the traditional relationship between classification and compensation has deteriorated considerably; for by executive order all job titles exclusively represented are excluded from the city's career and salary plan for purposes of fixing pay. This exclusion covers a majority of the city's employees. Since some local union leaders believe that classification has outlived its usefulness for pay purposes, they see union bargaining strength as the ultimate determinant of salaries.

Such is not the case under federal labor contracts. CSC classification standards still govern the job descriptions and ratings of white-collar workers, and blue-collar positions are also rated according to agency classification criteria. Pay-fixing procedures in the federal service mean that no pay changes can occur because a union is able to bargain over the classification of a position or group of positions, and this has continued to be true under the EMC program. Under the program, however, contracts were able to provide a formalization of the regular classification and classification appeals procedures through which unions might influence the grading of positions. To some this seemed a possible channel through which classification decisions could be swayed.

Final authority remained incontestably in management's hands, however. And it was the intention of the Nixon Administration to insure that it remained there. In the hearings prior to issuance of E.O. 11616 amending the Nixon order, it was recommended that the subject of job classification be placed within the scope of negotiation and grievance procedures. The Federal Labor Relations Council, however, contended it was not at that time appropriate to act on the issue.[42]

Federal agreements opened up two avenues of approach to classification. First, they provided for direct dialogues between union and management on policies concerning the classification system generally. Second, they formalized procedures under which dissatisfied individual employees could appeal their job descriptions and ratings with the aid of union representatives. As to the first approach, the NAGE agreement with the FAA expressed the union's desire for notice and communication by stating that "The Employer agrees to notify the Union of reclassification changes in positions in the unit, as soon as he is officially advised of such changes." [43]

The 1967 Goddard Space Flight Center agreement went further, stating that reclassification involving classes of positions in the unit would be discussed with the MTC and its affiliated unions prior to official action and that the employer would discuss any question concerning the titling of positions in order to establish clear and descriptive titles and improve the classification system.[44] Some contracts actually permitted the union to institute general reviews and committed the employer, in broad terms, to cooperate with union efforts. The 1964 Langley Research Center contract declared:

> "The Union may initiate a request for review within broad areas of classification, pay levels, or ratings. In connection with such requests, the Union may meet with appropriate officials of the Employer to discuss pertinent facts and information. The Employer agrees to transmit formal documents which the Union may submit concerning such matters to the NASA Headquarters along with recommendations, if any, which the Employer may deem necessary or desirable. A copy of any recommendations made by the Employer will be furnished to the Union." [45]

In the 1967 Long Beach Naval Shipyard agreement with the Technical Engineers, management agreed to notify the union

---

[42] Federal Labor Relations Council, *Report and Recommendations on Labor-Management Relations in the Federal Service,* June 1971, p. 14.

[43] Federal Aviation Agency, *Agreement,* between FAA Eastern Region Airways Facility, Boston, Mass., and NAGE, Local R1-78, 1966, Art. XIII, Sec. a.

[44] National Aeronautics and Space Administration, Goddard Space Flight Center, *Agreement,* 1967, Art. XIX, Secs. 2, 3.

[45] National Aeronautics and Space Administration, *Basic Agreement,* between Langley Research Center, Hampton, Va., and IAM, Local 892, AFL-CIO, 1964, Art. XVIII, Sec. 3.

whenever a classification-act position was to be changed to a lower grade level. The union could then make representations and submit supporting evidence regarding the adequacy or fairness of position classification standards. The employer agreed to take appropriate action and to advise the union accordingly.[46]

An agreement between the Office of the General Counsel of the NLRB and the independent union representing professional field examiners and field attorneys did not reserve the classification rights specified by management in many other contracts. Instead, it emphasized joint union-management action, burdening management with the obligation of initiating action and providing necessary documents. Current and revised job descriptions were to be furnished to all new and old employees and to the union. Management also was required to make available to the union all position classification standards and other necessary evaluation material to enable it to consult effectively on studies to establish or change the status of positions.[47] The agreement also clearly denominated classification as a negotiable item.[48]

Among the reasons which unions give to justify an active union role in classification procedures is protection of the individual employee against unfair job descriptions. To avoid unfairness, some contracts call for an annual review of each position. A common provision permits either the employee or the union to request a position evaluation whenever it is believed that there are severe inconsistencies between a job and its official description.[49] The most advanced clauses provide for union participation in both formal and informal position reclassification processes.

---

[46] U.S. Department of the Navy, *Agreement*, between Long Beach Naval Shipyard and American Federation of Technical Engineers, Local 174, AFL-CIO, 1967, Art. XV, Secs. 2, 3.

[47] National Labor Relations Board, *Agreement*, between General Counsel and NLRB Union, 1966, Art. XIX, Sec. 2.

[48] *Ibid.*, Sec. 1.

[49] E.g., U.S. Treasury Department, *Labor-Management Agreement*, between Bureau of Engraving and Printing and Printing Pressmen's Union No. 1, IPPAU, AFL-CIO, 1965, Art. 16, Sec. 4.

Chapter XIII

GRIEVANCE AND DISCIPLINARY PROCEDURES

A. DEVELOPMENT OF GRIEVANCE PROCEDURES

When the Kennedy order brought grievances within the scope of collective bargaining, it initiated a course of events that eventually redefined grievances and revised the procedures for their resolution. New terminology evolved to describe grievances arising solely out of the federal labor agreements. The fundamental CSC standards governing traditional individual employee grievances were bargained over and modified. The scope of permissible negotiations on grievance procedures was successively broadened by the three ensuing executive orders, No. 11491, No. 11616, and No. 11838, enabling negotiators to write increasingly sophisticated procedures geared to agency, union, and employee needs.

Changes resulting from the EMC program must be seen in relation to the history of grievance administration in the federal service. Some of the major dissatisfactions over federal grievance handling were stated more than 20 years ago by Louis J. Van Mol of the TVA. Commenting upon a study by the Federal Personnel Council, Van Mol found general agreement that federal grievance machinery was too cumbersome. Management believed the procedures were loaded in favor of the workers, while employees believed they favored management. Unions saw the procedures as stacked in favor of the government. Both unions and management agreed that final decisions too frequently failed to state clearly the grounds for determination.[1]

In the early 1950s the union role in the grievance process was minimal. Grievance resolution was primarily an employee-management matter, with the worker sometimes permitted to have the union represent him. This approach became obsolete as labor agreements came more and more to govern employee-manage-

---

[1] Louis J. Van Mol, *Effective Procedures for the Handling of Employee Grievances* (Chicago: Public Personnel Association, 1953), pp. 2, 3.

ment and union-management relations. Since disputes over individual grievances sometimes actually involved much more than the interests of a single worker, labor settlements under the Kennedy order developed formal grievance machinery. In addition, since the definition of a grievance and, indeed, day-to-day adherence to the terms of the agreement depended on contract interpretation, procedures for settling contract-interpretation disputes were also developed.

Under E.O. 10988 and E.O. 11491 negotiated grievance provisions stressed two points, the preservation of the individual employee's rights as traditionally protected in existing machinery and an active union role in grievance handling. Most contracts permitted union representation if desired by the worker. Many also provided for union participation whether requested or not if a case called into question any general policies contained in the negotiated agreement. On this point, Warren Irons, former executive director of the CSC, declared that of the union's dual roles, its role as a grievance representative was generally of more value to federal employees than its role as negotiator.[2] This declaration may not have sat very well with union leaders concerned primarily with advancing effective collective bargaining in the program's early years. However, it reflected an emerging official CSC position of accepting a large measure of union participation in the grievance process.

Under the Kennedy order there developed a problem that resulted in dual systems for grievance administration. As collective bargaining progressed, negotiated grievance machinery was inaugurated, expanded, and written into contracts. However, to preserve all legally established procedures and abide by the minimal requirements of CSC standards necessary under E.O. 10988, the employee could select either the negotiated grievance system or the agency-CSC system, a practice which created much confusion and duplication of effort.

The use of arbitration presented another area of controversy. Prior to the EMC program CSC grievance procedures contained no provision for arbitration. The Kennedy order permitted only advisory arbitration and restricted its application to the interpretation or application of negotiated agreements or agency policy.[3] Over the years recommendations to expand the scope of arbitration and make it binding increased. To date, CSC policy as ex-

---

[2] Warren B. Irons, *Speech*, before the Federal Bar Association, April 8, 1965.
[3] E.O. 10988, Sec. 8 (a) (b).

pressed in the *Federal Personnel Manual* has not included arbitration as a part of the grievance process or the appeals procedures following agency adverse actions in disciplinary proceedings.[4]

During the first decade of the EMC program, federal labor agreements varied in content but adhered essentially to the substance and sometimes the wording of Section 8 of the Kennedy order.[5] It was plain that during this early period the basic character of grievance clauses soon crystallized, varying relatively little among the agencies except when changed by overall policy. The manner and extent to which grievances were bargained over and adopted during this crucial, initial time pointed up the varying degrees of agency acceptance of the new policy. Bargaining over grievance procedures in the first years after the promulgation of the Kennedy order quickly revealed major issues of controversy, some of which were not acted on until the Nixon orders.

As of mid-1965, studies by the BLS and The Bureau of National Affairs, Inc., found that only two thirds of the contracts analyzed included procedures for handling employee complaints. Although some accords relegated the issue to supplementary agreements, the fact that one third of the basic contracts did not reflect the CSC acceptance of negotiated grievance procedures emphasized the task still remaining for union negotiators. Federal management has not yet adopted union participation in its entirety, although over four fifths of the 1971 contracts studied by the BLS contained negotiated grievance procedures.[6]

The 1970 Metal Trades Council agreement at the Pearl Harbor Naval Shipyard was typical of those accords which retained

---

[4] U.S. Civil Service Commission, *Federal Personnel Manual*, Chaps. 752, 771, 772, January 3, 1972; May 25, 1972.

[5] E.O. 10988, Sec. 8 (a) (b) : "Agreements entered into or negotiated in accordance with this Order with an employee organization which is the exclusive representative of employees in an appropriate unit may contain provisions applicable only to employees in the unit, concerning procedures for consideration of grievances. Such procedures (1) shall conform to standards issued by the CSC and (2) may not in any manner diminish or impair any rights which would otherwise be available to any employee in the absence of an agreement providing for such procedure.

"Procedures established by an agreement which are otherwise in conformity with this section may include provisions for the arbitration of grievances. Such arbitration (1) shall be advisory in nature with any decision or recommendations subject to the approval of the agency head; (2) shall extend only to the interpretation or application of agreements or agency policy and not to changes in or proposed changes in agreements or agency policy; and (3) shall be invoked only with the approval of the individual employee or employees concerned."

[6] *Government Employee Relations Report*, No. 92 (1965), pp. x-1–x-12; U.S. Department of Labor, Bureau of Labor Statistics, *Collective Bargaining Agreements in the Federal Service, Late Summer 1964*, BLS Bulletin No. 1451, 1965, pp. 35–37, 56–64; *Collective Bargaining Agreements in the Federal Service, Late 1971*, BLS Bulletin No. 1789, April 1973, p. 71.

the dual system—that is, permitted use of either the negotiated procedure or the agency procedure prior to E.O. 11616. It gave the employee an option but protected the union's role throughout. It provided:

> "Before processing a grievance . . . an employee shall first exercise his right to choose whether to pursue the grievance through the procedure set forth in this Article or through the standard Navy grievance procedure. The employee's choice at this point shall be irrevocable. If the employee selects the standard Navy procedure, he shall have the right to choose a representative of his choice and the Council will have the right to have a representative present at any formal hearing held and to make the Council's views known at an appropriate time. If the negotiated procedure is selected the employee shall be represented by the appropriate Council Steward or a representative designated by the Council . . . ." [7]

Even if the employee dropped his grievance the union could still pursue it if it involved "a significant issue of general application." [8] Similar provisions appeared in most MTC agreements.

B. JURISDICTION

In the first stages of the EMC program, defining grievances was necessary to establish the range of issues to be considered or excluded from procedures. Negotiators had to deal with two major categories. First, there were the traditional employee grievances for which machinery had already been provided in CSC regulations. Many contracts generally used the wording in the Kennedy order or the *Federal Personnel Manual* to define such grievances. The FPM called an individual employee grievance a matter "of concern or dissatisfaction to an employee if the matter is subject to the control of agency management." [9] This definition excluded a wide variety of disputes, as will be seen. The second major category included those grievances that arose out of the application or interpretation of agreements. Such grievances could be brought by unions, individual employees, or groups of employees.

FPM definitions and policies frequently appeared in contracts whose grievance machinery lacked detail and did not permit arbitration.[10] On the other hand, agreements with more detailed procedures typically outlined the scope of grievance coverage, and

---

[7] U.S. Department of the Navy, *Agreement*, between Pearl Harbor Naval Shipyard and Honolulu Metal Trades Council, 1970, Art. XIV, Secs. 3, 6.

[8] *Ibid.*, Art. XVIII.

[9] U.S. Civil Service Commission, *Federal Personnel Manual*, Chap. 771, Sec. 3-2, May 25, 1971.

[10] *Government Employee Relations Report, op. cit.*, p. x-3.

their grievance machinery considered both individual grievances and questions of contract interpretation. For example, the definition in the first contract between the St. Lawrence Seaway and the AFGE was most comprehensive, specifying that:

"Grievances within the meaning of this agreement shall consist of matters of personal concern to the employees . . . such as working conditions and environment, allegations of unfair treatment, interpretation or application of the Corporation's personnel policies and practices, and the provisions of this agreement or other administrative action except adverse actions . . . ." [11]

Although few contracts drew a distinction between employees and unions in their grievance disputes with management, the trend toward separate grievance systems progressed. Some contracts, such as the AFGE's Field Labor Lodges' agreements and the Naval Air Station accord at Virginia Beach, established two separate and equally detailed procedures, one for traditional grievances and one for union disputes over contract interpretation.[12]

After the adoption of E.O. 11491, there was further divergence between "employee" grievance procedures and procedures for handling union grievances. One 1972 AFGE accord specified that the procedures for union grievances could not be used for adjusting individual dissatisfactions.[13] Generally, union grievance provisos tended to eliminate the appeal steps in the traditional procedure, to rely more upon negotiation than upon formal hearings and decisions, to resort more often to the "binding" arbitration permitted by E.O. 11491, and to reduce the time period necessary to resolve the dispute.

The range of grievable issues was often restricted, particularly in the more detailed agreements. Typical of this approach was the 1967 agreement between the Long Beach Naval Shipyard and the American Federation of Technical Engineers, which provided as follows:

"Appeal from the following types of actions are [sic] specifically excluded from this procedure: 1—Reduction in force 2—Position Classification 3—Performance ratings and performance rating warn-

[11] St. Lawrence Seaway Development Corporation, *Memorandum of Agreement* with AFGE, Lodge 1968, March 21, 1964, Sec. 27.
[12] *Government Employee Relations Report, op. cit.,* p. x-4; U.S. Department of Labor, *Agreement,* with AFGE, National Council of Field Labor Lodges, Renewed 1970, Art. 16.
[13] U.S. Department of Health, Education and Welfare, *Master Agreement,* between Bureau of Retirement and Survivors Insurance and National Office, AFGE, 1971, Art. XXVIII, Sec. h.

ings 4—Alleged discrimination because of race, creed, color, religion or national origin 5—Incentive awards 6—Adverse actions under security regulations and failure to be cleared to perform duties of a confidential and sensitive nature 7—Nonselection for promotion when the sole basis for the grievance is an allegation by the employee that he is better qualified than the person selected 8—Letters of caution or requirement 9—Suspensions of more than 30 days, demotions, reductions in rank or compensation, separations or removal actions." [14]

Negotiated grievance procedures could deal only with those areas that lay within agency management's discretionary authority and for which no other official system of review had been established by law or CSC regulation. Law, CSC regulations, and other official procedures took precedence over the negotiated contract.

C. INITIATION AND REPRESENTATION

Setting the procedures for grievance administration automatically involved the rights of all the parties—the employees, the employer, and the union. The individual's right to initiate his own case and control its presentation was protected in the majority of contracts. Generally, either an employee or a group of employees could commence a grievance proceeding and select a representative, if one was desired. The representative did not necessarily have to be a union agent. The Kennedy and Nixon executive orders specified that preexisting employee rights could not be impaired by contract. The union's primary interest still lay in defending the employee's cause whenever possible and in promoting machinery to resolve union disputes with management under the contract. The strong AFGE Field Labor Lodges agreement was most explicit in the enumeration of employee rights. To assure a fair hearing for the employee, the agreement called for quick attention, prompt consideration of grievances, representation, official time for case preparation, written grievances, personal appearances before a grievance officer or arbitrator, agency payment of necessary travel expenses, and written decisions.[15] These provisions controlled each stage of the grievance procedure at progressively higher appeals levels.

This AFGE agreement was representative of the majority of contracts providing comprehensive union participation clauses.

---

[14] U.S. Department of the Navy, *Agreement,* between Long Beach Naval Shipyard and American Federation of Technical Engineers, Local 174, 1967, Art. XXI, Sec. 3. Presently excluded areas are to be found in the *Federal Personnel Manual,* Chap. 771, Sec. 3-2 (b).

[15] U.S. Department of Labor, *Agreement,* with AFGE, National Council of Field Labor Lodges, 1966, Art. 15, Secs. a, b, c, g, h, j, k.

Its provisions constituted a virtual summary of the major union rights that were sought in detailed accords. In certain respects, it was strongly pro-union. For example, a preliminary statement declared that grievance adjustments were not to conflict with the terms of the agreement; this amounted to a "subject" clause to govern grievances.[16] In addition, a strongly worded provision on representation suggested that the union would act as the employee representative in most grievance cases, since the burden was placed upon the employee to select another representative or act as his own.[17]

Provisions allowing the employee freedom to choose his own representative present a real threat to the union's position as an effective representative. Such provisions foster worker independence from unions and lead naturally to the question of whether there is a need to have a union at all. Moreover, they tend to undercut a major function of labor unions—grievance representation. Grievance representation, perhaps more than any other task, has built up unions' protective image, an image that must be continually renewed. Even more threatening to an exclusively recognized union than loss of its prerogatives is the ever-present possibility that rival unions, vying for leadership in an internal struggle, may lure away members with their allegedly superior ability to process grievances.

To assure the union presence throughout the grievance process, the AFGE compact required that notice be given the union within one workday of receipt of a written grievance. When the union was selected to act for the employee, all management communications had to be transmitted through the union representative to the grievant or simultaneously to the grievant and his representative. Where the union was not selected as the representative, it still had to be given the opportunity to be present at all discussions between the parties. When the employee was to be counseled by his supervisors on matters that were likely to lead to disciplinary action, he was entitled to have his shop steward or another union agent present at the discussion. In fact, the conference was to be scheduled so that the union representative could be present.[18] Under the provisions of E.O. 10988, the union could make oral presentations in advisory arbitration proceedings and was entitled to receive copies of all recommendations made by arbitrators or grievance officers.[19]

---

[16] *Ibid.,* Sec. a.
[17] *Ibid.,* Sec. b (1) .
[18] *Ibid.,* Secs. b (2) , b (3) .
[19] *Ibid.,* Secs. g, k (3) .

D. PROCEDURES

The effectiveness of grievance administration hinges largely upon the clarity with which its procedures are spelled out in the contract. Labor and management have long agreed that the essential ingredient of good grievance machinery is a clear statement of its basic components, including processing time, the use of written documents, and the graduated steps in the procedure.

It is vital that the contract require the grievance to be reduced to writing at some point in the proceeding. Very few federal labor contracts have called for a written complaint at the employee's first informal consultation with his immediate supervisor. The reasons for this are obvious. In the first place, the largest percentage of dissatisfactions can and should be resolved at this early stage if there is good faith and a real desire to make the agreement operative. The less formality, the better.

If a grievance cannot be resolved through discussion, then it enters the formal stage of the grievance process, which at some point requires submission of a written complaint. Written submissions are necessary to clarify issues and present basic facts so that the grievant, his coworkers, and the union have a clear understanding of the case.

Many contracts require that the grievant follow a set format in documenting his case. Among the declarations he sometimes must make are the following, as stipulated in a 1964 NASA/IAM agreement:

> "If the employee is not satisfied he reduces his complaint to writing either on the form mutually agreed to by the Employer and the Union or in other suitable form. Such grievance must contain the following information: 1—a statement indicating his decision to process his grievance either through the negotiated grievance procedure or the NASA Grievance Procedure; 2—a statement presenting, in concise manner, details concerning the grievance; 3—a statement outlining the corrective action desired; and 4—the name of the representative, if any." [20]

Other agreements require additional information, including identification, the signatures of the grievants, and a summary of all the efforts that have previously been made to resolve the complaint informally.[21]

The time factor is of utmost importance in the grievance proc-

---

[20] U.S. National Aeronautics and Space Administration, *Basic Agreement*, between Langley Research Center, Hampton, Va., and IAM, Lodge 892, 1964, Art. XX, Sec. 4b.

[21] See, for example, National Labor Relations Board, *Agreement*, between the General Counsel of the NLRB and the NLRB Union, 1966, Art. XV, Sec. 10.

ess. Both labor and management agree on this point, and for good reason. According to the late A. Andras, labor member of the Canadian Public Service Staff Relations Board:

> "The element of time is important to avoid hasty decisions as well as to avoid the irritation of prolonged delay. It follows, therefore, that the parties should seek to provide a grievance procedure which gives either side a reasonable time to examine a grievance and to arrive at a conclusion; to decide whether the grievance should be carried a step further or be withdrawn as the case may be. There should be a time limit at each step . . ." [22]

Unclear time limits for initiation and processing of complaints have caused serious defects in the grievance process. Unions believe the lack of fixed time limits leads to management procrastination in settling, meeting over, or even answering complaints, thus defeating the purpose of negotiated grievance machinery. Management has also expressed concern over the absence of time limits for each step in the procedural ladder, noting that the passage of time may make it very difficult to ascertain the true facts.[23]

To meet such complaints, some detailed accords specify fixed times for initiating the first informal consultations over grievances, which may start anywhere from three to 30 days after the contested event. Most grievance provisions set a period of 10 or 15 days during which the complainant must request a discussion with his supervisor or lose the right to have his case considered.

Detailed agreements also set time limits, ranging from one to 10 days, for complainant appeals at the second and third steps. At the second step, the time limit commonly is three or five days, while five or 10 days is the general rule at the third step. In agreements with up to six appeal steps, time limits in steps four to six usually range from one to five days.[24] Many contracts have incorporated flexibility into grievance procedures by allowing time extensions by mutual agreement if warranted by extenuating circumstances.[25] A good number of contracts also place time limits upon management responses to complaints.

The number of procedural steps in the grievance system is a major consideration. A. Andras of the Canadian PSSRB reflected

---

[22] A. Andras, "Concepts of a Collective Agreement Between a Government and a Government Employees' Association," in *Collective Bargaining in the Public Service* (Ottawa: Canadian Labour Congress, 1961) , p. 14.
[23] *Government Employee Relations Report, op. cit.,* p. x-6.
[24] *Ibid.*
[25] National Aeronautics and Space Administration, Langley Research Center, *Agreement,* 1964, Art. XX, Sec. 5.

sensible thinking from the standpoint of personnel administration when he stated that grievance machinery should be as simple or as complex as the circumstances warrant. The technicalities of the sequential appeals ladder must reflect the operational structure of the agency itself. Andras noted that if there is an extensive hierarchy of management authority, the grievance procedure should match that hierarchy—that is, there should be enough appeal steps to process a complaint successfully from one management level to another until a mutually agreeable decision is achieved.[26] He cautioned, however, that "The union on its part must be able to match the managerial hierarchy with one of its own so that officers of equal status on both sides can discuss the grievance with respect to one another's authority." [27]

While Andras' remarks are well taken, it must be remembered that too complicated a system can be just as dangerous as one that is oversimplified. In forming a grievance system the prime goals remain clarity, speed, and simplicity as adapted to a particular agency's operations.

From the diversity of types of grievance systems, certain patterns have emerged. Among other things, there appears to be a general relation between the size of a unit and the extent of formalization of its grievance machinery. The larger the federal agency, the more precise are the details of its appeal procedures.[28]

In accordance with best practices in private industry and the public service, the first step is nearly always an informal, face-to-face discussion of the complaint by the worker, his representative, and the immediate supervisor at the workplace. This procedure serves to resolve minor problems quickly and to select only the more serious complaints for further consideration.

As has so often been stated in the field of administrative regulation, informal procedures constitute the "lifeblood" of the administrative process. A Marshall Space Flight Center accord brought supervisors above the employee's immediate superior into the informal steps by stipulating:

> "The employee must first informally discuss his complaint with his immediate supervisor, and attempt to resolve the complaint through this method. (In the event that his complaint involves his immediate supervisor, the first contact may be with the next level supervisor.)
> "If necessary, the employee and his immediate supervisor should

---

[26] A. Andras, *op. cit.*, p. 14.
[27] *Ibid.*
[28] *Government Employee Relations Report, op. cit.*, p. x-7.

also hold informal discussions with higher level supervisors, and members of the Personnel Office." [29]

In the 1966 NLRB General Counsel's contract, informal procedures could go as high as the regional director.[30] However, such provisions were in the minority.

If there is no informal settlement, succeeding steps offer an avenue of appeal to higher managerial levels. If contracts stipulate the use of agency appeal procedures, successive steps generally are not described in detail. Where grievance machinery is negotiated, however, the most frequent series selected is an appeal ladder of three steps, with final recourse to arbitration.

The number of steps depends primarily upon the structural organization of the agency. The agreements of the National Maritime Union plainly show how operations dictate the number and form of procedural steps. Reflecting practices on private vessels, the federal NMU contracts followed chains of command and made provisions for grievance hearing committees. Twelve NMU agreements examined by the BLS called for six or seven appeal steps, a grievance-hearing committee, and advisory arbitration.[31]

The NMU used the factfinding-committee method extensively, adopting it in agreements with the Jacksonville, Philadelphia, Buffalo, Mobile, and Portland Army Engineer Districts, among others.[32] Steps leading up to the appointment of a grievance-hearing committee involved discussion by the grievant, first, with his immediate supervisor; next with his department head; and finally with the ship's master. Failing resolution at the third step, the master was to appoint a committee to handle the case.

The grievance-hearing committee consisted of

"one department head and three additional members, all of whom shall be from departments other than appellant. Two of the additional members shall be members of the Union. The committee will conduct the hearing and investigate the complaint. Within five working days after the conclusion of the hearing, the committee

---

[29] National Aeronautics and Space Administration, *Agreement,* between Marshall Space Flight Center, Huntsville, Ala., and AFGE, Lodge 1858, 1965, Art. VI, Secs. 3a, b.

[30] National Labor Relations Board, General Counsel's Office and the NLRB Union, *Agreement,* 1966, Art. XV, Sec. 9.

[31] U.S. Department of Labor, Bureau of Labor Statistics, BLS Bulletin No. 1451, pp. 60-61.

[32] As in many such National Maritime Union contracts, these provisions appeared in much the same form in the following agreements:
Army Engineers District, Mobile, Ala., 1965; same, Jacksonville, Fla., 1965; same, Buffalo, N.Y., 1964; same, Philadelphia, Pa., 1965; Military Sea Transport Service, Atlantic Area, 1963; U.S. Department of Commerce, Coast and Geodetic Survey, 1965.

will submit to the Master a copy of the hearing record and the committee's findings of facts." [33]

The hearing report was to be submitted to the employee, the union, and the master, who was to render a decision. A dissatisfied employee could appeal at the district level in a fifth step. The sixth step was a meeting of district representatives with the parties, and the seventh step was a request for advisory arbitration.[34]

The question of who has final decision-making authority in the grievance process is extremely important. Resolution of grievances under the Kennedy order was a matter for unilateral management decision. Committees or arbitrators could only make recommendations to management. The locus of executive authority varied in different collective agreements, ranging from installation head to regional, bureau, and department heads. Although advisory procedures operated well and added vitality to the grievance system, union leadership still desired an independent appellate authority. Their feeling was heightened by the fact that agency grievance decisions were truly final, unlike adverse-action decisions, which could be appealed directly to the CSC.[35]

Generally, collective bargaining over grievances under E.O. 10988 achieved favorable results. It is true that many grievance provisions incorporated into contracts were already amply provided for in the *Federal Personnel Manual*. But the introduction of advisory arbitration was a substantial accomplishment, and the very presence of unions in the grievance procedure worked considerable change within the limitations of policy and regulations.

E. ADVISORY ARBITRATION

Although it had been used in the 1930s by the TVA and the Interior Department, advisory arbitration did not become widespread in the federal service until the advent of E.O. 10988. A pattern of collective bargaining incorporating advisory arbitration as the final step in grievance machinery appeared early in the EMC program and continued until the revisions of the Nixon orders. A 1964 BLS study of 209 agreements disclosed that two thirds of the 96 accords creating grievance procedures provided for advisory arbitration.[36] While the final decision still remained with execu-

33 U.S. Department of the Army, *Agreement*, between Army Engineers District, Portland, Ore., and National Maritime Union, 1964, Art. V., Sec. 4.

34 *Ibid.*, Steps 4, 5-7.

35 U.S. Civil Service Commission, *Federal Personnel Manual*, Chap. 771, Subchaps. 2-18, 3-15, May 25, 1971.

36 U.S. Department of Labor, Bureau of Labor Statistics, BLS Bulletin No. 1451, p. 62.

tive authority, management accepted the third-party decision in the overwhelming majority of cases going to arbitration. Nevertheless, the few instances in which installation officers overruled arbitrator's awards served as sharp reminders of the reserved management powers protected by the Kennedy order.

Negotiated grievance-arbitration procedures in the federal agencies closely resembled their counterparts in private industry. However, two major differences between private- and public-sector procedures lay in the limited scope of public-sector arbitration and the insistence upon its advisory nature. The usual practice was for arbitrators to be designated on an ad hoc basis as the need arose. Prior to the Nixon orders, the parties initially endeavored to select the arbitrators. If unsuccessful, they generally resorted to the professional services of organizations such as the American Arbitration Association or, more often, the Federal Mediation and Conciliation Service. Contract clauses usually allowed for the use of government facilities and government time to conduct the hearings. No loss of pay or leave time was to be incurred by any of the parties or witnesses for participation in arbitration proceedings. As in private industry, fees were shared by both sides; however, limits often were placed on fee amounts.[37]

Some agreements were quite specific as to the arbitrator's jurisdiction. Many simply repeated the broad limitations stipulated in E.O. 10988. Thus, the NASA Goddard agreement specified that such arbitration "shall extend only to the interpretation or application of agreements or agency policy and not to changes in or proposed changes in agreements or agency policy."[38] Other accords spelled out the arbitrator's restrictions, as in the case of the 1965 Red River Army Depot's compact:

"The arbitrator's award is subject to the provisions of existing or future laws, regulations and policies.
"The arbitrator shall have no jurisdiction over promotions.
"The arbitrator shall have no power to add to or subtract from, to disregard or to modify any of the terms of this or any agreements made by the undersigned parties.
"It is understood by the parties that any and all arbitration proceedings are:
(1) Advisory in nature to the Depot Commander.

---

[37] Typical of the comprehensive agreements that have been written for both blue-collar and classification-act units were the accords effective through 1970 at the Charleston Naval Shipyard. See U.S. Department of the Navy, *Agreement,* between Charleston Naval Shipyard and Charleston Metal Trades Council, 1968, Art. XXIII, Secs. 1-5.

[38] U.S. National Aeronautics and Space Administration, Goddard Space Flight Center, *Agreement,* 1967, Art. XXIV, Sec. 5 (2) .

(2) Shall not extend to changes in or proposed changes in agreements or depot policy." [39]

Some unions chose not to include arbitration in their early contracts. NMU agreements, for example, postponed adoption by the consistent use of a standard clause inserted at the end of the grievance procedure that provided:

> "Until such time as additional experience is gained by both parties under the operation of this agreement, it is resolved that the subject of advisory arbitration of grievances not be included in this agreement. Should future experience show an appreciable number of unreconcilable differences, this matter may be reopened . . . ." [40]

Acquired expertise soon led to arbitration adoption.

It should be noted that private-sector labor relations practice strongly influenced the adoption of arbitration machinery in federal grievance systems. The 1965 BNA survey referred to in this section revealed that almost two thirds of the contracts containing grievance arbitration were written by the traditional craft unions which had concluded similar agreements in private industry. Thus, public-employee unions wrote only a third of the arbitration clauses in the accords.[41] From 1965 to 1970, advisory-arbitration provisions were the general rule in contracts of all types of unions. However, management's reluctance in the early and mid-1960s to bring third parties into their labor relations contributed to the growing union discontent later expressed before the presidential study committees.

F. DISCIPLINARY ACTIONS AND APPEALS

The attitude of federal unions towards disciplinary actions was formed in private industrial labor relations. Yet the government's attitude toward disciplinary actions differs in several respects from that of private industry and is conditioned by unique concerns, such as the need for political neutrality and the maintenance of national security. In private industry, unions traditionally have striven to govern disciplinary procedures through the basic grievance machinery in the collective agreement. While the

---

[39] U.S. Department of the Army, *Agreement,* between Red River Army Depot and International Chemical Workers' Union, Local NR 750, 1965, Art. IX, Sec. 2, b-e.

[40] U.S. Military Sea Transportation Service, Gulf Subarea and NMU, 1963; U.S. Military Sea Transportation Service, Atlantic Area and NMU, 1963; U.S. Department of Commerce, Coast and Geodetic Survey and NMU, 1965.

[41] *Government Employee Relations Report, op. cit.,* p. x-9.

evolution of employee rights in the collective agreement in some cases ended periods of arbitrary and discriminatory action, it also created new problems. Some contracts appeared to give employees vested rights to their jobs. Disciplinary actions—firing, suspension, demotion—were viewed by some as challenges to these rights. The potential for loss of seniority rights, pensions, and fringe benefits spurred unions to insist on contract provisions that would guarantee the organization's right to challenge all disciplinary actions.[42] Due process became essential.

In the early 1950s Neil Chamberlain observed that private-sector labor unions already had successfully established a joint interest in discipline control. This was not done through detailed contract provisions covering discipline *per se*. Although contracts affirmed the right to punish for just cause as a reserved management prerogative, they also secured for unions the right to protest adverse actions through the grievance procedure. As a result, there developed over the years a considerable body of principles and practices governing employee discipline, deriving not so much from contracts as from precedents set by successive decisions handed down in grievance processes that included binding arbitration awards. The store of arbitral decisions in discipline cases closely approximated a body of "common law" in industry.[43]

Public-sector unions sought, therefore, to secure special handling of disciplinary actions within negotiated grievance procedures. They wanted special clauses to govern dismissals and other penalties. For example, they sought.provisions which required notification to the union of every dismissal and which permitted the employee time to file a grievance before the dismissal. They also called for reinstatement with full back pay if a dismissal was found to be without merit—a practice commonly found in private sector collective bargaining agreements. Union success in establishing such provisions has been on state and local levels rather than on the federal level.

Management retains full control of federal adverse action proceedings. Unions participate less in such federal proceedings than they do in private-sector disciplinary actions. Federal procedures controlling disciplinary actions are delineated in the rules and regulations of the Civil Service Commission and the various agencies. These regulations govern violations of civil service stat-

---

[42] Richard A. Lester, *Labor and Industrial Relations* (New York: The Macmillan Co., 1954) , p. 163.

[43] Neil W. Chamberlain, *Collective Bargaining* (New York: McGraw-Hill, 1951) , pp. 323, 324.

utes, agency regulations, required norms of conduct, and standards of performance. Union contracts cannot contravene statute or regulation. Federal agreements, therefore, have not succeeded in changing the basic regulations governing adverse actions in any measurable degree—assuredly not to the extent accomplished in private labor relations.

Unlike the private sector, the federal labor relations system treats grievances and disciplinary proceedings separately, and has provided two independent procedures for their administration.[44] Although there has been some agitation to combine grievances and disciplinary actions, the Kennedy, Nixon, and Ford executive orders have preserved and advanced the CSC's policy of maintaining their basic independence from each other.

Separate nomenclature was also fostered by this policy. In the Federal Government grievances are defined essentially as employee dissatisfactions. Adverse actions include removals, suspensions for more than 30 days, furloughs without pay, and reductions in rank or pay.[45] Letters of reprimand or suspensions of 30 days or less are considered disciplinary actions; however, these minor actions may be handled through grievance procedures as well as through disciplinary procedures.[46]

Appeals from adverse actions and grievance proceedings also differ. Grievance machinery contains all appeal steps, which lie entirely within an agency. On the other hand, appeals from adverse-action decisions may be made within the agency and to the CSC. That there should be appeals from adverse actions but not grievance decisions appears to be due partially to the fact that, generally speaking, an employee does not suffer any great material loss if faced with a negative grievance determination, whereas he suffers severe material penalties from adverse actions.

The *Federal Personnel Manual* set a minimal number of criteria for the adverse-action process itself, which required notification to the employee of the proposed adverse action, an oral or written answer to charges from the employee, and notification to the employee of the administrative decision. Provisions were made to help the employee understand and implement his rights in adverse-action proceedings. Such provisions were broadened through agency collaboration with employee organizations.

The dual system of adverse-action appeals developed partially

---

[44] U.S. Civil Service Commission, *Federal Personnel Manual,* Part 752, January 3 1972; Chap. 771, May 25, 1971; Part 772, September 22, 1971.

[45] *Ibid.,* Chap. 752, Subpart B, January 3, 1972.

[46] *Ibid.,* Subpart C.

as a result of the dissatisfaction which had arisen over the inequity created by Section 14 of the Veterans' Preference Act of 1944 giving veterans the right of appeal to the CSC in disciplinary proceedings. Executive Order 10987 [47] requiring agencies to establish administrative review systems was intended to give non-veterans the same appeal rights as veterans. An employee could appeal directly to the CSC or move first through his agency and then appeal to the CSC under certain circumstances. Rulings incorporated into the *Federal Personnel Manual* in 1971 permitted the inclusion of advisory arbitration as a part of the negotiated agency appeals system.[48] If an agency desired to expand employee rights, there was no federal policy to prevent its doing so.[49] Indeed, many agencies so acted through consultation and negotiation with exclusive representatives.

In adverse-action proceedings, as in grievance proceedings, union concerns center around notice and participation. At the outset of the EMC program, the incidence of negotiated disciplinary procedures and advisory arbitration was low in union agreements. Whereas two thirds of the agreements in the 1965 BLS survey had grievance clauses, only one fifth had clauses dealing with union functions in adverse actions. In the 1971 BLS survey one fourth of the contracts studied had negotiated adverse-action clauses. Many agreements simply relied upon agency procedures. In a large number of contracts with extensive grievance procedures, the only reference to adverse actions was found in exclusions that specifically removed disciplinary proceedings from the grievance machinery.[50]

Under the EMC program, bargaining over disciplinary procedures could go beyond the scope of CSC regulations. Federal unions had varying degrees of success in such bargaining. Many agreements left the ultimate decision on union notice and representation to the employee under fire. An early Machinists' contract with the Federal Aviation Agency base in Oklahoma City typified those contracts in which management retained control in adverse-action provisions. The contract was silent on union notice or observers and relied primarily upon governing regulations. In fact, it made no reference to the union whatsoever:

---

[47] E.O. 10987, *Agency Systems for Appeals From Adverse Actions*, January 17, 1962.
[48] U.S. Civil Service Commission, *Federal Personnel Manual*, Chap. 771, Subchap. 2, Secs. 15-18, May 25, 1971.
[49] *Ibid.*, Chap. 771, Subchap. 1, Sec. 2.
[50] U.S. Department of Labor, Bureau of Labor Statistics, BLS Bulletin No. 1451, pp. 35, 36; BLS Bulletin No. 1789, 1973, p. 44.

"This Article shall be applicable to adverse actions as follows: Removal for cause; Suspension for more than thirty days; Change to lower grade for cause.

"Any employee in the unit receiving a letter of proposed adverse action shall have the right to an informal meeting with the Deciding Official prior to the issuance of a final notice of adverse action. In exercising this right to a meeting the employee must within ten days after receipt of proposed adverse action, notify the Deciding Official that an informal meeting is desired. The Deciding Official, upon receipt of notification that a meeting is desired, will schedule such meeting not less than one working day nor more than three working days after receipt of the request.

"Conduct of the Meeting: In the process of the informal meeting the Deciding Official shall provide the employee, who may be accompanied by his designated representative, the right to present information or introduce witnesses in his behalf. Such witnesses shall be limited to a reasonable number sufficient to establish a point.

"In the event the employee wishes to pursue the matter further he shall be entitled to the Agency and Civil Service Commission Appeals procedures provided by regulations." [51]

Provisions here for employee representatives and witnesses went beyond the minimal requirements in the FPM. If the union was to be the appellant's representative, its role was governed by agency regulations, not by a negotiated procedure.

While most agreements provided for direct union notification of proposed adverse actions, many contained some sort of restriction. Even some highly advanced agreements, such as the NASA Goddard contract, made no mention of union notification, stating only that:

"In all cases of proposed suspension, discharge, or other formal disciplinary action by the Employer against any Employee covered by this agreement, the Employer agrees to notify the Employee of his right to be represented, or not represented, by the Council or any other authorized representative of his choosing." [52]

An agreement at the Trenton Naval Turbine Test Station avoided union notification through negative language. It provided simply that the union president was to receive a copy of all letters of reprimand or proposed suspensions of 30 days or less. Its grievance exclusions eliminated all major adverse actions, and the cited cases were the two types of minor adverse actions that could be conducted through grievance machinery. Thus, there

[51] Federal Aviation Agency, *Basic Agreement*, between Aircraft Services Base, Oklahoma City, and IAM, Lodge 960, 1964, Art. XV, Secs. 1-3.

[52] National Aeronautics and Space Administration, Goddard Space Flight Center, *Agreement*, 1967, Art. XVII, Sec. 1.

was no notice requirement for major actions.[53] And even in the case of minor adverse actions, notice would not be forthcoming if "The action is based on 'security' or 'morals' or divulging information which would, in the judgment of the Employer, violate the privileged information relationship between the Employer and Employee." [54]

It was quite common for management notification of the union to depend upon employee consent. Thus, in an IAM agreement at the Langley Research Center a written employee request could prevent union notification.[55] One Navy accord allowed for automatic direct notice to the union but stipulated that "Specifications of charges on disciplinary actions will be provided the shop steward only upon written authorization of the affected employee." [56] A clause which appeared in many Metal Trades Council and other blue-collar agreements provided for notice to the union of hearings even if notice of proposed adverse actions had not been required. It stipulated: "When any employee of the unit requests such a hearing, the Employer agrees to notify the Council at the same time the employee is notified of the date set for the hearing." [57]

The personal and privileged character of adverse actions provided sufficient cause for management to hedge upon the issue of union notification. This consideration was exemplified by the Charleston Naval Shipyard-Metal Trades Council contract, effective through 1970. Union notice and participation hinged upon employee consent. The agreement established a specific form for notifying employees of their right to representation by the Council, chief stewards, stewards, or any other employees during preliminary investigations and throughout the disciplinary proceedings. If the worker declined representation, he could also request that no personal or confidential documents be furnished to the union. If, however, he chose a representative, the representative was to receive the notice of the investigation and other pertinent data.[58]

---

[53] U.S. Department of the Navy, *Negotiated Agreement*, between Naval Air Turbine Test Station Trenton, N.J., and IAM, Lodge 176, 1965, Art. VII, Sec. 2, Art. IX, Sec. 1.

[54] *Ibid.*

[55] National Aeronautics and Space Administration, *Basic Agreement*, between Langley Research Center, Hampton, Va., and IAM, Lodge 892, 1965, Art. XII, Sec. 1.

[56] U.S. Department of the Navy, Defense Printing Service, Navy Publications Printing Service Office, *Agreement*, 1966, Art. XXX, Secs. 1-3.

[57] U.S. Department of the Navy, *Agreement*, between Puget Sound Naval Shipyard and Bremerton Metal Trades Council, 1965, Art. XVI, Sec. 1.

[58] U.S. Department of the Navy *Employee-Management Cooperation Agreement*, between Charleston Naval Shipyard and Charleston Metal Trades Council, 1968, Art. XVI, Sec. 1, Appendix II.

Unions are vitally concerned with having their observers present at all stages of the adverse-action process. Observers are particularly desired at the more formal proceedings when the employee has chosen some representative other than the union. Thus, an agreement at the National Institutes of Health in Washington provided for a union observer at formal hearings in the event the union was not selected as the employee representative.[59] The Technical Engineers' accord with the Supervisor of Shipbuilding at Camden, N.J., stated:

> "that in accordance with regulations the Union shall be entitled to have an observer at hearings conducted by the Hearing Advisory Committee and he may make a statement of the Union's views concerning the case for the record. The statement shall be made at a time determined by the Chairman of the Advisory Hearing Committee. The Union will commit its observers at such hearings to treat information received concerning the employee as privileged and private to the employee." [60]

Similar committee mechanisms were found in many accords. This device not only provided for observers but also afforded the union an additional avenue of participation through the selection of committeemen, an important gain. The patterns for selection followed those set earlier for forming wage-survey and grievance committees. The 1966 Charleston Shipyard accord advanced the cause of greater Union-management mutuality in administering the agency system through its provision that:

> "The Council may submit to the Employer a list of at least twenty-five employees in the unit and the Employer agrees to select from this list at least ten employees to serve as members of Hearing Advisory Committees for disciplinary actions proposed to be taken against employees in the unit. . . . No more than one employee in the unit will be assigned to any Hearing Advisory Committee. No employee may serve on any committee to consider a case with which he has any connection." [61]

A 1968 contract at the Charleston Shipyard effectively insured a union presence during disciplinary appeals. The compact allowed minor adverse actions—letters of reprimand and suspensions of 30 days or less—to be appealed entirely under the negotiated grievance procedure. However, more serious disciplinary

---

[59] U.S. Department of Health, Education and Welfare, *Negotiated Agreement*, between National Institutes of Health and Washington Area Metal Trades Council, 1966, Art. XVII, Sec. 2.

[60] U.S. Department of the Navy, *Agreement*, between Supervisor of Shipbuilding, Camden, N.J., and American Federation of Technical Engineers, Local 198, 1964 Art. XV, Sec. 2.

[61] U.S. Department of the Navy, Charleston Naval Shipyard, *Agreement*, 1966, Art. XV, Sec. 3.

cases could also be appealed at specific stages of the negotiated grievance machinery. Union observers were assured for both minor and major proceedings; for even if the employee elected to process his appeal via the Navy procedure, the union was to be

"permitted to be represented by one observer at hearings of disciplinary and adverse actions involving employees in the unit when the employee does not desire to be represented by the Council, even if the employee's representative is an Officer, Steward or other official of the Council. The observer may make the views of the Council known at the appropriate time." [62]

This provision secured the presence of union observers at appeals hearings whose result might well affect the entire unit.

Very few agreements made the negotiated grievance procedure applicable to appeals from adverse actions. During the first few years of the EMC program, though, some confusion arose over the possibility that negotiated grievance procedures might be used for adverse-action appeals. The wording of the first IAM accord at the Naval Ordnance Plant in York, Pa., for example, left little room for dispute. It stated without qualification that:

"In all cases of suspension, discharge or other disciplinary action . . . disciplinary action must be for just cause, and the employee may exercise his rights under the grievance and arbitration procedures of this Agreement." [63]

This clause gave the union a greater role as employee representative until it was weakened by Navy action. According to William Ryan, former president of IAM District 44, four months after the contract at York was signed the Navy revised its regulations, putting final determination of all adverse actions of 30 days or over under the coverage of the Navy Civilian Personnel Instructions. This automatically took major adverse actions out of the contractual area since the union could not bargain to change rules and regulations.[64]

Executive Order 10987 provided that agencies could, entirely at their discretion, negotiate advisory arbitration into their adverse-action appeals procedures. Among the first agencies to do so were the Post Office, HEW, and the Smithsonian Institution.

The Civil Service Commission had recommended that more disciplinary cases be subject to negotiations, and certain agencies,

[62] U.S. Department of the Navy, Charleston Naval Shipyard, *Agreement,* 1968, Art. XVI, Sec. 4.
[63] U.S. Department of the Navy, *Basic Agreement,* between Naval Ordnance Plant, York, Pa., and IAM, Lodge 174, 1963, Art. XVIII.
[64] William H. Ryan, *Interview,* Washington, July 28, 1964.

including the Navy Department, revised their policies in some of their accords, adopting negotiated systems to a degree. In only a few agreements, however, were substantial attempts made to incorporate the features of the negotiated grievance and arbitration procedures into adverse-action provisions. In the exercise of their discretion, agency negotiators varied the degree of union participation, representation, and the use of grievance machinery or advisory arbitration. If weak in negotiated disciplinary procedures, contracts did at least indicate that greater mutuality in disciplinary proceedings was feasible and, indeed, was being encouraged.

The Civil Service Commission was well aware of the conflicting desires and continuing problems involved in grievance and adverse-action administration. As in other areas, it had conducted internal studies with an eye to improving procedures. In early 1967, the CSC issued staff proposals to adopt a single-hearing disciplinary-appeals procedure in order to eliminate the diverse situations arising from a system in which appeals could be taken to the agency, the Commissioner and, in some instances, to both. It sought to develop a simplified and uniform system of appeals that would apply to all agencies.[65]

Unions harbored some strong reservations about CSC staff proposals. Their views closely resembled the arguments later offered in opposition to the promotion revisions. The Government Employes' Council, for example, sought to protect whatever gains had been achieved through collective bargaining. The GEC feared that the proposals would remove adverse actions entirely from the negotiation table contrary to the spirit of the Kennedy order and would inhibit further experimentation with the administration of disciplinary action.[66]

When in 1968 the Commission set requirements for agency appeals from adverse actions, it adhered to the essentials of due process. Acting in accordance with the provisions of E.O. 10987, the CSC set minimum standards for agency and/or Commission appeals procedures. Detailed criteria controlled notice, written appeals, employee representation, full and fair hearings, impartial hearing committees, witnesses, records, and written reports. The nonnegotiated agency system offered the employee an initial choice of appeal to the agency or to the Commission. If he appealed first to the Commission he was foreclosed from the agency system. If he appealed first under the agency machinery and his

---

[65] *Government Employee Relations Report,* No. 179 (1967), p. A-7.
[66] *Government Employee Relations Report,* No. 192 (1967), pp. A-12, A-13.

agency had only one appellate level, he could still appeal to the Commission. If the agency had two levels of appeal, the employee had the choice of using the second agency level or going to the Commission for final decision.[67]

G. RECOMMENDATIONS FOR CHANGE AND E.O. 11491

On balance, unions believed considerable inroads had been made into management prerogatives in the areas of grievances and discipline. They also contended, however, that reform and improvements in the EMC program were still needed. This was apparent from union testimony before the Johnson Review Committee.

The lead was taken by the AFL-CIO, and union officers generally supported its stand, as spelled out by George Meany. Meany's prime recommendations stipulated that:

"Negotiated grievance procedures should automatically preclude the use of agency procedures contained in the personnel manual; all grievances and appeals should be subject to the negotiated procedure except when special procedures were required by law and that grievance arbitration should be final and binding."[68]

These proposals embodied policies that unions had tried to achieve through negotiation, but with only partial success.

The preclusion of agency grievance procedures was unanimously supported by AFL-CIO affiliates. Collective bargaining would be meaningless, they held, if unions were unable to represent and protect their workers in effecting contract enforcement. Where an agency had permitted negotiated grievance procedures, unions saw no need to retain separate agency procedures. Maintenance of "dual" grievance systems, it was believed, indicated a lack of good faith on the part of the agency in its formal relationships with both union and employees. The union should represent all workers in the unit.[69] Dual grievance systems were viewed as inconsistent with union representation rights, tending to erode them and to undermine the validity of the negotiation process.[70] To improve working conditions by contract without providing an effective procedure for resolving disputes over interpretation or

[67] U.S. Civil Service Commission, *Federal Personnel Manual*, Chap. 771, Subchap. 2 (1-10), August 16, 1968; May 25, 1971.

[68] George Meany, President, AFL-CIO, *Statement*, before President's Review Committee, October 23, 1967, p. 10.

[69] John F. Griner, President, American Federation of Government Employees, *Statement*, before President's Review Committee, October 23, 1967, p. 12.

[70] Government Employes' Council, *Statement*, before President's Review Committee, October 24, 1967, p. 4.

application would render agreements meaningless.[71] Insistence
that an employee be allowed to choose between agency and negotiated grievance systems was viewed as a remnant of "paternalistic policy" that considered unions as outsiders in the worker-man-
agement relationship.[72]

The limited scope of cases covered by negotiated appeals
machinery, particularly adverse-action procedures, came in for
sharp criticism. It was considered unfortunate and contrary to the
principles of collective bargaining that so many matters were
excluded by the Kennedy order and agency regulations.[73] The
Machinists recommended that existing exclusions be removed from
negotiated grievance machinery, thus expanding coverage to include position-classification cases, major adverse-action appeals,
and complaints regarding alleged violations of law and Civil Service Commission or agency regulations. They also considered union-
management disputes over contract interpretation or application
as proper subjects for grievance machinery even if they did not
involve grievances of individual employees.[74]

Perhaps the strongest union arguments were presented in support of final and binding arbitration of grievances and adverse
actions. It was believed that the Kennedy order had not gone far
enough in providing only advisory arbitration; binding arbitration could add strength and validity to its policies.[75] In support
of their case, unions pointed to situations in which local management had not accepted advisory arbitration awards that in no way
conflicted with existing law.[76] Although most federal officials did
not reject advisory arbitration awards, the instances of rejection,
it was believed, emphasized the ineffectiveness of the system.
Some unions reflected on the system's one-sidedness, observing
that unions and employees had no right to refuse a third-party
award.[77] The Metal Trades Department cited instances in which
arbitrators' opinions conflicted with rulings of the Comptroller
General or agency officials simply did not have the authority to
comply with the award. The MTD called for the removal of technical impediments to compliance with awards unless the awards
clearly violated the law, and it suggested that legislation be pro-

---

[71] B. A. Gritta, President, Metal Trades Department, Statement, before President's Review Committee, October 23, 1967, p. 7.
[72] George Meany, Statement, op. cit., p. 9.
[73] B. A. Gritta, Statement, op. cit., p. 6.
[74] W. H. Ryan, as National Coordinator, Government Employees Department,
IAM, Statement, before President's Review Committee, October 23, 1967, p. 6.
[75] E. C. Hallbeck, President, United Federation of Postal Clerks, Statement,
before President's Review Committee, October 25, 1967, p. 9.
[76] W. H. Ryan, Statement, op. cit., p. 6.
[77] Government Employees' Council, Statement, op. cit., p. 4.

posed, if necessary, to permit the payment of monies under such impartial decisions.[78]

John Griner of the AFGE was particularly vehement on the issue of advisory arbitration, terming it worthless. When local officials rejected awards and then were upheld at higher levels, he stated, the inevitable result was a loss of confidence in management. Griner recommended a simple two-step procedure for compulsory binding arbitration. First, a Labor Department mediator would seek a voluntary settlement. Failing this, the parties would resort to binding arbitration by professional arbitrators.[79]

According to George Meany, the federal arbitration experience had so far evidenced "a great deal of maturity on both sides, management and labor." Meany noted that an analysis of federal arbitration cases revealed "an amazing similarity to the practices in private industry in regard to subject matters, percentage of cases lost by the union and also the attitude of management towards the arbitrator's award." He concluded, therefore, that the prohibition against final and binding arbitration should not be continued.[80]

The Review Committee [81] made recommendations that incorporated many union aspirations. The Nixon Study Committee also considered labor's proposals for grievance and appeals reforms. Here, as elsewhere, the Study Committee report [82] relied, to a degree, upon the language and policies of its predecessor, but by no means did the Study Committee affirm all of the Johnson-Wirtz Review Committee's proposals. Some of the Review Committee's major ideas were firmly rejected in the Nixon Report and E.O. 11491. Nevertheless, in the main the reforms accomplished by the Nixon Study Committee had to be considered by the unions as a beneficial forward step.

Both committees decided not to differentiate between union grievances involving disputes over application or interpretation of the agreement and employee grievances arising from individual dissatisfactions. Union and employee grievances were still grouped together by the Nixon Committee when it affirmed the Wirtz Report's proposal for more binding arbitration to help re-

---

[78] B. A. Gritta, *Statement, op. cit.*, pp. 7, 8.
[79] John F. Griner, *Statement, op. cit.*, pp. 13, 14.
[80] George Meany, *Statement, op. cit.*, p. 10.
[81] President's Review Committee on Employee-Management Relations in the Federal Service, *Draft Report*, April 1968, in U.S. Department of Labor, *56th Annual Report*, 1969, Attachment B, pp. 11, 12.
[82] President's Study Committee, *Report and Recommendations, on Labor-Management Relations in the Federal Service*, August 1969.

solve such cases.[83] At no time did either committee's report suggest separate treatment for each category. Other problems appeared to be of far more pressing importance. Executive Order 11491 specifically cited both union and employee grievances as proper subjects for the same grievance machinery.[84]

There was also considerable unanimity on the need to eliminate the dual system of grievance machinery. Both committees agreed that union and agency procedures concurrently available should be replaced by a single grievance system for all employees covered by an agreement in an exclusive unit. While neither committee desired to perpetuate the dual system developed under the Kennedy order, the Review Committe appeared to support a greater degree of union exclusivity than the Nixon Committee. So long as the negotiated procedure preserved all the material rights available to employees under the CSC standards, the Review Committee recommended that it "should be the exclusive procedure available to the employees in the unit." [85] The Study Committee also found merit in a single negotiated grievance system but softened the wording of its recommendation to allow management more latitude. It thus made exclusive adoption of a grievance system a proper subject for collective negotiation.[86] E.O. 11491 stipulated that if negotiated grievance procedures conformed to law and to CSC and agency standards, they would be the exclusive machinery "when the agreement so provides." [87] Depending on the relative strength and desires of the parties, therefore, a dual or a single system could be chosen. Management was still free to bargain on the issue. The Review Committee proposal, if adopted, would have permitted only the negotiated system.

Union aspirations were also met on the issue of advisory versus binding arbitration. Both committees felt the need for a clear statement that arbitration procedures were appropriate for the resolution of disputes over contract interpretation and application and the resolution of employee grievances. Unlike the Johnson Committee, the Nixon Committee did not apply the same approach to adverse-action appeals.[88] Its views differed from those of the Review Committee on several aspects of the adverse-action appeals procedures. On the subject of arbitration in principle

---

[83] Review Committee, op. cit., pp. 14-15; Study Committee, op. cit., pp. 50-51.
[84] E.O. 11491, Sec. 13.
[85] Review Committee, op. cit., pp. 12-13.
[86] Study Committee, op. cit., p. 50.
[87] E.O. 11491, Sec. 13.
[88] Review Committee, op. cit., p. 14; Study Committee, op. cit., p. 50.

there was no divergence. The Study Committee affirmed the views of its predecessor by reporting:

"We find that arbitration of grievances has worked well and has benefited both employees and agencies. Many thousands of grievances have been settled without referral to arbitration. In those instances in which the grievance was referred to arbitration, the arbitrator's decisions have been accepted most of the time." [89]

The Review Committee's report exhibited some similarity to the AFL-CIO's official position on arbitration. Both the Review Committee and the AFL-CIO laid great stress on the private labor relations experience and sought greater adherence to arbitration awards. The need for more binding arbitration was also supported by the Study Committee, which asserted that arbitrators' decisions should be accepted by the parties. Both committees agreed to set standards and procedures that would help insure fuller effectuation of decisions. Since in a few instances agencies had unilaterally rejected or modified awards, both committees recommended that challenges to arbitrators' awards "should be sustained only on grounds similar to those applied by the courts in private sector labor-management relations." [90]

Procedures for the consideration of such exceptions were to be developed by the Federal Labor Relations Council, as discussed in Chapter VI. The committees believed that referral to higher authority should first be attempted if an award appeared unacceptable. Exceptions were to be taken quickly by notifying the other party, the head of the agency, and the national union president of the full nature of the objections to the award. If the problem was not resolved internally by the highest agency and union officers within a reasonable period of time, either side would have the right to appeal to the FLRC.[91] If a case went to the Council, the latter would review the record, consider the briefs and any other pertinent information, issue its decision, and publish the decision in the *Federal Register*.[92]

The new procedures as embodied in E.O. 11491 had much to recommend them, although they fell short of the final and binding arbitration sought by the unions. E.O. 11491 set forth a procedure which, as a practical matter, has had the same effect as final and binding arbitration.[93] While it motivated agencies to

[89] *Ibid.*
[90] Review Committee, pp. 12, 15; Study Committee, pp. 50-51.
[91] *Ibid.*
[92] E.O. 11491, Sec. 14.
[93] Review Committee, *op. cit.*, p. 15; Study Committee, *op. cit.*, p. 51.

accept an arbitration award rather than face the prestigious FLRC, it fully met the needs of sovereignty, for the final determination was still to be made by management officials. From the union point of view, although the Nixon order failed to achieve final and binding arbitration, its arbitration provisions constituted a fair and rational compromise.

The Johnson and Nixon Committees diverged over the issues of unification of grievance and appeals systems and union representation. The attitudes of the Study Committee may be viewed as presaging the major procedural revisions of the second Nixon order. These attitudes led to a further separation of the grievance systems and the removal of traditional employee grievances and adverse actions entirely from the scope of collective bargaining.

The Johnson Committee recommended the establishment of a single system for all grievances and appeals procedures within an agency. It would have permitted arbitration, reduced the number of levels of appeal, and prohibited duplicate channels of review. This unified system emulated established private-sector practice and was supported vigorously by the labor witnesses before the Review Committee. Supported by hearing testimony, the Review Committee believed that the CSC should have proceeded to implement the proposal to the extent feasible by law.[94]

The Study Committee, however, took the opposite tack. Noting that the CSC had considered extensively and had rejected the idea of a unified system, the Committee declined to recommend its reconsideration. The CSC had concluded that the "extensive and varied appeal rights available to federal employees by law" made it impracticable to unite grievances and appeals systems.[95] Indeed, the revised FPM provisions of 1971 and 1972 strengthened the existing division.[96] Accordingly, the Study Committee declared that if a single system fulfilled all the statutory requirements for adverse-action appeals, it would seriously hamper the processing of the majority of ordinary working-conditions grievances and lesser disciplinary cases. The legal necessities of such cases would be burdensome and inappropriate in the simple and direct procedures available in negotiated grievance systems. In view of these factors the Nixon Committee advocated continuance of the separated system already in effect. The Committee's proposals were "aimed at improving separately the agency adverse action appeals

---

[94] Review Committee, *op. cit.*, pp. 11, 12.
[95] Study Committee, *op. cit.*, p. 49.
[96] U.S. Civil Service Commission, *Federal Personnel Manual*, Chaps. 752, 771, 772.

system and the grievance system." [97] Executive Order 11616 carried the separation of the system a step further.

The Study Committee failed to treat the question of union representation in grievances and appeals in depth. The Review Committee, on the other hand, had gone to some lengths to preserve a union presence in grievances, appeals, and personnel policies and practices that might affect general working conditions in a unit. The Committee also believed that the exclusive representative should be permitted to negotiate the mechanics for individual presentation of grievances in cases where arbitration was not invoked. The decisions of cases in which the exclusive representative did not enjoy an unqualified right to be present were not to be binding on other employees in the unit.

These and other precautions were clearly enumerated in the Wirtz report.[98] Nevertheless, they were omitted from the Study Committee's recommendations and discussion. Formal comment may have been considered superfluous since union representation had been amply developed in the contracts and was also well provided for by the CSC's standards for agency systems. However, the Study Committee's failure to comment on an issue that had been probed by the Review Committee and was of such vital concern to labor indicated a change in emphasis.

H. THE EFFECT OF E.O. 11616

In 1971 the Federal Labor Relations Council initiated "an intensive review of the whole subject" of grievances and arbitration, from which it concluded that substantial changes were warranted.[99] Of the revisions made by E.O. 11616, perhaps the most far-reaching were those concerning grievances and appeals.[100] Basically, the second Nixon order continued the trend toward separated systems. It excluded numerous areas from negotiated grievance and appeals systems, restricting these areas to the CSC's statutory procedures. It also limited grievance representation by the exclusive union.

Unlike the previous Kennedy and Nixon orders, E.O. 11616 distinguished traditional employee grievances from union disputes arising from application and interpretation of agreements.

---

[97] Study Committee, *op. cit.*, p. 50.
[98] Review Committee, *op. cit.*, pp. 13-14.
[99] Federal Labor Relations Council, *Labor-Management Relations in the Federal Service, Amendments to E.O. 11491, with Report and Recommendations,* Washington, August 1971, pp. 4-5.
[100] E.O. 11616, Secs. 6, 7 (d) (1), 13, 14.

All disputes over the interpretation and application of agreements were to be treated under the grievance procedure negotiated by the exclusive union, while employee grievances were taken out of collective bargaining and made grievable only under the agency statutory system that conformed with CSC standards. Prior practice had permitted a dual system of negotiated and agency procedures to handle such grievances. Thus, traditional grievances joined the statutory appeals procedures already excluded from negotiated grievance machinery by E. O. 11491. This separated system was further institutionalized through the differentiation of union and employee grievances, the latter administered by the agency system, the former by negotiated machinery.

The FLRC's rationale in support of these moves was not without merit. The Council noted that the "persistent dissatisfactions" with grievances and arbitrations were rooted in the "confusing intermixture of individual employee rights established by law and regulation with the collective rights of employees established by negotiated agreement." The result was an overlapping and duplication of rights and remedies; negotiated grievance systems often had requirements that obstructed the effective handling of grievances.[101]

The Council believed that existing practice forced difficult and confusing decisions on a grievant. Under CSC rules only an employee or a group of employees could file a traditional "employee" grievance, which could involve the application of law, regulation, agency policy, or the collective agreement. The employee also had to decide on his representative, if any, and on whether to invoke arbitration or, if a dual system was in effect, under which system he was going to proceed. On the other hand, union "disputes," including their arbitration, were limited to the application or interpretation of the agreement.[102]

The Council recommended that the scope of the negotiated grievance procedure be delineated to remove confusion. Henceforth there was to be only one negotiated grievance and arbitration procedure for disputes over the interpretation and application of the collective agreement. Unlike negotiated machinery written under prior executive orders, this machinery would not have to conform to CSC regulations. The parties might bargain, for example, over the nature and scope of the system, the costs of arbitration, and so on. The exclusive union would possess full

---

[101] Federal Labor Relations Council, *op. cit.*, p. 5.
[102] *Ibid.*, pp. 5-6.

authority and responsibility for grievance processing on the negotiated conditions of employment. Only the exclusive union could represent a grievant under the procedures. If an employee did not want union representation, management still would be accessible for adjustment of the grievance. Executive action would have to conform to the terms of the agreement, however, and the exclusive representative would have the right to be present at the adjustment.[103]

As to contract disputes, the changes wrought by E.O. 11616 placed the exclusive union in a more authoritative and flexible position, but it was radically weakened in the area of "employee" grievances. Executive Order 11616 clearly affirmed the employee's rights to choose his own representative in the grievance and appellate actions that were now to be conducted only through agency-CSC systems. This held true regardless of whether the employee was in an exclusive unit or not.[104]

Executive Order 11616 fully implemented the Council's recommendations, and the *Federal Personnel Manual* was accordingly revised to remove employee grievances from negotiated procedures.[105] Section 13 of E.O. 11491 was entirely rewritten and expanded, and Section 14, providing for the arbitration of grievances, was revoked.[106] This meant that arbitration systems for employee grievances that had been developed through collective bargaining would have to be scrapped, since arbitration was not a part of the CSC's grievance system. If questions arose as to whether a case was grievable or arbitrable under negotiated procedures, they were to be determined by the Assistant Secretary of Labor for Labor-Management Relations.

Unions argued that E.O. 11616 was retrogressive as a result of its reduction of the union presence in grievances and appeals. To the extent that grievances and appeals were removed from collective bargaining, this argument is valid. Nevertheless, it is abundantly clear that, whether by collective negotiations or unilateral action by the agencies and the CSC, union representation and participation in grievances and appeals has been promoted under the EMC and has been expanded and retained as a continuing federal policy. Returning employee grievances and appeals to FPM procedures does not automatically eliminate the union pres-

---

[103] *Ibid.*, pp. 6-8.
[104] E.O. 11616, Sec. 7 (d) (1) .
[105] U.S. Civil Service Commission, *Federal Personnel Manual,* FPM Letter No. 771-6, November 19, 1971.
[106] E.O. 11616, Secs. 13, 14.

ence. Any reading of the *Manual* and agency regulations will reveal innumerable occasions for union action. There is nothing to prevent an agency from continuing the procedures evolved over the years under collective negotiations, even if those procedures have been removed from the scope of negotiations. Retrogressive policy revisions would simply be bad human relations. Many agencies have continued established practices and will continue to deal sensibly with their exclusive representatives.[107] As long as basic employee rights and CSC policies are not transgressed, there is no reason why agencies cannot pursue a liberal labor relations policy in grievances and appeals.

Nevertheless, to the extent that E.O. 11616 has returned these areas to management control, union dissatisfaction will increase, and unions will agitate for grievance procedures that surpass those attained prior to the order.

I. PROSPECTIVE ALTERNATIVES

Since the promulgation of E.O. 11616 two developments have occurred that could profoundly affect the nature of future grievance procedures. These occurrences have followed diametrically opposed courses. The first, the 1971 Postal Service Agreement, came only one month after E.O. 11616, yet it severely reversed the direction of this Nixon order. The second, E.O. 11838 of 1975, served to strengthen prior Nixon policies.

The Postal Reform Act made possible machinery that resembled private industrial practice as closely as any public grievance and disciplinary procedures reasonably could.[108] As a result of comprehensive federal collective bargaining, a single grievance-arbitration process was established covering individual grievances, union disputes over interpretation of contracts, and employee disciplinary proceedings, all ending in binding arbitration.[109] This unified structure eliminated the prior practices of allowing a dual system of "agency" and "negotiated" procedures under a single contract, of separating grievances from adverse actions, of divorcing traditional employee grievances from union disputes over contract interpretation, and of excluding all statutory grievance and adverse action procedures from the bargaining process. Recent postal contracts have provided for a strong union pres-

---

[107] Thomas A. Milazzo, Labor Relations Officer, Civil Service Commission, New York Region, *Interview,* June 6, 1972.

[108] Public Law 91-375, 91st Cong., August 12, 1970; 39 U.S.C. Sec. 1206.

[109] U.S. Postal Service, *Working Agreement,* July, 1971, Arts. XV-XVII.

ence and a streamlined arbitration process[110] and are giving rise to a new body of precedents under binding arbitration.[111]

Unlike the Postal Agreements, President Ford's E.O. 11838 made only evolutionary changes in the grievance processes established by earlier executive orders. In its report prior to the order, the Federal Labor Relations Council made no attempt to change the federal practice of mandatory exclusion from negotiations of all matters for which statutory appeals procedures already existed.[112] Nevertheless, since E.O. 11616 had limited negotiation to "grievances over the interpretation or application of the agreement," confusion persisted over the concept of mandatory exclusions, which included, among other things, what was vaguely termed "any other matters." [113] This catch-all proviso had caused considerable difficulty, particularly in regard to negotiations over pertinent agency rules and regulations.

The FLRC accordingly sought to clarify the terminology relating to federal negotiating policy. The Ford order discarded the vague phraseology of E.O. 11616 and simply granted the power to negotiate grievance and arbitration procedures subject only to the mandatory exclusions.[114] Thus, any unexcluded matter such as agency rules, regulations, or policies, even if unmentioned in the contract, could be brought within the negotiated grievance procedure.

Both unions and management strongly supported the Ford order, which unquestionably broadened the scope of grievance negotiations as already defined.[115] However, there are still great disparities between federal policy and the policy of such systems as the Postal Service. Whether these will be lessened must wait upon more fundamental executive or legislative action.

---

[110] U.S. Postal Service, *National Agreements,* July 1973 and July 1975, Arts. XV-XVII.

[111] National Association of Letter Carriers, *Bulletin,* No. 17, June 9, 1972.

[112] Federal Labor Relations Council, *Labor-Management Relations in the Federal Service, Amendments to E.O. 11491, with Report and Recommendations,* Washington, February 1975, pp. 44-50.

[113] E.O. 11616, Sec. 13.

[114] E.O. 11838, Sec. 14 amending E.O. 11491, Sec. 13

[115] *Government Employee Relations Report,* No. 592 (1975), pp. A-8, A-14.

CHAPTER XIV

THE RESOLUTION OF IMPASSES

The first decade of the federal labor relations program saw a significant change in executive policy towards bargaining impasse procedures. Starting from a position of outright opposition to third parties in dispute settlement, national policy evolved to a position of acceptance of the major aspects of factfinding and arbitration as reflected in the establishment of the Federal Service Impasses Panel (FSIP). Throughout this evolutionary period national policy stressed the primacy of negotiations over reliance upon a procedural crutch that could seriously weaken the bargaining process.

In 1961 the Kennedy Task Force recommended that methods "other than arbitration" be devised to help resolve negotiation deadlocks. It did not choose to amplify this recommendation but stated simply that possible settlement techniques should be negotiated on an agency-to-agency basis. Its prediction that the need and concern for impasse procedures would mount as the EMC program developed was fully realized. However, what the Task Force wanted most was individual experimentation based upon the diversity of each agency's requirements. In support of its position, it emphasized the problems usually associated with the use of arbitration. For example, the temptation of inexperienced negotiators to relinquish responsibility to a third party was considered a serious obstacle to the building of mutual relationships and the evolution of realistic negotiating practices.[1]

The Task Force also sought support in the traditional argument of the unique nature of government employment. It declared:

"The important differences between the nature of negotiations between employees and management in the private economy, as against most parts of the Federal Government, and the relative lack of experience in any form of employee-management negotiations on the part of most Government officials and employees, leads the

---

[1] President's Task Force on Employee-Management Relations in the Federal Service, *Report,* November 30, 1961, pp. 18, 19.

268

Task Force to feel that the arbitration of negotiations impasses is not an appropriate technique for general adoption by the Federal Government at this time." [2]

To insure this prohibition, the Kennedy order permitted only advisory arbitration in its grievance machinery provisions. Advisory arbitration was limited specifically: "to the interpretation or application of agreements or agency policy and not to changes in or proposed changes in agreements or agency policy. . . ." [3]

In recommending such a limitation, the Task Force reflected the traditional thinking of the time, as exemplified by the National Civil Service League's 1960 policy statement that "Binding arbitration, as we know it in industry is rarely possible in public employment for no arbitration award can supersede government."[4]

The evolution of this policy was described in a statement by H. T. Herrick, labor relations director of the Atomic Energy Commission and former general counsel of the Federal Mediation and Conciliation Service. Herrick, who was closely involved with E.O. 10988 at its inception, disclosed at a 1967 seminar of the Federal Bar Association that the final decision of the Task Force on arbitration was made on the advice of the Justice Department. That agency had advised the Task Force that a serious constitutional problem regarding the delegation of authority would develop if arbitration were to be fully adopted, particularly in regard to grievances and unfair labor practices. This position enjoyed strong support from the Civil Service Commission and the Defense Department.[5]

A. THE CONTINUING PROBLEM

Negotiation deadlocks almost immediately generated a considerable amount of argument for and against a revision of E.O. 10988. CSC Chairman Macy acknowledged deep union concern over this issue when he reported on the progress of the EMC program to President Johnson in 1964. He stated the Commission's basic position and conceded that:

"Probably the most significant change proposed is a recommendation by some organizations that the Order be amended to provide for the arbitration of negotiation impasses. Both the Department of

---

2 *Ibid.*

3 E.O. 10988, Sec. 8, (b) (2).

4 National Civil Service League, *Employee Organizations in Government,* New York, 1960, Sec. X.

5 H. T. Herrick, *Address,* to Seminar, "Collective Bargaining in the Federal Service," Federal Bar Association, Washington, D.C., April 18, 1967; *Interview,* March 11, 1964.

Labor and the Commission oppose this recommendation because arbitration of negotiation impasses in the Federal Service would weaken the obligation of the parties themselves to reach agreement across the conference table. The present program permits use of alternative procedures such as fact-finding, mediation or referral to higher authority within the agency. Their potential value has not yet been explored." [6]

The extent of union concern over impasse policy was demonstrated in AFGE president John F. Griner's reaction to Macy's report. Griner claimed there had been enough experience with existing negotiation rules to prove them inadequate for "true give-and-take bargaining." In many instances reasonable union proposals were met with summary management rejection, and meaningful negotiations were at an end.[7] As to Macy's argument that existing alternatives had not been explored, Griner responded:

"These procedures are virtually meaningless. In one Agency, for example, fact-finding is used when a negotiation impasse is reached. The fact-finding board makes its report without any recommendation. Then the parties go back to the bargaining table and if after a month no agreement is reached the point at issue is dropped. . . .

"Referral to higher authority is another deadend street. The disinclination of higher management to accept a union proposal which local officials rejected is nothing short of monumental. On the contrary, what happens much more often is that union proposals accepted by local management are ordered stricken from the contract by higher agency authority. .Mediation, as it has been practiced in the government, has meant little more than fact-finding. And Agency management does not have to submit negotiation impasses to mediation. They can and do refuse.

"Submitting negotiation impasses to advisory arbitration would not be a radical step. This is exactly the procedure used now when there is a dispute over a bargaining unit. It has worked well and should be extended to negotiation impasses. The Executive Order can never even begin to reach its full potential until a system is established for solving negotiation impasses that gives unions at least an impartial hearing on these proposals." [8]

Craft unions were as dissatisfied as the AFGE. In November 1964, Paul R. Hutchings, research director of the Metal Trades

[6] Office of White House Press Secretary, *Press Release,* exchange of letters between the President and John W. Macy, Jr., January 25, 1964. See also W. B. Irons, "Employee-Management Cooperation: The Federal Program in Perspective," *Public Personnel Review,* July 1964, p. 148. Irons stated that these techniques had not been tested to the point where it could be said that they were insufficient.

[7] John F. Griner, "Changes in Operating Labor Policy Needs," *The Government Standard,* February 21, 1964.

[8] *Ibid.*

Department, AFL-CIO, presented his union's position at a Navy seminar on negotiations. He pointed out that the Department of Defense and the Navy Department, as well as the Civil Service Commission, had called for the use of third parties, from within or without, for developing facts or for advisory mediation of deadlocked disputes. Yet, he noted:

> "it has thus far been impossible for any of our Councils in the various naval activities to get agreement from their activity heads to use mediation or fact-finding in connection with resolution of deadlocks in negotiations. . . . The abject refusal by activity heads to agree to such methods in all instances has meant that labor organizations in their negotiations with naval activities are very frequently faced with the dismal prospect of either capitulating and accepting unsatisfactory clauses in their collective bargaining agreements or having no agreements whatsoever." [9]

Hutchings declared that the MTD expected management to "require or, at least, affirmatively encourage, the use of an impartial third party to develop the facts or to mediate on deadlocked issues." [10]

B. A. Gritta, then president of the Metal Trades Department, felt there was a complete blank on the subject of impasses in the Kennedy order. He complained that since the union could not strike, union representatives were severely restricted; they could only present their proposals to management and had to accept management's final decision. He believed that alternatives to bargaining standoffs had to be provided. Disagreeing with Macy's view that the unions themselves had not developed alternative measures as much as they might, he identified the problem as agency unwillingness to agree to permitted alternatives. Interestingly enough, the MTD at this time preferred to emphasize advisory mediation over arbitration. [11] Gritta publicly stated the MTD position in March 1965, declaring that as the number of exclusive recognitions multiplied, negotiation impasses had become an increasing problem. He called for the establishment of mediation and factfinding panels. [12] William Ryan of the IAM basically supported Gritta's declaration, stating that it was primarily the mutual-consent requirement that frustrated mediation. Too often, he

---

[9] Paul R. Hutchings, *Remarks,* to Seminar on Negotiations, U.S. Navy Department, Office of Industrial Relations, November 17, 1964, as reported in *Government Employee Relations Report,* No. 63 (1964) , p. D-3.

[10] *Ibid.*

[11] B. A. Gritta, *Interview,* Washington, D.C., July 20, 1964.

[12] B. A. Gritta, *Remarks,* before Society for Personnel Administration, March 15, 1965, as in *Government Employee Relations Report,* No. 80 (1965) , p. A-11.

believed, local negotiators who refused mediation were controlled by higher authorities.[13]

Management was not entirely at fault, however. Unions also had been lax in promoting wider use of resolution devices in the first three years of the EMC program. This was true even though Secretary of Labor Goldberg, the Task Force Chairman, had praised the mediation which resolved serious differences between his department and the AFGE and led to the first agreement under the Kennedy order.[14]

In 1966, CSC Executive Director Oganovic reiterated the Commission's basic stand but implied that under pressing circumstances some changes might occur. He rejected compulsory arbitration and decried the lack of efforts to exhaust other problem-solving techniques, noting the encouragement given the agencies to make greater use of mediation and other methods. He foresaw improvement as the parties gained greater negotiating experience, but cited the shortage of "available mediators who are knowledgeable in this highly specialized field of public employee unionism." [15] On this point he concluded that "If it appears that real impasses are developing on matters of real substance, then it may be necessary to develop a body of trained personnel for mediation or fact-finding work." [16]

He did not develop this suggestion, and whether he meant to suggest the need for a formal panel of mediators appointed by some central organization or was merely commenting upon the general need for public service mediators was not fully apparent.

In early 1964 in a letter to President Johnson, Gritta had proposed setting up a panel or commission made up of highly qualified impartial observers to resolve impasses. This panel would have recommended solutions for deadlocked negotiations after it had investigated all the facts and issues.[17]

It is now possible to observe how the elements of present federal impasse policy were beginning to coalesce even in the mid-1960s. The evolutionary process was unfolding long before the issuance of E.O. 11491. After an undeniably slow start, attempts were made to develop a variety of impasse procedures in agreements under the Kennedy order. These fell into three categories:

---

13 W. H. Ryan, *Interview*, Washington, July 28, 1964.

14 Arthur J. Goldberg, *Statement*, accompanying the signing of the agreement between Department of Labor and AFGE, Lodge 12, August 9, 1962.

15 Nicholas J. Oganovic, *Address*, at the Conference on Public Employee Labor Relations, New York State School of Industrial and Labor Relations May 12, 1966.

16 *Ibid.*

17 B. A. Gritta, *Interview*, Washington, July 20, 1964.

mediation, factfinding, and referral to higher authority. Some accords combined and varied elements from each procedure. As the EMC program grew, increasing numbers of contracts included impasse provisions.

B. MEDIATION

Mediation and factfinding generally were not included in the early contracts. Some installations delayed their full acceptance despite the exhortations of agency directives and the CSC. CSC and Navy policy supported joint factfinding committees, mediation, and higher referral for operating units. In 1966, this policy was officially embodied in the CSC's *Federal Personnel Manual*. The Commission considered impasse techniques to be valuable instruments for facilitating negotiations and strengthening the entire federal program, and recommended greater use of such techniques, alone or in combination.[18]

A Bureau of Labor Statistics survey of the first two and one-half years of the EMC program disclosed that only five Army contracts and one Navy accord provided for factfinding. Only six Army agreements and two Navy contracts had mediation provisions. Most other agencies presented a similar picture.[19] This weak showing appeared to bear out the complaints of the blue-collar union leaders and Chairman Macy's chidings of agency heads for their hesitancy to utilize new methods.

The reluctance to accept third-party assistance may simply have reflected the intransigent attitude of certain military men that was seen from time to time in federal labor relations. Most defense installations maintained a policy of unilateral management control of final decisions in negotiations. It was not unusual for certain Defense Department contracts, comprehensive and detailed on many other negotiable items, to fall decidedly short on impasses. Relatively few MTD, IAM, AFGE, or NAGE agreements in the defense agencies contained meaningful impasse clauses well into the 1960s.

Typical of defense agency agreements was the noted second-round accord at the Charleston Naval Shipyard. This was the first agreement negotiated with the aid of the FMCS. The Metal Trades Department and the Bureau of Ships had to resort to me-

---

18 U.S. Civil Service Commission, *Federal Personnel Manual System*, FPM Letter 711-3, February 7, 1966.
19 U.S. Department of Labor, Bureau of Labor Statistics, *Collective Bargaining Agreements in the Federal Service, Late Summer 1964*, BLS Bulletin No. 1451, August 1965, pp. 52-54.

diation after several months of fruitless bargaining. The final contract was an object of satisfaction to both union and management, which voiced their approval of the mediation machinery. Mediation resulted in a highly improved agreement, worded in clear, positive terms.[20] Yet this accord, like most MTD-Navy agreements from this period, did not contain any provision for the resolution of future impasses. Even the third compact at the Charleston Naval Shipyard, effective through 1970, failed to include an impasse clause, though it added many other major improvements.

The early reluctance to accept impasse provisions was not confined to the defense agencies. Only one fourth or 52 of the 209 accords surveyed by the BLS in 1965 established factfinding machinery. A far smaller number—24, or about 11 percent—called for mediation procedures.[21] This pattern indicated that individual installations intended to follow the central policy laid down by their highest agency authority. Thus, 29 or three fifths of the factfinding contracts were in the Veterans Administration.[22] VA units simply adhered to the policy established in the VA *Personnel Policy Manual* and emulated the suggested contract clause that made the inclusion of a method for resolving impasses mandatory.[23]

Central policy also accounted for the fact that a sixth of the factfinding and half the 24 mediation accords were in the Interior Department. The Interior Department, with a long history of mediation and arbitration in its bargaining, also set national guidelines, through its departmental manual, which was revised to comply more fully with E.O. 10988. The manual eliminated arbitration by requiring that basic agreements incorporate the following provisions:

> "Methods of settling disputes concerning negotiable items (exclusive of arbitration procedures) by mediation, conciliation or similar measures agreeable to employees and management. Arbitration procedures for this purpose are not authorized by E.O. 10988." [24]

Interior Department impasse experience under the Kennedy order had a double-edged meaning for the whole federal estab-

---

[20] *Government Employee Relations Report,* No. 124 (1966) , p. 21.
[21] U.S. Department of Labor, *op. cit.,* pp. 53-54.
[22] Veterans Administration, *Personnel Policy Manual,* Chap. 20, Par. 19b (7) , 20; Veterans Administration, Office of Assistant Administrator for Personnel, *The Basic Agreement,* June 1963, p. 4.
[23] *Ibid.*
[24] U.S. Department of the Interior, *Departmental Manual,* Employee-Management Cooperation, Chap. 711, Subchap. 7, Sec. 5J, January 7, 1966.

lishment. On the one hand, the ban on new arbitration procedures was a setback for impasse collective bargaining. On the
other hand, Interior's policy of continuing arbitration procedures
wherever established by pre-Kennedy order contracts significantly
influenced future developments in national impasse policy. Prior
to E.O. 10988, under Interior's liberal labor policy, unions had
succeeded in negotiating a system with arbitration that was "final
and binding on both parties upon approval by the Secretary."
How the system worked was described by Newell B. Terry, Interior's Personnel Director:

> "When an issue arises, which cannot be resolved by the
> individuals directly involved, the agreements outline a process
> whereby a settlement can be reached. Initially in such cases, the
> matter is referred to a higher echelon. If no settlement results, a
> mediator is brought in to attempt to bring agreement. A negative
> result at this stage causes the appointment of a 'board of arbitra-
> tion'. Each party selects one member, and the two men thus se-
> lected choose a third member. The resulting three-man panel hears
> the arguments pertinent to the dispute and incorporates their con-
> clusions in a recommendation submitted to the Secretary for ap-
> proval. This process is utilized when an impasse is reached on con-
> tract negotiations, as well as in settling grievances." [25]

A standard mediation-arbitration clause was found in practically all advanced Interior contracts prior to E.O. 10988. The accord between the Bureau of Reclamation's Boise-Minidoka
Projects in Idaho and the International Brotherhood of Electrical
Workers was typical. The mediation-arbitration clause read as fol-
ows:

> "When agreement is not reached in direct negotiation upon rates
> of pay or working conditions affecting employees covered by this
> agreement either party may invoke the services of a mediator to be
> selected jointly by the parties. The mediator shall use his best efforts
> to bring the parties into agreement by mediation.
>   "If such efforts to bring about an agreement through mediation
> are not successful, the Union and the Region shall submit their
> controversy to arbitration and each of the parties shall appoint an
> arbitrator, and those two arbitrators shall, with the help of the me-
> diator, endeavor within five days to agree upon a third arbitrator.
> If the parties are unable to agree upon an arbitrator, the mediator
> shall then appoint such arbitrator. The decision of the majority of
> said arbitrators shall be final and binding on both parties upon ap-
> proval by the Office of the Commissioner of Reclamation.
>   "The expenses of mediation and arbitration, including the com-

---

[25] Newell B. Terry, "Collective Bargaining in the U.S. Department of the Interior", *Public Administration Review*, Winter 1962, Vol. XXII, No. 1, pp. 21, 22.

pensation and expenses of any mediator or arbitrator (other than one solely representing the Union or the Region) shall be borne equally by the Union and the Region." [26]

Identical clauses had been written into other contracts, before 1962. However, after the issuance of E.O. 10988 and in accordance with CSC's language and the modified departmental manual, at least one basic agreement was revised by amendment to remove its arbitration provisions. Although mediation was retained, arbitration was most often displaced by referral to higher authority for final and binding decision. The Bureau of Mines' agreements with the Oil, Chemical, and Atomic Workers Union adopted mediation alone. Although its multiplant Helium Activity in the Southwest had signed successive agreements since August 1952,[27] the September 1964 accord provided only that:

> "Both parties recognize the desirability of obtaining impartial assistance in the settlement of disagreements that may arise. When a decision by the General Manager, Helium Operations, relative to a grievance or in connection with negotiable matters is not satisfactory the Grievance Committee or Negotiating Committee concerned may within 10 days request mediation of negotiable items in dispute or a grievance. The mediator shall be furnished all information and correspondence pertinent to the dispute at hand for study. Both parties will have full opportunity to present information pertaining to the disputed issue. When the mediator has the full facts, the parties will cooperate with him in generally acceptable practices of mediation to bring them into agreement." [28]

The mediator was to be selected with the aid of the FMCS, much as arbitrators are selected for other contractual purposes.[29]

A great loss from the union standpoint was the prohibition of arbitration in all contracts negotiated after the Kennedy order. A standardized impasse clause was developed to incorporate mediation and resort to higher authority. This provision, with remarkably little variation, was included in most Interior accords under E.O. 10988. It was typified by the IBEW accord with the Bureau of Indian Affairs' Flathead Irrigation Project in 1967, which declared:

> "When agreement is not reached in direct negotiation upon rates of pay and working conditions affecting employees covered by this

---

[26] U.S. Department of the Interior, *General Employee-Management Agreement,* between Bureau of Reclamation (Region 1), Boise-Minidoka Projects, and IBEW, Local 283, AFL-CIO, February 21, 1961, Art. VII, Secs. 7.1, 7.2, 7.3.

[27] U.S. Department of the Interior, *Basic Labor Agreement,* between Bureau of Mines, Helium Activity and Oil, Chemical and Atomic Workers International Union, AFL-CIO, 1952, 1961, 1964.

[28] *Ibid., Agreement,* 1964, Art. VI, Sec. 1.

[29] *Ibid.,* Sec. 2.

agreement, either party may invoke the services of a mediator to be selected jointly by the parties. The mediator shall use his best efforts to bring the parties to agreement by mediation.

"If efforts to bring about agreement through mediation are not successful, the dispute shall be submitted by the parties to the Commissioner of Indian Affairs for consideration of the merits and his decision shall be final and binding on both parties to the dispute. Copies of briefs, documentary evidence, statements by the mediator or other materials filed with the Commissioner as pertinent to the dispute by either the Area Director or the Union shall be furnished to the other party in the dispute." [30]

Expenses were to be borne equally by the parties. Almost identical clauses appeared in agreements covering a variety of agencies and many unions. Many of the contracts were first accords written under the Kennedy order.[31]

The evolution of this clause indicates with striking clarity how central agency policy can control contract writing at the installation level. Although Interior continued to have some of the most comprehensive agreements, the loss of advisory arbitration in so large a number of new accords constituted for the unions a decided lessening of collective bargaining alternatives in a highly controversial area.

It was significant that, despite E.O. 10988, advisory arbitration clauses still continued in effect in about half of the Interior agreements. Approximately 24 accords, including all the contracts of the Bonneville Power Administration and the Alaska Railroad and many contracts in the Bureau of Reclamation, contained some advanced form of arbitration and/or mediation procedure.[32] The nature of the machinery varied only slightly from that already described as typical in the Bureau of Reclamation's Region 1 agreement. The continuance of this policy was made possible by a departmental interpretation of Section 15 of the Kennedy order. Section 15 specifically declared that: "Nothing in this Order shall be construed to annul or modify or to preclude the renewal or continuation of, any lawful agreement heretofore entered into between any agency and any representative of its employees." [33]

---

[30] U.S. Department of the Interior, *Basic Agreement,* between Bureau of Indian Affairs, Flathead Irrigation Project, Montana, and IBEW, Local 768, AFL-CIO, 1967, Sec. 11.

[31] E.g. U.S. Department of the Interior, Bureau of Indian Affairs, *Basic Agreement,* with Employees Council of USMV North Star III, 1963.

[32] E.g., U.S. Department of the Interior, *Collective Agreement,* between Bonneville Power Administration and Columbia Power Trades Council, AFL-CIO, 1945, revised 1964, Art. 9.

[33] E.O. 10988, Sec. 15.

After years of mutual agreement with the unions over the importance of their impasse machinery, Interior was understandably reluctant to abandon arbitration. There was a strong belief that advisory arbitration had a rightful place in federal labor relations and should, therefore, be retained in existing agreements. The policy of the Task Force was interpreted as not being intended to cause unnecessary upheavals or to disturb existing successful relations. Interior believed that Section 15 of the order could accommodate its established practices and those of other agencies such as the TVA. Hence the Department elected to renew all existing arbitration-mediation clauses. It does not appear that any major problems resulted from this policy. As previously noted, the continued and successful use by Interior of arbitration carried great weight in contemplated policy revisions. And in the end, the theoretical essentials of Interior practice were incorporated in E. O. 11491.

Mediation provisions in other agencies were varied but generally included the main features of the revised Interior clauses. The first accord under the Kennedy order at the Tobyhanna Army Depot declared:

> "When an agreement is not reached in direct negotiations as provided by CPR E6.3, (4c), both parties shall request a third party from within the Federal Government for the purpose of mediation; said party shall be mutually acceptable to both parties." [34]

More detailed and comprehensive was the agreement between the Labor Department and the AFGE covering the Department's field services. The agreement first defined an impasse in specific rather than general terms, thus clarifying for the parties exactly what constituted a deadlock. Moreover, the agreement did away with the potentially crippling requirement of mutual consent for the initiation of the impasse procedure. Either party could invoke mediation, and in accordance with accepted practice, the services of the Federal Mediation and Conciliation Service were utilized. [35] Sophisticated provisions were included to promote collective bargaining by the parties, and costs came in for unusual treatment. The accord concluded:

> "The above does not preclude either party from presenting, in the interest of reaching agreement, a substantive counter proposal

---

[34] U.S. Department of the Army, *Labor Agreement*, between Tobyhanna Army Depot, and AFGE, Lodge 1647, AFL-CIO, May 31, 1963, Art. VIII.

[35] U.S. Department of Labor, *Agreement*, with AFGE, Council of Field Labor Lodges, AFL-CIO, August 30, 1966, Art. 13, Secs. a, b, c.

at any stage in this procedure that would continue negotiation without the assistance of mediation.

. . . . .

"The costs of the mediator, and necessary administrative costs incurred by the mediator will normally be shared equally by the parties except that a different cost sharing ratio may be jointly agreed upon by the parties when they agree to enter mediation. The cost of travel of Union representatives shall be borne by the Council." [36]

Such mediation accords increased at a rapid pace. According to the 1973 BLS study of collective bargaining agreements, mediation clauses tripled, rising from 11.5 to 33.1 percent of the agreements reviewed. The incidence of clauses on factfinding and referral to higher authority remained at about 25 percent.

C. FACTFINDING

More agreements relied upon factfinding than upon mediation procedures to resolve impasses in the early years. This was particularly true of agreements covering blue-collar and mixed units. As noted, many of the factfinding procedures were found in VA contracts as a result of VA national policy. These procedures commonly utilized a committee of three members, but in some cases committees were to be composed of equal numbers of management and union representatives. The contract at the VA hospital in Tuscaloosa, Ala., provided for a five-man factfinding committee.[37] Certain agreements restricted committee membership to agency employees; others, by remaining silent on this point, permitted the use of outside observers.

The VA center in Reno, Nev., provided for submission of oral and written briefs. Failing resolution of the deadlock, the committee's findings and the parties positions were to be submitted to the center director for decision.[38] Both the Tuscaloosa and the Reno contract reserved the power of decision at the installation level to management; there was no appeal to higher levels of VA authority.

The contract between the National Association of Internal Revenue Employees and the IRS in Newark did not specify the number of committee members. It merely called for an equal number of employees to be appointed by each party, all of whom together would select an additional member as chairman. The

---

[36] *Ibid.*, Secs. d, e, f.

[37] Veterans Administration, *Basic Agreement,* between VA Hospital, Tuscaloosa, Ala., and AFGE Lodge 131, 1963, Sec. IX.

[38] Veterans Administration, *Basic Agreement,* between VA Center, Reno, Nev., and AFGE Lodge 2152, 1964, Art. XI.

impasse machinery in this contract coexisted with that already established by the Internal Revenue manual. Thus, if the negotiated factfinding machinery failed, the impasse provisions in the manual went into effect.[39] In a highly management-oriented accord at the Atlanta Army Depot in 1965, specific time limits were set for the factfinding and negotiation functions. A fixed cutoff date was set for negotiations in the event of an insoluble impasse, and no provision was made for appeal to a higher authority.[40]

A few clauses went beyond mere factfinding and gave joint committees the power to submit recommendations in addition to their findings of fact. Thus, the AFGE accord at the National Zoological Park declared: "The fact-finding committee shall ascertain the facts involved and submit its findings and recommendations to the negotiating parties." [41] Since there was no contractual stipulation that the committee be made up of unit employees, the procedure in this AFGE accord approximated private-sector labor relations practice in that it combined elements of factfinding, mediation, and conciliation by outside parties. In the event of a continued impasse, the accord further provided that the dispute was to be referred to the Assistant Secretary of the Smithsonian Institution for an advisory opinion.[42]

D. REFERRAL TO HIGHER AUTHORITY

The technique of referral to higher authority was provided either as the sole medium of appeal or as a step preceding or following mediation or factfinding. Characteristic of this mode of settlement was an emphasis upon concerted efforts to complete negotiations and resolve differences at the lowest possible levels. In the majority of cases the decision of the highest executive named was binding on the negotiating parties.

As in grievance procedures, the levels of impasse appeals normally reflected the organizational structure of the agency. At one Marine Corps Base, provisions for appeal to higher authority through appropriate channels reflected the military chain of command. In the event of an impasse, since the management team

[39] U.S. Treasury Department, *General Agreement*, between Internal Revenue Service, Newark District, and NAIRE, Chapter 60, 1965, Chapter VII ,Secs. 5, 6.

[40] U.S. Department of the Army, *Agreement*, between Atlanta Army Depot, Ga., and Building Service Employees' International Union, Local 534, 1965, Art. VI, Secs. 3, 4, 5.

[41] Smithsonian Institution, *Agreement*, between National Zoological Park and AFGE Lodge 2463, 1966, Art. XXV, Sec. 2.

[42] *Ibid.*, Sec. 3.

was led by the Base Chief of Staff, the first appeal lay to the Commanding General of the Base. If no resolution could be achieved at this level, the union would next appeal to the Marine Corps Commandant. If still dissatisfied, it could appeal to the Secretary of the Navy, whose decision was binding on all parties.[43]

The AFGE effectively wrote two impasse procedures into its national accord with the Meat Inspection Division of the Agriculture Department's Agricultural Research Service. The machinery was geared to the authority levels and hierarchical structure of the organization. Thus, the first procedure covering station or local agreement deadlocks provided for informal appeals to the division level. If the impasse continued, written appeals would next be made to the Administrator, ARS, at the Service level for final decision. The second impasse procedure pertained to issues involving the basic agreement. If the matter in dispute was within the delegated authority of the Service, the impasse could be appealed to the director of personnel for final decision. If the issue involved a departmental matter, impasses could be referred by the union to the Assistant Secretary for Administration for final determination.[44]

The 1968 National Postal Agreement's rather detailed impasse procedures reflected the organizational structure of the Postal Service.[45] If an impasse was reached on a particular proposal, the local installation head and union representatives were required to report it to the regional level. After the first 14 days and at the conclusion of local negotiations, impasse items were to be submitted to the regional director of industrial relations and the regional union representatives for joint consideration. A regional-level resolution within 15 days was binding on the local parties.[46]

If no resolution was reached at the regional level, regional officers and union representatives were to refer the impasse promptly to the national level. There it was to be considered by the appropriate national exclusive unions and the Deputy Assistant Postmaster General, Bureau of Personnel. A decision reached here within 15 days was to bind the local negotiators. If no decision was reached at the national level, the impassed issues were to

---

43 U.S. Marine Corps., U.S.M.C. Base, Twentynine Palms, Calif., *Agreement*, 1965, Sec. 6.2.

44 U.S. Department of Agriculture, Agricultural Research Service, *Agreement*, 1964, Secs. 7.2, 7.3.

45 U.S. Post Office Department, *Agreement*, with the seven major postal unions with national exclusive recognition, 1968, Art. VII, Sec. 18.

46 *Ibid.*

be considered deadlocked and would not be subject to further negotiation during the life of the local agreement.

The old POD impasse provisions contained more than simple referral to higher authority. They actually set forth graduated steps for continued negotiations conducted by higher level officers on both sides of the bargaining table. Management retained final authority, however, since impasse items were simply dropped from negotiations if not quickly resolved at the national level.[47]

Mediation was optional for national negotiations over the postal accord. Impasse items were to be temporarily set aside while agreement was reached on as many negotiable items as possible. Then if further efforts to settle the remaining issues were unavailing, either party could request mediation under the auspices of the FMCS. The mediator was given rather broad powers not only to bring the parties together but to use "any and all means he deems advisable providing he makes no public report or evaluation on the issues nor any public statement or findings of fact." Finally, if mediation failed, impasses were to be referred to the Postmaster General, whose decision was to be final. The concerned unions could submit briefs and documents and meet with the Postmaster General to aid in resolving the deadlock.[48]

It is apparent from an examination of "higher authority" clauses that their popularity was due, in no small degree, to the definitive manner in which they placed final decisions squarely in executive hands. This was entirely in keeping with the spirit of the Kennedy order. Employee organizations voiced their preferences for outside mediation and arbitration but would always accept higher authority rather than no impasse procedures at all. The success of referral to higher authority hinged largely upon management attitudes. If the unions believed their submissions would be reasonably considered, the end purpose of the machinery would be fulfilled.

E. PRESSURES FOR REFORM AND THE FEDERAL SERVICE IMPASSES PANEL

Public pronouncements from almost all quarters generally agreed that serious reforms of impasse procedures were needed. After four years of the EMC program, CSC Chairman Macy remonstrated over the severe lack of agency acceptance of prob-

---

47 *Ibid.*
48 *Ibid.*, Art. XI, Secs. B, 1-6.

lem-solving techniques short of arbitration. A strong proponent of mediation and factfinding, he was constrained to admit:

"because the use of mediation is optional with agency management, little use is being made of this effective instrument of cooperation.

"The same goes for the use of advisory arbitration in unfair labor practice cases, and grievances and adverse action appeals." [49]

Herein lay a great weakness of the Kennedy order. In its reluctance to dilute any of the reserved, legal authority of employing agencies, it neglected to require the use of conciliation techniques. It could have done so without vitiating management's final power.

Union dissatisfaction over this weakness did not diminish over the years. Voicing the displeasure of the national officers of the AFGE with the overriding authority vested in management by existing arrangements, Clifford B. Noxon, executive vice president of the AFGE, declared:

"There cannot be realistic collective bargaining where management makes the final decision and there is no appeal to an impartial board. In our opinion, government operates under a paternalistic system which labor unions have constantly opposed and will continue to oppose." [50]

The Committee on Law of Government Employee Relations of the American Bar Association observed in August 1967 that most government agencies still did not permit an outside party to be involved in collective bargaining.[51] In 1966, the Committee had reported that very few federal collective bargaining agreements made any provision for deadlocks in negotiations. It had called for greater encouragement of such provisions and, if necessary, revision of the program machinery or the Kennedy order itself.[52] Its call was heeded.

Considerable argument had developed over the years concerning the place of impasse procedures in the EMC program. While in his capacity as executive director of the CSC, Warren B. Irons declared that issues considered impasses in government were frequently unrelated to vital matters. He considered some deadlocks

---

[49] John W. Macy, Jr., *Address*, before Federal Personnel Management Conference, San Francisco, October 29, 1965, as reported in *Government Employee Relations Report* No. 112 (1965), p. D-3.

[50] Clifford B. Noxon, *Address*, to Army Civilian Personnel Officers' Conference, November 1965, in *Government Employees Relations Report*, No. 115 (1965), p. A-9.

[51] American Bar Association, Section of Labor Relations Law, Committee on Law of Government Employee Relations, *Report*, "Federal Employee-Employer Relations," 1967, p. 178.

[52] *Ibid.*, pp. 134-135.

trivial, the result of poor handling by management; there were very few real impasses in the federal service. Irons believed that major issues which created impasses in private industry, such as wages, overtime, leave, insurance, and the like, could not be the cause of federal stalemates since these were controlled by statute.[53]

The relative importance of items creating deadlocks is, however, a matter of value judgment and differing standards. Although the proportion of impasses to the number of signed agreements was very small, the existence of a stalemate was a frustrating experience for the parties involved. Some of the differences that could complicate negotiations were described in a CSC progress report. Among them were the issues of conflict of interest of union officers, failure for over a year to agree on a union-requested safety procedure, disputes over the definition of a negotiable issue, alleged management delays and hostility to the bargaining process, and disagreements created by strongly held views on the substantive contractual issues.[54]

The ABA's Committee on Law of Government Employee Relations deemed the impasse issue significant enough to warrant a major revision of the federal labor relations program. Reviewing the advantages of each impasse technique, the committee recognized that the FMCS was handicapped by having neither the official jurisdiction nor the appropriated funds necessary to service federal stalemates. The FMCS was well able to supply lists of available mediators with whom the parties could contract on an individual basis. Indeed, more mediation was recommended in the belief that persuasion and appraisal by outside parties would be fruitful for those directly involved.[55]

The ABA committee suggested that impasses be submitted to advisory arbitration. Since this device was precluded by Section 8 (b) of the Kennedy order, obviously the section would have to be amended. It was the committee's belief that making arbitration advisory in character would not weaken it. This conclusion was based on the relative success of advisory arbitration in appropriate unit determinations under Section 11 of the order. Finally, the committee advised that negotiated agreements should include

53 Warren B. Irons, *Address*, Conference on Employee-Management Relations, Bureau of National Affairs-Federal Bar Association, Washington, April 18, 1965, in *Government Employee Relations Report*, No. 83 (1965), p. D-2.

54 U.S. Civil Service Commission, Bureau of Inspections, Analysis and Development Division, *Summary Report on Employee Management Cooperation*, March 1967, p. 5.

55 American Bar Association, *op. cit.*, 1966, p. 135.

a provision permitting either party, at its option, to resort to any or all of the suggested impasse techniques.[56] Such a broad provision was not unreasonable, since its breadth gave it the flexibility to deal with the unique problems of different agencies.

As already noted, substantial weight was placed on the continued success of arbitration procedures in the Interior Department. Carried forward in spite of the Kennedy order, such procedures were included in about half of Interior's agreements, and had been successfully used in wage and other disputes.

The need for a revision of impasse machinery was constantly being pressed in Congress. The bills of Representatives William F. Ryan[57] and Dominick V. Daniels[58] typified the proposals to revamp impasse machinery submitted in Congress before the Nixon reforms. These bills, many aspects of which were later to be found in E.O. 11491, proposed set procedures for mediation and binding arbitration whenever deadlocks occurred in federal collective bargaining. Use of the FMCS was to be an integral part of the labor relations programs of all government agencies. In addition, a new federal agency, to be known as the Government Labor-Management Relations Panel, would decide all disputes as yet unresolved. This panel, whose makeup reflected suggestions from many quarters over the years, would have comprised a chairman and from four to eight additional members appointed by the President.

Amid growing concern over whether reforms would be worked by legislative or executive means the cycle of events leading to E.O. 11491 was begun. Management and labor testimony before the Johnson Review Committee generally favored reform, and this testimony influenced the findings of the Nixon Study Committee and the form of the resulting new federal impasse program.

Presenting the AFL-CIO's position on impasse machinery, George Meany stressed the ineffectiveness of collective bargaining in the absence of adequate techniques for resolving impasses. He declared:

> "We believe that it is essential to devise an impartial and orderly procedure to settle unresolved disputes in the federal service which can be an effective substitute for the right to strike. Otherwise, the right to organize and bargain collectively loses substance and becomes an empty force." [59]

---

[56] *Ibid.*

[57] H.R. 4281, 89th Cong., 1st Sess., 1965, H.R. 3393, 90th Cong., 1st Sess., 1967.

[58] H.R. 460, 90th Cong., 1st Sess., 1967.

[59] George Meany, *Statement,* before President's Review Committee, October 23, 1967, p. 11.

The AFL-CIO recommendations called for increased reliance on mediation and the establishment of a Federal Services Disputes Panel empowered to make final and binding decisions. A simple two-step procedure called first for mediation by a commissioner appointed by the FMCS. If this failed, the proposed disputes panel, made up of two members each from labor and management and an impartial chairman, all appointed by the President, could be called in by either party. The panel would attempt to resolve the dispute through voluntary efforts, including further mediation. If these efforts failed, it would then hold hearings and make a final, binding decision.[60]

Meany added that the parties should have the right to employ specific techniques to settle disputes, including binding arbitration or factfinding plus public recommendations. At the same time, he cautioned against the use of compulsory arbitration, which the AFL-CIO also opposed in private industry. Meany's emphasis, rather, was on a "voluntary acceptance of permanent arbitration machinery by both parties." [61]

Management attitudes toward impasse resolution were varied. There was general agreement, however, that final and binding arbitration should not be permitted. This was understandable. At one point, Anthony Ingrassia, then representing the Post Office, condemned compulsory arbitration, whether advisory or binding, as tending to stifle collective bargaining. He believed that trilateral settlements would be as unpalatable as unilateral settlements to union representatives. Maturing relationships and the expansion of existing techniques would better serve the achievement of bilateral agreements.[62]

These views, based essentially upon the original Task Force objections to advisory arbitration, were supported by the Treasury Department. According to a Department spokesman, management and union inexperience in bargaining would be perpetuated by reliance on the crutch of arbitration. Rather, he recommended more extensive use of mediation, factfinding, and higher level review.[63] Most agencies did not deal with the arbitration issue extensively, but emphasized instead a continued reliance upon the three accepted resolution techniques.[64]

---

[60] *Ibid.*

[61] *Ibid.*

[62] Anthony F. Ingrassia, Director, Civil Service Commission—Office of Labor-Management Relations, Labor Relations Division, Post Office Department, *Statement,* before President's Review Committee, October 26, 1967, p. 9.

[63] Bernard J. Beary, Treasury Department, *Statement,* President's Review Committee, October 25, 1967, pp. 11, 12.

[64] Eugene T. Ferraro, Deputy Under Secretary, Department of the Air Force,

At the other end of the spectrum, certain agencies lauded the benefits derived from advisory arbitration. The General Services Administration's representative, for example, declared:

"We would have no objection to the establishment of an official agency with skilled mediators and arbitrators knowledgeable in the laws, regulations and other special conditions of Federal employment, who could render assistance in resolving disputes and deciding unfair practice complaints." [65]

Consistent with its experience and progressive attitude, the Interior Department came out four-square for advisory arbitration. Newell B. Terry felt that the EMC program had reached a point of maturity warranting third-party advisory arbitration as "a practical and necessary" next step after mediation. Above all, he wanted its adoption to be left to the negotiators. Terry believed conditions were particularly favorable for instituting his proposal. There was a solid corps of highly qualified arbitrators at hand, and their effective handling of Section 11 unit cases had demonstrated their ability to advise on bargaining deadlocks.[66] He concluded:

"We can recommend no better substitute for the denial of strike action in the Federal service than impartial third-party intervention in disputes concerning negotiable matters. We feel that responsible union representation and progressive principles of management should embrace that doctrine as essential to the vitality of stable relationships and the traditional concept of fair play in modern industrial relations." [67]

The Johnson Review Committee steered a sensible course between the extremes of union and management positions on advisory arbitration. What had proved valid in the past it retained, and where innovation was justified by progress, it clearly outlined practical alternatives.

The Review Committee shared the Kennedy Task Force's earlier concern over excessive reliance upon third-party intervention. It was convinced that procedures too easily available for resolving negotiation deadlocks could result in continuous resort to outside assistance in lieu of serious negotiation. It echoed the sentiments of the AFL-CIO when it declared that "agreements voluntarily

Statement, before President's Review Committee, October 26, 1967, p. 8; Department of the Army, *Statement,* pp. 4-5; R. S. Driver, Assistant Secretary, Navy Department, *Statement,* pp. 3, 5.

65 U.S. General Services Administration, *Statement,* before President's Review Committee, October 24, 1967, p. 6.

66 Newell B. Terry, Director of Personnel, Department of the Interior, *Statement,* before President's Review Committee, October 27, 1967, pp. 10, 11.

67 *Ibid.*

arrived at through a free collective bargaining system are the hallmark of the industrial democracy enjoyed in this country." This principle was fully concurred in by the Nixon Study Committee.[68]

In fact, the principle of voluntary collective bargaining justified both committees' insistence that resolution devices that had been used successfully in the past should continue to be utilized.[69] Indeed, the reports of both committees were almost identical in philosophy and recommendations. The Nixon Study Committee, however, was considerably more concise and forceful than was the Review Committee in presenting proposals geared to administrative clarity and efficiency. Its task was eased, of course, by the prior work of the Review Committee. Nevertheless, in its full application of the FMCS to federal labor relations and the institution of a separate Federal Service Impasses Panel it surpassed its predecessor in the vital area of disputes resolution.[70] The Review Committee had proposed that functions later given the FSIP be simply part of the responsibility of the Labor Relations Panel it had envisioned. As the Study Committee's proposal was embodied in E.O. 11491, however, the FSIP became a separate unit within the Federal Labor Relations Council.[71] This removed any possible doubt or confusion over the locus of authority, and satisfied the need for a central, third-party agency to settle disputes.

The FMCS was fully recognized by the Nixon Study Committee for its past contributions. Although its mediation function had been limited and experimental, its success was lauded as demonstrating that use of the Service's facilities "should be expanded to the maximum extent possible." The Study Committee therefore proposed that the full range of FMCS mediation services, including preventive mediation, be made available to federal negotiators, who, however, would be free to make use of other third-party mediation on a cost-sharing basis.[72] This approach is reflected in E.O. 11491.[73]

Any doubts as to when a deadlock occurred were removed by

---

[68] President's Review Committee on Employee-Management Relations in the Federal Service, *Draft Report*, April 1968, in U.S. Department of Labor, *56th Annual Report, 1969*, Attachment B, pp. 16, 17; President's Study Committee, *Report and Recommendations on Labor-Management Relations in the Federal Service*, August 1969, pp. 44-45.

[69] Review Committee, p. 19; Study Committee, p. 45.

[70] Study Committee, *op. cit.*, pp. 43-48.

[71] E.O. 11491, Sec. 5.

[72] Study Committee, *op. cit.*, pp. 45-46.

[73] E.O. 11491, Sec. 17.

the definition of "impasse" offered by the Study Committee and contained in E.O. 11491. A deadlock occurred only when voluntary efforts such as direct negotiations, full referral to higher authority, mediation by the FMCS, or other third-party action had failed. At such time either negotiating party could request the assistance of the Federal Service Impasses Panel.[74] This was a major step forward. Mutual consent was no longer a prerequisite for the initiation of resolution procedures. Unilateral "inaction" could no longer block the settlement of a dispute.

Some of the most substantial policy changes brought about by E.O. 11491 were in the area of factfinding and arbitration.[75] The Review Committee had limited the resort to these techniques by predicating their use upon specific agreements between the parties.[76] The Study Committee, in its attempt to preserve the prime responsibility of the parties themselves to negotiate settlements, recommended that factfinding and arbitration be available only if "authorized by governmental authority" separate from the negotiating parties.[77] On its further recommendation a separate governmental authority—the Federal Service Impasses Panel—to deal with the problem of dispute settlement was established under E.O. 11491.[78]

Under FSIP regulations, when negotiations reach an impasse one or both the parties, the FMCS, or the executive secretary of the FSIP may request that the FSIP take jurisdiction of the dispute. The request is docketed with the Panel and an initial inquiry is made by an FSIP staff member.[79] This is essentially an informal inquiry into the merits of the case utilizing face-to-face contacts and oral and written communications with all parties concerned in the deadlock. After the Panel has received and analyzed the report, it determines, first, whether it will assume jurisdiction and, second, what steps should be taken to resolve the deadlock.[80]

The FSIP, sitting *en banc,* participates at every step of the proceedings. If the Panel deems jurisdiction warranted, it may au-

---

[74] Study Committee, *op. cit.,* p. 46; E.O. 11491, Sec. 17.

[75] Study Committee, *op. cit.,* pp. 44, 46-47; E.O. 11491, Sec. 5. See also Ed. D. Roach and Frank W. McClain, "Executive Order 11491: Prospects and Problems," *Public Personnel Review,* July 1970, Vol. XXXI, No. 3, p. 199.

[76] Review Committee, *op. cit.,* p. 18.

[77] Study Committee, *op. cit.,* pp. 44-45.

[78] E.O. 11491, Sec. 5.

[79] Federal Service Impasses Panel, *Rules of Procedure,* October 16, 1970, Sec. 2471.6. They were amended one year later.

[80] *Ibid.;* see also David T. Roadley, Executive Secretary, FSIP, *Interview,* February 18, 1972.

thorize one of several alternative impasse procedures. If it believes that negotiation efforts were not fully exhausted, it may simply return the dispute to the parties for further bargaining.[81] Thus, application to the FSIP provides no assurance that the burden of reaching agreement will automatically be lifted from the negotiators' shoulders. The Panel may suggest mediation or other voluntary procedures to assist the bargaining.[82] At this point, issues presenting the question of negotiability are seprated for handling in accordance with the procedures of Section 11 (c) of E.O. 11491. The FSIP retains control over other disputed issues.[83]

The intent of the Nixon order was clearly to promote the use of voluntary factfinding procedures. The Study Committee was emphatic on this point, and the experience of the FSIP to date reflects a close adherence to this intent. If the Panel determines upon factfinding, a Panel member or a staff member of the FSIP may be tapped for the job. Usually only one is chosen, although FSIP rules allow the use of several factfinders. The factfinder may conduct a prehearing conference before presiding at a formal hearing. The procedures of formal hearing closely approximate those typically seen in any labor arbitration regarding, for example, testimony, depositions, witnesses, records, briefs, and general hearing conduct.[84] All of the procedures of the FSIP meet the due-process requirements of notice and representation.

The factfinder, after receipt of briefs or transcripts, submits his report to the Panel, which reviews the history of the impasse and the factfinder's submissions, and issues its own report and recommendations to the negotiating parties.[85] The parties then have 20 days to consider the Panel's recommendations. They must tell the Panel whether they have used the proposed recommendations in whole or in part as a basis for resolving the impasse.[86]

The factfinding efforts of the FSIP were successful from the start. Between 1970 and 1973, 96 disputes were submitted to the Panel. Of these, only 17 went through all the steps described above. In 15 of the 17 protracted cases, the recommendations of the Panel were accepted in toto, while in the remaining two disputes Panel recommendations were used as the basis for final set-

---

81 Federal Service Impasses Panel, Sec. 2471.6 (a) (2) .

82 *Ibid.*, Sec. 2471.6 (a) (3) .

83 *Ibid.*, Sec. 2471.6 (b) .

84 *Ibid.*, Secs. 2471.7-2471.9.

85 *Ibid.*, Sec. 2471.11.

86 *Ibid.*, Sec. 2471.12.

tlement. All in all, this constituted a commendable record, particularly in view of the newness of the program.[87]

E.O. 11491 provided for an additional step if the parties refused to accept the Panel's recommendations. In such a case the Panel was empowered to "take whatever action it deem[ed] necessary to bring the dispute to settlement."[88] In the first few years of its life, the Panel did not use this power. But in July 1974 a landmark was passed when it determined to take final action and issued a decision and order in a negotiation dispute.[89] The dispute involved temporary promotions at the General Services Administration in Washington, D.C. Howard W. Solomon, FSIP's executive director, cited the decision as important because it was "the first time the Panel . . . had to settle a negotiation impasse by issuing a final and binding decision." The FSIP order demonstrated to Solomon that:

"E.O. 11491 provides for finality in the procedures set forth therein for resolving negotiation impasses. More specifically, the authority of the Panel to take action which is 'necessary' and 'appropriate' to resolve a dispute includes the authority to issue a final decision."[90]

This decision has far-reaching implications for the entire federal establishment. It shows that a form of final and binding arbitration has been worked out through the procedures of the FSIP. In all likelihood, however, the FSIP will continue to stress its factfinding procedures, and the voluntary efforts of the parties will remain the principal avenue for impasse resolution.

Executive Order 11491 also empowered the Panel to authorize voluntary binding arbitration, but this impasse mechanism has not been utilized. The Study Committee's intent was plainly that factfinding become the chief instrument for impasse resolution. The FSIP rules are broad enough to encompass the use of binding arbitration since they provide for "other voluntary arrangements."[91] In allowing such leeway, however, the Panel had in mind the needs of the almost 150,000 federal employees working outside the continental United States.[92] In any event, the develop-

---

[87] Federal Service Impasses Panel, *Report*, July 1, 1970—December 31, 1973, Washington, 1974, pp. 6-9.

[88] E.O. 11491, Sec. 17; Federal Service Impasses Panel, *Rules of Procedure*, October 16, 1970, Secs. 2471.12, .13.

[89] Federal Service Impasses Panel, *In re General Services Administration, Region III and Local 2151, AFGE*, Case No. 73, FSIP 18, July 11, 1974; see also FSIP, *Release* No. 41, July 19, 1974.

[90] Howard H. Solomon, *Letter*, July 19, 1974.

[91] Federal Service Impasses Panel, *Rules of Procedure*, October 16, 1970, Sec. 2471.6 (4).

[92] David T. Roadley, *Interview*, February 18, 1972.

ment of an instrument of final resolution in the FSIP, described above, should lessen possible pressures for the use of outside arbitration.

The comprehensiveness of the FSIP's procedures has obviated the need for extensive impasse clauses in contracts. A simple clause such as the following is now typical of federal contracts: [93] "When voluntary arrangements, including the services of the FMCS or other third-party mediation, fail to resolve a negotiation impasse, either party may request the Federal Service Impasses Panel to consider the matter."

In its operations, the Panel has reported several administrative problems stemming primarily from the inexperience of labor and management alike. Some negotiators are still unsure of the Panel's role and are as yet insecure with its procedures. Difficulties can arise through some parties' failure to provide complete background data on negotiations during the early inquiry stage. At the factfinding hearing itself, insufficient acquaintance with the procedural rules for presenting a formal case can cause delay and uncertainty. As a result of certain misconceptions the Panel's functions are confused with those of other labor relations units. Above all, some negotiators still erroneously think the Panel is going to complete their job of bargaining.[94] It is plain that the shortcomings mentioned here are to be expected of any new program and that time is necessary for familiarization with the FSIP impasse machinery.

F. THE FUTURE OF ARBITRATION

Arbitration, whether voluntary or compulsory, has had a checkered history in the public service. Initiated primarily at the local level, it has generally been considered destructive of serious collective bargaining.[95] Yet it may prove to be the only acceptable alternative to the public strike.

Resort to compulsory arbitration has been more common in Canada than in the United States. Under the Canadian Public

---

[93] E.g., see U.S. Department of Commerce, *Agreement,* between ESSA, National Ocean Survey and National Maritime Union, 1970, Art. IX, Sec. A; U.S. Department of the Navy, *Agreement,* between Military Sealift Command, Atlantic, and National Maritime Union, 1971, Art. VII, Sec. D.

[94] U.S. Civil Service Commission, Office of Labor-Management Relations, *Federal Labor Management Consultant,* Vol. 1, No. 5, August 6, 1971, p. 2.

[95] See City of New York, Department of Labor, *Unresolved Disputes in Public Employment,* Monograph Serial L.R. 9, December 1955; S. J. Frankel and R. C. Pratt, *Municipal Labour Relations in Canada* (Montreal: Industrial Relations Centre, McGill University, 1954) , Chap. IV; S. J. Frankel, *Staff Relations in the Civil Service* (Montreal: McGill University Press, 1962) , pp. 188-193.

Service Staff Relations Act of 1967, a bargaining agent may choose either the "strike route" or arbitration before serving a notice to bargain upon an employer.[96] Prior to passage of that act, compulsory arbitration for decades was required for the resolution of fire and police disputes. In Quebec, statutory compulsory arbitration has been used generally in government employment since 1944.[97]

Rarely employed in the United States, compulsory arbitration was accepted by New York City, with its highly unionized work force, in 1972. Whether its use will diminish the number of public strikes in New York remains to be seen. It may cause the parties simply to go through the motions of bargaining in the knowledge that decisions ultimately will be made by a third party. Arbitrated settlements may well exceed those that otherwise would have resulted from negotiations—a result that could compound the financial problems now being experienced by the city. Most municipal labor leaders in New York opposed the introduction of compulsory arbitration, just as management and union leaders have opposed it at the federal level. The possibility that compulsory arbitration will become the rule in the federal service is remote, if it exists at all. Yet its use at the local level is remarkable and bears watching.

Procedures under the Postal Reorganization Act of 1970 have important implications for the nonpostal federal establishment. The 1970 act prescribed binding arbitration as an integral part of a total impasse procedure, which included extensive negotiation and factfinding with recommendations.[98] The parties are required to bargain for at least 90 days before the dispute-resolution process begins. If an agreement is not reached during this period, a factfinding panel of three members is appointed under the leadership of the director of the FMCS. The panel's investigation and report are to be completed in 45 days. If no settlement can be reached as a result of the panel's efforts, a second round of negotiations lasting 45 days is commenced.[99] If there is still no settlement, a three-member arbitration board is established to render a binding award. The board is selected in the usual manner, except that it may not include anyone who served as a member of the factfinding panel. All items in dispute after the second phase of negotiations must be submitted to arbitration. If the parties

96 Public Service Staff Relations Act, 15-15-16 Eliz. II, Ch. 72, Secs. 36, 49 (1) .
97 Frankel and Pratt, *op. cit.*, pp. 66-82; Frankel, *op cit.*, pp. 15-20.
98 Public Law 9-375, 91st Cong., August 12, 1970; 39 USC Sec. 1207.
99 84 Stat. 735-736 (1970); 39 USC Sec. 1207(a), (b), (c).

cannot agree on the framing of the issues, the factfinding panel makes the submission to the arbitration board.[100]

The entire process may take as long as 225 days, which may seem excessive. Yet the system clearly is superior to that of the old Post Office Department under the EMC program. Even if the full time is used, the present system is still simpler, more predictable, and ultimately more manageable than the former system, which involved postal union efforts in Congress to achieve pay increases or other benefits. It generally took longer to submit bills, defend them at committee hearings, lobby their passage through the House and the Senate, and then weather the possibility of a presidential veto.

In the historic bargaining that culminated in the first Postal Service agreement in July 1971, the statutory procedures were almost exhausted, falling just short of arbitration. The possibility of a third-party determination forced crisis bargaining that produced a contract in the final hours. These negotiations were fraught with bitterness. There were accusations of management bad faith and constant threats of strike action. Most union leaders, however, sought to lay the foundations of a constructive relationship with management by giving the new procedures a fair trial. It appears that a great deal was learned by both sides in these negotiations. In April 1973, second-round negotiations commenced in an atmosphere of comparative good will, and in two months a national agreement was concluded by direct bargaining.

It is conceivable that the disputes-resolution machinery of the Federal Service Impasses Panel, especially its power to issue binding orders, may satisfy both management and unions in the federal service. But if the unions develop serious misgivings over the effectiveness of the FSIP, the postal impasse procedures and other facets of the Postal Reorganization Act may serve as precedents for government-wide collective bargaining reform.

---

[100] 84 Stat. 736; 39 USC, 1207 (c) , (d) .

Chapter XV

THE TENNESSEE VALLEY AUTHORITY

The Review and Study Committees given the task of reassessing national labor policy considered the recommendations of all interested parties. Their assessment of federal labor relations would have been incomplete without a consideration of the more unconventional federal agencies, since the broad labor relations experience of such agencies could provide possible guidelines for new policy.

The Tennessee Valley Authority and the Interior Department, especially its Bonneville Power Administration, have long occupied a unique position in the government labor field. The Kennedy Task Force had observed that the TVA and certain units of Interior had developed ties between unions and management that were close to full-scale collective bargaining relationships.[1]

The Task Force noted that the more closely the function of a federal agency approximated that of a private organization, the more closely its labor relations were patterned upon the private model. Since suggestions for change, particularly from the labor quarter, increasingly resemble the approaches of the general labor movement, it is essential to examine agencies whose labor policies and contracts are similar to those of private-sector organizations. Their experience, both prior to and under the EMC program, might point to a future line of development for all federal installations.

At its founding, many dispensations were granted the TVA, which protected its independence as a "business-type" government corporation. However, the TVA cannot be fully compared with a private corporation having complete freedom in labor matters. The TVA fulfills a service function as an installation of the Federal Government. All its labor agreements specify that the parties recognize the TVA as an agency of the U.S. Government. Its workers are paid as employees of a federal executive arm.

---

[1] President's Task Force on Employee-Management Relations in the Federal Service, *Report,* November 30, 1961, p. 3.

TVA labor policy was the result of a clear congressional intent in the Tennessee Valley Authority Act of 1933 to provide the organization the flexibility necessary to do a complicated job. Having much of the freedom enjoyed by management in private industry, TVA's management could develop a personnel system relatively independent of Civil Service Commission restrictions. The only injunctions placed upon the TVA were a requirement for merit and efficiency in appointment and promotion and a prohibition upon political considerations in personnel actions.[2]

A question might, therefore, arise as to whether the TVA's merit requirements were hindered by its labor policy. Harry L. Case, a former director of personnel for the TVA, declared that the TVA's merit policy differed from the personnel policy of other government agencies since the responsibility for personnel decisions was placed in a directing board and not in an independent commission. The TVA's practices, Case said, were at least as successful as those of other agencies as "reflected in the fact that no political consideration has ever affected the appointment, promotion, or retention of a TVA employee."[3]

It would appear that the TVA's merit system did not suffer any measurable deterioration by reason of its advanced labor relations program. Practically all of the TVA's employees are covered by its civil service merit provisions. All of its current labor contracts include clauses restating the TVA Act's official stand on merit, efficiency, the prohibition of political tests, racial discrimination, and nepotism. A degree of preference for union members is provided in the contracts, as will be discussed later.

The Tennessee Valley Authority Act of 1933 was almost entirely silent on the issue of labor relations. Within the two years, however, the TVA Board of Directors had issued an Employee Relationship Policy based on both employee and management views. As described by Otto S. Beyer:

> "This policy was not something distilled out of the superior wisdom of 'top' management and handed down to the men and women of TVA for their guidance and edification. Rather, it was the result of a great deal of deliberation and consultation in the course of which anyone who had any legitimate interest whatsoever in TVA's human relations was given an opportunity to participate. All up and down the valley the employees of TVA, the officers of the local unions to which they belonged, and their international

---

[2] Tennessee Valley Authority, *Working with TVA,* Knoxville, Tennessee, July 1952, p. 19.

[3] Harry L. Case, "Cornerstones of Personnel Administration in TVA," *Personnel Administration,* Vol. 33, January 1949, pp. 14-15.

labor representatives, as well as members of TVA's local and departmental supervisory staff and top management, met and expressed their views, ideas, and feelings as to what ought to constitute a guide to govern relations between labor and management." [4]

The 1935 Employee Relationship Policy affirmed the sovereignty concept for the TVA as an agency of the U.S. Government. The TVA had, therefore, to adhere to national policy and to submit to final control by the Federal Government. However, within statutory limitations, it could formulate a progressive labor program.[5] It was thus among the first federal agencies to recognize formally accepted labor relations terminology and practice when it declared: "For the purposes of collective bargaining and employee-management cooperation, employees of the Authority shall have the right to organize and designate representatives of their own choosing." [6]

Contributing to the TVA's stable labor relations were a number of factors, not the least of which was the strength of the craft unions in the power industry. The prevailing-rate principle applied throughout TVA installations. Employee- management cooperation was inseparably related to the growing strength of unions in the valley generally and in the TVA in particular. Furthermore, unlike the Atomic Energy Commission or NASA, the TVA decided early to employ its own workers and not to contract out to private corporations. Direct management contact with the labor force was thus assured. On the union side, the AFL sent out its best labor leaders to organize the valley region and to establish the TVA Trades and Labor Council in 1937. In time, recognition was granted to the Council on the basis of majority representation, and a collective bargaining relationship was created that has successfully endured. In 1940, after the final phases of formal negotiation were completed, a General Agreement was entered into between the TVA and the TVA Trades and Labor Council (TVATLC).[7] This is essentially the same agreement that remains in effect today after several major revisions. There are 16 craft unions in the Council.[8]

From the inception of the TVA's labor relations program,

[4] Otto S. Beyer, *Remarks,* Supper Meeting of the Central Joint Cooperative Committee, Wilson Dam, Ala., September 10, 1946, pp. 1, 2.

[5] Tennessee Valley Authority, *Employee Relationship Policy,* August 28, 1935, p. 4.

[6] *Ibid.,* Sec. 3, p. 5.

[7] Harry L. Case, *Democracy in Administration: A Study of Personnel Policy in TVA,* Tennessee Valley Authority, May 1954, pp. 29, 30.

[8] Tennessee Valley Authority, *General Agreement and Supplementary Schedules Covering Annual Employment,* between TVA and TVA Trades and Labor Council, 1940, revised 1951 and 1964.

there was a deep commitment on the part of both management and labor to the collective bargaining process.[9] Management negotiated agreements with two major groups. In addition to the craft-union Council, there was a Salary Policy Employee Panel (SPEP) representing five white-collar unions. For a variety of reasons it took the white-collar employees longer to organize and bargain than it did the blue-collar employees. There was, for example, a good deal of overlapping of appropriate bargaining units. Between 1941 and 1943, white-collar unions gained limited recognition. In late 1943 these unions decided to emulate the craft-union Council and formed the SPEP, which was quickly recognized as their sole collective bargaining agent. In 1950 the SPEP negotiated a basic agreement which remains in effect after several revisions.[10]

The basic bargaining techniques adopted resembled craft-union practices in private industry and were later emulated by other federal agencies, particularly the Interior Department. According to Louis J. Van Mol, negotiating with separate blue-collar and white-collar unions, the Council and Panel, held distinct advantages. In its search for the best possible appropriate unit, TVA's management attempted to avoid selecting either a single agency-wide unit on the one hand or many smaller units on the other. With the Council representing all of the craft bargaining units and the Panel negotiating for all white-collar units, the advantages of an agency-wide unit were preserved along with the flexibility to negotiate individual unit issues as they arose. Of course, separate negotiations could neither contravene the general agreement nor deal with issues that applied to all member unions. The dual recognition at the TVA placed a burden upon the unions to maintain peaceful and stable inter-organization relations in order to present a consistently solid front to management. Consequently, it minimized executive involvement in inter-union disputes.[11] Under the Kennedy order an attempt was made, particularly in the Metal Trades Department contracts, to mitigate the impact of such disputes by incorporating extensive jurisdictional disputes clauses.

---

[9] Louis J. Van Mol, "The TVA Experience," in *Collective Bargaining in the Public Service: Theory and Practice* (Chicago: Public Personnel Assn., 1967) , p. 89.

[10] Tennessee Valley Authority, *Articles of Agreement and Supplementary Agreements,* between TVA and Salary Policy Employee Panel, 1950; revised 1955 and reaffirmed 1964, Art. I.

[11] Van Mol, *op. cit.,* pp. 90, 91.

A. THE TVA LABOR CONTRACTS

The terms of the agreements negotiated with the Council and the Panel exceeded the policy requirements of the Kennedy order in a number of particulars. For example, they reflected a positive policy towards the promotion of union organization quite unlike the national policy of neutrality. This policy was inherently bound up with the question of union security in the federal establishment. The Kennedy Task Force had insisted that the union shop and the closed shop were inappropriate in the federal service, and in fact, in 1935 the TVA, in Section 4 of its Employee Relationship Policy, had made a neutral declaration on the open shop. But although it declared that joining or refraining from joining a union would not be required as a condition of employment, transfer, promotion, or retention in service, the Authority conducted its labor relations in an atmosphere which encouraged union membership.[12]

The unions wanted more security than that afforded by a declaration of neutrality. They first pressed their demands for a closed or union shop in 1938 and have continued these demands to the present. Although neither closed nor union shop was ever granted, a degree of preference for union members in personnel selection was written into TVA agreements, which amounted to strong union support. In compliance with the law, the accords stipulate that selection must be based upon merit and efficiency. However, union membership is designated as a prime factor in evaluating merit and efficiency. This policy is quite forcefully declared in the TVA Trades and Labor Council contract, which states, in regard to selection for appointment, promotion, demotion, transfer, and retention:

> "Membership in unions party to this agreement is advantageous to employees and to management, and employees are accordingly encouraged to become and remain members of the appropriate unions. Such membership is a positive factor in appraising relative merit and efficiency. Accordingly, within the limits permitted by applicable laws and Federal regulations qualified union members are selected and retained in preference to qualified non-union applicants or employees." [13]

The white-collar contract goes beyond mere membership to encourage employee participation in union activities through a clause recognizing union activities as a means of "improving rela-

---

[12] Sterling D. Spero, *Government as Employer* (New York: Remsen Press, 1948), p. 368. Reprinted Carbondale, Ill.: Southern Illinois University Press, 1972.
[13] TVA, *General Agreement, op. cit.,* Art. III, Sec. 2.

tions between management and employees and promoting employee efficiency and understanding of TVA policy, thereby contributing to the accomplishment of TVA objectives." [14] Not only are membership and participation positive factors to be considered in selecting employees for promotion, transfer, or retention; but the evidence of such participation is solely that which is submitted to the TVA by the employee's union.[15] At one point the white-collar contract actually states: "The TVA encourages employees to join the Panel organizations which represent their positions." [16]

In view of this managerial policy and the obvious benefits of union membership, it is no wonder that union strength is pronounced in the Authority. Perhaps the last chapter on union security at the TVA has yet to be written; however, the policy of union preference within existing rules has defused the issue. According to Personnel Director Harry Case, management took union membership almost for granted, and it was rarely an issue.[17]

The TVA compacts differ widely from the usual agreements written under the federal EMC program on the issues of management prerogatives and union participation in management functions. The provisions and policies of TVA accords are far more permissive than those of other federal agencies in regard to union participation. Unlike agreements with extensive subject clauses and management prerogative provisions parroted from the Kennedy and Nixon orders, TVA agreements merely recognize the TVA as an agency of the government, which must, therefore, operate within the limits of its legally delegated authority.[18] The Panel agreement notes, in addition, that this ultimate authority cannot be surrendered and that all parties are engaged in a program devoted to the public interest.[19] The agreement goes no further, however. Unlike other federal agreements, it does not attempt to limit the scope of bargaining by listing nonnegotiable areas. According to Van Mol, TVA management tried to break itself of the habit of viewing labor relations in terms of its own prerogatives. It attempted, rather, to

"maintain the attitude that [it would] negotiate on any matter up to that point where negotiations encroach upon those responsibil-

---

[14] TVA, *Articles of Agreement, op. cit., Supplementary Agreement 5,* Sec. B.
[15] *Ibid.*
[16] *Ibid.,* Art. II, Sec. C.
[17] Harry L. Case, *op. cit.,* pp. 31, 32.
[18] TVA, *General Agreement, op. cit.,* Art. II, Sec. 1.
[19] TVA, *Articles of Agreement, op. cit.,* Art. II, Sec. A.

ities which law or regulation confers solely upon management—responsibilities management cannot share with the unions. . . ." [20]

The extent of union participation in personnel matters is quite remarkable. Although management has the final say in initial appointment, it cannot hire any candidate who is unwilling to abide by the agreement. The unions are actually involved in the hiring process through membership in a Joint Committee on Employment Qualifications which resolves issues in regard to the qualifications of job candidates—a formidable spur towards union membership.[21] In the promotion process, the factors of union membership, seniority on the job, and promotion from within are guiding principles.[22] The Panel agreement, moreover, provides for extensive procedures for announcing vacancies and governing transfers. Special consideration is given to employees with TVA-service-connected disabilities. One may say that no contract written under the Kennedy and Nixon executive orders can begin to approach the Panel accord in the degree of participation it allows unions in the areas of appointment, promotion, tenure, demotion, suspension, or reduction in force.[23]

The TVA was also ahead of the times in allowing unions a greater voice in determining wage rates and worker classifications. While there is far more mutuality and equality in decision-making than previously as a result of the joint committee system in force, management still retains final authority at the highest levels. For example, a Joint Classification Committee handles matters relating to the classification of trades and labor positions. It is composed of four union representatives and four alternates appointed by the Council president and four representatives and four alternates appointed by the director of personnel. The Committee has extensive procedures for maintaining the classification plans fairly. Its final reports are binding on the TVA upon approval by both the personnel director and the Council president.[24]

The wage-determination process is also a cooperative venture. The personnel director and the Council president act as co-chairmen of the wage conferences assembled to dispose of all requests for wage-rate revisions. A Joint Committee on Wage Data, consisting of not more than five members chosen by TVA manage-

20 Van Mol, *op. cit.*, pp. 89, 90.
21 TVA, *General Agreement, op. cit.*, Art. III, Sec. 4.
22 *Ibid.*, Supplementary Schedule A-III.
23 TVA, *Articles of Agreement, op. cit.*, Supplementary Agreements 5-10.
24 TVA, *General Agreement, op. cit.*, Supplementary Schedule A-I, Sec. **B.**

ment and an equal number representing the union, is appointed to review wage data submitted by the parties, hear oral statements, and report its findings to the wage conference. The co-chairmen arrange for general negotiating sessions to expedite the work of the conference. Joint committee reports are not binding upon the TVA or the Council until both agree upon them. When both sides have agreed to rate revisions, new supplemental wage schedules are submitted to the TVA board of directors for approval and implementation. If there is still a dispute as to what the prevailing rate should be, the question is referred to the Secretary of Labor for a final and binding decision.[25]

The entire rate-setting process may be described as a form of collective dealing within the wage-survey mechanism with a high degree of mutual and equal participation in fixing the prevailing rate, subject to executive approval. The heavy use of union representatives in the rate-setting process does not seem to have jeopardized management's rights or efficiency. There is little doubt that the employees are convinced of the efficacy of the process.

The Panel agreement for white-collar workers also provides for mutual resolution of difficulties that arise in the related fields of classification and pay. Unions may request new or changed classification standards, and provision is made for joint meetings and conferences. Requests for the review of actual position classifications are processed administratively through extensive grievance machinery. Classes and class series are assigned to specific salary schedules by the Joint Salary Schedule Committee, whose prime function is in reality pay determination.[26] The principles governing the classification plan, position allocation, job descriptions, and reclassification are written into the negotiated agreement.[27]

The provisions in the Panel and Council agreements that control annual hourly, overtime, shift differential, holiday, callout, relief-shift pay rates, and within-grade rate increases have far more substance than those found in agreements under the Kennedy and Nixon orders.[28] It may well be that other federal agreements eventually will incorporate the classification and pay provisions of the TVA accords to a greater degree. Many of these provisions have already been incorporated in the Coordinated Federal Wage System.

[25] *Ibid.*, Art. VIII, Supplementary Schedule A-II, Secs. A, B.
[26] TVA, *Articles of Agreement, op. cit., Supplementary Agreement 2*, Secs. A, B, F.
[27] *Ibid.*, Secs. A, C, D, E.
[28] *Ibid.*, Supplementary Agreement 4, and TVA, *General Agreement*, Art. VIII, Supplementary Schedules A-II, A-VI, A-XII, A-XIV.

One of the central means for promoting union and management understanding has been the joint union-management cooperation programs created by the Authority. These programs recognized and relied upon the contributions of employee organizations. Well-directed and centralized, joint cooperation programs have achieved an impressive record of successes in improving job efficiency, morale, health, and safety.[29]

Council and Panel agreements provide for a Central Joint Cooperative Committee or Conference and for Local Joint Cooperative Committees or Conferences. The Panel agreement best illustrates how these committees operate. To participate in the Panel Conference Program, employees must join the unions represented in the Conference. The Conference statement of objectives which follows has served as a model for similar committees established in other federal programs:

> "Cooperative conferences consider such matters as strengthening the morale of the service; improving communications between employees and management; conserving manpower, materials and supplies; improving quality of workmanship and services; eliminating waste; promoting education and training; correcting conditions making for grievances and misunderstandings; safeguarding health; preventing hazards to life and property; improving working conditions and encouraging good public relations." [30]

Conferences do not deal with items subject to negotiations or covered by grievance procedures.[31]

The Central Joint Cooperative Conference is composed of six employee representatives designated by the Panel and six representatives designated by TVA management. The director of personnel and one employee representative serve as co-chairmen. Meetings are scheduled on call, and all actions must be based on mutual consent. The Central Conference develops guidelines for the entire program and supervises the formation and maintenance of local conferences, reviewing and coordinating their activities. It discusses major TVA programs and policies and maintains communication channels with employees through, among other things, the publication of a monthly news bulletin.[32]

Local joint cooperative conferences are made up of three or

[29] National Civil Service League, *Report on Employee Organizations in Government*, New York, 1960, p. 21. See also Arthur A. Thompson, "Employee Participation in Decision Making: The TVA Experience," *Public Personnel Review*, Vol. 28, No. 2, April 1967.

[30] TVA, *Articles of Agreement, op. cit., Supplementary Agreement 13*, Sec. C.

[31] *Ibid.*

[32] *Ibid.*, Sec. D.

more management representatives and an equal number of employees appointed by the unions. Meetings are held on a continuing basis and are scheduled at regular intervals, typically once a month. They are informally conducted with few procedural formalities. Decisions are not dependent upon strict parliamentary procedures. Rather, there are continuous, frank, and full discussions on issues until a consensus is attained, if possible. The conclusions reached are not binding but sometimes need follow-up action. Management and unions must report whether they have taken suggested actions, giving adequate explanations for their decisions.[33] Similar though not identical provisions appear in the Council contract.

These TVA programs have had a substantial impact on agreements under the EMC program. A 1965 BLS study reported that approximately one fourth of federal accords established some form of cooperative committee system. By 1972 almost one half of the contracts provided for cooperation committees. In large degree, the objectives and procedures of these committees resembled those of the TVA committees.[34]

The TVA was the first federal agency to apply third-party procedures to impasses. When TVA negotiations reach an impasse on matters of pay, hours, and other working conditions, a mediator jointly selected from a panel of five candidates may be called in. If the deadlock continues the mediator must endeavor to induce the TVA Trades and Labor Council and TVA to submit the controversy to voluntary arbitration. Each party selects one arbitrator, and the mediator selects the third. Once voluntary arbitration has been chosen, the decision of the majority of arbitrators is final and binding upon both parties. This provision does not conflict with the agreement's initial clause limiting its legally delegated authority, since the TVA may refuse to submit to arbitration.[35]

Both the Council and the Panel have written arbitration into their agreements as the last step in their grievance procedures. The decision of the impartial arbitrator must be accepted by both parties as final and binding.[36] Decisions need not be referred

33 *Ibid.*, Sec. E (1-7) .

34 U.S. Department of Labor, Bureau of Labor Statistics, *Collective Bargaining Agreements in the Federal Service. Late Summer 1964.* BLS Bulletin No. 1451, 1965, pp. 49, 51; *Collective Bargaining Agreements in the Federal Service, Late 1971,* BLS Bulletin No. 1789, 1973, pp. 62-64.

35 TVA, *General Agreement, op. cit.,* Art. XIV, and TVA, *Articles of Agreement,* Art. VI, Secs. B, C.

36 TVA, *General Agreement,* Supplementary Schedule A-IX, Sec. C (4) , and TVA *Articles of Agreement, Supplementary Agreement* II, Sec. E.

to a higher authority for adjudication. Binding arbitration can be invoked to determine appropriate bargaining units and, if the unions involved agree, for the settlement of jurisdictional disputes.[37]

The TVA has never had to invoke the impasse arbitration procedure. In cases of a wage deadlock, the TVA Act requires the Secretary of Labor, acting essentially as an arbitrator, to resolve the dispute. The Secretary's services have never been called upon. The absence of impasses may be ascribed to the TVA's long history of excellent labor relations and to the familiarity of the parties with outside collective negotiations and their confidence in each other's competence and good will.

B. EMPLOYEE ATTITUDES

The cooperative attitude of TVA's executives throughout the Authority's history has resulted in increased union representation and a joint committee system governing a great variety of working problems. The question naturally arises as to whether management's attitude has benefited the TVA. One test of this question would lie in the Authority's operational success, and there is general agreement that the TVA's operations have succeeded. Another test lies in the attitude of the employees themselves.

A revealing employee attitude survey was conducted among TVA's white-collar workers by Arthur Thompson and Irwin Weinstock, of Virginia Polytechnic Institute. The study covered 911 TVA employees, or nearly 17 percent of the nonmanagerial white-collar group, and its findings held significant implications for the Authority and for the entire federal program.[38]

Thompson's and Weinstock's survey found strong support in the white-collar group for unions and the concept of collective bargaining. Sixty-six percent of the respondents agreed that membership in an employee organization improves relations between management and the workers; almost 75 percent disagreed with the proposition that union membership results in a loss of individual prestige. Almost two thirds expressed the view that employees and management would get along worse if there were no employee organizations, while less than 6 percent said that the TVA would be a better place to work if there were no unions. More than 80 percent of the respondents were agreed that when employees are directly affected, employee representatives should

---

37 TVA, *General Agreement, op. cit.,* Arts. IV, VI.
38 Arthur Thompson and Irwin Weinstock, "White Collar Employees and the Unions at TVA," *Personnel Journal,* Vol. 46, No. 1, January 1967, pp. 14-21.

be consulted before management changes its policies or procedures. Other responses indicated favorable employee estimates of the contributions and performances of their specific employee organizations.[39]

Thompson and Weinstock reported that attitudes toward union performance grew more favorable as length of service increased. Older people, possibly influenced by their seniority benefits, exhibited greater union support. The opposite was true of education; the more formal education an employee had, the less likely was he to view unions positively. There were no significant differences between the responses of men and those of women.[40]

The survey findings clearly showed that the traditional hostility of white-collar employees toward unions was not shared by the TVA employees, among whom there were many professionals. Thompson and Weinstock attributed this fact to the organizational climate existing in the TVA, in which professional development, close identification with management and increased opportunity for promotion are compatible with employee participation in union activities.[41]

Although in some respects the TVA experience is unique, Thompson and Weinstock believed that certain of their survey findings might be said to have relevance for other agencies. For example, they concluded that the creation of a collective bargaining environment through favorable management attitudes is more important than employee attributes. They also determined that white-collar resistance to unions may be expected to diminish in an atmosphere where participation in union activities is consistent with the achievement by white-collar employees of their personal goals. Finally, they believed that the prime ingredient for the success of public service labor relations may be management's desire to work affirmatively with employee organizations.[42]

---

[39] *Ibid.*, pp. 16-18.
[40] *Ibid.*, pp. 18-20.
[41] *Ibid.*, p. 20.
[42] *Ibid.*, p. 21.

CHAPTER XVI

THE INTERIOR DEPARTMENT—
BONNEVILLE POWER ADMINISTRATION

The Department of the Interior and in particular its Bonneville Power Administration (BPA) served as models for many of the contract innovations that occurred under E.O. 10988. Prior to the EMC program, the labor relations practices of the Interior Department and the BPA were substantially more advanced than those of most other agencies. After the Kennedy order, the format and policies of Interior and BPA contracts became models for negotiations in other arms of the Federal Government.

The true measure of the Interior Department's success is that it achieved its record of collective bargaining completely within the confines of the labor relations policy imposed by the executive branch of the government. Unlike the Tennessee Valley Authority or the Government Printing Office, the Interior Department was not the object of special legislation that permitted unusual powers or liberties in its conduct of labor relations. The Interior Department is not an independent agency or government corporation with unique privileges or freedoms. Whatever advances in collective bargaining it obtained were secured through executive policies administratively instituted through normal channels and within the management discretion of departmental officers.

The independence that Interior allowed its various bureaus and services increased the individual administrator's ability to carry out his own labor policy. Thus, the Department's National Park Service hewed to the line of orthodoxy,[1] while the Bureau of Mines, the Bureau of Reclamation, and the BPA negotiated contracts to rival the TVA's.

The BPA undoubtedly was influenced by the TVA's experience. In turn, it was the BPA that pioneered collective bargaining processes for the rest of Interior. In 1945, it wrote its first

---

[1] U.S. Department of the Interior, National Park Service, *Employee Handbook,* In-Service Training Series, Revised 1958, p. 55.

agreement along the private industrial lines adopted in the TVA. This agreement established a contract pattern subsequently followed by other major Interior agencies and ultimately adopted by many federal departments and agencies under E.O. 10988. The BPA's labor relations practices were probably of greater importance than those of the TVA; for, unlike the TVA, which is a business-type corporation, the BPA lies entirely within the executive branch.

The Interior Department officially supported unit heads who desired greater union participation in labor relations policy making. The labor relations policies set forth in the departmental manual were the result of an extensive union and management study undertaken by Interior in conjunction with a committee of the Government Employes' Council, representatives of more than 20 national and international unions, the Civil Service Commission, and the National Federation of Federal Employees. A departmental declaration in 1959 stated:

> "The policies emphasize the desirability of frequent consultation and close cooperation with labor representatives of employees and restate formal collective bargaining procedures which have been an important part of the Department's wage program since 1948." [2]

The Bonneville Power Administration was the first Interior Department agency to develop collective bargaining policies. Unions in the BPA early expressed their desire for more collective negotiations. As the Senate reported in 1951:

> ". . . skilled craftsmen began to ask why they could not confer with management at Bonneville through union representatives as they were accustomed to do with management in the private utilities of the northwest. It did not make sense to them that the federal government, which encouraged private industry to bargain collectively with their employees, should not be willing to use the same method in a public enterprise which was in competition with private undertakings." [3]

To initiate labor-management consultation, the Columbia Power Trades Council was formed along the lines of similar councils in the Northwest. Labor-management relations, however, were continued much as before on an informal discussion basis. Unions viewed their position within the BPA as deteriorating rather than improving. By 1944, after seven years of conventional

---

[2] U.S. Department of the Interior, *Labor Relations Policy, Departmental Manual,* January 1959, Chaps. 376.1, 376.2, Foreword.

[3] U.S. Senate, Committee on Labor and Public Welfare, *Labor Management Relations in the Bonneville Power Administration, Senate Report No. 192,* 82nd Cong., 1st Sess., March 1957, p. 17.

dealing, it had become apparent that a new approach to labor relations was necessary for the BPA. Although strikes, stoppages, or slowdowns never occurred, a critical period was clearly in the offing. Management had to choose between the status quo and the adoption of more formal collective bargaining procedures.

The administrator of the BPA, Dr. Paul J. Raver, wished to meet with the employees to explore possible avenues of fuller co-operation. The Columbia Power Trades Council named a union committee to meet with Dr. Raver in December 1944. A month later Raver named a management counterpart to seek out means of establishing sound labor relations. The bargaining committees met and negotiated for several months in an atmosphere of conscious, studied cooperation. Proposals and counterproposals were submitted, and it was noted that:

> "[The initial exchange of ideas] dispelled any doubt on the part of the unions as to the readiness of Bonneville to work out a sound relationship. Discussions and conferences proceeded not as if labor was trying to pry something out of a reluctant management but rather as if both were faced with a common problem: How best to carry on their future relationship so that the interests of employees, management and the public would be effectively served." [4]

Newell B. Terry, Interior's director of personnel, has observed that the resultant BPA agreement of 1945 remained the only formal contract in the Interior Department for some time, while its legal and practical aspects were being examined for possible application in other bureaus. He related that collective bargaining was greatly encouraged by an opinion handed down in September 1946 by the Acting Solicitor and approved by the Secretary of the Interior. It stated that the Reclamation Bureau, Bonneville Power Administration, and other Interior bureaus were empowered to enter into collective bargaining agreements with unions on matters within agency discretion. On this basis, a labor policy statement was issued in 1948 by the Interior Department and accepted by the agencies. The Reclamation Bureau subsequently negotiated a collective agreement with the craft workers at the Grand Coulee Dam and at other projects. In time, other bureaus and services followed suit.[5]

The BPA's bargaining system as revised in 1959 called for two fundamental types of agreements never before used in an executive department. These were the Basic Labor Agreements, concerned primarily with matters of broad principle, policy, and pro-

---

[4] *Ibid.*, p. 19.

[5] Newell B. Terry, "Collective Bargaining in the U.S. Department of the Interior," *Public Administration Review*, Winter 1962, Vol. XXII, No. 1, pp. 20, 21.

cedure, and the Supplementary Labor Agreements, which covered a wide variety of issues in greater detail. This arrangement is now seen in many federal agencies. Under the Kennedy order, the early "preamble" type of basic agreement often restated the *Federal Personnel Manual* and order policies while other types of contracts provided for substantial union participation in personnel decision making.[6] In Interior and under the EMC program, supplementary agreements to a high degree regulated the adjustment of wage rates, working rules, general working conditions, grievance procedures, and the checkoff of union dues, to cite but a few of the areas of coverage. The BLS reported that by late summer of 1964, the parties to 30 of the 208 nonpostal contracts it surveyed had negotiated supplementary agreements.[7] Thus, although a majority of federal accords today incorporate the provisions of basic and supplementary agreements in a single collective bargaining document, the dual format of the Interior Departments has nevertheless enjoyed broad acceptance.

The BPA's Basic Agreement was revised in 1958 and 1960, prior to E.O. 10988, and there have been several revisions since.[8] The contract is automatically renewable and many supplementary agreements have been negotiated over tne years. It should be understood, however, that the government-wide application of the Kennedy and Nixon executive orders had a considerable effect upon Interior's policies and contracts in certain areas.

Many of the BPA's basic labor policies were clearly incorporated in the federal program. Of great significance was the manner in which the BPA agreement overcame the issue of sovereignty, the perennial obstacle to collective bargaining. First, as in the TVA agreements, a clause specifically recognized the BPA as an agency of the U.S. Government charged with fulfilling public purposes. The clause was immediately followed, however, by a provision which declared that cooperation on the basis of mutual understanding "arrived at through the processes of collective bargaining is indispensable to the accomplishment of those public purposes." [9]

Constitutional objections were overcome by contract require-

---

6 See Chapter X.

7 U.S. Department of Labor, Bureau of Labor Statistics, *Collective Bargaining Agreements in the Federal Service, Late Summer 1964*, BLS Bulletin No. 1451, 1965, p. 64.

8 U.S. Department of the Interior, Bonneville Power Administration, *Basic Agreement*, with Columbia Power Trades Council, 1945, 1958, 1960, 1964, 1968, 1969, and to date.

9 U.S. Department of the Interior, Bonneville Power Administration, *Basic Agreement*, 1969, Art. 5, Secs. 5.01, 5.02.

ments that all basic agreements had to be approved by the office of the Secretary of the Interior before becoming effective.[10] Such approval was not required for supplementary agreements, which, of course, could not conflict with the basic agreement. Generally they were approved by the administrator. A subject clause recognized the paramount position of federal laws, executive orders, secretarial instructions, and related policies and regulations. If new laws, regulations, or policies conflicting with the agreement were adopted, procedures were established to interpret their possible effects upon the terms of the agreement.[11] Clauses and related provisions that reserved management prerogatives became, in essence, policy models for statements of rights under the Kennedy order and were widely adopted in other federal contracts.

In Interior, therefore, the Secretary is not the negotiating party; his subordinates are. Under governing provisions, however, he is not bound by a contract until he approves it, and he can revise his position by writing new regulations after his approval. Unions consider this condition to be a major threat to "true" collective bargaining.

The BPA agreements surpass most federal contracts in a number of areas, but do not go as far as TVA accords. On the question of union security, the departmental manual, both before and after the Kennedy order, prohibited any union-membership requirement for employment, transfer, or promotion.[12] This prohibition was similar to the later Task Force policy against union or closed shops in the federal service. The BPA's agreements did not make use of the strong TVA language encouraging union membership, but they were not silent on the subject of union security. They guaranteed all the individual employee's rights and privileges later specified in E.O. 10988,[13] but, unlike the contracts written under the Kennedy order, they contained a strong pro-union clause which stated: "It is recognized that membership on the part of employees covered by this agreement in the unions affiliated with the Council is helpful in accomplishing the purposes of the administration." [14] The contract also required that supervisors refrain from discouraging union membership.[15]

10 *Ibid.*, Art. 2, Sec. 2.02.

11 *Ibid.*, Art. 1, Secs. 1.01, 1.02.

12 U.S. Department of the Interior, *Labor Relations Policy, Departmental Manual,* December 22, 1958, Part 376, 1.5c, and *Departmental Manual,* January 7, 1966, and June 29, 1970, Part 370, 2.1c.

13 U.S. Department of the Interior, Bonneville Power Administration, *Basic Agreement,* 1969, Art. 13, Sec. 13.01.

14 *Ibid.*, Sec. 13.02.

15 *Ibid.*

Even in the galling area of conflict of interest, Interior's revised departmental manual protects the rights of management officials to be union members as long as they do not take an active leadership role in the union organization or in actual negotiations that might conflict with their management function.[16] This provision is far clearer and more permissive than its forerunner prior to the Kennedy order, which, as written, could have been interpreted to bar union membership entirely. Such an interpretation would have dealt a blow to traditional craft groups whose journeyman members often move to supervisory positions.

The BPA agreements had provisions emphasizing the collective bargaining process and union participation in cooperative programs and grievance procedures. Many of these provisions, particularly those concerning joint-cooperation committees and grievance machinery, became the models for similar clauses in other federal contracts. The root influences were obvious, for Interior considered as a major element of its program "The adaptation to departmental operations, whenever feasible, of significant and important policies and practices accepted by a large segment of American industry and labor." [17]

The BPA accords were forerunners of the Kennedy order's policy permitting advisory arbitration as the final step in grievance procedures. Advisory arbitration was a radical departure from conventional federal practice. As spelled out in the 1969 BPA contract, the appeals ladder contained four steps. The first step was informal discussion with the immediate supervisor. Next came an appeal to the area manager or branch chief. The third step was an appeal to the administrator or to the joint grievance board, made up of four members (two appointed by the Council and two by the administrator), which after hearing submitted recommendations to the division chief. Finally if there was still no resolution, the grievance board could be requested to appoint an arbitrator to make recommendations to the administrator, whose decision was final and binding on all parties.[18] The BPA experience was innovative and led to changes in grievance arbitration policy, which may be seen in the many agreements negotiated under the Kennedy order.

The BPA 1969 agreement declared that pay rates and working

---

[16] U.S. Department of the Interior, *Departmental Manual,* June 29, 1970, Part 370, 2.1.B.

[17] *Ibid.,* Part 370, 1.2H.

[18] U.S. Department of the Interior, Bonneville Power Administration, *Basic Agreement,* 1969, Art. 12.

conditions were to be determined "through the process of collective bargaining between the Council and the Administrator." [19] Two negotiating committees of five members each were to be appointed by the Council and the administrator. Other union representatives could also attend negotiating conferences. While the prevailing-rate principle applies in the BPA, the procedures adopted by the BPA for fixing wage rates resembled the bargaining practices of private industry far more than even the most advanced forms of wage-survey provisions in the contracts under the Kennedy and Nixon orders. This was particularly true before the adoption of the Coordinated Federal Wage System in December 1967.

The contractual procedure for negotiating pay rates began with the executive secretary of the Council and BPA's labor relations officer, assisted by additional staff, acting as a joint factfinding committee to obtain the data necessary to determine rates established by collective bargaining for similar work in the relevant geographical area. This was in marked contrast to the usual wage-survey provisions negotiated under the Kennedy order prior to 1968, which made extremely limited use of union-appointed data gatherers, observers, and alternates. The committee's findings were used by the negotiating committees in framing recommendations for submission to the administrator. Even the wage rates for new classifications established between negotiating conferences were to be bargained over by the territorial representative of the respective craft union, the executive secretary of the Council, and the BPA's labor relations officer.[20]

BPA's wage rate provisions came as close as was possible, given the limits of federal labor relations policy, to private industrial collective bargaining over this most difficult of negotiable issues. This was evident despite the fact that the administrator retained final authority. Other federal agencies did not involve unions in wage surveys and wage negotiations to the extent that the BPA did. The Coordinated Federal Wage System was introduced in part to enhance union participation in wage setting and to rationalize pay negotiations.

It has been noted that Interior's departmental manual protected provisions for advisory arbitration of bargaining impasses against new prohibitions of E.O. 10988. Such provisions were to continue in effect in agreements negotiated prior to July 1,

---

19 *Ibid.*, Art. 8, Sec. 8.01.
20 *Ibid.*, Art. 8, Secs. 8.02, 8.03.

1962.[21] This reservation of rights flew in the face of the language and policy of the Kennedy order, which specifically excluded advisory arbitration as a medium for resolving deadlocks. The relative success of Interior's standard mediation-advisory arbitration clause no doubt helped bring about the revisions of impasse policy effected by E.O. 11491. The binding arbitration of TVA agreements also served as a significant model for the Nixon order.

The BPA's mediation-advisory arbitration method has successfully averted serious deadlocks over the years. This was demonstrated by the fact that in 1967, for the first time in the BPA's history, a three-man arbitration panel was convened to hand down an award pertaining to wage rates for trades and craft employees. After one month of negotiations in May 1967, all outstanding contractual issues were resolved, with the sole exception of wage rates. The mediation requirement was quickly dispensed with after one session with an FMCS mediator. On submission to arbitration, an award was quickly handed down after a hearing on June 27, 1967, to establish the wage rates for the contract year ending June 30, 1968.[22]

The successful conclusion of this single resort to advisory arbitration in over 20 years of collective bargaining emphasized the unfortunate loss of this technique to agencies under the Kennedy order's policy. Its use in BPA agreements did not threaten ultimate management authority. Although at one time it was honestly believed that advisory arbitration would impede the development of the collective bargaining abilities of all the parties, such an objection cannot be effectively raised today after many years of EMC experience. The Johnson Review Committee's final recommendations called for mediation combined with strong arbitration provisions. In time, E.O. 11491 corrected the Kennedy order's oversight by establishing the Federal Service Impasses Panel.

---

[21] U.S. Department of the Interior, *Departmental Manual,* January 7, 1966, Part 370, 1.4.

[22] U.S. Department of the Interior, Office of the Secretary, "Arbitration Award in Negotiation Impasse—Bonneville Power Administration," *Personnel Management Bulletin,* No. 67-143 (711), July 19, 1967, p. 2.

CHAPTER XVII

THE POSTAL SERVICE

A. LABOR RELATIONS UNDER THE KENNEDY ORDER

The traditional activists on the federal scene, the postal unions, were a major force in the drive towards a new national labor policy. They led the way in operationally implementing the Employee-Management Cooperation program. With a strong history of unionism behind them and the largest membership when the Kennedy order was issued, they were among the first to adapt swiftly to the new system. In the number of exclusive agreements and employees covered, they quickly approached their full potential.

In the early years their leadership was emulated somewhat by the defense-installations unions with similar labor backgrounds, although a great number of blue-collar workers were still to be organized and integrated into the system. This task was systematically accomplished by active affiliated and independent unions. Classification Act employees were so thinly organized in 1962, however, that the prospect of their involvement was staggering in its proportions. Yet they too progressed at a steady rate. It appears that the postal unions soon reached a stabilized plateau in developing their representation function while the two other categories had to apply considerable efforts to achieve continuing growth. Thus, after more than a decade of formal federal labor relations, the postal unions could boast the strongest national exclusive agreement and the widest representation in what was now their independent labor program. What is particularly pertinent here, however, is that they were the first to act in a meaningful manner prior to and under the Kennedy EMC program.[1]

This development was not unexpected. Congress had long felt the strength and influence of the postal unions. Their concerted efforts in securing postal pay raises were persistent and resource-

---

[1] U.S. Civil Service Commission, Office of Labor Management Relations, *Union Recognition in the Federal Government—November 1969,* Washington, April 1969, pp. 1, 20.

315

ful. They mounted relentless pressure to enact some form of labor-management relations bill into law long before the March 1970 stoppages. Although unsuccessful in this, their persistence in successive Congresses after World War II helped coalesce a growing consensus among the legislators for some positive action.

For 15 years, proposals such as the Rhodes-Johnston bill gained real momentum as a result of their efforts to establish official procedures for recognition and collective bargaining. These pressures did not diminish. Dissatisfied with the Johnson and Nixon Administrations' failure to innovate, they added their support to various bills, including one endorsed by the AFL-CIO and submitted by Committee Chairman Thaddeus J. Dulski.[2] This bill had called for a Federal Service Labor-Management Relations Board. They, as always, simply utilized the legislative route protected in the Kennedy order to achieve goals that appeared to be improbable by executive action. In retrospect, it is almost universally accepted that President Kennedy's appointment of his Task Force was motivated by similar pressures. His executive order was in part precipitated by the possibility that congressional action might foist on federal management a comprehensive, formal system of labor relations it was not fully prepared to accept. Wilson Hart has pointed out that during the 1958 hearings on the Rhodes bill, 21 congressmen supported the measure while not a single member testified against it.[3] It was for good cause, therefore, that President Jerome J. Keating of the Letter Carriers reflected on signing the first national postal agreement that "such triumphs are never instantaneous creations. They never spring complete and perfect from the brow of any individual. Years of campaigning on the part of the postal unions preceded the event."[4]

In implementing the EMC program, some unique conditions faced the Post Office Department. Delivering the mail constitutes the major "industrial" enterprise in the federal establishment. POD's essential "business-type" function lay at the root of the perennial recommendations to make it a government corporation. In addition, it was among the first to act nationally under E.O. 10988. This situation naturally lent itself to comparison with those in the Tennessee Valley Authority and the Interior Depart-

[2] U.S. House of Representatives, Committee on Post Office and Civil Service, *H.R. 12349*, Rep. Dulski, 91st Cong., 1st Sess., June 24, 1969.

[3] Wilson R. Hart, *Collective Bargaining in the Federal Civil Service* (New York: Harper & Bros., 1961), p. 144.

[4] Jerome J. Keating, "Message to All Members of the National Association of Letter Carriers," *The Postal Record*, April 1963, p. 33.

ment. Although similar in their business and service operations, the labor relations histories of TVA and Interior reflected different management attitudes. TVA was empowered as an independent corporation to adopt any labor policy it desired and chose the private industry model. Interior, unlike TVA, had to function under civil service requirements, yet it sought to emulate TVA's precedent. Both agencies attained labor records unique in the federal service.

The Post Office Department, on the other hand, never adopted a management attitude countenancing agency-wide, formal labor relations procedures. It had never fully accepted collective bargaining. There had been sporadic, localized agreements. Too often, however, labor relations rested upon the views of postmasters like Burleson. Thus, POD approached implementation of the Kennedy order with something of an empirical vacuum in labor-management relations. It lacked the history of ongoing collective bargaining that characterized the major federal utility enterprises. Its unions relied more on Congress for basic redress of grievances. Yet when the Task Force study was being conducted, the Post Office was the largest single employer in the country, public or private, and had the greatest number of employees belonging to unions.

It was now to be seen whether the initial enthusiasm of the postal unions could be translated into successful collective bargaining. Something more than enthusiasm would be necessary in a tough negotiating situation. Even more determinative would be the attitudes and actions of postal management. It was operating in a collective negotiations context for the first time under strong executive direction. Both sides rose admirably to the initial tasks. This was quite a change from the strong establishment opposition, for example, to the Rhodes bill.[5] It soon became apparent that top postal management recognized the facts of departmental union life and was prepared to carry out the dictates of the Kennedy order.

The Labor, Agriculture, and Post Office Departments all showed an early willingness to effectuate the program. This reflected the sympathetic views of Secretaries Goldberg and Freeman and Postmaster General Day. POD's task was the greatest by far. But as Wilson Hart has observed, the attitudes of key officials such as Day, Assistant Postmaster Murphy, and Deputy Postmas-

---

[5] Wilson R. Hart, *op. cit.*, p. 144.

ter Brawley compared favorably with their aggressive union counterparts. He commented further:

">. . . it may be expected that true collective bargaining will become a reality in the Post Office Department in a short time and the limits of its potential will be quickly probed. If it proves conspicuously successful in the Post Office Department, the effects on the other departments, their employees and their unions is bound to be profound." [6]

The Department proceeded to conduct the largest union representation election of its kind in the history of the country. On July 1, 1962, when all the votes were in, about 367,000 workers had participated, and the six major postal unions were granted national exclusive recognition as expected. Another, smaller union, the Mail Handlers, was granted national exclusive recognition in December 1964 and became a party to the national agreement in February 1965.[7] Negotiations began in mid-October 1962, and after five months the first National Postal Agreement was signed on March 20, 1963. Strong bargaining teams repre-

---

[6] Wilson R. Hart, "Government Labor's New Frontiers Through Presidential Directive," 48 *Virginia Law Review* 906-907 (1962).

[7] The unions that received national exclusive recognition on September 11, 1962, and were covered by the first national postal agreement are listed according to the number of employees included in their respective units as of November 1970. These were the last statistics gathered prior to establishment of the U.S. Postal Service. See U.S. Civil Service Commission, Office of Labor-Management Relations, *Union Recognition in the Federal Government; Statistical Report and Listings by Agency—November 1970*, Washington, June 1971, pp. 33-34, 250-252.

	Number	%
United Federation of Postal Clerks (AFL-CIO)	301,078	42
National Association of Letter Carriers (AFL-CIO)	203,823	28
National Rural Letter Carriers Assoc. (Ind.)	31,134	4
National Association of Post Office and General Service Maintenance Employees (AFL-CIO)	25,665	4
National Federation of Post Office Motor Vehicles Employees (AFL-CIO)	12,781	2
National Association of Special Delivery Messengers (AFL-CIO)	5,882	1
National Association of Mail Handlers, Watchmen, Messengers and Group Leaders (AFL-CIO)	44,234	6
Total under National Postal Agreement	624,597	87

These statistics showed the number of employees then covered in exclusive units but did not necessarily indicate the full picture of postal union strength. Here the checkoff is a useful additional indicator. As noted in Chapter XI, four independent unions that received national formal recognition in 1962 and 1963 were among the leaders in union dues allotments. Thus, as of January 1968 the National Postal Union had 58,487 allotments; the Postal Supervisors, 27,852; the Postal Alliance had 25,210; and the National League of Postmasters counted 8,300 checkoffs. These increased in following years and indicated clearly the comprehensive extent of postal unionism. See U.S. Civil Service Commission, Office of Labor-Management Relations, *Voluntary Union Dues Allotments in the Federal Government, 1968*, Washington, 1969, p. 22.

sented the six unions and the Department. POD faced a mammoth task, yet the elan with which it carried it out elicited approving comment even from some union leaders.[8] The American Bar Association's first appraisal of the EMC program recognized management's formidable efforts, declaring, "In little more than a year the Post Office Department has completely overhauled its labor relations . . . and has embarked on local negotiations in over 20,000 post offices across the land."[9]

Under decentralized agency administration, POD was able to set the nature and number of its units and agreements. EMC criteria for fixing appropriate units and recognizing unions sought flexibility to serve the particular needs of each agency. Post Office policy reflected this intent. The national, regional, and local structure of the department and the functional nature of its major unions influenced its bargaining processes. POD accordingly established units along functional lines, and thousands of agreements were concluded at local post offices with the exclusively recognized craft unions. At post offices where industrial-type organizations held exclusive recognition, the organizations bargained for their covered crafts. Representation by the National Postal Union in Manhattan and the Bronx typified this situation.

The system adopted by the Post Office resembled the proved Interior procedures in general outline. Here again a basic contract was concluded in the form of the National Postal Agreement. Supplemental agreements for particular crafts covered such items as "heavy duty compensation," seniority, and tools for vehicle maintenance personnel. Above all, the National Postal Agreement fixed the essential provisions that governed problems of a national nature. These would control issues pertaining to essentially similar operational matters in most local post offices. Being subject to the national contract, local accords would have considerable portions of their substance foreordained. In addition, particularly under the last POD 1968 accord, extensive provisions were set forth governing local negotiations and implementation of the agreement. Although exclusive recognition could be granted at the regional level, agreements were not negotiated there. The regional level had important functions to insure that

---

[8] Jerome J. Keating, *op. cit.,* p. 33.

[9] American Bar Association, Labor Law Section, Committee on Law of Government Employee Relations, *Report,* Chicago, 1963, pp. 140-141. Permission to reprint this article was obtained from the ABA and its Section of Labor Relations Law, 1969.

local agreements conformed to the national contract. It had a role in the processing of grievances and unfair labor practice charges.

Finally, several independent postal organizations enjoyed the benefits of Kennedy-type national formal recognition in the years before the mergers. They were not signatories to the national agreement. For example, from September 1962 through the Nixon orders the National Postal Union and the National Alliance, the latter predominantly black and increasingly militant, had consultation rights. The National League of Postmasters and the National Association of Postal Supervisors had national formal recognition from April 1963.

Four basic national agreements were concluded under the EMC program.[10] The first three were considered to be of a continuing nature under which the provisions of the prior accords were brought forward with modifications. It became quickly apparent in the 1967-68 negotiations, however, that management had adopted a far tougher bargaining posture, a basic element of which was the requirement that all former agreements, both national and local, legally end as of December 5, 1967. The third contract had been extended to this final date to permit five more weeks of bargaining. For reasons deemed vital by the Department, its negotiators insisted that the fourth round of talks start with a fresh slate. Many existing provisions were continued by mutual assent. However, it was clear that bargaining for 1968 on all accords, including the thousands of local contracts, would have to start from scratch.

Management was so committed to its negotiation proposals that mediation was invoked for the first time to resolve the inevitable impasses. POD was especially concerned about the processing of adverse actions and reassignments. In retrospect, however, what occurred during the fourth negotiations was part of an evolutionary process. There is little doubt that for contracts written under the Kennedy order, the basic postal agreement was an enviable model. Nevertheless, for both the postal unions and management, the period from 1962 to 1967 was one of phased development and

---

[10] The first basic agreement was signed on March 20, 1963, effective April 1, 1963. The second was concluded June 18, 1964, to run to October 31, 1965. The third national accord was signed August 31, 1966, to terminate on October 31, 1967. The last accord, reflecting the intense negotiations and mediation that surrounded its signing, was the first with a two-year duration period. Signed February 9, 1968, effective March 9, 1968, its termination date was set for March 8, 1970. It was terminated as to prior character by the March 1970 disturbances. The agreement of July 20, 1971, differed widely in substance and was to remain in effect for two years through 1973. This first accord under the new Postal Service was followed by a national agreement effective through July 1975.

self-discovery. It was an educative process. The obvious change in atmosphere of the 1967-68 bargaining was noted by Executive Vice President Don E. Dunn, who led the United Federation of Postal Clerks' negotiating team. He recognized that "the earlier sessions were a 'growing up' time for everyone concerned—a period in which we were operating under a continuation of the 1963 agreement." [11] Management was also "growing up." POD felt that perhaps too much had been given up over the years, particularly in the local post offices. It believed that a greater share of bargaining power should be afforded the local postmaster; that management prerogatives should be clearly stated and preserved. The resulting impasse was almost unavoidable in this maturing process. Indeed, the successful use of mediation was itself a forward step in that process.

To the unions, POD's new approach exhibited a "take-it-or-leave-it attitude." [12] They believed the Department's proposals were retrogressive and hindered the advance of sound labor relations. The UFPC's official organ commented, in retrospect, that it was clear from the very start that "the possibility for normal give and take was tenuous at best." Where management had the advantage of the prerogative provisions of the order, the unions decried their lack of "muscle" without the strike weapon. [13] After the five-week extension expired, Postmaster General Lawrence F. O'Brien incorporated the terminated accord into the postal regulations rather than permit another extension. He said this was necessary to protect the employees' "rights and guarantees while we try to achieve a new agreement." [14] Even this action was viewed with suspicion. As the UFPC viewed it, once management let the negotiating period expire, then as long as it met its obligation to communicate and exchange information, it could issue new instructions or amend the Postal Manual at will. [15]

Department negotiators were particularly dissatisfied with Article X, governing adverse actions, which permitted actual disciplinary proceedings only after decision at the first level of appeal. This would often be handed down two or three months after the employee's first notice of the projected adverse action. The resultant delay was deemed harmful to the maintenance of proper discipline, to the morale of dutiful workers, and to efforts to im-

---

11 *The Union Postal Clerk,* Special Issue, March 1968, p. 3.
12 *Ibid.,* p. 4.
13 *Ibid.*
14 *Government Employee Relations Report,* No. 222 (1967) , p. A-3.
15 *The Union Postal Clerk, op. cit.,* p. 4.

prove the postal service. POD proposed, therefore, to speed the disciplinary process. Postmasters would be given authority to suspend accused employees for up to 10 days within 48 hours of the alleged offense. An arbitrator would then be selected by both parties to hear the case. His decision would be binding if the Postmaster General failed to invoke his power of final review in 10 days—a power, O'Brien pointed out, that he would be most reluctant to assert if the changes were made.[16]

Management's concern in this area was deep-rooted. To Oscar Liberman, director of industrial relations for POD's large New York region, adverse actions were a "big nut" in the bargaining. He saw management's desire to renegotiate these provisions as a basic effort to retain necessary managerial prerogatives. In Liberman's view, the Department perhaps had bargained away too many of its rights and now wanted them back. Particularly as to adverse actions, he believed, management had to have more elbow room to operate efficiently.[17] This concern over control of discipline was emphasized by Postmaster General O'Brien when he accepted mediator James Holden's recommendation that the existing provisions be retained intact in the new agreement. He declared, "The capacity to deal promptly with patent insubordination is vital to the operation of an efficient postal service . . . and I continue to believe that our present procedures are in need of improvement." [18] Clearly, the last chapter was yet to be written on discipline and other crucial issues.

The disagreement over reassignment of employees centered around transfers from nonmail processing facilities to post offices and assignments from a railway postal unit to stationary facilities. Usually employees come into post offices and work up to regular positions. A "bumping" controversy was the obvious result. Pay difficulties arose if railway clerks at pay level five were to be transferred to a post office where most clerks were at pay level four. The Department sought to acquire greater flexibility in the transfer process, while the unions wanted the power to contract over bumping rights at the local post office.[19] The problems inherent in this area were particularly galling to management. If

---

[16] *Government Employees Relations Report,* No. 222 (1967), p. A-3.

[17] Oscar Liberman, Director, Industrial Relations, New York Region, POD, *Interview,* January 16, 1968.

[18] Lawrence F. O'Brien, Postmaster General, quoted in the *Union Postal Clerk,* March 1968, p. 1. See U.S. Post Office Department, *Basic Agreement,* March 9, 1968, Art. X.

[19] *Government Employee Relations Report,* No. 222 (1967), pp. A-3, A-4, and No. 231 (1968), p. A-2.

the rules on reassignment were not renegotiated, "a chaotic mess" would result for both labor and management. Conditions literally forced the need for change. Oscar Liberman cited the difficulties encountered when POD's discontinuance of certain railway services necessitated the reassignment of 1,000 employees. If Article XII of the agreement were not revised to provide for such contingencies, the result would be chaos.[20] When finally negotiated, the 1968 agreement contained some provisions increasing management's authority over the reassignment process, although not as much as it desired.

The Post Office's use of a mediator in the 1967-68 negotiations was itself an important precedent. In the 1966 accord a provision for optional mediation of negotiation impasses was agreed to at the national level only. Specific negotiation procedures were set forth. If both sides agreed that an impasse existed, the item was to be set aside until all other negotiable issues were resolved. Another attempt would then be made to break the deadlock. If this failed, either party could request the aid of the Federal Mediation and Conciliation Service. The postal agreement procedures, however, differed from the usual E.O. 10988 accords in that privacy was to be observed throughout. The mediator was precluded from making any public statement on any aspect of the negotiations. If unsuccessful in his efforts, his report and recommendations were to be made privately and confidentially to the Postmaster General, whose decision remained final.[21]

In 1967, after more than three months of bargaining, about 26 negotiable issues had been satisfactorily settled. However, vital questions still unresolved required that the optional mediation procedure be invoked. The UFPC believed the appointment of veteran federal mediator James Holden produced a brighter atmosphere and evidenced a "real change of attitude"; that management could not "browbeat him into making recommendations necessarily suitable to its viewpoint." [22] The contract procedures were followed, and PMG O'Brien accepted Holden's recommendations fully. Having previously expressed a partiality to binding arbitration in employee appeals, the Postmaster General was influenced, to some extent, by his feeling that the concept of third-party intervention was itself on trial.[23]

---

[20] Oscar Liberman, *op. cit.*
[21] U.S. Post Office Department, *Basic Agreement,* effective September 24, 1966, Art. XI.
[22] *The Union Postal Clerk, op. cit.,* p. 4.
[23] *Government Employees Relations Report,* No. 231 (1968) , p. A-1.

In the 1968 basic agreement, innovations were introduced that affected negotiations at the local level to a far greater extent than any of the three previous national accords. Management preroga- tives were stated in no uncertain terms. This was done by posi- tively defining the scope of consultation in language which en- hanced local management's power of final decision over what items were negotiable or nonnegotiable. In the previous agree- ments, the first five articles had included all the fundamental pol- icies of the Kennedy order that were required in all accords. As by far the most substantive contracts, the postal agreements set forth these provisions in great detail. The basic clauses governed recognition, purpose, management rights, and organization and employee rights. Although clearly delineated in the national agreements, the writing of these preliminary ground-rules clauses in local contracts previously had been left to the local negotiators. The 1968 accord radically altered this practice by removing the new ground-rules provisions of the national agreement, with their stricter limitations, from the local bargaining process. The exten- sive procedures governing local negotiations explicitly declared that:

> "Both parties, when formulating proposals or counter proposals shall consider that Articles I through V of this Agreement are not subject to local negotiations, except that the local agreement should identify the parties to that agreement." [24]

The result necessitated a revised strategy for local exclusives in negotiating items previously included in the first five articles and gave rise to vehement protests, particularly from the independent unions, that hard-won gains were being vitiated.

The reasoning behind POD's approach was stated by Anthony F. Ingrassia, then director of the Department's Labor Relations Division, before the 1967 President's Review Committee.[25] His testimony virtually anticipated the wording of the new limita- tions. Ingrassia held that in negotiating local agreements, conces- sions had been made that constituted serious incursions into man- agerial areas. He attributed this to a basic confusion over the intended meaning of the scope of negotiation and the matters to be subjects for consultation. To Ingrassia:

> "Confusion on consultation may stem from misinterpretation of the emphasis on 'cooperation' in the Executive Order. Union repre-

---

[24] U.S. Post Office Department, *Basic Agreement*, effective March 9, 1968, Art. VII, Sec. A (13) .
[25] See Chapters XIV, XX.

sentatives sometimes take this to mean they have become 'co-managers' of an agency or installation. This, of course, was never intended.

"Somehow this confusion must be cleared up, along with delineating the scope of negotiation." [26]

There is little doubt that the 1968 agreement proceeded "to clear up the confusion" as the Department defined it.

Essentially, POD believed that the frustration unions expressed over the scope of negotiations derived from their inability, by law, to bargain over the bread-and-butter issues of pay, hours, and fringe benefits. Unions were, therefore, seen as extending negotiations over personnel policies, practices, and working conditions by interpreting consultation to mean bargaining on these issues. Management believed, of course, that much of this was within its executive prerogatives and thus nonnegotiable. As Ingrassia put it, negotiable items were subject to both negotiation and consultation, with the difference lying in the type of recognition granted.[27] He might have added that it depended also upon management's view of an item's negotiability. Nevertheless, he sought to distinguish between negotiation, which implied "a good faith attempt at agreement by both parties," and consultation, which required "only management consideration, in good faith, of union views before making decisions." [28] Ingrassia stressed that:

> "Consultation is a never-ending problem. Management often thinks unions try to twist consultation into negotiations, using the consultative process to delay or prevent the issuance of policy statements unless the union position is recognized; unions often think management makes a sham of consultation, merely informing them of matters affecting personnel policies, practices and working conditions after all decisions have been made." [29]

The 1968 accord transformed these departmental views into firm contractual clauses that bolstered management rights in the consultative process. Article IV, Section D, had been a fairly innocuous provision allowing for the exchange of information in aid of greater understanding and cooperation. Revised and expanded in 1968, it defined consultation, its scope, and management's rights thereunder. POD's apprehensions were thus substantially resolved. As generally understood, the scope of negotiation and consultation remained the same, and what was

---

[26] Anthony F. Ingrassia, *Statement,* before President's Review Committee, October 26, 1967, p. 7.

[27] *Ibid.,* pp. 6, 7.

[28] *Ibid.,* p. 7.

[29] *Ibid.*

nonnegotiable did not necessitate consultation.[30] The clause required only that management seek out and sincerely consider union positions on impending actions concerning personnel policies, practices, and working conditions that management had the right to take under its reserved authority. Agreement before final executive action was unnecessary.

As noted, the revised Article IV removed from local negotiation many diverse items previously included in the first five articles. Exclusives such as the Postal Clerks accepted this change as merely a refinement of the previous accord but recognized the heavier responsibility now devolving upon local negotiators. The UFPC, for example, advised local bargainers to review their agreements immediately. They now had to sift out of the five nonnegotiable articles any previous gains and place them in other, more appropriate articles, new articles, or in supplements to the local agreement.[31] The new negotiations were to have a different set of ground rules. The more vehement opponents of the national agreement declared that whatever local unions had accomplished in the preceding few years was "out the window." Morris Biller of the large and then-independent Manhattan-Bronx Postal Union scored the five nonnegotiable articles as the "biggest gains for management." Article IV was specifically singled out for it:

> ". . . puts it positively clear that management makes the final decisions relative to tours, basic work weeks, quotas, etc. As a matter of fact reduction of preferred assignments becomes a purely informational matter. Management doesn't even have to consult on this. It needs only to inform labor well in advance of its plans. Period." [32]

The fact that local departmental negotiators enjoyed greater authority only emphasized the major bargaining task that lay ahead. Local union negotiators still retained the right to bargain on a substantial number of issues. Twenty-five provisions in 11 articles of the national agreement were specifically reserved for local negotiations. Local bargaining began on April 1, with a negotiations deadline set for May 17, 1968. A wave of bad-faith-bargaining complaints ensued, however, and the deadline was extended to July 1 since nearly 60 percent of the local post offices still lacked negotiated agreements.

---

[30] U.S. Post Office Department, *Agreements between POD and Seven Employee Organizations with Explanation of Changes, 1966 and 1968,* March 1968, Art. IV, Sec. D(1)(a).

[31] *The Union Postal Clerk, op. cit.,* p. 2.

[32] Morris Biller, President, MBPU-NPU, *The Union Mail,* March 1968, p. 3.

The Letter Carriers, Postal Clerks, and NPU among others complained that the stern new face presented by local management had resulted in arbitrary determinations of nonnegotiability, particularly over union proposals to continue provisions already present in previous accords. Union accusations of bad-faith bargaining and antilabor attitudes led to a series of protest demonstrations and picketing at major post offices. The stubborn management approach was attributed by the unions in part to the labor-management training conferences convened by Postmaster General O'Brien at the University of Oklahoma in early 1968. There, it was alleged, postmasters and labor relations experts were encouraged to take a tough stand in local dealings. The unions charged that a national breakdown of local negotiations had resulted from management's "hard-nosed" attitude. They accused management negotiators of "hiding behind the broad umbrella of Section 13 of Article VII . . . which states that nothing can be negotiated that conflicts with law, POD regulations or conflicts with, repeats, rewords or paraphrases the National Agreement." [33]

Negotiations proceeded amid considerable acrimony. They were reported broken off in New York, Detroit, Boston, and Saginaw, Mich. The New York postal unions took their grievances to their congressional representatives, including Chairman Dulski of the House Post Office and Civil Service Committee. A meeting with Postmaster General W. Marvin Watson (who by then had succeeded O'Brien) was promised as soon as possible to consider the situation. The Postal Clerks filed formal charges of unfair labor practices. By the May 17 deadline about 5,000 items were declared nonnegotiable or had reached an impasse. Of some 6,000 post offices, only about 2,500 had concluded local agreements.[34]

Under such conditions the locus of bargaining authority had to be transferred to the national level. By September 4, about 4,700 local accords had been renegotiated, but over 1,200 postal installations were still without new agreements. Under the basic contract, of 8,514 issues that had reached an impasse, 2,777 were resolved at the regional level and 1,927 at the national level; the great majority of them were declared nonnegotiable. This left about 3,810 entirely unresolved items.

Postmaster General Watson, however, felt he had acquired first-hand knowledge of the local differences after attending the

---

[33] *Government Employee Relations Report,* No. 227 (1968); No. 240 (1968); No. 242 (1968); No. 244 (1968).

[34] *Ibid.,* No. 242 (1968); No. 244 (1968); and No. 246 (1968).

national conventions of the major unions. Immediately thereafter, he called for top-level conferences with national exclusive representatives and formulated a comprehensive policy to govern the hamstrung local negotiations. The new policy statement consolidated the 8,514 issues into 33 principal items. All local negotiators were required to review settled accords and revise them in accordance with the new policy. The revised position on negotiability or nonnegotiability was, of course, to govern the settlement of agreements in installations where bargaining had been entirely unsuccessful.[35] The Postal Bulletin on Local Negotiations covered contested items affecting overtime, training, assignment of substitutes and ill and injured workers, details, patron complaints, the use of unsafe vehicles, holiday assignments, facilities for union meetings, and other items of particular concern to local installations.[36]

Most union leaders were pleased, and it was expected that the remaining local contracts would be concluded within several weeks. The parties were afforded the flexibility of "a reasonable time" in which to accomplish this end.[37] As a result, local bargaining impasses were resolved in fairly short order.

The harsh aftereffects of these events, however, cannot be denied. The trying experiences of the fourth-round negotiations caused union leaders to call more frequently for a federal labor relations law to govern negotiability. Of greater significance, the residual feelings undoubtedly contributed to the accumulation of tensions that culminated in the 1970 strike.

Definite counterreactions were registered among the local postmasters. They had seen their local accords superseded by policy directives from above and felt themselves seriously weakened in the bargaining process. After all, *they* had to live with the contract. At their annual convention, therefore, the National Association of Postmasters called for a greater participation in decision-making. They felt themselves unprotected when controlling decisions were made at the regional and national levels. As Anthony Ingrassia noted, higher level decisions are made on the basis of what is deemed best for the local installations; they are decisions that cannot satisfy all postmasters.[38] The 1968 experience, nevertheless, was a major step in the continued progress of

---

[35] *Ibid.,* No. 263 (1968), pp. A-1, A-2.

[36] U.S. Post Office Department, *Postal Bulletin,* No. 20664, September 19, 1968, pp. 3-5.

[37] *Government Employee Relations Report,* No. 263 (1968), p. A-1.

[38] *Ibid.,* No. 265 (1968), pp. A-3, A-4.

postal bargaining. There is little doubt that the expertise of both sides was considerably enhanced.

The immensity of POD collective bargaining was demonstrated by the last statistics gathered while still a department. By November 1969, as noted, seven national exclusive and four national formal recognitions had been granted. In addition, 24,608 local exclusive units and 7,834 local formal units were recognized. Approximately 6,100 supplemental local agreements were negotiated.[39] Eighty-seven percent of all postal employees were covered by exclusive recognitions.[40] Another significant indicator of the Department's leadership position in labor matters was the check-off data. The projected annual dues withholding for 1968 covered 448,545 employees, double that of the Defense Department, the agency with the next largest number on check-off. The actual amount of monies withheld, $12,096,428, came to more than one half of all the dues checked off for the entire federal establishment. If Defense Department deductions are excluded, the postal unions received three times as much in withheld dues as the unions in all of the remaining federal agencies combined.[41] This has contributed greatly to their financial and organizational stability.

B. THE PATH TO REFORM

The record of the old Post Office Department under the EMC program should not be underestimated. Its achievements over the years were manifested in strong national agreements and extensive collective bargaining. These exemplified the commendable advances in labor relations accomplished since 1962. It would have been naive in the extreme, however, to assume even in 1969 that all was well in postal employment. Dissatisfaction on both sides continued over many issues. The original Task Force had disclosed that strong antagonisms already existed in POD. Testimony revealed that many postal workers were discontented with labor relations before the Kennedy order.

The Bureau of Inspections in the Civil Service Commission saw the EMC program as a beneficial influence. It described consultation and cooperation as more firmly entrenched and labor-

[39] U.S. Civil Service Commission, Office of Labor-Management Relations, *Union Recognition in the Federal Government-Statistical Report and Listings by Agency, November 1969*, Washington, June 17, 1970, p. 234.

[40] *Ibid.*, p. 13.

[41] U.S. Civil Service Commission, Office of Labor-Management Relations, *Voluntary Union Dues Allotments in the Federal Government, 1968*, Washington, 1969, p. 1.

management relationships as more productive. Employees and unions were gaining increased confidence. Some managers saw their jobs as more "difficult" but conceded that increased attention paid off in better personnel management.[42] Reviewing the atmosphere of dealings in the year 1965-66, the Bureau reported a generally favorable climate at the local level. In very few instances did relationships deteriorate to a point that seriously hampered dealings. However, the Bureau noted that "even though the overall picture of employee-management relationships was generally good, friction continued to be reported." [43] Personality conflicts arising out of union aggressiveness or management antagonism strained relations. Other contributory factors were the lack of program understanding in some union leaders and management's unfamiliarity with the national accord.[44]

Even where favorable labor relations existed, criticism and complaint were still evident. To unions, management's attitude sometimes appeared to be "negative, dictatorial, or inconsiderate." There were allegations of supervisors' harassment of union leaders. Delays in management decision-making were attributed to the failure of local officials to act without consulting higher authority. Grievance handling was too slow. A too-liberal interpretation of the term "emergency" permitted supervisors to do nonsupervisory work. On the other hand, managers criticized union leaders because of their excesssive concern with "petty, insignificant problems." They decried excessive union concern over program operations deemed outside the area of negotiability.[45] Similar complaints were later cited by the President's Commisssion on Postal Organization.[46]

The bargaining difficulties of 1968, the recurring job actions in 1969, and the 1970 strike caused these serious underlying discontents to surface. Widespread dissatisfaction with the 1969 4.1-percent pay increase further spurred employee unrest. These events emphasized the need for reform, but how reform would be achieved remained in doubt. Executive action was momentarily expected. New legislation conceivably could affect the entire federal labor structure. Some believed that a reform of the postal

---

[42] U.S. Civil Service Commission, Bureau of Inspections, Analysis and Development Division, *Summary Report on Employee-Management Cooperation,* March 1967, p. 23.

[43] *Ibid.,* p. 21.

[44] *Ibid.*

[45] *Ibid.,* p. 22.

[46] Report of the U.S. President's Commission on Postal Organization, *Towards Postal Excellence,* Washington, 1968, p. 20.

service alone would be senseless if unaccompanied by revision of the general labor relations system.

The widening debate over postal incorporation provided a major arena for airing strongly held contending views. Labor issues stood high among them. Establishing a government corporation to run the postal service was a question of formidable consequence to the public, to Congress, to the Department, and to over 700,000 postal workers. Declaring that "total reform of the nation's postal system is absolutely necessary," President Nixon termed such action to be "one of the most significant proposals that will be made in the entire period of this Administration."[47]

The undeniable difficulties and persistent problems in postal operations are not within the purview of this study. The intent here is to examine the reform issue primarily in terms of its relevancy to postal labor relations.[48]

Agitation for a corporate revision was generally couched in terms of an "inevitable impending crisis." The vast postal "deficit," the disastrous October 1966 breakdown in Chicago at the world's largest post office, poor working conditions, and archaic patronage practices were all cited as harbingers of catastrophe. Similar criticism was levelled against POD's labor practices.

During his tenure as Postmaster General, O'Brien appointed what he described as a "small, very confidential task force within the Department to study the overall structure of the post office" and to recommend to him "whether it would be feasible to convert the postal service into a government-owned corporation." This was a group of four young executives in their early thirties or under, none of whom were career postal employees. They considered and rejected the possibilities of reform both within the existing departmental structure and under a private postal system, opting instead, in a March 1967 report to O'Brien, for the corporation solution. In a confidential memo to President Johnson, O'Brien then proposed that the Department be taken "out of its present context entirely." He called for establishment of the corporation and abolition of the office of Postmaster General.[49] President Johnson appeared interested and on April 8, 1967, ap-

---

47 *The New York Times,* May 28, 1969, pp. 1, 20.

48 For definitive treatments of postal history and operations under POD, see Sterling D. Spero, *The Labor Movement in a Government Industry* (New York: MacMillan, 1927; reprinted, New York: Arno Press and New York Times, 1971), and Gerald Cullinan, *The United States Postal Service* (New York: Frederick A. Praeger, 1973).

49 Lawrence F. O'Brien, "How the Post Office Plotted Suicide," *Washington Post,* August 18, 1968. This excellent article intimately described the internal development of O'Brien's efforts and their reception when finally publicized.

pointed his Commission on Postal Organization headed by Frederick R. Kappel, a retired Chairman of the Board of A.T. and T. It has been noted that the background of the Commission members, the majority of whom were from the business community (General Electric, Bank of America, Campbell Soup, Federated Department Stores, Cummins Engine Company), necessarily would predispose the Commission to turning the service into a profit-making business.[50] AFL-CIO President George Meany was the sole labor member.

C. THE KAPPEL COMMISSION RECOMMENDATIONS

The Commission on Postal Organization submitted its report to the President in June 1968. Concluding that the service was incapable of meeting the demands of a growing economy and expanding population,[51] it called for a wholly owned government corporation, chartered by Congress and operating on a self-supporting basis with a nine-man board of directors. The corporation was to act immediately to improve the quality of service and the working environment of postal employees. Obsolescent and inefficient facilities were to be replaced. All appointments and promotions in the postal system were to be on a nonpolitical basis. Postal employees were to be transferred with their accrued Civil Service benefits to a new postal corporation career service. The new board, after hearings by expert rate commissioners, was to establish fair postal rates, subject to congressional veto.

Long-term benefits, in the Commission's view, would be a dependable, fairly priced postal service, fully responsive to the needs of the public. It would be a soundly financed, self-supporting system with better working conditions and career opportunities for postal employees. Considerable attention was devoted to providing the workers with pay comparable to that in private industry and greater opportunities for real collective bargaining.[52]

The corporation proposal appeared too simplistic. Most assuredly, some of the Commission's major recommendations were long overdue, particularly those for capital improvements and freeing the service from political patronage.[53] Indeed, in February

---

[50] Robert Sherrill, "Bring Back the Pony Express," *New York Times Magazine,* November 3, 1968, p. 112.

[51] Report of the U.S. President's Commission on Postal Organization, *op. cit.,* p. iii.

[52] *Ibid.,* pp. 1-6.

[53] The National Civil Service League, for example, had for many decades been totally committed to ridding the Post Office of spoils. One of its most forceful declarations was a Policy Statement issued in September 1966, entitled "Abandoning Patronage in Postal Appointments." It sought full merit standards for appointing postmasters and rural letter carriers.

1969 President Nixon and Postmaster General Blount acted to remove politics as a factor in the appointment of postmasters and
rural letter carriers.[54] However, there was opposition to the corporation plan, particularly from some members of former Democratic administrations. The Commission Report also noted
George Meany's reservations. Meany agreed with the goal of modernizing the service and improving working conditions. But, he
said, "the status of the Post Office as a Cabinet Department has a
positive value that should not be discarded lightly." [55]

Successive Democratic Postmasters General differed greatly as
to the plan's advisability. President Kennedy's first Postmaster
General, J. Edward Day, one of the original members of the
EMC Task Force, testified at great length with knowledgeable arguments in opposition to a postal corporation.[56] O'Brien's successor, PMG W. Marvin Watson, denied the existence of a crisis.
Watson also disagreed with the Kappel group's argument that
inefficiencies were wasting one billion dollars annually. To him
POD was not in serious trouble; its problems could be resolved in
five years if the Department were only supplied the necessary
hardware. As he put it: "We know exactly what needs to be
done." [57]

Robert Sherrill's perceptive article in *The New York Times*
noted that the supporters of O'Brien "swear that President Johnson was on the verge of approving the Kappel report as soon as it
came out and Watson persuaded him not to." [58] Whatever the
reasons, Johnson did not receive the report with great enthusiasm. Quite the contrary, he reacted noncommittally, asking the
Postmaster General and Budget Director to review what he
termed the "sobering judgment" of the Commission and report
back to him.[59] Later, however, he endorsed the corporation in
principle.

A consensus in Congress was also lacking. O'Brien noted that
reaction to his proposals on Capitol Hill was "predictably
guarded." Despite some endorsements, the predominant view in
both the House and the Senate was that further study was

---

[54] *Government Employee Relations Report,* No. 283 (1969) , pp. A-3, A-4, A-5.

[55] Report of U.S. President's Commission on Postal Organization, *op. cit.,* p. 2.

[56] J. Edward Day, *Statement on Proposals for Post Office Reorganization,* before
the U.S. House of Representatives, Committee on Post Office and Civil Service,
July 31, 1969.

[57] Robert Sherrill, *op. cit.,* p. 90.

[58] *Ibid.*

[59] David R. Jones, "Johnson is Noncommittal on a Postal Corporation," *The New
York Times,* July 17, 1968, p. 20.

needed.[60] Congress, reluctant to relinquish power and sensitive to union desires, continued its noncommittal attitude when President Nixon submitted his 1969 reforms.[61] Recognizing there was little chance of its passage that year, government officials were reported girding for a tough selling job in the Congress and a long-term fight.[62]

The New York Times recognized these facts of political life. Favorably disposed to the Nixon plan, which was fundamentally the same as the Kappel Commission's, *The Times* chided Congress for being swayed by the "pressures of vested interests" and attributed the unions' coolness to the prospect of losing their "leverage on Congress where sheer numbers have made them an effective lobby. . . ." [63] It also recognized, however, that major unions were supporting other postal reform bills, particularly Representative Dulski's bill, H.R. 4, which would have accomplished many of the aims of the Nixon plan without revising POD's status.[64]

Indeed, the postal unions could hardly dispute the Kappel Commission's labor relations findings. What they did fear was a total reform that might automatically include a new labor relations system inconsistent with the growing militancy of postal employees; particularly as these workers now defined "real" collective bargaining. The unions dearly wanted to retain their traditional avenue to Congress and to use it for expanding their rights and benefits.

The Kappel Commission had not painted a picture of amicable labor relations under the EMC program. It had cited in detail the numerous dissatisfactions already delineated in this chapter.[65] Without passing on the merits of the varied grievances of both sides, the Commission had deemed it "nevertheless clear that the relationship between labor and management in the Post Office is generally unproductive." [66] In summarizing its findings, the Kappel group had concluded that:

> "Despite six years of experience under Executive Order 10988 and some positive results, relations between postal unions and management have been less than a success judging from frequent com-

---

[60] Lawrence F. O'Brien, "How the Post Office Plotted Suicide."

[61] U.S. House of Representatives, *Postal Service Act of 1969*, H.R. 11750, 91st Cong., 1st Sess., May 28, 1969.

[62] Robert B. Semple Jr., "Nixon Proposes U.S. Corporation for Mail Service," *The New York Times*, May 28, 1969, p. 1.

[63] "Hope for the Mails," *The New York Times*, May 28, 1969, p. 46.

[64] *Ibid.*, p. 20.

[65] Report of the U.S. President's Commission on Postal Organization, *op. cit.*, pp. 19-20, 117-119.

[66] *Ibid.*, pp. 21-22.

plaints by both groups. Labor and management have seriously questioned the good faith of the other. . . . It is understandable that differences are bound to exist between the management and employees of any organization, particularly one as large as the Post Office Department. However, the frequency and intensity of the complaints presented to this Commission indicate a serious gulf between the parties." [67]

D. CONGRESSIONAL MANEUVERING OVER REFORM

The Commission's reasoning and recommendations, with minor variations, formed the basis of the Nixon proposals. In his Message to Congress accompanying the Postal Service Act of 1969, the President echoed the concern for the "rightful aspirations of our postal workers." He decried their inferior working environment, calling for true comparability with private industry and an employee voice in determining working conditions. Although he spoke only of the postal service because of its unique character, he nevertheless proposed changes long sought by unions for the entire government. These included new and extensive collective bargaining rights. For example, he declared there would be

> "for the first time in history, true collective bargaining in the postal system. Postal employees in every part of the United States will be given the statutory right to negotiate directly with management over wages and working conditions. A fair and impartial mechanism—with provision for binding arbitration—will be established to resolve negotiating impasses and disputes arising in labor agreements." [68]

Nevertheless, sharp differences arose between the Administration and the postal unions as to each's interpretation of "true collective bargaining."

A bill introduced by Representative Udall (Dem., Ariz.) embodied the President's proposals. The corporation concept, now made more palatable by a new title, the United States Postal Service, would be run by a nine-man board of directors. Seven part-time directors would be appointed by the President with Senate confirmation. They would then select an eighth as Chief Executive Officer, who, in turn, would choose a Chief Operating Officer. These two directors would serve full time with pay and tenure fixed by the seven. Their basic corporate powers would be

---

[67] *Ibid.,* pp. 119-120.
[68] U.S. President Nixon, *Message on Reform of the Nation's Postal System,* 91st Cong., 1st Sess., House Document No. 91-121, May 27, 1969.

similar in a general way to those enjoyed by the corresponding officials in the Tennessee Valley Authority.[69]

The bill's personnel provisions would expand collective bargaining, by statute, to cover a new merit system outside the regular civil service. All accrued rights under civil service or existing contracts would continue in effect until changed through collective bargaining. Compensation, benefits, and other terms and conditions of employment were to be determined by the board of directors in accordance with the principles of collective bargaining laid down in the Taft-Hartley Act and new provisions for resolving bargaining impasses. The prohibition against strikes and the affidavit requirements were specifically retained by cross reference to applicable laws.[70] The management rights provision closely resembled the required E.O. 10988 clause; however, it too would now be subject to collective bargaining.[71]

It was reported that Administration supporters of the bill were relying heavily on its impasse arbitration proposals to overcome the major opposition expected from the postal unions; that these would "set some of labor's fears to rest." [72] But this was not the case. The unions, still bridling over retention of the strike prohibition, believed the arbitration provisions to be illusory. They also contended, contrary to the Administration's view, that "true collective bargaining" was impossible without the strike weapon. They insisted that if there was to be a postal corporation, postal workers should be given the right to strike.[73]

The opposition of the Letter Carriers, Postal Clerks, and National Postal Union was supplemented by that of the Government Employees' Council, which unanimously resolved to "disapprove wholeheartedly" the proposal on much broader grounds. It felt that the postal service, being the basic means of communication in the nation, should not be removed from the control of the people through their representatives in Congress. It saw the corporation directors exerting absolute and arbitrary power over rates, salaries, and quality of service in contravention of the con-

---

[69] U.S. House of Representatives, *Postal Service Act of 1969, H.R. 11750,* 91st Cong., 1st Sess., May 28, 1969, Ch. 2, Secs. 202-210.

[70] *Ibid.,* Chap. 8, Secs. 801-807, Chap. 2, Sec. 209.

[71] *Ibid.,* Chap. 8, Sec. 806 (b) .

[72] *The New York Times,* May 28, 1969, p. 20.

[73] See James H. Rademacher, President, National Association of Letter Carriers, "Postal Corporation—Everybody's Nightmare," *The Postal Record,* July 1969, pp. 4-5, and Morris Biller, President, then MBPU-NPU, "Postal Service Corporation—And What It Will Mean to You", *The Union Mail,* June 1969, p. 4.

stitutional system of checks and balances.[74] Great concern was also expressed by most unions over the possible threat to their members' civil service status.

On the other hand, strong union support was registered for Representative Dulski's bill, H. R. 4.[75] He had introduced it on the first day of the 1969 Congress after lengthy study of the Kappel Commission report. He believed his proposal would:

> "do everything that is claimed for a corporate entity—and all within the framework of the historic philosophy and the fundamental principles of our government.
>
> "It would preserve the traditional character of the postal service as a direct duty of Government—a duty to be carried out by placing responsibility on an executive department and giving the department the authority and flexibility it must have to carry out that responsibility." [76]

He conceded the need for radical changes but cautioned against cures that might be worse than the illness. Every necessary reform, he asserted, could be accomplished "more quickly and effectively within the present framework of government" and "without the inevitable disruption and turmoil involved in a changeover to a corporation." [77]

Dulski contended that H. R. 4 would meet most of the Kappel Commission recommendations. To make the service self-supporting, his bill provided that the Department would use its own revenues to pay its expenses free of restrictive limitations. Postal rates would be set by a Commission on Postal Finance reporting to the President, whose recommendations in turn would be passed on by Congress. All political influences in the appointment of postmasters would be prohibited. A Postal Modernization Authority operating under the Government Corporation Control Act would have extensive powers to update the system.[78]

Representative Dulski considered his labor relations reforms to be the most critically needed improvements. He saw them establishing a clearly defined, workable charter for postal labor that embodied "all of the essential policies, principles, practices and procedures that have been adopted in modern progressive private enterprise." [79] Elements of this charter included compulsory arbi-

[74] Government Employes' Council, *Resolution on the Postal Corporation*, February 11, 1969.
[75] U.S. House of Representatives, *The Postal Reform Act of 1969*, H.R. 4, 91st Cong., 1st Sess., January 3, 1969.
[76] 115 *Congressional Record* H75 (1969).
[77] *Ibid.*
[78] H.R. 4, Titles II, IV, V, VI.
[79] 115 *Congressional Record* H76 (1969).

tration and the effective settlement of appeals and grievances, exclusive recognition for employee unions, separate consideration for supervisors' organizations, and codes of fair conduct for both labor and management.[80] The enactment of so comprehensive a system of rights, Dulski reasoned, would ensure maintenance of "the traditional policy of the great postal employee unions that they do not ask, and do not want, the right to strike."[81]

The lines were thus drawn some four months before the outbreak of the March 1970 postal strike. Legislative efforts during this time were hampered and delayed by intense congressional in-fighting. All concerned elements were involved—the national exclusive unions and the independents, the AFL-CIO, the President, the Post Office Department, large corporate postal users, and the National Right to Work Committee, to cite some major influences. Legislative dickering and bargaining proceeded at a furious pace, and the possibility of postal labor relations attaining statutory regulation became inextricably enmeshed with pay bills, retirement bills, and executive labor orders.

In October 1969 the Administration bill, H. R. 11750, was blocked in committee. Passage of any pay bill then became increasingly dependent upon some union acceptance of postal reorganization. It was quite clear that the President was not going to permit a pay raise without such acceptance. The rationale was that only through reorganization could savings be realized that would justify wage increases.

In December, sharp disagreements over the federal pay bill ensured that no more action would be taken until Congress met again in 1970. Change was in the wind, however. In a meeting with the leader of the Carriers, the President retreated somewhat from the corporation concept. Instead, an independent "authority" of considerable power would be the quid pro quo for a better postal pay package.[82] For a time union acceptance of this compromise seemed likely. But opposition gradually developed, in part because of a presidential decision to defer a comparability pay increase automatically due on July 1, 1970, to January 1971. Chairman Dulski of the House Post Office Committee then stated his intention to push H. R. 4, a bill Nixon was committed to veto.

All of this was too little and too late for the disgruntled mem-

---

[80] H.R. 4, Title VII.

[81] *The Postal Record*, July 1969, p. 31.

[82] James Rademacher, "President's Biennial Report," *The Postal Record*, September, 1970, pp. 17-18.

bership of the urban New York Carrier locals. Strike sentiment was growing, not only because of the lack of a valid pay bill but also because of the scant consideration being afforded regional wage differentials. On March 12, 1970, the House Post Office Committee voted out a substitute bill presented by Rep. David Henderson of North Carolina. It established a Postal Authority and provided for retroactive pay increases, real collective bargaining, and most of the provisions of the original pay bill. Congressional sentiment for its passage appeared quite favorable, but the impending strike destroyed its chances.

Whatever its other consequences, as related in Chapter XVIII, the national postal stoppage of March 1970 forced a reappraisal of the entire Post Office situation at the highest levels of authority. There were negotiations between Secretary Shultz, Postmaster General Blount, and Assistant Secretary of Labor W. J. Ussery and George Meany and James Gildea of the AFL-CIO and the postal union leaders. Finally, postal operations were restored, and by April 2 the negotiators had hammered out a Memorandum of Agreement that formed the basis for statutory reform—the Postal Reorganization Act of August 12, 1970.[83] Reform and pay problems were treated in the same measure. The concept of the postal service and wage increases of 14 percent were the final results.

Despite an apparent consensus among Administration and labor leaders on eventual goals, immediate enactment was not forthcoming. Once again legislative maneuvering and lobbying delayed passage of the law almost five months. On April 3, the President's message to Congress calling for an immediate 6-percent increase was couched throughout in terms of needed postal reorganization.[84] His major message on postal reform, delivered April 16, 1970, set forth the essentials of the proposed act: convert the Post Office Department into an independent establishment in the Executive Branch, provide for collective bargaining over pay and working conditions, increase postal pay by an additional 8 percent, and compress the time to reach the top salary scale for most postal jobs from 21 to 8 years.[85] It was plain from the publicity attending the message that Mr. Nixon saw postal reform as an historic accomplishment of his Administration.

---

[83] See Chapter XVIII. See also Memorandum of Agreement in U.S. House of Representatives, Committee on Post Office and Civil Service, *Hearings on Postal Reform*, H.R. *17070*, 91st Cong., 2nd Sess., April 22, 1970, pp. 2-3.

[84] *The New York Times*, April 4, 1970, p. 13.

[85] U.S. House of Representatives, *Message of the President*, 91st Cong., 2nd Sess., April 16, 1970, Document No. 91-313, p. 1.

There was a new unanimity on the Hill. A bill, H. R. 17070, was introduced by Chairman Dulski and Representatives Udall, Corbett, and Derwinski that embodied the Administration's program as negotiated with postal labor.[86] Several others of similar nature were introduced.[87] Congress appeared quite willing to implement the accord that ended the strike. The media expressed support and encouragement for postal improvement. Hearings began almost immediately, and for a while it appeared that both Senate and House bills might be passed by the end of May. This was not to be.

Considerable delay and difficulty were caused in the Senate by the Cambodian intervention. Senate business was seriously disrupted by the acrimonious and vehement debate. In addition, the National Right to Work Committee again brought all its guns to bear to prevent any major form of union security from being adopted in the Federal Government. The original House bill did not contain any provision preserving the right to refrain from union activity. This was true also of the Senate bill, S. 3842, as passed, and thus it would have been possible to contract for a union shop in those states without "right to work" laws. However, just as their past efforts had helped forestall union security by executive order for the whole federal establishment,[88] the Right to Work Committee effectively lobbied to prevent its adoption by statute.[89] Again they were successful. The House bill as finally passed contained a provision stating that "Each employee . . . shall have the right . . ; to refrain from any such activity, and . . . shall be protected in the exercise of that right." [90]

Despite a filibuster threat, such language did not appear in the final Senate bill. However, in sending its bill to a joint conference committee, the House overwhelmingly adopted a resolution offered by Representative Henderson barring the House conferees from retreating from the final House position on union security. If there was to be any postal legislation at all, it was plain that the union shop would have to go.

Efforts had also been mounted in both the House and the Senate to substitute bills that would have afforded independent un-

---

86 U.S. House of Representatives, Committee on Post Office and Civil Service, *The Postal Reorganization and Salary Adjustment Act of 1970, H.R. 17070,* 91st Cong., 2nd Sess., April 20, 1970, Committee Print No. 13.

87 H.R. 17071, H.R. 17072, H.R. 17082 and H.R. 17144.

88 See Chapter VII, Sec. A.

89 U.S. House of Representatives, Committee on Post Office and Civil Service, *Hearings on Postal Reform,* 91st Cong., 2nd Sess., April 27, 1970, pp. 193-195.

90 84 Stat. 737; 39 U.S.C. Sec. 1209 (c) , August 12, 1970.

ions better consideration and recognition in the proposed reforms. Primarily involved here was the National Postal Union, industrial in character and the third largest postal organization. Not fitting the definition of a "national exclusive union" under the executive orders, it had been precluded from the strike-ending negotiations.[91] The Senate bill would have perpetuated this condition; however, the conference committee adopted the House position that appropriate unit issues should be left entirely to the NLRB.[92]

After three weeks of consideration and many meetings, the conference committee reported favorably on the bill, and during the first week of August both the House and the Senate passed H. R. 17070 as amended and sent it to the President for signature.[93] With great fanfare Mr. Nixon signed the bill into law on August 12, 1970. The old Post Office Department of 181 years' duration was marked for total reorganization.

E. THE POSTAL REORGANIZATION ACT OF 1970

Before a considerable audience which included six former Postmasters General, the President lauded the bipartisan character of the postal reform drive. He described the landmark legislation as "historic" and stated "that hundreds of thousands of people in the Post Office can look to a better future, . . . and as the future is better for them it means better service for the American people."[94] After some five years of operation, it can be argued whether progress has been made toward both these goals.

The Postal Reorganization Act created the U.S. Postal Service as an independent establishment within the executive branch of the Federal Government. Although not a corporation or "authority" as earlier proposed, it is not far removed from the original concept in structure, operations, and purpose.[95]

The major policies enacted seek to provide a tenured manage-

---

91 U.S. House of Representatives, Committee on Post Office and Civil Service, *Hearings on Postal Reform*, Testimony of David Silvergleid, President, National Postal Union, and Morris Biller, President, Manhattan-Bronx Postal Union, 91st Cong., 2nd Sess., April 27, 1970, pp. 113-141.

92 U.S. House of Representatives, *Conference Report on Postal Reorganization*, 91st Cong., 2nd Sess., Report No. 91-1363, August 3, 1970, pp. 18-19, 81-82.

93 The Senate passed H.R. 17070 on August 3 by a vote of 57 to 7. The House approved the measure on August 6 by a vote of 339 to 29. Both were roll-call votes.

94 *New York Times*, August 13, 1970, pp. 1, 35.

95 See U.S. House of Representatives, Committee on Post Office and Civil Service, *Hearings on Postal Reform, op. cit.*, for detailed comparisons of H.R. 17070 with the "corporation" Udall bill H.R. 11750 and the Dulski "authority" bill H.R. 4, April 22, 1970, Serial No. 91022, pp. 62-82.

ment free of political considerations. Indeed, postal operations have been substantially removed from congressional control. The Postmaster General, no longer a cabinet member, is independent of the President, the Congress, and the Bureau of the Budget (OMB). Peformance, not politics, is to determine tenure.

The Postal Service is directed by an 11-member Board of Governors. Nine members are appointed by the President with the Senate's consent. Not more than five of these may be from the same political party, and all serve staggered terms. The Board selects the Postmaster General and its own Chairman. Both the Board and the Postmaster General choose the Deputy PMG, who also serves as a Board member. The Board determines the number of Assistant Postmasters General needed, and the PMG has the authority to hire and fire them.[96] The Act specifically states that, with few exceptions, oral or written recommendations from Members of Congress, state or local officials, or political party officials shall not be considered in hiring, promotion, or transfer of postal employees.[97] The machinery is there to make the Postal Service free of politics. Whether this is achieved will depend upon the people who administer the law.

A Postal Rate Commission of five presidential appointees was established as another independent agency of the executive branch. On request of the Postal Service, the Rate Commission, after hearings and due process, submits to the Board its recommendations on changes in postal rates or fees. The statutory intent is to have rates and fees provide sufficient revenue so that income and appropriations, as nearly as practicable, will equal the costs of maintaining and developing the Postal Service.[98] These procedures clearly take from Congress its traditional authority to determine postal rates and classes of mail.

An Advisory Council was established to consult with and advise the Postal Service on "all aspects of postal operations."[99] A body of 13 members with the Postmaster General as chairman and the Deputy PMG as vice chairman, it is made up of presidential appointees from the sectors most vitally concerned with the mails. Four members are chosen from nominees of labor unions granted exclusive bargaining rights; four members represent the

---

[96] 84 Stat. 721; 39 U.S.C. Sec. 204; Conference Report on Postal Reorganization, *op. cit.*, p. 80.

[97] 84 Stat. 729; 39 U.S.C. Sec. 1002; Conference Report on Postal Reorganization, *op cit.*, p. 81.

[98] 84 Stat. 760; 39 U.S.C. Secs. 3621-3628.

[99] 84 Stat. 722; 39 U.S.C. Sec. 206; Conference Report on Postal Reorganization, *op. cit.*, p. 80.

major mail users, and the remaining three are appointed to represent the public at large.[100] This hardly amounts to a massive representation of the public interest. In the last analysis, whether the public will truly be served will hinge upon the attitudes and actions of those who administer the new machinery. It is one thing to pass a law; it is another to administer it.

The law brought many other new policies. The 8-percent retroactive pay increase was finally achieved;[101] wage schedules were compressed to eight years for the maximum pay;[102] the concept of pay comparability with the private sector was achieved;[103] and the proposals for a self-supporting postal system and a postal career service were adopted. In the area of finance, the Postal Service was empowered to issue up to $10 billion of bonds to carry on modernization and capital improvement.[104] In addition, because of the public service costs entailed in maintaining effective mails nationwide, and particularly in communities where local post offices are not self-sustaining, federal subsidies were allotted through 1984. Appropriations for fiscal 1972 through 1979 were to be 10 percent of the 1971 POD appropriation. Thereafter such subsidies are to be paid on a declining basis.[105]

These reformed administrative structures and service policies directly and vitally affect labor relations in the Postal Service. Indeed, perhaps the greatest innovations of all, in the long run, will be the reforms wrought in postal labor-management relations. It was, after all, the breakdown in this area that spurred adoption of the entire program. It is of prime importance, therefore, to consider the public labor law revisions of the Act not only in terms of the Postal Service but all public employment.

To George Meany, the law was unique in that it was the product of genuine collective bargaining between the executive branch and the duly elected representatives of the workers involved.[106] This was seen as "sound evidence that the democratic process of collective bargaining can and does work in a free country, between the government and its workers as well as between private employers and their workers." There was little doubt as to his overall intent. He declared:

---

[100] *Ibid.*
[101] 84 Stat. 784; 39 U.S.C. Sec. 3061, Subsec. 9 (a) .
[102] 84 Stat. 785; 39 U.S.C. Sec. 3061, Subsec. 10 (b) .
[103] 84 Stat. 719; 39 U.S.C. Sec. 101.
[104] 84 Stat. 710; 39 U.S.C. Sec. 2005.
[105] 84 Stat. 743; 39 U.S.C. Sec. 2401.
[106] These, of course, were the affiliated national exclusives under E.O. 11491.

"We in the AFL-CIO hope to be back . . . in the very near future, urging adoption of a measure that will ensure genuine collective bargaining for all aspects of government employment for all civilian workers in the federal government.

"We think this bill is only the beginning. We are convinced that the other federal employees also must have a right to economic self-determination and to the democracy of the collective bargaining table.

"As we see it, Congress is today paving the way for a new day in federal employment relationship—a good day, too long delayed."[107]

In its essentials, the Postal Reorganization Act embodied the major elements of the Memoranda of Agreement between POD and the seven national exclusives. When over 90 percent of the striking postal workers returned to the job, collective bargaining began in earnest. Meany convened the postal union leadership to help unify their positions and presentations. His assistant, James Gildea, was selected as the unions' major negotiator. There followed a crucial period of intense bargaining from March 25 to April 2, with the pay issue a major stumbling block. The first Memorandum of Agreement came with acceptance of the 14-percent pay-increase package.[108] Both sides then returned to the bargaining table to implement, in greater detail, the structure and policies of the postal reorganization. Within two weeks, negotiations culminated in a new Memorandum of Agreement, signed at AFL-CIO headquarters, that formed the basis of the Act.[109] Each stage of these consecutive negotiations was widely publicized in the media and received public presidential blessings. A major goal of most federal unions was momentarily to be achieved, at least for the postal workers—labor relations governed by statute.

In the President's message, the prime criterion for the new system was the framework of collective bargaining and its labor regulatory procedures that had long prevailed in the private sector.[110]

Thus the national labor code evolved over the years under the Wagner Act and its Taft-Hartley and Landrum-Griffin Law amendments was now to apply to the USPS.[111] Postal unions determine compensation, hours, benefits, and terms and conditions of employment through collective bargaining. Grievances and ad-

107 U.S. House of Representatives, Committee on Post Office and Civil Service, *Hearings on Postal Reform,* 91st Cong., 2nd Sess., April 23, 1970, p. 85.

108 *Ibid.,* p. 2.

109 U.S. Senate, Committee on Post Office and Civil Service, *Hearings on Postal Modernization,* S. 3613, 91st Cong., 2nd Sess., April 23, 1970, p. 1083.

110 U.S. House of Representatives, *Message of the President,* 91st Cong., 2nd Sess., April 16, 1970, Document No. 91-313, p. 3.

111 84 Stat. 737; 39 U.S.C., Sec. 1209.

verse actions under the agreement are subject to negotiation.[112] The National Labor Relations Board alone supervises representation elections and enforces the unfair labor practice provisions of the private-sector labor law.[113] Methods had to be provided to resolve bargaining impasses since the prohibition against all federal strikes is still enforced. To placate the growing union sentiment for the right to strike, the Act provides factfinding procedures and then binding arbitration if the bargaining impasse persists for 180 days from the start of negotiations. Negotiations were to begin immediately upon enactment.[114]

On the controversial issue of appropriate unit, the Senate amendments had the NLRB selecting only craft national units to receive exclusive recognition while the House bill applied no such restrictions. The conference committee adopted the House provisions in the belief that it was more desirable to leave unit determination "entirely in the judgment of the NLRB than to predetermine such matters in any way." Its intent was to allow this to be done "on the basis of the same criteria applied by the Board in determining appropriate bargaining units in the private sector." [115] Supervisory and managerial personnel were excluded from the collective bargaining process but were assured pay differentials over their subordinates. Their associations, however, were provided consultation and participation rights in the planning and development of their pay policies, fringe benefits, and related programs. [116]

The House effort to provide pay comparability on an area wage basis was not included in the final bills.[117] This rankled urban postal locals bridling under the economic inequalities of the high living cost regions. Indeed, all parties saw shortcomings in the Act, in its infant administration. Nevertheless, its validity as a pioneer effort is unimpeachable. Senator Gale McGee, chairman of the Senate Post Office and Civil Service Committee, was not off the mark when he referred to the collective bargaining agreement of April 16, saying: "That formula signed there may well become a model for all branches of the Federal Government." [118]

112 84 Stat. 735; 39 U.S.C., Sec. 1206.

113 84 Stat. 735; 39 U.S.C. Secs. 1204, 1209.

114 84 Stat. 735; 39 U.S.C. 1207; see also Chapter XIV for a description of the use of these procedures in the first USPS negotiations.

115 84 Stat. 733; 39 U.S.C. Sec. 1202; Conference Report on Postal Reorganization, op. cit., pp. 81-82.

116 84 Stat. 731; 39 U.S.C. Sec. 1004; Conference Report on Postal Reorganization, op. cit., pp. 82-83.

117 Ibid., p. 81.

118 U.S. Senate, op. cit., p. 961.

F. POSTAL BARGAINING AND CONTRACTS

The details of the first-round negotiations in the Postal Service have been set forth in Chapter XIV. The first Working Agreement was reached July 20, 1971. [119] It replaced the old POD accords and implemented pertinent provisions of the Postal Reorganization Act. The second round of negotiations presented an entirely different face of postal collective bargaining. Three months from the start of negotiations on April 19, the National Agreement was signed on July 21, 1973, effective through 1975.[120] As in the private sector, experience and communications acquired in the school of hard bargaining and contract administration was having its eventual effect—more mature negotiations.

The bread and butter issues union leaders sought so long in "true collective bargaining" achieved prominent attention now under the reorganized postal system. Wages, hours, and working conditions—traditional labor areas—some previously governed by statute, became bargainable items, unfettered by prior laws. (Yet it must be emphasized that within the relatively limited scope of the EMC program, the four agreements written with the Post Office Department were among the most substantive and detailed in the entire federal establishment. From the very outset the importance of the first postal accord was recognized as the contract of largest employee coverage with a single employer in the United States. It was a major bellwether and guide for all agencies in the infant program.)

With "private sector" bargaining assured under the Postal Reorganization Act, negotiations over pay, for example, were attacked with a vigor born of long-term complaint and short-run crisis. Wage issues were the most pressing. In the large urban areas they were the prime spur to the strike. Agreement on an immediate rise of 6 percent and a subsequent increase of 8 percent was a requisite for strike settlement. Assurance that collective bargaining for future pay increases would be guaranteed by statute was another. In addition several other important pay policies that were to be effectuated by negotiation were written into the law. Most were achieved, some were not.[121] However, it was felt that, after two rounds of Postal Service bargaining, economic

---

[119] U.S. Postal Service, *Working Agreement* with seven national exclusive representative unions, July 20, 1971.

[120] U.S. Postal Service, *National Agreement* with four national exclusive representative unions, July 21, 1973.

[121] National Association of Letter Carriers, "Another Union-Made Pay Raise," *Bulletin,* No. 15, July 22, 1974.

comparability had been reached. The 1973-1975 accord achieved substantial economic parity.

The first Postal Service Agreement saw a basic salary rise for the 18-month period of $1,416, or 67 cents per hour. This included a $166 cost-of-living allowance based on the BLS Consumer Price Index. In addition, a $300 transition bonus was paid, bringing the total increase to $1,716 per postal worker. By January 1973, therefore, an employee at the first step of Level 5 in the pay schedule, the basic starting-salary position, was paid $8,488 while a veteran at the top of that level (Step 12) earned $11,073. In sharp contrast, the pre-strike scale provided a starting salary of only $6,176 and a maximum salary, after 21 years, of only $8,442. The negotiated increases in some instances were delayed under the government's stabilization program, but in the end they were fully paid.

The National Postal Service Agreement of 1973-1975 pressed pay comparability still further. It provided two across-the-board yearly salary increases. A $700 rise (34 cents hourly) became effective on July 21, 1973, with another across-the-board increase of $400 (19 cents hourly) on July 20, 1974. The preexisting cost-of-living adjustment of $166 was fully incorporated into the base annual salary, and other arrangements were made to determine future cost-of-living allowances. The new formula for such allowances is free of any "cap," and under no consideration can adjustments result in salary decreases. New COLA calculations were scheduled for six-month intervals over the life of the contract—four adjustments. Base salary schedules are increased one cent for every full 0.4-point increase in the National Consumer Price Index for Urban Wage Earners and Clerical Workers.[122]

The 1973 postal bargaining, for the first time, achieved substantial improvements in the area of fringe benefits. During the EMC years fringes were not negotiable items. So also, in spite of the drawn-out negotiations of 1970-71, no major changes were worked by the first Postal Service contract in this vital area. Arrangements that had evolved through statute and administrative action were retained in full in the 1971 accord. Thus union demands for change in such areas as health insurance, life insurance, retirement, and workmen's compensation were not agreed upon. Regarding all of these, the new agreement affirmed that the USPS would continue funding or administration " . . . at the current level for the duration of this agreement." [123]

---

122 *Ibid.*, Art. IX, Secs. 1, 2, 3.
123 U.S. Postal Service, *Working Agreement,* July 20, 1971, Art. XXI, Secs. 1-4.

Not so in 1973. Union demands for 100-percent employer financing were not fully agreed to. However, fringe benefit-improvements rightly could be termed a "significant break-through." [124] Whereas the previous employer share of health insurance premiums had been 40 percent, the new contract increased this by 15 percent in July 1973 and by a further 10 percent in July 1974.[125] On the subject of life insurance, it was provided that, as of July 20, 1974, the Postal Service would pay 100 percent of the cost; previously the employer share had been one third. No radical revisions were made in retirement or injury compensation. However, these provisions were worded to insure USPS compliance with any changes effected by union efforts before the Congress. Thus the employer continues to pay 50 percent of retirement costs and the full cost of injury compensation as required by law.[126] Since the Postal Service must comply with the regulations of the Office of Federal Employees Compensation, injured employees are now guaranteed their choice of doctors.[127]

Indeed, as John Cramer emphasized in the Washington Star-News, collective bargaining has enabled postal workers to surpass the white- and blue-collar employees of the Federal Government in both pay and fringe benefits. As to wages, postal clerks and letter carriers achieved parity with GS-5 white-collar workers upon the establishment of the USPS. Cramer pointed out, however, that as of July 1973, a Level 5, Step 6, clerk or carrier reached $10,509, while a GS-5, Step 5, received $9,127, a difference of $1,382. By mid-1974, moreover, the postal employee's advantage had increased to $1,982. The implications of such widening differences are self-evident.[128]

G. CONTINUING AREAS OF BARGAINING FRICTION

The pay issue that continued to rankle postal unions was the question of area wage differentials. As noted, the higher costs faced by urban postal workers were the prime impetus behind the national strike, and the large city locals maintained that consideration had to be given in the new contracts to these higher living costs. A confrontation between city and national union leadership developed, with debate often bitter and acrimonious.

---

[124] National Association of Letter Carriers, *Bulletin*, No. 15, July 2, 1973.

[125] U.S. Postal Service, *National Agreement*, July 21, 1973, Art. XXI.

[126] *Ibid.*

[127] *The Postal Record*, July 1973, p. 7.

[128] John Cramer, "Recent Gains Put Postal Workers in Catbird Seat," *Washington Star-News*, January 12, 1974, p. A-2.

National officers of both the NALC and APWA were inclined to consider the entire picture and the total membership. Wage increases were negotiated, therefore, in terms of the national working force regardless of regional cost-of- living variations. Thus urban union leaders and members believed themselves to have been sold short since uniform national pay increases, no matter how favorable, must inherently create inequities.

The failure of the first two national agreements to provide for area wage differentials contributed to internal union disputes over ratification of the tentative agreement of July 1973. In the APWA, opposition to to the national accord was led by the powerful New York Metropolitan Area Postal Union. It voted against ratification, and in the National Rank and File Bargaining Advisory Committee, for example, the contract was accepted only after considerable oratory and vote-switching.[129] The Minority Report of the National Ratification Committee of the Letter Carriers cited the failure to achieve area wage differentials, which it claimed would benefit 80 percent of the carriers, as a major reason for rejecting the contract.[130] Eventually the NALC ratified by a margin of more than two to one. [131] In both major postal unions the possibility of a national strike if the accord was not ratified undoubtedly influenced the final outcome. To urban postal unions, the logical path then appeared to be renewed vigor and determination in pressing their petitions before the NLRB for area exclusive representation and collective bargaining.

Important areas of negotiation were developed in the two USPS agreements in a manner fully comparable to the private sector. In addition to wage security, job security was shored up and protected. Chapter XIII has catalogued in some detail how the expanded grievance-arbitration and disciplinary procedures worked to protect an employee's position on the job. Indeed, these provisions are comparable to any other labor contract in fairness, coverage, and advanced procedures. The ban on layoffs or reductions in force in the 1971 agreement was retained through 1975 despite efforts by management to secure greater leeway in laying off junior employees. [132] The NALC's Rademacher reflected union sentiment in declaring that retention of the no-layoff

---

[129] In the APWA, the national membership overwhelmingly voted six to one for ratification: 119,922 for and 21,958 against the agreement. *The Union Mail,* July-August 1973, p. 1.
[130] National Association of Letter Carriers, *Bulletin,* No. 15, July 2, 1973.
[131] *The Postal Record,* August 1973, pp. 4, 6; the NALC ratification vote was 93,216 in favor and 41,454 against. *Postal Record,* p. 6.
[132] U.S. Postal Service, *National Agreement,* July 21, 1973, Art. VI.

clause was a strike issue.[133] In addition, craft unions had long been concerned over supervisors in the smaller post offices who often did bargaining-unit work. The 1973 accord clearly forbade such supervisor activity except in emergencies or when it normally fell within their own job description responsibilities.[134] The proviso alone will not effect compliance. This is perhaps one of the more patent instances of a provision whose impact will depend primarily upon enforcement and administration.

Technological innovation is recognized by all parties and the public as vital and overdue in the Postal Service. To American organized labor such changes always pose a threat to job security. Since change is inevitable, unions have evolved diverse formulae to soften its effects in private industry. With the USPS committed to a long-term modernization program of considerable proportions, the danger of postal job elimination became very real indeed, particularly to the crafts. Accordingly, it was agreed that unions at the national level must be informed as soon as practicable, but no less than 90 days in advance, of the purchase and installation of any major new equipment. At the national level, a Joint Labor-Management Technological or Mechanization Changes Committee was established, representing both sides equally, in order to resolve all issues presented by such contemplated changes. If questions remain unresolved after a reasonable period of operations, they are to be submitted to arbitration under the grievance-arbitration machinery. The 1973 accord further provided that any arbitration of this type was to be given priority in scheduling.[135] Long-run problems must undergo periodic reviews by a Blue Ribbon Committee established in that contract. The Committee is charged to consider the long-range impact of technological changes while they are still in the planning stages.[136]

Any new jobs created by modernization must be offered to present employees who can be trained to do them. If a job is eliminated, the worker who cannot be placed in another position of equal grade must nevertheless receive pay-rate protection. Pay protection was assured only for the term of the agreement in the 1971 accord. In the second contract the worker received rate protection so long as he kept on bidding for jobs at his former pay

---

[133] *The Postal Record*, July 1973, p. 4.
[134] U.S. Postal Service, *National Agreement*, July 21, 1973, Art. I, Sec. 6.
[135] *Ibid.*, Art. IV, Secs. 1, 2.
[136] *Ibid.*, Art. IV, Sec. 4.

level—a far more reliable basis for maintaining his job and pay security.[137]

Major criticism of these provisions hinged upon the inability of local leaders to deal with operational changes that have their greatest impact in employee dislocation at the local level. Such problems are resolved nationally without, perhaps, the major local input seen as necessary, particularly by local memberships. It was also believed that far-reaching changes of so vital a nature should be resolved through collective bargaining only and not via the grievance-arbitration procedures. In any event, the problem is recognized, is being faced, and is subject to a procedure that is binding on all parties.

All major items covered in the POD agreements were dealt with, and most were considerably expanded. Union representation was emphasized; the appointment, payment, and rights of stewards were specified in detail.[138] Joint Labor-Management Committee meetings were set for national, regional, and local levels. A National Blue Ribbon Labor-Management Committee, composed of the national presidents of the unions and the Senior Assistant PMG for Employee and Labor Relations and other top postal officials, was mandated to hold quarterly meetings to discuss, explore, and consider policy matters of substantial national concern.[139] Checkoff was expanded to credit union and group automobile insurance deductions.[140] Pay and retirement benefits for employees on full or part-time leave for union business were amply protected.[141] Work week, work schedules, overtime assignments, Sunday premium pay, and night shift and wash-up time were defined and their administration clearly detailed.[142] Typical were the guarantees of four hours' and eight hours' work or pay for workers called in outside their regular work schedule or work day, respectively.[143] Job safety received particular attention. Since July 1973, every installation of 50 or more employees has had a Joint Labor-Management Safety and Health Committee. A Regional Joint Committee for each postal region meets regularly. The Postal Service agreed to comply with the Office of Federal Employees Compensation and the Occupational Safety and Health

---

[137] *Ibid.,* Art. IV, Sec. 3.
[138] *Ibid.,* Art. XVII, Secs. 1-4.
[139] *Ibid.,* Art. XVII, Secs. 5, 6.
[140] *Ibid.,* Art. XVII, Sec. 7.
[141] *Ibid.,* Art. XXIV, Secs. 1-5.
[142] *Ibid.,* Art. VIII, Secs. 1-7, 9.
[143] *Ibid.,* Art. VIII, Sec. 8.

Act. Finally, procedures for assessing and reporting health hazards and maintaining safety precautions were enumerated.[144]

Although postal negotiations have advanced considerably since the EMC program, bargaining and implementation of postal agreements will require the continued and unremitting attention of both sides, particularly in the early years. In essence, the USPS is moving through a period of transition that is fraught with potential difficulties for its labor relations. In the metamorphosis from a governmental to a proprietary undertaking, management will naturally assume more of the private-sector attitudes associated with industrial corporations. This is to be expected and will be necessary to effect the massive operational changes without which modernization is impossible. The transitional stage will see considerable efforts to exert management prerogatives and discretion with ever greater flexibility and scope. These actions will strike at some of the core interests of organized labor—job security, craft bargaining units, working conditions, and the like.

One aspect of the problem is the degree of local participation permitted under the accords. The National Agreement sets the basic terms, and local negotiations are relatively limited. This is not much of a problem for the smaller post offices. Large locals in the urban centers, however, are vitally concerned with technological or policy changes that could, for example, create major personnel dislocations for which local leaders must answer. The contract procedures were not able to prevent a four-day shutdown in January 1974 at the New York Bulk and Foreign Mail center in Jersey City, the largest such bulk mail installation in the world. The Postal Service instituted changes in the two basic work shifts (7 a.m. to 3:30 p.m. and 3:15 p.m. to 11:45 p.m.) and called for new reporting times of 10:15 a.m. and 7 p.m. , respectively. The rescheduling was predicated on the need for better service, economy, and energy conservation.

Efforts under the established machinery failed to resolve the problem, and on January 21 the new shifts were ordered. Resentment and dislocation ensued since many of the 2,000 workers at the installation, some long-term veterans, travelled considerable distances to reach the facility. Members of the Metro Area Postal Union reported to work at the old reporting times and were not permitted entrance. There followed accusations and counter accusations of illegal lockout and work stoppage, court actions for injunctions ordering a return to work, possible contempt citations,

---

[144] *Ibid.,* Art. XIV, Secs. 1-8.

violence, and some arrests. Finally, by order of a federal district court, the original shifts were restored pending resolution of the dispute through court-ordered binding arbitration. A week of mandated negotiations had failed to settle the disruption. Such labor disputes will continue to arise and must be expected as so vast an operation as the USPS changes form.

The degree of union participation in decision-making that is written into the postal agreement merits comparison with the best accords in industry. Few federal contracts under the presidential orders can approach it in scope and substance. Nevertheless, it remains important to postal management that its basic right to manage and direct be kept intact in the coming years of change. Management prerogatives will have to be exerted, sometimes with far-reaching effects upon working personnel. Postal agreements must recognize that this necessary function will create dislocations and must, therefore, provide improved means for resolution. Even more important, perhaps, there must be a willingness on the part of union and postal leaders to work together and make the collective bargaining structure work.

H.   THE USPS—DIRECTIONS IN PROSPECT

The benefits and disadvantages of the corporate entity in government have been fully debated in the literature of public administration. It has generally been weighed in a balance pitting autonomy in aid of efficiency against public accountability and service. The postal-corporation dispute generated deep conceptual and immediate practical problems. Herbert Emmerich believes that the "public" should be emphasized in public administration; that the practice of public administration, in its broadest sense, comprises "all executive acts, subject to political control, performed by public agencies, officials, or employees." [145] He lists the government corporation first among the "sacred white cows of public administration" that *de facto* or *de jure* have achieved a degree of exemption from executive and legislative controls.[146]

Emmerich recognizes the special problems that arise when such exemption is afforded to an essentially revenue-producing organization. Business motivations can overwhelm the service funtion. He cautions:

---

[145] Herbert Emmerich, "The Scope of the Practice of Public Administration," *Theory and Practice of Public Administration—Scope, Objectives and Methods*, American Academy of Political and Social Science and American Society for Public Administration, Monograph 8, Philadelphia, October 1968, pp. 95-96.

[146] *Ibid.*, p. 96.

"The drive for revenues by an aggressive management may distort its programs and cause it to neglect needed services which are less profitable. Its autonomy may render the corporation immune to policies and programs of elected officials. . . ."[147]

Indeed, it was the overwhelming preoccupation with revenues, the need to break even, and the alleged postal "deficit" that both spurred and confused the ongoing debate. The self-supporting, break-even argument was strongly criticized in terms of the philosophy of service to the public. Former Postmaster General Day, for example, considered this the greatest flaw in the Kappel Commission's approach. Just as a state university should not hobble its educational program by the limitations of its meagre student tuition fees, so the Post Office should continue its policy of setting postal goals and priorities first, even if federal tax revenues have to supplement the postal budget. Day drew a comparison with metropolitan transit systems, used by all and paid for mainly by user charges, yet supplemented by general tax revenues.[148] Unlike the Kappel Commission, Day believed that the "deficit" was due primarily to rising costs and not inefficiency. His principal dispute with the Commission was over its "top priority emphasis on the break even goal, rather than on service as the top consideration." [149] Day testified that if the service factor were fully recognized, "the so-called 'deficit' of the Post Office will be as irrelevant as the deficit of the Department of Interior or of the Veterans Administration."[150]

To Robert Sherrill, the Kappel reasoning would justify tolls on all federal highways and user fees on canals and rivers maintained and dredged at great national expense. Farmers would pay for the numerous services provided them free or at low subsidized prices. He could not understand the obsession with the extra postal cost of $1 billion over its $6 billion income, when billions in the defense budget were "acknowledged to be no more than subsidies for defense industrialists" and "many billions are paid to farmers for crop subsidies and for not planting anything." [151] Indeed many have long considered the postal "deficit" a fraud; Congress arbitrarily appropriated a sum and if user charges exceeded it, the result was called a "deficit." The Reorganization Act, itself, does not reform this aspect. It anticipates continuing deficits and provides for their payment through 1984.

---

147 *Ibid.*, pp. 96-97.
148 J. Edward Day, *op. cit.*, pp. 10-12.
149 *Ibid.*, pp. 12-13.
150 *Ibid.*, p. 27.
151 Robert Sherrill, *op. cit.*, pp. 112, 114.

Experience with other autonomous public authorities leaves much to be desired. Their example presents no sovereign solution to operational problems. Too often, they have exhibited a tendency to operate irresponsibly on a business aggrandizement basis. In New York City, the Port Authority has branched out into gigantic, office-building construction. For years it pursued an energy-wasteful, anti-mass-transit policy, making insufficient attempts to solve the region's suffocating traffic and transit problems. These apparently were subordinated to business interests. The New York Triborough Bridge and Tunnel Authority rationalized building a Columbus Circle Coliseum as one of its functions.

Nor has the private-sector corporation insured efficiency when operated in the public service. We need only note their gross failures in railroad service, breakdowns and lack of planning for growth in the telephone system, and recurring power shortages, as well as blackouts over whole regions of the country. Failure to anticipate what has been obvious for decades and a callous attitude towards the consumer have characterized our oil and energy companies. Yet the private corporation is offered as the model to be emulated in government.

On the federal scene, the Tennessee Valley Authority is consistently cited as an exemplar of successful corporate operations in the public interest. No such analogy can be made for the Postal Service, however, because of important underlying dissimilarities. As former PMG Day testified, the TVA and other government corporations were established primarily to start new enterprises. None were set up to take over the functions of a major, ongoing federal agency. Moreover, the TVA is essentially an electric utility; there have been both public and private power companies for years, with no real problem in covering costs.[152] Above all, power utilities like the TVA are not labor intensive, quite unlike the Postal Service, which, despite all attempts at mechanization, will continue to require a high level of human effort.

The analogy to the TVA is, unfortunately, even less valid in the crucial area of labor relations. To assume that advances in collective bargaining would automatically flow if only the corporate structure of the TVA were adopted for the Postal Service is to ignore the truths of their labor histories. Their long-term records of employer attitude could not be more different. From the TVA's start, its officials were not simply tolerant of unions. They

---

152 J. Edward Day, *op. cit.*, p. 33.

went out of their way to encourage a union presence in the Authority. The cooperative nature of its labor policy, in turn, attracted the best leadership the union community could muster. This management approach, consistently maintained, helped assure the best in personnel relations over the years. It was an attitude born of the idealism of Senator Norris and the labor policies of the New Deal. As such, it was a unique administrative effort, led by outstanding people, dedicated to the success of a regional, multipurpose service undertaking, who knew that amicable labor relations were essential to that success.

The labor history of the postal system in its early years and sporadically since has presented a classic example of the hard-line approach. The Kennedy program unquestionably worked major improvements. Nevertheless, the cooperative attitude that prevailed in the TVA, even if present at the highest levels of the old Post Office Department, would have taken years to permeate down to all levels of its nationwide management structure. In spite of the EMC program advances, some antagonistic labor relationships of the pre-Kennedy years were perpetuated, as was amply noted by the Kappel Commission. The substantial breakdown of local negotiations in 1968, the 1970 strike, and the dilatory 1971 bargaining and local disruptions since are simply manifestations of an adversary atmosphere. Should one assume that incorporating the system would reverse such tendencies?

The TVA possessed an innate desire to work with labor. The Postal Service, open to the lures of business goals, might assume the none-too-cooperative attitudes that have often characterized private industry. In any event, TVA-type labor relations can be possible in the USPS only after there are fundamental changes in attitude at all levels of the Service.

Operational difficulties have not diminished. Customer mail costs have soared along with the economy and the 10-cent stamp may double by 1984. Postal-worker morale has been seriously shaken by personnel policies of retrenchment, job freeze, overtime, and mechanization in the face of an ever-increasing volume of mail. The public, never overly enamoured of the system, increasingly complains of sharply deteriorating services—reduced mail deliveries, lost articles, and unwarranted delays. Private express delivery and mail companies are cutting sharply into USPS potential revenues and present a serious threat to the federal system. Yet commercial and private users, in search of consistency and reliability, will turn to them in increasing numbers unless radical improvements are soon effected.

It is against this background of structural, operational, and labor problems that the future policy of the USPS will have to be determined. Inseparable from that policy will be the question of whether the "service" or the "business" concept is to prevail.

If the decision is to adhere to the break-even, business concept, management may continue to retrench on services, economize on staff, and extend the utilization of existing personnel. In such an event, labor difficulties will proliferate. If future emphasis turns towards greater service above all other considerations, however, there are several alternatives. The USPS could then expand and develop programs for greater efficiency and modernization and achieve the best possible service even if it does not break even. It could come to Congress for the necessary appropriations, a responsibility legislators appear fairly willing to assume. This may involve greater congressional input and oversight but could avoid increased labor disruptions and service deterioration. A working combination of both concepts would be highly desirable. The danger most scrupulously to be avoided is a policy enabling business motivations to overcome the bedrock purpose of the system —public service.

PART IV

PROBLEMS AND POLICIES

CHAPTER XVIII

THE STRIKE ISSUE

In the private sector the right to strike is regarded as so basic a factor in the maintenance of a free society that public authorities have shown extreme reluctance to interfere in strikes even when the interruption of vital services is involved. Attempts to protect the public against such stoppages have largely taken the form of seeking to discourage or postpone strikes through mediation, fact-finding, voluntary arbitration, and "cooling-off" periods. It is sought, above all, to encourage further tries at settlement.

The Railway Labor Act (RLA), the last of a long series of enactments beginning in 1888 to discourage railway strikes, provides for mediation, factfinding, and voluntray nonbinding arbitration, together with a 60-day no-strike period. The Taft-Hartley Act permits the government, where it deems vital national interests to be involved, to seek an injunction postponing a strike for 80 days. In both cases the ultimate right to strike remains. Even in wartime the government has been reluctant to curtail the right to strike. The War Labor Disputes Act, passed during World War II, provided for waiting periods and government-supervised strike votes but did not deny the right to strike after these procedures were exhausted.

Only in the case of the railroads has the government taken action to stop strikes, and then only when nationwide tie-ups were threatened. Where strikes occurring after the procedures of the RLA had been exhausted were of a local or limited nature, the Federal Government made no attempt to interfere. Congress denied a request of President Harding to prohibit rail strikes when the shopmen walked out in 1922. In 1946, when the nation experienced its first nationwide rail tie-up, the Senate refused to accede to President Truman's proposal to end the strike by drafting the strikers into the armed forces.

When a nationwide strike threatened in 1962, President Kennedy obtained the passage of the country's first compulsory arbitration law. Its duration, however, was limited in time, and its coverage extended only to the key issue in dispute, the elimination of locomotive firemen. In the face of a nationwide strike threat in 1967, Congress twice extended the no-strike waiting period. When, after the second extension expired, a strike began on several roads and threatened to spread to the whole country, Congress reluctantly passed legislation providing for a new round of collective bargaining, mediation, and factfinding. In the absence of agreement, a settlement was to be imposed by a factfinding panel.

This novel procedure, condemned as compulsory arbitration by union leaders, differed from conventional compulsory arbitration. No quasi-judicial body and no formal arbitration procedures were involved. The provision for an ultimate imposed solution was intended to force a negotiated settlement rather than an arbitral finding and award in lieu of one. This procedure, upon which the Congress seems to have stumbled, may well prove an effective one for the resolution of negotiation impasses in the public service. In 1970, President Nixon had Congress impose a settlement by law. The agreement had been negotiated by the four shopcraft unions, but their members rejected it and threatened to strike after the expiration of a 37-day strike moratorium passed by Congress. The legislation enforced the negotiated agreement and forbade any stoppage during its term.

The reluctance to limit the right to strike in the private sector does not extend to the public sector. There, on the contrary, the maxim "one cannot strike against the Government" is invoked. This policy, which began with the rise in the postal service of organizations composed wholly of federal employees, represented a departure from the labor policies prevailing in federal industrial plants. There the resort to strikes and political pressure by workers, organized along with private employees in the unions of their trades and crafts, was taken for granted. A distinction was drawn between "workers who are following a trade or vocation which is not exclusively the performance of a governmental function . . . (who) happened to be associated with the government for the time being . . . and men whose employment is strictly limited to a governmental function, who are part of the government itself." [1]

This distinction, however, is no longer drawn. The government now applies its no-strike policy to every category of federal worker. It makes no distinction among charwomen, clerk-typists,

---

[1] U.S. House of Representatives, Committee on Reform in the Civil Service, *Statement of Assistant Postmaster General Stewart*, 62nd Cong., 1st Sess., 1911, pp. 48-49.

arsenal machinists, and policemen. The policy does not, however, completely protect government operations against interruptions or curtailments, for it applies only to government employees and not to employees in privately owned services upon whose continuity federal services depend. The no-strike policy applies to postal employees but not to telephone workers; to Commerce Department clerks but not to the drivers of milk or produce trucks; to customs guards but not longshoremen; to revenue cutter crews but not to the crews of harbor tugboats.

This apparently inconsistent policy is founded on the assumption that while strikes by private employees may inconvenience the public, dislocate the economy, and even interfere with government operations, they do not represent the direct defiance of public authority imputed to strikes by government employees. Strikes by the latter are regarded not as labor disputes but as attacks upon the authority of the state and thus as assaults upon the foundations of public order.

A. WORK STOPPAGES UNDER PROHIBITORY STATUTES

One of the most significant aspects of civil service no-strike policy was the extent to which it was accepted by the unions of civil employees. Every employee organization with a membership confined to federal workers was committed to a no-strike policy by constitutional provision or in other ways. Chairman John W. Macy, Jr., called this no-strike tradition "a principal characteristic of federal employment . . . based on law." [2]

Macy referred to a 1955 law forbidding strikes,[3] which barred as a felony striking, asserting the right to strike, or belonging to an employee organization that asserted the right to strike. Punishment under the law could range up to a $1,000 fine or imprisonment for a year and a day or both. Federal strike policy, however, long antedated this act. Every administration since Theodore Roosevelt's had, by presidential statement or departmental declaration, denied the right of federal employees to strike. Yet, aside from two laws passed in the wake of the Boston police strike and affecting Washington, D.C., police and fire fighters,[4] there was no legislation expressly forbidding federal strikes until after the end of World War II.

The strike issue arose in Congress during consideration of the Lloyd-LaFollette anti-gag bill. The legislation finally enacted,

---

2 John W. Macy, Jr., "Employee-Management Cooperation in the Federal Service," *Proceedings*, Industrial Relations Research Association, 1966, p. 62.
3 Public Law 330 (1955).
4 41 Stat. 364 (1919) and 41 Stat. 398 (1920).

while indicating congressional disapproval of strikes, stopped short of forbidding them. The Act guaranteed the right of postal employees to belong to labor organizations "not affiliated with any outside organization imposing an obligation or duty upon them to engage in any strike, or proposing to assist them in any strike against the United States." [5] There were also a number of other statutory provisions which, though not enacted as antistrike measures, affected the right to strike. One imposed fines and imprisonment upon persons conspiring "to commit any offense against the United States"; [6] another law made it a punishable offense "knowingly and willfully to obstruct or retard the passage of the mail." [7]

This provision was once invoked to punish 25 postal workers who resigned in protest over the discharge of three of their fellow workers. These were individual resignations directed at the postmaster at Fairmont, W. Va., who, according to the employees, was "incompetent, inconsiderate and discourteous" and had threatened his critics with dismissals "all along the line." There was no evidence that the employees were using their resignations in an attempt to enforce their demands upon their employer—that is, as a substitute for a strike. [8] Nevertheless, they were charged with "conspiracy to obstruct the mails." Since they had no funds or organization backing, they entered pleas of *nolo contendere* and were let off with nominal fines. [9] It is questionable whether the employees' action was an attempt "knowingly and willfully" to "obstruct or retard the passage of the mail," but their plea made it impossible to test the issue in the higher courts.

The question of whether federal mass resignations are actually strikes has never been judicially decided. The issue was discussed at length by Members of Congress, representatives of the AFL, and postal officials at the anti-gag hearings in 1911. Secretary Morrison of the AFL defended the right of "one man" or "a thousand men" to resign. Joseph Stewart of the Post Office Department insisted that a mass resignation was an instrument of coercion and a conspiracy against the United States. [10]

Although the procedure in the Fairmont case precluded a deci-

---

5 37 Stat. 555 (1912).
6 35 Stat. 1098 (1909).
7 35 Stat. 1127 (1909).
8 U.S. House of Representatives, Committee on Reform in the Civil Service, *Hearings*, 64th Cong., 1st Sess., April 7, 1916, pp. 28-32.
9 *Ibid.*
10 U.S. House of Representatives, Committee on Reform in the Civil Service, *Hearings*, 62nd Cong., 1st Sess., May 1911, p. 80.

sion in a higher court, the Supreme Court subsequently did pass judgment on issues bearing upon strikes by federal employees. In 1946 the United Mine Workers struck the soft coal mines. Under authority of a law passed during the rearmament period preceding Pearl Harbor, the President was given authority to seize and operate strike-bound plants necessary to the national defense. Acting under this authority, the President seized the coal mines and ordered the miners back to work.

In other instances of plant seizure, the workers bowed to the maxim "one cannot strike against the government" and went back to work. President John L. Lewis of the Mine Workers refused to accept the "fiction of seizure" and continued the strike. When the United States obtained an injunction against the strike, Lewis insisted that the war, though legally only suspended by an armistice, was actually ended and that the injunction violated the Norris-LaGuardia Anti-Injunction Act. Lewis and the union were held in contempt and fined heavily. The Supreme Court modified the fines but sustained the government's contention that the seizure was legal and that the anti-injunction law did not apply to government operations.[11] The doctrine that strikes against the government are ipso facto enjoinable was thus established.

Its wide acceptance notwithstanding, groups of employees have at times challenged the government's no-strike policy when traditional organization methods and tactics seemed frustratingly slow. This happened during the periods of especially active suppression of employee organization, as exemplified by the Post Office's anti-gag campaign, the Taft "take up the slack" orders, and Postmaster General Burleson's economy and anti-union efforts in the Wilson Administration. During the Taft years there were rebellions when small groups of railway mail clerks refused to take on extra runs and threatened mass resignations. During the regime of Postmaster General Burleson, when post-World War I prices were rapidly outstripping wages, the National Federation of Post Office Clerks, at its 1919 national convention, seriously considered the repeal of the no-strike clause in its constitution. Said Thomas F. Flaherty, leader of the union:

"Strikes are a last resort. Should the time come—and I hope it will not—when we exert the limit of our legislative resources in seeking legislative relief and fail to gain our just ends, then a strike

---

[11] United States v. United Mine Workers of America, 330 U.S. 258, 67 S.Ct. 677 (1947).

would be justifiable. I can conceive circumstances when to refrain from striking would be cowardly. There are far worse things than a strike. One is supine submission to injustice. Have no patience with those who say that postal employees cannot strike. There is a constitutional inhibition against involuntary servitude."[12]

Yet, Flaherty warned, "the strike is no short cut to the postal millenium," adding that the Federation had not yet exhausted its resources in seeking legislative relief.[13] The convention committee assigned to the problem nevertheless reported in favor of eliminating the restriction, and most of the delegates appeared to favor the change.

President Gompers of the AFL was in the hall listening intently to the discussion while waiting to address the delegates. He began his address saying that although he had no intention of criticizing the actions of the convention, he did want to say that "at this moment in the life of organized labor it is well for us to exercise the most extreme care." [14] Secretary Flaherty blocked repeal by obtaining the passage of a resolution calling for a referendum on the proposition within a month, far too short a time to air the issue adequately. In a light turnout, a repeal was favored by a majority but less than the two thirds required to change the union constitution.

This was as close as any federal employee union came to ending its no-strike policy until the Communist-dominated United Public Workers of America stumbled into a confused situation after the close of World War II. The UPWA was formed by the merger of the State, County, and Municipal Workers and the United Federal Workers. While the constitution of the merged union stated: "It shall not be the policy of this organization to engage in strikes as a means of obtaining its objectives," [15] a subsequent section provided that "no local union may resort to strike action without submitting such proposed action to the international president." [16] Locals violating the provision were subject to suspension.

This aroused Congress and led to antistrike legislation. The union's executive board, meeting in an emergency session, declared that the strike procedure applied only to locals of state, county, and municipal employees and not to federal employees.

---

[12] *Union Postal Clerk,* October 1919, p. 213.
[13] *Ibid.*
[14] *Ibid.*
[15] United Public Workers of America (CIO), *Constitution,* Art. II, Sec. 2.
[16] *Ibid.,* Art. VIII, Sec. 15.

The union, the declaration concluded, "never contemplated a strike against the Government of the United States and never asserted nor does not now assert the right to strike against the Government of the United States." [17]

The statement complied with the new antistrike legislation and permitted the UPWA to continue to function in the federal service. The legislation, introduced by Senator Joseph Ball of Minnesota in the form of riders to appropriation bills, made it illegal to use any of the funds appropriated to pay the salary of any employee who belonged to an organization "asserting the right to strike against the United States." The employee was required to file an affidavit with his department head declaring that he was not a member of such an organization, would not join such an organization while in federal employ, and would not strike against the United States.[18]

The next year this provision was superseded by the following section of the Taft-Hartley Act:

> "It shall be unlawful for any individual employed by the United States or any agency thereof including wholly owned government corporations to participate in any strike. Any individual employed by the United States or by any such agency, who strikes, shall be discharged immediately from his employment and shall forfeit his civil service status, if any, and shall not be eligible for reemployment for three years by the United States or any such agency."[19]

This section remained in effect until 1955 when it was superseded by the present act, which returned to the declarations and affidavits required by the earlier Ball riders. Criminal penalties were provided for violations.

These stringent provisions put an end to federal strikes in the only areas where the weapon was actually used, namely, in the industrial services. David Ziskind listed 19 strikes by craft unions in naval establishments between 1835 and 1920 and five in army arsenals between 1893 and 1918.[20] He overlooked one of the most important, the Rock Island Arsenal strike shortly after the Spanish-American War;[21] a seven-week strike by the Bookbinders Union in the Government Printing Office shortly after the government purchased the plant in 1861; and another by the

---

[17] Sterling D. Spero, *Government as Employer* (New York: Remsen Press, 1948), p. 200. Reprinted Carbondale Ill.: Southern Illinois University Press, 1972.
[18] Public Law 419 (1946).
[19] Public Law 101 (1947).
[20] David Ziskind, *One Thousand Strikes of Government Employees* (New York: Columbia University Press, 1940).
[21] Sterling D. Spero, *op. cit.*, pp. 94 ff.

printers in 1866.[22] Ziskind listed five strikes on the Barge Lines
of the Inland Waterways Corporation in 1937 and 1938, and 46
on the railroads during World War I while they were operated
by the U.S. Railroad Administration. This is particularly significant in the light of the rail workers' strict observance of the no-
strike and compulsory arbitration laws passed during the Kennedy and Johnson administrations. A number of work stoppages
in the arsenals and navy yards were not reported as strikes. They
were referred to as "sitting on the fence." The officers in charge
much preferred settling their employees' complaints and restoring
operations to asserting their authority and making big issues of
the incidents. From time to time, before the Ball provisos, the
TVA had experienced and quietly settled a number of jurisdictional disputes.

The 1946 Ball provisos were challenged twice. In November
1946, several hundred employees of the Inland Waterways Corp.
struck. When Senator Ball demanded their immediate discharge,
the Department of Commerce, the corporation's parent agency,
assured him that the law would be enforced. The incident ended
with the discharge of a few of the strike leaders. If the requirements of the law had been met, the operations of the corporation
would have been crippled.

B. CONTEMPORARY STRIKE POLICY AND PRACTICE

It is strange, despite the strong antistatist attitude which pre-
vails in the United States, that opposition to government strikes
should be so great and antistrike laws so severe. Italy, France, and
other European countries guarantee the right of public employees to strike. The right is exercised freely though usually in the
form of brief demonstration strikes seldom lasting more than a
day in vital services. More recently strikes have continued for
longer periods.

In Great Britain the right to strike is guaranteed to employees
in the nationalized industries and is frequently used. Stoppages in
the coal mines can be counted by the hundred each year. There
have been several rail strikes as well as strikes in the light and
power industries. Employees of the nationalized industries have
not exhibited the relative acquiescence of the established British
Civil Service, which has a strong antistrike tradition. Yet even in
the regular service there was a strike of many days' duration by
postal workers in the summer of 1964. It caused havoc in the

---

[22] *Ibid.,* pp. 85-86.

mail service and took weeks to straighten out. This was the first strike by regular civil servants since a postmen's walkout in 1890 and a telegraphers' strike in the 1870s.

In early 1970 the British Post Office endured the longest and largest strike in the United Kingdom since the General Strike of 1926. The Post Office was made a Public Corporation in October 1969, and the British Union of Post Office Workers alleged that industrial relations had deteriorated under the changed management. Pay impasses led to the record 47-day stoppage involving more than 200,000 postal workers. All Post Office deliveries of letters and parcels ceased completely in Britain and to overseas points; telephone and telegraph services were reduced to the barest essentials. It was the view of Norman Stagg, of the Union of Post Office Workers, that the strikers were strengthened in their resolve by great financial support from international postal and nonpostal unions. Postal unions in Europe, the United States, and the underdeveloped nations donated more than $100,000. Other British trade unions and the public contributed some $600,000.[23] Whether the strike was a success or failure depends upon the views of those making the judgment.

Canada has had several postal strikes, recent ones occurring from 1968 through 1974. A strike also was called on the government-owned Canadian National Railways in 1966. All these stoppages were treated as labor disputes similar to those in private industry rather than as attacks upon the sovereignty of the state and assaults upon the public order.

Recent Canadian experience has provided an object lesson for American federal unions. The leaders of public-employee unions in this country observed with envy when Parliament passed the Public Service Staff Relations (PSSR) Act in 1967.[24] As noted, there are good reasons for considering this law in the American context. Although smaller, the Canadian federal establishment possesses similarities in function and organization that invite comparison wth the Federal Government. American unions in their own legislative proposals sought the establishment of an independent agency such as the Canadian Public Service Staff Relations Board. Of particular interest on this side of the border was the provision under which Parliament granted most federal workers the right to strike. [25]

---

23 Norman Stagg, Deputy General Secretary, Union of Post Office Workers, U.K., "British Post Office Strike Details," *Postal Record*, May 1971, p. 9.
24 Public Service Staff Relations Act, 15-15-16 (Elizabeth II) (1967).
25 *Ibid.*, Chap. 72, Secs. 2, 36-38, 49, 79, 101-104.

Actually, its acceptance in Canada was logically to be expected. Just as our federal laws reflect the general development of public strike policy in the United States, so the Canadian statute reflects such development in Canada. Thus it incorporated the comparatively permissive practices that already obtained in many areas of the Canadian public service. The Heeney Committee, whose two-year study formed the basis for the PSSR Act, had necessarily addressed itself to the strike issue. Even though convinced that "a strike would be quite indefensible and a lockout unthinkable" in many parts of the public service, the Committee decided against statutory prohibition. The report of this committee declared: "Looking at the recent history of the Public Service, we concluded that it would be difficult to justify a prohibition on the grounds of demonstrated need." [26] Historical experience and accepted practices were also cited as precedent by PSSR Board Chairman Finkelman:

> "In Canada this development is not looked upon as being quite so radical as it may be in the United States. In Canada, collective bargaining in the public sector was in operation in local government as early as 1943, at first under a local option provision but ultimately on a compulsory basis, generally speaking under the same rules and conditions as apply in the private sector, and this included the right to strike." [27]

In their final form the impasse provisions accommodated the two major approaches to the problem. The Heeney Committee, in compliance with the views of most employee organizations, recommended binding arbitration, and the government agreed. It appeared, however, that the Canadian postal workers opposed binding arbitration. In this they were supported by some other labor spokesmen. [28] The postal employees wanted the strike option and threatened to strike if it was not included. Under these circumstances, the government satisfied both approaches by "including in the legislation an alternative process of dispute settlement directly comparable to that provided [in the federal legislation applicable to the private sector]." [29] Thus the legal "strike route" was finalized.

---

26 Preparatory Committee on Collective Bargaining in the Public Service, *Report*, Queen's Printer, Ottawa, 1965, p. 36.

27 Jacob Finkelman, Chairman, Public Service Staff Relations Board, "Canada's Bold Experiment," *Address*, before Public Personnel Association, Seminar on Negotiating with Organized Public Employees, Albany, New York, April 23, 1968, pp. 1-2.

28 *Ibid.*, pp. 12, 13.

29 Canada, Special Joint Committee of the Senate and House of Commons on Employer-Employee Relations in the Public Service of Canada, *Proceedings*, pp. 204-205, cited in *Ibid.*, pp. 11-12.

The choice of alternatives was bound to the certification and bargaining process. After a bargaining agent has been certified, it must first select its preferred settlement process before it can serve the employer with a notice to bargain.[30] The two alternatives are referral of the dispute either to binding arbitration or to a conciliation board. If the first is chosen, the union may not call a strike, nor may the employees in the unit engage in a strike. If conciliation is selected the employees with certain exceptions "may ultimately engage in a strike to enforce their 'demands.' "[31] The chairman has rather extensive control over the appointment of conciliation boards and may even refrain from doing so if he feels, after consulting the parties, that such a board is unlikely to assist in resolving the dispute.[32] Where a board is established it has 14 days to submit its report to the chairman. This period can be extended. Once the report is submitted, however, a lawful strike may be called after seven days from the receipt of the report. If the chairman notifies the parties that he does not intend to appoint a conciliation board, a lawful strike may take place immediately.[33]

The law does not confer an unlimited right to strike. Chairman Finkelman specified that organizational strikes are unlawful and that no employee can strike until a bargaining agent is certified for his unit. No strike may occur during the life of a collective agreement or an arbitration award, during the period of an arbitration option, or during the conciliation process of the "strike route." Finally, no employee whose duties are deemed necessary to the public safety or security may lawfully strike. A little over 13 percent of the federal employees in certified units were so categorized by the Board during its first year of operations.[34]

Has this relative permissiveness sparked a rash of federal stoppages? Admittedly, it is too soon to discern trends. Nevertheless, experience thus far would indicate a union reluctance to strike. Of the 64 units that made the choice by November 1968, 56 units covering 84,000 employees opted for binding arbitration. Only eight units comprising 33,000 workers chose the "strike route,"

---

[30] Public Service Staff Relations Board, *Analysis of the Public Service Staff Relations Act*, Ottawa, 1968. PSSR Act, Secs. 36, 49 (1), at pp. 15-16.
[31] PSSR Act, Secs. 2 (a), 101 (1) (b).
[32] *Ibid.*, Sec. 78 (1) (b).
[33] *Ibid.*, Sec. 86 (1), p. 33, and Sec. 101, p. 34.
[34] Jacob Finkelman, Chairman, Public Service Staff Relations Board, "Collective Bargaining in Federal Public Service—The Basic Legislation in Canada," *Address*, before Joint Conference in Collective Bargaining in Federal Public Service, AFL-CIO and Canadian Labour Congress, Niagara Falls, Ontario, November 19, 1968, pp. 19-20.

and one of these units—the postal operations—accounted for 25,000 of that number.[35] Thus, as Finkelman anticipated, most unions will select arbitration.[36]

This situation prevailed for the first five years of the Act's operations. However, during its fifth year ending in March 1972, there was a pronounced swing to the conciliation-board option, notably by the Public Service Alliance of Canada, bargaining agent for seven units in the operational category. This shift involved approximately 27,000 workers and was significant if it signalled a trend. During this time the Public Service Alliance had publicly criticized the Act's restrictions on the subject matter upon which the Arbitration Tribunal could make an award.[37] Quite possibly discontent over the arbitral powers of the Tribunal motivated the change to the conciliation option.

The first lawful strike under the PSSR Act occurred in mid-July 1968, when the postal workers went out. The considerable publicity it received was undoubtedly attributable to the nature of postal operations. This is one of the relatively few federal services that provides direct, daily contact with the public. Since the Canadian postal employees had struck illegally three years earlier, it is not unreasonable to assume that the situation was closely observed by the American postal unions and management. Subsequent events in the United States would support this assumption.[38]

Even though this strike was legal, it was reluctantly started. William Kidd, an official of the Canadian Union of Postal Workers, indicated that there was much soul-searching in Ottawa before it was called. But he asked rhetorically, "What power do the workers have other than withholding their labor?" Kidd emphatically stated that the unions were not going to enter into the next negotiations with any preconceived intent to strike again, only to resolve the disputes.[39]

The strike was led by the Council of Postal Unions, comprising the Canadian Union of Postal Workers and the Letter Carriers Union of Canada, and lasted 22 days. A 15.1-percent wage increase

[35] *Ibid.,* p. 10.

[36] Jacob Finkelman, "Canada's Bold Experiment," *op. cit.,* p. 13.

[37] Public Service Staff Relations Board, *Fifth Annual Report* (Ottawa: Information Canada, 1972), pp. 12-15.

[38] American interest in the Canadian Postal System is a continuing one. As late as May 1974 the National Association of Letter Carriers appointed a committee to investigate Canadian developments. See *Postal Record,* June 1974, pp. 38, 43.

[39] William B. Kidd, Field Officer, Canadian Union of Postal Workers, *Remarks, Panel Discussion of Joint Conference on Collective Bargaining in Federal Public Service,* AFL-CIO and Canadian Labour Congress, Niagara Falls, Ontario, November 20, 1968.

spread over 26 months and many important nonmonetary gains were won, causing the unions' leaders to term the contract "in essence palatable and livable." [40] Twenty-four thousand postal workers had gone out. With the strike in its twelfth day, they began to feel the pinch in their pocketbooks when the first post-strike checks containing only two or three days pay, minus deductions, were issued. Yet in Toronto they refused to cross their own picket lines to collect even these meager amounts. Their union local offered to pay for the rent and groceries of needy strikers. In contrast to public sentiment during many local service strikes in the United States, there was little public outcry over the halt in mail service. Many Canadian businessmen showed great inventiveness and resourcefulness, renting U.S. post office boxes and using the telephones, telegraphs, and special air delivery services. [41] Throughout the strike the government maintained a hands-off policy. Canada's iconoclastic Prime Minister Pierre Trudeau apparently considered the occasion an appropriate time to visit the Canadian Arctic. When he returned he declared that Parliament would not interfere with the strike, [42] although he had previously expressed serious reservations about public strikes.

In 1970, postal workers adopted a new stratagem. They did not pursue a prolonged total shutdown. Service was stopped for a few hours at a time or for a day or for several days at a time, the pattern varying from city to city and from region to region. Intermittent stoppages, strikes, and sitdown demonstrations continued for over three months until a pay settlement was reached.

In the United States although opposition on the part of local governments to strikes has been just as great as in the federal service, neither the injunctive powers of the courts nor legislation carrying heavy penalties has been able to prevent increasing resort to the strike. Municipal strikes became more frequent after World War II and multiplied remarkably during the 1960s. In the year 1966-67 alone the Bureau of Labor Statistics recorded 181 government strikes involving 132,000 employees and costing 1.23 million man-days. This was one fifth the working-time loss in the private sector. Teachers accounted for a majority of the strikes, and there were frequent stoppages in the administrative and protective services. [43] The BLS also noted that from 1958 to

---

[40] *Canadian Labour,* Vol. 13, No. 9, September 1968, p. 9.
[41] *New York Post,* July 29, 1968, p. 26.
[42] *Ibid.*
[43] James T. Hall, Jr., "Work Stoppages in Government," *Monthly Labor Review,* July 1968. See also *Government Employee Relations Report,* No. 253 (1968), p. C-1.

1968, government strikes rose from 15 to 254 per year; workers involved rose from 1,700 to 202,000; and man-days lost, from 7,500 to 2.5 million.[44] Assistant Secretary of Labor W. J. Usery, Jr., reported that 380 public-sector strikes affecting more than 200,000 workers occurred in 1969.[45]

This pronounced trend has continued apace. Strikes have taken place in every part of the country and in every type of service— among garbage collectors, welfare workers, teachers, nurses, doctors, firemen, and police. Continued opposition notwithstanding, the strike has now become an established factor in municipal labor relations.

C. FEDERAL FERMENT IN THE 1960s

All of these developments here and abroad had their inevitable effect on the attitude of federal employees. The law prohibiting even the assertion of the right to strike did not prevent thinking and speaking. Sentiment took more solid shape when unions started revising the traditional no-strike pledges in their constitutions. The American Nurses Association reversed a no-strike policy of some 18 years when its 1968 convention officially left the strike decision to individual nurses groups and state nurses associations.[46] The National Education Association finally rejected its no-strike pledge in 1967, offering financial aid, legal advice, and staff experts to local affiliates forced into unavoidable strikes. This policy was affirmed in 1968 and proposals were made to increase dues to maintain a defense fund.[47] In 1968 the International Association of Fire Fighters dropped its 50-year-old constitutional restrictions on strikes. A 10-man factfinding commission appointed in 1966 had reported that the no-strike provision was "sensible and enforceable" only where there was "an established procedure for redress of grievances and timely, amicable settlement of disagreements relative to wages and working conditions." The convention even rejected its recommendation that fire services be withheld only when such procedures were unavailable.[48]

More powerful federal unions, particularly the postal organiza-

---

[44] U.S. Department of Labor, Bureau of Labor Statistics, *Work Stoppages in Government, 1958-1968*, Report No. 348, Washington 1969, pp. 1, 9.

[45] William J. Usery Jr., Assistant Secretary of Labor, *Address*, before 47th Biennial Convention of the National Association of Letter Carriers, Honolulu, Hawaii, August 16, 1970, *Proceedings*, p. 8.

[46] *Government Employee Relations Report*, No. 246 (1968), p. A-1.

[47] *Ibid.*, No. 252 (1968), pp. B-3, B-4.

[48] *Ibid.*, No. 232 (1968), p. B-5; and No. 259 (1968), p. B-1.

tions, were equally a part of this movement. After much discussion, action was taken in August of 1968,[49] when the postal clerks, the National Postal Union, and the letter carriers either dropped or acted to drop their no-strike provisions from their constitutions. Though the possibility of such action had long existed, the successful settlement of the Canadian postal strike on August 8, 1968, may well have been the catalyst spurring final decision.

Over the years the late President E. C. Hallbeck of the United Federation of Postal Clerks supported the right to strike in local government services but refused to "assert" it in federal employment. Postal-clerk sentiment was divided on the issue when it was raised at the 1966 national convention. When the issue was presented again in 1968, disagreement had pretty well dissipated. By a voice vote after less than an hour of debate, the 165,000-member UFPC became the first major federal government union thus to alter its constitution. It removed the no-strike clause on the ground that it was "superfluous" under existing federal law. The amending resolution made it clear that the federation did not assert the right to strike but was merely cutting out the provision since federal antistrike statutes eliminated its need.[50] Although other impasse legislation was recommended, the implication was clear on the change of sentiment.

Sidney A. Goodman, president of the National Postal Union, was far more accusatory. He declared:

"But the biggest myth of all, I now speak as an individual, is the prohibition of the right to strike. What is really wrong with labor-management relations in the program? There are no countervailing forces, there is no balance. It is just that simple. Before us stands an inevitable dynamic which must take the form of paternalism and it does not serve even management, if it is self-respecting, in the long run . . . .

"There is not, never has been, never will be any substitute for the right of employees to withhold their labor as a method of advancing their interests." [51]

Thus, the NPU also continued the trend. Its 1968 convention

---

[49] See John Cramer, "Postal Unions Revolt Over Strike Law," *Washington Daily News*, August 26, 1968. Also in *Postal Record*, October 1968, p. 23.

[50] United Federation of Postal Clerks, *Federation News Service*, Convention Bulletin No. 2, August 13, 1968. Article II, Sec. 3 of the Constitution had previously read: "We recognize the fact that legislation and not strike is the last resort in the adjustment of our grievances, and, therefore, we oppose strikes in the postal service." It was amended to read simply: "We recognize the fact that legislation is the last resort in the adjustment of our grievances."

[51] Sidney A. Goodman, President, National Postal Union, *Remarks*, to Federal Bar Association, Seminar on Collective Bargaining in Federal Service, Washington, April 18, 1967, p. 10.

voted to drop the sentence in Article II of its Constitution that stated, "We are opposed to strikes in the postal service." Led by its president, David Silvergleid, it overwhelmingly passed a resolution to seek the "legal right" to strike.[52] The National Association of Letter Carriers, in convention, did not act to change its charter immediately. Instead, it passed a resolution instructing its national officers "to investigate fully the legal and legislative technicalities involved so that government employees may be accorded the right to strike by the Congress" and "to study the feasibility of removing the no-strike oath that we are now required to take as a condition of employment." This action was taken, the resolution stated, because the letter carriers were "disenchanted and impatient with the inordinately slow progress of legislative campaigns continuously waged by the NALC year in and year out." [53] Litigation was started to clarify judicially the strike-oath and right-to-strike issues.

The American Federation of Government Employees, a major proponent of change through legislation, declined to take similar action. Revisionary resolutions had been unsuccessfully introduced at every recent convention of the AFGE, except in 1966. A lively discussion ensued at the 1968 meeting, but only 25 percent voted for amendment. President Griner, a moderate on the issue, emphasized that such declarations could only hurt relations with Congress and were useless anyway in the face of the law. On the other hand, a major competitor, the new independent National Association of Government Employees, became the first large nonpostal union to delete the no-strike pledge. The action was taken by acclamation and without debate.[54] When the issue was raised again at the 1970 AFGE national convention, the no-strike clause was dropped from the constitution after less than five minutes of debate.

These developments did not go unnoticed by the Civil Service Commisssion or the Post Office Department. They were well aware of the convention actions, the increasing militancy of federal unions, and the labor unrest on the state, local, and Canadian scenes. Wilfred V. Gill, then director of the Commission's Office of Labor-Management Relations, noted this on several occasions, stating, "We view this seriously but so far without alarm. . . . The fact is there has been no great problem—despite some erroneous

---

[52] Manhattan-Bronx Postal Union, NPU, "Convention KO's 'No-Strike' Clause," *The Union Mail*, September 1968, pp. 4-5.
[53] *Government Employee Relations Report*, No. 259 (1968) .
[54] *Ibid.*, No. 262 (1968) , pp. A-1, A-2; No. 263 (1969) , p. A-8.

reports in the press and alarmist remarks by uninformed observers." [55] Nevertheless, the CSC felt constrained to guide the agencies informally on how to deal with threatened or actual strike or picketing conditions.

Compared to other jurisdictions, the Federal Government had been relatively free of labor disruptions under the Kennedy order. Strikes and picketing had been rare, but the rumblings were there. In 1962 a jurisdictional dispute at the TVA resulted in a strike that kept some 2,600 employees out of work for a number of days. The Authority promptly invoked the law, obtained an injunction, and fired the 81 sheet metal workers who went out. Here, unlike the strikes against the Inland Waterways Commission, the numbers were small enough to make enforcement possible.

Two incidents involving the antistrike laws occurred in Europe. In 1964 a strike by teachers in a school for children of American military personnel was narrowly averted by firm action by the Department of Defense. In an earlier incident the government backed down and overlooked the violation of the law when several hundred Italians employed by the U.S. Government refused to sign the no-strike pledges required by the 1946 legislation. The requirement seemed incomprehensible to these Italian workers, whose own government guaranteed the right to strike to all workers, including public employees.

The Civil Service Commission has reported more recent strike situations and related incidents. During the Christmas rush of 1967, letter carriers were offered overtime work at the Newark, New Jersey, Post Office to help with the holiday mail. Carriers from the more remote stations, discontented because they received no overtime, conducted a protest march to the main post office. The president of the NALC local in Newark then announced, "OK, all carriers out." Thereupon, 82 men left their work without permission and joined the demonstration. The Post Office Department suspended the local president for 28 days for "disrupting postal service" and "bringing the agency into disrepute." No action was taken against the demonstrators since it was not clear whether they knew they were acting without authority, being on voluntary overtime. In October 1968 a stoppage of some three days by about 50 cafeteria employees occurred at the San Francisco Naval Shipyard. Since the employees were paid with

---

nonappropriated funds, their status under the no-strike statute was in doubt. This fact and the fact that management had not informed them of the law were mitigating circumstances. They had not signed the no-strike pledges. As a result, the Navy Department merely suspended them for one day and docked their pay for the unworked time and cautioned them against future stoppages.[56]

One major picketing incident occurred when 25 off-duty Weather Bureau workers demonstrated before the New York City Weather Bureau Office. Arising out of impasses in negotiations over work scheduling, overtime, and promotions, the protest received much publicity in the mass media. Since picketing in certain situations is a violation of the Code of Fair Labor Practices, a hearing was held, in which the union refused to participate. The Weather Bureau then declined to discipline the individual employees, apart from reprimands, but levied 10- and five-day suspensions against the union officers leading the demonstration. Its action was based on the reasoning that only the organizers of the protest were cognizant of the difference between labor-management-dispute picketing and other types of off-duty actions.[57]

Numerous incidents involving near-stoppages, questionable picketing, and threats of strikes and picketing were warded off by executive measures. The CSC reported that nine situations involved possible stoppages and strike threats while eight cases concerned demonstrations or threats of picketing. Harassment by employees took the form of "working to rule," stay-at-home sick demonstrations, and strike rumors. Variations of the mass-sick-call technique were used by the overseas teachers in Europe, VA nursing assistants, letter carriers in Brooklyn and Akron, and postal clerks in Buffalo. VA interns conducted a "heal-in" in Washington, D.C. Air traffic controllers allegedly staged a working-to-rule slowdown. A "stay-home-sick" work stoppage was carried on by nursing assistants and dietary workers at St. Elizabeth's Hospital in Washington, D.C.[58] It is significant to note the CSC's observation in recounting these incidents that:

> ". . . Generally, the employees were aware of the penalties of the anti-strike law, but in view of the success experienced by public employees in striking in defiance of law in local jurisdictions,

---

[56] U.S. Civil Service Commission, Office of Labor-Management Relations, *Strikes, Picketing and Associated Incidents under Executive Order 10988, 1962-1968,* Washington, 1968, pp. 3-4.
[57] *Ibid.,* pp. 5-6.
[58] *Ibid.,* p. 6.

there was some inclination to test militant tactics in the federal service."[59]

Picketing occurred at the Social Security Payment Center in Philadelphia, and demonstrations were mounted by teachers in Madrid, Spain, VA nurses in California, letter carriers in Akron, and postal employees in the Bronx and Manhattan. For a variety of reasons, incidents of potential picketing and demonstrations took place at the Philadelphia Post Office, the General Services Administration in Baltimore, and the Marshall Space Flight Center in Huntsville, Ala.[60]

The situation among the air-traffic controllers has proved particularly troublesome to the Federal Aviation Administration. Federal antistrike laws have not been able to prevent a series of stoppages by these highly trained professionals. However, the statutes have helped get them back to work. The nation is well aware of the crisis in the air transport industry. With its unprecedented growth have come grave problems of insufficient airfields, control centers, and passenger facilities, accompanied by intense air and noise pollution. Air controllers' attitudes reflect these problems. In addition to the usual demands for better pay and working conditions, they have sought better facilities to reduce air congestion and an increase in the number of controllers. They claim the intense pressure of working under present conditions promotes serious physical and mental illness. The situation is further complicated by the fact that controllers are represented by three different organizations, the Air Traffic Controllers' Association (ATCA), the National Association of Government Employees, and the relatively new and militant Professional Air Traffic Controllers' Organization (PATCO).[61]

In the summer of 1968 PATCO was primarily responsible for the work-to-rule slowdown that quickly created air traffic jams. The organization was also the prime mover in the "sick-out" of June 18 and 19 in 1969, which created serious national and international disruptions. Evidently emulating the action of some controllers in Denver and Kansas City, many at the FAA control room in Islip, Long Island, called in sick. The Islip center is a crucial one, responsible for air traffic over some 40,000 square miles around the New York City region. The press reported that "air travel throughout much of the nation was turned into near chaos"; the country's air transport system was "crippled"; the "impact of their 'sickness' was felt from California to Europe, but it was at its worst in New York"; "more than 1,000 New York airline flights were delayed, some as long as four hours." Three hundred flights were cancelled.[62]

A striking fact was that a national disruption could hinge upon the action of only about 250 men. Of the approximately 14,000 FAA air traffic controllers, it took only some 150 in New York and 100 others in control centers across the nation to tie up air travel from coast to coast.[63] As a result, the FAA suspended controllers who could not substantiate their illnesses and revoked the checkoff privileges of PATCO for its involvement in the slowdown.

When a similar sick-out occurred in 1970, the effects were far more extensive. For approximately three full weeks from March 25 to April 15, large numbers of employees failed to man control consoles and radar screens. Although there were contradictory reports, more than 1,800 controllers probably were absent when the sick-out was at its peak, while about 1,200 were absent on an average day—a far more substantial proportion of the 14,000 controllers than were involved in the 1969 action.

Occurring during the Easter season, the slowdown affected the public and the airlines greatly. Unlike other stoppages, this one did not enjoy measurable public support. The slowdown was occasioned by the transfer of three PATCO members from their center in Baton Rouge, La., an action that was viewed as harassment and part of an overall plan to defeat the union, which was trying to regain recognition. PATCO demanded that a mediator be appointed to resolve the dispute, but the FAA rejected the demand. Nothing would be done until the men came back.[64]

FAA Administrator John H. Shaffer regarded the sick-out as a strike in contravention of law. Over 15 legal proceedings were instituted before different courts to force a return to work. After one week, injunctions and contempt judgments coupled with instructions to return from the union's head began to ease the disruptions. Substantial sick-out persistence in a few of the crucial centers, however, was enough to prolong national slowdowns for another two weeks. The Justice Department was reported to be concerned over the lack of uniformity in the decisions handed down by different district courts. Court punishments varied and the justices restricted efforts by the FAA to punish the men. This

---

[62] *The New York Times*, June 20, 1969, pp. 1, 82; July 2, 1969, p. 86.
[63] *Ibid.*, July 2, 1969, p. 86.
[64] *Ibid.*, March 27, 1970, pp. 1, 14.

was deemed an improper judicial interference in enforcement of what was essentially an agency personnel policy and an agency responsibility.[65] A distinct possibility exists that judicial resolution of future federal strikes could also include specific formulas for enforcement in conflict with government personnel policy.

Although the FAA discharged many controllers—the first such action under the labor relations program—a substantial number were returned to duty. Rigid enforcement of the law in this case would have had dire consequences. Controllers are not easily replaced. Even prolonged suspensions would have been unwise. The shortage of air traffic controllers is quite serious, and Congress has moved to increase the number of controller positions. The wholesale firing of scarce trained personnel is not the kind of tactic to be embarked upon lightly.

D. MANAGEMENT FACES THE GROWING PROBLEM

The CSC recognizes that great care must be exercised by management, for not all actual or potential instances of protest are punishable as strikes or breaches of the Code of Fair Labor Practices. The constitutional protections of free speech and assembly are directly involved. Employees are not to be disciplined for demonstrating for higher wages through legislation or for civil rights. Therefore, the Commission has cautioned agencies to be sure that the employee action was intended as a coercive means to influence a labor-management dispute before taking disciplinary measures.[66]

The dominant feature of the overall federal picture has been labor peace. Observers generally have concurred with Wilfred Gill's assessment that "On the whole, it is a remarkable record of responsible labor-management relations, and reflects great credit upon the unions, employees and federal officials for their respect for law and the public service to which they are committed." [67] In truth, the relatively minute proportion of man-days lost in the Federal Government under the Kennedy order compared well to the total loss of time in all public service strikes. There was no assurance, however, that this would continue in the future.

The potential for danger was clearly recognized by the Commission. Gill had earlier stated: "In a work force of nearly three

---

[65] *Ibid.*, April 30, 1970, p. 70.

[66] U.S. Civil Service Commission, Office of Labor-Management Relations, *op. cit.*, p. 7.

[67] Wilfred V. Gill, *Statement*, before the House Subcommittee on Postal Operations, April 25, 1969, pp. 19-20.

million you have to bank on the possibility that anything can happen and be prepared to deal with it." [68] The Commission reported that more demonstrations were to be expected. It continued:

> "The incidents show that there is a restlessness and heightened militancy among federal employees which can burst forth into strike action. The attitude of the public is such, as evidenced by successful strikes in some local jurisdictions, that public denunciation may fall, in some circumstances, not on the strikers but on management that barricades inaction or indifference behind an anti-strike law."[69]

This last reference indicated a readiness on the part of the Commission to cooperate with unions and employees in averting possible disturbances. At the same time there was a basic commitment to enforce the law. The Commission considered the best approach for dealing with local disruptions to be

> ". . . (a) early warning, (b) prompt management action telling employees and the union that a strike will not be tolerated, and (c) an indication of a willingness to look into and correct employee complaints. In some cases, a call to the union's national office provided the leverage needed to stop the walkout."[70]

Variations of this basic strategy worked successfully for certain incidents but not so well for others. Statutory obligations must be enforced. Nevertheless, the approach of the Commission in a strike situation appears not to have been the hard-nosed "no retreat" attitude that was manifested by many employers in the early stages of union organization in the private sector. In its work with the agencies, the CSC recommended firmness but insisted that they show a real desire at all times to maintain a fruitful dialogue with the unions on disruptive problems, with an eye to their resolution.

The Commission has acted in an advisory capacity on the strike issue. In time more formal, official directives may be issued. As yet no official guidelines have been published for agency use, but the CSC has orally and informally advised the agencies on projected strategy whenever actual or possible disruptions have occurred.[71] As Gill has said, "we need to be ready to cope any-

---

[68] Wilfred V. Gill, *Remarks, op. cit.*, p. 5.
[69] U.S. Civil Service Commission, Office of Labor-Management Relations, *op. cit.*, pp. 7, 8.
[70] *Ibid.*, p. 7.
[71] *Ibid.*, p. 9.

where with possible need for emergency action to maintain operations and replace personnel." [72] Accordingly, the CSC has made staff studies, conducted training courses, and generally managed to stay on top of potential crises by maintaining immediate contacts with affected agencies and following up any incident reported in the news media.

Civil Service Commission advisory guidelines emphasize advance preparedness, union-management cooperation to avert or terminate disruptions, and firm agency strategy in strike situations. Accordingly, the CSC cautioned agencies to "maintain an intelligence system to give advanced warning of any impending strike or picketing." Prompt preliminary reports were to identify the participants, determine the degree of union implication, and try to detect whether the potential situation was planned— whether it was led by individuals, a group, or a union.[73] Unions would undoubtedly use less complimentary terms for "intelligence system."

Actual violations of law were to be discouraged by the use of preventive measures. Agencies were enjoined to discover the causes for individual or union discontent on one hand and, on the other, to set right unreasonable local management attitudes that contributed to the dissatisfaction. They also were urged to seek the aid of local and national union leaders to aid in resolving problems without concerted action. At the same time, the agencies could inform the leadership of their intention to enforce the strike prohibitions. Since notice is an important factor in justifying punitive action, employees were to be advised beforehand by all possible means that any stoppages or demonstrations in whatever guise would be treated as violations. The possible consequences to the workers were to be conveyed in a manner that would establish "the psychological certainty that the penalties of the law will be invoked." [74] Contingency plans for continuing operations were to be formulated, including the possible replacement of personnel. In the event of strike action, agencies were advised to seek court injunctions against disruptive picketing, report the circumstances to the Justice Department, and take whatever punitive actions were prescribed under laws and regulations.[75]

---

[72] Wilfred V. Gill, *Remarks, op. cit.*
[73] U.S. Civil Service Commission, Office of Labor-Management Relations, *op. cit.,* p. 10.
[74] *Ibid.,* pp. 10-11.
[75] *Ibid.*

The Commission's task in setting policy was not an easy one. Considering statutory restrictions, CSC policy was not unreasonable; it was conciliatory when possible, yet committed to the law. It contained elements of both the harsh and the more cooperative approach. However, the final strategy decisions still remained an agency prerogative. Since decentralization was a major feature of the federal program, each agency could select, in varying degree, those CSC proposals it deemed appropriate to its situation. Thus, concerning the strike issue, decentralization allowed the possible perpetuation of established agency attitudes.

The contingency plan for work stoppages issued by the Post Office Department in July 1968 received particularly wide publicity.[76] This was due to the compelling interest of the postal unions, the largest in the federal service, and the fact that mail delivery constitutes the major daily consumer contact service provided by the Federal Government. The POD contingency plan rather closely followed the guidelines set down by the Civil Service Commission. Illegal activity was defined broadly to include all of the actions discussed in this chapter. Instructions were specifically delineated for officials at the local, regional, and headquarters levels. At the local level, directions resembled the procedures followed in gathering the evidence necessary to make a prima facie case in a court of law. Direct return-to-work orders were to be made by supervisors to show clear evidence of a wilful intent to stop working. Officials were urged to attempt to take photographs of the participants in action and to collect any other evidence in the form of handbills, notices, and flyers. Attempts were to be made to get union help in resolving difficulties. However, postmasters were cautioned not to "make any commitment to the union leaders to secure their cooperation." [77]

Union reaction was immediate. The next month saw the dropping of the no-strike constitutional pledges. The postal-union press railed against what it termed the Department's "strike jitters." The contingency plan was termed "intimidation, pure and simple"; "through this threatening memo, the Post Office Department has barricaded itself behind the safety of governmental authority waiting for a volcano to erupt." [78]

Opportunities to implement the contingency plan were plenti-

---

[76] U.S. Post Office Department, *Memorandum—Contingency Planning for Work Stoppages,* Washington, July 15, 1968. Also reported in *Government Employee Relations Report,* No. 261 (1968) , pp. G-1, G-4.

[77] *Ibid.,* pp. 2-4.

[78] *The Union Mail,* September 1968, p. 3.

ful after President Nixon's executive order raising federal postal pay by 4.1 percent, effective July 1, 1969. Dissatisfaction was rife, particularly in New York City. The major postal unions had been supporting a pay bill that called for a starting salary of $7,500, rising to $10,000 over five years. The new pay raise provided a scale ranging only from $6,176 to $8,422. Three days later 3,000 demonstrators were reported protesting before the Manhattan General Post Office. There was a simultaneous march by some 1,500 postal workers before the Grand Central Post Office, and a demonstration occurred also in the Bronx. All three employee actions received wide coverage in the media. The picket signs were vehement in their denunciation of the pay hike.[79] Even so, up to this point such demonstrations fell into the category of free speech.

It was another matter only 11 days later, however, when all but some half dozen of the letter carriers and clerks at the Kingsbridge Post Office in the Bronx staged a sick-leave call-in. There was a delay of mail deliveries, and service windows in the post office were closed. The Letter Carriers' local and the Manhattan-Bronx Postal Union did not authorize any action; however, it was clear to all that both unions had been active in the agitation for higher wages.[80] The contingency plan was evidently activated immediately. Supervisory personnel were called in to maintain normal service. An investigation was begun "to determine the extent of actual illness." Suspensions were promised where appropriate. The New York regional headquarters warned that "an alert" on the case was being sent to the U.S. Attorney's Office.[81] The "ill" employees were reportedly given 24 hours to answer charges that they were engaged in concerted action to withhold services.[82] The next day, July 2, 1969, the Bronx postmaster announced the suspension of 56 letter carriers and 16 clerks pending investigation. Gustave J. Johnson, then president of the Letter Carriers' Branch 36, called the suspensions "overreaction" and "violations of due process"; many of the absent workers, he added, had validating doctors letters.[83] Morris Biller, president of the MBPU, declared he would fight the suspensions of the 16 clerks he represented in the courts.[84]

The investigative process did not appear to blunt the disrup-

---

79 *The Union Mail,* June 1969, pp. 1, 5.
80 *The New York Times,* July 2, 1969, p. 10.
81 *Ibid.*
82 *Ibid.,* July 3, 1969, p. 50.
83 *New York Post,* July 3, 1969, p. 8.
84 *The New York Times,* July 3, 1969, p. 50.

tions. On the contrary, sick calls spread to the Throggs Neck Branch in the Bronx, where on the day of the 72 suspensions 16 of the 36 letter carriers gave notice they were ill and did not report for work.[85] Branch 36 and the MBPU had now tasted involvement in postal stoppages.

E. THE POSTAL STRIKE OF 1970

Previous strikes were as nothing compared to the postal upheaval of March 1970. It was the first truly national federal strike, and its ramifications will be felt for years by the entire federal establishment and by local governments. It raised new questions of rights, strikes, and collective bargaining, many of which still remain unanswered.

The strike should have come as no surprise. The indications were undeniable, the rumblings too plain to be passed off simply as employee unrest. For too many years postal workers had been grossly underpaid. The mass media, even those elements that condemned the action, recognized this fact. Postal employees were aware that far higher salaries had been achieved by illegal strike action by sanitation men and other workers at the local levels. In the city areas where living costs were high the presence of such wide pay differentials added fuel to the fire. It was common knowledge that many letter carriers moonlighted on one or more extra jobs; some even received welfare benefits. Postal workers of many years' standing contemplated resigning to apply for city sanitation jobs. The President himself acknowledged the disparity and the unfair difficulties it created. National postal union leaders had been warning POD management for years of potential strikes. It was thought by some that the Administration might well have welcomed a local strike to emphasize the need for postal reorganization.

The pay issue coupled with executive and legislative haggling over the form of the new postal corporation was the immediate cause of the walkout. Details of the bills presented and executive negotiations have been examined in Chapter XVII. Postal workers viewed proposals for a postal corporation with skepticism, since it would deprive the unions of their powerful influence in Congress. At least congressional connections had provided a channel for grievances that had led to some results in the past. Suffice it to say that dissatisfaction over the 4.1-percent pay increase in 1969 and demands for an area wage formula, a compression of

---

[85] *Ibid.*

the steps to top-level postal pay, and a substantial pay increase were the major striker complaints.

The postal unions generally had supported Representative Dulski's bill (H.R. 4) and had opposed the Nixon-sponsored H.R. 11750 on postal reorganization.[86] The incendiary spark was a substitute bill for H.R. 4 proposed to the House Post Office and Civil Service Committee by Rep. David Henderson of North Carolina. It combined a modified corporate reform proposal with a 5.4-percent increase and was voted out of committee on March 12, 1970. On the same day, at a heavily attended monthly meeting of Branch 36, the membership charged the rostrum upon learning of the committee action, and demanded that President Gustave Johnson set a date for a strike vote. Herman Sandbank, executive vice president of the local, saw this as the "crescendo" of a militancy among Branch 36 members that had been rising for over 20 years.[87] On March 17 a strike vote was conducted by Johnson. Reported Sandbank: "Many of our members saw a long delayed dream come true when the vote was announced at 1,555 in favor of a strike and 1,055 against." [88] There was quick action. The strike began officially about two hours later at 12:01 a.m., Wednesday, March 18. Not all of the members voted, but they abided by the results, and during the strike almost 100 percent stayed out.

Solidarity in the metropolitan region was remarkable. President Jack Leventhal of Branch 41 (Brooklyn) of the NALC had his 3,600 letter carriers join the 6,700 of Branch 36 on their very next tours. The Brooklyn local of the UFPC shut down its general post office almost immediately. The walkout spread to surrounding counties and on March 18 not a single letter carrier reported for work in New York, Brooklyn, and various localities on Long Island and in northern New Jersey. On the same day, strike votes were taken in Westchester, Rockland, and Orange Counties near New York City and adjacent communities in Connecticut.

The powerful MBPU, with 26,000 members working in almost all the postal crafts, also acted. It had supported the strike from the outset by respecting picket lines. On March 18 President Biller was mandated by a stormy membership meeting of some 6,500 workers to call a strike vote. Balloting on March 21 produced a margin of 10 to one for immediate strike action.[89]

---

86 See Chapter XVII.
87 New York Letter Carriers, *Outlook*, March 1970, p. 1.
88 *Ibid.*
89 *The Union Mail*, April 1970, pp. 3-5.

The POD secured court injunctions against the unions involved, but none returned to work. Mail service in the metropolitan region was virtually paralyzed.

The strike spread to other population centers. Services in the Northeast were virtually in suspension, while all areas curtailed services under POD embargoes to prevent impossible backlogs. Mass walkouts occurred in Chicago, the main east-west hub, as well as Buffalo, Philadelphia, Cleveland, Detroit, Milwaukee, Akron, Pittsburgh, St. Paul, Minneapolis, Los Angeles, and San Francisco. The POD reported that only seven regions in the South and Midwest were unaffected. Although figures varied, it was estimated that around 200,000 postal workers had gone out from coast to coast. POD contingency plans to meet potential crises were never patterned to cope with a cessation of such proportions. The damages and inconveniences suffered by government, business, industry, and the general public were devastating.

All the inputs of decision-making in the Federal Government were involved in the strike's resolution. Congress refused to be pressured into further consideration of pay or reform bills so long as the strike continued. Postmaster General Blount took an equally adamant position, refusing to discuss any terms of settlement until the men returned to work. The leaders of the seven national postal unions with exclusive recognition did not support the local walkouts. Necessarily having to concern themselves with total national membership desires, the legal sanctions under E.O. 11491, and the federal antistrike statutes, they notified their striking locals to return to work and attempted to resolve the difficulties by bargaining with the Administration. Letter Carrier President Rademacher especially was condemned for not calling a national strike. On March 20 he had sought a consensus from the NALC by convening a meeting in Washington of 300 presidents of his largest locals.[90] In the interim, President Nixon, concerned with the crippling effects of the strike, directed Secretary of Labor George Shultz to begin negotiations with Rademacher and the other nationally recognized postal-union leaders. As a result, an outline for further substantive negotiations was agreed upon. Rademacher's local presidents almost unanimously authorized him to start bargaining but set a five-day limit for negotiations. Shultz was the ideal negotiator for the Administration. His attitude, born of a background of enlightened labor relations and

[90] James H. Rademacher, "President's Biennial Report," *Postal Record*, September 1, 1970, pp. 21-25.

business administration, contrasted sharply with the obduracy of Postmaster General Blount. Both men were in agreement, however, that there could be no negotiations until the strikers returned to work. National union leaders sought to get the men back to work with the hope of getting the negotiations rolling.

After a preliminary meeting between Secretary Shultz and the seven exclusive unions, a back-to-work movement began. However, though service was gradually restored in the rural and suburban communities, service in the majority of urban centers remained drastically curtailed. There was some talk of a national AFL-CIO action in support of the postal workers if agreement was not concluded before the five-day negotiation period ended. On Monday, March 23, with the return to work gathering momentum in the rest of the nation, the New York area was still tied up.

Such was the background of President Nixon's momentous action of mobilizing the armed forces to move the mail in New York City. In a national television address the President reiterated the willingness of the government to begin negotiations if the men returned, and told of his troop activation to restore the postal service in New York City. He clearly implied that, if necessary, such military action would be taken in other important cities. On the same day he proclaimed a state of national emergency and by executive order authorized the Secretary of Defense to utilize units of the armed forces or National Guard as necessary to restore essential services.[91] This was the first use of troops to quell a federal public-workers strike.[92]

---

[91] *New York Times,* March 24, 1970, p. 34.

[92] Such action has traditionally been considered anathema by organized labor. Since the historic Boston Police Strike of 1919 its use in a public-sector labor crisis has been equally reviled by government employee unions. Great publicity was afforded Governor Coolidge's use of the State National Guard to put down the Boston strike. It has been clearly pointed out, however, that his action was unnecessary, coming after the mayor had already restored order with police volunteers, nonstriking police, and the Boston militia. Nevertheless, he reaped much political capital from his action, enhancing the reputation that led him to the White House.

The Boston episode left a feeling of disquietude about the use of troops at the local level that has persisted to this time. When a sanitation strike in New York City reached emergency proportions threatening the health of the public in 1968, Mayor Lindsay asked the governor to call out the State Guard. Rockefeller refused to do so because of the strife he believed such action would bring to the city. The well-organized and numerous municipal unions were most vehement in their opposition to such drastic measures. So also did organized labor, in and out of public service, decry the President's use of troops in the postal crisis. There is always the cry of "scab" and "strikebreaker," just as there are considerable segments of the public who breathe easier knowing the military is always available to meet a public crisis.

For more on the Boston Police Strike, see Sterling D. Spero, *Government as Employer,* pp. 277-284.

The estimated 25,000 soldiers, airmen, and reservists were inexpert and slow in sorting the mail and performing the myriad tasks of the striking professional postal workers. But their effect was undeniable. On March 24, when about 90 percent of the postal workers had returned to their jobs, Blount announced that enough workers were on the job for bargaining to begin. Gustave Johnson in conjunction with Morris Biller thereupon ordered the Branch 36 letter carriers and the MBPU back to work. On the afternoon of March 25 the strike was over in New York City.[93]

We have seen the far-reaching effects of the strike in the passage of the Postal Reorganization Act with its historic postal reforms and greater collective bargaining for postal unions. What must also be appreciated were the immediate events that led to and followed the termination of the strike. When the leaders of the seven exclusively recognized unions sat down with Secretary Shultz to set the ground rules for bargaining, an historic precedent was established. Negotiations with postal officials began in earnest and finally resulted in a Memorandum of Agreement, signed by Blount and the seven union leaders, that included a general wage increase, a joint commitment to postal reform, private-sector-type collective bargaining, and a compression of the wage schedule from 21 to eight years.[94] For the first time, leaders of federal unions that did not legally possess a right to strike sat down with administration officials and negotiated a collective bargaining agreement under conditions almost identical to those in private industry. It was unfortunate that the trauma of national emergency spurred the event, but labor history has invariably been written in an atmosphere of economic strife reflecting changing times.

F. REASSESSMENT OF THE PUBLIC-SECTOR STRIKE

Events of recent years have forced a reappraisal of the strike issue in government service. Many old and several new approaches in theory and practice have been put forward as possible panaceas. Relaxation of the basic no-strike statutes at all levels of government does not appear in the offing. Indeed, the reverse trend is quite apparent, as witness the increased severity of strike penalties under the New York Taylor Act. When that law was

---

[93] New York Letter Carriers' *Outlook*, March 1970, p. 1; *The Union Mail*, April 1970, p. 3.

[94] U.S. House of Representatives, Committee on Post Office and Civil Service, *Hearings on Postal Reform*, 91st Cong., 2nd Sess., April 22, 1970, Serial #91-22, pp. 2-3.

appealed to the Supreme Court upon several constitutional issues, review was denied "for want of a properly presented federal question." [95] The Supreme Court has for some 40 years considered the state police power, exerted for the general welfare, to be superior to private rights in most matters of labor regulation. This applies to unions as well as management.[96] Local courts continue to enjoin stoppages deemed contrary to the public interest. Finally, the favorable public attitudes which are the essential ingredients for support of any major legislative change are often lacking.

A new look at the federal antistrike statutes was forced by union litigation. The postal unions, fulfilling convention mandates to test the laws in court, attacked their basic constitutionality. The major targets of the unions were the employment oath and the provisions forbidding the strike itself, the assertion of the right to strike, or membership in an organization that asserted the right to strike.[97] The NALC with the aid of the American Civil Liberties Union moved against the affidavit requirement and the prohibition against asserting the right to strike. Union counsel condemned these as infringing upon First Amendment freedoms—particularly free speech—and abridging the civil liberties of postal employees. Initiated before the postal strike, the case was decided in the union's favor by the U.S. District Court for the District of Columbia.[98]

In a declaratory judgment proceeding Judge Gesell spoke for the three-judge court on applying the "chilling effect" doctrine to federal practice. Recent decisions, he recognized, had held that where the freedoms of expression and association were concerned "the threat alone of loss of job, criminal sanction or other penalty may inhibit, or 'chill' their exercise and thus require court intervention to preserve them." As applied to federal procedures, he declared:

"The oath is a condition of employment for all postal employees. Who can ever say whether it may inhibit persons from joining a collective bargaining agent through which they might more effectively work for improvements in the terms and conditions of their employment. The statute and oath combined may also inhibit a variety of other activities, on and off duty, protected by the First Amendment, including legislative effort on behalf of the right to

[95] DeLury, et al. v. City of New York, 394 U.S. 455 (1969).
[96] Lincoln Federal Labor Union v. Northwestern Iron and Metal Co.; Whitaker v. North Carolina, 335 U.S. 525, 23 LRRM 2199 (1949).
[97] 5 U.S.C. §3333; 5 U.S.C. §7311; 5 U.S.C. §8315; 18 U.S.C. §1918; E.O. 11491, Secs. 2 (e) (2), 19 (b) (4).
[98] National Association of Letter Carriers v. Blount, etc., 305 F. Supp. 546 (D.D.C., 1969).

strike, group discussion, and legitimate protest short of an actual strike. By contrast, similar activities opposing the right to strike are in no way inhibited or restricted."[99]

Using the ordinary meaning of the word "asserts," Judge Gesell rejected government arguments and followed the major thrust of recent Supreme Court decisions "striking down employment oaths and legislation which compel, or, by vagueness, may well result in abandonment of constitutionally guaranteed rights."[100] The court accordingly struck down the employment oath and the words "or asserts the right to strike" from the U.S. Code as violative of the First Amendment. All existing executed oaths were declared without force and effect.[101]

The government appealed the case to the Supreme Court, which agreed in April 1970 to pass on the lower court decision. However, once the postal strike subsided, the preliminary negotiations were concluded, and the U.S. Postal Service was established, the government showed no further interest in pressing the appeal. In September 1970 it was quietly dropped.[102] It can only be surmised whether the accommodation was part of the postal negotiations or a result of the government's belief that it would not prevail. This was tantamount to accepting the unconstitutionality of an oath that prohibited "asserting" a right to strike. In August 1971, E.O. 11616 revised Section 2 (e) (2) of the Nixon order removing the prohibition against recognizing any union that asserted the right.[103] This section, at least, was not to be a part of the federal labor relations program.

The statutory prohibition against strikes in the Federal Government, however, was a different matter. The United Federation of Postal Clerks sued in the U.S. District Court for the District of Columbia, seeking to invalidate the laws preventing federal employees from striking.

The UFPC contended that the right to strike was a "fundamental" right constitutionally protected and that abridgment of the right violated the First Amendment and denied federal workers equal protection of the laws. The laws also were attacked as being "vague and overbroad" and thus violating the due-process clause in the Fifth Amendment. On March 3, 1971, a three-judge

---

99 305 F. Supp. at 549.
100 305 F. Supp. 550.
101 305 F. Supp. 550-551.
102 *New York Times*, September 2, 1970, p. 34.
103 E.O. 11616, Sec. 2 (e) (2) ; Federal Labor Relations Council, *Labor-Management Relations in the Federal Service, Amendments to E.O. 11491 With Report and Recommendations*, Washington, August 1971, p. 3.

court unanimously denied the union's claim to a constitutional right to strike.[104] In tracing the evolution of strike legality the court began with the conspiracy doctrine, which at common law was successfully used to deprive workers in private employment of the strike through much of the industrial revolution. At common law neither private nor public workers had any such constitutional right. The court noted that it took a law, the National Labor Relations Act, to protect fully the right of private workers to strike and concluded: "It seems clear that public employees stand on no stronger footing in this regard than private employees and that in the absence of a statute, they do not possess the right to strike." [105] Noting that Congress has always treated public workers separately and uniquely, the court declared:

> "Given the fact that there is no constitutional right to strike, it is not irrational or arbitrary for the Government to condition employment on a promise not to withhold labor collectively, and to prohibit strikes by those in public employment, whether because of the prerogatives of the sovereign, some sense of higher obligation associated with public service, to assure the continuing functioning of the Government without interruption, to protect public health and safety or for other reasons."[106]

The strike was intended to equalize bargaining power in the private sphere, the court observed, but it was not intended to be used to influence the political decisions of the government in allocating its resources. Since Congress has the obligation to ensure that the government's machinery runs without interference, it was "a reasonable implementation of that obligation" to prohibit strikes by federal employees.[107] The claim of vagueness was likewise rejected.

Circuit Judge J. Skelly Wright, concurring, nevertheless expressed several misgivings. He questioned the flat ban on federal strikes under the due-process clause of the Fifth Amendment, and voiced some doubt about the majority view that the strike was not a fundamental right. The right to organize labor unions has been adjudged a fundamental right protected by the First Amendment, he noted, and the right to strike seemed "intimately

---

[104] United Federation of Postal Clerks v. Blount, 325 F. Supp. 879 (D.D.C., 1971).
[105] The court noted two federal decisions in this area. In *Amell* v. *U.S.*, 384 U.S. 158, 161 (1965), the Supreme Court "spoke approvingly of such a restriction" and in *TVA* v. *Local Union No. 110, Sheet Metal Workers*, 233 F. Supp. 997 (D.C. W.D.Ky.1962), a District Court invoked the predecessor statute to the one in issue (5 U.S.C. Sec. 118, p-r) to enjoin a strike by federal workers.
[106] 325 F. Supp. at 882.
[107] 325 F. Supp. at 884.

related" to this. A union that could neither strike nor threaten to strike might "wither away in ineffectiveness." This is not to say that the right to strike is co-equal with the right to organize labor unions, but "the right to strike is, at least, within constitutional concern and should not be discriminatorily abridged without substantial or 'compelling' justification."[108]

Judge Wright, therefore, considered the main issue to be whether there was justification to deny federal workers what was guaranteed in the private sector. He suggested that the union's argument that many federal services are not essential whereas some private services are essential "cast doubt on the validity of the flat ban on federal employees' strikes." "In our mixed economic system of governmental and private enterprise," he noted, "the line separating governmental from private functions may depend more on the accidents of history than on substantial differences in kind."[109]

These reservations, however, did not prevent Judge Wright from agreeing with the end result. His final comments summed up the courts' attitude toward public strikes:

"As the majority indicates, the asserted right of public employees to strike has often been litigated and, so far as I know, never recognized as a matter of law. The present state of the relevant jurisprudence offers almost no support for the proposition that the government lacks a 'compelling' interest in prohibiting such strikes. No doubt, the line between 'essential' and 'non-essential' functions is very, very difficult to draw. For that reason, it may well be best to accept the demarcations resulting from the development of our political economy. If the right of public employees to strike—with all its political and social ramifications—is to be recognized and protected by the judiciary, it should be done by the Supreme Court which has the power to reject established jurisprudence and the authority to enforce such a sweeping rule."[110]

The devastating effect of this decision on the legality of public strikes at all levels of government was self-evident. It was the avowed purpose of the UFPC, with NALC support, to seek a reversal of the decision before the Supreme Court.[111] Prudence would have dictated some caution; the make-up of the Court clearly pointed to a maintenance of the status quo. The decision was affirmed on appeal by a six-to-one vote, with Justice Douglas alone dissenting.[112] This Supreme Court pronouncement rein-

---

[108] 325 F. Supp. at 885.
[109] 325 F. Supp. at 885-886.
[110] 325 F. Supp. at 886.
[111] *The Postal Record,* May 1971, p. 6.
[112] UFPC v. Blount, 404 U.S. 802 (1971).

forces all state and local no-strike statutes. It is in accord with public opinion toward public strikes, and means there is little prospect for passage of permissive legislation in the near future. The outlook for proposals to permit postal workers to strike by amending the Postal Reorganization Act is similarly dim.[113]

On the strike issue, therefore, the sovereignty concept remains a potent factor. The public feels put upon when daily services are curtailed by disruptive strikes. Rank-and-file union members in the private sector are very often among those who criticize public strikers. There is an undeniable tendency for the public to feel a proprietary interest, much as any employer.

In Canada, the growth of collective bargaining and relaxation of the strike ban was in large part due to an erosion of the sovereignty doctrine. The Honorable C.M. Drury, president of the Treasury Board of Canada, the principal agent of the employer in collective bargaining, pointed out that since World War II, Canadian governmental experience brought a growing awareness to both sides "of the practical problems that must be faced in any systematic effort to reconcile differing interests and points of view."[114] Highly pertinent to this discussion was his conclusion that "it brought about critical changes in atmosphere and mood. The cloak of sovereignty was still available, and was still used, but it was worn with a growing sense of unease. In point of fact, it was becoming threadbare and going out of style."[115]

Although sovereignty has lost much of its power to prevent advanced forms of collective bargaining in the United States, it is still among the arguments against any relaxation of the strike ban. The American public has not yet reached the point where it will accept public strikes. Nevertheless, the doctrine has become decidedly tarnished even here. Its deterioration was hastened by increased statutory acceptance of public collective bargaining and the trauma of public strikes at the state and municipal levels.

It would be naive to assume that the rapidly rising trend of civil service stoppages will reverse itself. Ours is a pluralistic society of many groups, each striving in its own fashion to improve its economic position. Each claims to be acting in the public interest, but when pressed it acts in its own interests even if the public

---

113 U.S. House of Representatives, Committee on Post Office and Civil Service, *H.R. 11535*, 92nd Cong., 1st Sess., November 1971.
114 The Hon. C. M. Drury, President, Treasury Board, Canada, "The Future of Labour-Management Relations in the Public Service of Canada," *Address*, to Joint Conference on Collective Bargaining in Federal Public Service, AFL-CIO, CLC, Niagara Falls, Ontario, November 20, 1968, pp. 3-4.
115 *Ibid.*, p. 4.

suffers. Public employees and their unions are no exception. As a practical matter, given no alternative, they will strike. In recent years, for example, nurses and school teachers—conforming, proper, respected, even docile—have engaged in numerous costly and dangerous illegal strikes. As to the statutes, if those they regulate do not generally accept their regulation, they will be as effective as the fugitive slave acts and prohibition.

The retention of antistrike laws remains a highly charged issue, particularly among the unions. Supporters of these laws, for example, Professor George W. Taylor, cite the existence of such statutes in most jurisdictions. In any event, at common law, such disruptions are enjoinable.[116] Furthermore, the whole question of strike avoidance must inevitably involve considering the several alternatives for impasse resolution.

There is one approach that conceivably could produce some revision of strike statutes. This is the proposal set forth by Theodore W. Kheel and others that emergency provisions such as those in the Taft-Hartley Act be applied to the public service. Kheel saw the greatest chance for averting strikes in the fullest adoption of collective bargaining with all its appurtenances. He considered arbitration workable, but he did not see it as ending public labor strife.[117] He declared:

> "I believe, rather, that we should acknowledge the failure of unilateral determination, however disguised by unreal promises of joint negotiation, and turn instead to true collective bargaining, even though this must include the possibility of a strike. We would then clearly understand that we have no alternative except to improve the bargaining process and the skill of the practitioners to prevent strikes. . . . For too long our attention has been directed to the mechanics and penalties rather than the participants and the process. It is now time to change that, to seek to prevent strikes by encouraging collective bargaining to the fullest extent possible."[118]

Kheel suggested, for the few types of strikes that could seriously disrupt public welfare, legislation permitting injunctions followed by a Taft-Hartley type of emergency procedure. If impasse persisted, the legislature could consider the possibility of ar-

---

[116] George W. Taylor, *Remarks,* Governor's Conference on Public Employment Relations, New York, N.Y., October 15, 1968, as reported in *Government Employee Relations Report,* No. 267 (1968), pp. 6-1, 6-2.

[117] Theodore W. Kheel, *Statement,* to Federal Bar Association Briefing Conference on Collective Bargaining in Public Employment, San Francisco, California, January 24, 1969, as reported in *Government Employee Relations Report,* No. 282 (1969), p. F-5.

[118] *Ibid.*

bitration. But Kheel did not envisage collective bargaining as doing away with all strikes. He believed simply that penalties and complicated third-party proposals had failed, that compulsory arbitration cannot always succeed, and so "we should give bargaining in the public sector the same try it has with beneficial results received in the private sector." [119]

The most realistic concern for the public safety might be found in legislation that in no way differentiated between strikes in the private and public sectors. Such a law would ask only: "Would a strike affect the public interest?" A statute applying Taft-Hartley procedures to all strikes would be fair and conducive to full collective bargaining. Exceptions subject to a strict strike ban would be police, firemen, and prison guards. Such an approach would be similar to the Canadian model. Though there would be no guarantee, awareness on the part of public employees of their responsibilites probably would result in fewer public strikes. The public strike ban has been lifted to a limited extent in at least two states, Hawaii and Pennsylvania. Enacted in July 1970, the Pennsylvania statute affected some half a million public employees and workers in nonprofit institutions. These workers for the most part may strike, but stoppages that might endanger public health and safety still are prohibited. Policemen and firemen already were covered by a binding-arbitration law.[120] Statutes such as those in Pennsylvania and Hawaii are breaches in the solid wall of general prohibition, but they do not represent the beginning of a trend.

There are several factors that are likely to inhibit strikes by federal unions. First, aside from the postal service, there are relatively few services where a strike would have an immediate impact on the general public comparable to the "job actions" of almost any group of city or state employees. Second, federal unions have developed effective legislative lobbies which enable them to turn to Congress when galling issues stymie relations with management.

Finally, there are many who believe that federal collective bargaining can serve as an example to the rest of the community for the orderly settlement of employment problems without resort to industrial warfare. Not everyone accepts resort to strikes, even in the private sphere, as inevitable or desirable. The head of one of the largest unions in the class-conscious British labor movement

---

[119] *Ibid.*
[120] *The New York Times,* July 24, 1970, p. 19.

has said that the strike, especially in services upon whose continuity society depends, is becoming an instrument of increasingly questionable value. Indeed, it was a Labour Government that sought legislation to control wildcat strikes threatening the nation's delicate economic position. Provisions against strikes are an essential part of the Conservative Government's Industrial Relations Act of 1971.[121]

In the coming period of change the need for mutual understanding between labor and management will be greater than ever before. If the Federal Government is to set an example of resolving labor disputes without resort to strikes, cooperation must be of the highest order. The public interest must remain a prime consideration. The strike is an admission of failure by the parties. To union leaders in the general labor movement, it is an action of last resort. As former Chairman Macy said in one of his last addresses while in office:

> "You know well that responsible unions in the private sector are as fully concerned as management in preserving the economic health of the employer and industry. The cooperation we seek in the public service is of the same order: preservation of the public's confidence in the service of its government, in its efficiency, its productivity and its responsiveness to the public will."[122]

---

[121] Industrial Relations Act, Chap. 72 (Elizabeth II), 1971.

[122] John W. Macy, Jr., Chairman, Civil Service Commission, "Public Employee Labor Relations in a Changing Society," *Address*, before Joint Conference on Collective Bargaining in Federal Public Service, AFL-CIO, CLC, Niagara Falls, Ontario, November 20, 1968, p. 5.

Chapter XIX

THE GOVERNANCE OF FEDERAL WAGES

The perennial controversy over government pay policy that pits the doctrine of the model employer against the prevailing-rate principle no longer has practical significance. The large place federal employment holds in the national labor market and the size of its payroll have rendered the model-employer doctrine all but obsolete.

The principle of prevailing rate of pay has been established for more than a century in the government's industrial services. Although it served as a rough guide in setting blue-collar salaries under various classification acts, it was not until the passage of the Salary Reform Act of 1962 that the prevailing-rate principle was explicitly extended to nonindustrial employees. Provisions in the Salary Reform Act required that the salaries of classified employees should "be reasonably comparable with those paid in private industry." [1] The Act required the President to make recommendations to Congress for federal pay changes based upon annual surveys by the Bureau of Labor Statistics that compare federal and private compensation.

A. WAGE BOARDS AND PREVAILING RATE

Setting skilled and unskilled workers' wages in the federal industrial services at prevailing rates has been practiced since the mid-1830s, when trade unionism first developed in the navy yards, arsenals, and public works. The first legislative recognition of this practice came in 1861. Today the pay of industrial or blue-collar employees is set under the authority of several different statutes. An act passed in 1862 governs the pay of civilian employees in the navy yards. [2] The Kiess Act of 1924 relates to employees of the Government Printing Office. [3] The Tennessee Valley Authority Act of 1933 requires payment of "not less than

---

[1] Public Law 87-793 (1962).
[2] 12 Stat. 587 (1862).
[3] Public Law 276, 68th Cong., 1st Sess., Ch. 354, 1924.

prevailing rates" for work done for the corporation by contractors. It also requires that where work "is done directly by the corporation, the prevailing rate of wages shall be paid in the same manner as though such work had been let out by contract." [4] A section of the Classification Act of 1949 exempts "employees in recognized trades or crafts, or other skilled mechanical crafts, or in unskilled, semi-skilled or skilled manual labor occupations" from its provisions and requires that their compensation "shall be fixed from time to time as nearly as is consistent with the public interest in accordance with prevailing rates." [5] There was a similar provision in the Classification Act of 1923, and before that prevailing-wage requirements were written into various appropriations acts.

The determination of prevailing rates is commonly referred to as a "wage board" procedure regardless of whether the determination is actually made by wage boards, by joint conference as in the Government Printing Office, or by collective bargaining as in the TVA and the bureaus of the Department of the Interior.

When Congress first recognized the prevailing-rate principle in the navy yards, it left the setting of wages to the commandants of the various installations. To assure a greater degree of uniformity the Act of 1862 required the ultimate approval of rates by the Secretary of the Navy. Within these requirements, wage rates were to be based upon "private establishments in the immediate vicinity of the respective yards," yet were to be "consistent with the public interest." [6]

In 1864, under instructions from the Navy Department, the first wage boards were appointed by the commandants of the various yards. At first these boards included naval officers and civilians, but they were shortly reorganized to consist only of officers. Departmental instructions required the commandants to post the wage scale recommended by the yard board "so that workmen may examine it and state their views on it to the commandant." [7]

This employee role in wage determination continued until the Spanish-American War of 1898. The expanded operations of the war brought large numbers of new workers, many of them union members, into the navy yards. Dissatisfied with their ex-post-facto role, employees at several yards asked to present their views to

---

[4] Tennessee Valley Authority Act, 73rd Cong., 1st Sess., Ch. 32, 1933.
[5] Public Law 429, 81st Cong., 1st Sess., Ch. 782, Sec. 202 (7) , 1949.
[6] 12 Stat. 587 (1862) .
[7] Joseph P. Goldberg, "The Government's Industrial Employees; Part II," *Monthly Labor Review,* Vol. 77, March 1954, p. 249.

the local wage board in the course of its work rather than after the recommendations were reported. The requests were granted, and in short order consultations with employee representatives during the wage-fixing process became widespread. Such consultation on a local and informal basis continued until the rapidly changing needs of World War I compelled the creation of emergency machinery to coordinate Army and Navy wages.[8] An Arsenal-Navy Yard Adjustment Commission representing the Departments of Labor, War, and the Navy was set up.

The Navy centralized its wage fixing by adopting the rates set from time to time for private shipyards by the Shipbuilding Labor Adjustment Board. The Arsenal-Navy Yard Adjustment Commission held informal conferences and approved the navy awards almost as a matter of course.

In the Army, authority to pay prevailing rates was derived from various separate appropriation acts covering its Ordnance Department and other industrial bureaus. These bureaus were administered on a highly autonomous basis. Suspicious of central wage fixing, the Army sent its staff man on the joint Arsenal-Navy Yard Adjustment Commission to make his own investigations and hold hearings at the several arsenals. His results were then reported to the joint commission, which, as in the case of the Navy, gave them its formal approval. Despite their different methods, army and navy wage rates tended toward uniformity.

The War Department devised a method known as the Balderson plan, under which locality wage boards, composed of departmental representatives in the area, made prevailing-rate surveys. Established craft distinctions were bypassed so that, according to the Department, wages might be set on the basis of the job rather than the craft name. A number of key jobs were used as a basis of comparison with all other jobs for such factors as experience, training, skill, responsibility, physical demands, and working conditions.[9]

When the plan was first presented, a union official with long service as a representative of skilled workers in the military departments condemned it as "a complicated way of cutting unions out of the wage fixing process." [10] Official union protests were followed by a series of conferences at which modifications were pro-

---

[8] See Sterling D. Spero, *Government as Employer* (New York: Remsen Press, 1948), pp. 432-438. Reprinted Carbondale, Ill.: Southern Illinois University Press, 1972.
[9] Donald A. Rutledge, "Civilian Personnel Administration in the War Department," *Public Administration Review,* Winter 1947, p. 57.
[10] Sterling D. Spero, *op. cit.,* pp. 437-438.

posed that sought to preserve craft identities and give the unions a recognized role in the wage-fixing process.[11]

The War Department, however, refused concessions. Its wage procedure, with requirements and modifications, not only remained in effect but became essentially the model for wage-setting procedures in the Air Force and a number of agencies employing blue-collar employees.

The Army and Air Force set their rates under the supervision of an Army-Air Force Wage Board of six, three designated by the Secretary of each service. This joint board was assisted by a Technical Staff which actually ran the wage-fixing process, prescribing the details of methods and procedures to be followed in the field under the guidance of published official *Instructions for Locality Wage Boards*. Locality wage boards were made up of officers of local installations and chaired, wherever possible, by a member of the Technical Staff, or where this was not possible, by someone designated by the Staff. The locality boards were assisted by statisticians and classification and personnel technicians. Appeals from local decisions went to the Technical Staff and were formally approved by the Army-Air Force Wage Board.

The Navy had its own machinery. Its procedures read:

"The successful completion of a wage survey requires the coordinated effort of the Office of Industrial Relations (OIR), the cognizant Area Wage Classification Office (AWCO), the naval activities in the area and the Area Wage Survey Committee (AWSC)." [12]

Wage surveys were authorized by the OIR and were conducted under procedures set forth in the regulations by Area Wage Survey Committees designated locally and operating under the general supervision of the Area Wage and Classification Office. As in the case of the Army-Air Force Wage Board, meticulously detailed procedures were handed down from the departmental offices defining the locality limits, the jobs and firms to be surveyed, and the statistical procedures to be followed.

There was a difference in spirit, rooted in long practice, however, between the Navy and Army-Air Force attitudes toward employee participation in the rate-determination procedure. Years ago the president of District 44 of the Machinists noted this difference, declaring that Army authorities "apparently still resent the interference of organized labor in their affairs," and while

---

[11] District Lodge 44, IAM, *Proceedings*, 1945, pp. 69-71.

[12] U.S. Department of the Navy, Office of Industrial Relations, *Department of the Navy Policies and Procedures for Wage Fixing*, 1955, p. 5.

they were ready to listen and at times act upon union suggestions, "an effort is continuously made to impress upon us that they are not making arrangements with us."[13] The Navy, on the other hand, had "evidenced a willingness to recognize and enter into the consideration of all grievances with representatives of the employees. . . ."[14] The Metal Trades Department, which enjoys great strength among Navy Department workers, has consistently lauded the Department's policy of cooperation. This long-established Navy practice sought informally and otherwise to consider union views and advice before instituting major personnel policy changes.[15] Indeed, the degree of collective cooperation achieved over the years between the Metal Trades Department and the Navy probably underlay the MTD's reluctance and anticipated difficulties in implementing the new wage-board systems in the Department. Similar approaches were not prevalent in the Army and Air Force, although the Technical Staff did informally exchange nonconfidential wage information with union representatives.

At the local level, the Navy provided for the appointment of employees as observers on Area Wage Survey Committees where "such action is considered necessary to meet a local employee-relations need."[16] Provision was also made for the appointment of employees as data collectors. Although the unions in fact, though not in name, usually nominate the observers and data collectors, the effectiveness of these designees as representatives of their fellow workers was greatly limited by the requirement that they "maintain the confidence of all wage data they see in the same manner as all other persons participating in the survey."[17] This requirement in effect made them arms of the employer. Although the data they saw were of vital concern to all the workers, they were forbidden to share their information with their fellows.

Instructions provided for the Army-Air Force Wage Board stated that

> "only authorized locality wage board members may attend its final meeting since the rates paid by individual companies will be discussed. The chairman, however, will be available after the final

---

[13] District Lodge 44, IAM, *Proceedings*, 1915, p. 20.

[14] U.S. Congress, House of Representatives, Committee on Labor, *Hearings*, April 17, 1914, p. 54.

[15] See Sterling D. Spero, *op cit.*, pp. 432-438; and Joseph P. Goldberg, *op. cit.*, pp. 249-251.

[16] U.S. Department of the Navy, *op cit.*, p. 6.

[17] *Ibid.*, p. 7.

meeting to meet with employees and their representatives to discuss the survey in general terms." [18]

There was no provision for observers on locality boards. Although employees could serve as data collectors, there was no specific provision for such designation. The regulations stated that data collectors were "representatives of the Secretaries of the Army and the Air Force." [19]

Both services provided for hearings at the local board level where employee representatives could testify. Both provided for appeals to the national level. Under the Army-Air Force procedures, such appeals were, for practical purposes, decided by the Technical Staff, although a further appeal could be taken to the joint Army-Air Force Wage Boards. Final appeals in the Navy went from the Office of Industrial Relations to the central Navy Wage Committee, on which unions had been represented by their own nominees since the end of World War I. The Committee consisted of five members appointed by the Secretary. Two were nominated by the OIR, one each by the presidents of the Metal Trades Department of the AFL-CIO and the Government Employees Department of the International Association of Machinists, the successor to the Old District 44. A fifth membership rotated among the various Navy bureaus.

Other agencies employing blue-collar workers followed the Army-Air Force wage-fixing model. Among them were the National Aeronautics and Space Agency, the Treasury and Agriculture Departments, and a group of cooperating agencies which included the Veterans' Administration, Health, Education and Welfare, the General Services Administration, and a number of smaller agencies.

Union-management consultation under wage-board procedures was actually more substantial than the descriptions of the formal processes indicated, particularly in the Navy. The locality wage boards met with trade-union spokesmen, and although observers and data collectors were designated on the basis of their ability and knowledge rather than as employee representatives, they were nevertheless still usually union nominees.

The legal independence of their operations notwithstanding, the procedures of the various agencies were informally coordinated, especially where their facilities were situated in the same or nearby labor-market areas. The Bureau of Labor Statistics also

---

[18] U.S. Departments of Army and Air Force, *Instructions for Locality Wage Boards,* December 1963, p. 10.
[19] *Ibid.,* p. 7.

played a significant coordinating role, making data collected in its community and industry surveys available to interested federal employing agencies.

The basic difference between the statistical rate-setting methods of the Army-Air Force and its emulators on the one hand and the Navy on the other was that the latter still based its averages on established craft designations, while the former classified jobs into labor grades cutting across craft lines.[20]

B. BLUE-COLLAR AGREEMENTS UNDER E.O. 10988

Since E.O. 10988 was implemented within the framework of the existing wage-board systems, it is important to consider whether contractual developments stemming from it worked any significant change in the wage-determination process. As has been noted, the issue of pay-fixing in the federal service remains a fundamental question in the eyes of union leaders.[21] They speak with feeling of some future time when "true" collective bargaining will be achieved through the mutual negotiation of pay schedules, when its inclusion as an accepted negotiable item is beyond question. It was also pointed out in Chapter V that the statutes governing blue-collar compensation permitted great executive discretion; there could as easily and as legally have been collective negotiation as the wage-board system. Thus, the pay-fixing procedures chosen by management in the TVA and the Interior prior to the Kennedy order closely approximated collective bargaining. They included extensive negotiation of prevailing rates and resulted in signed agreements.[22] Practice varied in the remaining agencies from consultation to greater participation, as in the Navy. Changes continued to be made administratively despite the unending stream of legislative proposals to revise the wage-board structure. The present Coordinated Federal Wage System is the direct result of presidential and Civil Service Commission actions.

To what extent, therefore, did the Kennedy order influence the blue-collar wage system? Were unions empowered to achieve greater participation in the rate-fixing process by contract? Indeed, some changes towards expanded participation at the installation level were effected. However, there was no official and substantial movement to raise the wage-board system in any particular

---

[20] U.S. War Department, Wage Coordinating Board, *Report on Locality Wages,* 1947.
[21] See Chapter II and Chapter V, Section **B**.
[22] See Chapters XVI, XVII.

agency to the status of a negotiable issue. To a large extent the agreements concluded under E.O. 10988 reflected and incorporated preexisting agency practices. Management retained the unilateral control of the wage systems it enjoyed prior to negotiations.

Nevertheless, much was gained in that the contracts specifically formalized pay policies and practices. They served formally and officially to incorporate union views in the administration of pay policy. Provision was made for the participation of unions in framing practices with respect to overtime, holidays, shift differentials, hazardous work, and the like, even though agency regulations clearly covered these issues.

The precise areas that were agreed to by management in wage-survey administration can be reasonably defined. The constant pay pressures that motivate union interest in wage-survey procedures cannot be ignored except at the risk of serious conflicts. Many union leaders and observers maintain that extensive union participation in the survey method in a sense constitutes a significant form of collective bargaining on wages. Thus, if data collectors are picked by unions and they fully satisfy union interests in selecting the firms and positions for comparison, there is little doubt that the final wage scale will reflect union influence. It may be said, however, that under the Kennedy order, even though hundreds of contracts provided for some form of union participation in wage surveys, management retained ultimate control over the entire process with little or no formal commitment to appoint union members as such to wage-survey boards.

The salient forms of participation that were agreed to in the more advanced contracts are as follows: Unions were granted the right to request that area full-scale and wage-change surveys be conducted when significant industry wage raises had taken place in the survey area. Such requests were to be promptly considered.[23] Most blue-collar contracts now require the employer to communicate immediately with the union on receipt of notification that a full-scale wage survey has been planned or ordered for an area in cases where the survey was not requested by the union. Reasonable efforts are to be made to advise the union at least 10 days or two weeks before the survey is to begin. The union may then request the collection of industry data on any upgraded rating not scheduled for survey but which the union

---

[23] U.S. Department of the Navy, *Agreement,* between Charleston Naval Shipyard and Charleston Metal Trades Council, February 29, 1968, Art. XXVI, Sec. 1.

believes is out of pay alignment.[24] Many contracts granted the union the right to submit lists of union-member nominees for the post of data collector. Management generally agreed to consider the names submitted but practically always emphasized impartiality and merit as the only grounds for choice. Any aspect of mutual bargaining was downgraded by precise clauses on this point.[25]

Thus the majority of survey-participation clauses assured only that the union nominees would be considered but not necessarily selected by the employer.[26] What the unions succeeded in formalizing in most such accords was the assurance that the wage board would include a reasonable number of employees from the unit whether they were union members or not. Thus the board was not to be entirely management oriented.

An interesting compromise accord reached in the 1968 Charleston shipyard agreement granting partial preference declared:

"When data collectors are requested by the Area Wage Survey Committee, the Employer agrees that fifty per cent of the total number will be from among qualified employees of the unit. In selecting data collectors, the Employer agrees to consider first those qualified employees whom the council may nominate." [27]

In certain rarer instances there was outright agreement to appoint a union member to the wage board. Thus, the 1965 NASA Space Flight Center at Huntsville, Ala., actually agreed that members were to be selected on their merits without regard to organized groups, " provided, however, that at least one qualified person, who is also a member of the union will be included on the locality wage survey board." [28] However, even when this action was taken, data collection as a union function was forcefully deemphasized. Thus, the contract further provided:

"Every Marshall Space Flight Center member of the board shall act only in his capacity as a member of the board. He shall not act in the capacity as the representative of any organization. Further, any and all information gathered by any member is the property of

24 U.S. Department of the Navy, *Agreement,* between Navy Marine Engineering Laboratory, Annapolis, Md., and IAM Lodge 174, March 7, 1966, Art. X, Secs. 3, 4.

25 U.S. Veterans' Administration, *Basic Agreement,* between VA Center, Reno, Nev., and AFGE Lodge 2152, June 23, 1965, Art. 14, Sec. B.

26 U.S. Department of the Navy, *Negotiated Agreement,* between Naval Air Turbine Test Station, Trenton, N.J., and IAM Lodge 176, April 1, 1965, Art. XXII, Sec. 3.

27 U.S. Department of the Navy, *Agreement,* between Charleston Naval Shipyard and Charleston Metal Trades Council, February 29, 1968, Art. XXVI, Sec. 3.

28 NASA, *Agreement,* between George C. Marshall Space Flight Center, Huntsville, Ala., and AFGE Lodge 1858, November 4, 1965, Art. XXII, Sec. 2.

the wage board and shall not be conveyed to any unauthorized person who is not a member of the board." [29]

Under such circumstances, there was little possibility of the wage-board method's becoming a viable form of collective dealing.

A more frequent provision which met with far greater management acceptance pertained to the appointment of union observers to the wage survey. Representative of this arrangement was the following stipulation in the Philadelphia Naval Supply Depot accord:

"[W]hen the wage data and related recommendations are being reviewed by the Food Services Board, . . . the Union shall designate an observer to be present and to make further oral and/or written presentations for consideration by the board." [30]

Very often, detailed provisions were set forth governing the appointment and conduct of union observers.[31] Although observers do not have the power of data collectors, they do constitute a means for presenting union views. Some contracts provided that the "kick-off" meeting of the wage survey could be attended by a union representative.[32]

A most effective means of influencing wage surveys is to help decide which companies and position titles are to be investigated. Obviously, the selection of firms with high pay rates set by collective bargaining agreements in surrounding industry means that wage findings for comparable jobs will be commensurately high. Even though the exact wording might vary, most blue-collar survey clauses contained provisions for the consideration of, but not necessarily the acceptance of, union-suggested firms.[33]

One IAM agreement spoke in the broadest terms of union recommendations:

"The Employer will forward promptly to the Area Wage Survey Committee any request submitted by the Union for the addition and/or deletion of industry firms to be surveyed, the addition and/or deletion of job ratings to be surveyed and the expansion or contraction of the area to be surveyed." [34]

---

[29] Ibid., Sec. 3.

[30] U.S. Department of the Navy, Negotiated Agreement, between Naval Supply Depot, Phila., Pa., and Laborers' Local 1041, December 20, 1965, Art. XV, Sec. 3.

[31] U.S. Department of the Navy, Negotiated Agreement, between Naval Air Turbine Test Station, Trenton, N.J., and IAM Lodge 176, April 1, 1965, Art. XXII, Sec. 4.

[32] U.S. Veterans' Administration, Basic Agreement, between VA Center, Reno, Nev., and Lodge 176, April 1, 1965, Art. XIV, Sec. C.

[33] Ibid., Art. 14, Sec. D.

[34] U.S. Department of the Navy, Agreement, between Navy Marine Engineering Laboratory, Annapolis, Md., and IAM Lodge 174, March 7, 1966, Art. X, Sec. 2.

However, nothing definite was promised except, as in the Philadelphia Naval Supply Depot accord, that the employer would consider the inclusion of the union-submitted firms and the union's recommendations concerning the adjustment of pay rates for individual occupations.[35]

It should be noted that in none of the cited agreements did management relinquish final authority over the specific selection of firms, positions, and areas to be covered. Its prerogatives in the general conduct of the wage survey remained unimpaired.

Many wage-survey clauses also contained provisions for union review and appeal of the survey committee's findings. This essentially confirmed existing practices in most wage-board systems. Thus, the Huntsville NASA Center agreed that upon completion of the survey the leading management representative on the survey board was to consult with the union representatives to review the results.[36] More precise language was to be found in contracts written by the Lithographers. For example, their Defense Printing Service accord forthrightly states: "The Union reserves the right, however, to appeal the findings of the Interdepartmental Lithographic Wage Board in the event the Union feels there has been an error in compiling or in the collection of the data."[37]

Formal contract and actual practice can be and often are two entirely different matters. The maxim that a law is only as good as its administration has its counterpart here. It is evident that the cited contract provisions left unions with the powers of suggestion, recommendation, and consultation but without any substantial and formal power for influencing the wage survey. Yet in fact they may not have been totally without power. The granting of effective participation must ultimately rest with management. If the agency adopted a cooperative attitude toward acceptance of union views in the survey, the existing contracts provided sufficient channels for the presentation, consideration, and discretionary acceptance of union submissions. Under such an administration the survey became to a large extent a mutual undertaking. If management sought to retain complete control over the ultimate conduct of the survey, there was little in the contracts to prevent it. Thus, it was up to the agency whether administration of per-

---

[35] U.S. Department of the Navy, *Negotiated Agreement,* between Naval Supply Depot, Philadelphia, Pa., and Laborers' Local 1041, December 20, 1965, Art. XV, Sec. 2.

[36] NASA, *Agreement,* between George C. Marshall Space Flight Center, Huntsville, Ala., and AFGE Lodge 1858, November 4, 1965, Art. XXII, Sec. 4.

[37] U.S. Department of Defense, *Agreement,* between Defense Printing Service, Wash., D.C., and Lithographers Local 98-L, May 17, 1966, Art. VIII, Sec. 2.

haps the most basic issue—the setting of wages—was to be a mutual decision or essentially unilateral.

C. DISCONTENT OVER WAGE ADMINISTRATION

Both management and labor were dissatisfied with existing wage-board practices. Certain glaring inequities in the system kept the issue of realistic prevailing-rate measures before the Post Office and Civil Service Committees of both houses. Wage disparities refuting the concept of equal pay for equal work were well known to the Civil Service Commission and the Bureau of the Budget. However, it was the concern of the federal blue-collar worker and his union representatives, affiliated and independent alike, that led to greater reform. Protecting their various interests, which were based upon their relative strength in the major blue-collar agencies, certain unions disagreed over the best machinery to bring about the desired changes.

Above all, there can be little doubt that the unions' sense of frustration was heightened by their failure to advance in pay matters, while gaining diverse and substantial concessions in other major areas under the EMC program. In the absence of collective bargaining over wages, the traditional blue-collar unions strove to develop as close an approximation as possible of private-sector wage scales by means of wage-survey participation. In agencies where cooperative management had helped maintain an agreeable *modus vivendi,* unions believed that they had achieved an effective form of representation comparable to collective bargaining in the private sector. However, this was not enough. B. A. Gritta of the Metal Trades Department reflected the views of the established crafts when he stated at the 1965 convention that:

> "We vigorously contended that participation in wage surveys and in the determination of wage rates should properly fall within the scope of the bargaining rights of the labor organizations which federal workers designate as their exclusive bargaining representatives."[38]

Much that had happened under the Kennedy order underlay labor's insistence on participation guarantees. As has been pointed out, essential unilateral management control was never really relinquished. Indeed, certain management officials were concerned about any trend toward "excessive" union participation in wage setting. This fear was expressed, to a degree, in re-

---

[38] B. A. Gritta, *President's Report,* Proceedings of the 52nd Convention, Metal Trades Department, AFL-CIO, San Francisco, December 6, 1965, p. 27.

trenchment by management. Such action was entirely possible as a matter of executive discretion, for the Kennedy order added no new limitations to the wage-board system.

Some blue-collar unions had achieved a certain degree of participation prior to the order. Relatively expert in contract writing, they were sometimes successful in achieving their objectives in the first contracts written under the program. However, it was the perception of some union officials that an initially cooperative attitude on the part of management was soon replaced with a hard-nosed determination to give nothing away.[39]

One instance of management discretion in the pay area was found in a contract change on wage-survey participation. Among the first agreements the International Association of Machinists signed was one which it considered to be among the best in the early months of the program. The agreement was arrived at between IAM Lodge 830 and the Naval Ordnance Plant in Louisville, Ky., in December 1962. It provided, in addition to the usual rights to request and review notice of pending surveys, that the union was to submit a list of names of employees in the bargaining unit for use by the employer in conducting the wage survey. Of those selected from the list by both parties, the Navy was to choose one employee to serve as a member of the area wage subcommittee and another to serve as an alternate. Even more sweeping was the agreement to select from the remaining names at least 50 percent of the total number of data collectors and a reasonable number to be trained as alternates.[40] The union thus was actually to have a voting member on the wage board. This agreement embodied much of the practice that had been built up over the years at the installation.[41]

Indicating a more conservative management approach, the second agreement entered into by the same parties about a year later removed the clauses for extensive union participation. Prompted by provisions in the Naval Civilian Personnel Instructions, the Office of Industrial Relations amended the existing contract to provide only for a union list of observers without voting power. As to Area Wage Survey Committee members and data collectors, the second accord clearly stated that they would "be se-

---

39 Interview with William H. Ryan, president of District 44, IAM, and Leo C. Sammon, business representative, Washington, July 28, 1964.

40 U.S. Department of the Navy, *Basic Agreement*, between Naval Ordnance Plant, Louisville, Ky., and IAM Lodge 830, AFL-CIO, December 20, 1962, Article VII.

41 Interview with William Ryan, *op. cit.*

lected on the basis of their qualifications to assist in collecting local wage data without reference to affiliation or nonaffiliation with any organization." [42] This complied fully with Navy instructions. However, because of the "new relationship between management and employee organizations" deriving from the concept of exclusive recognition, the Navy instructions were modified "to permit and to encourage granting an exclusively recognized employee organization the right to nominate the activity's observer on an Area Wage Survey Committee." [43] Even the appointment of a union observer was made to depend, in part, upon the proportion of wage-board employees in the activity the union represented.[44] This did not apply to survey committee members or data collectors. The degree of collective participation in the wage issue was thus clearly a matter of executive discretion.

The experience of the National Maritime Union combined a lack of participation with glaring pay disparities. The NMU, limited in matters closest to the workers, also felt the lack of "real" collective bargaining since it could not negotiate in its usual way. It charged that, on occasion, the Army-Air Force Wage Board would refuse to listen to union comments, complaints, or the NMU's own statistical findings—that, in essence, union members could not participate on this board. Less vehemence was expressed about the Navy procedures governing the Military Sea Transportation Service.

At some agencies the NMU conducted its own wage surveys and found rates to be below even those paid by certain other federal employers. Unable to negotiate, the union claimed that its threat publicly to expose substandard wages and poor wage calculations was the cause of substantial pay increases in the Corps of Engineers and Coast and Geodetic Survey. However, the NMU lamented that this was not the proper way to get things done. Its officers much preferred the tried procedures of collective bargaining.[45]

The NMU found that existing wage-board practices created serious pay inequities, often in contiguous areas. One such instance occurred for vessels operating on the Mississippi River. Sal-

---

[42] U.S. Department of the Navy, *Basic Agreement,* between Naval Ordnance Plant, Louisville, Ky., and IAM Lodge 830, AFL-CIO, February 13, 1964, Article VII.

[43] U.S. Department of the Navy, Office of Industrial Relations, *Analysis of Negotiated Agreements,* OIR Notice #12721, December 18, 1963, Sec. 3 (b) (3).

[44] *Ibid.*

[45] Interview with Peter Bocker, Vice-President, and Shannon Wall, Secretary-Treasurer, National Maritime Union, New York, July 8, 1965. (Wall became president of the NMU in 1972.)

aries based on surveys that included Arkansas were lower than those paid workers across the river in Tennessee. Thus the government, it was held, could take advantage of lower wages in favorable labor markets. On another occasion, the transfer of a dredge from the Great Lakes region to the Galveston, Texas, Corps of Engineers operations during the winter months resulted in pay differentials among unlicensed marine personnel.[46]

Government as well as labor was well aware of discrepancies such as those just described and their debilitating effect on efficiency and morale. Characterizing pay inequities in 1968, CSC Chairman John W. Macy, Jr., said:

> "Today there are approximately 800,000 wage employees of more than 50 agencies in well over 300 separately identified localities. They have been paid under a veritable hodge-podge of widely differing agency policies which have resulted in baffling differences in pay for people doing identical work in the same wage area.
> "Thus, the so-called 'wage board system' has been up to now, not one but a great many different systems.
> "A janitor working for one agency in one city was being paid $2.40 an hour—and his counterpart, working for another agency in the same city was getting $1.61. A difference of 79 cents an hour, of $31.60 a week, of $1,643 a year." [47]

The CSC, accordingly, engaged in corrective action. Elements in the Bureau of the Budget and Civil Service Commission considered revising prevailing wage-board practices. Meanwhile, legislative proposals were advanced in Congress. At this point, serious differences arose among the unions.

D. THE COORDINATED FEDERAL WAGE SYSTEM

1. Labor and Management Positions on Administrative Reform

General unions such as the American Federation of Government Employees and the National Federation of Federal Employees supported the idea of a central wage board. These organizations, having embarked on a new and militant campaign of representing blue-collar workers and counting among their membership many lesser skilled personnel, believed that the existing wage practices helped the established craft unions. The AFGE, preferring the congressional route over the executive, submitted bills in consecutive years calling for a five-man Federal Departmental Wage Board appointed by the Secretary of Labor. The

---

46 *Ibid.*
47 John W. Macy, Jr., "Coordination Comes to the Wage System," *Civil Service Journal,* Vol. 8, January-March 1968, p. 3.

Board would include two members representing employee organizations with substantial federal membership. It would also establish a Wage Review Committee to adjudicate appeals from disputes that arose in the field. The AFGE also called for an Employee Advisory Committee of 11 members, three of whom would be chosen from among nonsupervisory employees. Bona fide organizations would nominate four members as their representatives. Essentially, the bills called for greater union representation in a new wage system applying uniform and consistent standards to pay and position classification in all departments and agencies.[48]

The IAM and the Metal Trades Department, however, did not favor drastic changes. When William H. Ryan testified before the House Subcommittee on Compensation about the IAM's views on Administration pay proposals, he sought to remove the consideration of wage-board practice from any review of federal pay systems. Maintaining the soundness of existing arrangements, he stated that the encouragement of a "central wage fixing authority for blue collar workers" would be "fraught with cumbersome procedures and delays, and not immediately responsive to the changing needs of the agencies." [49]

President Gritta of the Metal Trades Department took a similar position at the union's 1965 Convention:

> "We went on record as opposing any efforts by the Administration through the Bureau of the Budget and the Civil Service Commission or other agencies to emasculate effective collective bargaining through the destruction of our rights to effectively participate in wage surveys and to further remove wage determinations from the bargaining table through the use of a single wage survey and central wage board system." [50]

It was apparent that diverse claims in favor of the central board or the status quo were defended essentially upon similar arguments of greater union participation and more collective bargaining.

In response to President Johnson's request for union consultation on possible revisions, these two basic demands remained the unanimous position of the AFL-CIO's Committee on Wage De-

---

[48] U.S. House of Representatives, Committee on Post Office and Civil Service, 89th Cong., 2nd Sess., H.R. 16302, "Wage Board Rate Determination and Adjustment Act of 1966," introduced by Mr. Flynt, July 18, 1966. Titles III, IV, V. An almost identical bill was introduced in 1965.

[49] Statement of William H. Ryan, reported in, Government Employee Relations Report, No. 93 (1965), p. A-3.

[50] B. A. Gritta, op. cit., p. 27.

termination. Its statement to the Civil Service Commission came out foursquare against legislative or administrative action to set up a central wage board for ungraded employees. The difficulties of total wage-board reform, it believed, might promote hasty determination. However, the essential view of all the unions concerned was expressed in the statement that:

"We believe that any coordination of the wage determination systems should provide for the greatest possible participation of the workers, through their recognized labor organizations and should approach collective bargaining practices in private industry as closely as possible. Therefore, following the letter and spirit of E.O. 10988, including specifically its preamble clause and its Section 15, we believe that any changes in the present methods and procedures for wage determination should clearly establish and promote the basic principles of union participation and collective bargaining at all steps and levels of job classification, wage-survey and wage-setting processes.

"The last AFL-CIO convention on December 13, 1965, unanimously declared its support for the principle of equal pay for equal levels of skill and called for 'true collective bargaining' between unions and federal agencies under the present wage determination systems. The AFL-CIO position is that job classification, wage surveys and wage determinations should properly fall within the scope of the bargaining rights of the labor organizations which federal workers designate as their collective bargaining representatives." [51]

President Johnson formally initiated operations to coordinate federal wage-board activities by issuing two directives on November 16, 1965. First, he reminded the heads of the executive departments and agencies of their differing pay practices and wage rates for the same trades and labor jobs in the same localities. Perturbed by these inequities, he asked that they join together "in the development of common job standards and wage policies and practices which will insure interagency equity in wage rates based upon statistically valid wage surveys." The two guiding principles in this task were to be:

"(1) wages shall be fixed and adjusted from time to time as nearly as is consistent with the public interest in accordance with prevailing rates and

"(2) there shall be equal pay for substantially equal work, and pay distinctions shall be maintained in keeping with work distinctions." [52]

[51] AFL-CIO Statement to Civil Service Commission, March 18, 1966, reported in, *Government Employee Relations Report*, No. 133 (1966), pp. A-7, E-1.

[52] U.S. President Johnson, *Memorandum*, For the Heads of Executive Departments and Agencies on Coordination of Wage Board Activities, November 16, 1965.

There was little innovation in the President's declaration, which restated long-accepted principles of pay theory and practice. However, he did call for consultation with the representatives of employee organizations in the development of a new coordinated system.

In directing collective action to develop a common federal wage system, the President was concerned with the diverse practices governing the 617,000 federal employees whose annual payroll totaled over four billion dollars. The President assigned CSC Chairman Macy the responsibility for leading the collective effort and consulting with the appropriate employee organizations. Macy was to keep the President informed of significant developments and to report on the "corrective actions adopted." [53]

Within two days, an Interagency Advisory Group met to discuss the presidential directive and heard Civil Service Commission representatives on the basic scope, objectives, and direction of the proposed coordination. The CSC moved quickly to solicit the views of the affected agencies, some of which had serious misgivings about aspects of the proposals. Preliminary drafts of guiding policies, which also included the CSC's preferred directions for the new system, were sent to the departments for consideration and comment. [54] Answering departmental reports were received, meetings held, and intensive staff studies and analyses made, whereupon the CSC forwarded copies of its "Proposed Program for Coordinated Federal Wage Administration Applying to Trade, Craft, and Laboring Positions" [55] to the departments. This was done prior to final issuance of the new and presidentially approved Coordinated Federal Wage System on December 1, 1967. [56] After two years of considering union and management views and preparing the system, the program was scheduled to take effect in mid-1968. Implementation was to take two years, on an area-by-area basis, as new wage schedules grounded on full-scale surveys under the system were established. [57]

During the period of preparation extensive union submissions were made to the CSC reflecting the views already described. Ad-

[53] U.S. President Johnson, Memorandum, For Chairman Macy on Coordination of Wage Board Activities, November 16, 1965.

[54] U.S. Civil Service Commission, Bureau of Policies and Standards, *Staff Proposals for Guiding Policy Statements for Development of Coordinated Federal Wage System, September 1, 1966.*

[55] U.S. Civil Service Commission, *Proposed Program for Coordinated Federal Wage Administration Applying to Trade, Craft, and Laboring Positions,* April 1967.

[56] U.S. Civil Service Commission, *Federal Personnel Manual,* Coordinated Federal Wage System, Chap. 532, December 1, 1967.

[57] John W. Macy, *op. cit.,* p. 20.

ministrative action, however, did not lessen the AFGE's reliance upon possible legislation, particularly a new wage-board bill introduced by Senator Monroney. AFGE President Griner claimed that there was no friction between his union and the AFL-CIO, that they agreed upon the same objectives but were simply following different routes. The AFL-CIO spokesman, on the other hand, emphasized the progress made in cooperation with the CSC and the expectation that reform would be brought about administratively far more quickly and effectively.[58]

Certain agencies and departments expressed apprehensions about the alleged salutary effect the changes would have upon existing collective bargaining relationships. The Interior Department had already experienced under the Kennedy order what it considered to be a serious curtailment of its collective bargaining advances. The arbitration of negotiation impasses was viewed as one of the more constructive features of Interior's labor history, yet under the Kennedy order future accords could not include such arbitration. Indeed, it was only upon Interior's insistence on interpreting Section 15 of the order that existing collective bargaining practices were retained.[59] Interior expressed concern that innovations under the new wage program would have the same effect on its institutionalized wage practices.

Negotiated and other specialized pay schedules are of utmost importance to agencies such as the TVA, BPA, and the Alaska Railroad that fix pay through collective bargaining. In the preliminary draft of the CSC's guiding policies submitted for discussion purposes, however, the preferred policy was that:

> "Present agreements between the agencies and employee organizations for wage fixing through collective bargaining . . . would be continued at least for the time being, including negotiation of future wage adjustments for the employees now covered by these agreements. However, no new agreements would be entered into between the agencies and employee organizations which provide for wage fixing through collective bargaining procedures for areas, installations, activities, or groups of employees not now covered by such agreements."[60]

No alternatives were offered for discussion purposes.

Newell B. Terry, Interior's personnel director, believed that such an innovation posed a serious threat to existing practices and the spirit of E.O. 10988. Continuation of existing contracts

---

[58] *Government Employee Relations Report*, No. 207 (1967) , pp. A-5, A-6.
[59] See Chapter XVI.
[60] U.S. Civil Service Commission, *Preliminary Staff Proposals*, September 1, 1966, Sec. X, pp. 9-10.

was mandated by Section 15 of the Kennedy order preserving the renewal and continuation of lawfully negotiated agreements. But Terry was disturbed by the possible prohibition upon future negotiation of such accords. He noted that in 1962 Interior had had 26 labor agreements protected by Section 15. Since then an additional 23 accords had been negotiated that followed accepted Interior practice by "containing procedures for wage-rate fixing under collective bargaining within the principle of prevailing locality rates."[61] Obviously, this ongoing trend could be substantially hindered by new limitations. Terry informed the CSC that:

"In our opinion, the negotiation of wage rates is by far the most important single privilege that a union with exclusive recognition can enjoy under E.O. 10988. We think that privilege should be preserved as an effective means of employee participation in fixing terms and conditions of employment, and that it need not create an inconsistency in the coordination objectives of the Commission."[62]

The foreclosure of new wage negotiations was thought to impair sound employee-management relations. Said Terry:

"There is an obvious injustice and inequity in not allowing additional groups of employees . . . the same rights and privileges for meaningful negotiations on wages that are accorded the pre-existing units. This points up a basic conflict with the primary objective of E.O. 10988.

"Rather than jeopardize the employee-management cooperation program by providing a diminishing role for employee organizations, we think the Commission should undertake to resolve the apparent conflict by providing procedures and guidelines under which unions can play a more significant role in these matters. We think that unions will not, nor do we think they should be satisfied for long with a program which provides for exclusive recognition of their right to represent employees and then limits them to negotiate only on the trivia of their relationship with management."[63]

In defense of collective bargaining on pay scales, agencies such as Interior received strong support from the AFL-CIO. In March 1967 the AFL-CIO specifically called for the retention and continuation of wage negotiation practices in such federal activities as the "TVA, Bonneville Power Administration, the Southwestern Power Administration, the Pacific Northwest Power Rate Schedule, the South Atlantic Power Rate Schedule, Department

[61] Letter from Newell B. Terry, director of Personnel, Interior Department, to O. Glenn Stahl, director, Bureau of Policies and Standards, Civil Service Commission, October 3, 1966, pp. 1-2, in Department of Interior, *Personnel Management Bulletin,* No. 66-137 (532), October 10, 1966, p. 2.
[62] *Ibid.*
[63] *Ibid.*

of Interior Bureau of Reclamation projects and other Interior Department projects, the Canal Zone Governnment, the Panama Canal Company, the Alaska Railroad and where the Army Corps of Engineers has established a practice of setting rates based upon private utility company rates." [64] It called also for the retention of collective bargaining practices for workers in the Government Printing Office, as provided by the Kiess Act, and for the craft and skilled employees in the Treasury's Bureau of Engraving and Printing whose wages were administratively based upon GPO wages. All other wage-board employees of the Bureau were to be covered by the new system. To be excluded were those special trades, crafts, and occupations where law or industry and past agency practice created special circumstances calling for separate schedules.[65] The AFL-CIO believed these practices approximated "as closely as possible the collective bargaining rights enjoyed by workers in private industry" and were "in line with the letter and spirit of E.O. 10988." [66]

CSC's revised proposed program of April 1967 gave no ground, still insisting that no new agreements providing for collective bargaining be written. It proposed that only existing agreements be continued "until the whole matter of negotiated schedules can be fully studied after the common system is in full operation." [67] To this Interior replied:

> "We agree with the decision to exclude negotiated wage schedules from the coordinated program 'at least for the time being.' We are, however, deeply concerned over the predetermination that no new agreements may be entered into . . . The study proposed by the Commission may be years in the making. To preclude new contracts until the study is completed is, in effect, prejudging the practice. We recommend that agencies which are now negotiating wage rates with employee organizations be authorized to continue the practice as an exclusion from the unified program until the study is completed and all factors considered in terms of the concept of E.O. 10988." [68]

The action finally taken under the new program reflected several possible attitudes. First, it evidenced a willingness in the CSC to allow for the apprehensions of established labor and manage-

---

[64] AFL-CIO, *Statement, Wage Board Conduct of Locality Wage Surveys*, March 21, 1967, Appendix A, p. 8.

[65] *Ibid.*

[66] *Ibid.*

[67] U.S. Civil Service Commission, *Proposed Program for Coordinated Federal Wage Administration*, April 1967, Section II, pp. 14-15.

[68] U.S. Department of the Interior, Report to Civil Service Commission on Revised Politics, *Personnel Management Bulletin*, No. 67-116 (532), June 12, 1967, Sec. I, p. 1.

ment bodies. Second, it reflected a readiness to permit existing practices to continue, at least to a degree. As stated by the CSC:

> "Nothing in the Coordinated Federal Wage System restricts any independent agency or agency subdivision within a governmental department which engages in collective bargaining in connection with wage fixing from continuing such practices until such time as an opportunity is presented to the National Wage Policy Committee for consideration and recommendation." [69]

Macy viewed this decision as not inconsistent with the major objectives of the program. The Commission was primarily concerned with establishing common wage schedules, that is, the "regular" schedules covering most wage-board workers, which were now also to include laundry, food service, and custodial employees. With initial efforts thus concentrated, the special and negotiated systems would be studied individually only after the general system had been established.[70] As Macy noted, "these excepted categories seldom cause interagency differences." [71]

In addition, there was no inconsistency about collective bargaining. The new system was a form of general application of aspects of the negotiated systems. Differences between them were essentially in comparative pay levels. Exclusion, in essence, amounted to preserving established collective bargaining where labor-management relations had become an important agency institution.

2. Union Participation

In its final form, the new Coordinated Federal Wage System covered all wage-board employees in the executive agencies. This included most trades, crafts, and labor employees outside the postal field service. Certain agencies not in the executive branch were encouraged to adopt the new system to the degree that it was consistent with their blue-collar pay policies. These included the Government Printing Office, the Library of Congress, the Administrative Office of the United States Courts, the District of Columbia Government, the Botanic Garden, and the Capitol Architect's Office. Totally excluded were those agencies exempt by statute from the general classification and pay law. These were the TVA, the Alaska Railroad, the Virgin Islands

---

[69] U.S. Civil Service Commission, Coordinated Federal Wage System, *Federal Personnel Manual*, Chap. 532, Subchap. 2-4.

[70] U.S. Civil Service Commission, *Proposed Program*, April 1967, p. 1.

[71] John W. Macy, Jr., *op. cit.*, p. 6.

Corporation, the Atomic Energy Commission, the Central Intelligence Agency, the National Security Agency, and the Panama Canal Company.[72]

As has been noted, implementation was to be delayed for the agencies with advanced collective bargaining. It was also decided to continue certain existing special pay schedules possessing unusual characteristics which militated against inclusion in the regular pay plan. These special pay schedules involved activities long identified with particular private industries. They were the special schedules governing the printing and lithographic trades, motion picture production, officers and crew members of vessels and floating plants, hydroelectric power plants, radio broadcasting, communications and piece rates. Their inclusion was also to be delayed pending further study and separate decision until such time as the newly established National Wage Policy Committee could consider them and make recommendations.[73]

The Coordinated Federal Wage System retains final authority for administering pay in the government, an authority exercised by both the Civil Service Commission and the operating agencies. Nevertheless, to conform with the stated objectives of the program, a substantial degree of union participation in decision making and in its functional operations has been written into the system. The new structure generally has been praised by union leaders, particularly President Meany of the AFL-CIO.

On the national government-wide level, the Civil Service Commission provides the leadership for establishing and operating the system. It is the chairman who, after proper consultation, determines the basic policies, practices, and procedures of the program. Among its many staff and operating functions, the CSC must define the boundaries of the individual local wage areas. It also designates the lead agency which, as the major local employer of wage-board workers, will have the primary responsibility for the wage surveys, data analyses, and pay schedules for each specific wage area. The Commission must set the requirements for the design and accomplishment of wage surveys and pay schedules. It must establish occupational groupings and a job-grading system with appropriate standards. A system for employee job-grading appeals must be provided along with rules governing pay administration for individual workers who are, for example, appointed, transferred, promoted, or demoted. The Commission

---

[72] U.S. Civil Service Commission, *Federal Personnel Manual*, Chap. 532, Subchap. 1-3 (d) ; Subchap. 2-1.

[73] *Ibid.*, Chap. 532, Subchaps. 2-2, 2-3, 2-4.

is charged with authorizing additional pay for work under severe or hazardous conditions. Most important, it can authorize special rates or schedules when competitive factors prevailing make this necessary to retain qualified personnel. Finally, the CSC conducts the audits and inspections necessary to insure full compliance, and generally endeavors to keep the system abreast of wage developments in the private and public sectors.[74]

The unified system of wage administration with its high degree of joint union-management action is seen to best advantage by examining its organizational structure and survey operations. At the government-wide level, a National Wage Policy Committee consisting of 11 members was established. Five management members from among those federal departments and agencies that employ large numbers of wage-board employees were appointed by Chairman Macy.[75] All were top-ranking officials in charge of civilian personnel. Four members, overwhelmingly representing the views of the established crafts, were designated by AFL-CIO President Meany.[76] Not appointed initially was AFGE President Griner. It is a fair inference that his omission was attributable to AFGE's industrial-union approach and its position on the projected wage-board machinery, but in any case Griner was appointed by Meany soon thereafter to fill a vacancy.

In addition, Macy was charged with selecting, on a rotating basis, one independent employee organization to designate the fifth labor member. He chose the National Association of Government Employees, which named Manuel Donabedian, its national vice president. NAGE's blue-collar membership in exclusive units was more than 12,000 greater than that of any other independent. Finally, Macy selected Wilfred V. Gill, his own assistant, as the chairman. All appointees serve at the discretion of their respective designating authorities, who in turn are responsible for their salaries.[77]

The main purpose of the National Wage Policy Committee is to consider new or revised basic policies and procedures for the system and to make recommendations to the CSC chairman. The

---

[74] *Ibid.*, Chap. 532, Subchaps. 3-1 (a) , 4-3 (a) (b) .

[75] Carl W. Clewlow, Department of Defense; Francis C. Hadro, Veterans' Administration; Robert H. Huddleston, General Services Administration; Charles F. Mullaly, Department of the Army; and Robert H. Willey, Department of the Navy.

[76] B. A. Gritta, Metal Trades Department; George J. Knaly, International Brotherhood of Electrical Workers; William H. Ryan, International Association of Machinists; and Andrew J. Biemiller, AFL-CIO Legislative Director.

[77] U.S. Civil Service Commission, *Federal Personnel Manual*, Chap. 532, Subchap. 3-1 (b) . Also, Metal Trades Department, "National Wage Policy Committee," *Pamphlet*, 1968, p. 24.

Committee fulfills the need for obtaining the views of both unions and agencies on a continuing basis. It was envisioned as a chairman's advisory committee that would study and present its views on possible policy changes in the coordinated program. As such it satisfied union desires to be heard at the highest levels. Although it was scheduled to meet at the call of its chairman from time to time, any member could request a meeting at any time to consider policy matters.

It is at the agency level, mainly, that the objective of regional wage coordination is served. The heads of each federal department and agency still have ultimate authority to fix the pay of their wage-board employees. However, the Civil Service Commission, having delineated the local wage areas, designates a lead agency for each area, generally its largest blue-collar employer. The lead agency then has full responsibility to administer the local wage surveys and fix the pay schedules for all agencies in the effected area. Collaboration with the Bureau of Labor Statistics is required in areas where the latter already conducts surveys, thus avoiding duplication of effort, particularly on employer contacts. Upon completion of a survey, all other agencies are supplied copies of the lead-agency wage rates for their individual application. All requirements of the Coordinated Federal Wage System must be adhered to throughout the survey process.[78]

Union-management cooperation is provided at this level by Agency Wage Committees. Every federal unit designated as a lead agency is called upon to establish an Agency Wage Committee of five members. Two labor members are selected by the head of the union with the largest number of wage-board workers under exclusive recognition in the lead agency. The union has this authority for a minimum of two years. The head of the lead agency appoints both the Committee chairman and its two management members. Although this follows the committee pattern and appears to weight decisions in favor of management, union participation at least has official sanction and the potential for influencing the decisions of the agency head is there.[79]

Agency Wage Committees advise the lead agency on local survey procedures. With Local Wage Survey Committees, they select the areas in which they desire to participate in planning and reviewing full-scale surveys and recommending wage schedules. For such local areas, the Committee makes recommendations

---

[78] U.S. Civil Service Commission, *Federal Personnel Manual,* Chap. 532, Subchap. 3-2 (a) .
[79] *Ibid.,* Subchap. 3-2 (b) (1) .

to the lead agency when the latter does not choose to accept the recommendations of the Local Wage Survey Committee. When the Local Wage Survey Committee has completed its work, the Agency Wage Committee considers the survey data and the Local Committee's report, recommendations, analyses, and proposed schedules, including any minority report filed by a labor member. It then submits recommended wage schedules to the pay-fixing authority. A majority Committee vote carries. However, minority members may file reports with the Committee recommendations.[80]

At the local level, each federal installation, under agency headquarters direction, has the ultimate responsibility of setting the category, titles, and codes for its wage-board jobs and of seeing that its wage-board employees are properly paid. Under the new system if a unit is designated by the lead agency as the host installation, it must also supply the support facilities and clerical assistance for the Local Wage Survey Committee. All federal units in the wage area are required to cooperate in providing the necessary members and data collectors for the local committee.[81]

In the last analysis, it is the Local Wage Survey Committee that is primarily responsible for the depth survey work. During the program's preparatory stages, a larger role was envisaged for the Bureau of Labor Statistics in the survey process. In its final form, however, the system's provisions speak mainly of "collaboration" with the BLS, a point which will be discussed later. Local Wage Survey Committees are established for every wage area where there are 400 or more wage-board workers and the total number of such employees in exclusive units in all activities in the area is equal to 10 percent or more of the number of wage-board personnel in the largest such local employer, with a minimum of 150 workers. Each such committee has three members. One member is appointed by the lead agency in the area. The labor member is appointed by his employing agency, but only after the union with the largest number of local wage-board personnel in exclusive units recommends him. The same agency and union must provide these members for a minimum period of two years, which is equivalent to the wage-determination cycle; and no change may be made while a survey is going on. The chairman is appointed by the lead agency. All members receive their regular pay while engaged in committee activities.[82]

---

[80] *Ibid.*, Subchap. 3-2 (b) (2) .
[81] *Ibid.*, Subchap. 3-3 (a) .
[82] *Ibid.*, Subchap. 3-3 (b) (1) .

The primary function of the Local Wage Survey Committee is to gather the required wage data and forward it to the proper authorities. Once a survey is completed, the committee submits the data to the lead agency for analysis and refers it to the Agency Wage Committee where appropriate. Along with the comparative wage findings, it also forwards to the lead agency a narrative report of its activities, decisions, and recommendations in respect to submissions presented to it by interested parties. The report also includes the reasons upon which decisions and recommendations were based.

The committee is responsible for conducting hearings at which information and recommendations may be presented by labor unions and other concerned groups. It is charged with fixing the number of data collectors needed and providing for their necessary training and supervision. When differences arise among data collectors over the comparability of job matches, discriminatory rates, or administration of the policies and procedures in the manual, the committee makes its decision and refers its recommendations to the lead agency. The committee makes the preliminary employer contacts unless this has already been done in the course of regular BLS analyses in a particular wage area.[83]

The use of the Bureau of Labor Statistics in the coordinated program appears to have undergone a metamorphosis. Union desires for direct employee participation with management in the wage process and not with another federal agency such as the BLS may have contributed to this change. The proposed program of the Civil Service Commission in April 1967 spoke in terms of appointing a "wage survey agent" for each wage area to carry out the surveys. The survey agent was to be responsible for the design and accomplishment of statistically valid wage surveys in accordance with prescribed procedures.[84] A major role for the BLS was foreseen, and logically so, since it was widely engaged under existing agency wage programs in such surveys. As envisioned by CSC:

> "The ultimate objective is to utilize BLS as the survey agent in as many areas as possible under the coordinated federal wage program. However, pending development of standard procedures to provide for employee participation that is both meaningful and consistent with the objectives of the program, the kind of employee participation in wage surveys continues to be governed by policies and practices of the individual agencies. . . ." [85]

---

[83] *Ibid.*, Subchap. 3-3 (b) (2) .
[84] U.S. Civil Service Commission, *Proposed Program,* April 1967, Sec. V, p. 22.
[85] *Ibid.*

The CSC described an extensive experimental plan under which employees, as members of local wage-survey advisory groups, would work with the BLS as survey agents throughout the data-gathering process. These procedures were to be tested over a two-year period in areas where the BLS already conducted surveys. The intent was to achieve an orderly expansion of the BLS survey role, and only in areas where this was not feasible would a lead agency be designated as a wage-survey agent.[86]

In the new wage system's final form the reference to official "wage survey agents" was deleted. Instead, there was merely a call for coordination with the BLS in areas where it was engaged in wage operations. This cooperation takes the form primarily of joint visits to employers by committee and BLS data collectors. Contacts and arrangements are made by the BLS. During the collection, the BLS records the data; however, the committee representative transcribes the data to committee forms. Attempts are made to reconcile differences over job comparability that arise between the two. However, it is the committee representative who reports the wage data and any unresolved differences to the committee.[87] It is possible that eventually the BLS will play a greater role in the program. There is much to be said for such a development in terms of increasing expertise, eliminating duplication of effort, and promoting uniformity. However, any such innovation will have to be accompanied by safeguards for continuing union participation if the objectives of the program are to be met.

The new system more than amply incorporated provisions for union participation in the collection process. Whereas procedures under the Kennedy order had failed to provide for union-chosen committee members, data collectors, observers, and alternates uniformly at all blue-collar installations, the new system made such participation official. In this regard, once the Local Wage Survey Committee has determined the number of necessary data collectors, half of them are selected from a list of federal workers recommended by the qualifying labor union, and the other half are chosen from among employees recommended by local federal activities.[88] This procedure actually provides more stability than suggested by the AFL-CIO, although perhaps it is less representative. The AFL-CIO recommended that only 50 percent of the

---

[86] Ibid., pp. 22-23 and Appendix C, pp. 1-7.
[87] U.S. Civil Service Commission, Federal Personnel Manual, Chap. 532, Subchap. 5-2 (c).
[88] Ibid., Subchaps. 3-3(b)(2), 5-3(e)(1).

labor data collectors be recommended by the union with the largest number of wage-board employees in exclusives, with the remaining 50 percent of the labor data collectors chosen from among the other organizations holding exclusive recognition.[89] No such distinction was drawn in the CSC's final directions.

Specific criteria are provided for choosing data collectors. Participants must be knowledgeable in matters of occupational job content and federal wage administration, objective, unprejudiced, and open-minded. Also needed is the ability to communicate and maintain good relations, along with the balance and maturity necessary to deal with private industrial executives as equals. Survey data are to be kept secret, and both unions and management are called upon to cooperate in imposing discipline for improper disclosure.[90]

The satisfaction of the AFL-CIO and most affiliated unions with the organization of the new structure is understandable. They had suggested other plans but were fairly well satisfied with the format and functions the provision made for union participation in the wage process. They would have preferred that the chairmen of the committees at all three levels be chosen jointly and not by management alone.[91] This might have resulted in neutral participants' holding the swing vote but would also have been in conflict with the program's intent to retain pay authority under management control.

In their final form, the wage schedules and job-grading system of the new program retained much that was deemed appropriate in the old agency systems. The intent of the CSC was more than the elimination of agency differences in pay schedules and grading structures. The principle of a common pay system is best served by endeavoring to pay the largest possible number of employees from the same regular pay schedules. Special schedules, it was felt, should be restricted to those instances required by law or prior practice, or where absolutely necessary to hire and retain qualified workers in a competitive market. The CSC sought simplicity, uniformity, and comprehensive application. It believed the continuation of pay practices followed by most agencies would reduce the difficulties of conversion by minimizing change.[92]

---

[89] AFL-CIO, *Statement, Wage Board Conduct, op. cit.,* p. 7.

[90] U.S. Civil Service Commission, *Federal Personnel Manual,* Chap. 532, Subchaps. 3-3 (b) (2), 5-3 (e) (2) .

[91] AFL-CIO, *op. cit.,* pp. 1, 3, 5.

[92] U.S. Civil Service Commission, *Proposed Program,* April 1967, p. 11.

Three regular schedules were, therefore, established, a nonsupervisory schedule, a supervisory schedule, and a leader schedule. The regular nonsupervisory schedule, covering the largest number of blue-collar workers, consisted of 15 grade levels, and was the pay structure already applicable to the majority of employees paid under the Army-Air Force system.[93]

The coordinated system provides for equal gradations of skill and pay ranges for each of the grade levels, though variations may be necessary to conform to particular local industrial wage patterns. All three schedules are provided with three step rates of pay for each grade. The middle or second step is based upon the prevailing-rate pay line, while the first and third step rates are 4 percent below and above the second rate, respectively. Other alternatives considered ranged from a 5-percent step interval to the single prevailing-rate system for each grade used in the Interior Department. Under the new system, employees are hired at the first rate and advanced automatically, upon satisfactory work performance, to the second rate after 26 weeks. After 78 weeks of creditable service at the second rate, they are advanced to the final pay rate. Each regular wage schedule also contains separately stated night-shift differentials based upon the prevailing rates paid by local industry.[94]

Regular leader schedules of 15 grades and supervisory schedules of 17 grades were established with grade structures similar to those used in the Army and Air Force Departments. Leader and supervisory schedules were initially to be determined by means of established formulas providing specified pay differentials above the rates of nonsupervisory personnel. It was stated that these formulas, when used in conjunction with separate leader and supervisory grading plans and structures, would provide rates comparable to their counterparts in private industry.[95] However, it was also made clear when the system was introduced that the leader and supervisory schedules were temporary. The Commission and Defense Department, it was pointed out, were engaged in a comprehensive study of pay and evaluation practices for similar groups in private industry, which, when finished, would serve as a basis for review and appropriate modification of the evaluation structures and pay differentials of the supervisory and leader groups.[96]

---

[93] U.S. Civil Service Commission, *Federal Personnel Manual*, Chap. 532, Subchap. 4-2.

[94] *Ibid.*, Subchaps. 4-1, 4-2.

[95] *Ibid.*, Subchap. 4-1 (c).

[96] U.S. Civil Service Commission, *FPM Letter*, No. 532-2, December 1, 1967, pp. 1-2.

Surveys under the program are to be comprehensive and adaptable to particular conditions. As CSC Chairman Macy put it:

> The industrial coverage of regular wage surveys will encompass most manufacturing, transportation, and communications concerns, public utilities, wholesale trade, and real estate operators who both own and maintain office buildings." [97]

In recognition of the increasing competition among governmental employers, the system calls for exceptions to be made in the basic policy of surveying only private establishments. In adapting to these circumstances:

> "State and local governmental activities may be appropriate for inclusion in a regular local wage survey when the area involved has limited private industry employment and a high concentration of such governmental employment exerts a major influence on the overall level of rates prevailing in the local wage area." [98]

Full-scale surveys are to be made every second year, with interim surveys in the alternating years.[99]

In the job-grading system adopted, the Commission's official guides for coding and identifying positions were to be continued for occupational grouping until new occupations were formally established. Bench-mark positions, referred to as key ranking jobs, were selected to measure the relative worth of different lines and levels of work and to control the alignment of grade levels in all job-grading standards. Procedures were established to maintain the currency of the key ranking jobs. Agencies and unions are to consult and cooperate in any special factfinding studies undertaken to change the key ranking jobs. They also are expected to consult extensively with the Commission in its work of developing and revising job-grading standards.[100] A job-grading method similar to that of the Army and Air Force was adopted, except that it was a factor-comparison method without point ratings. Grading is based upon the total job. However, four major factor definitions are used to identify the nature of the position in comparing jobs—skill and knowledge, responsibility, physical effort, and working conditions. There is a separate grading plan for supervisory and leader jobs.[101] Procedures are provided for the appeal of the grade, title, or series assigned to any employee's

---

97 John W. Macy, Jr., *op. cit.*, p. 6.

98 U.S. Civil Service Commission, *Federal Personnel Manual*, Chap. 532, Subchap. 5-3 (c) .

99 *Ibid.*, Subchap. 5-3 (d) .

100 *Ibid.*, Subchaps. 6-2, 6-3, 6-4.

101 *Ibid.*, Subchap. 6-5.

position. The appellant first must exhaust the job-grading appeals machinery established internally by all agencies, after which he may further appeal a negative decision before the Commission for final and binding resolution.[102]

E. THE PAY IMPLICATIONS FOR ALL FEDERAL EMPLOYEES

Macy saw implications in the new coordinated system that transcended the furtherance of union-management pay cooperation. He believed that the designation of a lead agency and local survey committees to determine the pay for all units provided "a new mode for interagency cooperation." [103] As a result of these innovative features, agencies would acquire a greater knowledge of each other's missions and operations within the context of the entire federal personnel program. He also believed that the new system, together with the legislation of 1967 giving full pay comparability to the white-collar workers, marked a new period of executive salary administration:

> "We now have a common base for evaluation and ranking of jobs, both wage system and General Schedule, for the establishment of rates of pay—and a unity of principle in the administration of all Federal pay systems."[104]

For organized labor in the Federal Government—at least wage-board workers—the new system did much to remove the complaint that they were essentially barred from negotiating on the bread-and-butter issue of pay. Prevailing-rate procedures have always been well received by labor at all levels of government. It is a major means by which the benefits of collective bargaining can be projected on the government scene, enabling the "mixed" unions to see the fruits of their private-sector bargaining extended to their government members. Above all, the union participation in the prevailing-rate procedures constitutes an immediate and direct element in the process that is not wholly unlike collective negotiations.

With these benefits have come the obligation for unions and management alike to develop new skills and adopt new attitudes. In this regard, Harry A. Donoian, a perceptive observer of the federal scene, has commented:

> "This participation by the unions puts important responsibilities on their shoulders. They must recruit and train personnel to func-

---

[102] *Ibid.*, Subchap. 7.
[103] John W. Macy, Jr., *op. cit.*, p. 8.
[104] *Ibid.*

tion as data collectors and as local wage survey committee members. They must keep a watchful eye on the development of the area wage schedules. They must provide counsel on how the system can be improved and point out shortcomings in particular instances. The executive agencies and the CSC, on the other hand, must make at least an equal effort to learn how to deal, on the basis of equality, with federal employee unions at all levels of the federal government." [105]

Just as the establishment of the EMC program spurred massive efforts on both sides of the bargaining table to acquire vital negotiating skills, so the new federal wage system has created the need for pay-setting expertise. Federal unions must establish pay research and training units comparable in skill to full-time government bodies concerned with pay and classification.

Establishing the coordinated wage system did not proceed without some difficulty despite the projected time tables for implementation. Unions still found serious shortcomings in the program. There was at least one labor walkout, and criticisms were levelled by unions with particular membership and organizational problems. Federal management, conditioned for years to operating under fixed job standards, grade levels, and data-finding procedures, did not find it easy to adapt. Factors causing delay were organizational inertia and the reluctance of established groups to risk changes in their vested interests.

Congress maintained close scrutiny over federal pay issues. This interest surfaced in the Federal Pay Comparability Act covering white-collar workers and in the blue-collar pay fight of late 1970. Strong evidence of basic union acceptance of the new blue-collar plan appeared in H.R. 17809, which was vetoed by President Nixon on January 1, 1971. This labor-supported legislation, which incorporated certain policies and procedures which were quite similar to the Coordinated Federal Wage System, would have established statutory machinery for setting blue-collar wages.

What the President particularly disliked were the pay increases resulting from a fourth step rate that would have been added to the wage schedules. He believed the existing wage system already possessed the flexibility necessary to insure that wage-board employees received periodic adjustments, and that there was no need for legislation to maintain comparability with private industry. His primary reason for vetoing the bill, however, was that it would provide excessive pay increases. Defending his action,

[105] Harry A. Donoian, "A New Approach to Setting the Pay of Federal Blue Collar Workers," *Monthly Labor Review*, April 1969, p. 34.

which was vigorously protested by unions, the President asserted that federal blue-collar workers' pay was already 4 percent above prevailing rates and that they had received average annual wage increases of 9.5 percent in fiscal 1969 and 8.1 percent in fiscal 1970.[106]

The passage of the Federal Pay Comparability Act [107] in 1971 did not alter the tradition whereby white-collar pay was fixed by Congress. Essentially, the Act carried forward the philosophy of the 1962 legislation. What it did absorb from the blue-collar experience, however, was an increased union input in pay determination for over 1.3 million white-collar workers under the General Schedule. The new pay system did not provide for the degree of union participation enjoyed by wage-board employees. But for white-collar employees this was a major new formalization of their pay input. In addition, many of their union representatives, those who would actually participate in the new system, had freely crossed craft lines and, therefore, had acquired valuable blue-collar experience.

Although the Act incorporated the concept of union participation in fixing white-collar pay, the new system remained essentially one of executive decision-making at the presidential level, with the union function essentially an advisory one. As in the 1962 law, the prime objectives were comparability with private industry and equal pay for equal work. To accomplish these the President was to appoint an "agent" to report annually on comparable salary rates and make recommendations for appropriate adjustments.[108] For 1971 and 1972 the Act specifically named the chairman of the CSC and the director of the Office of Management and Budget to act jointly in the agent capacity.[109] Eventually proposed adjustments would be based on a review of comparative wage surveys of the Bureau of Labor Statistics, primarily its National Survey of Professional, Administrative, Technical, and Clerical Pay.[110]

The agent was empowered to appoint a Federal Employees Pay Council as the major vehicle for union participation. The Council is composed of five members representing substantial numbers of federal employees under the statutory pay systems. Only three Council members may come simultaneously from a single federa-

[106] U.S. Civil Service Commission, Bureau of Policies and Standards, *Operations Letter*, No. 530-3, January 29, 1971.

[107] 84 Stat. 1946 (1971) ; Public Law 91-656.

[108] 84 Stat. 1946; 5 U.S.C. Sec. 5305 (a) (1971) .

[109] 84 Stat. 1952; 5 U.S.C. Sec. 5308 (1971) .

[110] U.S. Civil Service Commission, Bureau of Policies and Standards, *op. cit.*, p. 2.

tion or affiliation of employee organizations.[111] Chairman Hampton and Director Shultz accorded AFL-CIO affiliates three seats. The two remaining seats went to the two independents with the largest white-collar membership, the National Federation of Federal Employees and the National Association of Internal Revenue Employees.[112]

To a degree the Council's input approximates that of the blue-collar workers in several aspects. Both the Council as a whole and its individual members may present views and recommendations on the coverage of the BLS surveys relied upon. Recommendations may be made as to occupations, establishment sizes, industries, and geographic areas used—in short, factors similar to those considered in the Coordinated Federal Wage System. The Council may examine and question the processes used for comparing federal pay rates with their private enterprise counterparts. It may also make recommendations as to the adjustments necessary to achieve comparability. The President's agent is enjoined to meet with the Council and report its views to the President for decision. He is also required to consider and report on the views submitted by any organization not represented on the Council.[113] Obviously, reporting is not equal to deciding. If the union role is substantial and consistent in determining the factors deciding pay adjustments, a form of pay negotiation has been achieved. However, not only is the Employees Pay Council playing essentially an advisory role, but the agent's reporting procedure is subordinate to still another consultative body, the Advisory Committee on Federal Pay, whose members may or may not be from the labor community.

The statutory intent is that the Advisory Committee on Federal Pay be made up of three members selected by the President for "their impartiality, knowledge and experience in the field of labor relations and pay policy." It is a permanent, independent establishment with a chairman and all members eventually serving six-year terms. With support services and an administrative staff of its own, the Advisory Committee is to review the agent's report, gather its own data, and submit its own report to the President, who may then issue a final executive order adjusting pay in the salaried systems. The President, however, can also decide to use a statutory option empowering him to submit his own alternative plan if demanded by national emergency or economic

---

111 84 Stat. 1946; 5 U.S.C. Sec. 5305 (b) (1971).
112 U.S. Civil Service Commission, *News Release,* February 5, 1971.
113 84 Stat. 1947; 5 U.S.C. Sec. 5305 (b) (1971).

conditions. If he believes the general welfare makes it inappropriate to adopt the recommended adjustment, his alternative proposal may be sent to Congress and eventually become effective. If either House should reject his alternative during the first 30 days of continuous session, however, the regular comparability adjustment would become effective.[114] This option procedure was used by President Nixon in connection with his national wage-freeze program.

In terms of its fostering of participative labor relations, the Federal Pay Comparability Act falls short of blue-collar procedures and is hardly comparable with those of the Postal Service. Admittedly, the controlling factors in white-collar pay determination differ. On the one hand, there are no all-powerful "mixed" craft unions of white-collar workers that effectively control a limited supply of highly specialized workers. Such a condition could force a "bargaining-type" prevailing-rate procedure for salaried employees. On the other hand, the impact on the national economy of pay increases for so large a group of employees is so great that a strong argument can be made for keeping such increases discretionary. The result is a system which permits an increased degree of union consultation, but not to an extent that would, for example, deter the unions from going directly to Congress for pay adjustments.

In the TVA and Postal Service white-collar employees achieved equality with their blue-collar co-workers by means of procedures approximating private enterprise pay-determination systems. Under the Coordinated Federal Wage System, the CSC moved in this direction by endeavoring to accommodate the legitimate desires of blue-collar employees as far as possible within the context of an executive personnel system. For the approximately 1.3 million federal employees under the General Schedule and other salary systems, the prospects for such participation in the near future are dim.[115]

---

[114] 84 Stat. 1948; 5 U.S.C. Sec. 5305 (b) (1971).

[115] BLS Bulletin No. 1789, April 1973, reported in its survey of 671 contracts that 10 percent of the accords specifically permitted union requests for interim wage surveys and 28 percent repeated the guarantees of the new federal wage system for union participation. As was to be expected, most such clauses were found in the defense agencies and the VA.

Chapter XX

THE LIMITATIONS ON COLLECTIVE BARGAINING

The Kennedy Task Force and order set fixed boundaries within which the Employee-Management Cooperation program was to operate. These ground rules brooked no departure from the concept of sovereignty. Ultimate responsibility for personnel matters was retained in the executive. In support of this executive authority, the managerial prerogatives specified for the new system, on balance, far exceeded the diminishing managerial privileges of the private sector.

Questions involving managerial prerogatives, departmental approval of local agreements, the permitted scope of negotiations, and the overriding authority of personnel statutes were disturbing to union leaders from the program's inception. These were the limiting aspects of the system which they believed prevented real collective bargaining. Their desire to minimize such restrictions in E.O. 10988 augmented the general sentiment for overall reforms in the entire program.

The restrictive features of the EMC program were discussed by unions and management before the President's Review Committee in 1967, and were included in the Kennedy Task Force report and order because of the inherent separation of functions characteristic of the Federal Government. Both documents expressed concern for fulfilling the missions of government in the public interest and preserving the merit system. Therefore, many features regularly bargained over in private industry, being determined by law, were deemed nonnegotiable. In the final analysis, no changes were permitted in subject areas where Congress had already acted. In addition, no changes were to be effected by negotiation in areas where management was required to act in the public interest. This maintained executive superiority in its appointed sphere within the tripartite system.

A. THE BOUNDARIES FOR COLLECTIVE ACTION UNDER THE KENNEDY PROGRAM

Provisions for maintaining the separation of powers, managerial prerogatives, and the merit system appeared, primarily, in the areas that dealt with exclusive recognition and the scope of permissible consultations and negotiations. No agreement could conflict with laws, regulations, government-wide policies, or congressional authority.[1] The report suggested that each exclusive recognition agreement include a statement specifying that officials and employees involved in the contract's administration were to be governed at all times by the provisions of all applicable federal laws and regulations. These were to include policies set forth in the *Federal Personnel Manual* and in agency regulations, all of which were to be regarded as paramount.[2] A "subject to" clause was then suggested, which was later incorporated in almost every agreement signed under the Kennedy order. It became de rigeur in contract-writing to conform with the Civil Service Commission's recommendations as set forth in the *Federal Personnel Manual*, training institutes, and materials.

The Task Force recommendation on the scope of consultations emphasized the limitations on administrative discretion beyond the legal restrictions described above.[3] It noted that employers in the Federal Government generally cannot negotiate on pay, hours of work, and most fringe benefits since these are fixed by law. It cautioned further that negotiable matters were to be restricted to those lying solely within the executive's administrative discretion—that is, in the authority remaining to the negotiating manager after effect was given to the law, executive orders, and agency policies. It specifically ruled out negotiation of all matters concerning the agency's mission, its budget, its organization, the assignment of personnel, and the technology of performing the agency's work.[4]

Managerial protections were incorporated into Sections 6 (b) and 7 of the Kennedy order. Section 7 satisfied the needs of sovereignty by requiring the approval of the agency head or his representative of all basic or supplemental agreements. It called for a "subject to" clause recognizing the superiority of all existing or future laws, the *Federal Personnel Manual*, and so forth.

---

[1] President's Task Force on Employee-Management Relations in the Federal Service, *Report,* November 30, 1961, Sec. B (3) , p. iv.

[2] *Ibid.,* p. 16.

[3] *Ibid.,* p. v.

[4] Task Force, *op cit.,* pp. 17, 18, and E.O. 10988, Sec. 6 (b) .

In addition, it laid out managerial prerogatives with great particularity.[5] Section 6 (b) described the extent to which executive discretion was to limit the scope of negotiations.[6] As we shall see, the exact wording of these provisions was duplicated in the negotiated accords. Clauses insuring management rights, executive approval, and statutory superiority (Section 7) were included in every agreement in the 1965 BLS study. Clauses setting bargaining areas and executive discretion (Section 6 (b)) were written into four out of five of the contracts studied.[7] The 1973 BLS review disclosed no radical departure from the provisions.[8]

The preservation of managerial prerogatives created discontent among the unions, primarily for two reasons. First, unions contended that the independence of each agency in the program's decentralized administration permitted management to restrict the area of negotiation at the very outset simply by fixing the items of negotiability in advance. This power was guaranteed under Sections 6 (b) and 7. Such actions, it was held, tended to vitiate the program. Some critics declared that "true" collective bargaining would never be attained until the full negotiation of wages, hours, and fringe benefits based on the industrial model was permitted. Second, the unions argued that management conceivably could agree to terms on a particular matter and then renege, overriding the agreement by revising the agency's rules or regulations on the point at issue.

Under the Kennedy order practically all agreements were made subject to laws and regulations. The National Basic Agreements in the old Post Office Department represented a major departure from this practice, however. After including the stock clause required by Section 7 (1), these agreements enunciated the superiority of the earlier National Basic Agreements over the *Postal Manual* by specifically providing that "To the extent provisions of the Postal Manual which are in effect on the effective or renewal date of the agreement are in conflict with this agreement, the provisions of this agreement shall govern." [9]

The 1968 postal agreement went a step further. It reaffirmed the union's right to claim that a management action violated the

---

5 E.O. 10988, Sec. 7 (1), (2).

6 *Ibid.*, Sec. 6 (b).

7 U.S. Department of Labor, Bureau of Labor Statistics, *Collective Bargaining Agreements in the Federal Service—Late Summer 1964*, Bulletin No. 1451, August 1965.

8 ———, *Collective Bargaining Agreements in the Federal Service—Late 1971*, Bulletin No. 1789, April 1973, pp. 10-11.

9 U.S. Post Office Department, *National Basic Agreement*, with the six major postal unions, March 20, 1963, Art. XXVI. Repeated in 1964, 1966, and 1968.

contract even if management promulgated the new regulation after the effective date of the agreement. If the new regulation was determined to be contrary to the agreement, the regulation had to be rescinded within 10 days. Only the personal intervention of the Postmaster General could continue the regulation in effect. Residual authority was thus retained, but the clause remained a powerful protection against arbitrary action.[10]

B. THE LABOR APPROACH TO SCOPE OF NEGOTIATIONS

It became abundantly clear in the 1967 testimony before the Review Committee that five years of experience had wrought little change in basic attitudes. In the main, both management and the unions continued adamant in their traditional approaches. Practically all the unions called for a reduction in the limitations on collective bargaining by an enlargement of the scope of negotiations. On the other hand, the majority of employing agencies stood firm on their rights. They steadfastly maintained that past experience and their continuing executive function militated against any sharing of the responsibility in certain basic areas. Only the TVA, NLRB, and Interior Department expressed views favorable to a reassessment and possible expansion of the scope of bargaining. In their testimony, these agencies relied considerably upon their sophistication in labor relations.

Any widening of the scope of negotiations hinged upon acceptance of change on four major points: the preservation of executive discretion (Section 6 (b)) ; the requirement of departmental contract approval (Section 7) ; the recognition of laws and regulations as paramount (Section 7 (1)) ; and the maintenance of extensive management prerogatives (Section 7 (2)) .

The union position, as stated by George Meany, was developed by a committee of leading labor union officials and was supported by all AFL-CIO unions with a major involvement in the Federal Government.[11] The Committee report formed the basis of Meany's testimony.[12] On the areas at issue the AFL-CIO recommended that, contrary to the limitations of Section 6 (b) , "all matters with respect to personnel policies and practices and

---

10 U.S. Post Office Department, *National Basic Agreement,* with the seven major postal unions, March 9, 1968, Art. XXVI.

11 George Meany, President, AFL-CIO, *Statement* before President's Review Committee, October 23, 1967.

12 AFL-CIO, "Program to Improve Collective Bargaining in the Federal Service," September 28, 1967.

matters affecting working conditions should be negotiable items as long as they are not inconsistent with present and future laws." [13] As officially worded these areas were negotiable "so far as may be appropriate subject to law and policy requirements," [14] present and future.[15]

According to the AFL-CIO, "To achieve genuine collective bargaining it is necessary to widen the scope of collective bargaining and to enlarge the authority of local activity management." [16] In this regard the Federation saw agency policies barring installation managers from negotiating on matters not within their administrative discretion as "perhaps the most stringent curtailment of bilateral collective bargaining." It emphasized that local administrative discretion was fixed by agency regulations that could be unilaterally established, amended, or abolished by the agency. Unions with national exclusive recognition could negotiate to the fullest degree, for at this level the agency head had the executive discretion to revise the personnel manual accordingly. However, this was not the case for the local installation manager, who was subject to regulation changes from above.[17] This disparity was held to be discriminatory. Meany concluded, "It is clear that collective bargaining with the Federal service has not yet become fully accepted. Unfortunately agency regulations do not now leave room enough for genuine bilateral negotiations." [18]

Two proposals for the enlargement of local administrative discretion were therefore submitted. First, Meany recommended that "when agreements are negotiated at the local level satisfactory assurance should be given that those negotiating for the local activity or installation have the necessary authority to negotiate and sign an agreement." [19] Second, the Section 7 requirement of agency approval of negotiated agreements should be abolished. The AFL-CIO considered it most frustrating, to union and local management alike, for an agency head to withhold contract approval after both parties had conducted long and trying negotiations and finally had hammered out an agreement. It believed that contract clauses too often were vetoed by top management not because they were in violation of law or regulation but because

---

13 *Ibid.,* pp. 5-6.
14 E.O. 10988, Sec. 6 (b) .
15 E.O. 10988, Sec. 7 (l) .
16 AFL-CIO, *op. cit.,* p. 6.
17 *Ibid.,* pp. 5, 6.
18 George Meany, *op. cit.,* p. 8.
19 *Ibid.*

the agency, as a matter of policy, disapproved of a specific clause.[20] "By affixing their signatures to the terms of a negotiated agreement," the Federation declared, "the parties have concluded a binding contract. The veto right of 'higher authority' makes a travesty of collective bargaining." [21]

Finally, the AFL-CIO took a forceful stand on the question of management rights. Meany counseled that the last sentence of Section 6 (b) and all of Section 7 (2) be amended "to guarantee the rights of unions to protect the workers they represent." [22] He was careful to differentiate among the specific managerial areas protected in Section 6 (b). Thus, unions were not to be concerned with the mission of an agency, its budget, or its organization since these were not related to personnel policies or working conditions.[23] However, in line with labor policies applied to similar problems in private industry, he remonstrated:

> "[W]e are concerned with the assignment of personnel and the technology of performing work because both matters affect directly the jobs of the employees, particularly of those who are being displaced by automation or other technological changes.

> "We do not deny the right of an agency to assign personnel or to introduce new machines and working processes. But we do want to assure the right of the union to negotiate protections for workers adversely affected by personnel policies, changing technology, and partial or entire closing of an installation." [24]

The AFL-CIO program strongly urged the deletion of the extensive enumeration of management rights in Section 7 (2). It noted that even though most of its provisions were governed by statute and that E.O. 10988's wording was mandatorily to be included in every contract many agreements nevertheless contained provisions governing some of those very items. "There is no reason," it concluded, "why these matters cannot be subject to negotiation within the framework of these laws." [25] Indeed, most accords that included detailed provisions—those pertaining to, among other subjects, promotion, transfer, classification, assignment, demotions, reductions in force, and disciplinary proceedings—indicated a growing union participation in management functions. The AFL-CIO position pointed out that such contract clauses did not take away from management any rights

---

[20] AFL-CIO, *op. cit.,* p. 7.
[21] *Ibid.*
[22] George Meany, *op. cit.,* p. 9.
[23] *Ibid.*
[24] *Ibid.*
[25] AFL-CIO, *op. cit.,* p. 8.

it held according to law. They merely dealt with the application of management's decision "by determining bilaterally how this decision can be carried out fairly and justly, protecting the interests of the employees in the bargaining unit." [26]

C. THE SPECTRUM OF MANAGEMENT ATTITUDES

Unlike most employing agencies, the TVA emphasized that collective bargaining can work only when the management negotiator possesses the actual power to commit his agency. Aubrey Wagner, chairman of the TVA board of directors, pointed out that negotiated changes are reviewed or approved by the TVA Board "only if they are of major policy significance." [27] A team approach insured that management was involved in all commitments. Thus, top management was assisted by persons who, "geographically and functionally, are close enough to all local situations to know what TVA needs in order to effectively perform its work." [28]

The Interior Department was adamant on the need for change. Newell Terry saw nothing in Section 6 (b) to inhibit any federal agency from sharing administrative personnel decisions with unions on a continuing, bilateral basis. Section 7 obviously curtailed "free collective bargaining" in proclaiming the paramount importance of pertinent laws. Terry was in full agreement with this; however, he saw serious defects in the emphasis upon overriding agency regulations and heavily enumerated management prerogatives.[29] He admonished that:

> "With major variations among agencies as to degrees of delegations of authority to management at the bargaining unit levels, we are concerned that the vitality of meaningful negotiations and employee-management cooperation at local installations will be severely drained by the cumulative effect of such restraints." [30]

Terry suggested that one valid approach would be "to encourage a concerted effort in the federal service to refrain from overregulating exact terms and conditions of employment at the headquarters level and to allow greater freedom at local levels to negotiate rules and regulations suitable to the practical operat-

---

[26] *Ibid.*

[27] Aubrey J. Wagner, Chairman, TVA Board of Directors, *Statement,* before President's Review Committee, October 19, 1967, p. 7.

[28] *Ibid.*

[29] Newell B. Terry, Director of Personnel, Interior Department, *Statement,* before President's Review Committee, October 27, 1967, p. 7.

[30] *Ibid.*

ing situations." [31] Field levels could be delegated broader authority so that management bargainers could satisfactorily conclude
agreements. In Interior, he noted, negotiators follow three basic
guidelines. First, items specifically covered by statute are excluded
from negotiation since executives have no discretion as to them.
A second group of issues, also covered by law, nevertheless permits a degree of administrative judgment and is therefore negotiable. Finally, a third group, discretion over which lies
primarily in the hands of management, constitutes the issues and
items for continuing meaningful negotiations. [32] Terry observed
that among many other issues, Interior always had included the
negotiation of wage rates for blue-collar workers in the third
category. He considered such wage negotiation "by far the most
important single privilege that a union with exclusive recognition
can enjoy under Executive Order 10988." [33] He urged a government-wide expansion of the scope of negotiable items, accompanied by a parallel de-emphasis of unilateral personnel management regulation. [34]

The majority of federal executives, however, adhered un-
swervingly to a policy of "no retreat" on managerial prerogatives.
They vigorously opposed any major expansion of the scope of
negotiations. This was forcefully evidenced before the 1967
Review Committee when the Navy spokesman declared "that the
'management rights' clause is so fundamental that any report
covering actions of the Committee should reaffirm the integrity
of these rights." [35] The Air Force cautioned that "These rights
must continue to be emphasized in view of the provisions of some
negotiated agreements which appear to have eroded these management prerogatives." [36] In the same vein was the Army's testimony:

> "There has been a continual clamor from the unions regarding
> the limited scope of negotiations in the federal sector. Our view is
> that there should be *no change in the scope of negotiations* as
> presently described in E. O. 10988. Any desirable changes in the
> scope of negotiations can be made through agency administrative
> processes under the Order. We make this recommendation because

---

[31] *Ibid.*, p. 8.

[32] *Ibid.*

[33] *Ibid.*

[34] *Ibid.*

[35] Randolph S. Driver, Deputy Under Secretary of the Navy for Manpower, *Statement,* before President's Review Committee, October 1967, pp. 2-4.

[36] Eugene T. Ferraro, Deputy Under Secretary of the Air Force (Manpower),
Statement, before President's Review Committee, October 26, 1967, p. 10.

by and large, the union complaints are directed to things we can take action on if the local parties so request." [37]

Management was almost universally opposed to any tampering with agency authority at the headquarters level. Strong opposition was expressed to revising final agency approval or delegating more power to local negotiators. As the General Services Administration spokesman remarked:

"We agree that this criticism may be warranted and recognize that negotiations should be conducted at the local level on matters within local management discretion. However, many issues presented at field office levels will continue to require higher level review or approval because they pertain to matters that affect regional or national policies and regulations and cannot possibly be acted upon or negotiated at the local level." [38]

The GSA claimed that much of the problem stemmed from a lack of training and understanding of the program on the part of both union and management negotiators. It felt constrained to criticize the practice of union locals of circumventing prescribed procedures by referring local problems to national agency and union levels for solution.[39]

To the Air Force, management's ability to operate in an effective and expeditious manner required that the interpretation of agency regulations or the negotiability of union proposals be determined at the agency headquarters level.[40] The Treasury Department also emphasized "that the preservation of management rights should not be in question" but called for a greater clarification of these rights. It sought a clearer definition of negotiable matters. This troublesome problem was seen as becoming more critical as negotiations became more sophisticated. A clearer expression of intent, it was held, would serve to speed mutual accommodation, relieve frustrations, and provide greater uniformity among federal agencies. According to a Treasury spokesman, "management wants to feel that it understands clearly where the line of demarcation is, so that the matters in which it can properly deal with employee representatives are clearly known to both parties." [41]

---

[37] D. M. Atkinson, Acting Chief, Labor Relations Branch, Department of the Army, *Statement,* before President's Review Committee, October 1967, p. 8. (Emphasis added.)

[38] General Services Administration, *Statement,* before President's Review Committee, October 1967, p. 5.

[39] *Ibid.*

[40] Eugene T. Ferraro, *op. cit.,* p. 13.

[41] Amos N. Latham Jr., Director of Personnel, Treasury Department, *Statement,* before President's Review Committee, October 1967, pp. 9-10.

The Post Office Department was understandably concerned with the scope of negotiations. By November 1967, it had granted over 24,000 local exclusive recognitions and had negotiated over 13,000 local agreements. These totals far exceeded those in other federal agencies. The POD's concern was evidenced in the broader play it gave to this issue before the Review Committee. The POD noted that local contracts took effect upon signature by both parties. However, they could be invalidated later by higher level, joint union-management representatives, with the Department always retaining final authority. Anything provided in local contracts found in conflict with law, regulations, or the National Agreement was to be invalidated and removed. It was noted that in the third round of local negotiations after the 1966 National Agreement, over 6,000 local contracts were reviewed, and 2,839 clauses were declared invalid by the joint union-management procedures provided for at the regional level by the postal agreement. In addition, 196 clauses were sent on to the national level for final review, although the POD spokesman did not clarify how many of these were invalidated.[42] With the fourth round of local negotiations running their course under the 1968 National Agreement, the problem of negotiability was, if anything, decidedly aggravated.

The views expressed by the Post Office in 1967 in essence called for maintenance of the status quo. A clarification and definition of the rights of the parties was called for within the context of applicable requirements.[43] Anthony F. Ingrassia, then director of POD's Labor Relations Division and later director of the Office of Labor-Management Relations of the Civil Service Commission, described the cause of growing frustrations to be the divergent union and management interpretations of identical provisions and purposes of the program. Overlapping language in the Kennedy order made it possible, if carried to extremes, for a union to insist that everything was negotiable and for management to claim that almost nothing was negotiable.[44]

Definitely presaging the harder attitude that according to the postal unions characterized management in the 1967-68 negotiations, Ingrassia adopted a traditional approach. He would not condone removing the management-rights clause from the order and deemed essential the retention of higher level review. He

---

[42] Anthony F. Ingrassia, Director, Labor Relations Division, Post Office Department, *Statement,* before President's Review Committee, October 26, 1967, p. 8.
[43] *Ibid.,* pp. 7, 14.
[44] *Ibid.,* p. 5.

said that "to do otherwise would be to put the stamp of approval on any actions taken by installation management under the mistaken impression they are within their scope of authority." [45] The possibility of expanding local authority was not mentioned. Whether contracts were to be reviewed before or after becoming effective was viewed as unimportant so long as higher level review was maintained.

The scope of negotiations was a serious stumbling block in the 1968 local postal bargaining. Amid an atmosphere of picketing and demonstrations before the Manhattan and Bronx Post Offices, it was claimed that local bargaining had been broken off in Boston, Detroit, and Saginaw, Mich., in addition to New York City. The Letter Carriers, the Postal Clerks, and the National Postal Union reportedly charged local postmasters with failing to bargain in good faith by rejecting as not negotiable suggested provisions already agreed to in past contracts.[46] These 1968 occurrences illustrated the impotence of local union bargainers when management chose to follow narrow boundaries in defining negotiability. They doubtless added to the frictions culminating in the national postal strike of March 1970.

D. THE JOHNSON REVIEW COMMITTEE

When the President's Review Committee was established, negotiability was quickly recognized as a major problem issue. The limitations on bargaining had been amply described in the press. For example, *The New York Times* had commented that:

"The federal managers generally are reluctant to surrender management prerogatives to the unions, and the unions, in turn, accuse them of refusing to honor the Executive Order. But because the unions cannot strike, federal managers have the last word in most disputes." [47]

In April 1968, when all concerned were momentarily expecting a White House statement based upon a detailed Committee report, information was informally publicized by "authoritative" sources close to the group. Very little was said about the scope of negotiability. It was reported only that the Committee "would broaden the area of negotiations." [48] Some recommendations on pay fixing

---

[45] *Ibid.*, p. 8.
[46] *Government Employee Relations Report*, No. 242 (1968), p. A-1.
[47] David R. Jones, "Rights for Federal Workers Weighed," *The New York Times*, October 23, 1967.
[48] Joseph A. Loftus, "Panel Supports Arbitration for Federal Workers," *The New York Times*, April 11, 1968.

were anticipated,[49] but these would, in any case, be supplanted by the new Coordinated Federal Wage System. Predictions were ventured that negotiability might be expanded to include job assignments resulting from technological change, retraining, transfers, and related matters. [50]

When the Committee's draft report was finally made public in early 1969, it appeared that negotiation limits and management rights had received considerable attention.[51] Although the draft report was unofficial, it was an accurate barometer of how far management was willing to go in expanding this area.

The Review Committee gave the limitations on collective bargaining close scrutiny. The substantial portion of the report devoted to this issue incorporated many of the views of both unions and management. The final product, however, traced an independent path, acceding to union demands where possible and vigorously maintaining executive privileges where these were deemed essential. Specific recommendations were proposed to govern the scope of bargaining, management rights, the delegation of authority, and the approval of agreements.[52]

The Committee's concessions to the unions on the scope of bargaining corresponded with the positions taken by the AFL-CIO. Thus, the report recommended that Section 6 (b) of the Kennedy order be modified and clarified. Its stated intent was to provide for "the negotiation of appropriate protective arrangements for employees adversely affected by the realignment of work forces or technological change." [53] The unions had sought the right "to protect the workers they represent" and to negotiate on all issues involving personnel matters. They were concerned over the adverse effects on employees of certain operational decisions.[54]

The general union approach was that all matters in Section 6 (b) should be negotiable unless barred by law. However, the approach recognized the right of an agency to assign personnel and to introduce new technological advances. What unions sought in these instances was an opportunity to participate in the adjustment process when, for example, automated devices were brought in or installations were partially or totally closed down.[55] While

49 Ibid.
50 Joseph Young, "The Federal Spotlight," The Washington Star, April 19, 1968.
51 U.S. President's Review Committee on Employee-Management Relations in the Federal Service, Draft Report, April 1968, in U.S. Department of Labor, 56th Annual Report, 1969, Attachment B.
52 Ibid., pp. 33-43.
53 Ibid., p. 33.
54 George Meany, op. cit., p. 9.
55 Ibid., pp. 8, 9.

executive decisions to effect such changes are not negotiable, the resultant problems often are. As the draft report noted, promotion, demotion, and training procedures necessitated by such managerial innovation are negotiable and indeed had been bargained over in numerous instances.[56]

The Review Committee's recommendation, therefore, called for a clarification of Section 6 (b) that would substantially relieve union concerns. It sought to remove the confusion surrounding the phrase precluding negotiation over an agency's "organization and the assignment of its personnel." This had been interpreted as involving, for example, the detailing of workers and overtime and shift assignments. What was really intended was a reservation of the agency's right to set its own organizational staffing patterns. The Committee proposed, accordingly, that a new phrase be substituted clarifying the agency's control over "its organization and the numbers, types and grades of positions included in each organizational unit." [57] This would preserve the right of management to initiate the work processes or organizational changes it deemed essential to productivity.

Furthermore, the Review Committee report recognized the legitimate union concern for its protective function in the event of technological changes. It suggested the addition of a clause permitting negotiations as to the plans and means to meet technological innovations that could adversely affect the work force. The clause was later adopted in its entirety.[58] Thus the distinction was maintained between managerial authority over organization and the traditional union position that organizational changes, particularly during the adjustment period, were essentially personnel matters and therefore subject to collective bargaining.

E. THE NIXON STUDY COMMITTEE AND E.O. 11491

The approach of the Nixon Study Committee to the limitations of collective bargaining was for all practical purposes in accord with that of the Johnson group. Indeed, the entire section of the Study Committee's report entitled "Negotiation and Administration of Agreements" duplicated with little variation the language and rationale of its predecessor. It is thus quite reasonable to conclude that many of the changes effected by E.O. 11491 were first put forward by the Committee chaired by former Labor Secretary Wirtz. Certain changes in wording and provisions reflected the

---

[56] Review Committee, *op. cit.*, p. 34.
[57] *Ibid.*, pp. 34, 35.
[58] Review Committee, *op. cit.*, p. 35.

business-administration approach of the Study Committee but the bases for actions finally taken stemmed from the offerings of the prior report. It too acceded to many union desires; nevertheless, like the Johnson-Wirtz Review Committee before it, the Nixon group did not envision any major limitation of executive authority. The scope of collective bargaining was clarified, further defined, and broadened to some degree; policies to ease the mechanics of bargaining were instituted.

In accordance, therefore, with the rationale of the Study Committee, E.O. 11491 more precisely defined the limitations on scope of negotiations and administration previously found in Sections 6 (b) and 7 (2) of the Kennedy order. The parties were required to negotiate "in good faith." The superiority of laws and regulations, including the *Federal Personnel Manual,* published agency policies, and controlling agreements at a higher level in the agency, was detailed in an expanded subject-to clause.[59] The scope of negotiations was clarified by language that removed previous confusing elements but added another exclusion, "internal security practices." On the other hand, the scope of negotiations was broadened, as recommended by all, to permit mutual accords to handle technological change. Section 11 (b) of the Nixon order read:

> "In prescribing regulations relating to personnel policies and practices and working conditions, an agency shall have due regard for the obligation imposed by paragraph (a) of this section [the subject-to clause]. However, the obligation to meet and confer does not include matters with respect to the mission of an agency; its budget; its organization; the number of employees; and the numbers, types, and grades of positions or employees assigned to an organizational unit, work project or tour of duty; the technology of performing its work; or its internal security practices. This does not preclude the parties from negotiating agreements providing appropriate arrangements for employees adversely affected by the impact of realignment of work forces or technological change." [60]

On the management-rights issue there was far less union accommodation. Both the Review Committee and the Study Committee rejected union suggestions that the management-rights provisions of Section 7 (2) be deleted. The AFL-CIO had claimed that these matters were governed by law anyway, and that considerable bargaining had been conducted over these items within the legal framework. While accepting the AFL-CIO's position, the

---

[59] E.O. 11491, Sec. 11 (a) ; President's Study Committee, *Report and Recommendations on Labor-Management Relations in the Federal Service,* August 1969, pp. 32-35.
[60] E.O. 11491, Sec. 11 (b) ; Study Committee, *op. cit.,* pp. 34-35.

Review Committee nevertheless insisted upon the continuance of the management-rights statement in the Kennedy order and the agreements. It believed there should be continued recognition of management's responsibility to carry out its mission in the public interest in accordance with laws and regulations. The management-rights statement in Section 7 (2) was to be modified only to conform it to the terms and conditions of the collective bargaining agreement.[61] The Nixon Study Committee made no such recommendation. Management rights were not subordinated to the "terms and conditions of the agreement." Accordingly, E.O. 11491 retained the original management-rights wording of the Kennedy order.[62]

There were minor changes, however, dealing with tne subject-to clauses that had proved so galling to the unions. Both the Johnson and Nixon committees noted the unions claim that agencies changed their regulations to nullify contract provisions previously approved by the negotiating parties. The Nixon Committee agreed, therefore, that the administration of contracts should be governed by agency policies and regulations in effect when accords were approved. This was apparently a step forward since it did protect an accord from agency regulation changes during the term of the contract. E.O. 11491 provided that administration of an agreement should be subject only to published agency policies and regulations in force at the time of contract approval. Administration also would be subject to future "agency published policies and regulations required by law or by regulations of appropriate authorities, or authorized by the terms of a controlling agreement at a higher agency level."[63] But as to regulation changes promulgated by the agency alone the negotiated agreement would prevail.

Such protection would cease, however, upon termination of the agreement. The Nixon Study Committee pointedly emphasized that at the time of renewal or renegotiation the contract had to be conformed to current agency regulations. Only when management had renewed or granted an exception to presently existing regulations could this be avoided.

The problem of delegation of authority to local installation officials also drew the attention of the Johnson and Nixon Committees, both of which called for an increase in the bargaining

---

[61] Review Committee, *op. cit.*, pp. 35-36.
[62] Study Committee, *op. cit.*, p. 41; E.O. 11491, Sec. 12 (b) .
[63] E.O. 11491, Sec. 12 (a) ; Study Committee, *op. cit.*, p. 41; Review Committee, *op. cit.*, p. 37.

power delegated to local managers on personnel matters. Both Committees recommended that agencies "should not issue over-prescriptive regulations, and should consider exceptions from agency regulations on specific items where both parties request an exception and the agency considers the exception feasible." [64]

The Committees' proposals, which sought to ameliorate union dissatisfactions with the scope of negotiations, were, however, hedged with provisos that helped preserve management control. One such proviso was that agencies should grant requests for exceptions "where practicable." [65] Decisions on the scope of negotiations remained, therefore, unilateral in nature. They were still to be made on an essentially decentralized basis despite the new centralized administration. Agency discretion was to determine whether exceptions would be granted at all. Although the Nixon Study Committee agreed that "fruitful negotiations can take place only where management officials have sufficient authority to negotiate matters of concern to employees" and although it recommended increased delegation of negotiating authority, it firmly believed "that agency regulatory authority must be retained." [66]

The machinery established for impasses on negotiability reinforced the ultimate control of national government officials over the scope of bargaining. There is little doubt that the negotiability-impasse proposals were a step in the right direction. For the first time, formal machinery was set up to deal with such impasses. Nevertheless, a strong element of unilateralism was retained. Agencies could maintain recalcitrant positions if they so desired. Both Committees were hopeful that if local negotiability impasses arose and the union enjoyed national consultation rights, deadlocks could be resolved at the national level. If the local dispute was over a union proposal deemed contrary to law or agency regulations, the union could submit the question to agency headquarters for determination. Regulatory authority was clearly preserved since it was stipulated that the decisions governing agency regulation interpretations by the agency head were final. If the union believed, however, that the agency head's interpretation of his own regulations violated any law, regulation, or the executive order, it could appeal to the Federal Labor Relations Council. If an agency head believed that a union proposal violated such laws and regulations, the proposal also could be put before the Council for resolution. If a negotiability dispute arose

---

[64]Review Committee, *op. cit.*, p. 38; Study Committee, *op. cit.*, p. 36.
[65] Review Committee, pp. 37, 38; and Study Committee, p. 36.
[66] Study Committee, *op. cit.*, p. 35.

over interpretation of a controlling agreement reached at a higher agency level, it was to be resolved under the procedures of that agreement, or according to agency regulations.[67]

E.O. 11491 fully incorporated these proposals. The Nixon order still retained ultimate executive authority, but at least the final review was made outside the agency, assuring greater impartiality and giving decisions some precedent value.

The intention of the Review and Study Committees was to foster greater local discretion and authority in collective bargaining. Their recommendations may not have gone as far as some labor leaders had desired, but they represented an honest effort to improve the bargaining process. They proposed that national consultation and the granting of exceptions from agency regulations serve as the means by which agencies "to the extent possible, should attempt to increase the authority of local managers to accomplish the purposes of the Order consistent with the public interest and the maintenance of the efficiency of the government operations entrusted to them." [68]

Further recommendations sought to give teeth to proposals to promote local responsibility. For example, once a question of legality or contravention of agency policy had been disposed of through the newly established impasse procedures, the installation officials would be required to negotiate on the issue. If the union then thought that local bargainers were acting arbitrarily or in error in refusing to negotiate, it would be permitted to file an unfair labor practice complaint against the offending parties.[69]

The Nixon Study Committee agreed that much could be done "within agencies to improve the bargaining process." [70] In essence, it addressed itself to union complaints that management negotiators often lacked authority to commit an agency and that agencies sometimes attempted to create confusion over the true locus of authority. Mistrust and bad faith inevitably resulted when local officials interrupted bargaining to telephone headquarters on a negotiability question. Unions wanted a clear understanding as to who could commit an agency on specific bargaining issues. Both review groups believed that the suggested machinery would provide a formal procedure under which exclusively recognized unions could appeal questions of negotiability "during negotiations." [71] If used effectively, this machinery should improve the

---

[67] *Ibid.*, p. 37.
[68] Review Committee, *op. cit.*, p. 39; Study Committee, *op. cit.*, p. 36.
[69] Study Committee, *op. cit.*, pp. 37, 38, 39, 40.
[70] *Ibid.*, p. 38.
[71] Review Committee, *op. cit.*, p. 40; Study Committee, *op. cit.*, p. 38.

bargaining process by blocking dilatory tactics and forcing agency decisions to be arrived at openly. The power to press an unfair labor practice charge against an official who will not bargain over an item adjudged negotiable or who interprets the management-rights clause capriciously or erroneously may act as a powerful spur to more meaningful local negotiations.

Both the Johnson and Nixon Committees adhered to the fundamental premise that "the requirement for agency approval is necessary and should be continued." They so held in spite of lengthy union complaints that the approval requirement too often resulted in unwarranted delays or in needless or arbitrary revisions of local contracts. Union dissatisfaction was justified in such instances, they conceded. They could not, however, countenance proposals to eliminate the approval provision entirely, restrict the scope of review, or fix time limitations for approval or disapproval. The committees believed the dissatisfaction might well evaporate as greater sophistication in the administration of the federal program was achieved.[72]

Strict adherence to agency-head approval was, nevertheless, tempered by suggestions intended to rectify its more glaring deficiencies, such as conformance with statutory or published agency policies and with the regulations of other proper authorities.[73] With the possible grounds for disapproval restricted to the highest levels, it was hoped that excuses for delay and obstruction would become far less plausible.

The intent of such suggestions was to speed the approval process. The Johnson Review Committee was quite explicit on this point. Without actually chiding management, it cautioned: "It is, of course, expected that agencies will move expeditiously on contract approvals. They should facilitate the process in order to afford the parties the immediate benefits of the negotiated agreement." [74] This admonition was missing from the Study Committee Report, which simply called for approval of local agreements according to the procedures set forth in the higher level controlling agreement or under agency regulations.[75] Although this revision could conceivably expedite the approval process, uncooperative executives could still delay approval since, as stated in Section 15 of the Nixon order, the procedure still allowed individual discretion. This policy was reversed when President

---

[72] Review Committee, *op. cit.*, pp. 41, 42; Study Committee, *op. cit.*, pp. 39, 40.
[73] Study Committee, *op. cit.*, p. 40.
[74] Review Committee, *op. cit.*, p. 43.
[75] Study Committee, *op. cit.*, pp. 40-41.

Ford's executive order E.O. 11838 changed Section 15 and speeded up procedures by setting a 45-day time limit for agency head approval of negotiated agreements.

F. THE CHANNELS FOR PROGRAM EXPANSION

It has become increasingly evident that some government officials, particularly those responsible for the program, are adopting attitudes supporting certain labor proposals for change. Some officials also have been moved to comment on the scope of negotiation. Assistant Secretary of Labor Thomas R. Donohue, for example, mirrored management's changing sentiments when he declared:

> "The bitter, early struggles between unions and management in the private sector should have no counterpart in the new public unionism of today. Public management must turn its thoughts to how to widen, rather than limit the scope of labor-management relations. If public managers consciously set out to develop consultation and try to share personnel policy-making with their employees, a new form of industrial relations will emerge—a form or system based upon a broad cooperative bond, as opposed to an atmosphere of conflict. An indifferent public manager can be assured that his attitude will help produce the hard, militant attitude of unionism which was fostered by the anti-union employer in the private sector."[76]

The limitations upon collective bargaining are too oppressive to be maintained without serious union reactions. Union efforts to broaden negotiability through collective bargaining legislation may increase as the expectation of presidential action decreases. Far more portentous is the fact that, whether out of desperation or as the result of evolutionary change, the traditional federal union view of strikes is undergoing reevaluation. The strong positions taken by the postal unions since 1967 have resulted in the removal of no-strike clauses from their constitutions. The American Federation of Government Employees and the American Postal Workers Union, among others, now seriously question the denial of the strike. The 1970 postal strike offers the best evidence of this attitude. Professional organizations such as the American Nurses Association and the National Education Association have officially acted to support strike action.

Legislation following the postal stoppage has had a powerful impact upon the rest of the federal establishment. Officials cannot

---

[76] Thomas R. Donohue, Assistant Secretary of Labor, *Speech*, to United Federation of Postal Clerks, Minneapolis, Minnesota, August 12, 1968, in U.S. Department of Labor, *Press Release* No. 8897, p. 5.

help but be impressed by the extensive scope of negotiations permitted under the Postal Reorganization Act. Since the Postal Service now falls under the jurisdiction of the NLRB, the entire body of labor law governing unfair labor practices in private industry can be brought to bear on postal management, particularly if it fails to bargain in good faith.

The Civil Service Commission, well aware of the Postal Service developments, also knows of the frustrations that can result from limitations on bargaining power. Anthony Ingrassia, director of the CSC's Office of Labor-Management Relations, has consistently recognized the severe curbs under which government negotiators must labor. Nevertheless, he has stressed the importance of crediting the advances made within these limits. Communications have improved, union representatives have much more input on personnel policies, and except for the bread-and-butter items, as Ingrassia pointed out, "federal agreements cover every subject imaginable." [77]

Yet Ingrassia emphasized that E.O. 11491 still "imposes further restrictions on the scope of bargaining—distinguishing it in substantial measure from that in the private sector." These restrictions generally fall within three areas—customary management rights, legislative restrictions, and the limitations needed to protect and insure the merit system and uniform employment conditions.[78] Ingrassia has noted that frustrations over the narrow scope of negotiations create "dual but opposite pressures"—pressures to delegate authority down to the actual bargaining level and pressures to push the level of negotiations to the locus of ultimate authority. The result has been a "limited willingness to delegate and a corresponding push by unions for bigger and bigger units with the ultimate national exclusive recognition (agency-wide) achieved in a few instances." [79] Above all, Ingrassia has said that the Federal Government must accommodate its collective bargaining practices to those in the public sector. For this the executive order was the best vehicle, although legislation remained a possibility. Either way, both unions and management should emphasize problem-solving techniques, not assume adversary roles. Finally, Ingrassia has called for increased union input in major policy developments of the federal program.[80]

---

[77] Anthony F. Ingrassia, "Widening Dimensions of the Federal Bargaining Table," *Civil Service Journal*, Vol. 12, No. 1, July-September 1971, p. 2.

[78] Anthony F. Ingrassia, "The Maturing Federal Labor-Management Relationship," *Civil Service Journal*, Vol. 12, No. 4, April-June 1972, p. 6.

[79] *Ibid.*, p. 10.

[80] *Ibid.*

In July 1972, following a CSC "scope of bargaining" project, a series of tentative proposals was submitted to concerned federal agencies and unions for their comments prior to possible adoption. If adopted they would expand the scope of negotiations to allow unions greater bargaining opportunity in, among others, the following areas: merit promotion requirements and procedures, the length of probationary and trial periods, regulations covering incentive awards, CSC regulations carrying out basic reduction-in-force requirements, criteria for permitting withdrawals of resignations or applications for optional retirement, the distribution of health insurance literature, and annual leave regulations.[81]

The scope-of-bargaining project dealt with CSC policies alone and not with statutory or executive order requirements. Negotiations would be expanded by clarifying certain CSC regulations and requirements, eliminating others, and providing new alternatives for still others.[82] Although this effort was viewed as only slightly broadening the scope of negotiations,[83] it did reflect a commendable CSC intent to move on the issue in its accustomed evolutionary manner.

This project represented one of the major inputs into the intensive Federal Labor Relations Council review that culminated in President Ford's E.O. 11838, promulgated in 1975. The Council's report recognized that higher agency regulations had acted as a bar to broader local negotiations and chided both management and labor for failing to request exceptions from such regulations when they conflicted with local bargaining proposals and were "not critical to effective agency management and the public interest." [84] President Ford's executive order seeks to ameliorate this situation.

E.O. 11838 provides that only those internal agency regulations for which a "compelling need" exists may bar negotiations over a conflicting proposal in local bargaining.[85] The Council is authorized to establish specific criteria to define "compelling need," and procedures are to be established for requesting regulation exceptions in bargaining. Under amendments to Sections 11 (a) and 11 (c) of E.O. 11491, if local bargaining proposals run afoul of higher agency regulations, the new rules would allow

---

[81] U.S. Civil Service Commission, *News Release*, July 5, 1972, pp. 1-2.
[82] *Ibid.*
[83] See Mike Causey, *The Washington Post*, July 6, 1972, p. H5.
[84] Federal Labor Relations Council, *Labor-Management Relations in the Federal Service—Amendments to E.O. 11491 with Accompanying Report and Recommendations*, Washington, February 1975, pp. 31-32.
[85] E.O. 11491 as amended by E.O. 11838, Sec. 11 (a) .

their negotiation when the higher regulations are not critical to agency functions. In such a case the labor union may, unilaterally or jointly with management, request the agency head for an exception to the regulation for bargaining purposes. If denied by the agency head, appeals over nonnegotiability and "compelling need" lie to the Council itself under the existing appeals machinery. To avoid a multiplicity of challenges, and in recognition of the great importance of regulation exception requests, such appeals may be filed only by the national president of the labor union concerned or his designee.[86] The Council intent is not to dilute agency regulatory authority by these amendments but to retain it. Its aim is simply to delineate "the levels of internal agency regulations which may bar negotiation" and thus eliminate "the confusion and anomalies previously encountered." [87]

The changes embodied in E.O. 11838 will eliminate much of the confusion that has surrounded the scope-of-bargaining issue. The locus of bargaining authority will be somewhat clarified. The definition of "compelling need" may take some time to crystallize, however, since the Council will settle disputes on a case-by-case approach once the basic criteria have been set. The fundamental statutory limitations on bargaining still control. Nevertheless, within the executive structure of the federal program, the Ford order has considerably broadened the scope of local negotiations over personnel policies, practices, and working conditions.

---

[86] Federal Labor Relations Council, *op. cit.,* pp. 30-31, 38, 39.
[87] *Ibid.,* p. 36.

CHAPTER XXI

THE ADMINISTRATION OF FEDERAL
LABOR RELATIONS

A. THE FIRST DECADE

The administrative structure of the federal labor relations program underwent considerable change in its first 10 years of existence. Modifications were effected in response to the legitimate complaints of both management and labor. Federal unions expressed relatively little dissatisfaction during the initial stages of implementation of the Kennedy order. Their grievances quickly proliferated, however. Unions found particular fault with the administrative procedures of the EMC program. Management also expressed a desire for change before both the Johnson and Nixon Committees, but discontent over labor relations administration developed as a predominantly union complaint, and so it remains today.

Over the years, union-sponsored bills to revise the system were introduced with little effect. Some success was achieved in the postal reorganization, which brought the USPS within the NLRB's jurisdiction. For the remainder of the federal service, however, underlying disenchantment with the organization of the labor relations program tended to amplify an already considerable array of problems.

From the outset inherent factors inhibited the federal program. The intended purpose of the Kennedy order was that all actions taken should be those permissible under executive authority alone. New legislation and funding of new agencies were neither sought nor desired. Support facilities were to be provided by existing federal institutions. This policy was adhered to fully by the Johnson and Nixon Administrations. Thus, by insistence upon strict retention of labor relations within the executive branch alone, the possibility of legislative innovations in basic policy or administrative machinery was removed.

Labor relations administration was subject to varying degrees of executive unilateralism. Such unilateralism was probably strongest from 1962 to 1969, when, as a result of the Nixon

457

order, the EMC program under E.O. 10988 was essentially decentralized, with administration left in large part to the individual agencies. During this period, the Civil Service Commission
and the Department of Labor supervised the labor relations
program. Among other things, they were responsible for setting
central agency guidelines, interpreting overall policies, and providing training. Although the Labor Department established procedures for the resolution of appropriate-bargaining-unit disputes
through arbitration, the executive authority of the individual
agency remained the final determinant. In the event of disputes,
the decision-making process rested essentially in the hands of the
executive officers of both the central and the operating agencies.
Such a distribution of authority brought on conflicts with the
federal labor unions. Disputes over policy and administration
were aggravated by union belief that final decisions could be
unilateral. Although the Kennedy order adopted much of the
language and philosophy of the National Labor Relations Act,
it omitted the essential ingredient—labor relations regulation by
the NLRB.

There was much validity, particularly early in the program,
in the arguments against a central authority patterned on the
NLRB. The new legislation needed for creation of such a board
could conceivably have deprived the executive of considerable
authority over its own personnel. This it was not prepared to
relinquish. Furthermore, some federal administrators were not
kindly disposed to increased unionism. A far greater proportion
were simply unprepared for the rigors of collective bargaining
and contract administration.

A review of background factors indicates that the seeds of
centralization were present even during this early period of
greater agency autonomy. For one thing, the overall functions
of the CSC and the Labor Department assumed increased importance over the years. A major leveller was the requirement
that all agencies abide by the *Federal Personnel Manual*. Executive Order 10988 gave the CSC a new array of responsibilities
in the labor area, which were expressed centrally through the
FPM; and their effects were manifested in the agencies accordingly. These new duties coincided naturally with the traditional
functions of the Commission. As it already was doing in other
personnel areas, the CSC was now to fulfill the staff function in
the field of labor relations, as mandated in Section 12 of the Kennedy order.[1]

---

[1] E.O. 10988, Sec. 12.

Under Chairman Macy, Wilfred V. Gill, L. David Korb, and others the CSC rose to its tasks in a relatively untried area. Existing offices, such as the Bureau of Policies and Standards and the Bureau of Inspections, were utilized, and others, such as the Employee-Management Relations Section, were created. Louis D. Wallerstein, as Chief of the Labor Department's Division of Federal Employee-Management Relations, worked closely with the CSC throughout. Willem B. Vosloo, in his study of the EMC program in its early years, fully credited the CSC's supervisory and coordination efforts. He described how:

"The Commission met the leadership needs of the program implementation phase by giving technical advice and assistance to agencies regarding program interpretation, assistance in the training of managerial personnel, dissemination of information; and by coordinating agency officials responsible for program supervision. Generally speaking, the Commission took the position that it was responsible for assuring a balanced implementation of the Order, assisting the departments and agencies in seeing that the program be administered in accordance with the provisions of the Order, and reporting to the President on program progress and deficiencies." [2]

Since these responsibilities were specifically delegated in Section 12 Vosloo emphasized that:

"The Commission did not view itself as a neutral party in disputes between agencies and employee organizations. On the contrary, its advice and assistance were in the nature of guiding departments and agencies in their dealings with employee organizations. Its role in relation to employee organizations has not been clearly defined either internally or externally." [3]

For the unions, this situation became more vexatious as the years progressed. They mistrusted what they viewed as a lack of administrative neutrality in the CSC. Union leaders, imbued with traditional labor concepts and not fully aware of the Commission's essential personnel role, could not accept its basic position. They saw the CSC simply as another element of the federal employer. The Commission endeavored to consult with union leaders over many proposed changes in wage fixing, grievances, adverse action, and promotion plans. Nevertheless, the Commission's prime function was to help management conduct the program in accordance with the order. This was fully admitted by the CSC. [4]

---

[2] Willem B. Vosloo, *Collective Bargaining in the United States Federal Civil Service* (Chicago: Public Personnel Association, 1966), p. 85.
[3] *Ibid.*
[4] U.S. Civil Service Commission Office of Labor-Management Relations, *The Role of the Civil Service Commission in Federal Labor Relations* (Washington: U.S. Government Printing Office, 1971), p. 20.

The substantive limitations on collective bargaining, innate in order provisions, were supported by the CSC and the Labor Department. To unions, particularly when disappointed or disgruntled over negotiations with operating departments, such support was seen as further weakening a collective bargaining process already inferior to the process in the private sector. Unions believed that staff agencies, acting unilaterally from within the executive branch on behalf of negotiating departments, necessarily perpetuated the weak bargaining program. Involvement in the actual bargaining process was not alone at issue here; impartial administration of the preliminary and supportive procedures underlying collective bargaining was seriously brought into question.

The need for impartiality was recognized by Chairman Macy when the Standards of Conduct and Code of Fair Labor Practices were first issued in 1963.[5] He asserted that with decentralization

---

[5] Section 13 of the Kennedy order established a Temporary Committee on the Implementation of the Federal Employee-Management Relation's Program, composed of the Secretary of Labor as chairman, the CSC chairman, the Secretary of Defense, and the Postmaster General. Its purpose was to advise the President and submit to him proposed Standards and a Code to be prepared by the Labor Department and CSC. On May 21, 1963, President Kennedy approved the Standards of Conduct for Employee Organizations and the Code of Fair Labor Practices in the Federal Service.

In essence, the Standards of Conduct drew from the general requirements of the Labor-Management Reporting and Disclosure Act of 1959. In the Code, the Temporary Committee sought to adopt only what it deemed appropriate to the federal service from the unfair labor practices defined for private management in the 1935 Wagner Act and for labor and management in the 1947 Taft-Hartley Act. Language and policies reflected the general labor law. Although both Standards and Code were purposely kept simple, it was anticipated that difficulties in interpretation and enforcement would still arise. See Civil Service Commission, *Federal Personnel Manual Letter*, No. 711-2, August 30, 1963, pp. 1-3.

Labor could hardly contest the Standards, which called for democratic internal union operations, periodic elections, protections for individual union members' rights, fiscal integrity, financial accounting, and prohibitions against conflicts of interest among union officers. Failure to correct violations could result in denial, suspension, or withdrawal of recognition. As in the Landrum-Griffin Act, persons affiliated with Communist or other totalitarian movements and those identified with corrupt influences were precluded from holding union office. See Civil Service Commission, Bulletin No. 711-3, June 5, 1963, Part A.

The Code adopted the principal unfair labor practices of the private sector. Management and unions were prohibited from interfering with employees' rights assured by the order. Agencies were not to encourage or discourage union membership through hire or tenure, etc. They could not sponsor, control, or assist any employee organization. Disciplinary or discriminatory measures against any employee for acting under the order, Standards, or Code were prohibited. Failure to accord recognition when appropriate and refusal to negotiate or confer as required by the order were also proscribed. Union unfair labor practices included attempts to coerce or discipline any union member so that his duties as a federal employee were hindered, discriminatory union membership practices, and engaging in any strike, work stoppage, slowdown or picketing as a substitute for a strike. Finally, unions with exclusive recognition were required to accept any person in an appropriate unit as a member so long as he was willing to pay his fees and dues and met reasonable occupational standards required for membership. See Civil Service Commission, Bulletin No. 711-3, June 5, 1963, Part B.

"the Standards and Code very cleary—like the Order itself—place responsibility on the agencies and management chain of command for administration of the program and for resolution of any disputes that may arise in the course of the program." [6] Final responsibility for decisions rested with the agency heads. Nevertheless, management was expected to act impartially in enforcing standards of conduct for the labor unions that operated directly under it. The fair labor practice code was promulgated for labor and management alike. With unilateral administration, however, an agency could claim that a union with which it was negotiating had committed an unfair labor practice and then determine the validity of the complaint. Management was thus in a stronger position than the union, since the case could constitute an added bargaining point. An adverse decision could result in suspension or withdrawal of exclusive recognition. If the labor union saw fit to lodge an unfair labor practice complaint against management, the result could be even more incongruous since management would be able to pass judgment on its own alleged violation.

Primary enforcement of the Standards and Code was to be accomplished informally. In regard to violations of the Standards of Conduct, management, if requested by the union, could convene a hearing before decision. It was not required that formal hearing procedures be specified in agency regulations since it was thought such a process would "very likely never or rarely" have to be applied. Third-party participation in a Standards case could occur only if the agency desired it, and then only to a limited

---

Aside from important procedural changes, E.O. 11491 worked several substantive enlargements on both the Standards and Code. Thus in 1970, Landrum-Griffin-like requirments for filing financial reports, bonding labor officials, and meeting election standards were included in the Standards. See E.O. 11491, Secs. 18 (a) (b) (c) , (d) (6) . Unlike the experience in private industry under Landrum-Griffin, federal unions of all sizes and types complied swiftly. It was reported that as of June 30, 1972, 3,605 active nonpostal unions had reported to the Office of Labor-Management and Welfare-Pension Reports in the Labor Department. This compared well with the 3,380 exclusive bargaining units in the federal service by November 1971. It was deemed an "impressive beginning" in fulfilling the new responsibilities. See U.S. Civil Service Commission, Office of Labor-Management Relations, *Consultant*, No. 15, August 4, 1972, p. 4

The Nixon order also increased the number of union unfair labor practices without revising those for management. Substantive additions provided that unions could not fine or take economic sanctions against a member as punishment for or to hinder his performance or productivity. Unions may not condone a strike or prohibited picketing by failing to take affirmative action to prevent or stop it. Unions are now also barred from refusing to negotiate or consult if so required by the order. Age and sex were added as prohibited discriminations in union membership. See E.O. 11491, Sec. 19 (b) . While E.O. 11616 made several revisions in their procedure, the substantive content of the Standards and Code was not modified.

[6] John W. Macy, Jr., "Introduction to the Standards and Code," September 12, 1963, in U.S. Civil Service Commission, *Operations Letter*, No. 711-1, October 29, 1963, p. 3.

degree. Before instituting any proceedings against a union and before taking final action against an employee organization, the agency could consult with the Secretary of Labor. That was all it could do, however, for the final decision, after such consultation, lay with the agency head alone. From this determination there was no appeal.[7] Indeed, it was reported that in the eight years of E.O. 10988 no Standards case actually did progress to the formal stage.[8]

Unfair labor practice cases have been far more numerous than Standards cases over the years. The Kennedy program allowed for little outside participation in such cases. Unlike the practice in Standards cases, although informal and hearing procedures were required of agencies, the Code of Conduct did not provide for consultation with the Labor Secretary before final determination. Once again, this determination was the agency head's alone, and it was nonappealable. Because code violations sometimes were also "grievable" actions for which procedures already existed, two enforcement procedures were possible under E.O. 10988. Use of one precluded resort to the other. Outside impartial participation was available to the extent that advisory arbitration was used in the grievance procedure. In adverse action cases, an appeal could be made to the CSC. In all other code cases, however, the agencies established hearing procedures for enforcement which, though informal, provided for due process before impartial hearing officers. However, these officers still were responsible directly to the agency head; and when the agency head made his decision, it was final and binding. Neither the Labor Department nor the Civil Service Commission was empowered to review a final decision of a department head in any unfair labor practice case.[9]

Thus, not unexpectedly, by 1967 there was almost total agreement in labor testimony before the Johnson Review Committee that Standards and Code administration was unfairly unilateral. The Civil Service Commission later noted that these programs were "administered by each department and agency for its own employees. Agencies, thus, in resolving disputes often found themselves playing both the role of employer and a 'little NLRB.' "[10]

---

[7] U.S. Civil Service Commission, *Federal Personnel Manual Letters*, No. 711-2, August 30, 1963, pp. 10-12.

[8] U.S. Civil Service Commission, *The Role of the Civil Service Commission in Federal Labor Relations*, op. cit., p. 33.

[9] U.S. Civil Service Commission, *Federal Personnel Manual Letter*, No. 711-2, August 30, 1963, pp. 18-21.

[10] U.S. Civil Service Commission, *The Role of the Civil Service Commission in Federal Labor Relations*, p. 33.

The myriad problems that underlay representation disputes and the diverse confrontations they generated in unit determination were also left to departmental discretion. Detailed guidelines for setting appropriate bargaining units were prepared by the Labor Department and distributed and interpreted by the CSC to aid the agencies.[11] These were based primarily upon the appropriate-bargaining-unit rules developed by the NLRB. Nevertheless, jurisdiction was again laid entirely in the hands of agency management. Assistance from central sources was extended by the Kennedy order, which stipulated that the Labor Department should provide requesting parties FMCS arbitrators to advise on the determination of appropriate bargaining units and to conduct representation elections.[12] Advisory arbitration was helpful in bringing expertise to an area new to personnel administrators. Literally thousands of exclusive units had to be determined, and in almost all instances where advisory arbitration was invoked it was adhered to by management. Nevertheless, the complex problem of determining the appropriate unit for purposes of collective bargaining was left for unilateral agency determination. This, far more than the Standards and Code cases, was a source of union dissatisfaction since it involved recognition itself.

Unquestioned progress was made under the EMC program in successfully establishing exclusive bargaining units. But union statements before the 1967 Johnson-Wirtz Review Committee were particularly centered on processing delays and the lack of policy uniformity throughout the government. The National Maritime Union discovered that various people in federal agencies interpreted the same language of the Kennedy order differently, "depending upon whom we talk to." It took one agency 10 months "to render the simplest of decisions—who would be included in a bargaining representation unit." [13] John Griner of the AFGE deplored the lack of uniformity in interpreting the entire order. He noted that since each agency could interpret "as would suit its needs . . . we have about 58 different interpretations from 58 different agencies . . . . As an example, the four principal arms of the DOD have separate and distinct interpretations." [14] B. A. Gritta of the Metal Trades Department

11 U.S. Civil Service Commission, *Federal Personnel Manual Letter*, No. 700-1, April 24, 1962.

12 E.O. 10988, Sec. 11.

13 Rick Miller, V.P., National Maritime Union, *Statement*, before President's Review Committee, October 24, 1967, p. 6.

14 John F. Griner, President, AFGE, *Statement*, before President's Review Committee, October 23, 1967, p. 15.

was concerned over the processing of all representation issues. He stated:

> "The failure of the Executive Order to provide for any administrative agency to handle problems of appropriate bargaining units, elections, etc., and the cumbersome Section 11, Arbitration Proceedings required for the establishment of bargaining units, coupled with the unrealistic initial approach by many federal agencies to appropriate bargaining unit questions, made it necessary for us to arbitrate a long line of cases to establish the appropriateness of bargaining units of wage board workers. . . ." [15]

The question of unfair labor practices was seen as inextricably bound up with the need for third-party intervention. To John Griner, the absence of third-party intervention was the cause of delay and bias in administration. In his testimony in support of recommendations for an impartial board, he claimed that 10 or 12 unfair labor practice cases were pending before different agencies, some for almost a year. "Without doubt," he declared, "the agencies are dragging their feet and doing nothing to resolve these charges." [16] In some cases where the allegations had been sustained, no definite action was taken against the person charged. "A mere slap on the wrist appears to suffice," said Griner. "The employee and/or labor organization involved is left holding the bag. We have some cases where the same violations by the same person occurs [sic] two or three times—about all we get is the equivalent of 'so sorry.' " [17] In another case the charge was readily admitted as true, yet it took nine months for any action. The AFGE's position was "that so long as the agency has control of processing unfair labor charges against it or its management officials, we will not get speedy action from them." [18]

The position of the AFL-CIO, presented by George Meany and endorsed by AFL-CIO affiliates, called for establishing a Federal Service Labor-Management Relations Board. The IAM felt that if government executives reserved a significant area of management rights and prerogatives, ". . . then such labor-management relationship should guarantee an unbiased method of resolving disagreements in the absence of any economic sanctions." [19] Roy Hallbeck of the Postal Clerks believed that it would be contrary to human nature to expect management to act entirely without

---

[15] B. A. Gritta, President, Metal Trades Department, *Statement,* before President's Review Committee, October 23, 1967, p. 3.

[16] John F. Griner, *op. cit.,* p. 14.

[17] *Ibid.,* pp. 14-15.

[18] *Ibid.,* p. 15.

[19] W. H. Ryan, National Coordinator, Government Employees Department, IAM, *Statement,* before President's Review Committee, October 23, 1967, p. 9.

bias.[20] James Rademacher of the Letter Carriers scored the conflict-of-interest problem in interpreting and administering the entire order and noted a critic of the system who compared it to "Walter Reuther seeking a final determination from the President of the Ford Motor Company." [21] George Meany, in stating the need for an impartial, independent board, declared that the very concept of collective bargaining refuted the possibility that an agency head could remain neutral in a labor relations dispute.[22] Although there was considerable division among management witnesses on the issue, several important and deeply involved federal units supported the idea of an independent board. Among these were the Departments of the Army, Navy, and Interior.[23]

Studies conducted in both the Johnson and the Nixon Administrations took considerable notice of the criticisms outlined above. Their result was E.O. 11491. The Nixon order wrought many important policy changes, but its organizational modifications restructured the entire operation of the program. This was due in no small degree to the Nixon Study Committee's effort to be responsive to reasonable proposals from all sources in its attempt to upgrade the EMC program. Substantial concessions were made to union views. Administrative changes certainly were in order. What revisions were effected in administration, however, were built upon a compromise of management and labor concepts as to the proper status for a labor regulatory body.

The Nixon order required the Federal Labor Relations Council to give centralized direction to the entire EMC program. The FLRC was not the independent regulatory agency sought by the affiliated unions. The union-proposed board would have consisted of five members nominated by the President and confirmed by the Senate and would have approximated the NLRB in independent status and powers. The Review Committee had suggested an agency or panel similar to the FLRC which would have included the NLRB chairman. However, this and other specific

---

[20] E. C. Hallbeck, President, UFPC, *Statement,* before President's Review Committee, October 25, 1967, p. 3.

[21] J. H. Rademacher, Vice-President, NALC, *Statement,* before President's Review Committee, October 26, 1967, in *Postal Record,* December 1967, p. 19.

[22] George Meany, President, AFL-CIO, *Statement,* before President's Review Committee, October 23, 1967, pp. 12-13. The AFL-CIO-sponsored Federal Service Labor-Management Relations Board would have had the power: (1) to define appropriate bargaining units; (2) to determine majority status of a labor organization; (3) to determine the eligibility of an organization as a bona fide labor organization; (4) to decide on unfair labor practice charges; and (5) to interpret the meaning and application of the executive order. See AFL-CIO *Program to Improve Collective Bargaining in the Federal Service,* September 28, 1967, pp. 12-13.

[23] See President's Review Committee, *Statements,* Department of the Army, p. 7; Department of the Navy, p. 5.

references to administrative aid from the NLRB were not retained by the Study Committee. The Council had central authority, but its members were drawn from the executive branch and it remained an integral part of the executive branch, an element of government-wide executive management.

The Study Committee fully realized the need for overall central authority and more impartial, third-party handling of labor disputes.[24] The Federal Labor Relations Council therefore was empowered to administer the entire labor relations program, make definitive interpretations of any provision in the order, and decide major policy issues. It was to prescribe regulations and report to the President on the progress of the program. The FLRC was given broad discretionary power to act as the final appeals body for certain labor disputes. Appeals to it could be made from decisions of the Assistant Secretary of Labor for Labor-Management Relations, which covered several of the major areas of union complaint. It could review exceptions from arbitration awards and disputes over whether an issue was negotiable in terms of being contrary to law, regulations, or a controlling agreement.[25] The Committee believed that such a body of high executive officials would "ensure the desired balance of judgment and expertise" in the personnel and labor areas.[26]

In response to the demands for impartial administration of disputes, the Committee turned to the Assistant Secretary of Labor for Labor-Management Relations. The Department of Labor, through its Office of Federal Employee-Management Relations in the Labor-Management Services Administration, was already engaged in servicing the EMC program. Established in August 1963 to carry out Section 11 of the Kennedy order, this office had been actively providing machinery for advisory arbitration to help resolve disputes over representation units for exclusive recognition. It already had handled requests for arbitrators in cases arising out of representation elections and had provided other arbitration-related services.[27] With the changes in policy under E.O. 11491, the Assistant Secretary was given full authority to decide unit and representation disputes. His responsibility now covered supervising elections, certifying their results, and deter-

---

24 President's Study Committee, *Report and Recommendations on Labor-Management Relations in the Federal Service*, August 1969, pp. 6-8.

25 E.O. 11491, Secs. 4, 11 (c).

26 Study Committee, *op. cit.*, p. 8.

27 U.S. Department of Labor, Labor-Management Services Administration, *Summary of Activities of the Office of Federal Employee-Management Relations Under E.O. 10988* (Washington: U.S. Government Printing Office, 1963).

mining what unions were entitled to national consultation rights under FLRC criteria. To refute claims of bias, jurisdiction over all Standards and Code cases was transferred from the agencies to him, thus giving him the power to decide all cases of unfair labor practices and violations of the Standards of Conduct. He was given the right to issue cease and desist orders to recalcitrant agencies or unions and to require that their affirmative action conform to the order.[28]

The Study Committee believed that having "administrative" disputes determined by "an official who is independent of the parties and is assigned this responsibility by the President" would materially improve the program by providing impartial action, fairness, and effectiveness in administering federal labor relations. It was believed that the Assistant Secretary's judgments could, in time, build up a body of precedent for the guidance of the parties in avoiding actions that might contravene policy or create conflict.[29] Indeed, a kind of "common law" of federal labor relations could be developed from decisions of the FLRC, the Assistant Secretary, and the Federal Service Impasses Panel.

Executive Order No. 11616 went even further to place unfair labor practice cases solely within the jurisdiction of the Assistant Secretary. This order was intended to strengthen third-party handling and to insure that only the Assistant Secretary's decisions and FLRC appeal opinions would be considered binding precedents in unfair labor practice cases. Any disputes processed by other means were not to be deemed unfair labor practice cases. Under E.O. 11616, an employee could now opt to handle a dispute as either a grievance or an unfair labor practice case. His decision was final and precluded his use of the alternative.

E.O. 11616 gave the Assistant Secretary exclusive power to build a "body of precedent" for the Code of Fair Labor Practices. Proposals had been offered to establish an independent office for the prosecution of unfair labor practice complaints, but the Council chose to rely on executive procedures. In this regard, its recommendations were adopted in full by President Ford in E.O. 11838. The executive order increased the Assistant Secretary's power considerably, authorizing him to conduct independent investigations of unfair labor practice cases to help determine whether there is a reasonable basis for complaint. It allows him to make the initial decision over negotiability in unfair labor practice cases where it

---

28 E.O. 11491, Sec. 6.
29 Study Committee, *op. cit.,* pp. 25-26.

is charged that the acting party has unilaterally changed personnel policies, practices, or working conditions and is, therefore, refusing to consult, confer, or negotiate. The adversely affected party may appeal his ruling to the Council. The Assistant Secretary also was given exclusive authority to decide whether a grievance involves a matter subject to statutory appeal procedure. All remaining disagreements over the grievability or arbitrability of an issue may be submitted by the parties either to him or to an arbitrator.[30]

Although the CSC and the Labor Department adjusted their organization and functions to meet rapidly changing needs and policy revisions, it was quite plain by the mid-1960s that the rapid growth of federal unionism and its resultant demands for greater CSC services necessitated change. Labor relations could no longer be treated as just another element in the traditional galaxy of personnel administration functions. It required more attention than that which it received from a single section in the Bureau of Policies and Standards. Accordingly, in November 1966, the Office of Labor-Management Relations (OLMR) was created in the Office of the CSC chairman, with Wilfred V. Gill, assistant to the chairman, as its director and L. David Korb as assistant director.[31]

Under E.O. 11491, however, the overall functions of the CSC were transferred to the Federal Labor Relations Council. At the same time other activities were expanded. The order emphasized centralized technical guidance and advice to the agencies but moved away from centralized policy making and interpretation. The order stressed the FLRC's information and training functions. For example, working with the Bureau of Training, the FLRC helped establish a Labor Relations Training Center in November 1970, with courses on collective bargaining and other activities in the field. E.O. 11491 required the Office of Labor-Management Relations to review and evaluate the program and from time to time help prepare reports to the Council such as those previously made to the President.[32] Under E.O. 11616, these activities were to be conducted in conjunction with the newly established Office of

[30] Federal Labor Relations Council, *Report and Recommendations on Labor-Management Relations in the Federal Service,* June 1971, pp. 8-10; _____, *Labor-Management Relations in the Federal Service, Amendments to E.O. 11491 With Report and Recommendations,* Washington, February 1975, pp. 44-53, 58-64; E.O. 11616, Sec. 10 amending Sec. 19 (d) ; E.O. 11838, Secs. 4, 13, 14. See also *Government Employee Relations Report,* No. 582, February 10, 1975, pp. 1, A-14 A-15.
[31] U.S. Civil Service Commission, *The Role of the Civil Service Commission in Federal Labor Relations,* pp. 34-37.
[32] *Ibid.,* pp. 52, 54.

Management and Budget because of OMB's great responsibility for executive management.[33] Indeed, the new partnership of the OMB and CSC could evolve as the prime source of executive policy in federal labor relations.

Since the CSC chairman was now also chairman of the Council, the OLMR was transferred from his office to that of the executive director of the CSC. With Gill now serving with the Council, Anthony F. Ingrassia became director of the OLMR.

Although the Federal Labor Relations Council was granted full central authority, it was cautioned by the Study Committee "to use calculated restraint in exercising its responsibilities so as to leave the agencies and labor organizations to work out their differences to the maximum extent possible without damaging the overall program." [34]

Prior to the issuance of E.O. 11616 in August 1971, the FLRC, as is customary, held extensive public hearings on federal experience under E.O. 11491. Sixty-five people involved in various aspects of federal labor relations testified or submitted papers. The Council met 18 times in executive session to consider major policy changes. The resultant E.O. 11616 worked no major changes in overall administrative structure. Indeed, as noted, third-party operations of the Assistant Secretary of Labor were further strengthened. The system was working well and effectively in terms of the envisioned needs of the federal establishment. The testimony of John A. McCart of the Government Employes' Council, a major association of the AFL-CIO government unions, was representative of labor views presented in the public hearings. McCart recognized the "advances incorporated in the revised policy" in E.O. 11491,[35] but from his vantage point as a labor representative he was critical of various facets of the EMC program. On program operations he cited "[i]mpartial administration of the entire policy"as "a matter of continued concern" since 1962. Noting the makeup of the Council, he was perturbed that the "obligation of overseeing the program falls upon three of the highest level management officials in the executive branch." He questioned the fact that one of the agencies represented on the FLRC administered the general personnel program for all agencies.[36] Citing the inaccessibility of Council members, he declared:

33 E.O. 11616, Sec. 25.

34 Study Committee, op. cit., p. 8.

35 John A. McCart, Operations Director, Government Employes' Council, AFL-CIO, Statement of the GEC, before the Federal Labor Relations Council, October 7, 1970, pp. 2, 6.

36 Ibid., pp. 3-4.

"It is our considered judgement that creation of the three member Council simply disperses among three Federal agencies functions performed previously by the Civil Service Commission alone. The concept of impartial oversight of the Federal Government's labor policy for its own workers has not been adopted." [37]

McCart concluded by commenting on an observation that the FLRC was never intended to be impartial, saying that the GEC was "at a loss to understand the failure to create an independent board." [38] Apparently "internal independence" within the executive branch was not enough for labor spokesmen. They still desired a regulatory body completely independent of the executive. Nevertheless, after the FLRC conducted its second general review of the entire federal program, no change was effected in the fundamental administrative structure. For some 18 months during 1973-1975, the Council sought to determine whether basic changes were needed. Recounting statistically the considerable advances of the various regulatory units established under E.O. 11491, it concluded that "progress can be seen in the operations under the order and in many ways the order is functioning smoothly." Accordingly, President Ford's E.O. 11838 retained the full power and structure of the FLRC as set forth in the Nixon orders.[38]

B. STATE AND CITY LABOR ADMINISTRATION IN THE UNITED STATES AND CANADA

A number of alternatives are available in determining the form that administration shall take. Three of these are, first, to keep administration within the executive authority; second, to incorporate the administration of public labor relations into the jurisdiction of existing private-sector labor relations and mediation agencies; and third, to establish new independent bodies that deal only with the public sector.

As public unionism gained strength and became an integral facet of the changing social climate of the 1960s, each of these administrative systems was brought into play at the state level and in Canada. The experience thus gained has considerable relevance to federal labor relations and must influence its development over the long run.

The states in the 1960s saw the development of new labor power and the willingness of legislatures to deal with it. In 1960-61, the

---

[37] *Ibid.*, p. 4.

[38] *Ibid.*, E. O. 11491 as amended by E.O. 11838, Secs. 4-6; Federal Labor Relations Council, *Labor-Management Relations in the Federal Service, Amendments to E.O. 11491 With Report and Recommendations*, Washington, February 1975, pp. 1-4.

author, in cooperation with the National Civil Service League, conducted a survey of public labor relations at all levels of government.[39] The state returns indicated a general pattern of statutory silence on the permissibility of collective bargaining itself. Only 11 states had taken a legislative stand on the issue. It would be most generous to say that many returns indicated that the term "collective bargaining" did not enjoy general acceptance or respectability.[40] At the time, Wisconsin had recently acted to guarantee municipal employees the rights to organize, confer, and negotiate.[41] This was the first instance of major state labor relations law for the public sector. Through a remarkable *volte-face,* within one decade it could be reported by the American Bar Association that 40 states had enacted laws permitting some degree of public employee union activities. Of deeper significance, 23 of these statutes could be classified as comprehensive legislation covering state and/ or local government workers.[42] Variations existed among the states in employee coverage as well as in the administrative machinery for implementing the statutes. But the force and substance of these trends appeared to indicate still further evolution of the state labor relations process.

Administration of these programs at present lies squarely in the hands of executive authority in the majority of state jurisdictions. Twenty-seven states do not have comprehensive coverage nor do all those possessing advanced programs provide neutral governing agencies. As in the majority of county and city governments, in most states labor relations are administered by various combinations of civil service commissions and/or departments of labor, specially appointed executive officers, or ad hoc agencies. Therefore, there is assuredly no lack of precedent for the retention of executive control of labor program administration. But, interest-

---

[39] Murray B. Nesbitt, "The Civil Service Merit System and Collective Bargaining," (unpublished Ph.D. dissertation, Graduate School of Public Administration, New York University, 1962).

[40] *Ibid.,* pp. 132-138.

[41] Wisconsin Statutes, Ch. III, Subch. IV, Sec. 111.70; Laws of 1959, Ch. 108, Sec. 1.

[42] *Government Employee Relations Report, Reference File,* Section on Issues and Techniques, and *Report* of the American Bar Association, Committee on State Labor Law, 1967-1970, cited in U.S. Department of Labor, Labor-Management Services Administration, *Collective Bargaining in Public Employment and the Merit System,* by Jerry Lelchook and Herbert J. Lahne (Washington, 1972), pp. 30-32. States generally covering all public employees are Alaska, California, Delaware, Hawaii, Kansas, Massachusetts, Minnesota, Missouri, Nebraska, New Jersey, New York, Oregon, Pennsylvania, Rhode Island, South Dakota, Vermont, Wisconsin; New Hampshire's coverage applies mainly to state employees while municipal workers are covered by state laws in Connecticut, Maine, Michigan, Nevada and Washington. Several states have special statutes governing public utility and transport workers, teachers, police, firemen, university, and hospital personnel.

ingly, it is just this form of control from which the major state and city programs appear to be departing. The greatest and most varied substantive changes have occurred in those industrialized states and populous cities where private-sector union values and political muscle can be brought to bear.[43]

In passing it should be noted that the larger cities are no longer alone in advancing labor relations. In 1972 the Bureau of Labor Statistics reported over three fifths of the 2,064 cities surveyed in one study had union representation and collective bargaining agreements. The study included municipalities with as few as 10,000 people. Spurred by permissive legislation, unions had become very real factors in negotiation. The BLS study noted that recent years had seen a shift in union organizing activities away from the great municipalities with their large civil services bureaucracies to the smaller cities.[44]

In several states, by the simple process of nondifferentiation between public and private employees, state statutes made available to the state civil service and its unions the facilities of the labor boards and commissions established to service the private sector. State conciliation, mediation, and arbitration agencies in some cases were also allotted these added responsibilities. Thus, for example, Massachusetts' State Labor Relations Commission oversees public service recognition, certification, appropriate unit, and unfair labor practice cases, while the State Board of Conciliation and Arbitration must use its impasse machinery to resolve public employment deadlocks. Similar provisions apply in Connecticut, Delaware, Rhode Island, and Wisconsin.[45]

The Wisconsin experience with impartial administration of public labor relations was not only a pioneer experiment at the state level but also a prime example of the total incorporation of public-sector jurisdiction into existing private labor relations machinery. A 1959 law extended coverage to municipal employees only; in 1968 another labor relations law brought in state employees.[46]

Arvid Anderson, who left the Wisconsin Employment Relations

---

[43] For comprehensive coverage of the modern scene at local levels, see: Streling D. Spero and John M. Capozzola, *The Urban Community and its Unionized Bureaucracy* (New York: Dunellen Publishing Co., 1973). See also *Municipal Collective Bargaining Agreements in Large Cities,* Bureau of Labor Statistics, Bulletin No. 1759, 1972.

[44] Richard R. Nelson and James L. Doster, Bureau of Labor Statistics, "City Employee Representation and Bargaining Policies," *Monthly Labor Review,* November 1972, pp. 43-46, 50.

[45] Jean T. McKelvey, "The Role of State Agencies in Public Employee Labor Relations," *Industrial and Labor Relations Review,* Vol. XX, January 1967.

[46] Wisconsin Statutes Annotated, Title XIII, Ch. III, Subch. IV, Sec. 111.70.

Board to become chairman of New York City's Office of Collective Bargaining, has described the WERB's handling of the public sector. The statutes, he said, "tied in with administrative machinery provide a rather well-structured framework within which municipal employees and their employers are authorized to carry on relations on an organized, systematic basis." [47] The law guaranteed the right to join, organize, and be represented by labor organizations and the right to refrain from union activity. It also contained a list of labor practices reminiscent of federal law applicable to unions and employers. A 1962 amendment named the WERB as the administrator of the act, with, among other things, the responsibility of enforcing the prohibited practices code and determining questions of representation on the petition of either union or employer. In addition, the WERB determined appropriate bargaining units and certified exclusive bargaining representatives, and was empowered to use its mediation and fact-finding services in public labor disputes. Its final orders were subject to judicial review.[48]

The WERB proved highly flexible and effective in dealing with public-sector labor disputes. Comparable success had been achieved two decades earlier in Canadian cities and provinces. After passage of the Wagner Act in the United States, similar statutes were enacted in the provinces, but municipal employees were not excluded from coverage. Soon after World War II nearly all the provinces had passed public-service labor relations laws to cover municipal employees.[49]

The basic aspect of Canadian labor relations practice pertinent to U.S. state practice is the refusal to distinguish between municipal employers and private employers. Thus, in most cases city collective-bargaining relations and disputes can be regulated legally by provincial labor relations boards. And while not all provincial employees enjoy the liberality and administrative independence provided municipal workers, as Richard D. Salik has pointed ed out:

"The most significant feature of municipal labor relations in the 10 provinces of Canada is the envelopment by the labor relations

---

[47] Arvid Anderson, "Legal Aspects of Collective Bargaining," in *Developments in Public Employee Relations,* Kenneth O. Warner, Ed. (Chicago: Public Personnel Association, 1965), p. 136.

[48] *Ibid.,* pp. 136-137.

[49] Statutes of Saskatchewan, 1944, Ch. 69; Revised Statutes of Quebec, 1941, Ch. 167, 169; Statutes of Alberta, 1947, Ch. 8; Revised Statutes of British Columbia, 1918, Ch. 155; Revised Statutes of Ontario, 1951, Ch. 194; Statutes of Manitoba, 1947, Ch. 43; Statutes of New Brunswick, 1952, Sec. 1 (4); Statutes of Nova Scotia, 1947, Ch. 3.

acts controlling private industry. Provincial employees, for the most part, find relations with the provincial employer regulated by public service or civil service acts." [50]

C. THE PROVINCE OF SASKATCHEWAN—THE EXPERIMENT THAT LASTED

The prairie province of Saskatchewan represents a particularly successful experiment at the provincial or "state" level. It was the first region to bring private-sector advantages to both provincial and city employees.

The Saskatchewan public labor relations program was launched with the support of the provincial government itself. For many years Saskatchewan had been a major stronghold of the New Democratic Party, formerly the Canadian Commonwealth Federation. The CCF's fundamentally socialist stance had resulted in a long tradition of cooperation with the Canadian labor movement and passage of enlightened labor legislation. When the CCF came to political power in 1944, it seemed only appropriate that, in this labor-oriented atmosphere, the benefits available to workers generally should be afforded employees of the state itself. Accordingly, the Trade Union Act of 1944 granted full organizing and bargaining rights to all government employees. Interestingly enough, by Section 2 (6) of the Act "Her Majesty in the right of Saskatchewan" was defined as an "employer" within the meaning of the law. [51] Thus a true sovereign legally relinquished the then-vaunted immunity of the sovereignty doctrine.

Independent administration of the labor relations program was assured under the jurisdiction of the Saskatchewan Labour Relations Board, an impartial panel similar to the American NLRB. Under the Act it had responsibility for protecting rights and providing the legal framework for collective bargaining. On occasion, it has also selected appropriate bargaining units and certified unions as exclusive representatives, to the disenchantment of both the government and unions alike. [52]

Negotiating machinery was clearly patterned on the Whitley

---

[50] Richard D. Salik, "A Digest of Provincial Labor Laws Governing Municipal and Provincial Employees in Canada," *Personnel Report No. 664* (Chicago: Public Personnel Association, 1966) , p. 2.

[51] S. J. Frankel and R. C. Pratt, *Municipal Labour Relations in Canada* (Montreal: Industrial Relations Centre, McGill University and Canadian Federation of Mayors and Municipalities, 1954) , pp. 5, 6, 21.

[52] Saul J. Frankel, *Staff Relations in the Civil Service: The Canadian Experience* (Montreal: McGill University Press, 1962) , pp. 212-215.

Councils.[53] Thus, bargaining is conducted between a staff side and a government side. The staff side, composed of a half dozen or more persons, forms a negotiating committee drawn from leading members of the Executive Board of the province's single largest employee organization. Although the Act calls for a Cabinet member to make the agreement, the chief negotiator and head of the government side is the chairman of the Public Service Commission (PSC). Other negotiating committee members are from the Public Service Commission and operating departments concerned in the negotiations. The PSC chairman is best qualified to head the committee since he is the most intimately involved in personnel administration. As in the United States, any agreement must receive final executive approval, in this case, from the Cabinet. Indeed, the Cabinet itself has in some instances negotiated with the staff side to iron out last-minute deadlocks. If an impasse remains, a board of conciliation may be convened, or if mutually agreeable, the issues may be submitted to arbitration. Failing this, the employee association may legally resort to the strike, although this is viewed by unions as a last resort.[54]

The Province of Saskatchewan has entered into collective bargaining agreements since 1948. Both unions and management have fixed rights. While management is not statutorily required to contract, there must be compliance with the procedures normally expected of private employers in good-faith collective bargaining.[55] But by no means has the system vitiated management's power to negotiate from strength and principle.[56]

It was clear from the outset of the Saskatchewan labor relations program that all were anxious for the new venture to succeed. The major political parties and the civil service association were well aware of the program's experimental character and the attention it was attracting throughout Canada and the United States. In his study of the Canadian Civil Service Frankel emphasized that the election of a government favorable to trade union aspirations con-

---

[53] Since 1919, Whitley Councils in Great Britain have successfully used this basic procedure for joint negotiations and consultations. See: Leonard D. White, *Whitley Councils in the British Civil Service* (Chicago: University of Chicago Press, 1933) ; James Callaghan, *Whitleyism, A Study of Joint Consultation in the Civil Service* (London: Fabian Research Series, No. 159, 1953) ; H. M. Treasury, *Staff Relations in the Civil Service* (London: Her Majesty's Stationery Office, 1958) .

[54] Saul J. Frankel, *op. cit.*, pp. 218-228. See also Howard A. Scarrow, "Employer-Employee Relationships in the Civil Services of the Canadian Provinces," *Canadian Public Administration*, J. E. Hodgetts and D. C. Corbett, Eds. (Toronto: Macmillan Press, 1960) , pp. 389-391.

[55] Howard A. Scarrow, *op. cit.*, pp. 390-391.

[56] Hugh M. Morrison, "Personnel Panorama-1960; Canadian Provincial Developments," *Public Personnel Review*, Vol. XXII, No. 1, January 1961, p. 11.

tributed to the program's success. The government attitude of sympathetic cooperation ". . . helped to produce the atmosphere and machinery which contributed to the apparent success of the experiment." [57] Frankel and most observers agree that the labor relations system and the process of collective bargaining have proved themselves and can stand on their own merits apart from party politics.

D. THE POSTAL SERVICE BEFORE THE NLRB—THE PRIVATE-SECTOR AGENCY

Saskatchewan showed the importance of political motivation and support in achieving sweeping changes in labor relations administration. In the United States, the drastic reorganization that created the Postal Service and placed it squarely within the NLRB's jurisdiction demonstrated the same thing in a wider arena. Mushrooming political clout, born of labor crisis, was finally sufficient to force the passage of the kind of labor law the majority of postal unions had long sought. The end result was the largest single instance in the United States of totally independent administration of a public labor relations program by means of existing private-sector regulatory machinery.

On July 1, 1971, the vast postal establishment became subject to the National Labor Relations Act and certain other federal labor legislation. Under the reorganization, accordingly, the National Labor Relations Board's jurisdiction enveloped the Postal Service. Over the years the Board had extended its coverage to quasi-public employers such as hospitals and universities, none of which generated as many cases as the new postal organization.

The NLRB appeared able to handle the new case load without any serious problems. New funds were allotted to help meet the expected influx of cases. The Board's regular procedures for handling unfair labor practice charges, representation proceedings, unit determinations and elections were made applicable to postal disputes.

The heavy postal case load undoubtedly helped bring about changes in the NLRB's Office of the General Counsel. It was reported that the sheer volume of work entailed in increased cases and changes in the composition of the case load significantly added to the "complexity and scope" of the General Counsel's Office. The 36th Annual Report declared that:

---

[57] Saul J. Frankel, *op. cit.,* p. 233.

"Recent years have seen the extension of the NLRB jurisdiction to the Postal Service with sizeable increases in the proportion of unfair labor practice charges involving highly complex factual and legal issues, in the percentage of charges found to be meritorious and the number of petitions filed by respondents in Board cases seeking appellate court review." [58]

This was the NLRB's sole acknowledgment of the ramifications of the postal reorganization. The NLRB *Report* stated that by July 1972 the internal reorganizations intended to facilitate case processing in the General Counsel's Office had "proven very encouraging." [59] In short, the addition of a large segment of the federal establishment had not created any administrative difficulties that could not be reasonably overcome.

By far the largest number of postal cases were unfair labor practice charges. Literally thousands of such charges alleged that the USPS had violated Section 8 (a) (5) by refusing to bargain in good faith, particularly during the first round of local negotiations starting in February 1972 under the first National Working Agreement of the Postal Service. It was reported that the Letter Carriers alone, surpassing all other postal unions, filed charges in the thousands. [60]

Representation disputes were far less numerous but perhaps had greater implications for the national bargaining structure. It was soon clear to the seven unions enjoying national exclusive recognition that NLRA coverage also carried certain disadvantages. The exclusive bargaining status of these unions could now be challenged by competing unions in accordance with the procedures and administrative criteria developed by the NLRB since 1935. This was entirely in keeping with the NLRB's common law of exclusive representation for appropriate bargaining units. Six exclusive representation petitions were submitted almost immediately after the Postal Service was created. [61] They came primarily from the militant independents and branches of the postal craft unions seeking area wage differentials. Thus, the large metropolitan branches of the National Postal Union sought local or regional appropriate bargaining units. If the Board, following its private-sector standards and criteria for appropriate units, had authorized such units, these powerful unions might well have displaced the exclusives on the local level. This would have undercut the

---

58 U. S. National Labor Relations Board, *36th Annual Report,* Fiscal Year 1971, in *Labor Relations Year Book—1972* (Washington: BNA Books, 1973) , p 239.

59 *Ibid.*

60 Mozart G. Ratner, "Report of the General Counsel," NALC, *The Postal Record,* August 1972, p. 53.

61 *Ibid.*

system of national collective bargaining that had governed postal workers since 1962.

Even after the National Postal Union became an integral part of the merged American Postal Workers Union, regional councils in the urban areas still pressed their petitions before the Board for area appropriate bargaining units. Their underlying motives were essentially economic. Spurred by the same causes that sparked the 1970 strike, postal workers in the heavily industrialized and unionized metropolitan regions complained of wages far lower than those in private industry and usually much lower than those of their fellow public workers in state and city government. Urban postal workers had to survive in the highest cost-of-living areas, yet under national bargaining they were bound, essentially, to national wage scales, which did not provide for area wage differentials.

In the New York City region the movement for higher wages was led primarily by the Manhattan-Bronx Postal Union, comprising many crafts and Branch 36 of the Letter Carriers. MBPU submitted a petition to the NLRB to establish an appropriate bargaining unit for the "metro" area.[62] The petition was hotly contested by both the USPS and the national leadership of the National Association of Letter Carriers and the APWU, who were committed to preserving the national bargaining structure. Procedural and legal infighting prolonged the case well beyond the second round of postal negotiations that resulted in a new two-year National Working Agreement in 1973. The Postal Coordinated Bargaining Committee comprising the four national exclusives attempted to negotiate more effective area wage considerations but to no avail. The second postal contract, effective through 1975, thus offered no national formula to cause urban postal workers to relent in pressing their case before the Board. The concept of area bargaining involved more than a simple pay issue to the MBPU, which at this time was renamed the New York Metro Area Postal Union in keeping with its bargaining aspirations. As Morris Biller pointed out, if the union won, the entire gamut of negotiable items would come under local negotiations, including "retirement, insurance benefits and a grievance and seniority program that would fit [union] needs."[63]

The Board was also involved in the efforts of the predominantly

---

[62] See New York Metro Area Postal Union (formerly Manhattan-Bronx Postal Union), APWU, *The Union Mail*, July 1971, April-August 1972; New York Letter Carriers, Branch 36, NALC, *Outlook*, October 1971, March-April 1972.

[63] New York Metro Area Postal Union, APWU, *The Union Mail*, May 1972, p. 3.

black National Alliance of Postal and Federal Employees to secure recognition as the exclusive representative of its members on a less than national basis. Despite the presence of the national exclusives, these efforts went on through Alliance-instituted unfair labor practice and representation cases.

On the national scene, a decision was handed down by the NLRB that was immensely significant for the vast number of postal unfair labor practice cases. It was discovered, almost immediately after Board coverage was extended to postal employees, that being governed by private-sector rulings could be quite disadvantageous. On August 20, 1971, in an unfair labor practice decision, the Board held that if a union agreement contained a procedure for final, binding arbitration of disputes arising under the contract, that procedure must be followed, rather than the procedure stemming from an unfair labor practice charge under Section 8 (a) (5) of the Act alleging that the employer had refused to bargain collectively in good faith. This was a reversal of a position of many years standing.[64]

The employer in the case, the Collyer Insulated Wire Company, changed the wage rates of some employees during the term of the contract. The International Brotherhood of Electrical Workers claimed this violated Section 8 (a) (5) since the employer had taken unilateral action and thus had refused to bargain on so vital an issue. The controlling contract contained grievance-arbitration machinery. By deferring to the arbitration clause, the Board relieved itself of the responsibility of handling such cases whenever an arbitration clause existed. Contractual rather than Board procedures were now to govern.

This unprecedented decision affected hundreds of similar private-sector cases. For the postal unions, the holding was particularly ominous since Article XV of their National Working Agreement contained precisely the kind of grievance-arbitration provision involved in the *Collyer* case.

Joseph S. Smolen of the National Association of Letter Carriers closely examined the implications of the decision and concluded that postal workers and unions would suffer "great damage" from the decision, that it would make postal management "very bold in violating labor contracts which contained arbitration clauses." He cited the February 1972 local negotiations in which alleged management lack of good-faith bargaining was widespread. Smolen declared that "with over 100,000 instances" of such violations, un-

---

[64] Collyer Insulated Wire Co., 192 NLRB No. 150 (1971), 77 LRRM 1931.

der the NLRB policy management could flood the arbitration procedures with so many cases that "the arbitration policy would have worked too slowly to be of any use or any benefit to letter carriers." [65] He pointed out that the NLRB's machinery far surpassed that of arbitrators in force and effect, among other reasons because of the Board's power to issue subpoenas and cease and desist orders.

The U.S. Supreme Court has yet to pass judgment on the Board's *Collyer* doctrine. The doctrine has, however, been upheld by several U.S. courts of appeals.[66]

What do these developments during the short period of NLRB postal coverage signify? Primarily, they mean that with the benefits of administration by an independent regulatory agency, the newly initiated postal unions must also accept the risks of independent regulatory procedures. The unions have alleged that the Board is not impartial—that the three-to-two, management-oriented *Collyer* decision was authored by Nixon appointees, while the two Democratic appointees dissented vigorously. In addition, the Board's General Counsel, actively enforcing the deferral-to-arbitration policy, also was a Nixon appointee. This is extremely important since under Section 3 (d) of the Taft-Hartley Act he has "final authority" over the issuance of unfair labor practice complaints and other general administrative powers that make him far more formidable than any of his counterparts in other independent agencies.[67]

Charges of partisanship, however, are nothing new to regulatory agencies. Since their inception these agencies, particularly the NLRB, have been accused of favoring one side or another. A special House committee appointed to investigate the Board in 1939 portrayed it as a radical body, partial to certain labor unions, and biased against employers.[68] Senator Taft (Rep., Ohio) charged that the Wagner Act Board was made up of "people who regarded themselves as crusaders to put a CIO union, if you please, in every plant in the United States." [69] On the other hand, the Eisenhower Administration was accused of making conservative appointments. Senators Douglas (Dem., Ill.) and McNamara (Dem., Mich.) de-

[65] Joseph S. Smolen, Director of Training and Union Development, NALC, "Protecting Your Rights," *The Postal Record*, October 1972, p. 30.

[66] Nabisco, Inc. v. NLRB, 479 F.2d 770, 83 LRRM 2612 (CA 2, 1973); Associated Press v. NLRB, 85 LRRM 2440 (CA DC, 1974); Enterprise Publishing Co. v. NLRB, 85 LRRM 2746 (CA 1, 1974).

[67] 61 Stat. 139, 29 U.S.C. Sec. 153 (1947).

[68] U.S. House of Representatives, Special Committee to Investigate the NLRB, *Final Report*, House Report No. 3109, 76th Cong., 3rd Sess., 1941, Part 1, pp. 149-152.

[69] 93 Cong. Rec. 7537-7538 (1947).

plored the "anti-labor background" of General Counsel T. C. Kammholz, who was vigorously opposed by the Chicago printing unions as strongly promanagement.[70] The current accusations levelled against the Board by organized labor do not break tradition.

The nature of the independent agency within the American system of separation of powers is such that political allegiance must be taken into account. Successive boards will vary their political hue as appointments reflect succeeding Presidents. The concept of bipartisan boards with odd-numbered memberships serving overlapping terms was intended to provide objective, impartial, and independent administration of a continuing national policy. In the main this goal has been achieved, although the agency structure is still susceptible to politically motivated decision making and, at times, undue influence. Nevertheless, the deficiencies of agencies as regulatory bodies are far outweighed by their virtues. The fundamental purpose of such agencies—to resolve as many disputes as possible informally through the administrative process—has been achieved remarkably well by the NLRB. The proportion of cases going to formal hearing and decision is but a small part of the great number of disputes that are processed and resolved without administrative trials.

Under the EMC program postal unions believed they were controlled by a powerful executive authority which determined the ultimate shape of their labor relations programs. Although possibly guilty of bias at times, the NLRB cannot be charged with exercising excessive authority over labor relations. It has remained, by and large, a truly independent agency, committed to enforcing a national policy formulated by Congress. Postal experience under the federal labor code has not been free of difficulty, but never were unions and management in the private sector entirely content with Board policies. Beyond any doubt, however, the NLRB in the few years of its coverage of the public sector has proved its ability to apply the private-sector labor code to a substantial segment of America's public service.

E. THE NEW YORK STATE PUBLIC EMPLOYMENT RELATIONS BOARD—THE PUBLIC-SECTOR AGENCY

Another trend worthy of consideration has loomed large on the public scene. Over the past few years the Council of State Governments has noted the significance of:

---

[70] *Labor Relations Reporter*, Vol. 35, pp. 179-181; *New York Times*, February 26, 1955, p. 6.

"the growing use of separate boards for the handling of public employment disputes and procedures, apart from facilities available for private sector disputes. Creation of such specialized organizational units in New Jersey, Nevada, Oregon and Vermont, aside from the Board established in New York by previous enactment, illustrated this trend." [71]

Carrying forward the trend, Minnesota adopted a broad collective bargaining act calling for a tripartite public employment relations board. A Kansas statute also created a separate agency.[72]

The distinguishing characteristic of these independent public employment labor boards, created under special acts whose labor policies are geared to the unique problems of public service, is the total separation of the public- and the private-sector jurisdictions. Rather than extending the jurisdiction of existing labor statutes and agencies, new labor laws and administrative agencies are being established to govern the public sphere. This new regulatory model not only conforms with the philosophy that essential differences exist between public and private employment but also provides the opportunity to write laws specially tailored to public-service needs.

In terms of the breadth of coverage, the foremost example of totally separated and independent administration is the system of the State of New York. There the passage of a Public Employees' Fair Employment Act in 1967 [73] ended some 20 years of confused and ineffectual attempts to regulate public labor relations peacefully. Prior to 1967, the law did not provide a framework within which public labor relations could flourish but, instead, imposed severe penalties for individual employees who went on strike. The old laws were almost unenforceable. The antistrike Condon-Wadlin Act was widely and seriously violated as unions in the state and particularly in New York City became increasingly militant. The situation bordered on the ridiculous when after each major strike the legislature would be forced to vote general amnesties and exemptions from the law. There was little choice, since inflicting statutory punishments would have served only to curtail public services or risk their total stoppage. A change was both inevitable and necessary. In New York City, by mayoral action, bargaining procedures had already been in effect for almost a decade.

---

[71] Council of State Governments, *Book of the States: 1970-1971* (Lexington, Ky., 1971), p. 498.

[72] _____, *Book of the States: 1971-1972* (Lexington, Ky., 1972), p. 510.

[73] New York Civil Service Law, Art. 14 (McKinney, 1967), Chapter 392 of the Laws of 1967. Amendments in 1969 prohibited employer and union improper practices and extended strike penalties to individual employees. Under 1971 amendments management and confidential employees could be excluded from the Act. Other amendments worked no substantial changes.

The state was clearly ready for a more compassionate and reasoned policy towards the public service.

The late George W. Taylor of the Wharton School chaired a committee of five well-known out-of-state authorities whose recommendations formed the basis of the statute which took his name.[74] It is true that this statute remained a vigorous antistrike law with severe financial and punitive penalties that could be exacted against unions, their officers, and their members. Loss of checkoff privileges was particularly damaging. However, the Taylor Act provided much that contributed to a healthy labor relations climate. For some time, the Act's antistrike aspects tended to overshadow its vital advances. Not only did it provide for basic representation and labor practices protections along with a separate administrative labor board but it instituted a detailed system for impasse resolution that included mediation and factfinding.[75] While strikes have by no means vanished, the Taylor Act's provisions have helped to diminish their intensity and frequency.

The Public Employment Relations Board (PERB) closely follows the pattern of the federal independent agency. It consists of three members appointed by the governor with the advice and consent of the senate. Only two may be of the same political party and all sit for overlapping terms of six years. Its extensive responsibilities include administering detailed representation and improper practices procedures; establishing panels to serve as mediators and factfinders; providing unions, employees, mediators, etc., with statistical data; acting as a clearing house for information concerning public employment throughout the state; and conducting studies and analyses of the major problems in representation and negotiations such as unit determination, scope of bargaining, etc. Its administrative and investigatory powers are comparable to those of the NLRB. It maintains a full complement of executive and hearing officers and technical advisers, conducts hearings and inquiries, and promulgates rules and regulations. It has full subpoena power over witnesses and documents, can elicit testimony under oath, and may receive from any state government such assistance, services, and data as it may need to function properly. To insure the PERB's independence of the CSC, all commission officers and agencies have been expressly forbidden to "supervise, direct or control" any of the PERB's functions or powers.[76]

---

[74] The Governor's Committee on Public Employee Relations also included E. Wight Bakke, David L. Cole, John T. Dunlop, and Frederick H. Harbison. Its *Final Report* was submitted March 31, 1966.

[75] Office of the Governor, *Memorandum of Approval*, Albany, April 21, 1967.

[76] New York Civil Service Law, Art. 14, Sec. 205 (1967) as amended 1969, 1970.

New York might simply have placed state and local employees under the jurisdiction of the State Labor Relations Board. It did not choose to do this, but utilized the separate public-service model instead, and it did so in a unique manner that allowed local authorities—counties, cities, incorporated villages—to create their own separate boards. The state legislature was well aware that New York City had a formal collective bargaining system and was just about to advance on its own to an even more structured labor relations agency. Accordingly, the Taylor Act specifically exempted the city from its application so long as the city's system was "substantially equivalent to the provisions and procedures" of the act.[77]

Even greater administrative flexibility was provided in the law for local governments. They were given a clear option to avail themselves of the services of the PERB or establish independent labor boards of their own. This unique provision multiplied the number of local labor relations boards. These "mini-PERB's," as they came to be called, were required to embody the rights and privileges set forth in the Taylor Act as well as its strike prohibitions. If a locality opted to handle its own labor relations, its projected procedures first had to be approved by the state PERB.[78] Localities might thus enact machinery for determining representation cases, resolving negotiation impasses, and deciding whether a labor organization had gone on strike in contravention of the law. They might also determine the penalty, if required. The parent PERB, however, retained authority to decide improper practices cases.[79]

Although over 30 mini-PERBs existed at one time, only 17 were operating by early 1973. Salaries and budget appropriations would indicate that only five of these were active boards. Ten acted on representation cases and seven resolved bargaining deadlocks. At least one strike was called in a mini-PERB jurisdiction.[80] It would appear that most localities prefer to rely on the umbrella state machinery. It is not unknown for miniboards to

---

[77] Ibid., Sec. 212.

[78] Ibid.

[79] New York State Public Employment Relations Board, PERB News, Annual Report Edition, Vol. 6, No. 2, February 1973, p. 7.

[80] Ibid. Mini-PERBs operated in the counties of Delaware, Monroe, Nassau, Onondaga, Suffolk, Tompkins, and Westchester; in the towns of Harrison, Hempstead, North Castle, North Hempstead, Oyster Bay, and Rye; and in the villages of Port Chester and Valley Stream. Surely their 1973 application at the village level would indicate a public maturity towards acceptance of the labor board model for the public service.

be done away with as soon as any truly major dispute arises.[81] Nevertheless, the statutory option for the creation of such boards is always available if a locality's labor problems become large enough to warrant separate administration.

It would be ostrich-like to deny the remarkable accomplishments of the PERB in its first five years. In 1967 only the approximately 300,000 New York City workers out of some one million public employees in the state enjoyed collective bargaining machinery. In five years this number tripled to 900,000 state and local employees organized in appropriate units and exerting their rights under the law. It was reported that of these, 280,000 were professional and nonprofessional employees of boards of education and 175,000 were local government workers. Approximately 600,000 belonged to public employee unions and associations.[82]

Although strikes continue to occur in New York State, their incidence and effect have been stabilized. PERB's record of accomplishment should lay to rest whatever fears persist as to a separate labor board's efficacy. While it is still developing, the New York PERB is accepted by all state parties concerned in its operations as an undoubted success.

F. THE NEW YORK CITY OFFICE OF COLLECTIVE BARGAINING—THE TRIPARTITE MODEL

Public administration in New York City traditionally has delivered a unique and broad array of benefits and services. The equally unique personnel problems attendant upon such services necessitate advanced, flexible solutions.

The dimensions of New York's public service are awesome. The number of citizens accommodated by the city, almost eight million, is more than double that of any other municipal government in the nation. With a civil service that numbered over 300,000 employees just prior to the 1975 fiscal crisis, New York City qualifies as the second largest public employer in the United States, surpassed only by the Federal Government.[83] This is attributable to the fact that it has a truly central metropolitan government. In most large American cities, the municipal government is but one of many local units providing traditional services. In New York, on the other hand, aside from the Port Authority

---

[81] New York State Public Employment Relations Board, *The First Five Years of the Taylor Law* (Albany, 1973) , p. 7.

[82] _____, *PERB News,* Vol. 5, No. 9, September 1972, p. 1; *PERB News,* Vol. 6, No. 2, February 1973, p. 1.

[83] New York State Study Commission for New York City, *Final Report,* New York, April 15, 1973, pp. 5-13.

and Waterfront Commission, the city government alone is responsible for services.[84]

According to the 1973 Scott Study Commission report, the comprehensiveness of New York's government is "almost unparalleled among American cities."[85] None can match its broad undertakings in welfare, health, and education. Some programs are mandated by state law, but in the last decade the city's own initiative fostered advanced public school projects, expanded a no-tuition city university with open enrollment and a major graduate school, and ran the country's largest day-care system.[86] The city government also had to contend with incredible poverty and drug addiction. By 1972, 1.2 million people, or one of every six inhabitants, were on the welfare rolls, and there were an estimated 150,000 addicts.[87]

The size and complexity of the megalopolis of New York are critical factors in public employee labor disputes. Since 1958 there has evolved a major labor relations structure that has brought many city workers the highest pay in the country for their classifications; higher than many private employers as to pay, pensions, and fringe benefits.[88]

The movement towards advanced labor relations was begun and fostered during the administration of Mayor Robert F. Wagner. In March 1958, the Mayor initiated a program, hailed as a "Little Wagner Act," that had been a feature of his election campaign.[89] Its many similarities to the national labor law somewhat justified its natural association with the progenitor of both the Mayor and the NLRB. City unions saw it as evidence of the city's "coming of age at long last in recognizing its responsibilities."[90] Wagner's historic Executive Order No. 49[91] declared collective bargaining to be city policy within the limits of state and city law.

---

[84] New York City, Temporary Commission on City Finances, *Municipal Collective Bargaining*, Staff Paper 8, New York, July 1966, p. 44. In comparison, in 1962, Chicago was served by 460 local governments, Pittsburgh by 358 and Los Angeles by 234 such units.

[85] New York State Study Commission for New York City, *New York City: Economic Base and Fiscal Capacity* (Syracuse, N.Y.: Maxwell School of Citizenship and Public Affairs, 1973), p. 2.

[86] ———, Final Report, April 15, 1973, pp. 19-23.

[87] *Ibid.*, p. 8, ff. 5-9.

[88] *Ibid.*, p. 22.

[89] *New York Times*, March 3, 1954.

[90] American Federation of State, County and Municipal Employees, New York City, *Press Release*, June 17, 1954.

[91] New York City, Office of the Mayor, *Executive Order No. 49—The Conduct of Labor Relations Between the City of New York and Its Employees*, March 31, 1958. See also New York City, Department of Labor, *Report on a Program of Labor Relations for New York City Employees*, June 1957.

The new system was quite similar to and, in truth, a forerunner of the federal program under E.O. 10988. Its administration and enforcement remained firmly under executive control. Remarkably broad and often undefined powers were given the Commissioner and Department of Labor to oversee the program. Its legal basis was entirely executive. No special, new administrative agency was created. The Commissioner was given the power to determine appropriate bargaining units, oversee representation procedures and elections, and certify exclusive bargaining representatives. Under certain circumstances he could vary the time, usually one year, that an exclusive representative was free from rival challenges. He could decertify a union as nonrepresentative.[92]

Under the Wagner order, a certified bargaining representative was the exclusive spokesman for all city employees in a particular job title. The scope of bargaining was quite broad; unions negotiated salaries, fringe benefits, promotions, and leave rules. In a resolution by the city CSC in 1961 bargaining was extended to include group classifications, normally a management prerogative. The usual procedure was for the union to bargain with a city negotiating team composed of officers from the Personnel Department and the Bureau of the Budget. The Commissioner of Labor and the agency involved were not supposed to participate in the negotiations. In most of the cases agreements were reached and implemented through normal CSC procedures. If a serious impasse resulted, however, the Commissioner of Labor could be asked to mediate, or he might simply proffer his services on his own initiative.[93] In crucial cases, therefore, he would be involved both at the outset and in the final stages. Unions and citizen groups had serious misgivings over the broad powers lodged in a single executive officer in the highly volatile labor area. These misgivings grew as the city labor relations program evolved over the next decade.

By 1961, continuing labor unrest created great citizen concern over the program's deficiencies. Criticisms were motivated by public interest; nevertheless, they coincided with the complaints of city unions with obvious vested interests. The prominent and independent Citizen's Budget Commission emphasized the flaws in the administrative structure and noted its failure to eliminate labor strife among the city's workers. It pointed out that within the

92 New York City, E.O. 49, Secs. 2-5, 8 (1958).
93 *Ibid.*; see also Murray B. Nesbitt, *op. cit.*, pp. 189-191; New York City Temporary Commission on City Finances, *op. cit.*, pp. 20-22, 25-29.

preceding year alone the police had engaged in a running battle with their superiors, and that teachers and museum workers staged one-day walk-outs. At various times City Hall was besieged and picketed by hospital workers, firemen, and sanitation workers over disputes ranging from "moonlighting" to the lack of collective bargaining.[94]

The gravamen of the Budget Commission's major complaint stemmed from the Department of Labor's unity of legislative, judicial, and executive functions. Yet the Department was authorized to administer and oversee partisan labor disputes through certifying representatives, processing grievances, and providing mediation. Unions could not forget that the Department itself, ostensibly impartial in these cases, remained an arm of the mayor. Accusations made against the Department charging that it was "prosecutor, judge, and jury" and prejudging decisions led to demands for greater separation of functions. The problem was compounded by the fact that a municipal agency was called upon to settle disputes where the city itself was a party. The Citizen's Budget Commission admonished that:

> "The objectivity of the Department in handling these matters has been assumed. On the other hand, labor union representatives have maintained that the City's Labor Department is actually serving in an inconsistent dual role; first as an agency of the City government with which they must bargain, and second as the disinterested 'third party' which sets the conditions under which bargaining will take place. The designation of bargaining units, which some City representatives may have originally believed to be a fairly routine ministerial matter for the Department of Labor has caused special difficulties. Whether justified or not, the suspicions which many employees feel about whether they get a full fair deal under the City's labor relations procedures have hampered the City's efforts by pay raises and better working conditions to achieve higher employee morale and efficiency." [95]

The question of independent, impartial administration was not a matter of theory to the city. Constant stress relationships, felt keenly by the unions, swelled their desire for administrative reform. This was so pressing and abrasive an issue that as part of the settlement of an unusually debilitating and destructive strike of welfare workers in mid-1965, it was agreed to conduct a full-fledged study of the entire labor relations machinery of the city. Accordingly, a Tripartite Committee on Labor Relations, com-

---

[94] Citizen's Budget Commission, Inc., *The City's Labor Relations Policies* (New York, 1961), pp. 3-6.
[95] *Ibid.*, pp. 6-7.

posed of representatives from city management, the labor unions, and the public, was assembled for this purpose.

In early 1966 the tripartite panel submitted comprehensive recommendations that were accepted by both the city and the unions representing a majority of the city employees.[96] This Labor-City Agreement served as the model for the quickly passed New York City Collective Bargaining Law and Mayor Lindsay's Executive Order No. 52 implementing the provisions of the law in 1967.[97] There was some question of the legality of a city law formalizing collective bargaining under controlling state statutes that were generally silent on the issue. This obstacle was removed by passage of the Taylor Act in April 1967. Indeed, the progress of events at the state and city levels coincided in both time and substantive reforms in so provident a manner that they were complementary and fully adapted to each other in administration and jurisdiction.

The basic purpose of the Lindsay order was to set "new procedures to govern collective bargaining in the public service, and particularly [to fill] the need for independent and impartial Tribunals to settle impasses arising in contract negotiations, unresolved grievances and representation issues . . . ." [98] The vehicle for accomplishing these goals is the New York City Office of Collective Bargaining. Two boards fulfill the OCB's functions. A seven-member tripartite Board of Collective Bargaining is composed of two labor representatives selected by the Municipal Labor Committee, a voluntary federation of municipal labor organizations; two city members chosen by the mayor; and three neutral members selected unanimously by the city and labor representatives. The three neutral members comprise a Board of Certification. Under the law, the individual elected as chairman of the Board of Collective Bargaining must also serve as chairman of the Certification Board and as the director of the entire OCB.[99] The chairman serves full time while the other impartial members work as needed on a per diem basis. The pay for the neutral members is shared equally by the city and the Municipal Labor Committee. The other board members serve without compensation.[100]

---

[96] Murray B. Nesbitt, "Who Works Where and Why—The City's Personnel System," *WNYC-TV*, New York, April 1967.

[97] New York City Administrative Code, Ch. 54; New York City Collective Bargaining Law (1967) ; New York City, Office of the Mayor, *Executive Order No. 52; The Conduct of Labor Relations Between the City of New York and its Employees*, September 29, 1967.

[98] New York City, E.O. No. 52, Preamble (1967) .

[99] New York City Administrative Code, Ch. 54, Secs. 1171, 1172. See also New York City, Office of Collective Bargaining, *Annual Report*, 1972, p. 24.

[100] *Ibid.*, Sec. 54-12.

The Board of Collective Bargaining can issue final decisions over what is bargainable under the Act, resolve disputes over the arbitrability of grievances, process improper practice cases against both the city and unions, and issue final and binding decisions on impasse recommendations. This last function is a powerful and innovative aspect of the Board's authority created by a 1972 amendment. The Board thus possesses final and binding control over negotiation deadlocks, a controversial power only beginning to gain acceptance in the public sector.[101]

OCB impasse machinery includes mediation, impasse panels, and grievance arbitration procedures. The chairman may designate a mediator to assist in negotiations on the request of either party or simply if he believes such action will aid settlement. If further action is needed, he may select an impasse panel at the request either of both sides or of the Board of Collective Bargaining. The panel has wide powers to mediate, conduct hearings, and do whatever is possible to resolve the deadlock. Its recommendations become final and binding if not rejected in a specific time. If either party refuses to accept the panel's recommendations, appeal is made to the Board of Collective Bargaining itself. After reviewing the recommendations the Board is empowered to hand down a final and binding decision. If it fails to do so in 30 days, the impasse panel's recommendations become final and binding.[102] While binding decisions are subject to full judicial review, the OCB's authority to make them constitutes a powerful form of impasse resolution.

The Board of Certification maintains the basic structure for city bargaining. Its functions are to define appropriate units, including the determination of managerial status; to certify majority representatives or exclusive bargaining agents; and to supervise representation elections impartially whenever disputes make them necessary. With regard to defining appropriate bargaining units, the Board adopted a policy in 1968, consistently followed since then, of "reducing the multiplicity of units fragmenting the bargaining process." This was seen as a means of strengthening negotiations and as a move to "impart greater stability to municipal labor relations." [103] To Leonard Irsay, OCB's information and research director, fewer appropriate units meant fewer bargaining sessions and far fewer contracts to hammer out.

---

[101] *Ibid.*, Secs. 54-5 (a) (1) (2) , 54-7; OCB, *op. cit.*, pp. 7, 24-25.

[102] *Ibid.*, Sec. 54-7 as amended; OCB, *op. cit.*, p. 25. See also *Government Employee Relations Report*, No. 461 (1972) , p. B-4.

[103] Office of Collective Bargaining, *Annual Report*, 1972, p. 8.

By the end of 1972, the OCB's policy reduced the number of certified units to 249, an overall drop of almost 36 percent from 1968. The reduction was achieved primarily through consolidation of existing units and the addition of new and formerly unrepresented titles to existing units.[104] Irsay noted that the first six months of 1973 saw a further reduction to 215 appropriate bargaining units. To him this indicated the success of the OCB in accomplishing one of its original goals, that of bringing order and rationalization to the entire collective bargaining structure.[105]

Without minimizing the intensity and seriousness of its strikes, it is possible to say that the City of New York fares quite well in a comparison of its work stoppages with public-employee strikes generally. In the first five years of the OCB, New York municipal strikes rose by only 11 percent over the previous five years (1963-1967). During this same period, strikes in state governments rose 267 percent and stoppages in local governments increased 217 percent. In 1972, there were but three stoppages in New York City, and only the strike against the Transit Authority created great public hardship and inconvenience. Statistics, of course, cannot measure the difficulties created by the 28 stoppages that occurred between 1968 and 1972. In retrospect, in three of those years there were only two to four stoppages and, generally, conditions in the city compared quite favorably to those elsewhere.[106]

Another factor of tremendous importance to the effectiveness of New York City's bargaining system was the city's action in establishing an Office of Labor Relations to negotiate forcefully and authoritatively on behalf of city management. Management's negotiating authority in the old city bargaining team was divided between the budget and personnel directors. Additional authority was lodged with the comptroller and the Labor Department. There was no clear line of responsibility; so it was not unusual for unions to approach the mayor's office itself, even while negotiations were in progress. The Office of Labor Relations was established to fix bargaining responsibility in a single agency speaking for the entire executive branch. Indeed, it was crucial that in an atmosphere of highly sophisticated labor in-fighting only industrial relations *experts* be recruited to meet the bargaining challenges. This was accomplished by the Office of Labor Relations. In city bargaining parties have often taken their

---

104 *Ibid.*, p. 8, Appendix, p. 21.
105 Leonard Irsay, Director of Information and Research, OCB, *Interview*, New York, N.Y., June 18, 1973.
106 Office of Collective Bargaining, *Annual Report*, pp. 20, 23, 24.

case directly to the mayor. Today, when dealing with the director of the OLR union negotiators are aware that they face a labor expert negotiating directly for the chief executive.

OCB Chairman Arvid Anderson has now experienced service with the two basic models for independent labor administration, the combined public and private jurisdiction of the Wisconsin Employment Relations Board and the separate public-sector model as exemplified by the OCB. Nevertheless, he generally does not favor one as unquestionably better than the other; under proper circumstances, either could be effective. In his view the NLRB's experience with the postal service has convincingly proved that a traditional board can exercise jurisdiction over public employees at the federal level.[107] Nevertheless, Anderson has strongly recommended that the New York City experience be considered a prime example for any jurisdiction embarking on a labor relations program. The OCB's great strength is the participatory, mutual-consent aspect of its administrative procedures. Of crucial importance is the fact that the Board's labor union representatives participate fully in the selection and financial support of the impartial members. They take part in the decision-making process, not only in cases before the Board but also in the selection of mediators, factfinders, and arbitrators. Such full participation has expedited their later acceptance of agency decisions and the recommendations of third-party intervenors selected to resolve impasses.[108]

The Office of Collective Bargaining unquestionably has achieved its goal of independent, impartial administration of a stabilized, ongoing collective bargaining process. Because of the consequences of almost any confrontation in New York City, the OCB's path will never be free of disruptive and widely publicized labor disputes. But it seems clear that if the OCB or a similar agency had not been at hand in recent years, the situation would have been immeasurably worse.

G. THE FEDERAL GOVERNMENT OF CANADA—THE PUBLIC SERVICE STAFF RELATIONS BOARD

Considerable attention has been given in this work to the federal experience in Canada. The reason is that several object lessons with application in this country can be drawn from the

---

[107] Arvid Anderson, Chairman-Director, New York City Office of Collective Bargaining, *Interview*, New York, N.Y., June 18, 1973.

[108] _____, "Public Employee Collective Bargaining: The Changing of the Establishment," *Wake Forest Law Review*, Vol. 7, No. 2, March 1971, p. 186.

Canadian experience. The similarities of both governments have prompted innumerable cross-references by many observers of the public labor scene.

Arguments to the contrary are always available. Can the problems of a federal service of about one-quarter million employees be compared with those of another of over ten times its size? [109] A more logical comparison might have been drawn, perhaps, to the New York City program, which, like the Canadian system, also bargains in terms of service-wide occupational groups and is, at least, reasonably comparable in size. Actually, the city's civil service exceeds that of Canada's entire federal government. Indeed, New York's Police Department, larger than an army division, surpasses in size the entire civil service of many major American cities and states. However, it is structure, policy, and administration that are the common denominators of fruitful comparison; qualitative not quantitative factors should prevail.

The established tenet of comparative public administration, that the civil service of one modern national society cannot be superimposed upon that of another, has applicability in this case. There are many social, historical, and political variations in the evolution of Canada and the United States that make for different national identities. But in the fields of personnel administration and labor relations it is remarkable how the similarities, on balance, far outweigh the differences. Canada and the United States have shared the same North American experience, a common law, the westward movement, and close cultural and racial affinities; their civil services bear equally great similarities. In both countries, from the depths of a patronage spoils era, merit-system concepts took hold. The independent civil service commission and its application of scientific personnel practices became the rule in both. Canada is one of the few nations to adopt the unitary job classification system so highly developed in the United States. The history of the labor movement in North America transcends the border. Just as many of Canada's industries are subsidiaries of American corporations, so most of its unions are affiliated with parent organizations in the United States. Modern labor legislation, labor boards, and regulatory procedures were adopted at federal and state-provincial levels by both countries

---

[109] This figure involves only those federal employees under the Public Service Staff Relations Act. The Canadian Government employs over 15,000 additional personnel in Crown Corporations such as the Canadian National Railway, Air Canada, and the Canadian Broadcasting Corporation whose labor relations are governed by general statute.

as they experienced equally the depressions, business cycles, and political upheavals that fostered such legislation. So also in the public labor sector, the municipalities and provinces were the experimental laboratories that pioneered eventual federal legislation. As in the United States, the federal government is the single largest employer. Its major federal strikes occurred among the same workers—postal employees and air traffic controllers. Many more such comparisons spring to mind, but these are sufficient to show the close parallel between U.S. and Canadian labor relations.

During the two decades following World War II, at a time when its postwar consumer demand, liberal immigration policy, and urban growth spurred an economic boom, Canada's federal service doubled in size.[110] There was a commensurate growth and consolidation of public service unions and associations. Just as in the United States, government attitudes and programs had to adapt to the changing labor scene.

The growth of Canada's federal service culminated in the appointment in August 1963 of a distinguished committee of senior civil servants "to make preparations for the introduction into the Public Service of an appropriate form of collective bargaining and arbitration. . . ." [111] Titled the Preparatory Committee on Collective Bargaining in the Public Service, it was chaired by A.D.P. Heeney, whose lifetime of service on the domestic and international scene and particular knowledge of personnel administration augured well for a substantive and comprehensive study.[112] It was just that. For two years the committee conducted intensive research into public-service labor relations of Canada, Britain, France, Australia, and the United States and the classification and pay systems in these jurisdictions. Its report of July 1965 contained its findings, recommendations, and a draft of proposed federal labor legislation,[113] which resulted within two years in the Public Service Staff Relations Act (PSSRA).[114]

---

110 H. W. Arthurs, *Collective Bargaining by Public Employees in Canada: Five Models* (Ann Arbor: Institute of Labor and Industrial Relations, University of Michigan-Wayne State University, 1971), pp. 7, 28.

111 Canada, Preparatory Committee on Collective Bargaining in the Public Service, *Report* (Ottawa: Queen's Printer, 1965), p. 1.

112 Mr. Heeney was Chairman of the Canadian Section of the International Joint Commission. He had served as ambassador to the United States and was Chairman of the independent Civil Service Commission for about two years. While he was Chairman, the CSC issued an historic report on the role of the CSC entitled, *Personnel Administration in the Public Service*, Ottawa, Queen's Printer, 1968. It led to reform legislation.

113 Canada, Preparatory Committee, *op. cit.*, pp. 17, 18.

114 Public Service Staff Relations Act; Statutes of Canada, 15-15-16, Eliz. II, Ch. 72 (1967).

Several factors unique to Canada presaged an eventual federal program. Municipal collective bargaining among some quarter of a million employees had been steadily developing since the late 1930s. Canadian municipalities are corporations created by the provinces and are governed under general provincial statutes. Accordingly, when provincial labor boards were established for the private sector, under laws emulating the Wagner Act, cities were not excluded. Municipal unions quickly moved to take advantage of the laws; and if they were certified by a Board, the municipal employer had to bargain with them. Such unions gained momentum during the full employment of World War II, and their growth since then has been termed "steady and impressive." [115] Thus, major collective bargaining in Canadian cities predated comparable American municipal development by at least 20 years. It was quite natural, therefore, that when the Preparatory Committee was appointed, it embarked upon an extensive review of the "principles underlying industrial relations law and practice in Canada and the experience of other public services in Canada." On reporting out a proposed federal statute, the Heeney Committee quickly concluded that

> "subject to such qualifications as may be necessary to protect the public interest and the sovereignty of Parliament . . . as far as possible, the system of collective bargaining and arbitration in the Public Service of Canada should be rooted in the principles and practices governing employee-employer relations in the Canadian community at large." [116]

Another aspect of the Canadian system quite unlike that of the American system of federal labor relations was the fact that a substantial number of Canadian federal employees enjoyed the fullest coverage allowed the private sector. These were the thousands of workers in the proprietary Crown corporations of the commercial, industrial, and financial type that are expected to be self-supporting.[117] In the United States, while it is true that in the TVA, some Interior Department units, and several other federal proprietary undertakings "relationships that are close to full scale collective bargaining . . . have been going on for years," [118] it is also true that these units are excluded from the

---

115 S. J. Frankel and R. C. Pratt, op. cit., pp. 2, 3; Canada, Preparatory Committee, op. cit., p. 20.

116 Canada, Preparatory Committee, op. cit., pp. 24, 25.

117 Ibid., pp. 4, 5; H. W. Arthurs, op. cit., pp. 13, 14; J. E. Hodgetts, "The Public Corporation in Canada," in Canadian Public Administration, J. E. Hodgetts and D. C. Corbett, Eds. (Toronto: The MacMillan Company, 1960), p. 188.

118 U.S. President's Task Force on Employee-Management Relations in the Federal Service, Report, November 1961, p. 3.

jurisdiction of the NLRB and so do not enjoy the complete benefits of the national legislation.

In comparison, Canadian federal labor legislation never differentiated between public and private proprietary corporations. In 1948, therefore, when the Industrial Relations and Disputes Investigation Act was amended, the new provisions also applied to such Crown corporations.[119] The Heeney Report remarked that by September 1963, about 140,000 people were employed by these commercial enterprises and already had the right to bargain collectively before the Canada Labour Relations Board. This figure represented more than one third of the total federal establishment of some 340,000 employees; and in several proprietary corporations bargaining agents were certified and collective agreements concluded.[120]

Although the Act applied to corporations, it excluded the rest of the federal establishment by exempting "employees of Her Majesty in right of Canada." [121] Saul Frankel has pointed out that when public employee associations intensified their pressures for collective bargaining in the 1950s, one major demand was repeal of this exclusionary proviso. However, the public associations now merged in the Public Service Alliance of Canada were divided on the issue of jurisdiction and administration. The Canadian Civil Service Federation, then some 75,000 strong, formally requested the government to consider abolishing the exclusion in 1957. The Civil Service Association of Ottawa and the Amalgamated Civil Servants of Canada, which represented some 30,000 employees and had been having jurisdictional problems with the Federation, took a different position. They informed the Secretary of State of their opposition and their belief that because of the "peculiar relationship between civil servants and their employer . . . a special procedure must be developed for bargaining between the Crown and its servants. . . ." The Professional Institute of the Public Service of Canada also opposed nondifferentiation and total inclusion in the private-sector machinery.[122] The Heeney Report took heed of this division and concluded that by about 1960, the view of those organizations that preferred a system "designed specifically for the public service . . . had become clearly predominant." [123]

---

[119] H. W. Arthurs, *op. cit.*, pp. 13, 14; J. E. Hodgetts, *op cit.*, p. 205

[120] Canada, Preparatory Committee, *op. cit.*, pp. 4, 5.

[121] Industrial Relations and Disputes Investigation Act, Statutes of Canada, 11-12, Geo. VI, Secs. 54, 55 (1948) .

[122] Saul J. Frankel, *Staff Relations in the Civil Service: The Canadian Experience,* *op. cit.*, pp. 18-19, 54, 132-133.

[123] Canada, Preparatory Committee, *op. cit.*, p. 18.

The Preparatory Committee was in full accord with this view and articulated its reasoning in what is perhaps the definitive statement on behalf of impartial administration. Noting that "third-party" functions in industrial relations law are normally divided between a labor minister and a labor relations board, the Heeney Report declared:

> "Although quite satisfactory in the private sector, where a government can stand between an employer and a group of organized employees in a position of impartiality, such a division would be open to question in the Public Service system because the Government *is* the employer and the Minister of Labour is a member of the Government. For this reason, the Preparatory Committee concluded that the administrative responsibility for the system, including responsibility for the provision of 'third-party' services, should be concentrated in an independent body." [124]

The Preparatory Committee seriously contemplated granting full jurisdiction to the Canada Labour Relations Board. But since it was concerned primarily with the "special character of the contemplated Public Service system and the multiplicity of functions to be performed in its operation," it believed that an arrangement of this kind would not be satisfactory.[125]

Jacob Finkelman was appointed chairman of the Public Service Staff Relations Board after years of distinguished service as chairman of the very active Ontario Labour Relations Board. He had also served as one of the advisors to the Preparatory Committee. His expertise in the private and public sectors was unquestioned. He recognized that certain aspects of the new Public Service Staff Relations Act might appear quite radical to American observers. Outstanding among these were the statutory right to strike in prescribed circumstances [126] and impasse arbitration that extended to wages and salaries. If a union chose the arbitration option and money or another award was handed down, the federal government was bound by the Act to honor the award. Specific remedies against any infringement of binding collective bargaining agreements were provided.[127]

In a major departure, many supervisory employees normally considered management personnel were not excluded from the Act.[128] Much of the problem over conflict of interest was thus

---

[124] *Ibid.*, p. 25. Italics as in original.
[125] *Ibid.*
[126] See Chapter XVIII.
[127] Jacob Finkelman, Chairman, PSSRB, "Canada's Bold Experiment," *Address,* to Public Personnel Association Seminar, Albany, New York, April 23, 1968.
[128] Stat. Can. 1966-67, c. 72, s2 (m) (p) (r) (u) .

eliminated. Even to the Hon. C. M. Drury, president of the Treasury Board, this reflected "the fact that supervisory and professional employees in the public service have been members of employee organizations for many years and have traditionally been represented by such organizations in discussions with the government. . . ." [129] Managers necessarily are excluded, but the overall provisions for supervisors are remarkable by U.S. federal standards. In many ways, the PSSRA's substantive provisions far exceeded the expected norms for labor laws and administration even in the private sector.

The implementation of the Act is entrusted to four administrative bodies. The Public Service Staff Relations Board bears the general operational responsibility for the law; a Public Service Arbitration Tribunal administers the impasse settlement provisions; a panel of Grievance Adjudicators provides for grievance arbitration; and the Pay Research Bureau, formerly in the Civil Service Commission, but now under the PSSRB, aids in the process of determining compensation. [130]

The PSSRB is a tripartite body that functions in a manner reminiscent of the New York City OCB—that is, on the basis of mutual consent. The principle of mutual consent has a long history in Canadian labor relations, and has been incorporated in much general legislation. Thus the best aspects of cooptation, a recognition of the importance and of the contribution of the concerned parties themselves, are utilized. Since both management and labor share responsibility in the decision-making process, they more readily accept the results of that process. The chairman and vice-chairman are the neutral members of the PSSR Board, while the PSSR Act provides that the other eight members "are to be representative in equal number of the interests of the employees and of the interests of the employer respectively." To maintain a balance, no member can be appointed for one side without an equal appointment for the other. [131] Accordingly, the employee members are selected from lists offered by the leading federal public unions and associations. However, consultation is sought from all concerned elements on the appointments of the impartial chairman and vice-chairman. [132]

---

[129] Hon. C. M. Drury, President, Treasury Board, "The Government as an Employer," *Canadian Labour*, Vol. 13, No. 9, September 1968, p. 23.

[130] PSSRB, *First Annual Report, 1967-1968* (Ottawa: Queen's Printer, 1968), pp. 16-20.

[131] Stat. Can. 1966-67, c. 72, s. 11 (4).

[132] Jacob Finkelman, Chairman, PSSRB, "Collective Bargaining in Federal Public Service: The Basic Legislation in Canada," *Address*, to Joint Conference on Collec-

The intent of the Act was to insure the objectivity, impartiality, and independence of the administrators. Therefore, in full compliance with the Heeney recommendations, it set fixed periods of appointment and ample provisions for secure tenure.[133] The neutral chairman and vice-chairman, who serve full time, are appointed for 10 years. They can be removed only "for cause" and only upon joint action by the Senate and the House of Commons.[134] The remaining eight members, who serve for seven years on a part-time basis also can be removed only "for cause," but this can be done at any time.[135] In Chairman Finkelman's view, all the members have performed with the impartiality sought in the new law. On considering their positions he was once moved to comment:

> "I am sure that, if any of you were permitted to sit in on the executive deliberations of the Board, you would find it very difficult to identify any of them, from the views that they express, with the interest that they were selected to represent. They quickly developed a degree of objectivity in their approach to their responsibilities which makes each of them equally the protector of the public interest in the best sense of the term." [136]

The functions of the PSSRB and the rights and privileges afforded employees, unions, and management under the PSSR Act are similar to those prescribed in most other labor relations statutes. The Board's major responsibilities are making unit determinations, certifying bargaining agents, deciding unfair practice cases, issuing declarations on the lawfulness of strikes, deciding questions of law or jurisdiction arising out of impasse arbitrations or grievance adjudications, and authorizing court prosecutions of violations of the Act.[137]

The PSSRB chairman has specific administrative duties for the two kinds of dispute settlement procedures used by the Board. The Public Service Arbitration Tribunal provides the dispute settlement services if the certified agent selects the arbitration alternative. The Arbitration Tribunal is a tripartite body. Its chairman, usually a distinguished jurist, must be acceptable to all parties. He is appointed for up to seven years on recommendation of the Board, which also appoints arbitrators representing

tive Bargaining in Federal Public Service, AFL-CIO and Canadian Labour Congress, Niagara Falls, Ontario, November 19, 1968, p. 21.

133 Canada, Preparatory Committee, op. cit., pp. 25, 26.

134 Stat. Can. 1966-67, c. 72, s. 11.

135 Ibid., s. 11 (3) .

136 Jacob Finkelman, op. cit., Joint Conference, p. 22.

137 PSSRB, First Annual Report, 1967-1968, pp. 12, 18.

labor and management to two panels for two-year terms. The particular Arbitration Tribunal chosen for a given dispute is composed of three members: the chairman of the Tribunal and one member from each panel selected by the chairman of the PSSRB. Tribunal awards are written in the form of an agreement and are final and binding on the parties.[138]

The bargaining agent may choose to select the alternative of conciliation and lawful strike. If it does so, the Board chairman must establish a tripartite ad hoc conciliation board, one member of which is nominated by each side, and the third chosen by the two nominees. The conciliation board submits findings and recommendations that may deter strike action. If the conciliation procedures described in Chapter XVIII do not succeed, employees not designated by the Board as necessary to the safety and security of the public may resort to a lawful strike.[139] If requested by the employer, the Board may determine whether a strike authorized by a union is lawful. If a strike is declared unlawful and the union or employees still act, they may be prosecuted. For prosecution, however, the consent of the Board must first be secured.[140]

The PSSRB has been given broad powers in grievance administration. It is authorized to enact regulations setting the internal grievance machinery for all federal employers, if the machinery is not established already by collective agreement. Beyond this, the Act provides for final and binding grievance arbitration through Grievance Adjudicators in the PSSRB. Adjudicators are appointed for up to five-year terms on the recommendation of the Board, and the Chief Adjudicator administers the system. Their decisions are enforced and reviewed only by the Board; no appeal may be made to the courts. Professor Arthurs, the Board's first Chief Adjudicator, regarded the Act's grievance provisions as quite liberal, yet at first employees and unions were slow to take advantage of them. By the end of the first five years of the program, however, a total of 607 cases had been referred to adjudication.[141]

There are two basic categories of adjudicable grievances under the Act. The first involves the interpretation of contracts and arbitral awards. Cases of this kind are by far the most numerous,

---

[138] Stat. Can. 1966-67, c. 72, s. 18, 63-76; Jacob Finkelman, *op. cit.*, Joint Conference, pp. 11, 12.

[139] Stat. Can. 1966-67, c. 72, s. 77-89; Jacob Finkelman, *op. cit.*, Joint Conference, pp. 13, 14, 19, 20.

[140] PSSRB, *First Annual Report, 1967-1968*, p. 40.

[141] H. W. Arthurs, *op. cit.*, pp. 50-52; Stat. Can. 1966-67, c. 72, s. 90-99.

427 such cases having been initiated in the first five years. The second category concerns grievances involving disciplinary actions such as discharge, suspension, or financial penalties—that is, adverse actions. Over five years, there were 180 such cases, of which 73 involved firings.[142]

During the first five years of the PSSRB's existence, over 98 percent of the federal public service achieved representation by certified bargaining agents with exclusive rights.[143] In the area of appropriate unit the record is equally impressive. In regard to appropriate-unit determination, the PSSRA provided that initially the Board should use as guides predetermined, service-wide, occupational groups that conformed to the new classification and pay system suggested by the Heeney Committee. Over the long run, the Board was to have more discretion.[144] The system closely approximated that of New York City, and, as in New York, an effort was made to stabilize and control the number and types of bargaining units. By 1972 the Board had processed 146 certification applications. All federal workers were represented by certified bargaining agents, except for about 2,000, or one percent of the entire establishment of some quarter million employees.[145]

Can the Board's accomplishments have significance for U.S. federal labor relations, considering the enormous disparity in the size of the U.S. and Canadian federal work forces? The answer appears to be yes, since the PSSRB has proved that it can efficiently handle the labor relations problems of a typically structured federal establishment. In the view of Professor Arthurs, a great strength of the Canadian system lies in the fact that labor relations administration is out of the control of the employer. In comparing the third-party activities of the Board, he stated:

"The Canadian arrangement is far more likely to win the confidence of public employees than the typical advisory body in the United States. Such bodies often created by executive order, depend for their very existence on the grace and favor of the appointing power, and public employees, not surprisingly, may sometimes feel that their recommendations are not completely unbiased." [146]

---

[142] PSSRB, *Fifth Annual Report, 1971-1972* (Ottawa: Information Canada, 1972), pp. 40-42.

[143] *Labor Relations Reporter*, Vol. 80, No. 25, July 24, 1972, p. 276.

[144] Jacob Finkelman, *op. cit.*, Joint Conference, p. 6; Stat. Can. 1966-67, c. 72, s. 26-32.

[145] PSSRB, *Fifth Annual Report, 1971-1972*, pp. 10, 102.

[146] H. W. Arthurs, *Collective Bargaining by Public Employees in Canada: Five Models* (Ann Arbor: University of Michigan-Wayne State University, 1971), p. 26.

H. THE ALTERNATIVES ON THE AMERICAN
FEDERAL SCENE

Public labor relations systems have long since survived their initial and transitional stages. Where adopted, these systems were speedily institutionalized in the 1960s. Questions of public acceptance were dispelled and more pressing issues have displaced them, among them the following: Do public unions have too much economic power? Have contract settlements approached irrational levels unconnected with productivity and delivery of essential services? Has the public interest become a minor consideration in bargaining? Can the political activism of federal employee unions tip deliberations in their favor? What social impact will public unions have?

These challenges inevitably must be faced in the coming decades. They have to a large extent replaced the burning issues of the early struggles for recognition. For many states and cities presently attempting to establish formalized labor relations systems, the problem will be one of catching up, of instituting the concepts and machinery proved successful in the labor relations milieu. A wide choice of systems is at hand, not only for new labor relations programs but also for existing programs concerned with administrative improvement. This section is concerned with federal management's attempt to accommodate the many contending elements in the labor relationship.

The first decade of the federal labor-management relations program was a period of advance and change. New collective policies altered the norms of federal employment, and their effects spread throughout the government. Total implementation of these policies, as occurred in Canada, was not achieved for all federal employees because of variations in size, geography, and diversity of both the government operations and the labor organizations competing for recognition. In some categories, notably postal workers, total implementation had always been the rule. Postal worker inclusion in exclusive units and under contract always varied from 85 to 91 percent.

Impressive gains have been made since 1961, prior to the Kennedy order, when for the entire federal establishment there were only 29 exclusive units, in the TVA and Interior Department, comprising approximately 19,000 employees.[147] As of November 1974, there were 3,483 exclusive units in over 50 different

---

[147] W. V. Gill, then Director, Office of Labor-Management Relations, CSC, *Statement*, before U. S. House of Representatives, Subcommittee on Postal Operations, April 25, 1969, p. 13.

agencies. In addition, the Postal Service recognized four national bargaining units and some 25,000 exclusive units in the local post offices. These covered 64 percent of the entire national workforce (excluding employees of the FBI, CIA, and NSA and foreign nationals employed outside the United States). Of the two million nonpostal employees, 1,142,419 were in exclusive units. These constituted 57 percent of all white- and blue-collar workers. In the 10 years following the Kennedy order, federal nonpostal employees covered by collective agreements increased almost sevenfold. Federal employers deal with about 90 national labor organizations and many local independents. There is a broad spectrum of bargaining units. Whereas the growing American Federation of Government Employees represents 650,038 people in 1,627 units, the International Typographical Union is certified for one unit with four employees.[148] In short, Vernon Gill had much evidence to justify his assessment that the federal policy was "sound in conception and has worked remarkably well in practice."[149] Despite drawbacks, the system's practical progress remains an incontestable fact.[150]

On the debit side of the ledger, by 1974, 36 percent of the federal workforce still remained without exclusive units and 51 percent of the nonpostal workers did not have a collective bargaining agreement. Of the 1,520,161 general schedule employees—the great majority of whom were white-collar workers—only 48 percent were in units and fewer were under agreements.[151]

Administrative models for the federal labor relations program have been described elsewhere in this book. None are totally applicable to the federal scene. Even if the remainder of the Federal Government were to follow the Postal Service's lead in accepting the NLRB's jurisdiction, most probably guidelines would be needed to alert the NLRB to differences in agency policy still held to govern public employees.

Legislatively, adoption of the single, private-sector board would entail the least administrative and financial problems. In mid-1972, Anthony F. Ingrassia, of the CSC Office of Labor-Management Relations, reflected the views of most observers in and out of management when he stated that legislative action was highly

148 U.S. Civil Service Commission, Report on Union Recognition in the Federal Service, Bulletin, No. 711-32, March 20, 1975, pp. 1, 10, 13-17, 21.
149 W. V. Gill, op. cit., pp. 2, 3.
150 See U.S. Civil Service Commission, Office of Labor-Management Relations, Reports on Union Recognition in the Federal Governments, 1963-1975
151 U.S. Civil Service Commission, Report on Union Recognition in the Federal Service, Bulletin, No. 711-32, pp. 1, 9, 11, 14.

improbable in the immediate future. Labor reform bills being submitted had little chance of enactment.[152]

Ingrassia noted, however, that further administrative changes could be effected by executive authority alone under the wording of Section 4 of E.O. 11491. Since executive action would have to be motivated by radical revisions of basic policy, it remained an interesting though highly distant possibility. Although the Federal Labor Relations Council is entirely composed of management officials, nevertheless under E.O. 11491 its character could be changed. As Ingrassia pointed out, there is power to appoint to the FLRC "such other officials of the executive branch as the President may designate from time to time." [153] There is no numerical limit. To make the Council more palatable to labor, the President conceivably could appoint new members to the FLRC who hold a federal appointment but who may have come from the ranks of labor or were picked for their acceptability to labor.[154] As E.O. 11491 was worded, the FLRC could not be made tripartite in nature. However, it remains possible, though improbable, that meaningful labor membership might be used to balance the Council in the cooptive tradition.

What type of regulatory agency might impart the greatest confidence and efficiency to federal labor relations? This is the question continually before federal labor administrators. It is of significance that John Macy, whose pioneering efforts as CSC Commissioner helped shape the EMC program during its formative years, has expressed an awareness of the general need for regulatory boards. On considering the basic needs of local labor relations, he cautioned communities facing up to the facts of public unionism that

"[A]s in the federal government there is an immediate need for the adoption of policy and practice to deal constructively with the aspirations and demands of these burgeoning labor organizations. . . . [A]n, agency, independent of executive discretion and subject only to court review should be created where none exists, to assure compliance with the basic principles of the program and to administer a code of public employee labor relations." [155]

---

[152] Anthony F. Ingrassia, Director, Office of Labor-Management Relations, CSC, *Interview*, Washington, July 6, 1972; see also *Labor Relations Reporter*, Vol. 80, July 24, 1972, p. 278, on the status of proposed legislation and the generally assumed improbability of passage.

[153] *Ibid.*; see also E.O. 11491, Sec. 4.

[154] *Ibid.*

[155] John W. Macy, Jr., *Public Service: The Human Side of Government* (New York: Harper and Row, 1971), pp. 141, 143.

Macy's admonition to local communities holds for the Federal Government as well since the basic problems of local and federal labor relations programs are the same.

There is little debate over whether the federal regulatory agency should be from the public or the private sector. After much discussion pro and con, most observers tend to believe that given the proper funding, personnel, and legislative guidelines, either the public or private model would effectively govern with independence and impartiality. More divergences actually have appeared over whether the agency should be tripartite or appointed by the executive or by independent citizens' groups. The size and scope of authority of an agency have come in for greater discussion than the basic need for an agency.

When the Postal Service came under NLRB jurisdiction, no change occurred in the antistrike ban. The strike prohibition probably will be continued whether the entire federal service comes under NLRB jurisdiction or a new federal labor agency is created. Continuation of this prohibition is an instance of how a particularized policy can be maintained regardless of the type of agency adopted.

Arvid Anderson believes that in the process of establishing new administrative procedures, the specifics of labor relations regulation had to be spelled out legislatively before the procedures went into effect. From his personal experience with the private- and public-sector models, he finds strong reasons for a separate agency to deal with appropriate-unit problems. He insists that the enabling statute must set down detailed standards and criteria for making unit determinations. Such determinations should be based on broad occupational groupings in both white- and blue-collar areas, such as skilled trades, technical groups, institutional services, protection services, and professionals. Declared policy should request that the agency recognize a smaller number of appropriate units in the best interests of all concerned with the process of collective bargaining. The law must define the scope of bargaining clearly and completely and must provide workable, trusted, and acceptable impasse procedures. In short, extensive statutory guidelines must be provided for any new agency or spelled out explicitly if the federal service is to enter the NLRB jurisdiction.[156]

Several practical reasons favor the establishment of a separate regulatory agency for federal labor relations. One, of

---

[156] Arvid Anderson, Chairman-Director, OCB, *Interview*, New York, June 18, 1973.

course, is that the NLRB is overloaded with case work. If the entire federal service came under its jurisdiction, the NLRB would be swamped. Moreover application of policies originating in private-sector disputes to federal unions would create dissatisfaction. Establishment of a separate agency would avoid the caseload problem and would permit the application of expertise to the special problems of the public service.

The public interest aspects of federal labor relations are as pressing as the national emergency situations that are specially treated under the Taft-Hartley Act. They too deserve to be afforded special treatment. Policies of personnel administration peculiar to the public and federal service would meet with fuller understanding. Merit, political activities, veterans' preference, and limitations of law are but a few of these. Furthermore, misgivings over private-sector collective bargaining and the penumbra of values it encompasses, which are still retained by some members of the federal executive corps, would be placated in part by reliance on an agency peculiarly geared to the public-service environment.

In 1973 federal unions renewed their efforts for legislative changes. The AFL-CIO and its affiliated public unions marshalled support for bills that would place the federal sector on as firm a statutory base as the national labor code affords private industry. Senate bill S. 351, which would have created a Federal Labor Relations Authority, was given strong and, at times, vociferous backing. Testifying before the Senate Post Office and Civil Service Committee, Kenneth Meiklejohn, representing the AFL-CIO, emphasized that only farm workers, federal employees, and most state and local civil servants were still denied general statutory protection of their labor relations rights. Under S. 351, the entire Federal Government and its employees except for the Postal Services would come under the new agency's jurisdiction.[157]

As expected, the Senate bill maintained the bar against strike activity; it provided for binding arbitration as an alternative, however. This provision approximates the finality procedures of the New York City OCB and the "arbitration route" of the Canadian PSSRB. In general, much is expected of the arbitration system as a viable alternative for protecting the public interest in the strike situation. The question is widely argued, but the supporters of arbitration insist that, where instituted, it has not destroyed public collective bargaining. Clyde Webber, president of the AFGE, maintained that S. 351 would bring about more

---

[157] *Government Employee Relations Report*, No. 506 (1973), pp. A-7, A-8.

genuine national exclusive bargaining units and would permit negotiations with department heads instead of subordinate levels: The limitations of the present system on bargaining, arbitrations, unit determinations, and grievances would be eliminated. Webber noted with approval the enforcement provisions of the statute—investigative and subpoena powers to be given the agency, greater access to the courts, and provisions for up to one year's imprisonment and $5,000 in fines for violations of the proposed statute.[158]

The labor-sponsored Federal Labor Relations Authority envisioned by S. 351 would be composed of a chairman and two other members, all of whom would be appointed by the President with the consent of the Senate. To eliminate partisan interests, members would be selected from a list of 10 candidates submitted by the American Arbitration Association. Just as in the Canadian federal service, the FLRA would be empowered to process unit determinations, unfair labor practices, and collective bargaining deadlocks. It is noteworthy that the AFL-CIO did not favor giving the NLRB jurisdiction over the federal sector, as it had done for postal workers in 1970. The Federation recognized the special nature of government service and the need to develop expertise in a special administrative agency.[159]

The AFGE, reflecting considerable misgivings among union elements, voiced particular concern over the designation of the director of the Office of Management and Budget as a full member of the Federal Labor Relations Council. E.O. 11616 had implemented the Council's view that the OMB should work very closely with the Civil Service Commission to provide policy guidance and review of labor relations management. Indeed, the OMB's major responsibility is executive management.[160] It was maintained that the OMB's management-oriented policy decisions involving reductions in force, personnel ceilings, the devaluing of grades in the classification system, and the contracting out of support services were not particularly conducive to good labor relations.[161]

The Federal Labor Relations Council was intended to supply the necessary administrative and policy-making authority to eliminate the inherent bias in agency-level administration.[162] The

---

158 *Ibid.*
159 *Ibid.*
160 Federal Labor Relations Council, *Labor-Management Relations in the Federal Service, Amendments to E.O. 11491 With Report and Recommendations*, Washington, August 1971, p. 13.
161 *Government Employee Relations Report*, No. 506 (1973), p. A-8.
162 Study Committee, *op. cit.*, pp. 7, 8.

injection of the OMB, however, emphasized the management nature of the FLRC. Surely, it was argued, in determining appeals from the Assistant Secretary of Labor and making interpretations and policy decisions, the OMB's management commitments would influence its Director's decisions on the Council. The OMB involves the President's office in the labor relations program intimately and directly and could easily become the shortest, most effective channel for intensifying the Chief Executive's control. Labor relations aspects would then necessarily take second place to presidential management considerations.

Thus the question of impartial and independent administration assumes even greater significance in the 1970s. Whether the proposed FLRA or the NLRB assumes the responsibility is secondary. Both regulatory agency models would fully accommodate the essential need for objectivity and independence in public labor administration. Because of the special nature of the federal structure, the separated public agency appears to hold greater promise. Perhaps improvements could also be made in the FLRA proposal. To have three impartial members, as recommended, would perhaps be to ignore an important aspect of labor-management relations, that is, the need of the parties to live together and accept decisions characteristic of the collective bargaining process.

This process, though certainly partisan, is essentially apolitical in the sense that there are no Democratic strikes or Republican adverse actions. The elements in conflict are public management and public labor. Economic and administrative considerations are at stake just as in the private sector. Yet because of the American preoccupation with politics, the usual method of seeking fairness on the part of independent regulatory agencies has been to create bipartisan boards and commissions. The current situation presents a unique opportunity to break with traditional administrative patterns. The contending parties, the "government side" and the "staff side," must be incorporated into the decision-making process. A tripartite authority composed of two or three impartial members and two panels with equal numbers of supporting members, one panel selected from the best of the federal executive corps and the other designated by a council of federal labor organizations, would bring to the regulatory agency additional channels of communication, fuller participation of labor and management, first-hand expertise, and a receptiveness towards mutually reached decisions. The winner would be the American people.

APPENDIX

LABOR-MANAGEMENT RELATIONS
IN THE FEDERAL SERVICE

Executive Order 11491, 34 Fed. Reg. 17605 (1969), as amended by
Executive Orders 11616, 36 Fed. Reg. 17319 (1971), and
11838, 40 Fed. Reg. 5743 (1975)

WHEREAS the public interest requires high standards of employee performance and the continual development and implementation of modern and progressive work practices to facilitate improved employee performance and efficiency; and

WHEREAS the well-being of employees and efficient administration of the Government are benefited by providing employees an opportunity to participate in the formulation and implementation of personnel policies and practices affecting the conditions of their employment; and

WHEREAS the participation of employees should be improved through the maintenance of constructive and cooperative relationships between labor organizations and management officials; and

WHEREAS subject to law and the paramount requirements of public service, effective labor-management relations within the Federal service require a clear statement of the respective rights and obligations of labor organizations and agency management:

NOW, THEREFORE, by virtue of the authority vested in me by the Constitution and statutes of the United States, including sections 3301 and 7301 of title 5 of the United States Code, and as President of the United States, I hereby direct that the following policies shall govern officers and agencies of the executive branch of the Government in all dealings with Federal employees and organizations representing such employees.

GENERAL PROVISIONS

Section 1. *Policy.* (a) Each employee of the executive branch of the Federal Government has the right, freely and without fear of penalty or reprisal, to form, join, and assist a labor organization or to refrain from any such activity, and each employee shall be protected in the exercise of this right. Except as otherwise expressly provided in this Order, the right to assist a labor organization extends to participation in the management of the organization and acting for the organization in the capacity of an organization representative, including presentation of its views to officials of the executive branch, the Congress, or other appropriate authority. The head of each agency shall take the action required

509

to assure that employees in the agency are apprised of their rights under this section, and that no interference, restraint, coercion, or discrimination is practiced within his agency to encourage or discourage membership in a labor organization.

(b) Paragraph (a) of this section does not authorize participation in the management of a labor organization or acting as a representative of such an organization by a supervisor, except as provided in section 24 of this Order, or by an employee when the participation or activity would result in a conflict or apparent conflict of interest or otherwise be incompatible with law or with the official duties of the employee.

Section 2. *Definitions.* When used in this Order, the term—

(a) "Agency" means an executive department, a Government corporation, and an independent establishment as defined in section 104 of title 5, United States Code, except the General Accounting Office;

(b) "Employee" means an employee of an agency and an employee of a nonappropriated fund instrumentality of the United States but does not include, for the purpose of exclusive recognition or national consultation rights, a supervisor, except as provided in section 24 of this Order;

(c) "Supervisor" means an employee having authority, in the interest of an agency, to hire, transfer, suspend, lay off, recall, promote, discharge, assign, reward, or discipline other employees, or responsibly to direct them, or to adjust their grievances, or effectively to recommend such action, if in connection with the foregoing the exercise of authority is not of a merely routine or clerical nature, but requires the use of independent judgment;

(d) [Revoked.]

(e) "Labor organization" means a lawful organization of any kind in which employees participate and which exists for the purpose, in whole or in part, of dealing with agencies concerning grievances, personnel policies and practices, or other matters affecting the working conditions of their employees; but does not include an organization which—

(1) consists of management officials or supervisors, except as provided in section 24 of this Order;

(2) assists or participates in a strike against the Government of the United States or any agency thereof or imposes a duty or obligation to conduct, assist, or participate in such a strike;

(3) advocates the overthrow of the constitutional form of government in the United States; or

(4) discriminates with regard to the terms or conditions of membership because of race, color, creed, sex, age, or national origin;

(f) "Agency management" means the agency head and all management officials, supervisors, and other representatives of management having authority to act for the agency on any matters relating to the implementation of the agency labor-management relations program established under this Order;

(g) "Council" means the Federal Labor Relations Council established by this Order;

(h) "Panel" means the Federal Service Impasses Panel established by this Order; and

(i) "Assistant Secretary" means the Assistant Secretary of Labor for Labor-Management Relations.

Sec. 3. *Application.* (a) This Order applies to all employees and agencies in the executive branch, except as provided in paragraphs (b), (c) and (d) of this section.

(b) This Order (except section 22) does not apply to—

(1) the Federal Bureau of Investigation;

(2) the Central Intelligence Agency;

(3) any other agency, or office, bureau, or entity within an agency, which has as a primary function intelligence, investigative, or security work, when the head of the agency determines, in his sole judgment, that the Order cannot be applied in a manner consistent with national security requirements and considerations; or

(4) any office, bureau or entity within an agency which has as a primary function investigation or audit of the conduct or work of officials or employees of the agency for the purpose of ensuring honesty and integrity in the discharge of their official duties, when the head of the agency determines, in his sole judgment, that the Order cannot be applied in a manner consistent with the internal security of the agency.

(5) the Foreign Service of the United States: Department of State, United States Information Agency and Agency for International Development and its successor agency or agencies.

(c) The head of an agency may, in his sole judgment, suspend any provision of this Order (except section 22) with respect to any agency installation or activity located outside the United States, when he determines that this is necessary in the national interest, subject to the conditions he prescribes.

(d) Employees engaged in administering a labor-management relations law or this Order shall not be represented by a labor organization which also represents other groups of employees under the law or this Order, or which is affiliated directly or indirectly with an organization which represents such a group of employees.

ADMINISTRATION

Sec. 4. *Federal Labor Relations Council.* (a) There is hereby established the Federal Labor Relations Council, which consists of the Chairman of the Civil Service Commission, who shall be chairman of the Council, the Secretary of Labor, the Director of the Office of Management and Budget, and such other officials of the executive branch as the President may designate from time to time. The Civil Service Commission shall provide administrative support and services to the Council to the extent authorized by law.

(b) The Council shall administer and interpret this Order, decide major policy issues, prescribe regulations, and from time to time, report and make recommendations to the President.

(c) The Council may consider, subject to its regulations—

(1) appeals from decisions of the Assistant Secretary issued pursuant to section 6 of this Order, except where, in carrying out his authority under section 11 (d), he makes a negotiability determination, in which instance the party adversely affected shall have a right of appeal;

(2) appeals on negotiability issues as provided in section 11 (c) of this Order;

(3) exceptions to arbitration awards; and

(4) other matters it deems appropriate to assure the effectuation of the purposes of this Order.

Sec. 5. *Federal Service Impasses Panel.* (a) There is hereby established the Federal Service Impasses Panel as an agency within the Council. The Panel consists of at least three members appointed by the President, one of whom he designates as chairman. The Council shall provide the services and staff assistance needed by the Panel.

(b) The Panel may consider negotiation impasses as provided in section 17 of this Order and may take any action it considers necessary to settle an impasse.

(c) The Panel shall prescribe regulations needed to administer its function under this Order.

Sec. 6. *Assistant Secretary of Labor for Labor-Management Relations.* (a) The Assistant Secretary shall—

(1) decide questions as to the appropriate unit for the purpose of exclusive recognition and related issues submitted for his consideration;

(2) supervise elections to determine whether a labor organization is the choice of a majority of the employees in an appropriate unit as their exclusive representative, and certify the results;

(3) decide questions as to the eligibility of labor organizations for national consultation rights under criteria prescribed by the Council;

(4) decide unfair labor practice complaints (including those where an alleged unilateral act by one of the parties requires an initial negotiability determination) and alleged violations of the standards of conduct for labor organizations; and

(5) decide questions as to whether a grievance is subject to a negotiated grievance procedure or subject to arbitration under an agreement as provided in section 13 (d) of this Order.

(b) In any matters arising under paragraph (a) of this section, the Assistant Secretary may require an agency or a labor organization to cease and desist from violations of this Order and require it to take such affirmative action as he considers appropriate to effectuate the policies of this Order.

(c) In performing the duties imposed on him by this section, the Assistant Secretary may request and use the services and assistance of employees of other agencies in accordance with section 1 of the Act of March 4, 1915, (38 Stat.1084, as amended; 31 U.S.C. § 686).

(d) The Assistant Secretary shall prescribe regulations needed to administer his functions under this Order.

(e) If any matters arising under paragraph (a) of this section involve the Department of Labor, the duties of the Assistant Secretary described in paragraphs (a) and (b) of this section shall be performed by a member of the Civil Service Commission designated by the Chairman of the Commission.

RECOGNITION

Sec. 7. *Recognition in general.* (a) An Agency shall accord exclusive recognition or national consultation rights at the request of a labor organization which meets the requirements for the recognition or consultation rights under this Order.

(b) A labor organization seeking recognition shall submit to the agency a roster of its officers and representatives, a copy of its constitution and by-laws, and a statement of its objectives.

(c) When recognition of a labor organization has been accorded, the recognition continues as long as the organization continues to meet the requirements of this Order applicable to that recognition, except that this section does not require an election to determine whether an organization should become, or continue to be recognized as, exclusive representative of the employees in any unit or subdivision thereof within 12 months after a prior valid election with respect to such unit.

(d) Recognition of a labor organization does not—

(1) preclude an employee, regardless of whether he is in a unit of exclusive recognition, from exercising grievance or appellate rights established by law or regulation, or from choosing his own representative in a grievance or appellate action, except when *the* grievance is covered under a negotiated procedure as provided in section 13;

(2) preclude or restrict consultations and dealings between an agency and a veterans organization with respect to matters of particular interest to employees with veterans preference; or

(3) preclude an agency from consulting or dealing with a religious, social, fraternal, professional or other lawful association, not qualified as a labor organization, with respect to matters or policies which involve individual members of the association or are of particular applicability to it or its members. Consultations and dealings under subparagraph (3) of this paragraph shall be so limited that they do not assume the character of formal consultation on matters of general employee-management policy *covering employees in that unit* or extend to areas where recognition of the interests of one employee group may result in discrimination against or injury to the interests of other employees.

(e) [Revoked.]

(f) Informal recognition or formal recognition shall not be accorded.

Sec. 8. [Revoked.]

Sec. 9. *National consultation rights.* (a) An agency shall accord national consultation rights to a labor organization which qualifies under criteria established by the Federal Labor Relations Council as the representative of a substantial number of employees of the agency. National consultation rights shall not be accorded for any unit where a labor organization already holds exclusive recognition at the national level for that unit. The granting of national consultation rights does not preclude an agency from appropriate dealings at the national level with other organizations on matters affecting their members. An agency shall terminate national consultation rights when the labor organization ceases to qualify under the established criteria.

(b) When a labor organization has been accorded national consultation rights, the agency, through appropriate officials, shall notify representatives of the organization of proposed substantive changes in personnel policies that affect employees it represents and provide an opportunity for the organization to comment on the proposed changes. The labor organization may suggest changes in the agency's personnel policies and have its views carefully considered. It may consult in person at reasonable times, on request, with appropriate officials on personnel policy matters, and at all times present its views thereon in writing. An agency is not required to consult with a labor organization on any matter on which it would not be required to meet and confer if the organization were entitled to exclusive recognition.

(c) Questions as to the eligibility of labor organizations for national consultation rights may be referred to the Assistant Secretary for decision.

Sec. 10. *Exclusive recognition.* (a) An agency shall accord exclusive recognition to a labor organization when the organization has been selected, in a secret ballot election, by a majority of the employees in an appropriate unit as their representative; provided that this section shall not preclude an agency from according exclusive recognition to a labor organization, without an election, where the appropriate unit is established through the consolidation of existing exclusively recognized units represented by that organization.

(b) A unit may be established on a plant or installation, craft, functional, or other basis which will ensure a clear and identifiable community of interest among the employees concerned and will promote effective dealings and efficiency of agency operations. A unit shall not be established solely on the basis of the extent to which employees in the proposed unit have organized, nor shall a unit be established if it includes—

(1) any management official or supervisor, except as provided in section 24;

(2) an employee engaged in Federal personnel work in other than a purely clerical capacity; or

(3) [Revoked.]

(4) both professional and nonprofessional employees, unless a majority of the professional employees vote for inclusion in the unit. Questions as to the appropriate unit and related issues may be referred to the Assistant Secretary for decision.

(c) [Revoked.]

(d) All elections shall be conducted under the supervision of the Assistant Secretary, or persons designated by him, and shall be by secret
ballot. Each employee eligible to vote shall be provided the opportunity
to choose the labor organization he wishes to represent him, from among
those on the ballot, or 'no union', except as provided in subparagraph
(4) of this paragraph. Elections may be held to determine whether—

(1) a labor organization should be recognized as the exclusive representative of employees in a unit;

(2) a labor organization should replace another labor organization as
the exclusive representative;

(3) a labor organization should cease to be the exclusive representative; or

(4) a labor organization should be recognized as the exclusive representative of employees in a unit composed of employees in units
currently represented by that labor organization or continue to be recognized in the existing separate units.

(e) When a labor organization has been accorded exclusive recognition, it is the exclusive representative of employees in the unit and is entitled to act for and to negotiate agreements covering all employees in
the unit. It is responsible for representing the interests of all employees
in the unit without discrimination and without regard to labor organization membership. The labor organization shall be given the opportunity
to be represented at formal discussions between management and employees or employee representatives concerning grievances, personnel
policies and practices, or other matters affecting general working conditions of employees in the unit.

AGREEMENTS

Sec. 11. *Negotiation of agreements.* (a) An agency and a labor organization that has been accorded exclusive recognition, through appropriate
representatives, shall meet at reasonable times and confer in good faith
with respect to personnel policies and practices and matters affecting
working conditions, so far as may be appropriate under applicable laws
and regulations, including policies set forth in the Federal Personnel
Manual; published agency policies and regulations for which a compelling need exists under criteria established by the Federal Labor Relations Council and which are issued at the agency headquarters level or
at the level of a primary national subdivision; a national or other controlling agreement at a higher level in the agency; and this Order. They
may negotiate an agreement, or any question arising thereunder; determine appropriate techniques, consistent with section 17 of this Order, to
assist in such negotiation; and execute a written agreement or memorandum of understanding.

(b) In prescribing regulations relating to personnel policies and
practices and working conditions, an agency shall have due regard for

the obligation imposed by paragraph (a) of this section. However, the obligation to meet and confer does not include matters with respect to the mission of an agency; its budget; its organization; the number of employees; and the numbers, types, and grades of positions or employees assigned to an organizational unit, work project or tour of duty; the technology of performing its work; or its internal security practices. This does not preclude the parties from negotiating agreements providing appropriate arrangements for employees adversely affected by the impact of realignment of work forces or technological change.

(c) If, in connection with negotiations, an issue develops as to whether a proposal is contrary to law, regulation, controlling agreement, or this Order and therefore not negotiable, it shall be resolved as follows:

(1) An issue which involves interpretation of a controlling agreement at a higher agency level is resolved under the procedures of the controlling agreement, or, if none, under agency regulations;

(2) An issue other than as described in subparagraph (1) of this paragraph which arises at a local level may be referred by either party to the head of the agency for determination;

(3) An agency head's determination as to the interpretation of the agency's regulations with respect to a proposal is final;

(4) A labor organization may appeal to the Council for a decision when—

(i) it disagrees with an agency head's determination that a proposal would violate applicable law, regulation of appropriate authority outside the agency, or this Order, or

(ii) it believes that an agency's regulations, as interpreted by the agency head, violate applicable law, regulation of appropriate authority outside the agency, or this Order, or are not otherwise applicable to bar negotiations under paragraph (a) of this section.

(d) If, as the result of an alleged unilateral change in, or addition to, personnel policies and practices or matters affecting working conditions, the acting party is charged with a refusal to consult, confer or negotiate as required under this Order, the Assistant Secretary may, in the exercise of his authority under section 6 (a) (4) of the Order, make those determinations of negotiability as may be necessary to resolve the merits of the alleged unfair labor practice. In such cases the party subject to an adverse ruling may appeal the Assistant Secretary's negotiability determination to the Council.

Sec. 12. *Basic provisions of agreements.* Each agreement between an agency and a labor organization is subject to the following requirements—

(a) in the administration of all matters covered by the agreement, officials and employees are governed by existing or future laws and the regulations of appropriate authorities, including policies set forth in the Federal Personnel Manual; by published agency policies and regulations in existence at the time the agreement was approved; and by subsequently published agency policies and regulations required by law or by the regulations of appropriate authorities, or authorized by the terms of a controlling agreement at a higher agency level;

(b) management officials of the agency retain the right, in accordance with applicable laws and regulations—

(1) to direct employees of the agency;

(2) to hire, promote, transfer, assign, and retain employees in positions within the agency, and to suspend, demote, discharge, or take other disciplinary action against employees;

(3) to relieve employees from duties because of lack of work or for other legitimate reasons;

(4) to maintain the efficiency of the Government operations entrusted to them;

(5) to determine the methods, means, and personnel by which such operations are to be conducted; and

(6) to take whatever actions may be necessary to carry out the mission of the agency in situations of emergency; and

(c) nothing in the agreement shall require an employee to become or to remain a member of a labor organization, or to pay money to the organization except pursuant to a voluntary, written authorization by a member for the payment of dues through payroll deductions.

The requirements of this section shall be expressly stated in the initial or basic agreement and apply to all supplemental, implementing, subsidiary, or informal agreements between the agency and the organization.

Sec. 13. *Grievance and arbitration procedures.* (a) An agreement between an agency and a labor organization shall provide a procedure, applicable only to the unit, for the consideration of grievances. The coverage and scope of the procedure shall be negotiated by the parties to the agreement with the exception that it may not cover matters for which a statutory appeal procedure exists and so long as it does not otherwise conflict with statute or this Order. It shall be the exclusive procedure available to the parties and the employees in the unit for resolving grievances which fall within its coverage. However, any employee or group of employees in the unit may present such grievances to the agency and have them adjusted, without the intervention of the exclusive representative, as long as the adjustment is not inconsistent with the terms of the agreement and the exclusive representative has been given opportunity to be present at the adjustment.

(b) A negotiated procedure may provide for the arbitration of grievances. Arbitration may be invoked only by the agency or the exclusive representative. Either party may file exceptions to an arbitrator's award with the Council, under regulations prescribed by the Council.

(c) [Revoked.]

(d) Questions that cannot be resolved by the parties as to whether or not a grievance is on a matter for which a statutory appeal procedure exists, shall be referred to the Assistant Secretary for decision. Other questions as to whether or not a grievance is on a matter subject to the grievance procedure in an existing agreement, or is subject to arbitration under that agreement, may by agreement of the parties be submitted to arbitration or may be referred to the Assistant Secretary for decision.

(e) [Revoked.]

Sec. 14. [Revoked.]

Sec. 15. *Approval of agreements.* An agreement with a labor organization as the exclusive representative of employees in a unit is subject to the approval of the head of the agency or an official designated by him. An agreement shall be approved within forty-five days from the date of its execution if it conforms to applicable laws, the Order, existing published agency policies and regulations (unless the agency has granted an exception to a policy or regulation) and regulations of other appropriate authorities. An agreement which has not been approved or disapproved within forty-five days from the date of its execution shall go into effect without the required approval of the agency head and shall be binding on the parties subject to the provisions of law, the Order and the regulations of appropriate authorities outside the agency. A local agreement subject to a national or other controlling agreement at a higher level shall be approved under the procedures of the controlling agreement, or, if none, under agency regulations.

NEGOTIATION DISPUTES AND IMPASSES

Sec. 16. *Negotiation disputes.* The Federal Mediation and Conciliation Service shall provide services and assistance to Federal agencies and labor organizations in the resolution of negotiation disputes. The Service shall determine under what circumstances and in what manner it shall proffer its services.

Sec. 17. *Negotiation impasses.* When voluntary arrangements, including the services of the Federal Mediation and Conciliation Service or other third-party mediation, fail to resolve a negotiation impasse, either party may request the Federal Service Impasses Panel to consider the matter. The Panel, in its discretion and under the regulations it prescribes, may consider the matter and may recommend procedures to the parties for the resolution of the impasse or may settle the impasse by appropriate action. Arbitration or third-party fact finding with recommendations to assist in the resolution of an impasse may be used by the parties only when authorized or directed by the Panel.

CONDUCT OF LABOR ORGANIZATIONS AND MANAGEMENT

Sec. 18. *Standards of conduct for labor organizations.* (a) An agency shall accord recognition only to a labor organization that is free from corrupt influences and influences opposed to basic democratic principles. Except as provided in paragraph (b) of this section, an organization is not required to prove that it has the required freedom when it is subject to governing requirements adopted by the organization or by a national or international labor organization or federation of labor organizations with which it is affiliated or in which it participates, containing explicit and detailed provisions to which it subscribes calling for—

(1) the maintenance of democratic procedures and practices, including provisions for periodic elections to be conducted subject to recognized safeguards and provisions defining and securing the right of individual members to participation in the affairs of the organization, to fair and equal treatment under the governing rules of the organization, and to fair process in disciplinary proceedings;

(2) the exclusion from office in the organization of persons affiliated with Communist or other totalitarian movements and persons identified with corrupt influences;

(3) the prohibition of business or financial interests on the part of organization officers and agents which conflict with their duty to the organization and its members; and

(4) the maintenance of fiscal integrity in the conduct of the affairs of the organization, including provision for accounting and financial controls and regular financial reports or summaries to be made available to members.

(b) Notwithstanding the fact that a labor organization has adopted or subscribed to standards of conduct as provided in paragraph (a) of this section, the organization is required to furnish evidence of its freedom from corrupt influences or influences opposed to basic democratic principles when there is reasonable cause to believe that—

(1) the organization has been suspended or expelled from or is subject to other sanction by a parent labor organization or federation of organizations with which it had been affiliated because it has demonstrated an unwillingness or inability to comply with governing requirements comparable in purpose to those required by paragraph (a) of this section; or

(2) the organization is in fact subject to influences that would preclude recognition under this Order.

(c) A labor organization which has or seeks recognition as a representative of employees under this Order shall file financial and other reports, provide for bonding of officials and employees of the organization, and comply with trusteeship and election standards.

(d) The Assistant Secretary shall prescribe the regulations needed to effectuate this section. These regulations shall conform generally to the principles applied to unions in the private sector. Complaints of violations of this section shall be filed with the Assistant Secretary.

Sec. 19. *Unfair labor practices.* (a) Agency management shall not—

(1) interfere with, restrain, or coerce an employee in the exercise of the rights assured by this Order;

(2) encourage or discourage membership in a labor organization by discrimination in regard to hiring, tenure, promotion, or other conditions of employment;

(3) sponsor, control, or otherwise assist a labor organization, except

that an agency may furnish customary and routine services and facilities under section 23 of this Order when consistent with the best interests of the agency, its employees, and the organization, and when the services and facilities are furnished, if requested, on an impartial basis to organizations having equivalent status;

(4) discipline or otherwise discriminate against an employee because he has filed a complaint or given testimony under this Order;

(5) refuse to accord appropriate recognition to a labor organization qualified for such recognition; or

(6) refuse to consult, confer, or negotiate with a labor organization as required by this Order.

(b) A labor organization shall not—

(1) interfere with, restrain, or coerce an employee in the exercise of his rights assured by this Order;

(2) attempt to induce agency management to coerce an employee in the exercise of his rights under this Order;

(3) coerce, attempt to coerce, or discipline, fine, or take other economic sanction against a member of the organization as punishment or reprisal for, or for the purpose of hindering or impeding his work performance, his productivity, or the discharge of his duties owed as an officer or employee of the United States;

(4) call or engage in a strike, work stoppage, or slowdown; picket an agency in a labor-management dispute; or condone any such activity by failing to take affirmative action to prevent or stop it;

(5) discriminate against an employee with regard to the terms or conditions of membership because of race, color, creed, sex, age, or national origin; or

(6) refuse to consult, confer, or negotiate with an agency as required by this Order.

(c) A labor organization which is accorded exclusive recognition shall not deny membership to any employee in the appropriate unit except for failure to meet reasonable occupational standards uniformly required for admission, or for failure to tender initiation fees and dues uniformly required as a condition of acquiring and retaining membership. This paragraph does not preclude a labor organization from enforcing discipline in accordance with procedures under its constitution or by-laws which conform to the requirements of this Order.

(d) Issues which can properly be raised under an appeals procedure may not be raised under this section. Issues which can be raised under a grievance procedure may, in the discretion of the aggrieved party, be raised under that procedure or the complaint procedure under this section, but not under both procedures. Appeals or grievance decisions shall not be construed as unfair labor practice decisions under this Order nor as precedent for such decisions. All complaints under this section that cannot be resolved by the parties shall be filed with the Assistant Secretary.

MISCELLANEOUS PROVISIONS

Sec. 20. *Use of official time.* Solicitation of membership or dues, and other internal business of a labor organization, shall be conducted during the non-duty hours of the employees concerned. Employees who represent a recognized labor organization shall not be on official time when negotiating an agreement with agency management, except to the extent that the negotiating parties agree to other arrangements which may provide that the agency will either authorize official time for up to 40 hours or authorize up to one-half the time spent in negotiations during regular working hours, for a reasonable number of employees, which number normally shall not exceed the number of management representatives.

Sec. 21. *Allotment of dues.* (a) When a labor organization holds exclusive recognition, and the agency and the organization agree in writing to this course of action, an agency may deduct the regular and periodic dues of the organization from the pay of members of the organization in the unit of recognition who make a voluntary allotment for that purpose. Such an allotment is subject to the regulations of the Civil Service Commission, which shall include provision for the employee to revoke his authorization at stated six-month intervals. Such an allotment terminates when—

(1) the dues withholding agreement between the agency and the labor organization is terminated or ceases to be applicable to the employee; or

(2) the employee has been suspended or expelled from the labor organization.

(b) [Revoked.]

Sec. 22. *Adverse action appeals.* The head of each agency, in accordance with the provisions of this Order and regulations prescribed by the Civil Service Commission, shall extend to all employees in the competitive civil service rights identical in adverse action cases to those provided preference eligibles under section 7511-7512 of title 5 of the United States Code. Each employee in the competitive service shall have the right to appeal to the Civil Service Commission from an adverse decision of the administrative officer so acting, such appeal to be processed in an identical manner to that provided for appeals under section 7701 of title 5 of the United States Code.

Any recommendation by the Civil Service Commission submitted to the head of an agency on the basis of an appeal by an employee in the competitive service shall be complied with by the head of the agency.

Sec. 23. *Agency implementation.* No later than April 1, 1970, each agency shall issue appropriate policies and regulations consistent with this Order for its implementation. This includes but is not limited to a clear statement of the rights of its employees under this Order; procedures with respect to recognition of labor organizations, determination of appropriate units, consultation and negotiation with labor organizations, approval of agreements, mediation, and impasse resolution; policies with respect to the use of agency facilities by labor organizations; and policies and practices regarding consultation with other organizations and associations and individual employees. Insofar as practicable, agencies shall consult with representatives of labor organizations in the formulation of these policies and regulations.

Sec. 24. *Savings clauses.* This Order does not preclude—

(1) the renewal of continuation of a lawful agreement between an agency and a representative of its employees entered into before the effective date of Executive Order No. 10988 (January 17, 1962); or

(2) the renewal, continuation, or initial according of recognition for units of management officials or supervisors represented by labor organizations which historically or traditionally represent the management officials or supervisors in private industry and which hold exclusive recognition for units of such officials or supervisors in any agency on the date of this Order.

Sec. 25. *Guidance, training, review and information.*

(a) The Civil Service Commission, in conjunction with the Office of Management and Budget, shall establish and maintain a program for the policy guidance of agencies on labor-management relations in the Federal service and periodically review the implementation of these policies. The Civil Service Commission shall continuously review the operation of the Federal labor-management relations program to assist in assuring adherence to its provisions and merit system requirements; implement technical advice and information programs for the agencies; assist in the development of programs for training agency personnel and management officials in labor-management relations; and, from time to time, report to the Council on the state of the program with any recommendations for its improvement.

(b) The Department of Labor and the Civil Service Commission shall develop programs for the collection and dissemination of information appropriate to the needs of agencies, organizations and the public.

Sec. 26. *Effective date.* This Order is effective on January 1, 1970, except sections 7 (f) and 8 which are effective immediately. Effective January 1, 1970, Executive Order No. 10988 and the President's Memorandum of May 21, 1963, entitled Standards of Conduct for Employee Organizations and Code of Fair Labor Practices and revoked.

RICHARD NIXON

THE WHITE HOUSE
October 29, 1969

TOPICAL INDEX